HISTORY
..of..
BARBOUR COUNTY, ALABAMA
..by..
MATTIE THOMAS THOMPSON

★ ★ ★

History brings to generations as they come and go,
The real facts and fancies, in printed story,
That glisten and shine bright, as they show
The deeds, that bring to men and women, glory
That lives on, as the years glide by;
The sad, the glad, that grips the heart
With memories that bring the song and the sigh,
From all, the writer of research seeks to impart.

★ ★ ★

EUFAULA, ALABAMA

Southern Historical Press, Inc.
Greenville, South Carolina

This volume was reproduced from
An 1939 edition located in the
Publisher's private Library

All rights reserved. No part of this publication may be reproduced,
stored in a retrieval system, transmitted in any form, posted
on to the web in any form or by any means without
the prior written permission of the publisher.

Please direct all correspondence and orders to:

www.southernhistoricalpress.com
or
**SOUTHERN HISTORICAL PRESS, Inc.
PO BOX 1267
375 West Broad Street
Greenville, SC   29601
southernhistoricalpress@gmail.com**

Originally published: Eufaula, AL. 1939
Copyright 1939 by:
Mattie Thomas Thompson
ISBN #0-89308-423-9
All rights Reserved.
Printed in the United States of America

FOREWORD

Although the world moves and we move with it, there is always the incentive, the limitation, the struggles and the victory, woven into a panorama that emblazens history.

From pioneer days to present times, Barbour County has played so conspicious a part in Alabama, and the entire South's history, that it is timely that the writer may reminiscent and sinking deep into the past, give to the reading world the story, so full of historical facts, unique setting, alluring romance and politics, painted red with the blood of the heroes of the War Between the States—and printed in never-fading letters on the books of the County throughout Reconstruction days .

Human imagination is never equal to the reconstruction of any great period, disaster or counterpart and no pen picture can represent the magnitude of any happenings in communities that history glorifies or reflects upon. Neither can any human transactions nor any traditions of heroism be accurately recorded unless stimulated and guided by research, by collaborator, who contributes the work of their research for publication.

When we contemplate the lives and acts of men, we should seek out the greatest and the best, but we should also not fail to remember that comparison aids conception—and since history is an inquiry, a written statement of what is known—a description of what has already taken place—and as Sir Francis Bacon said "makes men wise—the collaborator should have no omissions in the record presented of any research .

It concerns all readers to know that the writer of a history has given out genuine facts, thereby making the narrative twofold interesting .

With this solely in view, special pains have been taken to be accurate in all the family sketches and biographies .

They have been procured from the families direct and much of the data has been gathered from the files of old newspapers published in the County.

The articles contributed bear in each case the signature of the contributor.

INTRODUCTION

Barbour County was born in the pioneer days of Southeast Alabama, when over the land, there was glamor and urge, for the outreaching of the arm of progress, to lift from the lethargy—even though that lethargy was held by a strong romance that was so fascinating, the people were loath to let go entirely, although the progressive bee was buzzing in their ears daily.

There are none left to tell of those days, but fortunately there has remained, undimmed on time's pages, some hallmarks—and the first step in arranging for this history has been to go back to "First Settlement Days" when three tribes of Indians ruled supreme in this section of the state, which is now Barbour County.

After these tribes were sent by the U. S. Government to Indian Territory (now Oklahoma) a white settlement which had sprung up, grew with the years and they have passed along and have given to the South men and women whose memory is hallowed and blessed, who have been heroes and heroines in the face of every conceivable injustice and wrong and who have risen to the heights of personal integrity and intelligence "in times that tried men's souls," that have been the admiration of any citizeznship.

Barbour County has produced statesmen, politicians, lawyers, educators, governors, judges, senators, congressmen, merchants, farmers, and business men of the highest type and, last but not least, soldiers who were the heroes to whom we have sought to accord well merited honor never before given to them.

Their biographies in this history reveal their greatness.

DEDICATION

When "the morning stars sang together" it was a jubilation and the note that has sounded loudest down the centuries has been a refrain of "Achievement" that has made men and women great and their dwelling places redolent with history, calling forth the highest enconium from their descendents and a true and just relation concerning these people and places.

Nowhere in all the Southland has Gods' favor smiled upon, directed and carried through crisis, more dire as in Barbour County, nor has any county in any state in the whole United States given of her best more illustrious and distinguished citizenship to her honor and glory.

With this in mind I am dedicating this history to the men who made it "The Grand Old State of Barbour"—and feeling that the dreams of yesterday largely make our programs and acts of tomorrow. I hope to put into every line of it an incentive to inspire coming generations to aim high, as their predecessors did and accomplish even more with the aid of the advantages of the modern times, which those of former years did not have.

Mattie Thomas Thompson

INDEX

	Page
Chapter 1—Looking Backward	11
Chapter 2—Historical Facts About Towns	20
Chapter 3—Old Landmarks	30
Chapter 4—Bridges Across Chattahoochee River	37
Chapter 5—Barbour County's Great Men	46
Chapter 6—Indians In Barbour County	49
Chapter 7—Hotels	66
Chapter 8—Insurance and Banks	69
Chapter 9—Public Halls and Theatres	74
Chapter 10—Business and Industry	80
Chapter 11—Music and Libraries	91
Chapter 12—Writers In Barbour County	112
Chapter 13—Medical Profession—6 Great Doctors	130
Chapter 14—Historical Old Homes	144
Chapter 15—Faithful Old Servants	160
Chapter 16—County Officials	167
Chapter 17—Reconstruction Days	180
Chapter 18—Organization of Democratic and Conservative Party	184
Chapter 19—Sons of The South	190
Chapter 20—Reconstruction Facts	194
Chapter 21—Granger-Farmers' Alliance and Silver Question	207
Chapter 22—Military	214
Chapter 23—Veterans Who Received Cross of Honor	221
Chapter 24—Grierson's March Across Chattahoochee	231
Chapter 25—Address of The Fifty	245
Chapter 26—Newspapers	254
Chapter 27—Barbour County Schools	260
Chapter 28—Barbour County Churches	267
Chapter 29—Barbour County Cemeteries	290
Chapter 30—Barbour County Politics In 1884	293
Chapter 31—Disasters In Barbour County	305
Chapter 32—Unique Features in Barbour County	315
Chapter 33—Ten Lovely Old Ladies	321
Chapter 34—Old Settlers' Tea	326
Chapter 35—Pap Speight	329
Biographies	333 to 567

PART I

Chapter One

Looking Backward

Barbour County's glory began with its settlement, which was unique, romantic and illumines pioneer history, on through the Indian wars, the war between the states, Reconstruction days, when this section was the hot-bed of Republican invasion and carpet-bag rule; and the heroism of its loyal citizenship in the strife to clean County politics, are stories that emphasize the ascertion that "of Barbour's great men there could have been found no greater."

The County was named for James Barbour of Orange County, Virginia, who was a delegate to the assembly of 1796 and author of the Anti-dueling law, drafter of the Public Education Bill of 1812 and was chosen Governor of Virginia in 1812. His name was given to the County, not because of his high administrative connection, but because of an enviable personal character.

The Louisville section of the County, was settled by a colony of sturdy old Scotch men and women, who had been reared by the blue-stocking rule of, "going to bed Saturday evening at sundown, to begin to keep Sunday," and the community rapidly became staid Presbyterians of the "Elect" type, no better, to be found the world over.

Louisville was at that time in Pike County and was made the first temporary seat of County government, but in the early forties, the site was changed to Clayton where the first court house was built at a cost of $9,000.

Following the treaty with the U. S., made in 1832, in which the Indians gave up their lands that were above the Indian line, the Alabama Legislature organized Barbour County.

The act established that, the County provided that County Commissioners should select a site for the County seat which was to be moved from Louisville to Clayton. Jacob Utsey, Daniel McKenzie, William Cadenhead, William Norton, James A. Head, Green Beauchamp, Samuel G. B. Adams, Noah B. Cole, Robert Richards, and T. W. Pugh, were the Commissioners.

The site for the court house was selected, and in August,

1833, a deed was executed by heirs of Daniel Lewis, who had died before the execution was completd. (This deed to land on which Clayton Court House was built). It was to a committee composed of Beauchamp, Cole, Cadenhead, Head and William Loveless, for a lot upon which to build a courthouse and jail. Harrell Hobdy and Charles Lewis were witnesses to the deed.

The court house was completed in 1833 and was located on the northwestern corner of the present square. It was a one-room house about 20 feet square, of round logs "unarmed by any broad axe." There was one small window and a door at the Southeast end. Ryan Bannett was one of the men who could cut the four foot boards which served the building. They were secured from oak trees, which grew in the little stream just east of the present square. Thomas Warren superintended the building of this first courthouse.

The first Circuit Court assembled in Clayton in this house in 1834, with Judge Anderson Crenshaw and the same officers that had presided when the first County Court was opened at Louisville a year previous and the grand jurors were, William Beauchamp, Foreman, Henry Bizzell, Aaron Burlison, Ivey Cadenhead, Ariel Jones, Seaborn Jones, John McInnis, Daniel McLean, Benjamin D. Sellers, Thomas Warren, Hope D. Williams, Joel Winslett, Ezekiel Wise. Gary Motis was the bailiff.

The first case on the docket was a civil one, and was an appeal in the case of Duncan McRae vs. John McInnis. It was continued from court to court, and not settled until September, 1835. The judgement entries are in the hand writing of Jefferson Buford or George Goldwaiter.

The following is copy of the deed executed for the land on which the town of Clayton was laid out, and is from Deed Book A, page 309, in the Probate Office at Clayton, Alabama.
State of Alabama,
Barbour County

The following indenture, made this 29th day of December in the year 1836, made between Jacinth Jackson, Thomas E. Efurd, Amasa Lewis, Susan P. Keener and Charles Lewis, Commissioners for the County of Barbour—and their successors in office, of the one part, and Elliott Thomas of other part, witnesseth that ,the said Commissioners for the County aforesaid, for and in consideration of the sum of twenty six dollars to them in hand paid by the said Elliott Thomas, the receipt of which is hereby acknowledged, hath this day bargained and sold to the said John D. Thomas, heirs and assigns, one lot in the town of Clayton, known and designated in the plan of said town, as Lot No. 1 and Lot No. 40 to have and to hold the above recited lot and bargained premises together with all the appertainances thereunto. Bargain in anywise and in behalf of the said Elliott Thomas, his heirs and assigns forever and the said corresponders for themselves and their successors in office, doth covenant with the said Elliott Thomas and his heirs and assigns that they will warrant and defend the said lot and bargained premises against the claim of all persons whatsoever. In testimony whereof the correspondents have hereunto set their hand and seals this the day above written.

    Registered January 18, 1837.

                      JACINTH JACKSON (Seal)
                      THOS. E. EFURD (Seal)
                      AMASA LEWIS (Seal)
                      SUSAN F. KEENER (Seal)
                      CHARLES LEWIS (Seal)

    By order of Charles Lewis, Treas.

State of Alabama,
Barbour County.

    Personally appeared before me, James C. Coleman, Clerk of the County Court of said County, C. Lewis, one of the commissioners of the town of Clayton, to convey letters and acknowledges within deed to be made and executed by him forthe purpose herein mentioned this 1st day of December, 1837.

                Signed, JAMES COLEMAN, Clerk,
                            Circuit of Barbour County.

    Copied from Deed Book A, page 309 "Deeds."

    This is the land on which the town of Clayton is built.

    In the early seventies, as a convenience to citizens, who resided in the upper section of the County, a court house was built at Eufaula by the County, the City of Eufaula furnishing the lot on agreement that "they have control of Municipal offices in the building."

    A Probate office is maintained at Eufaula with a deputy Probate Clerk and County Court is held semi-monthly at Eufaula. The Circuit Court Clerk also has a deputy clerk at Eufaula, who maintains a separate Circuit Court office.

    All the other County offices are at Clayton.

    The County Board of Revenue (see Biography of C. S. McDowell in back of book) was established according to this bill, it is composed of the following members: W. A. Jackson, Clio, President; A. R. Wilkinson, Blue Springs; A. B. heimer, Eufaula; J. P. Smith, Baker Hill; G. J. Grant, Louisvile; G. C. Reeder, Sec.-Treas. Blue Springs Bank of Commerce, Clayton Depository.

FIRST SETTLEMENT

Barbour County was founded, from portions of Pike County and the Creek Indian cessions of 1932, which, although approved by the Legislature of this date, did not actually begin practical operations, until a year later.

It has retained its present shape, except small portions set apart to Bullock and Russell Counties.

The Creek Indians had ceded to the United States, a large tract of land occupied by them and on the meeting of the General Assembly of Alabama, following the signing of this Treaty, Governor Dale, in his message to the Legislature, explained that, "it was the duty of that body at that session, to lay off suitable and convenient counties and to establish a system of County organizations, so that protection as well as wholesome restraints, of our laws may be speedily introduced"—hence Barbour, was one of the first eight counties established, all but one, being in the area ceded by the Creeks —five of them lay along the Georgia border, viz: Barbour, Russell, Randolph, and Benton, now called Calhoun.

The records do not show who introduced the bill, the tenth section of which reads, that, "all that tract of land bounded as follows, from the Kendall Lewis old stand, to Pensacola Florida, along said road, till it strikes Pea river, thence down said river line to Dale County, thence along said line to the Chattahoochee river, thence up the said river to the beginning point, which shall form and constitute one separate and distinct County, to be called by the name of Barbour." The line 13 and 14 is about two miles north of the present site of Jernegan, Alabama and the lands in two townships, near the Chattahoochee river, were taken out of Barbour and put into Russell, in some re-adjustment of County lines after the "War Between the States." The area of the County is about 850 miles (so given by several records, but the present County Surveyor, G. B. Espy states that it is nearer 920.

In the Southwest quarter of the state, it is partly agricultural and partly timber region, having about 33,805 acres of forest land, 173,024 pasture land. Percentage of farm land in cultivation, 54.5; in cotton, 43; corn, 32; peanuts, 13; hay and other products, 7. Population (1930 census) 32,435. The soil is alluval subsoil, sandy and lies between the Chattahoochee and Pea rivers. Has large deposits of Bauxite, Fuller's Earth and Potters Clay. Several Companies now operate plants for the manufacture of the depositism and ship large quantities.

Sixty percent of the population, till the soil for a livelihood.

BARBOUR CENSUS

The first census of Barbour County, was taken in 1837, showing a population of 7348.

```
1840 .................................. 12,024
1850 .................................. 23,632
1860 .................................. 30,812
1870 .................................. 29,309
1880 .................................. 33,972
1890 .................................. 34,898
1900 .................................. 35,151
1910 .................................. 32,728
1920 .................................. 32,728
1930 .................................. 32,505
```

SOIL

The following Abstract of the reports of Judge H. D. Clayton of Clayton and Col. Hiram Hawkins of Hawkinsville, Barbour County; is taken from a report sent to State Geologist, Eugene A. Smith, in 1882.

(The region reported upon lies at the headwaters of the Choctahatchie river, and includes both the uplands and lowlands; also, the Chewalla lands are described.)

"No local causes influence the growth of cotton in the former region, but in the Cowikee lands the heavy dews are thought to be favorable to the growth. The uplands are gray to red in color, and mostly sandy and porus. The gray lands are about three-fourths and the red, about one-fourth of the area. The growth upon the gray land is a mixture of long-leaf pine, red, white, and post oaks, and hickory, and on that red land the same, with addition of walnut, persimmon, grapevines, chincapin, buckeye and the red soil is much stiffer than the gray and has a subsoil of sometimes very hard clay and sand underlaid frequently with a hard-pan at a depth of several feet.

"These soils are easy of tillage at all times, and produce the usual crops, being, however, best adapted to grain, potatoes and peas, although cotton forms at least half of the cultivated crops. The most productive height of the stalk is about three feet. About a fourth of this kind of land lies turned out, chiefly because since the war, negro laborers cannot be induced to care for the land and keep the ditches cleared out either on hillsides or in the bottoms, unless especially hired for the purpose, and this takes too much money from the owner of the land to justify him in so doing. On some farms where the negroes have become attached to the place, they can, by a little coaxing, be induced to keep up the land.

"When turned out fourteen or fifteen years and grown up in old field pines, lands will produce nearly as well as the fresh lands when reclaimed.

A great deal of injury is done both to hills and valley by washing and gullies. When the hillsides are turned out and grown up in pines, the valleys are improved, there being no washings from above.

The soil of the Cowikee lands in Barbour County (and the nearby counties of Russell and Bullock) is a sandy loam, alternating with a heavier clay, sometimes prarie-like loam, both more or less strong in lime. The color is usually gray or yellowish, and the subsoil is also of light color. The common growth is hickory, oak and long leaf pine. The three branches of Cowikee creek flow together, before reaching the river. On the north side of each, the land is comparatively level and the principal growth is pine; soil light-gray, chincapin, and hog-wallow. On these the cotton is small, but very prolific though most subject to rust after the land has been cultivated for a few years.

"On the South side of these streams, the soil is much stronger, with more lime, and produces a large cottonweed; it is also better for corn. In wet seasons the land is more difficult to till, but yields fine crops.

Cotton occupies four-fifths of the cultivated land, and the height of stalk at which it is most prolific is from three to four feet.

"About 10 per cent of the land lies out, but it does well when reclaimed. The soil washes badly on slopes, and valleys are injured, often to the extent of 10 per cent, by the washings from the uplands. Some slight effort has been made to check the damage by horizontalizing, hillside ditching, etc., and with good success.

"Barbour County is divided into two distinct parts. The Northern soils being calcareous with a substratum of marl and limestone and the Southern soils sandy, which has been pronounced some of the finest cottonlands in the state. This is due to the drainage of the three forks of the Cowikee creek. Low and flat, it has been called a Malaria district, therefore sparcely inhabited. The Southern half of the County, is notable for its beds of Tertiary formation with sands and loams of stratified drift. There Tertiary occasionally modify the soil the deficiency of lime and the high rolling Country, with freestone water makes this portion of the County, while not specially suitable to cotton, the free use of fertilizers necessary to a satisfactory yield.

"The bottom lands of the three or more miles of the eastern boundary of the Chattahoochee river are exceedingly fine.

"While the lower part of the County is of brown loams with oak, hickory and pine growth, yet the agriculture of Barbour County depends chiefly on the blue marls of the Cowikee and other drainages of the upper half of the County.

"Most of the cotton is raised in the upper area, but still there is no other section of the state, ranking higher in the production of cotton. These blue-marl lands of Barbour, Russell and Bullock Counties, have long shown that these lands are easily cultivated and that the soil ingredients are the best from many standpoints.

"From the drainage of these Blue-marl lands of the upper part of the County and the drainage area of the Chattahoochee river, there is shown an excess of sand among its surface materials and there are great, deep sand beds in Dale County and these same beds follow the Chattahoochee from Barbour County to the Gulf of Mexico."

During the early eighties, Mr. Benjamin Bibb Davis, a hardware merchant of Eufaula, (former citizen of Philadelphia, Pa.) was deeply interested in the soil of Barbour County, and inserted notices in the Eufaula Daily Times which aroused interest in this matter, all over the County, and resulted in many specimens of soil from different parts of the County, being sent to him, which, in turn, was sent by Mr. Davis to the Geological Survey Department of the State at the University of Alabama.

The following is a letter received by Mr. Davis relative to that matter which aroused enthusiasm at that time:

"Tuscaloosa, Ala.,
July, 2nd, 1884.

"Mr. B. B. Davis,
"Eufaula, Ala.
"Dear Sir:

"The marl inclosed in your letter of June 21st, contains a good deal of phosphoric acid and ought to be a good fertilizer, as it is, I should think. It holds from 1 to 2 percent of phosphoric acid. Where did it come from? If it is in the Tertiary formation, it will be particularly interesting. Please look further into this matter. The coal you speak of is, probably a very bituminous ignito, like one I have had lately from Marengo County.

"There is no test for Phosphoric acid which you could use without some experience in Chemical manipulation. The substance is pulverized—dissolved in nitric acid—filtered and treated with Molybrade of Ammonia—which gives a yellow precipitate if phosphoric acid be present.

"Yours truly,
Signed, EUGENE A. SMITH,
State Geologist.'

PECAN GROVES IN BARBOUR COUNTY

It is very probable that the first Pecan grove planted in Alabama was at Glennville (then Barbour, now Russell County). About 1836-37, when the village began to grow into the fine old town it became, some trees were planted, brought from South Carolina, and their size and age, indicate clearly their long life. They are still bearing.

In the early seventies, Capt. R. F. Kolb planted trees at his suburban home in Eufaula. Some years later, the late Robert Moulthrop planted a Pecan orchard at his estate 'Longview' 'overlooking the Chattahoochee river, kept in high state of cultivation by his son, Moss Moulthrop, which today is a beautiful park along "Riverside Drive". Mr. Albert Moulthrop, his son, at his farm, "Rockland," on the Western suburbs of Eufaula also has a large pecan grove of finest trees. In the long ago Major M. A. Brunson owned this farm and grew the finest fig orchard ever known in all this section. The old historic home, "Rockland," was burned recently.

Mrs. G. H. Davis grand daughter of Barbour County's great Confederate General Alpheus Baker, at her home two miles north of Eufaula, (formerly the historic old Fern Wood home) has one of the largest Pecan groves, all these planted about 20 years ago.

The Lampley Pecan orchard at "St. Francis" notable as an old Indian village, 3 miles from Eufaula, covers many acres, as does several other orchards at various of the Lampley farms in Barbour County.

The largest Pecan Industry in this section however, is the over three thousand acres in Pecans, planted by the Alabama Pecan Co., on the historic old Lore-Russell farm six miles South of Eufaula on the Clayton Highway. In about 1914 Mrs. H. C. Russell sold the fine old home and its thousands of acres of farm lands to the Alabama Pecan Co., composed of several families. that had moved here from Minnesota and other Northern points. Young trees were set out, seeds planted, and in a few years, this industry was in the full flush of success. Many new homes were built on the estate, and Barbour County received into her citizenship more than a half dozen fine families, who are now numbered among our most valued citizens. Among the number: Mr. F. C. Clapp, County Agent, who was reared on a farm. Born at Kasota, Minn., July 31st, 1888. He is a graduate of The University of Minn., and hold's a Master's degree in "Science of Soils." He directs the Barbour County Farm Bureau, and added to the benefits of that organization a group insurance with permanent disability clause, at a very low cost. He is a live, wide-awake, citizen and an asset to Barbour County.

The city of Eufaula, at the suggestion of Col. G. L. Comer, some years ago purchased from the Ala. Pecan Co., several hundred Fine Pecan Trees, planted along the side walks, parks, of the city, on the various streets, and today these trees are all bearing a fine yield of ' Stuart" and "Schly" nuts, that become the property of who ever picks them up off the ground, and the children on the streets usually keep them well cleared up.

FINE OATS IN BARBOUR COUNTY IN 1884

Cowikke, Ala.
May 22, 1884

Editor Times:

I saw in your issue of Tuesday 20th inst., a notice of some fine oats received by Mr. B. L. Jones of Batesville.

It affords me much pleasure to see the interest our leading farmers are already taking in this great cereal.

Said notice stated that the earliest variety was planted in January.

I hereby inclose you several heads that were sown February 2nd, on thin land, with ordinary manuring. The variety is the "Hill Oat" known to you as the "Hawkins Hill" oat, and they are undoubtedly a success, at least 4 weeks, earlier than the ordinary variety.

W. C. SWANSON.

From Eufaula Daily Times.

Chapter Two

Historical Facts About Towns In Barbour County

LOUISVILLE
By
A Louisville Citizen From the Clayton, Ala. Record

Louisville is one of the oldest towns in Alabama. In 1821 when Pike County was established the first County seat was Louisville.

For about two years following 1932 when Barbour was established, Louisville was the County seat of Barbour until the jail and Court house could be built at Clayton.

The first court house stood in what is now Mr. Will Bell's garden and was still standing in the memory of citizens now living in Louisville. The doors of the building were wide, hand-turned planks and had designs made on the doors with heavy nails thickly studded together.

The first settlers of Louisville had to go to Fort Gaines, Ga., to mill, until Hagler's Mill was built three miles east of Louisville. The first settlers in Louisville section mostly came from Georgia, North and South Carolina, and Virginia. They were large slave owners. The home making spirit of the pioneer woman is illustrated in the story of a prominent Louisville family who moved to this section from N. C. When the family packed their household goods to come to what was then a wilderness in South Alabama, the wife pulled up her rose bushes to bring with her. The husband thought that it would be impracticable to bring roses all the way from N. C., whereon the wife replied: "I will go with you into hardship, if you will in turn let me take my roses with me." This beauty loving spirit of the pioneer woman, is still alive in Louisville, for Louisville is a city of flowers.

In 1820 Louisville had four stores, in 1840, twelve stores. The first houses were built of logs. Louisville has always been noted for good schools. The M. E. Church was organized in 1820 and is one of the oldest churches in Barbour County. The Louisville Baptist Church was organized in 1896, and the Presbyterian in 1900. Louisville is supported by a good farming section and has always enjoyed a good mercantile trade. Daniel Lewis built the first house in Louisville and named the town Lewisville. It was never a large town but after the Railroad came in 1888, the town was incorporated and governed by a Mayor and Councilmen.

Among the first settlers were Lewis', Faulks', Grubbs', McSwains', Pugh Williams', McRaes', Lees', Shipmans', Burches'.

Bartley C. Williams was the first Postmaster at Williamston. Notwithstanding the fact that the first settlers of Louisville were old Scotch Presbyterians, the early Williamston settlers organized a Methodist church in 1823, which they named New Hope. A ground was prepared for Camp meetings and for many years this was a famous Camp Meeting ground, where devout worshipers came from all parts of Southeast Alabama. While "New Hope" church is extinct the old church cemetery is still there and often visited by sightseers.

The first recorded marriage in the county was that of Daniel McCall to Mary McDaniel, both of the Pea River Settlement. It is stated, that they had to go nearly to Franklin to find someone who could legally unite them in marriage.

Mr. Green Beauchamp, who wrote an early history of the county, said that it was at "Mount Pleasant, which was on the road from Louisville to Hobdy's Bridge, that John McNiel was buried." But Mrs. Addie McRae, who died at Clayton in 1932, aged 98, said "that it was on a road which ran from Joiner's Bridge north to Louisville—Hobdy's Bridge road." McNeil had one son, a physician, who died at Clayton in 1875 and seven daughters as follows: Mrs. John Windham; Mrs. Daniel Currie; Mrs. Emanuel Cox; Mrs. Harrell Hobdy; Mrs. Judge S. Williams; Mrs. Dr. E. M. Heron and Mrs. Lemuel Long, the latter killed in the Indian war of 1837. Curry was for years clerk of the session of Pea River Church. Heron was a pioneer physician of Louisville. Cox, Hobdy, and Williams, were Prominent planters. Mrs. Long, the last of the family, died at Louisville, 1891, at the age of 91. Jaon McNeill's descendants are numerous in Barbour County.

It is said there were settlers in the vicinity of Louisville as early as 1817 or 1818. By 1820 there were two stores and in 1821 it was made the County seat of Pike County of which was the lower part of Barbour County.

Dr. E. M. Heron and Dr. McRae, early physicians of Louisville, the former some years before his death stated that the original name was spelled Lewis, honoring the Lewis family, prominent in the early setlement, but from some unknown reason, the spelling was suddenly changed to Louis, instead of Lewis.

John G. Morgan was one of the early merchants. He had been sheriff of Henry County and was a blacksmith.

Rev. Jessee Burch, a preacher whom tradition says, with John McDonald and their families, formed a Methodist church and built a church house in the community near Louisville.

CLAYTON

The County Seat of Barbour County, was moved from Louisville in 1883, the commissioners deciding on the change, because of the central location.

Judge Siom L. Perry, at the regular Court session, over which he was presiding, ordered that the next term of Court be held there and this first court held in the court house, a square log structure, in March, 1834, with Judge Anderson Crenshaw presiding.

Although as early as 1818 there had been a few white immigrants passing through the section, stopping for months at a time, there was too much worry over the Indian proposition, for settlers to homstead, and it was not until about 1827, four years after Eufaula had been settled, that Captain S. Porter, an Indian trader's daughter, married Chilli McIntosh, son of the famous Indian Chief, and it was after the removal of the Indians from the County that real settlement of the town of Clayton began.

Deed Book No. 1 of the Orphan's Court in the Archives of the County shows that the land on which the city of Clayton was laid out was deeded by John DeLochiou and Elliott Thomas to five Commissioners who were the first settlers of Eufaula, 21 miles from Clayton. It is in the Central part of the County on the historic road from Hobdy's Bridge over Pea river to Eufaula on the Chattahoochee river.

The town was named in 1883 for Judge Augustine Clayton of Georgia.

This little town abounds in history, full of romance, tragedy, and has a political record that is as varied as it is colorful. Being the County seat, it has been the high point of the many happenings that have made the County's history both sensational and great. It is claimed there were settlers on the ridge between Louisville and Clayton as early as 1818, but the facts shown from Elliott, Johnathon and Jno. D. Thomas' old records, diaries, etc., show that there was practically no settlement until 1823. The first settlers on this ridge were: Luke Bennett and James Arthur. Today it is a beautiful, progressive town, with a handsome modern Courthouse, fine school house and several nice churches, Methodist, Baptist, Presbyterian and Episcopal, a library, banks and hotel, and Confederate monument. And on its streets in lovely homes reside some of the most distinguished families of Alabama.

Being the County seat proper the County jail is located at Clayton.

Among the first settlers were: William Beasley, John Beasley, Henry Black, Wilson Collins, William Cox, Jacinth Jackson, Daniel Lewis, Britt Atkinson, Randall Jackson. Most of these crossed the Chattahoochee at Eufaula on a ferry operated by the Indians. Atkinson became provoked at the ferry charges and quarreled with the Indians, striking a chief on the head with an iron stirrup, which ended the dispute. That night the women of the party were anxious, fearing the Indians treachery might attempt to harm them, but no trouble resulted.

Lewis located a mile west of Clayton and later donated the land upon which the courthouse was built (see deed). The Beasleys settled a mile east of what is now Pratt station and Jacinth Jackson settled west of what is now known as the Wash McRae place. Collins settled on the old Franklin road four miles east of Louisville.

Jim Beasley laid out the road from Clayton to Louisville. He was the grandfather of Hart Collins and Montfred Collins. There is a tradition that the hill upon which Jacinth Jackson built his house, was favorably considered at one time as the site for the County seat when Barbour County was organized.

The home of Matthew Fenn, descendant of Mark Williams was on the highway between Eufaula and Clayton. He also owned a large tract of land near Hobdy's Bridge.

The earliest settlers in the Pea River community were: Jessie Burch, Blake Jernegan, Alexander McCall, John McDaniel, John McInnis, Miles McInnis, Gilbert McEachern, John McNeill, and Joel Willis. In 1823 they built the Pea River Presbyterian Church, first worshiping under bush arbors. It is tradition that this is the mother Presbyterian Church of Barbour County.

Clio, Elamville, Blue Springs and Texasville were not developed until after the Railroad, Eufaula to Ozark, was completed. Since then these towns have rapidly grown. Texasville was named to honor Judge A. H. Alston. Clio's first name was Atkinson's head.

In the early seventies the cotton business in Barbour County was at its "crown and flower," and a few years after the building of the Vicksburg and Brunswich Railroad, Eufaula to Ozark, via Clayton, Louisville, Clio, Elamville, the immense Cotton business demanded Telegraph service, Eufaula to Clayton and Bunyan Davie there built a private Telegraph line between Eufaula and Claxton which years after was absorbed by the Western Union Telegraph Co., after it having been used as "connecting" line successfully a long time. In 1895 The Southern Bell Telegraph and Telephone Company built a long distance line to accommodate the cotton shippers and buyers, Eufaula to Louisville, and established an Exchange at Clayton to expedite the cotton business at this end of the county. The receipts from the Louisville Office during 1891 were very heavy.

BATESVILLE

For many years the largest voting Precinct, voting the largest number (consolidated with Glennville and Old Spring Hill) of any in the county was Batesville and the citizenship of that territory largely controlled the politics of the County because numbered among this citizenship were men of note who took active part in politics. It was also a religious section and there were four large churches, their pastors being the best in the state.

The Pine Grove Baptist Church, Old Providence Methodist Church, Batesville Church and Primitive Baptist Church and a religious atmosphere prevaded this section.

The early settlers were the Sylvesters, Irbys, Sparks, Engrams, Johnson, Whittington, Harwell, Lamar, Martin, Brown, Whigham, Doughtie, Boyer, Reeves, Thomas, Parker, Smith, Tyson. Cawthon, McLead, Foy, Wilson, Moore, Browder, Alston, Bates, Crimes, Ott, Pruitt, Margart, Otis, Weathers, Bush, Hill, Saunders, Norton, Cook, Lunsford, Worthington, Crawford, Woolhopter.

The land on which Old Providence Methodist Church was built, was donated by Edward S. Ott, who was the leading inspiration and example, for all the progress and fine citizenship that marked that locality. This historic old church was the place of worship of a consecrated band of christians whose descendants are outstanding today, wherever they are located.

BLUE SPRINGS

Blue Springs has always been an important farming section and famous for its great natural spring and pool, which for many years drew great crowds of visitors to the Blue Springs hotel and cottages there, seeking the pleasures of a watering place and the benefits of the curative powers in its water. It is seven miles from Clio. The pool is about 35 feet deep and into this pool flows a cold stream of water that spouts up and continually flows into this stream that empties into the Choctahatchee river.

Late years the hotel has not been kept open, but it is still popular and campers and pleasure seekers go there to spend their vacations in the cottages.

The section around Blue Springs was the home of some of the most prominent politicians of the County and always, at election time, there was much interest and sometimes excitement there. During campaigns it was a popular place to hold the speakings and candidates were always sure of getting together more listeners at Blue Springs than most any other place in the County.

Many memorable barbecues and picnics have been held there, and many of the distinguished politicians and speakers recall great times in that section in the eighties and nineties.

At a largely attended Convention held years ago in the northern part of the state, a distinguished Alabamian (not from Barbour) in a great speech on patriotism said, "Alabama is divided into three parts, North Alabama, South Alabama and Barbour County, from whence comes today, to this convention, six great men who have helped make it the grand old third Division of Alabama. Three Cheers for Barbour County." The speaker was Henry W. Hilliard.

AN OLD LANDMARK

Mr. Philip Johnston of Blue Springs was in town yesterday and being the oldest inhabitant in these parts, he was attacked by a Times man with the following result: Mr. Johnston is now in his 85th year and has been a resident of this county since 1822. He attended the first Court ever held in the County, which was at Louisville and was a member of the first grand jury, which found two bills; one for assault and battery; and one for adultry. He married early in life, and became the father of ten children. His wife died and he remained a widower for 15 years and at the age of 60 married a young woman of 22 to whom was born 9 children. He is hale and hearty and converses freely with evident relish of the early history of the County.

CLIO

Clio is situated on the East side of what is known as "Jugg Branch" and is a town of about 1000 population. When the Central of Georgia Railroad was extended from Clayton on to Ozark, in Dale County, in 1887, Old Clio was moved some distance that it might be nearer the railroad.

Clio's first merchant was Murdock Martin, one of the oldest settlers of the County, coming to Clio from the Louisville settlement. L. A. Hunt, Duncan McRae, Alex Shaw, were all early merchants.

The first hotel was run by Mrs. Mattie Hunt.

The Clio Banking Company was organized in 1905 by W. A. Arnold as President and the Farmers' Bank was organized by J. N. Stephens, Pres.

There are three churches at Clio: First built, Methodist; Presbyterian next in 1902 and later the Baptist.

In 1911 the County High School was built at Clio, at a cost of $12,500.00.

The first Mayor of the town was P. W. Shaw; the first Marshal H. C. Thompson.

The Telephone Exchange was established, 1907.

L. A. Hunt was the leading cotton factor in that section, and did a large business over Long Distance Telephone. The Long Distance Telephone service was stablishd by the Southern Bell Telephone and Telegraph Company in 1896, long before the Exchange, which was a private company, came.

When J. N. Strickland drove the first automobile down the Main street of Clio there was a sensation created. It was a Maxwell car.

Prominent business men of the old and new Clio were and are: Frank McRae, C. W. Knight, Baxters, Martins, Shaws, McInnis, Strickland, Faulks.

It is a delightful place to live.

GLENNVILLE

Beautiful for situation on the highest point in what was originally Barbour County, now Russell County, the reminders of this quaint old town stil remain. Time was, when it was a seat of wealth and refinement, its background was a cultured one and the very atmosphere breathes of the happiness of the old days, and the lines that have led from its old homes of wealth and culture have trailed to the far corners of the world. It was named for, and by, one of the oldest members of the Glenn family that has been distinguished and outstanding for many generations. (See Glenn biography).

The earliest settlers of Glennville community were, viz: A. C. Mitchell, Massimilon Glenn, Eugene Herndon Glenn, J. M. Raiford, George Thompson, Dr. Evans Dent, John Treutlen, Judge Cochran, MacGlenn, Dosh Glenn, William Ivey, Malichi Ivey, Walker Richardson, Douglass, Dr. T. C. Johnson, John Bass, Dr. Burke, Dr. A. W. Barnett, Dr. Darwin, Dr. Lomax, Railford Logan, Dr. Anslem Evans, Abner Bessey. The homes were the finest.

The Glennville Female College was on of the finest schools in the South at that time. Ranking A No. 1 in every way.

The St. Stephen Mission (Episcopal) at Glennville, is a branch of St. James Church at Eufaula. It was conceived and organized by Rev. C. M. Murry, Rector of St. James Church, and made possible by the interest and efforts of communicants of both of these churches.

Prof. and Mrs. Douglass, President of Glennville Female College, were the grandparents of Mrs. E. C. Motley of Eufaula, whose mother was Nellie Douglass, first wife of ex-Mayor R. A. Ballowe of Eufaula.

The homes in Glennville before the War Between the States, were said to be the finest in the state. It was the axe and torch, and thievery of the pilfers of the Union army that demolished and ruined that wealthy little town.

William Lee and William Smith were the owners of the first Stage Coach line through Barbour County.

That section of Russell County that was at one time a part of Barbour County may well be proud of her citizenry of that day and time. Among these the names of William Ingram, Edward Ingram, Dr. O'Neal, Scotts, Johnson, Thigpens, Jelks, Scarboroughs, Longs, McGoughs, Dawsons, Williamsons, Evans, Williams, whose descendants are valuable citizens of this section. The Glenns have given to the South more than a half dozen Methodist ministers, some of the leading lights in the denomination.

MAYORS OF EUFAULA

Up to 1857 the town was governed by an Intendant, whom the first records shows was Mark Williams, until he was succeeded in the late forties by George C. McGinty, who was followed by John McNab.

In 1857 Dr. William H. Thornton was elected Mayor, after the city Charter had been granted.

The following have served, viz.:

W. H. Thornton, G. Albert Roberts, J. C. Pope (acting in 1865), John G. Smith, Dr. Thornton again, Wells J. Bray, G. L. Comer, P. B. McKenzie, served ten years, Chas. S. McDowell, Jr., Geo. H. Dent, also served ten years, R. A. Ballowe, Charles G. Mercer, R. D. Thomas, H. H. Conner, Lee J. Clayton, E. H. Graves, and now Ernest Farrell.

For many years Thos. Cargill, followed by T. D. Patterson, was the town Marshall. The Chiefs of police have been Barney Rhody (ten years), Jeff N. Bradley (ten years), J. M. Huguley, Porter Hatfield, T. M. Brannon, H. T. Johnston, Jr., W. C. McGilary, Seth Speight, H. C. McCulloughs.

The City Clerks have been George C. McGinty, E. L. Catterville, George H. Sporman, A. A. Couric, T. C. Doughtie, and now for many years Mrs. R. M. McEachern (formerly Miss Ruby Dunbar) who has been acclaimed by many special expert auditors, "the most accurate and capable bookkeeper I ever checked."

EUFAULA INCORPORATED

Eufaula was incorporated December 19, 1857. Dr. W. H. Thornton, Mayor; George C. McGinty, City Clerk; Thomas Cargill, Marshal; Councilmen, G. A. Roberts, Hugh Black, N. M. Hyatt, Andrew McKenzie.

MAYORS OF CLAYTON

The Mayors of the town of Clayton in succession have been:

Capt. J. C. McNab, B. F. Petty, Dr. J. J. Winn, Judge A. H. Alston, E. Perry Thomas, Judge J. S. Williams, George W. Peach, T. M. Patterson, J. E. Martin, B. F. Kennedy, J. T. Floyd, J. S. Snead, A. J. Bethune, George A. Johnson, Jno. C. Martin, B. T. Roberts.

A. S. Borders, Jr., Mayor; Harrison Bonds, Marshal; J. B. Dykes, Night watchman.

Councilmen: J. N. Clements, S. P. Ventress, L. P. Ellington, Thomas Parish, H. M. Fenn.

City Attorney, Preston C. Clayton; City Clerk, Felix Ventress.

MAYORS OF LOUISVILLE

A. J. Lee, Sr., S. H. Hixon, H. Z. Norton, W. O. Bell, E. P. Grant, W. Z. Hartzog, W. H. McEachern, S. M. Greeb, J. M. Stephens, J. S. Douglass, D. R. Tillman, Judge M. L. Albritton, W. P. Patterson.

Present Officials: Mayor, Thomas D. Lee; Council Members, Dr. G. M. Harrison, B. D. Hurst, B. M. Grant, T. A. Norton, E. E. Bennett; City Clerk, E. P. Grant.

The members of the first County Council of Louisville were: The Lewis, Faulks, Grubbs, McSwain, Pugh, Williams, McRaes, Lees, Shipmans, and Birches.

NOTES FROM CLAYTON BANNER, 1853

"Major Jefferson Buford, who raised a company of emigrants to help colonize Kansas with pro-slavery people, left Montgomery with about four hundred men and had every reason to expect considerable accession to his company in Selma and Mobile. The probabilities are, that he will reach Kansas with no less than one thousand settlers. Whatever may be the outcome, the South owes a debt of gratitude to one, who in darkest hour, raised the Southern standard and freely risked everything in the Southern cause. The hopes and hearts of thousands go with him and his followers in this noble mission."

UNIQUE DEEDS

The lands deeded by the Indians and subsequently by the Government to Mark Williams and Durham and Floyd Lee at Eufaula were a stretch of three hundred and fifty feet below the present court house and two hundred feet west, was, at that time separate from what was then Irwinton proper. These deeds are still in the hands of heirs of these three settlers, have been passed upon legally and declared to be so written, that these heirs, if they saw fit, could reclaim these lands. An effort in this direction was made by the Lee heirs of Williams in 1891, but Jno. C. Thomas, one of the Williams heirs, interested himself in squelching the suit. (He was one of the principal heirs to gain by the suit) stating that the persons now owning these lands bought them in good faith and it would be dishonest to bring suit to recover them from these parties. The lands in question reach from the railroad tracks (former Wm. McLeod lands) to the home of J. L. Ross on Broad Street, the stretch reaching in width from the middle of Broad Street to middle of Barbour Street, taking in three of the best business blocks in the city.

The matter was agitated again, five years ago, an attorney from Mississippi, representing the Lee heirs, coming to Barbour county investigating, but the writer, standing firm on her father's decision in the matter, declining to surrender to this attorney papers she holds that would have aided him in filing these suits.

John McNeill was the first white man buried in Barbour County and he was buried at Pea river on his own plantation in 1833. It is recorded that Indians assisted in burying him and carved his coffin out of the trunk of a large oak tree.

His family moved to a farm, a mile west of Louisville, to be further away from an Indian village.

The children of the settlers of this particular section were: Mrs. Harrel Hobdy (Jane), Mrs. Emanuel Cox (Sarah), Mrs. Lemuel Long (Ann), Mrs. Judge Williams (Effie), Mrs. Windham (Eliza), Mrs. Curry Kate), Mary, first wife of Dr. Edward Heron and mother of Mrs. R. Q. Edmonson of Eufaula deceased, and one son Dr. John McNeill, who was a physician at Clayton many years.

Chapter Three
Old Landmarks

Stage Coaches in 1853, made a strictly "on time" schedule route, "Silver Run" (now Seale) to Apalachicola, Florida, and there was a branch line to Montgomery, out from this line.

Two Companies of Infantry and one of Cavalry were equipped and organized in Barbour for the Confederacy. The Cavalry was commanded by John M. Moore.

The first Saw Mill in Barbour County, was located near the Chewalla Creek in 1835 and was owned by John M. Moore.

In 1835 Mark Williams built "The Tavern", for a residence and a hotel.

"Pea River Tavern" and the "Rest" on the stage Coach route, was the saloon of J. G. L. Martin.

The first sporting place, was "Social Hall" near Glennville and had a $10,000 race track, built by the moneyed men of that section.

One day recently 500 home-cured hams raised in Barbour County, were sold in Dale County, bring 11-14. From 1882 Eufaula Times.

Barbour County Cotton receipts, for week ending December 9, 1884. 2541 bales against 2000 for the previous week. Receipts from September to December 9th—208,810 bales against 24,740 same time last year, 1836, showing increase of 2076 bales. The stock Thursday night was 3,670 bales—same time last year—4,831 bales.

OLD ROADS

On the "Pony Express", Nashville, Tenn., to Montgomery, Ala., J. L. Pugh and James Powell, pioneer builders of Montgomery, rode. This stage line first begun in Henry and Barbour Counties in 1835-36. The "Mail line', "Telegraph line", "People's line", and "Express Mail" operated from New York to New Orleans, La., passed through the Eastern boundary of Barbour County, crossing the Chattahoochee river.

Two hundred men and five hundred horses were used on this route. The earliest roads were mere paths or trails, hardly two feet wide and all streams had to be forded—and at the rainy season, were often impassable.

The second Federal road connecting Georgia with Alabama entered Alabama at Fort Mitchell (then in Barbour County) and went on to Fort Stephens, thence to Natchez, Miss. $12,400 appropriated by Congress for the opening of the "Natchez Trail"; and in 1938 Congress appropriated $79,565 for improving these roads.

In 1938, the upper Federal road" and extension of the Military Road from Pensacola, Florida, to Fort Mitchell, and from Tennessee to Louisiana.

This old Military Road had been begun by General Jackson in 1817 and was completed in 1820.

These were used for "Post Routes" on which Post Offices were established—the mail went on horseback in rainy weather and on stage coaches in dry weather.

The Indian Trails were a network of roads from town to town and settlement to settlement, of the upper and Lower Creeks on the Chattahoochee river.

The Creeks were the laregst tribe in the states of Alabama and Georgia. The Southern Trail "High Point Path" crossed the Chattahoochee river at "Shallow Ford" north of Atlanta, Georgia, an dthe Trail known as the "Trading Path" crossed the Chattahoochee river, below Columbus, Georgia, crossing from Stewart County, Georgia to Barbour County, Alabama, and many of the sites selected by the Indians for crossing the creeks and rivers and are now the sites of bridges over our railroads and highways.

In the early forties "Plank Roads" were laid over the bad places traveled, and from this came the term, "Plank Road". It was a Barbour County Senator, who in 1850 prepared a bill that led to the chartering of 25 "Plank Road Companies" in Alabama and from this, many Plank roads were built.

There were also "Turnpike" companies and the histories of the State of Alabama, all show that, since 1841, the good roads, Bridges, and taxation therefor, has been one of the most important questions before the Legislative sessions during the passing years.

When the stages began to carry passengers as well as mail, progression began to be visible everywhere and a speed of ten miles an hour was the usual schedule time allowed for.

Federal Roads connected Georgia and Alabama, entering Alabama at Fort Mitchell in Russell County and passed westward to Fort St. Stephens, later on to Natchez, Miss. The road from Pensacola to Fort Mitchell was the old Military Road of Jackson in 1817. Before 1840, there were three separate Coach lines. "The Mail", "Telegraph Line" and Peoples Line." Horses and drivers were changed every 12 miles. County roads were maintained by citizens of the Community, divided into sections. In pioneer days they were called "Pike Roads" in some places.

One of the old trail roads in Barbour County, is the road leading from Texasville to The White Pond, which must have been a great camping place for the Indians, because of the fish in the White Pond in Henry County. In 1860, there were signs of an old Indian village near there, and Mr. James Roberts, who owned a large plantation reaching to White Pond, in the late nineties, plowed up many mounds of Indian relics. This trail, through that section, became the highway from Dale County to Barbour, and was greatly travelled until the railroad from Eufaula to Ozark was built.

PLANK ROAD

We have hitherto unintentionally neglected to notice the completion of this enterprise. Recently the stockholders took hold anew of the work, which for awhile had been in part abandoned, and now have the road finished and in operation. It has been carried around the hill at the Bridge, instead of through it, as was at first attempted; and proves of incalculable advantage at a very small cost, to all who have hauling to and from the wharf. Those who have undertaken and completed the work certainly are entitled to the well wishes of the community; and we can now assure our friends in Georgia, that they need no longer fear encountering a muddy, boggy hill, in bringing their cotton and other produce into our markets. This road is not paved.—Clipped from "Spirit of the South", 1853.

When theearly settlers cut a road from Franklin in Henry County, it led westward into a dense wilderness, and these settlers cut their way to the Pea river and made astop at what is now Louisville. This old road ran by Richards Cross Road through Baker Hill to Williamston. It turned westward, passed through McSwean and Condry places, crossed the present road from Clayton to Texasville near the Floyd school and came into the Clayton and Louisville Highway near Bethlehem church, three miles from Louisville.

The Franklin road was the first road over which mail was brought into Barbour County. James L. Pugh, afterward U. S. Senator 25 years, as a young man, carried this mail from Franklin to Louisville.

Later in the fifties there was established a rural route of Stage Coach line over the road which had been an Indian trail, from Silver Run (Now Seal, Ala.) to Marianna Florida. and along this trail when used by the Indians, there were three Indian villages. After settlers took up lands in the Southern part of the County, the Indians withdrew to the northern part and a distinct line had been drawn, dividing the lands.

This line entered the county about one mile north of Mount Andrew, about six miles north of Clayton, passing just north of Baker Hill to the Chattahoochee river a few miles South of Eufaula. This line was called the old "Indian Boundary line," through the Ray and Espy places. After the Indians gave up their lands in the upper part of the County, Mt. Andrew, White Oak Springs and Fort Browder were settled. Mount Andrew was named for a distinguished Methodist Preacher.

Fort Browder was a Fort which was constructed as a protection against the Indians, after the Fort at Eufaula was built. It was on a high Hill above Batesville. The original White Oak Springs, was on the present highway, Clayton to Eufaula, half way between the two places. A post Office was established at this point as early as 1841 and A. B. Bushnas was Post Master 30 years.

RAILROADS

The nearest railroad to Barbour County, until the early fifties, was the Southwestern Railroad, which had a depot eight miles on the Georgia side coming from Macon, Georgia, to that point and a stage coach ran from there to Eufaula. From 1857 to 1860 there was a depot just across the river, where McKenzie's brick yard now is. In 1862 Mr. Robert Moulthrop came from North Haven Connecticut to work on a river bridge the Railroad was building across the Chattahoochee river to run their trains into Barbour County. He had only been here a short time when the Railroad turned down the Contractor and the bridge was turned over to him. He manufactured the brick for the piers and completed the bridge in late 1865, and Barbour County's first train rolled across into Eufaula. When the Southwestern Railroad's first depot at the extreme South end of Orange street was completed the station over the river was abandoned.

Early in the seventies, the Vicksburg and Brunswick Railroad began their line 21 miles down the County to Clayton and another fine depot was built on Union Street. In 1889 the present depot, the first of the modern ones built by the Central of Georgia Railroad, was built. The lots on which both the freight and passenger depots are built having been purchased from the William McLeod estate.

When the Old Montgomery and Eufaula depot was built in 1874, the M. and E. trains ceased to stop at Hoboken as was the case some years. During those years Hoboken was an incorporated town with a Mayor James Sherry, Marshal Wm. Courtney, and was a thriving little village.

Capt. Jno. O. Martin was agent for the M. and E. Railroad and the Agents for the Central of Georgia, which absorbed the old Southwestern and Vicksburg and Brunswick roads, Companies, have been D. Phelps, John G. Smith, C. I. McLaughlin, Dan Gugel, A. H. Stevens, C. C. Hanson, Seth Mabry, J. A. Hartszog, J. W. Edwards.

In 1888 the Central of Georgia Railroad was extended to Louisville and on down through Clio and Elamville in Barbour County, to Ozark in Dale County. The building of this Road to Ozark, proved an unfortunate move for the upper half of the county, in that this road, connecting at Ozark, with the Alabama Midland Railroad, carried the bulk of the retail trade, that had always come to Barbour County from Dale, Henry and Geneva, to Montgomery, Bainbridge, and later to Dothan, Ala. Barbour County assumed bonds for the building of this road, and yet has $750,000 worth of these to meet, after paying on the debt for nearly 50 years. The upper half of the County pays the larger percent of this debt annually, and instead of reaping a benefit, has lost all the trade enjoyed before the road was built.

Senator Morgan of Alabama, went to France to buy steel rails for this Alabama Midland Railroad because the low tariff made it possible for these rails to be imported from France cheaper than they could be manufactured at the steel plants in Alabama, which condition at that time was due to politics in the state, over which Barbour County representative citizens were worked up to fever heat. Congressman W. C. Oates undertook to help matters but did not get sufficient support in his efforts.

NOTES

In conversation with Mr. Thomas McRae of Louisville and Mr. R. M. McEachern of Eufaula, we learn that the original name given to the first settlement of Barbour County was "Williamston". The first settlers of that section of the County being William Williams, Jared Williams, Bartley C. Williams, William Bush, John Danner, Mr. Copeland, and the name Williamston was given to honor this family.

This family is possible a connection of Mark Williams, first settler at Eufaula, as the Williams' of that branch, had lived at St. George Island in the Gulf of Mexico off Port St. Joseph, and had been Gov. Light House Keepers, (father to son for nearly a hundred years). Mr. McRae states that Mr. Green Beauchamp crossed the Chattahoochee river at Fort Gaines, just across from the village of Franklin and settled in the Williams Community. He set up a store and his patrons were both Indians and settlers. The store was on the site where Jim Gilcrest now lives, near Wilkerson's X roads also called Ryan X road, between Eufaula and Clayton.

William Williams built and operated the first gin in Barbour County, and Danner, who, was a German, was the first blacksmith.

The road leading to Pensacola is thought to be The "Old Trail Blazed by Jackson's troops on his expedition to Pensacola, 1814, and took the name of "Three Notch" because troops passing through the forests, cut three notches on the trees at intervals that troops following them might have less trouble following the trail.

The point on this road where it touches Barbour County's original boundary, was near the site of "Three Notch" station on the Central of Ga. Railroad, between Midway and Union Springs.

The territory placed in Barbour County in 1832, lay partly in the already existing County of Pike, but more largely in that area lately ceded by the Indian tribes that dwelt in the section reaching from the river below Eufaula, to Columbus, Georgia.

It is a fact that Jackson's army passed up through Georgia, crossing the Chattahoochee river above Eufaula near Jernegan, and that on the trees in Clay, Randolph and Stewart Counties, Georgia, through which he passed, have "Three Notches, carved on them also, as a guide mark all along his route of march.

MAPS

At the Probate Office at Clayton, Barbour County, there are two most interesting Plat Books. I Vol. of 33 pages 17X14¼. A Township Plan of Plats of Barbour County.

Pinned to the first page of Vol. I, is the following telegram and letter:

"Montgomery, Alabama, April 22nd, 1869. B. B. Fields, Eufaula, Alabam, 12-25 P. M. Maps sent you ordered of Judge H. C. Russell. Price $107."

M. P. BLUE.
"Montgomery, Alabama,
April 23, 1869.

B. B. Fields, Esquire,
Eufaula, Alabama.

"Sir:

Under date of April 15th, Judge H. C. Russell of Clayton, Alabama, gave me order for Township maps of Barbour County, as required by section 95 of the Revenue Sa.

He requested me to send the book by express to you, which I have done. I telegraphed you yesterday, in which I stated the price of One Hundred and Seven, Dollars. Hoping the book will come safely to hand and prove satisfactory.

                Yours very respectfully,

                      M. P. BLUE, Sec'y of Grants.

Second Volume is 24 pages of Plats of Barbour. Both are heavy linen paper coated sheets bound in cloth.

FORT MITCHELL

Fort Mitchell is located on the Columbus, Georgia and Eufaula, Alabama, highway, 10 miles south of Columbus. From 1811 to 1837 it was a military establishment; and a United States Military Cemetery was located there. From 1805 to 1836, an Indian agency site and celebrated dueling ground. The remains of the Fort are still evident. In the Federal road at the Chattahoochee river crossing, is the site of the rendezvous of Confederate Soldiers of 1861. It is the site of a Celebrated Ball Ground play-ground of Indians in early historic days. The starting point for side trips to 18 Lower Creek Indian villages within 30 minutes auto drive. It is two miles from Coweta, the largest town of historic record in North America. Many visitors go to Fort Mitchell also Fort Benning, Georgia, and to Seale, Ala., the County seat of Russell County. Seale is a typical country town, and was formerly in Barbour County.

Chapter Four
Bridges Across Chattahoochee River

OLD AND NEW

There have been conflicting records as to the year the first bridge across the Chattahoochee river at Eufaula was built. Some records showing that a wooden bridge over the river at this point, was washed away previous to 1845, but this is an error, as the grandchildren of one ofthe four white men who first settled the town have in their possession payrolls for work done on the building of the bridge in 1837 and records show that, in 1840, there was a freshet known as the "Harrison Freshet," when steam boats passed around the bridge on the Georgia side, all the lowland on the Georgia side, being inundated by the overflowed river. The bridge was built in 1837, at a cost of $20,000.00, and was financed by Mr. Edward B. Young, President of the Gyrwinton Bridge Bank, the name of Eufaula having been changed to "Irwinton" to secure the influence of Senator William Irwin of Henry County, in getting steamboats to land at this point.

Old diaries show that Mr. Young owned the bridge ex-

Old Wooden Wagon Bridge

clusively at one time. He sold it to the city of Eufaula in 1845.

There was a town of the same name in Georgia, and on more than one occasion packages of money intended for Mr. Young's bank had been sent to the Georgia town of Irwinton. At that time there were more than twelve thousand negro slaves in Barbour County. Several hundred of them worked on building the bridge.

During the first years, it was a toll bridge, and the first bridgekeeper was Lochlan McLean (who held the position until early in the seventies). His daughter, Miss Lee Ellen McLean, when her mother, Mrs. Mary Lee McLean (daughter of Floyd Lee, first settler), died in the early 1900s, carried her remains to Crystal Springs, Miss., and has since resided there, where she inherited from her uncle, Quintillian Lee, one of the finest old mansions and plantations in Hindes County, Miss., to which place many of the Lee and Williams, of Barbour County family descendants, moved after the war between the states. The second Bridge-keeper was Jason Cleghorn. Following him came John Vaughn, who for many years was also sexton at the cemetery, and after his death his son, George Vaughan. After his death about 15 years ago, a special bridge keeper employed by the city, was discontinued and it was looked after by the wharf agent, Mr. J. N. Owens, employed by W. C. Bradley of Columbus, owner of the wharf for many years. It now belongs to the city, and there is no need for a keeper of the new steel bridge. The wharf was abandoned when steamboat traffic ceased.

During all the long years the "bridge keepers" resided in a little cottage at the approach to the bridge, at the foot of the hill on the Alabama side. Whenever the river reached high water mark, (as it usually does in the Spring) in the long ago, the steamboats had to tie up just below the wharf, because they could not pass under the old wooden bridge, even with their smoke stacks lowered.

Several times, one particularlly remembered, was in April, 1886, when the river was so high that boys in batteaux, could reach their hands through the cracks between the planks in the bridge floor and touch water.

In those old days between the seventies and eighties, during the cotton season, a line of heavily loaded wagons filled the bridge every day, coming to Eufaula, bringing cotton and going back. They carried merchandise bought with the money the cotton brought.

While the new bridge was in course of construction a Ferry (and a very unsatisfactory one) was used and the Georgia cotton was brought across the river (without cost) by the Central of Georgia Ry. Co.

When the old bridge began to show signs of being unsafe (after repeated repairs) Charles S. McDowell at that time Mayor of Eufaula, first conceived the idea of a new steel and concrete bridge; and in his mind, formulated a plan that he, after more than ten years, ultimately succeeded, against many odds.

When he was state Senator, he took up the matter with the Federal Government in putting it over and the result was, the state of Georgia, the state of Alabama and the Government each appropriated $12,500.00, but the expense went over those figures and the original amount was added to, until it reached $125,000.00. It was a gigantic task that Mr. McDowell undertook, and his labors, ultimately crowned with success, were unceasing and the great bridge, so fittingly named for him, is a lasting monument, to his interest in, and work for, his home town, county and state. When he was State Senator he introduced this bill, and against much opposition he put it over, and the stoy of the way he met and overcame this opposition being unique and interesting and filled with touches of humor. The new bridge was built several feet higher than the old one so that steam boats could pass under without even lowering the smoke stacks, but alas! The day of the steamboat has long since passed. There are hopes for a renewal of the river traffic, through the efforts now being made by 'The Chattahoochee Valley Association" to deepen the channel, build locks and resume boats to Apalachicola Bay and Port St. Joe, as a means of cheaper rates of freight transportation to Gulf ports of export and import.

This bridge is entirely of steel and concrete with concrete banisters and floor. On the Georgia side, the approach has been filled in to a gradual slope coming upto the long abuttment. The old piers were used, but were reinforced with many thicknesses of concrete. The entire bridge stands out maejstically, as a great piece of engineering and skilled workmanship.

The old "plank road" around the hill to the approach, on the Alabama side was paved by the Alabama Highway Company and the great "Jefferson Davis Highway", Washington, D. C. to New Orleans, crosses this bridge.

THE OLD WAGON BRIDGE AT EUFAULA

They are soon to tear it away,
    The old covered wagon bridge,
That has stood for many a day
    Across Eufaula and Georgetown's Chattahoochee ridge.

Over its time battered boards,
    Has rolled as the years have passed,

Georgia's harvests, in heavy loads,
   Going, sometimes slow and sometimes fast.

Around its colossal, ancient square piers,
   The muddy waters swiftly flow along.
And to cross it now, gives fears,
   Where oftentimes there was a song.

On the lips of those who gaily
   Rode over the river, to town
And carried back with them daily
   Their pay for peck and pound.

When the Spring floods have come
   And the roaring stream spread wide,
The old bridge has stood, like some
   Sentinel stationed above a danger tide.

To caution, direct and carry safe over
   By night and by day
Those who pass under its cover
   Be they life's December or May.

The oxen, the horse, the mule
   Have crossed, in creep, trot and run,
To saddest and jolliest tune
   And carried feather weight and ton.

Lovers, many, have stolen across it
   And were joined in wedlock,
Whether or not they were fit,
   Tomeet Life's every knock.

Slowly, funeral processions have rolled
   Over, carrying dear, beloved, dead,
While the old time bells tolled
   And Life's bitterest tears were shed.

Immigrants, in frame and covered wagons,
   Have trailed across it seeking places better
And here have gathered wagon tag ons
   Indian dogs, hound and setter.

Smoke stacks of steam boats, passing under,
   Have scraped its time worn floor,
When the Spring rains and thunder,
   Made the Chattahoochee rise and roar.

From its windows, latticed and cross-beamed,
   The lights by faithful George Vaugn tended
Far up and down the river gleamed,
   And by their glow, fisherman nets he mended.

It spans a curve under the bluff,
    Where the current is swift and rushes
Round the water stained piers rapid enough
    To sweep under, whatever its treachery clutches.

Time, decay and lumber trucks,
    Have made the old wooden bridge unsafe,
And despite the deep water sucks
    And the much money it takes,

A new bridge of cement and steel,
    Will take the old one's place,
And the fear we now feel
    As we ride across at snail pace

Will vanish like a morning cloud,
    As we fly in Packard or Fliver
So care free, happy and proud,
    With no trembling, no haulting or quiver.

It looks like a grey ribbon, stretched
    Over a moving bed of molten gold,
And fastened where, Spring has fetched,
    The green of Winter's cold—

To the end of the old "Plank Road"
    On the Alabama side, around the hill,
And to where you see many a "Ford,"
    As their occupants every day ride,

To and from the most historic city
    In Alabama or Georgia, no one will deny—
Over the old Bridge to which, it's a pity
    We'll soon, have to say goodbye.

                                M. T. T.

THE NEW McDOWELL BRIDGE AT EUFAULA

They've torn the old historic bridge away,
    And the new one has taken its place.
It's steele and cement, forever will stay,
    As the travel of time, it will face.

It majestically spans the Chattahoochee, high
    Up over the swiftly rolling stream,
And is the riveted and fastened tie,
    That holds the realization of a dream.

All our citizens well knew
    Would hold together two great states,
For a mutual interest, that not a few,
    But many could foster, despite the Fates.

A plan was figured out the money to get,
    And kept working until 'twas assured,
And when pessimists would fume and fret,
    Some smiled when other demured.

As Eufaula always does, she won,
    And the bridge is finished sure.
Thanks to Alabama's patriotic son,
    So able, so loyal and so true.

The old "Plank Road" too, is gone,
    And around the hill, its paved,
Complete, and travelers forlorn
    From the old road peril are saved.

The great girders that tower high,
    Swing out over head,
And the cement banisters, if you try
    To look over, hold you like lead.

Every fitted piece is modern plan,
    And skilled engineering put it there,
And as the laborers, every man
    Toiled faithfully, with no time to spare—

The power behind the enterprise
    Worked equally as hard against, funds diminished—
So it is no great surprise,
    That the bridge at last, is finished.

It is built many feet higher,
    From the water than the other,
So that steam boats, heavy and lighter,
    May pass under, without trouble further.

From the Bluff, Eufaula views it
    With pride, and as we celebrate
Has found it singularly fit
    To in these linves, just Elaborate—

By telling you that—"We needed it,"
    And "'twas gotten for us,"
And we can calmly, peacefully sit,
    As we ride across, without any fuss—

And rejoice in our past glory—
    Our present prosperity, that is yet
To be put into the long story
    History will tell of what we get.

                              M. T. T.

CHATTAHOOCHEE RIVER AND ITS TRAFFIC

The fact that the first thing conceived by the early settlers of Eufaula to promote their interests and advancement was steamboat service is significant, and from those days until 1922 the river has played a most important part in the business and social life of the city and citizens. General Irwin, whose name the city bore inthe thirties, years after, carried a boat load of cotton from his Henry county plantation to Columbus, sold it, and with the money in gold and silver, on his person was on board the steamer "Mary" enroute home and when the boat caught fire, he lashed the bag of money to his body and attempted to swim ashore, but the weight of it carried him down and he was drowned.

In October, 1865, Capt. Wingate, a resident of Eufaula, living at the old Wingate home on Eufaula Street, had just brought to this river a very fine steamboat, the "Alice," which on a down trip struck a snag tearing a hole in her hull. Capt. Wingate rushed below with pillows and blankets to stop the hold and never returned. His body was recovered afterward and he is buried in Fairview cemetery. His son, Mr. Charles Wingate, spent his life on this river. His daughters were belles in Eufaula society in the seventies and now live in neighboring cities. April 11th, 1883, the steamer "Geo. W. Wiley," struck the bridge at Ft. Gaines, when the river was very high, went to pieces and sank, all in thirty minutes. About one dozen persons were drowned. Among them Mr. Geo. Palmer, of Columbus, purser, and Mr. W. J. Rivers, second clerk, son of Rev. R. H. Rivers at that time pastor of the First Methodist church of Eufaula. When the boat was sinking he called out to a deck hand, 'Fouser," he knew well: "Save me, Fouser, for my wife and seven children's sake," but both went down and Mr. Rivers' body was later found, brought here and buried in the Eufaula cemetery.

One April 2nd, 1884, the "Rebecca Everingham" was burned to the waters edge at Fitzgeralds landing, above Florence, Ga., young Frank Lapham, a striker pilot, at the wheel with his father, proved himself a hero by jumping over board with a line, swimming to shore and "making fast" the burning boat. Several lives were lost, among them, Mr. J. C. Hightower, father of Mrs. N. Shelby, who ran back to his stateroom for something and perished in the flames. His charred body was never found.

The steamboat which all have perhaps been most familiar with the most interested in recent years, was the "Amos Hays." She was built at Jeffersonville, Ind., in 1883, under the personal supervision of Capt. T. A. Marcrum, familiarly called by his legions of friends "Capt. Bose," who was her largest stockholder, and master. Several Eufaulians also owned shares of her stock and she was a favorite with Eufaula shippers and Eufaula steamboat travelers. Very memorable to some are the "pleasure party trips," to the bay, on the "Hays." On her maiden trip up the river in August, 1883, her peculiar whistle broke up a negro camp meeting. A few miles below Columbia, Ala., on the Georgia side. This camp meeting was in full progress when the Hays blew to land at Columbia. It was a long trembling wierd sound, similar to the notes of a "caliope," and as the sounds drew nearer the camp ground, there was consternation, and the worshippers fled in double quick time, exclaiming, "A Wild panter" (panther) is after us." It was just daylight when it blew first for Eufaula and some of our citizens thought a circus had come to town unannounced. This whistle created too many sensations and Capt. "Bose" sold it to the steam tug "Lottie," at Apalachicola, Fla.

The most elegant steamboat ever on this river, was the Chattahoochee, owned by the "People's Line" at that time, 1880, called the "Plant Line." She was too large and handsome for our river and the "Plant System" transferred her to the St. Johns river.

But, to the traffic. In the days when Henry C. Hart was captain on the boats, thousands of bales of cotton were shipped to New Orleans and Savannah via Apalachicola. From 1870 to 1875 there was a through water rate from New Orleans and Mobile to Eufaula. The cotton rate was $1.50 per bale, Eufaula to Apalachicola. Capt. John O. Martin owned the wharf and Mr. T. E. Callen was the capable, accommodating and every way efficient agent from May 20th, 1870, to January 7, 1903, a period of 33 years. He has often been asked of late years "what was the old brick warehouse under the hill built for" but there are many who remember to have often seen it overflowing with freight in the seventies and eighties. Before Woods flour mills burnd July, 1884, there was often five and six hundred barrels of flour on the wharf at one time for shipment. Much cotton as late as 1885 was shipped to New York and Liverpool, by boat via Bainbridge, to Fernindenia, Fla. Tullis & Co., shipped thousands of bales up to Columbus to the Eagle and Pheonix Mills, this cotton being a special high grade for very fine cloth.

Merchants at Clayton, Ozark and Abbeville received New York and New Orleans, freight via Eufaula by boat, and it was stored in the old brick warehouse until the long train of wagons from these points (before the railroad was built) hauled it out. Every iron rail of the road from Eufaula to Clayton,, built in 1871 was received over Eufaula wharf from boat, shipped via Apalachicola.

Mr. Callen says he has often had fifteen hundred barrels and boxes of transfer freight on the wharf at one time.

The heavy business of his flour mills made it to Mr. R. J. Wood's interest to own the wharf and he purchased it from Mr. Martin about 1874 or 1875. Mr. Woods sol dit to Mr. F. W. Jennings and in 1890 Mr. Henry C. Holleman purchased it from Mr. Jennings.

The Alabama Midland railroad and other roads also tapping the river below Eufaula, killed the transfer business, and the compress here, virtually carrying the cotton to Savannah, cripped the river traffic.

In 1903 Mr. Holleman sold the wharf to Mr. W. C. Bradley, of Columbus, president of the Eufaula Grocery Co., and it is a significant fact that Mr. Bradley's interests along the river and at Columbus and Eufaula is a very strong factor in keeping active the river business. When Mr. Bradley bought the wharf, Mr. J. N. Owens, of Columbus, succeeded Mr. Callen as agent.

In 1922, traffic on the Chattahoochee river was abandoned. The old historic wharf torn away and the old days of "excursions to the Bay" and the freight and passenger traffic on two and sometimes three boats to Columbus and Apalachicola Bay each week, became only a glorious memory. Late years however, a project has been started, and has gained great headway, to secure an appropriation from the Government to Canalize the Chattahoochee and again have small passenger boats and great freight barges again opennig up a river trade. The Chattahoochee Valley Associaation is at the head of this Canalization, and opening up the Chattahoochee River is its prime object, beingto open a direct waterway freight service to foreign ports, from Atlanta and surrounding territory to deep water at Apalachicola and Port St. Joseph, Florida.

Barbour County citizens are actively aiding this project, which, if successfully brought about, will be the realization of the prophesy of the late Capt. T. A. "Bose" Marcrum, the most prominent and notable Steamboat Captain and financier that ever plied the Chattahoochee river.

The second object of the Chattahoochee Valley Association, is to build up and reestablish the farm and industrial interests along this river valley, hoping to restore the many fine farms that have been abandoned along the river banks.

Chapter Five

Barbour County's Great Men

Barbour County Statesmen of the past
Brave and true, are pinned high
On the wall of fame to last
As generations live and die.

John Gill Shorter was the Alabama War Governor, whose record as statesman has shone down the years, and his home was Barbour County. His diplomacy and forethought in those troublesome days, marked him great.

Augustus Holmes Alston was Judge of Probate of the County during the important days and years of rebuilding and the records show that his wisdom, tact and ability wrought great things, marking his administration and his labors, as possibly the most important of any man, who ever held office in the state.

A strict and careful investigation of every matter that came up, was always made by him personally, before acting upon its merits and otherwise in Barbour County, the race problem was most serious and it was no easy matter to handle the changing conditions, back from the reconstruction period, but Barbour County's great men DID handle it, in the face of blood and fire and her leaders, not once falling back, in their march forward, out of oppression and strife, into peaceful and law abiding success—but have written their own glory in acts of bravery and self sacrifice. See Biographies.

When the delegation to the Secession Convention in Montgomery were elected January 1, 1861, Alpheus Baker of Barbour County, was one of that number and his memorable addresses at the presentation of the Flag of the Confederacy, by Mrs. L. C. Tyler, March 4, 1861, was called a "masterpiece of brains and oratory." See biography.

The first Regiment of Alabama Infantry, that went to the front was commanded by Col. Henry D. Clayton of Barbour County.

The Governor of the State of Alabama, who is recorded the "State's greatest financial Governor" was William Dorsey Jelks of Barbour County, leaving more money in the state Treasury than any other Governor.

The greatest all-round business man, who was a success

[46]

to the letter as Governor of the State was Braxton Bragg Comer from Barbour County.

The man who occupied one of the highest places in the United States Senate for 25 years and was also notable as jurist, was James L. Pugh from Barbour County.

Governor William Calvin Oates, whose career as Governor of Alabama, was notable, was not a native of Barbour County, but was a resident of Barbour County when elected Governor, although originally from Henry County.

S. Hugh Dent, sixteen years in United States Congress from Montgomery County, was born and lived until middle age in Barbour County as did two young congressmen, from Florida, who were his schoolmates at Eufaula, the three serving in Congress at the same time. The other two were, Frank Clark, and Walter Kehoe. They met again together at the Celebration of Eufaula's One hundredth birthday, Home Coming in 1923.

Barbour County is very proud of these three Eufaulians.

Reuben F. Kolb, whose friends claim he was legally elected to the Governorship of Alabama, on the Populite platform and ticket, but counted out, was born in Barbour County and spent nearly all his life in the County, before moving late in life to Montgomery.

Charles S. McDowell, Jr., Lieut. Gov. of Alabama, and defeated for Governor in a campaign which outvoted him, by an unexpected vote, that is claimed was lax in Democracy, in its last minute to win, policies, overthrowing McDowell's, to the letter, Democratic platform.

Henry D. Clayton, Jr.,'s, long years as Congressman from the third Judicial Circuit, which includes Barbour, and later Federal Judge, was of Barbour County, bred and born.

Henry B. Steagall, that mighty power in Congress, one of the greatest Democratic forces of the hour, is Congressman from the Third Judicial Circuit, and is not Barbour born, but Barbour County claims him for her own by right of many things, chiefly personal friendship, and the pride that Barbour is a part of the District, that is served by so great a Democrat and brilliant and outstanding man of the day and hour.

Alto Vela Lee, that determined, forceful legal light, that made him not only a great lawyer and a prosecuting attorney, who always proved to the juries, he argued before, that "there were three things ,the Lord Himself did not know, viz.: the will of a woman"—"which side of a question would be popular," and "the verdict of a petty jury"—and he nearly always won. He was of "the grand old State of Barbour."

Barbour County's two Supreme Court Judges, A. A. Evans and E. Perry Thomas, knew the law like they did their own names, and were valuable citizens from Barbour County.

Captain A. S. Daggett, born in Washington, 1835, at his death, 1937, was said to be the oldest Army officer Veteran of the War Between the States.

He was in command of Company U Soldiers, stationed in Barbour County and the time of Reconstruction troubles of 1874. Brigadier General A. S. Daggett, owes his office as Brigadier General to Dr. Zadoc Daniel who was a Barbour County boy, in the sixties.

One day Captain Daggett mentioned that he contemplated quitting the service. Young Daniel replied, "You are a born Soldier, stand by the Army and you'll come out a Brigadier General some day. The prediction came true.

Dr. Zadoc Daniel married Laura, the daughter of Elias Kiels, another daughter, Alice, married a man named McNair.

BARBOUR COUNTY ACCLAIMED GREAT

It was at a memorable political meeting in North Alabama, many years ago, that a distinguished speaker from that section of the state, in the course of a speech, that was very notable. said: "Alabama is divided into three distinct parts, North North Alabama, South Alabama and Barbour County," and wound up his speech by adding—"When the Indians were sent from that section to the Government Reservation in Indian Territory (Now Oklahoma) that place was named Eufaula, Indian Territory, because the Indians sent there came from Eufaula, Alabama. Barbour is rich in her personal history, having given more illustrious men and women to the limelight of Politics, Literature, Music, Education, Philanthropy, to the Ministry, than any other county in all the South, including Governors, Senators and several Congressmen.

Some of the writers of Barbour County have reached the very highest in their line. Eufaula is an old beautiful, cultured city, sacred to the descendants of the men who were the first settlers.

Clayton, Alabama, also in Barbour County, shares alike in this glory of having produced great men and women.

Chapter Six

Indians In Barbour County

> The Indian brave with bow in hand
> And Arrow set, to swiftly fly,
> Resented the white man on his land,
> And often raised the "War Cry."

The Indian well deserves his name of warrior. Generally he prizes and values his honor, and the historical records show that most of the Indian chiefs have been honorable and full of valor.

From infancy, however, he has been taught that war was a business, and that he was born to be a victorious fighter.

He gloried in his forests and growing fields; was brave, but full of craftiness and strategy, but really never a thief, or dishonest, in a legitimate deal.

To him, war was serious and he prepared for it every day and hour of his life by dancing, drinking, what the Indians called "black drink," and by (religion to him) consulting the "Great Spirit."

He painted himself and bedecked his body, with feathers and bright emblems to make themselves look like the devils they were supposed to imitate, when fighting.

The warriors, thought more of fighting than working, and for a livelihood chose to hunt and fish, while the squaws stayed at home, tilled the soil and did the real work of the tribe, each doing their bit, not measured, but whatever they chose to do.

As husbands, and wives, generally, they were true to their mates and it was seldom that domestic trouble ever arose over unfaithfulness.

The Indians were revengeful, and never forgot an injury. They were fleet on foot, sneaking, but not liars.

They knew nothing of whiskey until the white man came among them, and, unfortunately, in some settlements there were a few of the low class whites, who bartered with the Indians and, giving them poor whiskey and imitating the white man, the "Fire Water" as they called it, wrought havoc among them for both Indians and whites.

Another unfortunate fact was that low class whites began intimate associations with the Indians.

When Andrew Jackson was elected President of the United States, about one fourth of the territory of Alabama was controlled (nominally) belonged to) the Indians: Cherokees, Chickasaws, Choctaws, Uchees, and Creeks, and the settlers had long wearied of living among them and of their dominations; and when there had been an inflow of over an hundred thousand people, by 1830, the lands these Indians held had become necessary to the whites and a demand was made: that the Indians be removed and Treaties of "Dancing Rabbit" (Creek, 1830; Cusseta 1832; and Echota, 1835) by which these Indains ceded their lands to the whites were made.

The question of the state vs. the Federal Government was the outcome of the Creek Cusseta Treaty, and there was grave controversy.

The settlers on Creek lands disregarded articles of the Treaty and many thousand settlers from other parts of Alabama flocked in.

So tense was the situation, in 1832 the United States Marshall, with troops from Fort Mitchell in Barbour County (Now Russel County) attempted to drive the settlers out and thereby created a very serious crisis. Congress was appealed to and protests made to the War Department. The question was whether or not thees lands had been purposely selected for the Indians—and white settlers were about to be moved off in a given time.

The County adjoining Barbour County (then not created) had white settlers living on lands claimed by Indians, and this enboldened others to homestead. And it was December, 1832, with these conditions existing, then "the state exerted its right over this territory (despite the Federal Government's claim) by creating nine new Counties of which Barbour County was one, which gave them legal right to negotiate Treaty with the Indians, which was done. "Some of the settlers were so lawless and so notorious that they had to be ejected, and one, Hardeman Owens, an official of Russell County (one of the Counties in the Creek Territory (then Barbour) and who was an outlaw and desperado among the Indians" (so said the Charleston Courier) "he refused to leave, and was kiled by troops sent to guard over him." This was one of the severe acts of these troops stationed at Fort Mitchell that created great exxcitement all over the state.

Gov. Gale was criticized for the state of things in Russell County (then Barbour) but he took a bold stand for states' rights.

When the State and Military Government heads clashed, and when the Federal Commandant at Fort Mitchell refused to turn over to the Sheriff of Russell County soldiers and officers indicted for the murder of Owens Gale was forced to send the details of the case to the War Department, and finally for consideration to President Jackson.

Gov. Gale, anxious to maintain peace, had early left orders that local militia be organized in the new counties "and begged the people to keep calm, urging the settlers to look to the Law for protection, and refrain from violence against the Indians." But they would not be calm. Mass meetings were held and men volunteered to go to arms if needed.

By December, excitement, both in Alabama and at Washington, were rife and the Nation, believed to be on the verge of war.

It was rumored that troops at Fort Mitchell were being reinforced to uphold the treaty and legislators were preparing Resolutions "enddangering the good principles of the Governor and authorizing him to see that the laws and justification of the state, be maintained in full force and effect in the said Counties."

The political result of this Creek Indian controversy was to produce friction among the leaders of the Democratic party, and to weaken Jackson's influence in the state (t(hese facts are obtained from some old records at Clayton, Alabama, court house, and are verified by facts related in Moore's history of Alabama.)

But the breech was closed. Gov. Gale turned over to the Whig party, becoming a Wrig elector in the "Log Cabin" and "Hard Cider" campaign of 1840.

It was clearly shown that Jackson's loss of prestige in the state and the progress of States' Rights sentiment resulted from the growth of the state, and the Creek Indain controversy, and gave Democrats not a little trouble in the middle thirties. (See Moore's History of Alabama.)

At first the Indians were friendly in their association with the white settlers in the villages along the Chattahoochee, but gradually they began to resent the intrusion of the whites, after some missionaries and land agents from the New England states and who were in sympathy with the Indains—and an appeal was made to the Government at Washington, seeking some redress for what they claimed was persecution.

United States troops were sent and the section was put under Military control. In many cases, whites were ordered out of the community.

These homesteaders scattered about in different sections of what is now Barbour County.

After a term of terror, when there was a conflict, known as the Indian War, and in 1827, a treaty was arranged with the Government, permitting the whites to buy land from the

Indians, but the three tribes, the Uchees, the Creeks, and Cherokees with Tecumsee (Jim Henry) and Tustunneegee chiefs again went on the warpath. From 1827 to 1835 the settlement went through, struggling from those early days, on through the years until 1846 and finally developed a real settlement of Barbour County in the face of innumerable hardships of living among Indians.

Chief Tustenuggee was their friend until the Creek war broke out in 1837, when there were days and months when the women and children had to be placed in a stockade which had been hastily and crudely built, and this reign of terror was not over for them until a second military detachment was sent for their protection.

Finally, the three chiefs, in a council of war against each other, made Tustenuggee, the Creek Chief known as "Billy Bow Legs," leader of the Clan that for a long time had been friendly to most of the whites.

These three notable warriors were honorable and honest, although ehere were many petty thieves (which was not always the case) among the majority of the Indians among these tribes, each of which spoke a different dialect. After the treaty of 1832 when war had broken out again, most of the whites along the west of the Chattahoochee went further west in the County.

About this time John Linguard Hunter from South Carolina had come to the County and was largely influential in having the Indains removed to the Indain Territory now Oklahoma.

Although sparsely settled until 1827, the town of Clayton rapidly progressed. As seen by the Deed, page xxxx the land it was built on was originally owned by Daniel Lewis, one of the original Louisvile settlers, and sold to the Commissioners by Eliott and John D. Thomas, who owned it at the time of sale, for a town site.

An early settler of Clayton was Captain S. Porter, an Indian trader. One of his daughters married Chillie McIntosh, son of General William McIntosh, the famous Creek Indian chief. When the Indians were moved to Indian Territory Reservation, Captain Porter and family accompanied them. Just a few years ago his grandson visited Barbour County.

The Porter property was purchased by members of the Fenn family at Clayton. Calvin Fenn, prominent Clayton citizen, was the great grandson of Mark Williams, one of the first settlers of the county at the village of Eufaula.

In 1838-39 a railroad was constructed from Iola, Florida, (58 miles) to St. Joseph on St. Joseph's Bay. A Mr. John Fountaine of Columbus, Georgia, was president of this road, which was built by his negro slaves. The object of its building was to reach deep water, whereby ships could come up to the docks. As it was, tugs and rafts had to convey from Appalachicola to deep water in East Pass.

This Road was successful mainly through the influence and efforts of Mr. Hunter who also had been the leading factor in the Indian movement matter. His grandson, John Linguard Hunter Hoole, son of Bertram and Viola Hunter Hoole, was one of the outstanding lieutenants of the Confederate Army, and his family has figured in all the later history of the County. The general names of all the creeks and rivers in the Chattahoochee Valley were given them by the whites, on account of their domiciles along the various rivers and creeks in Southeast Alabama, and NOT by the Indians, as has been claimed.

Some of these beautiful names were Cowikee, Okonee, Oketee, U-Fal-Ah, Chewalla, Choctahachee, Weelawnee. Jernegan was named for William Jernegan, a soldier among the troops, who crossed the Chattahoochee river in 1836, near the present McDowell bridge(which supplanted the old covered wagon bridge, famous in song and story.) He was stationed as a sentinel a short distance from the Chewalla creek—saw a flock of 35 deer rise from out of the bramble and run loping off. Venison was a staple diet and was dried and preserved in those days. After the troops captured the Indians and their chief, Tustenuggee (Billie Bow Legs) he, the chief, stated that he was watching from the top of a poplar tree, at the creek and demanded the venison he claimed the soldiers had stolen, claiming the deer as Indian property.

It is said that the scene on the ships at anchor at Apalachicola, with their cargo of Indians from Barbour County, was pathetic. The savages were awed at the spread sails, and uttered doleful lamentations, fearing they were being taken on the "big waters" to be drowned

After the removal of the Creek Indains, the development was as if by magic. (They were carried via New Orleans.)

INDIAN TRAILS AND MOUNDS

Many Indain villages, sites and Indain mounds in Barbour County still survive, giving evidence of the life previous to the white settlement.

Along the banks of the Chattahoochee river and its tributary streams, were the Lower Creek Indians, and the records of the County show much of the troubles of the whites with these Indians in 1836.

At a little Indian town, three miles northeast of Eufaula at "St. Frances" the people were armed, all work suspended and the women and children kept in the stockade.

This stockade was built on what is now Randolph street, on the lot afterwards owned for many years by Anthony and later Edward Stow.

An authentic story is told of how an 11-year-old boy, following his mother, who was fleeing with her small boy in her arms—was almost in the grasp of the Indian pursuing her—as she ran across a deep ravine (just below where the Compress now is) in an effort to reach the stockade. Close behind her the boy picked up a large rock, threw it directly at the Indian, felling him into the ravine and the mother and children, just did have tmie to reach the stockade and rush in before the Indains caught up with them.

At this old St. Francis site, there are numerous mounds, which have been evacuated and many relics secured.

On the Shorter river plantation, three miles from Eufaula, there were four mounds, from which Eli S. Shorter, Jon C. Thomas and J. H. G. Martin, as young lads, in the early fifties, dug out hundreds of arrows, flints, rocks and bushel sacks full of marbles of every conceivable kind, and it was the delight of these three boys; and also after they became men with families, to spend Sunday afternoons, strolling over the old grounds, all three of them students of Indian Lore.

Some of the valuable books they were wont to present each other in later life are still in the possession of this writer.

In the lower part of the County along the creeks are also many mounds. Along a trail that led from Uchee Shoals in Russel County near Columbus, Georgia, down the river, near Baker Hill, fifteen mies below Eufaula and 11 miles from Eufaula on the Clayton road is the remains of mounds at the Indian village "Boak," where a sick Indian saved the life of several whites because, he said, "The Great Spirit said I get well, if I no kill white man." Between Louisville and Hobby's Mill at the "Capel place," two miles east of Pratt's station, and at the Norton place, near Clayton, there are the remains of many mounds.

When the Indians were being collected by Government soldiers, to be carried to the boat to carry them down the river to Appalachicola, Florida, and from there to the Reservations, a young Indian girl was dropped by the squaw carrying her n her back, and she was found on the hillside, where the Indians had filed down to the wharf to embark.

She was taken in and cared for by a family named Robinson, who named her Ailsie. She grew up, married a negro, reared a large family and was for a lifetime a competent and worthy servant a nurse employed by the best families.

Her modest but picturesque home on Randolph street, built in the white resident section, being deeded to her by Mrs.

Robinson, who reared her. Her descendants are now respected colored citizens of the County.

THE CALL OF BLOOD

It is a sequel to fact ,that in 1876, when a tribe of wandering Indians did come back to this section and pitched their tepees in ' Bell's Grove" and among them were several of those sent to Indian Territory long years before who had come back to visit their old hunting grounds and that is how the Call of Blood was written for it is a true story.

It was a damp, cloudy day in early February, when a heavy mist hung over the Chattahoochee river, where it divides the states of Georgia and Alabama—and as a crude canoe drifted down the stream to a band where a big creek (Chewalla) empties into the river the four men who sat in the canoe, letting their paddles drag, in the water, Mark Willams suddenly cried out "look" as he spied the great bluff towering high above the clear water (now muddy red, from long years of cultivation of the land through which it flows)—that reflected the mossy banks and bare limbs of the trees that grew from under the bluff.

In the boat with Mark Williams were John DeLochiou Thomas, hero of the War of 1812 at New Orleans under General Coffee, a veteran of the war of 1812, William Ledbetter, Floyd Lee and the speaker's young son, Floyd Williams.

These men were enroute to Marianna, Florida, having journeyed from South Carolina.

As they looked on the high bluff, a desire to explore above it seized them and soon the canoe was run ashore and landed and the party climbed the bluff, to find a beautiful level plateau and a number of Indian tepees. The Indains greeted them kindly, but shyly. The result of this landing was that, three weeks later, the families of these men were brought from their immigrant camp, eight miles up the river on the Georgia side, and building of homes began, the former plan to go to Florida, having been abandoned.

A year went by, the association between the Indians was peaceable but not intimate.

One day several of the settlers sat outside the door of their newly built cabins—a young Indian girl strolled to the edge of the high bluff, and as she stood looking far off at the Georgia forest across the river that stretched to the eastern horizon, Ogo, a young Indain brave, rushed up to her, and snatching her from the slippery edge of the bluff, exclaimed "U-Fall-Ah." He had learned some words of the white man's language during the months he had listened to their talk. To him the girl was "you"—U—He had caught the meaning of "fall" and as the Indian always annexes "AH" to every exclamation, he gave utterance to a word that caught the ears of the whites and its euphony, appealed to them so much that right then and there, at the suggestion of John DeLochiou Thomas, the settlement was named Eufaula.

Not far away Floyd Williams, the young son of the first settler stood—and the beauty and grace of the Indian maiden so attracted his attention that for days he hung around her father's tepee, until one morning as she was carring faggots to light a fire under the great rocks that held the savory venison being roasted by the Indain women—he boldlyy approached and taking them from her said, "Let me help you." She looked shyly at him, blushed and handed the pieces to him. That was the beginning of our story. Never was there sweeter wooing—every evening brought him to her side—down by the spring, under the bluff, they sat together. He taught her his language, and she taught him hers. Her name was "Star Eye" and the light that shone in the limped depths of her eyes was very like unto, the bewitching starlight that is ever "the Light O' Love."

The day that Ogo had snatched her from the danger of falling over the bluff and the village had been named "Eufaula" the settlers had named her Eufaula, also.

Ogo had been her lover from youth, until Floyd Williams had taken her in his arms and said "Star Eye" you are mine" and she lifted her little brown hand to caress his cheek and nestled closer to him.

Behind the tall trees that grew near the mouth of the creeks where they had wandered and were so engrossed in their learning of "Love's Lesson," in all its fullness and sweetness that they failed to see Ogo as he stood with clinched hands and frowning face as he watched what showed him that Floyd had completely won "Star Eye," and the savage in him was thoroughly aroused and as he strode away into the forest, he planned in his heart diabolical revenge.

Spring time came. Floyd was busy chopping down trees to clear land his father was preparing to plant. Star Eye would slip away from the Indians and sit for hours watching him work.

The afternoon was waning and as the tree she was cutting fell to the ground ,one of the projecting limbs struck his shoulder, he reeled over insensible. When Star Eye saw that he was badly hurt she rushed wildly to the settlers' cabins for help. Ogo was secreted in the bush and was in the act of striking Floyd a deadly blow when Star Eye flew back and threw herself over Floyd as he lay prostrate. "Go, go," she cried. Ogo seized her roughly and said "I kill him, you take my Star Eye, I hate pale face. He take Star Eye away Ogo." By this time four of the white women arrived and helped lift Floyd and carry him to his father's cabin. Ogo enraged, sounded the war whoop and instantly the warriors gathered and began their war dance, full force. Star Eye fell down on her face before the Indian women feigning death. They threw a blanket over her and, leaving her, joined in the war dance. She lay there until she saw Floyd approaching.

After he had been revived by the white women, he had rushed in search of her—taking her by the hand he said, "Come," and they fled to the water's edge, soon unloosed the moored canoe, jumped in and rapidly rowed upstream toward Columbus, Georgia, Star Eye doing most of the paddling, as Floyd was too badly maimed to help much.

Night came on and by moonlight they hurried, fearful of being overtaken by the Indians on the war path. Daylight came and they kept on until late evening of the second day they landed—and leading the shrinking, frightened maiden by the hand, Floyd sought a Justice of the Peace. Curious crowds of passers-by stopped to see the Judge call in two witnesses. Very tenderly he drew her into his protecting arms, as the grey-haired old Judge pronounced them husband and wife.

Star Eye looked up into Floyd's face and said, "Star Eye go be white lady." Floyd was without even a hat and the strangely mated pair created a sensation, as they went hand in hand down Broad street.

In a confection store, near by, a kind-hearted clerk, who saw their plight, had given them lunch.

Floyd's uncle and aunt resided a few miles down the river, not far from the Georgia camp from which the South Carolina settlers had left when they moved to the village they named Eufaule—and it was mid afternoon the day they left the canoe again and wending their way through the woods to the old time "rail fence" that surrounded the cow pasture, they climbed over—Uncle Charlie, clothed in home-made overalls, was grinding his axe near the back door—Aunt Martha was "pipping" a hen on the door step when she spied the pair and cried out to her spouse, "Las honey, look, if it ain't Floyd and an Indian gal with him." The axe fell to the ground and the hen flew away, as the rustic old couple went to meet the younger ones. They greeted both cordially and Floyd tells them the story of their flight and the Eufaula settlement— their marriage and all the terrors of their escape.

Aunt Martha, who had been born with more than a balanced allowance of sentiment in her make-up, and who had been denied motherhood, found genuine joy in mothering the young Indian girl, and soon learned to love her very much.

Floyd was glad to accept Uncle Charles' offer to make him his farm foreman, and the year that followed was a very happy one for the four. Then one summer night, when the earth was wrapped in a dream of bliss—while the moon hung low and the mocking bird in the Cape Jasamine tree, trilled, until his throat almost bursted—"Star Eye" went drifting out across the bar and her spirit flew back to the mystic beginning —leaving Floyd's heart broken, with a tiny babe in his arms.

They called her "Star" for her mother and she grew to beautiful womanhood. At the old historic college on the high hill that overlooks the rolling Chattahoochee, she was educated and graduated with honors. Her classmates, Daisy, Laurie, Annie Laurie and Edna, loved her because she was the fairest among them.

Floyd Williams had succeeded financially and had, with his father, to whom he returned, built a lovely home on the bluff, near the spot where he first saw her mother, Star Eye, and his love for his daughter, whom he had reared without a mother's love and care, after Aunt Martha had been laid to beneath the tangle of honeysuckle vines—was the tenderest and deepest.

Twenty years had passed since her birth—the tribe of Indians to whom her mother belonged had long ago been sent to the U. S. Reservation in Indian Territory (now Oklahoma)—but one day as Star rocked on the porch of her home, an Indian Squaw, with a pappoose on her back, came in at the gate, and as she reached the steps, laid down her bundle of baskets and beads. Star was strangely interested in her and after buying a basket and string of beads, entered into conversation with her. She said, "I am of a wandering band of Indians camped about a mile from here in a grove where the high bluff ends and a broad field stretches from the grove to the river bank."

As Star and her father sat at dinner she said to him, "Father, I had a visitor this morning—an Indian woman with a little brown skinned baby tied to her back. She told me that there was an Indian camp in Bell's Grove." Won't you carry me there to see these strange people?"

Floyd's voice trembled and he was nervous and distraught as he falteringly said: "Indians are treacherous, filthy and dangerous. I would rather not take you to see them." Oh please do, father, she tearfully entreated. He had never denied her any request, and finally with great reluctance and sore misgivings, he consented. He was a busy man, but promised to carry her the next afternoon, which was Sunday.

"Star" was all eagerness to be off as soon as dinner was over. Despite his reluctance to carrying the daughter, whom he idolized, to see a race of people whom he dreaded to have her know anything of, he kept his promise to her and he could not shake off a strange eagerness that overtook him also, as he approached the camp.

Reaching there they found crowds of citizens whose curiosity had brought them to see the Indians—coming and going. While he stopped to pass a few words with a friend who greeted him, Star Eye crept near the edge of one of the tepees and suddenly a wrinkled old Indian woman took her by the hand, looked close into her eyes, exclaiming, "Mine Star Eye," and quickly drew her into the tepee.

Star was strangely drawn to this old woman, who hurridly told her the story of the Indan girl's marriage to Floyd Williams and said, "She was mine and you are my grand daughter." Peeping out of the tepee she saw Floyd as he talked to the white visitors and when she saw him start with fear when he found that Star was not beside him, she put her finger to her lips and said, "No tell him, come back here tonight. I will tell you all." Star answered, "Yes I'll come," and joined her father, merely saying, "How interesting the Indians are, father."

As they sat together in the twilight, she asked him numerous questions, some of which he answered, others which he evaded.

Next morning when he called at Star's door to awaken her, as was his usual custom, there was no response to his rap and opening the door he found that she was gone— Intuitively, he knew where. Rushing like mad to the camp, he found that the Indians had pulled down their tepees during the night and were far on their way. He knew that the "Call of Blood" had lured Star and that she had gone with the old grandmother, whom he had recognized.

Heart broken and humiliated, he sought the wandering band for months, found them hundreds of miles away, but Star and the old grandmother were not with them. The old woman had been shrewd enough to leave the other Indains and, by railway, had reached a hiding place in the Far West.

Time went on and she and Star joined another tribe and soon she became a teacher of Indian children. A young Missionary, William Ray, daily visited her at school and it was not long before her beauty and charm won his heart, and his integrity won hers. Often she told him of her girlhood home in the historic old town on the Chattahoochee river, that owed its existence to her grandparents both white and Indain. She wore the Indian dress now and she and her grandmother resided in a little cabin on the Indian Reservation. The trading post was not far away and one day, when an Indain boy brought some purchases from the Post, as she unwrapped the paper around them she read, "The Eufaula News," and her heart almost stopped beating, and she began eagerly reading. On the first page she saw, "Pioneer Citizen Dies.; Floyd Williams Buried in Old Family Cemetery Today Beside His Indian Wife."

She had saved the money the Government had paid her for teaching and she immediately took a train to carry her back to Alabama. When she stepped off the train that stopped on the Georgia side of the river near Georgetown, Georgia, the old carriage that had been the most elegant thing in the town happened to be at the station, and the old darky driver, Eugene recognized Star. Opening the carriage door he bade her step in. Quickly he drove her over the river to the old cemetery and she spent an hour kneeling beside the grave of her unknown mother and dearly beloved father.

The next day she returned to the West and soon after in a little chapel where William Ray preached, near her school, she gave her heart and hand to him in marriage.

Another year went by, the old grandmother passed on to the "happy hunting grounds" of her race—the Indian children were beginning to be taught in the schools of the whites and the waning of the needs emphasized another "Call of Blood," back to the white father's home and people—and the wedded pair came back to the old home on the bluff—the first residence (it still sands) that was built by Mark and Floyd Williams—and in the gathering twilight of many a summer evening passers along the bluff would see them sitting on the exact spot, where Ogo "snatched Star Eye from the edge of the bluff as she was about to fall.

Indian Chief Tustennuggee, known as Billy Bow Legs. was an Indian of superior ability. He was a born trader and when he reached Florida, it was said of him, "he sold many skins and pelts and was shrewd in his bargaining."

He was never accused of being in any way unfair and he demanded fair treatment from others.

He was quiet, dignified and eager to imitate the white man, in anything except attracting attention. It is related that despite the dispute, with the chief of another tribe in Barbour couny, when the argument was at its heat of the discussion was at its head he said, "I go," and with a look of disgust on his face, he walked out.

The Indain was not considered an exile.

Suspicious of the white man always, supposing that he wanted something from the Indian, he could never fully understand, however, what it was the white man wanted—and it is a noteworthy fact that the Indian, cruel as he was at times, it was solely because he believed that he had a grudge against the pale face, for taking the lands the Indian deemed were his own by right of first possession.

The Indian was not as, what we call a heathen, for he believed in the "Great Spirit" as directing the acts of man.

He was in a way superstitious, and he believed in all the traditions.

His religion was strict obedience to the laws of the "Great spirit" handed down to him.

The Creek Nations were the greatest traders of all the tribes in the South.

TUSTUNUGGEE—HOGO "BILL BOWLEGS"

When on his way, leaving the state, this warrior stopped at Tuscaloosa, and addressed the State Legislature, and his white audience with such dignity and eloquence that he left an almost unexplainable impression.

He said "I come brothers to see the great house of Alabama and the men that make the laws and to say farewell, in brotherly kindness, before I go to the Far West, where my people are now going. We leave behind our good will to the white people of Alabama who build great houses, and to the men who make laws. I say farewell to the wise men and to wish them peace and happiness in the country which my forefathers owned."

Moore states in his history that "the entire river banks of Alabama and Southwest Georgia are thickly dotted with Indian mounds and the trail of the Red Man is so definitely marked that his greatness can never be obliterated.

THE LAST INDIAN BATTLE IN ALABAMA

Fought March 25th, 1837

Battle of Pea River Swamp, in which Settlers Engaged Creeks, With Two Killed and Twenty-five Wounded. It Was the Result of Trouble, long brewing.

On March 225th, 1837, about three miles from Hobby's bridge on Pea River, between Troy and Louisville, the last battle between the white settlers and Indains was fought. While it was not the largest battle, it was one of the three greatest battles ever fought in Alabama. These three were: The capture of the Indian town of Maubila, or Desota, in 1850; the capture of Fort Mims in northern Baldwin County in 1813; and the battle of Horse Shoe Bend, in Tallapoosa, a few months later.

In the Chattahoochee Valley in 1936, trouble broke out on account of the encroachments of the whites, and the discontent of the Indians at these encroachments, and the proposal of the U. S. Government to transport them to the western Indain reservations.

The Creeks, always more or less warlike, formed lines along the Alabama and Georgia sides of the Chattahoochee river and in the spring of 1836, again went on the warpath. They burned homes, pilfered the settlers homes, and throughout all that section anxiety and dread enveloped the forest, to the extent that fear stalked broadcast.

Near the villages of Seale and Pittsview, the stagecoach had been attacked and several persons killed. Near Crawford, in Russell county today can still be seen the tombs of several killed by the Indians. In a cemetery near Three Notch and Union Springs there are a number of the tombs of settlers killed.

Homes of settlers in Glenville, which was then Barbour, but now Russell County, were burned, not even a cabin left in the whole settlement.

The town of Glenville was named for Rev. James Elizabeth Glenn. Algernon Sidney Glenn, who at 80 years of age, told the following story to his relative, Dr. James M. Glenn::

"After telling of the settling of Glenville, the troubles arising betwen the Indains and whites, in May, 1836, his father moved his family to Georgia, after being warned by a friendly Indian. William Flournoy was killed between Seale and Pittsview, the stage coach was attacked and homes in Glenville were burned. The old gentleman known far and wide as 'Capt. Buck Glenn' told of the family, returning to Glenville in October, 1836."

"After the trouble began, said he, "the governor sent troops to restore order, but upon returning to Glenville, we found everything burned, so we rebuilt our house in the same spot, almost directly across the road from the old Methodist church, and our second house was surrounded by split logs set on end with portholes through which to shoot, if we were attacked again."

Battle of Pea River

Were you in any of the battles with the marauding Indians, he was asked. "Yes, I was in the army as a member of the Barbour Rangers from Christmas, 1836, to March 25th, 1837, after the last battle was fought in Pea river swamp. I was less than 20 years of age and my older brother, Massillon, was a guide on the staff of Gen. Wingfield Scott who with General Jessup came to Alabama in connection with the Indian troubles."

The older brother of Mr. Glenn was one of the men who helped to frame a constitution for the state of Alabama during the perilous days of Reconstruction and had three or four grandsons in the world war, one of them dying while in service.

Mr. Glenn continued: "The U. S. troops who were sent to the scene of the trouble never had a battle with the Indians, although Gen. Jessup, with the forces, camped for a while between (Seale and Pittsview of today) and also at Creek Stand, Alabama, in Macon County. All the fighting was done by volunteers.

"In the fighting in Pea river swamp, there was a volunteer company from Franklin County, Georgia, and the Barbour Rangers, to which I belonged.

"The captain of the Barbour Rangers was William Wellborn; First Lieutenant, Patterson; Second Lieutenant, Cowan. Lieutenant Patterson was killed in the fight with the Indians at Martin's Creek near Midway in Bullock County and Lieutenant Cowan lost an arm there. Both were from Eufaula. I was not in that fight. There were only a few men in it. The Indians, who were in ambush, waited until our men were in the open field and then opened fire upon them. After this the Indians withdrew from Pea river.

"In pursuing them, we camped at Feagan's grove in front of Col. James Feagan's home in the northern adge of Midway. In following the Indians we tracked them by burned houses. At length we came to a house, which was still burning and we knew that the Indians were near. They were in the Pea river swamp above Hobdy's bridge, and before we attacked them they had already defeated a larger force of whites than we had.

"The swamp was inundated by high water and Indians were encamped on some high ground between the river and a large lagoon, that being the only high ground.

"A force of about 50 citizens was sent to cut them off. These were attacked by the Indians and driven back.

"Hearing the fighting, we dashed up. We were fighting Indian fashion from behind trees, bushes and other shelter. The Indians tried to flank us, so our line was extended from the river to the lagoon. We were in three hours and fifty-two minutes." 'You were the first man to kill an Indian, were you not?' he was asked. "No not the first. My first shot was too far and I made a miss. My second shot was when I saw the water shaking near a bush and an Indian was behind it. I fired at him and he fell dead.

"Young Wellborn, about my age, and a son of Capt. Welborn, our commander, was standing near me, standing behind a small poplar tree, and when he saw the result of my shot he unthoughtedly exposed himself a moment as he exclaimed, "Buck Glenn has killed an Indian." The next instant a bullet struck him in the head and he fell four feet from me writhing in death.

"I was down behind a palmetto bush and was not struck, though the bullets cut the limb of the trees above my head. I got one shot at the Indain who had shot young Wellborn. He was well concealed behind a large poplar about fifty yards away. Some also saw him and shot at him making him turn like a squirrel around a tree. I could see only his arm, but fired at that hoping to cripple him at least. He immediately disappeared from sight and I saw him no more.

"As long as my firing was going on I got along very well, but when there was a lull it was not very pleasant. Young Wellborn was not killed outright. When everything else was quiet, I could see the brave young fellow writhing in the agony of death and hear his groans as he lay there, almost right at me and I could feel that I would just about as soon be at home.

"Each of us had been supplied with 24 cartridges and after a while our ammunition was almost exhausted. Our officers knew that if we attempted to retreat we would be attacked by the Indians and overwhelmed so they decided to charge the camp. My older brother, Mack, was also in the fight and he was hit on the knee by a spent ball as we made the charge. About a half dozen of us volunteers went right through the Indian camp. We found the fires burning where they had been making bullets and found pewter plates being melted for the purpose, as they had run out of lead.

"Some of the Indains stood their ground bravely. A man from near Franklin County, Georgia, and I were together An Indian shot him in the arm and stood squarely. Another of our men shot the Indian down as he stood. "I killed one Indian as we went through the lagoon and tried to secure his gun, but could not on account of the depth of the water. But I secured his shot pouch, containing pewter bullets. In coming out of the fight my pants were as bloody as if we had been killing hogs.

"We had two men killed and about twenty-five wounded. The Indians were routed and we received honorable discharges."

Being asked what kind of guns were used he replied: "Flint lock muskets and they were very serviceable guns, shooting well. Each of us had 24 cartridges, each of which was wrapped in stiff paper, and consisted of a charge of powder, and three buckshot. We bit off the lower end of the cartridge, poured powder from it into the 'pan' under the hammer. Sparks fell into the powder in the pan and the fire, passing through a small hole into the barrel, fired the gun. It was all done in a flash. I went to the Indian

I had killed in the lagoon, and found a hole had been knocked in him, at least an inch in diameter. "However," he said smilingly, "after shooting a while, my shoulder was so sore from the kicking back of the gun that I could scarcely use my arm. The powder in the pan also had a way of flashing out, which was not very pleasant. The day of the Pea river fight, was the 25th of March, and there was a strong wind blowing from the northwest, and I lost all my eye brows and eye lashes by the flashing and blowing back of the powder in the pan of my gun."

The Indains who were driven out of Pea river swamp were on their way to Florida to join the Seminoles, among whom were already many of other Creeks from Alabama and while many persons in Alabama do not know it, Osceola himself, the noted chief of the Seminoles in Florida, was himself, having been born in Alabama on the Euhhaupee (U-Fowhy) creek some say, quite close to the present Clugh's Station on the Western railroad, near Chehaw, on the same creek. He was half white, and his English name was Billy Powell.

The present writer is personally acquainted with some of his great granddaughters. They are in Monroe County, Alabama, near the Baldwin County line. The writer also has been a guest in the home of two of the great granddaughters of the noted Creek chief, William Weatherford, or the "Red Eagle" as he is often called.

JAMES M. GLENN.

PART II

Chapter Seven

Hotels

The first hotel in Barbour County was the "Tavern," built by Mark Williams at Eufaula in 1827, for a residence, but used to accomodate the few travelers who passed through that section.

During the time that Eufaula was temporarily called "Irwinton" (changed back to its original name "Eufaula" in 1842.) It was the first house, other than log cabins, built in the newly settled village of Eufaula, and stands today, owned and occupied by Mrs. T. A. Mashburn. It has been kept in perfect repair through the years, always painted the original color first used. It is on Riverside drive, overlooking the Chattahoochee river, where Broad street turns to the bluff.

The next hotel was built on corner of Broad and Livingston streets, run by a man named Moore, and known as the "Howard House."

In the next ten years, the Central hotel corner of Broad and Eufaula street was built. It was managed by the following parties consecutively: J. D. Billings, S. Stuberfield, B. Bernstein, during the seventies. During the eighties, Bernstein sontinued and in the nineties J. H. Keho was manager, until the building was burned, and rebuilt by W. N. and J. H. Reeves and named "The Arlington," which was run by E. B. Freeman. The National Hotel was built by J. L. Ross and Robert Moulthrop, and run by Mrs. W. H. Locke with E. B. Freeman (who became "Mine Host" of the South as the years passed, as its first clerk.

The old "Chewalla House," corner of Broad and Orange streets, was run by A. J. Riddle for many years, later changed to the "St. Julien.' It had as managers, G. T. Long, who also managed the National a long time. For a long time Mrs. Ida Ross ran the National and after being closed for some time, was run 8 years by Mrs. W. C. Standifer.

Late years it has been used only as a store house, the upper stories and the lower story as bank offices. Now it is the New National owned by the Dean Estate and run by J. M. Cade.

The St. Julien, changed to the "New St. Julien," was run by the owner, Col. G. L. Comer for ten years, with different managers in charge. Among them Robert Brannon, who had been clerk many years, and Thomas Appling, also clerk, previously.

The building was torn away, when sold to the United States Government, the site used for the fine Post Office now serving Eufaula and surrounding territory

The old "Finnerty House" on Broad street, now used as a hotel was known for many years as the "Evans House," afterwards run by J. K. Sams, and now by Charles Ham.

Mr. E. B. Freeman came to Eufaula from Columbia, Alabama, in 1880 and to him is due the reputation of Eufaula as "the best hotel town in the South." At various times, he managed every first class hotel in the town. Coming as hotel clerk at the age of 18, in a few years he was manager of the "St. Julien, "Arlington," "New St. Julien," Eufaula, and after establishing such enviable reputation here, he was even more distinguished, and successful in careers at the following other hotels: "Anniston (Ala.) Inn, the "Caldwell," Birmingham, "Exchange" and "Windsor," Montgomery, "Dawson Inn," Dawson, Ga, then back to Birmingham to manage the "Hillsman," returning from Dawson to again manage the "Bluff City Inn, Eufaula, which was the original Central Hotel. He managed this hotel until his death, Sept. 3, 1919, when his mantle fell on his two sons, Edward B., Jr., and Walter S., who like himself, had grown up in the hotel business, assumed control and made their hotel and the name "Freeman," the first word in hostelry

They knew the business, loved it and were ambitious to keep it at the high point of perfection their father had always maintained.

The name "Freeman" is known by every traveling man in the country and for fifty years "Freeman's Hotel" has been the one sought by them for their stop over resting place. The traveling public became the family's warm, personal friends and their courteous accommodating service gave to them an enviable reputation as "mine hoste."

About four years ago Freeman Brothers sold out their hotel interests to Dr. J. L. Houston and retired.

Mr. Edward B. Freeman went into the insurance business as special agent for the Equitable Life Insurance Company and Mr. Walter S. Freeman, into the drug business, establishing the Eufaula Drug Company .

By their integrity and personality, both are making good in their new ventures and are first among Barbour County's most valuable citizens.

WHEELER HOUSE
Clayton, Alabama

The Eufaula, Louisville, and Columbus and Midway stages run to this House. Nov. 25, '58. 35tf.

EATING SALOON
—By—
B. A. THORN

The subscriber has opened an EATING SALOON on the east side of the public square, one door below the Post Office. Meals can be had at all hours of the day and night. He intends to keep the best the country affords, together with Fresh Oysters. He wishes it particularly understood that there is no Grocery attached to this Saloon. B. A. THORN. Clayton, Feb. 16, 1859. 45tf.

All records of the town of Clayton show that the principal hotel of pioneer days there was the Wheeler House, in the fifties and long before the Eufaula, Louisville and Columbus and Midway stage coaches ran to this house, which was one of their terminals.

For many long years, the "Hill House" was run by Mrs. Hill and daughters, and was a fine place. Then came the Enterprise Hotel, and now for nearly a half century, the Fryer House has been known all over the country. It was run many years by Miss Fryer, known to her friends and the traveling public as "Miss Dump," and her hotel was always "the best." Since her death, her brother has been proprietor, and this hotel still maintains its popularity.

Louisville—The hotels at Louisville are notable. For many years Mrs. Green was proprietor of the leading hotel.

Chapter Eight
Insurance and Banks
INSURANCE

> Insurance is a safe and wise protection against
> death and disaster of any kind, and should be
> a daily reflection throughout a lifetime.

The oldest insurance agency in Barbour County, possibly one of the oldest of the three oldest in the state, is the Dean Insurance Agency.

It was established in 1870 by Capt. Leonard Yancey Dean, a veteran of the War Between the States, who left an arm on the battle field, when he came forth maimed after that bitter struggle for home and the Southland.

Until about a year before his death, at the age of 89, this oldest agent, manager, wonderful business man and valuable, beloved citizen was actively engaged in this business, which his executive ability and genial personality had made through a period of over sixty years such a success as president of the Dean Agency, which comprised over an hundred thousand dollars worth of fire, accident, storm, burglar and life insurance, following the cyclone of 1919, when this Agency paid out large sums on policies made demandable by these casualties.

As a tribute to Capt. Dean's remarkable record, as adjustor and representative, he was the recipient of numerous trophies for his long service with the various companies he represented. Among these was a gold watch fob, for 40 years' service with the Fidelity-Phoenix Insurance Company and for 50 years with the same company, a beautiful clock. From Liverpool, London and Globe Agency a gold match case was given him in recognition of 60 years' service.

For a number of years, Captain Dean had associated with him G. B. Geothus, the firm name being Dean and Geotheus and later his brother-in-law, E. K. Cargill, and in later years his son, Leonard Yancey Dean, Jr.

Before his death, he sold the business to Mr. John R. Barr, one of the most capable and enthusiastic young business men in the County, who is carrying on, under the same old Dean programs and policies that have made the business so successful. Mr. Barr's slogan is "Go forward, never halting" and he is maintaining that strict business principal of "giving perfect service."

The Insurance business of Barbour County, is brim full of interest and color and includes the flattering records of other firms that have wrought the best and given luster to the glow of Insurance, in all its various and numerous phases.

The E. Y. Dent Insurance Co. had its inception and was born of the Insurance feature of the Eufaula National Bank, with Mr. E. Y. Dent Manager of the Agencies. Its life began in 18— and after this Bank ceased business in 1901, Mr. Dent continued the business, enlarging it. He knows the Insurance Business from every angle, and his record for ability, accuracy and knowledge in general of Insurance has enabled him to keep his Agency and Insurance business to a high standard that has not only held him his old business, but brings new daily. His slogan is "satisfaction" and he is holding fast to it.

The Sparks Insurance Agency is not so old in years, but is strong in every feature. It was established by H. C. and L. A. Sparks, young men who by indomniable will, strict integrity and application to business, have put their business at the very top. They represent the best companies and agencies and use the cleanest business policies. As sellers and dealers in the highest class Insurance they have used dignified, but attractive methods that have brought them business and success.

BANKS

> Gold, silver, currency and checks
> Play their part in life's drama,
> And the custodians of these, reflects
> The finance problems of Alabama.

The name of the "Bridge Bank" was changed to the "Young and Woods" Bank and finally was merged into the Eufaula National Bank.

The first bank established in Barbour County was the "Bridge Bank" in 1839 by Edward B. Young, who had come to Eufaula from New York, with his own capital, established this bank after, John W. Pettit, Representative from Barbour County had introduced a bill to establish a bank at Eufaula had failed. Mr. Young's project was a success, and it was the only bank in the County until John M. McNab, who had been in the County for some time, and was wealthy, built the fifty thousand dollar bank building still standing at the corner of Broad and Randolph streets and opened a banking business under the name of "The Eastern Bank of Alabama, in 1859. This was one of the four only banks then operating in Alabama. During the sixties he changed the name to 'The John

McNab Bank," which it bore until it was closed by the Hanover National Bank of New York March 31, 1891, after Mr. McNab's death, when his son-in-law, Dr. W. N. Reeves, was president. C. Rhodes was cashier from its opening to its closing March 31, 1891.

The People's Bank, with quarters on Hart's Block" was organized by Henry C. Hart, president, and A. A. Walker, cashier. It was popular but after a few years run it died February 16, 1869.

The Eufaula National Bank was the original "Bridge Bank, second name Young and Woods. S. H. Dent, president, and Edward B. Young, II, cashier, took charge after name was changed to "Eufaula National Bank." It did a great business for many years, but misfortunes came and it was also one of the unfortunate banks of the country to close in 1901.

The East National Bank was organized in 1886, capital stock $100,000, by John P Foy and J. L. Pitts and closed its doors July 1, 1929. It's closingg was a heavy blow to the business of this section. This bank was housed in the same building built by John McNab for the Eastern Bank of Alabama, and the bank that bore his name. It was used for banking purposes for nearly an hundred years. This banking business was sold by J. L. Pitts to A. H. Merrill.

The Commercial National Bank was organized in 1895, J. P. Foy, president, and C. P. Roberts, cashier. At his death W. D. Flewellen was appointed cashier. When President J. P. Foy died, his son, Humphrey Foy, succeeded him as president. The Commercial Bank closed its doors October, 1931.

The Bank of Eufaula was organized in 1906—$50,000 capital stock. W. L. Wild was president, G. L. Comer, vice president; chairmen were: George H. Dent, N. W. Roberts; cashier, C. E. Boyd, and board of directors, G. L. Comer, G. H. Dent, R. Moulthrop, C. L. McDowell, Jr., H. C. Hollemon, C. A. Loche, W. S. Britt, I. Neil, W. W. Roberts. This bank used the original E. B. Young and Eufaula National Bank building The bank closed its doors.

The Eufaula Bank and Trust Company was organized in 1925 with H. L. King, president; Chauncey Sparks, vice president, and R. C. Joiner as cashier.

Although the only bank in Eufaula, it handles the immense banking business satisfactorily and with success. L. Y. Dean, III, President (Recently elected).

The Clayton Banking Company was organized in 1887 by T. R. Parish, Sr., and has had many years of successful business. The original directors were viz (to come later)

The officials at present are T D. Grubbs, president; T. W. Parish, vice president; Thomas R Parish, cashier; directors,

T. D. Grubbs, E. W. Norton, T. W. Parish, Thomas R. Parish, E. W. Parish.

The Citizens Bank of Clayton was organized by J. J. Winn and J. E. Meadows. The directors were Dr. W. H. Wright, J. L. Pitts, T. E. Pitts.

The Barbour Bank at Louisville was organized by M. C. Bell, T. H. Blair and others.

The bank of Louisville was organized by Robert Flournoy and Frank Pierce.

The Clio Banking Company opened for business August 5th, 1905. The founders were J. D. Fuqua, president; B. I. Jackson, cashier, and C. J. Stephens, assistant cashier. Capital $50,000.

Some years later the Farmers' Bank was established at Clio with J. N. Stephens, president.

NOTES

BARBOUR COUNTY'S FIRST MANUFACTURING ENTERPRISE

Barbour County's first manufacturing enterprise was a "Wool Factory," owned and operated by Jonathan Thomas, one of the pioneer settlers. It was located three-fourths of a mile from the Barbour creek, near what is known as the "Mile Branch," and from the large herds of sheep he raised, he made the wool sheared into cloth and sold it far and near ... as it was the only "Wool Factory" in this section. He has several hundred descendants, who are citizens of Barbour County, scattered all over the County.

FIRST GAS PLANT

The first Gas Plant established in Southeast Alabama was built in Barbour county in 1884, owned by Captain John W. Tullis, progressive citizen, who afterwards, was president of the Eufaula Light and Power Company.

Mr. J. H. Hagerty was superintendent for many years. For some years the city of Eufaula municipaly owned the Light and Power Company, selling the plant to the Alabama Power Company.

BARBOUR COUNTY'S FIRST AUTOMOBILE

The first automobile ever brought to Barbour County was the little "Oldsmobile Buggy," in 1900, by Mr. James L. Ross, who purchased it from a Mr. Davis at Cuthbert, Georgia.

It created a sensation, when Mr. Ross drove down Sanford street, just as the school children had been dismissed, and they followed the "wonder," utterly astonished to witness the fulfillment of Old Mother Shipman's prophesy that "Carriages without horses shall go."

Soon after this Mr. Ross bought a fine touring car, Dr.

J. B. Whitlock bought a Chandler, Mrs. A. C. Mitchell and Dr. J. M. Reeves, buying fine cars of this make also. For over a year these were the only cars in the County, until Mr. J. A. Strickland of Louisville, bought a "Maxwell" and soon the little gasoline buggy that created such a sensation evolved into hundreds and now thousands of fine automobiles of every make, pattern and design desired are in use.

FIRST CIRCUS NOTES

The first circus that visited Barbour County was the great "Robinson Circus," in 1854. It created a sensation and when the parade marched through the streets of Eufaula, ropes had to be stretched to hold back the crowds.

Old residents have told that the negroes swarmed from hundreds of miles, and when daylight came the day of the circus, the road between Eufaula and Clayton was alive with a moving mass of humanity.

Chapter Nine

Public Halls And Theatres

FIRST COURT HOUSE

The first Court House built at Clayton was in 1854 at a cost of $9,695.

PUBLIC HALLS AND THEATRES

In 1866, John Hart, wealthy pioneer citizen, had sold his many slaves prior to emancipation, and with the more than $75,000 that they brought, he built Hart's Block, composed of ten stores, reaching from the corner of Broad and Eufaula streets in Eufaula, nearly to the corner of Barbour and Eufaula streets Above the six middle stores of this block, was the spacious hall or auditorium, used for all the dances, balls, banquets, theatres or public gatherings for many years.

The "Hart's Hall" was opened with a play in which Alice Oats, then in the hey day of her glory as an actress, and its historic walls held the secrets and the glories of long years, all to go up in flames, Nov. 24, 1904, when all of the block except the one street and rooms above on the Broad street corner, which stands today, as does the two last stores near Barbour street, small remains of the old "Hart Block."

Besides being used for theatrical purposes, it was the place where all the Balls, Church fairs and social functions of the community drew great crowds to make merry in the old days.

When the fine old Shorter mansion on the bluff was torn down, the superior material was used to build Shorter Opera House on Broad street. It was built by Kolb, Couric and Hayes, a large warehouse and cotton firm. Messrs. Kolb and Couric, being Shorter heirs, shared in the division of the large estate of General Reuben C. Shorter.

This opera house was one of the finest in the South, with its four handsome opera boxes, dressing rooms, and some of the most elaborate scenery.

For a long period of years, this opera house was run by Mr. P. H. Morris as manager, but its greatest glory was during the years that Mr. Jake Stern was manager, when all of the finest plays in the country played on its great stage, with Prof. Van Houten's Orchestra in the pit, and after his death the E. B. Young and Whitlock Orchestra. The great College Commencement Concerts, by Prof. Van Houten were given here, and one of the most memorable political gatherings within its walls was the county Democratic convention that met there in 1874.

When Rev. Sam Jones lectured there in 1895, the house was crowded to everflowing and the religious demonstration was one that will never be forgotten for soon after there was a revival at the First Baptist Church, and many new converts were added to the rolls of all the churches in the County.

Lawrence Barrett the great actor, played "Richileu" on the stage and declared to Manager Stern that the scenery was the most suitable to his great play that he had seen in any theatre in all the country.

The old curtain is still on the walls of Carnegie Library (a large part of it) preserved by the club women of the city, given to them by Dr. J. B. Whitlock, when Whitlock-Foy purchased the building, which was burned. The next opera house was built by the Eufaula Chautauqua (or Alabama Chautauqua) and after about ten years was sold and bought in by the Dr. H. M. Weedon estate, who held a mortgage on it

During its life, it was used as an opera house, and so called, after purchased by the Weedon estate.

It seated fifteen hundred people, and was a modern, first class opera house and theatre. During its entire existence it was used for a motion picture theatre, and for all other theatrical purposes. For a time it was used by both the First Baptist and First Methodist churches, while new church buildings of these two demonimations were being erected.

In 1924 the Eufaula High School Auditorium was built, a protentious building attached to the High School on Sanford street, with a seating capacity of 800, and since that time it has been used for the city, theatre, or opera house, purposes. It has beautiful, appropriate scenery for all occasions, and a large orchestra pit and a gallery; also a grand pipe organ, and is the home of the Concert Grand Mason and Hamlin piano owned by the Music Lovers Club of Eufaula and also the several school pianos, and those of Mrs. T. G. Wilkinson used with her splendid school orchestra of 40 pieces.

PICTURE THEATRES

The first moving picture theatre in Barbour County was the "Pictorium" owned and managed by Edward Black at Eufaula and was in the store on Broad street, known for many years as the "Shelly Jewelry store." It's life was short, but soon came the Vaudette, the A-mus-U and various others, until while manager of the Chautauqua Opera House, Mr. J.

M. Barr ran, for about three years, a splendid motion picture service that was Eufaula's and the surrounding territory's greatest pleasure asset. He sold out to a Mr. Jones from Florida, who in turn sold the Vaudette and Eufaula picture show privileges to Mr. M. G. Lee, and from that day until now, Eufaula has had the pleasure of the benefits of the best pictures released, all modern equipment, and perfect service, can give a town and community. After showing several years in the building in the National Hotel block, Mr. Lee purchased from the Jacob Ramser estate, adjoining the old Shorter building, two of the finest buildings on Broad street, and converted them into a perfectly equipped, modern motion picture theatre, and has given a "picture show" service that cannot be excelled anywhere, the large cities not excepted.

For many years, Mr. Lee has been claimed an esteemed, valuable citizen of Eufaula, although he calls Cuthbert, Georgia, home, having there and also at Dawson, Georgia, similar fine picture, theatres, run in connection with the Eufaula Theatre. He spends much time in Eufaula, where he has made a host of warm friends. He owns other real estate in Eufaula, among which are four fine stores on Eufaula street, situated in the old "Hart's Block," almost on the exact spot where the old historic "Hart's Hall," Eufaula's first hall of Amusement and theatre stood.

Recently he purchased from E. F. Espy the fine building next to the P. O. which he has transformed into the "Rex" Theatre, air conditioned, and fully equipped with opera upholstered chairs, giving to the public the same fine service that the "Lee" theatre has for so many years. The "Rex," will show a different run of pictures from that of the "Lee," both giving the very best released by the best filming companies.

The Lee Theatre under the management of Mr. J. R. Ivey, with Mrs. Ivey in the ticket office, and ticket taker and other assistants, Mr. and Mrs. Hester, Mrs. J. L. Barbaree and Mrs. E. T. Motley, is giving a service that can only be illustrated by the one word—Perfect. The lobby of the theatre is a beautiful, cosy place to linger and the pictures being shown to the audience bring pleasure, of higher education, benefits of travel, information, included in the news reels that is most instructive, and the news, that is full of all the high lights of the times, to say nothing of the beautiful pictures that brong forth romance, history and show human life in all its intricacies. The joy and relaxation found in these theatres are among the greatest assets to this section of Barbour County.

HART'S BLOCK GOES UP IN SMOKE
From the Eufaula Daily Times, Nov. 24th, 1904

The entire Hart's Block was destroyed by the fire Saturday night about ten o'clock. Hart's block was one of the chief sections of Eufaula's business center. How the flames originated or who first discovered them has not been learned, but several claim that they smelt the fire all afternoon, but could not locate it. It is believed that it started in store No. 2 upstairs and with almost incredible rapidity they spread and in the course of a few minutes the entire block was almost a seething mass of flames. The department responded quickly to general alarm, but it was soon seen that it was impossible to save anything in the whole block, except Petry and Stewart and Foy Grocery stores, and they were both badly damaged by fire and water.

The fire was the largest that has occurred here since September 15th, 1884, when the Compress and several houses were destroyed.

Nearly every man, woman, and child in the city were out to see the fire and remaining watching until it had been extinguished. While fighting the fire, Messrs. Ed Cargill, Ed Jones and Sid Hortman were injured by falling brick.

At about two o'clock the Eufaula Rifles were called out by the Mayor to protect the goods placed on the streets.

The Hart Block was owned by Scheur Bros. and Foy Bros. It was erected by Mr. John Hart, nearly fifty years ago at a cost of $750,000 and was a splendid piece of property

The burnt district will be rebuilt and you can put it down that it will be an ornament to the city, because, where a town has as much liberal-minded public-spirited citizens as Eufaula has, there is no danger of its declining or standing still—it's bound to go on and improve.

(Note 1936—The block has been rebuilt, with two handsome one-story buildings and between these and the remaining space next to the stores left that escaped total destruction is a new modern up-to-date filling station of unique architecture.)

The block was occupied by the following, viz.: No. 1, Petry-Stewart Furniture; No. 2, Charles Hart, grocer; Singer Sewing Machine;; Dr. Mangum office, upstairs; L. W. McLaughlin and Ready Dr. Medicine Company upstairs.

No. 3, H. B. Dowling Undertaking Establishment, upstairs unoccupied.

No. 4, Crawford's Bowling alley.

No. 5, 6, and 7, occupied by Foy Bros. and the upstairs over these comprised Hart's Hall and was occupied by the Eufaula Rifles Armory, splendidly fitted up as gymnasium, bath rooms, etc.

FIRE NOTES

'Twas said in the long ago that John Hart, the original owner, father of Henry C., William, B. Frank, Charles and Harrison Hart, sold all his negroes prior to 1866 and built this block, with the purchase money $75,000. Hart's Hall was opened by Alice Oates, then just beginning her career on the stage.

It has been the scene of hundreds of brilliant balls, bazaars, festivals, banquets, finest traveling plays, and all manner of mirth, through the passing years.

Religious services of all kinds have been held there. While the First Methodist Church was being built, the congrsgation worshipped there. Rev. E. L. Bounds, the pastor. Memorial services of many kinds have crowded within its massive doors. The tumbling walls today have echoed with sounds that every emotion can evoke, laughter, music, song, brilliant oratory, and some grief.

The late lamented Colonel Clement Clay Shorter said one night to a young girl he was dancing with—"some night this hall will be burned to ashes and some one will write of such scenes as this. How I should like to read it." (It was a Eufaula Light Infantry ball—the writer was the young girl) who 36 years later, is writing this history).

The Chattahoochee warehouse was known as "Hart's warehouse," which was burned in February 1885, the People's Bank which, dying, killed the finances of many Barbour County enterprises, were a part of Hart's Block.

Perhaps the most tragic event in the history of the block was an attempted burglary and midnight murder in this warehouse, some time in the seventies. A guinea bird was mistaken for a burglar, and actually killed for such.

Time was when every store in the block was heaped with goods of every kind. Stern's beautiful "Temple of Fashion" was always filled with ladies. In No. 3, during the late seventies, the Western Union Telegraph Co., Southern Express Co., Post Office, and Cotton Exchange lived together. The heads of these departments were close friends. Wood Guice, John C. Thomas, William A. Locke left the echo of many a joke in those walls. Reuben Kolb, L. H. Snead, Editor Shropshire will retrospect when they hear "Hart's Block was burned."

Hart's Block was built by Geo. W. Whipple, an architect and contractor of note in those days.

The warehouse on this block was occupied by Clark, Hart and Co., possibly at that time the largest cotton warehouse firm doing business in the state. The old Hart plantation in the Pine Grove section of Barbour County was sold by Major Hart to Mr. Johnathan Thornton, whose children still own it. Long years after, Capt. Henry Hart's daughter married Fred Thornton, youngest son of Johnathon Thornton, and they have lived on the old plantation near Batesville. Sallie Hart Thornton died, 1938.

Chapter Ten

Business and Industry In Barbour County

BARBOUR COUNTY'S DRUG STORE HISTORY

When William Eugene Besson was born in a stockade at Fort Gaines, Georgia, 25 miles from Eufaula, there was no such thing as a drug store in Barbour county His parents had come from France to America, and when he was 12 years old moved to Barbour County, and before he was 21 years old he was practically in charge of the City Drug store, at Eufaula, owned and run by McGinty and Smith, and in the sixties Eugene Besson had long been proprietor of this firm, which was merged into McGinty and Bullock Early in the seventies it was the "Besson Drug Store." After several years, Besson sold out to E. C. Bulloch, going to Montgomery,

E. B. WEEDON

DR. H. M. WEEDON

where he owned a drug store until his death, at a ripe old age.

Right after the war between the States, Dr. H. M. Weedon, who had come here to take charge of the Military hospital, having served at Pensacola, opened a drug business in the building on Broad street in Eufaula, which from that day, until this, had been used only as the Weedon and Dent Drug store, the last few years, being owned exclusively by Mr. E. B. Weedon, son of Dr. H. M. Weedon.

For over a half century, the firm of Weedon and Dent was the outstanding drug firm of Southeast, Alabama, owned by Dr. H. M. Weedon and his brother-in-law, Mr. George H. Dent. Associated with them for many years was a younger brother, Mr. Warren F. Dent, who went to Montgomery from Eufaula over twenty years ago and was a leading druggist there until his death.

The "Weedon and Dent Farmers Pills," made and patented by Dr. Weedon, made him famous all over the country. When Dr. Weedon died July 1st, 1898, E. B. Weedon bought the business which he ran until 1836, then becoming associated with Milton and Milton as prescriptionist. (A notable fact that Mr. John M. Milton, deceased, who had been pharmacist for the Old Bullock Drug store and its successors, had also been prescriptionist for the Weedon Drug store, and was the prescriptionist for Milton and Milton, of which firm he was original member, the same firm of which E. B. Weedon is now pharmacist The son of Mr. George H. Dent, Warren F. Dent, II, like E. B. Weedon, grew up in the drug business, and was prescriptionist in the firm of Beach and Dent, which succeeded Bullock.

Beach and Dent sold to Beauchamp and Hill, who sold to Milton and Milton, V. M. and J. M., two of the four brothers who had grown up in the drug stores of the city as prescriptionists.

After the death of V. M. Milton in 1935, the business was purchased by James H. Thaggard, who had previously been prescriptionist for J. P. Hill, and thus the long chain, unbroken, is reinforced and held to the old drug life and post of today by Weedon and Thaggard, being a culmination of the old Weedon and Dent—originally Beach and Dent; while the old Beauchamp and Hill, carried on by J. P. Hill after George A. Beauchamp retired, was purchased by Sim A. Thomas and now run as the Thomas Drug Co. These two have emerged, as you might say, from long lines of ancestry, while the Jackson Drug Co., established years later in the early 1900's by Albert Clayton, known as the Clayton Drug Co. It was then purchased by F. L. Warren and run as the Warren Drug Co., later becoming the Finn Drug Company and still later becoming the Finn Drug Company and still later Thaggard's Pharmacy. The business was purchased in June, 1924, by R. M. Jackson from Pugh Harris, who was at that time operating it as Harris' Pharmacy, having bought out Thaggard's Pharmacy some time before.

In 1924 it was purchased by Dr. R. M. Jackson, who, in addition to his large drug stock and prescription department, has placed his seed and flower business at the top in this County.

It is now the City Drug Store, owned by McKissick and Hughes.

All this drug story, linking the years, the business and then men who have conducted it is interesting, as well as unique, and brings the reader to the latest drug business, which stands out, absolutely new—less than five years old— the Eufaula Drug Co., owned by W. S. Freeman, who has as prescriptionist two young men, Arthur Fain and J. T. Mizelle, who are pharmacists of the new school, but not unmindful of the benefits of some of the old ideas mixed with the new, and are giving to the public a most gratifying and in every way a splendid service. This service has put the Eufaula Drug Co., while last on the honorable and enviable list, that has been notable throughout the years, first on the always desirable list of the new.

CLAYTON DRUG STORES

As far back as 1859, the record of Clayton's Drug stores shows that Dr. M. B. Fenn and Co. were leading druggists, and contemporary with that firm was the large firm of McNeill and Wise.

Later on there was the Clayton Drug Co., the drug store of Charles P. and John P. West.

The West Drug Store has always been popular in Clayton. It succeeded Fred Warren, then Jesse Hightower had a drug business, which he sold to Clayton and Warren.

Later there were the firms of Feagan and Brown and then the firm of Feagan and Meadows—then O. B. and J. G. Pruett—Grubbs and Winn—T. R. Parish—followed by Lamar Jennings, J. E. Parish, and still later Watkins and Green, succeeded by Dr. W. A. Smartt.

The firm of C. P. West was changed to West Bros., then to J. . West and then West and Robertson.

Again J. P. West and Company, and now this firm is C. T. Millburn, showing a long line of business changes.

The Clayton Drug Company was at one time owned by Elige Lingo, then E H. Waldon, then by Easterling, and now it is again the Clayton Drug Company owned by Rufus Little.

Clio—The first drug store at Clio was operated by Dr. Glover and now Clio boasts a Cash Drug store.

BARBOUR COUNTY'S LARGEST INDUSTRY

The second oldest and the largest industry in Barbour County, the Cowikee Mills, was established by John W. Tullis, president, and was known as the Eufaula Cotton Mills, with G. T. Marsh superintendent. The plant was operated successfully for a number of years, and was the pride of all this section, as it is today.

In 1909 the mill was sold to the late Governor B. B. Comer and with his son, Donald Comer, now president, and the name changed to "The Cowikee Mills," the entirprise includes Mills No. 1. (the original Eufault Cotton Mills with its extensive warehouses, offices and Mill No. 2 (which was originally the Chewalla Cotton Mills, organized and operated by John P. Foy and Clarence P. Roberts, then sold to B. B. McKenzie. Then it was sold to L. L. Conner who operated it until 1929, when it was purchased by the Comer interests (the Cowikee Cotton Mills Co.) and is now running full time employing over one hundred operatives. The Company also operates Mill No. 3 at Union Springs, Ala., making the group of three use approximately 10,000 bales of cotton annually in their manufacturing of cloth.

These mills also manufacture cotton yarns, cloth and rope. The three mills manufacture together 250,000 pounds of yarn annually.

Mill No. 1 at Eufaula, the original plant of the group, occupies a whole square block right in the business section of the city, gives employment to two hundred employees the year round and has an annual pay roll of $100,000. The lot, with the superintendent's fine home adjoining, fronting two streets, was originally the old John McNab place, later the Reeves home, built by John McNab, and his son-in-law, Dr. W. N. Reeves, and was and still is one of the old historic homes of the County.

Mill No. 2, one block away on Randolph street, is also built on the old historic site known as the Skillman home site, and adjoins the home of the late Charles C. Skillman, and his wife; Olivia Price Skillman. He was notable in Barbour County as the greatest horseman and she as the greatest singer that ever lived in the County.

When Donald Comer became president of the Cowikee Mills Co., he purchased the old historic Shorter-Welborn home on Eufaula street, just across the railroad from Mill No. 1, built a school house for children of the mill operatives, terraced the lawn and built an outdoor theatre, gymnasium hall, bathing pools, and equipped it with all the modern conveniences of an up-to-date Community House and Park. He also made possible the organization and maintenance of a fifty-piece band with paid instructor; the maintenance of a free kindergarten. Besides this wonderful community park; built a dozen or more tenant houses; paved the sidewalks of "Comer town," as the resident section occupied by employees is known, and every convenience for these operatives has been put in their reach.

The Mills maintain a 25-acre pasture for the milch cows of the employees, free.

There is also a baseball diamond nearby and a grandstand in **Comer Park**

The following have been the superintendents of the Cowikee Cotton Mills, consecutively: G. T. Marsh, J. F. White, C. F. Faulkner, R. D. Jones (superintendent 20 years,) died April 24th, 1929; O. F. Benton, present superintendent; Donald Comer, president; Comer Jennings, vice president and general manager; W. C. Glenn, secretary.

LONE OAK POULTRY FARM

Lone Oak Poultry farm owned and operated by Cowikee Mills Co., with T. J. Lockwood, manager, was established in 1925 not as a profit-making institution, but to show others that a profit could be made from poultry raised in this section of the country.

There are also 50 pens or more in which quail are raised on Lone Oak Poultry farm. They are sold in mated pairs to restock game preserves. Turkeys are also raised on Lone Oak farm, and the methods used by Mr. Lockwood have shown that "turkey raising" is most profitable and interesting.

Manager Lockwood has 4500 Leghorn breeders each year. He has entered his pens of white leghorns in contests for over ten years and the records are to be proud of. At the Alabama laying test in 1933 his pens laid 2536 eggs for an average of 253.6 eggs per bird.

The high hen laid 321 eggs for a point score of 323.05 or an average weight per dozen of 24.5.

Several years ago this farm sold a solid car load of laying pullets—1600 to be exact—to a northern customer. The largest order ever sent out from the South, that is on record.

Mr. Lockwood came to Eufaula from New Jersey, where he was born and reared. His father being a chicken dealer, he grew up in the poultry business. He is a past master in the great art, and most efficient.

There are sixteen buildings on Lone Oak farm, with a half dozen people employed to do the labor.

The incubator capacity is 10,000 eggs and in spring over two thousand eggs are sold daily.

The record of Lone Oak Poultry Farm has been an incentive and through its influence and example an interest has been stimulated all over the country, that has brought about a more universal poultry raising.

THE TELEGRAPH IN BARBOUR COUNTY

When the Georgia and Florida Telegraph Company was organized at Apalachicola, Florida, with William Wood as president, the line was constructed from Marianna, Florida, to Silver Run (now Seale, Ala.) via Tallahassee, Columbia, Alabama, Fort Gaines, Georgia, and Eufaula, Alabama, in 1853 and soon a line from Apalachocila to Marianna was added.

Mr. A. R. Stewart was sent here from Apalachicola and made manager. John C. Thomas, a lad of nine years, was employed as messenger and remained in the company's service until April 1st, 1888, retiring on account of bad health.

In 1861 Manager Stewart was displaced on account of politics and young Thomas, who as messenger, had learned the Telegraph business by actual experience, was appointed manager by LaFayette Howe, superintendent, and then sole owner of this company, having purchased it from the original company.

In 1865 the Federal Goverment seized these privately owned telegraph lines, offices and plant, and appropriated it to the service of the Government. No person who had not taken the oath of allegiance to the Federal Government could send or receive telegrams over these lines and at these offices Manager Thomas was forced to turn over the keys of the Eufaula office and he signed the oath of allegiance.

It is a fact, that Mr. Howe, the owner, was a union man from Michigan, and the keys were returned to young Thomas and he remained in charge as manager.

It is a fact, also, that the Government did not pay him one cent of damage or rental from the Government for this seizure and use of his property, although documents of promise to pay when the war was over were signed by officials and are still in the possession of the heirs of J. C. Thomas and LaFayette Howe, and a claim against the Government by these heirs has been presented to Congress three times in the past thirty years, but the loss of the original charter of the company by fire when the Franklin County, Florida Court House at Apalachicola was burned, proving the sale of said company's plant and business to said Howe, has been the only preventative, from these heirs being able to recover damages.

The Government abandoned these lines and service after the war between the States and the Western Union Telegraph Company took over and opened for business. Manager Thomas was retained by the W. U. Company. He was succeeded April 1, 1888, by Oliver T. Moore of Apex, North Carolina, who held the office of manager until 1893, being transferred from Eufaula to Macon, Georgia. The following managers served this office: Wood, Moore, Claud Mabry, then the managers have been, viz:

Miss Carrie Palmer (retired on pension in 1928.) Present manager is Mrs. Taylor.

During the seventies, Manager Thomas, Eufaula, and Mr. Bunyan Davie, Clayton, realized the need of Telegraph service between Eufaula and Clayton, on account of the enormous cotton business in Barbour County. Mr. B. Davie built a line from Eufaula to Clayton, established a "Connecting Lines Contact" with the Western Union. Later the Western Union Company took over the line appointing Mr. Davie manager at Clayton.

The telegraph business was extensive until the long distance telephone service in Barbour County was established, which greatly crippled all Western Union business.

Up to this time the Eufaula office had employed a manager, two assistant operators and three messengers, and the great amount of cotton business kept the lines always busy.

Now the business only warrants a manager and two messengers, but a good business maintains.

The First Telephone Talk Over Long Distance Was Between Georgetown, Georgia, and Eufaula, Ala.

Hearing Lowell Thomas, famous radio broadcaster's) reference to the birthday of the telephone (March 10th) recalled to mind one of the most interesting of the long line of recorded events that have made the County of Barbour and the city of Eufaula one of the most historical and every way notable, not only in the South, but in the entire United States.

And here is the unique "Telephone" story: :

In the early seventies, the late Dr. James W. Mercer, of Georgetown, Quitman County, Georgia, was one of the largest cotton planters and commercial dealers in southwest Georgia. He personally directed his immense general mercantile store, warehouses, bought and sold cotton and in order to keep directly in touch with the "Commercial News Department" he learned telegraphy, built a private line from Georgetown to Eufaula (a distance of two miles across the Chattahoochee river). He quickly learned to "send" perfectly but to be sure at all times, he procured an old time Morse Register to receive on instead of by ear.

Dr. Mercer's telegraph instructor was John C. Thomas, manager of the Western Union Telegraph office at Eufaula and so close was the friendship and intimacy between these two men that when Dr. and Mrs. Mercer went to the Centennial Exposition at Philadelphia in 1876 they were accompanied by young Thomas Randolph Rusk, adopted son of Mr. and Mrs. John C. Thomas, who had just graduated from the University of Georgia at Athens, and was chief operator at the Western Union Telegraph office at Eufaula.

Dr. Mercer and Dr. Alexander Graham Bell had met two preceding summers at watering places in Canada and they had become close friends and naturally through Dr. and Mrs. Mercer, thus thrown with Dr. Bell, the great inventor of the telephone, which was on display at the Centennial Exposition, young Rusk was closely associated with him during several weeks' stay in Philadelphia.

Securing his permission and with some blue prints and suggestions, also some remnants of material given him by Dr. Bell, this young man who was a deep thinker and scholar, who sought into things, came home to Eufaula and in a short time made (though some were crude) two telephones. Dr. Mercer used his private telegraph line that crossed the Chattahoochee river, and with one of these telephones in the Mercer store at Georgetown and the other in the battery room of the Western Union Telegraph office at Eufaula. Telephone service was actually carried on privately between Georgia and Alabama about a year before the first telephone in the United States was put into operation.

As soon as Dr. Bell's patent was obtained and telephones were manufactured, Dr. Mercer replaced the original "Rusk made" telephones with instruments rented from the American Bell Telephone and Telegraph Company and these instruments were still in use when the Eufaula Telephone Exchange was built in 1891, and Dr. Mercer was regularly enrolled as a subscriber to the Eufaula exchange, although living in Georgetown, Georgia, the Southern Bell Telephone and Telegraph Company running a new regular Exchange line to replace Dr. Mercer's original one.

It was during the years of association between Dr. Mercer and Dr. Bell that Mrs. Mercer (formerly Miss Anna Goode of Georgia) began to be troubled with a slight deafness and Dr. Bell, who was also deaf, kept in close touch with Dr. Mercer for many years, suggesting treatment, and she used a number of mechanical devices that he advised from time to time. She was benefitted to some extent by the personal experiences of the great electrical mind of Dr. Bell.

Thomas R. Rusk went to a high pinnacle in the telegraph world. He was manager of the Postal Telegraph Company at Columbus, Georgia. He taught a large class in Telegraph at the University of Georgia while he was a senior student there, and for many years was superintendent of the Southern Division of the Postal Telegraph Company, dying suddenly in his room at home in Augusta, while reading an electrical magazine. His foster mother consented to his being buried in Linwood cemetery, Columbus, on the family lot of Charles Phillips, of Columbus, instead of being brought home to Eufaula—because of the very warm friendship that existed between Mr. Charles Phillips and him during the years of his residence in Columbus and the fact that Mr. Phillips had also befriended him when a small boy at Marianna, Florida, and it was through this a warm friendship between Mr. Phillips and Mr. Thomas, that the latter adopted the lad at twelve years of age. He was an honor to, and greatly beloved by both the Thomas and Phillips families.

The assertion that the telephone connection between Eufaula and Georgetown was the first ever in the United States is made on the fact that the writer has in possession impression letter book copies of letters from said Thomas R. Rusk to Alexander Graham Bell, which reveal the fact that Mr. Bell wrote him, in reply to first notification that the phones he made worked on the Georgetown-Eufaula setup that, "Yours was the first—it will be four months yet before I test as far as two miles."

These phones made by Mr. Rusk were given to the late W. T. Gentry when he was manager of the Atlanta Telephone Exchange in 1892, and were shown to the managers of the Southern Bell Telephone and Telegraph Company at a managers and other officials convention held at Asheville, N. C., July, 1892, and the story was told by Mr. Gentry on this occasion.

Another spray of glory in Barbour County's having given to the world a citizen who made the telephone talked over a year before the inventor's was used.

BRAY HARDWARE COMPANY

There were four Bray Brothers, William H., John W., Nathan M., and Wells J. Bray. They were from New Haven, Connecticut, and when they came South and settled in Eufaula, they established the largest Hardware business in southeast Alabama.

Their large stores and warehouses occupied the block on which the National Hotel now stands, reaching from the corner of Broad and Randolph street to the alley beyond the Fire Department station.

Messrs. William, Nathan and Wells Bray managed the hardware store, while John W. managed the large tin shop.

The firm carried an immense stock of firearms and ammunition, the powder and loaded shells being kept in a brick and steel building at the end of Van Buren street, known as the "Magazine," and during Reconstruction days a guard was kept over this Magazine, for fear the carpetbaggers would blow it up. (See Riots in Barbour County page.)

The faithful porter, who as a young boy, went to work for "Bray's Hardware" as this store was called, spent his life in the business, when Bray Bros. retired from business, the next hardware business was that of Barnett and Ross, and this porter, Arnold Bloodworth, went with the new firm.

As the years passed on Mr. Barnett retired and the firm was J. L. Ross Hardware Company now owned by Mr. Kendall Ross, and for some time the Ross Hardware Company was the only Hardware store in Eufaula.

In 1899 a hardware business was opened by Foy Bros., with L. W. Foy, manager, and in looking about for a man to furnish the hardware experience, when the business began, a Mr. S. A. Bulloch, who was a graduate of Georgia Tech, was suggested and his services secured. Some time before 1915, Mr. H. C. Holloman, who had previously secured the business, sold his interest to Mr. Bulloch and the Eufaula Hardware Company was established with the following owners: S. A. Bulloch, A. C. Mitchell and A. E. Barlar, and like Bray Bros. was for so many years the Eufaula Hardware Company was and is today the largest business of its kind in southeast Alabama, a feature of which is its farm and mill supplies, that furnishes a large section adjacent to Barbour County, as well as the entire County.

The porter who served Bray Bros. throughout their long career, Arnold Bloodworth, also served Barnett and Ross, J. L. Ross, The Ross Hardware Company, The Foy Hardware Company, H. C. Holloman Hardware, and continued with the Eufaula Hardware Company until his death about eight years ago. He was a faithful servant who grew up in historic Eufaula, and was a novice in many kinds of workmanship.

He supervised the setting up of the first two coal grates ever used in Eufaula, one in a residence on Sanford street owned by Mr. Nathan Bray, and the other in the home of Mr. E. Stow on Randolph street in 1877.

At that time only anthracite coal was used (Mr. Stow using it in his large manufactures of several kinds) and it was hard to get a coal fire started by former wood users, and the lady who occupied the Bray house said to Arnold, "Could you make me a 'Blower' out of a piece of heavy tin?"

She drew a pattern on a piece of paper for him and he brought her the blower in a few days. The writer of this history is the daughter of that lady and today is using that same blower. It has been used constantly since the day it was delivered in 1897 and only has one hole about 5 inches long in it which does not interfere with its service.

The Eufaula Hardware Store was originally in the old Shorter Opera House building, which was burned a few years ago, and a commodious new building and warehouse replaces the old one.

Chapter Eleven
Music and Libraries In Barbour County

> There's music everywhere
> On earth and in the air.
> Where youth's at play,
> Where age's at stand,
> As we go, or stay
> There's melody at hand.

Since the day that four immigrants, rowing down the Chattahoochee River, perhaps caught the echo of the song of the woodland orchestra of birds singing, the notes of melody have become louder and stronger, until today real music, made by artists, is heard in the air, in the homes, in the churches, in the schools, on the streets, practically everywhere in Barbour County. It is real first class music for the musical advantages of Barbour County have been such, as to produce the best results.

Going back to the early fifties, Prof. John Van Houten came to accept a position as music instructor in Union Female College. He was born in Patterson, New Jersey, and at the age of 14 suffered an attack of sore eyes. The treatment his physician gave him destroyed his sight, and as he grew up his mother applied his portion of the fortune left by his father to his musical education, and personally carried him to Germany. There he studied under Litz and other of the great masters. Fate must have matched the man and the town, when he was led to accept the offer to come to Eufaula. The record of the later years proved that it did.

Although bred and born a Northerner, he had not been here long, when he had become, as it were, a "deeply died in the wool" Southerner. He loved the people and they loved him. He taught piano, violin and voice, to four generations of Barbour County girls, and they all idolized him. The concerts he gave were history making for the County. He played the organ in the Baptist church, weekly, had an unexcelled choir, played at the weddings and his orchestra was the pride of this section of the state. Most of the best teachers of the past 50 years and the finest singers and pianists were his pupils, who had added to his glory by the records of success they have made.

They have been: Singers—Callie Cargile Kolb; Sallie (Boykin) Bradley; Carrie (Malone) Doughtie; Eula (Beckham) Godwin; Emmie (Kolb) Richardson; Olivia (Price) Skillman; Retta (Thornton) Locke; Louise Shorter; Annie (Smitha) Reese; Minnie (Beay) Guice; Anna (Guice) Brannon; Anna (Sylvester) Edmnnds; Mattie (Thomas) Thompson; Ella (Spurlock) Grier; Eloise Buford; Alice (Shorter) Jelks; Effie (Jennings) Battle; Sallie (Jennings) Kendall; Fannie Kehoe; Lucy Glenn; Janie McNab; Amelia (Cargill) Callen. Pianists—Mamie (Rhodes) Long—on whose shoulders Prof. Van Huoten's mantle fell and she has carried it so grandly throughout the long years and is still holding his flame aloft—Islay (Reeves) Lampley;; Effie (Jennings) Battle; Annie (Jennings) Knox; Nellie Bray; Lily (Lightfoot) Bradley; Daisy (Lightfoot) Steagall; Mattie (Thomas) Thompson; Lillie (Jones) Head; Mary Jones.

The roster of Prof. Van's old orchestra was viz: A. W. Latimer, violin; Austin Cargill, fife; R. D. Shropshire, clarinet; Henry Heron, drums; E. D. Corker, cornet; J. K. Battle, cornet George W. Whitlock, flute; John B. Whitlock, base violin; Romeo Cargill, vioncella; L. J. Richardson, trombone; Robert W. Walker, basso.

In the early eighties, Mr. George W. Whitlock organizaed the E. B. Young orchestra. The members were G. W. Whitlock, first violin;; Prof. S. B. Becter, second violin; Prof. Barbe and J. B. Whitlock, violencello; James Dowe, pianist; Romeo Cargill, violin; Mott L. Pond, cornet;; Dr. Edgar Mitchell, clarinet; Robert Walker, trombone; E. D. Corker, cornet.

Barbour County's first music club was organized by Prof. Van Houten and was composed of the best singers in the town and his advanced pupils.

He stated on many occasions that after hearing the voices of the great singers of Europe, "the finest, sweetest and most perfect in every way was that of his pupil, Olivia Price Skillman, whom he taught and who sang alto in his choir and all his historic concerts. Her lovely voice gave joy through her life, even in extreme old age.

While Prof. Van Houten lived, he gave to the community what no man ever before or since has given.

The concerts he gave, every dollar (when an admittance fee was charged) went to Union Female College or some benevolent cause.

At one time he presented to the First Baptist Church a fine organ for which he paid $1000 and his generous purse was always open to charity. Besides his genius, he was a man of high and noble impulses—unable to see the beauties of this earth, he lived in a world of physical darkness, with only the sublime music in his soul to give him pleasure.

It was Christmas morning when his spirit winged its flight to the mansions above, and while Callie (Gargile) Kolb, whom he taught and loved, sang, with voice trembling and sweet, 'The Angels That Stand on the Heavenly Strand, Are Singing Their Welcome Home" to music that he composed, it was like the echo of the song of rejoicing "up there," and when his skilled fingers, touched the Harps of the New Jerusalem, the ecstacy of bliss, that thrilled him and the glorious halo of light and beauty that he beheld was compensation for the years his eyes saw only darkness on earth.

Among the violin players of the old days were Harrison Hart, Alfred Dickinson, George W. Whitlock, J. W. Hortman, Belle Hortman. In the next generation were Nettie Locke, John Reeves and then there came Nellie Wolff Beringer, a finished artist of today, a long time member of the Music Lovers Club. Today there are a dozen or more girls and boys of the Eufaula High school orchestra who play the violins, their instructor and director, Mrs. T. G. Wilkinson.

In 1906, Prof. S. V. DeTrinis came from Pensacola, Florida, where he was director of a Marine band, which he brought here to play at a Chautauqua. He was so impressed with the town and County and the musicians he met that he returned after a few months and organized a military band, which afterwards, was famous, as the 2nd Alabama Regiment band.

After several successful years at Eufaula Prof. DeTrinis went to New York where he opened a studio, returning to his first love of teaching violin. It was he, who first discovered the great talent of Miss Christine McCann (who has become famous as a violinist.) She is the daughter of Rev. and Mrs. J. E. McCann. It was while her father was presiding elder of the Methodist Eufaula district in Barbour county that she first began her violin career.

The Cowikee Mills band, directed many years by J. E. Simpkins and now by Alfred Beasley, has been the pride of Barbour County for nearly twenty years. It has been made possible through the influence and attitude of Donald Comer, president of the Cowikee Cotton Mills.

It is composed of about forty boys and girls and is a great asset to the community.

Since the days of the War Between the States, the Cargill family has been conspicious for their musical talent, inherited from Austin C. Cargill, fifer in the Confederate army.

All his sons were musicians and his daughters singers and pianists. His grandson, Elmer C. Cargill, is an exceptionally fine cornetist, and pianist, and for a time he played the cornet lead in Prof. DeTrinis' band, organizing an orchestra of his own, with his wife, Helen (Woods) Cargill, gifted pianist, that was the joy of the dancing set at the Country Club and elsewhere for years. The members of this orchestra were: Elmer Cargill, 1st cornet Marvin Tharp, 2nd cornet; J. T. Dunaway, slide trombone; Gladstone O'Byrne, taps and drums.

Later on came the Hortman Bros. with their fine orchestra, that traveled all over the South, carrying the musicians and their instruments, in a specially built trailer car.

Hobart C. (Puss) Hortman, was leader and Ambrose C. Hortman played both violin and saxophone. Dennard Engram was pianist (see Note D. Engram page); Simpson Foy, banjo; Levie H. Shelley, violinist; William Stewart, traps and drums. This was the first roster, but later for several years the band was increased to ten musicians, and different artists were employed from time to time by the Hortmans.

This orchestra was especially popular in Florida during the winter seasons. It ceased to exist three years ago, but was probably the most popular traveling organization in the South.

Up to the illness that overtook Prof Van Houten two years before his death Dec. 25, 1890, his "Chorus Club" had been the highest musical note in the County, and in 1892 Mrs. T. J. Simmons, wife of the president of Union Female College, organized the Eufaula Choral Society. This club was composed of all of the leading singers of Eufaula and several of them are charter members of the Eufaula Music Lovers Club which was organized in November, 1911, by Mrs. T. C. Doughtie. Carrie (Malone) one of Prof. Van Houten's pupils, whose voice was sweeter than any nightingale that ever trilled. Its First president was Mrs. E. Y. Dent (Annie McCormick) Dent. The directors of the Musci Lovers Club have been Mrs. C. S. McDowell, Mrs. T. G. Wilkinson, and now Mrs. L. Y. Dean, III.

The organists of the different city churches have been Baptist, Prof. J. C. Van Houten, Mrs. R. F. Kolb, Miss Emma Brooks, Miss Mattie Thomas, Miss Islay Reeves, and for all her life, except a few years that she resided in Columbus, Georgia, and Birmingham, Alabama, Mrs. E. T. Long (Mamie Rhodes) the musical genius, who is beloved as few women have been, has been the organist. To her the organ is a living human being almost and her music, while having all the finish of the classic artist, has a most unusual, harmonious touch, that any one who is familair with her playing, can recognize without seeing her at the instrument. She has played for forty years for the church, the dance, and all the social, patriotic, fraternal and civic entertainments in the

County, giving her services without one cent of pay. Only recently has she accepted a salary as organist.

During a period of 25 years, she played the accompaniments and helped coach 97 amateur concerts, plays, dramas, etc., all given for some benevolent purpose.

She is still the enthusiastic, musical note in Barbour County life she was forty years ago and is greatly beloved and appreciated. Recently she is being assisted by Julian Edwards, young High school boy who is a musical wonder. Failing health recently prevents her attendance at Church and William Cauthorn is now the capable organist at the First Baptist Church.

The organists of the first Methodist Church have been for long years, Mrs. W. C. Reese (Annie Smitha) and for more than forty years, Miss Lucy Glenn had, and like Mrs. Long at the Baptist, is still holding the position of organist. Mrs. C. S. McDowell and Mrs. J. R. Barr are fine organists and often supply for Miss Glenn.

The Presbyterian organists have been Mrs. J. C. Davis, Miss Nellie Bray (deceased) and Mrs. E. Y. Dent (Annie McCormick) who, after her children were grown up, studied music for the sole purpose of contributing her services as organist of this church. She became very proficient, and under her direction, the Presbyterian choir, was a joy to the church and the community. She was also a fiine pianist and was a great asset to the music of the community. Mrs. R. G. Wilkinson, Miss Mary Stewart and Mr. William Cawthon have been organists of this church.

At St. James Episcopal Church, Mr. J. H. Whitlock was the organist from the sixties until Mrs. P. H. Morris (Pauline Seymore) in the late eighties, succeeded him, and later years Mrs. Henry A. Dent (Etta Copeland) has been and still is organist. For quite a while Mrs. T. G. Wilkinson was organist. Miss Addie Skillman, now Mrs. Virgil Chandler, of Montgomery, was organist at one time and Mrs. C. A. Dantyler is now assistant to Mrs. Dent as organist.

One of the gifted musicians, of which Barbour is very proud, is Prof. Dennard Engram, son of Mr. and Mrs. H. D. Engram of Eufaula. After graduating at the University of Alabama, he went to New York and studied music under the best American artists at Columbia University and at famous artists' studios. Later he went to Italy and took post graduate courses, under several of Europe's most famous teachers. While in Europe he also studied the languages, receiving diplomas, that were most flattering to him, and now for a number of years, he has been Professor of Foreign Languages at the University of Alabama, where he is classed among the most capable instructors of that institution. As a musician he is rated among the best in America and Barbour County is very proud of his achievements.

As artist and teacher, pianist and soloist, Mrs. J. K. Battle (Effie Jennings), was brilliant in musical circles. Her pupils have all reached the most enviable heights as musicians and are monuments to her wonderful ability. Eufaula's musical page in Barbour County history glows with records of her concerts throughout her career.

Miss Emma Brooks (Mrs. O. Worthy) was for many years a teacher at Eufaula having her studio at Union Female College, and her pupils have all become fine musicians. Her sister, Mrs. Fanny Raleigh, also was a fine musician. Both of these artists furnishing, in the old days to Eufaula, the joy of their fine musical talent.

Organists at the Church of the Holy Redeemer have from time to time been: Miss Fannie Keho, Miss Nannie Blackmon (Mrs. H. C. Reynolds), Mrs. J. K. Battle, Mrs. J. M. Kemdall, (Sallie Jennings) Mrs. Fannie Raleigh, Miss Emma Brooks, Miss Mattie Thomas (Mrs. C. M. Thompson), Mr. Gladstone Obyrne, Mrs. D. T. Sheehan, Miss Margaret Hamilton and Miss Margaret Corcoran (Mrs. Emmett Jones).

All of these organists were Prodestants except Miss Keho, Mr. O'Byrne, Miss Hamilton and Miss Corcoran, and were paid organists.

The leading Vocalists in Eufaula today are Mrs. C. S. McDowell, Mrs. E. S. Shorter, Mrs. H. C. Glenn, Mrs. W. C. Flewellen, Mrs. M. W. Stewart, Mrs. T. G. Wilkinson, Mrs. Harry McCulloughs, Miss Hilda Glenn.

And last but far from least, is the Eufaula High School Orchestra of nearly fifty instruments and the High School Glee Club, both instructed by and directed by Mrs. T. G. Wilkinson, whose wonderful musical ability is the great musical asset that has kept Barbour County's stand so high musically and has given such joy.

This School orchestra ranks with the best in the land and the Glee Club is equally worthy of highest praise which both get from an appreciative public.

The leading Music teacher at Clayton, Alabama, has always been Miss Stella Davie and her pupils have gone out from year to year, spreading her fame as a musician and instructor. And among the fine singers at Clayton are Mrs. Guy Winn (Ellene Glenn).

During the seventies Miss Minna Collins of Clayton was the music teacher who, although blind, was an expert teacher and fine performer of organ and piano. She was the daughter of the late Hart Collins and sister of Jairus and Justice and Miss Lutie Collins of Clayton.

Miss Stella Davie is still teaching at Clayton and is

greatly beloved. She is a member of the notable Davie family of Barbour County, a sister of Mr. Bunyan Davie of Clayton, notable as one of the strongest forces and field workers of the Baptist Sunday School work of the State.

REVERIES OF PROF. VAN HOUTEN'S OLD VIOLIN

>Written by Mattie Thomas Thompson and read at an Alumni meeting of Union Female College at the Eufaula Chautauqua June, 1910.

Mr. Van's old Violin", I heard voices whisper, and the sound came to me as from the tomb of the past and gone. As my ear caught the strains, it called up the songs of many happy days, and I fain would give to you music that girds those olden days rememberances, sweet, as songs of birds that come unbidden. I would have these strains bring fondly back the old romances that sing themselves in your brain, until, life today, seems set to rhythm, and your souls to their refrain of mingled joy and sadness. Though the past is dead, it is not forgotten.

No, we never do forget. We let the years go by, wash them clean with tears, leave them to bleach out in the open day, or lock them carefully by, like dead friends' clothes, till we shall dare unfold them without pain, but we forget not, never can forget.

But before, my strings are swept to bring forth, unforgotten lays, suppose I tell many here, who do not know, a little about Mr. Van's old violin. I came to dear Eufaula, the fairest spot in all the world to call home, more than forty years ago. My Master, was refined, gentle and loving, as a woman. His softness and delicacy of touch, put his own aesthetic soul into my strings and my sweetest melody, was ever the inspiration of his great music mind.

I first grew familiar with his soft white hands, when the friend who was closer than a brother to him, and who loved him so well lay sick, and when for weeks daily he sat at this friend's bedside and played, for "Bonnie Annie Laurie I'd Lay Me Down and Dee," "The Mocking Bird." "Then You'll Remember Me" and "Home Sweet Home". It sent thrills to the heart that have echoed in the lives of two women here today, then not born.

The last time those dear fingers held my bow, my master was bowed with the weight of sorrow and suffering, and while his heart and body ached with, he said to this same friend of a life time (who had brought him a new string for me): "What may I give you tonight, John?" The answer was: "Weber", and he played "Von-Weber's Last Musical Thought." Soon after he grew too weak to hold me and I was laid away in the old red lined case, with the doe skin gloves, the silk handkerchief and my guard.

After a time it was my happy fate to fall into hands that hold me sacred because of what I had been to the old Master, for the link that binds him to the new one is friendship true. The Van Houten-Whitlock ties were the sweetest that ever existed between souls, alike to friendship drawn.

Far back in the unforgotten years, I wonder how many trips I made from the vineclad cottage on the hill to dear old Union Female College, lying in my red-lined case, in the foot of the old Scooped top buggy, that shaded my Masters' sightless eyes.

Uncle Randal, the faithful old valet and old John, the big Bay horse, that carried us, were a part of us, as completely as was my case, and his gold headed cane that always led him up the long walk from the gate to the front music studio in the old Union Female College.

Some are here today who know me well. My bow has beat time to their playing in the grand Commencement Concerts of those years.

> 'Some have gone to lands far distant,
> And with strangers made their home
> Some are gone from us forever,
> Longer here they might not stay,
> They have reached a fairer region
> Far away, far away."

I have rested beneath the classic chin, while those soft white hands picked out "Old Black Joe" and my bow drew out with sounds akin to pain:

> "A tear in every note,
> A sob in every strain,
> Soft as the shadows creep across
> The listless sea.
> Then You'll remember me."

In the music room, in the Chapel, in the First Baptist Church, in the old Shorter Opera House, I have led the orchestra that was Eufaula's pride, even as our High School orchestra is today.

Only four of the old number greet me. Austin Cargill's fife is silent and is in the Alabama room of the Confederate Museum at Richmond, Va., and he sleeps where the churchyard myrtles bloom above. A. W. Latimer's violin is unstrung, and he sleeps where the Georgia birds sing. Henry Heron, long ago beat his last tattoo and his drum is **muffled forever**. Only a short time ago, Robert D. Shropshire was laid to rest, "at home" in Fairview, and the clear sweet tones of his clarinet came back on memory's wings, as friends of other days stood around his open grave in the twilight. Romeo Cargill abides in Montgomery, but in his busy life, he no longer plays on his cello.

Robert Walker lives in Birmingham, but I do not know whether or not he ever now blows his trombone. (since deceased).

So gladly do I greet the other four, G. W. Whitlock, E. D. Corker, J. H. Whitlock and J. K. Battle. Long may they go close with me. (At date of this history all of these are dead, except Romeo Cargill.)

As I was carried along the street the other day I heard the cry of "Fish." My every fiber thrilled. I was again in the old buggy, with my master's supper, perching and floundering about my case, as we drove home in the evening. How fond of fish he was; how Will Cobb and Lexie Besson loved to go to the Barbour Creek Saturday morning, just to catch some fish for his dinner.

One day the express wagon left him a large shad, with no name of the sender attached, but in the mouth was a pill box and inside a $5.00 gold piece, with these words on a slip of paper: "A token for the Fishers' Horn Pipe" and "Money Musk" Friday night. John D. Roquemore was the sender, but Mr. Van never guessed until one day a wedding was announced.

One memorable day in 1865, there floated out on the breeze that blew over the western hills of our city the notes of "Yankee Doodle."

My master was sitting on the porch of Mrs. Hunter's home on Broad street. The mayor, Dr. Pope, rode by and said, "We have just carried the truce" to General Grierson. His men are coming down over the hill. At once my master called for me and although he was born in Yankee Land and had not been in the Southland long enough to love it as he learned to as the years passed and while the boys in blue marched by, to the music of "Yankee Doodle," he sat there and drew from my strings the sweetest strains of "Dixie," and "Old Folks at Home."

The closest friends I ever had were Callie Cargill Kolb and Belle Hortman. The one sang to me with a voice sweeter than any mocking bird's trill I ever imitated.

The other always strung me, and learned to play me, and very like her teachers' playing was hers. She, two, has gone home and methinks, teacher and pupil ,strike hands across the heavenly strings in exquisite notes of joy and praise.

More than eighteen years have passed since I joined in commencement exercises, and how glad I am to be here; so glad that she who is to hold me and draw forth my notes bears the name I knew so well, long ago. Others who bear it loved me much. You are bound to U. F. College by sweet young girl memories. I come to you with inspirations left in me by him, whose playing was "the sweetest ear ever heard." And though all unforgotten still and sweetly they be, I sigh as I sing these old songs. They are so dear to me.

Take me, I'll give you my best and with the melody of the happy long buried past, come back, in a flood of tender recollections that will make even sweeter the sacred memories of Dear Mr. Van.

Just after this was read, Mrs. Mamie Rhodes Long, piano, and Mrs. Genevieve Lockwood Dent, violin, played the old time airs here alluded to on this violin.

CARNEGIE LIBRARY, EUFAULA

Our fine, splendidly managed library building is the $10,000 gift of Andrew Carnegie. The site, and most of the books, were donated by the public spirited citizens of Eufaula. It was formally opened May 6th, 1904, by the Pierian Club, with the following trustees and officers: J. B. Whitlock, F. L. McCoy, C. A. Locke, J. P. Foy, George H. Dent, H. C. Holleman, Jake Stern, Mrs. L. D. Mitchell, Mrs. T. Miller. At the end of the first year the officers reported 2789 books on hand, over 7000 volumes circulated from the library and over 1,500 visitors. Each year to date shows increase of these figures. Mrs. Miller is still our untiring, efficient librarian and to her is due the praise for the great benefit and pleasure the library gives to our people.

Wednesday evening, May 6th, 1904, in response to a general invitation to attend a reception given by the Pierien Club, on the occasion of the formal opening of the new library building, society enmasse filled the large auditorium and thronged the reception halls and different apartments. The imposing exterior loomed up stately and grand, surrounded by silver leaf Elm trees, through which the approach lights shone brightly, throwing reflections varied over the snow white gravel walks, the red pressed brick walls, within elaborate ornamentation of yellow copings, balconies, plate glass windows, doors, etc. Grand without—substantial—even to everlasting (with the care as they abide their years, will give.) Within—"The scene of beauty, that remains a joy forever."

At the stairway landing—Mesdames Lillie Drewry Mitchell and Carrie Treutlin Foy, robed in soft white silken and lace gowns and rare diamonds, two women fit to grace a royal drawing room, greeted the arriving guests, with the cherry smile of cordiality which makes them society's favorites. Passing through the beautifully decorated and handsomely appointed apartments there were delightful greetings and welcome smiles from one after another of Pierian women, in brilliant costume, each wearing a "Pansy for thought," the Pierian flower tied with love knots of purple and gold, ribbons, Pierian colors.

Two thousand books given by Eufaulians adorn the walls. On a large table, all the periodicals of the day are found. One room is for children solely, and when the enthusiasm of the evening had waxed high, we saw small boys and girls turning pages, solemnly lost to what was passing around, so intent on the contents of these books. But to the auditorium, and the program—while Louie Dent and Miss Janie McNab brought march tones from the piano. The twenty handsome, cultured literary woman, took the front row of seats. The choir, mayor and council members of the library association, committee and speakers took their seats on the rostrum.

Rev. M. B. Wharton, D. D., invoked blessings, very applicable, after which Hon. Eli S. Shorter—whose deep, soft voice and distinguished bearing show—orator born, on behalf of the committee, in beautiful words their sentiment touching, delivered the building. Col. Shorter, whose heart throbs with every nerve that quivers too for Eufaula's betterment, eloquently paid tribute to those who deserve the laurels. While he gave true weight to all who had labored justly, he gave "highest honor where it lies," and his beautiful compliment to Mrs. Lillie Drewry Mitchell was voiced by every one who knew this noble woman and love her for all that she does." Her intelligence, culture, broad ideas, and indefatigable labors have made her honored and loved. Eufaula bows in reverence to such a woman.

To Dr. J. B. Whitlock, whose ingenious mind conceived Wednesday night's results, Col. Shorter paid an eloquent and very close fitting tribute to a man who puts his public spiritedness into every day life and help.

The speaker gave honor ,in words, that Eufaula join with him in sentiment and bow to Prof. McCoy's great executive ability in behalf, not only of his school, but of every Eufaula enterprise.

To Mr. A. L. Muir, editor of the Times, Colonel Shorter (in behalf of all Eufaula) tendered thanks, warm and sincere, for his personal influence, his pen which gave to the public that which kept alive the enthusiasm to bring success and finesse to the great undertaking. The Times is Eufaula's mouthpiece for it has told Eufaula much she has benefitted by and the generosity of its proprietor has long ago become known all over the community.

Col. Shorter took his seat, and Hon. George H. Dent introduced the speaker of the occasion, Rev. A. J. Messing of Montgomery. He held the large audience close, while with eloquence he told the ever-interesting stories of "Books, their writers, their themes, their morals; one after another he painted pictures most beautiful. He stated that historial, and philosophical writings were the most beneficial to society and, of course, best substitute for all other books." The address was beautiful, tender and heart touching.

The scholarly bearing, the enchanting voice and smooth fllow of grand thought, in distinct words, drew close attention, and the short histories of great men of ancient ages, and the beautiful reference of this distinguished Rabbi to "Him who suffered on Calvary," the thought, the words and the sentiment evoked showed the grand, broad mind of the speaker, as well as the tender feeling for all mankind ,whom he calls brother and friend.

Continuing on the address grew more beautiful, until the close, after a tribute to old Athens, the city of classics—culture —Dr. Messing closed amid hearty applause from those whose dormant souls had been awakened to all that is beautiful and makes happy.

Mrs. S. Oscar Williams, with voice sweeter than nightingale ever trilled, sang "May Morning;" Mrs. Thad C. Doughtie sang, as only she can sing, "Dixie Land," with full chorus, and as the rooms below began to fill, the "Pierian Women" in brilliant array served delicious Clayton punch, such as is never tasted wihout a thought of nector poured in amber cups in Oriental lands. The costumes of the Pierians were all elegant and beautiful, but among them Mrs. Edward Y. Dent, with black lace gown, jetted yoke with black velvet bands between shoulder and elbow, hair high on head with pompour and agriette—was a perfect duplicate of the Athenian royal lady and a more perfect costume could not have been devised for a beautiful Pierian woman of today. Mrs. Dent's personal beauty did honor to her costume. Passing on the robes, Mrs. Terese Mills was handing membership cards for signatures with her own gracious smile. Her election as Librarian is a happy one and another honor to Eufaula. Her cordiality, pleasantry and dignity will adorn the position, so unanimously tendered to her, without her application for same. Eufaula's thanks to these who secured the gift—and with one voice— may our library give us joy and gladness over!—Written by the author for the Eufaula Daily Times issue of November 9th, 1909.

Mrs. Teresa Miller was succeeded as librarian by Mrs. Willa Ethridge Barron and during her illness and death and after her death her sister, Mrs. Lucia Grosscup, held the position for a time.

Later Miss Jennie McRae was elected permanent Librabrian, and is still filling this important place, with ability and credit to the institution and herself.

She has put into use many novel ideas, that have helped the general service in many ways, in literary, financial and economic terms that have been for the progress of the town and for the pleasure and profit of the members of the Library Association.

Any afternoon that one may spend an hour in the library, they will see evidences of the fact that this library is one of the biggest assets of the city.

CLAYTON LIBRARY AND COMMUNITY BUILDING

One of the finest objectives of the WPA, in Barbour County was the assistance given to the town of Clayton and County of Barbour, in the building and establishment of a handsome brick Community building, which houses the Municipal offices and a splendid circulating and renting library which is presided over by Mrs. Robert Petty (Alma Peach,) a most capable and popular librarian.

This library, has been most fortunate in the donation of books to certain alcoves of shelves, named in memory of, and dedicated to distinguished persons and patriotic organizations.

In the alcove in memory the late Judge Augustus H. Alston is many fine volumes, donated by members of his family. The largest recent collection are fine books, among which are many of the classics, owned by the late Augustus H. Alston, Jr., who died in 1936, presented to the library by his sister, Mrs. Derrell J. Grubbs ((Lizie Drake Alston).

In the U. D. C. alcove are miscellaneous books, presented by the women of the U. D. C. of the County, and historical books of the Confederacy and history of the County during the War Between the States.

There is a fine picture of the 15th Alabama Regiment, with pictures of the late ex-Governor William C. Oates and the late Rev. DeBernie Waddell, at one time rector of Grace Episcopal Church, in the forefront.

This valuable and historic picture was presented to the library by the daughter of Rev. Waddell, Mrs. B. T. Roberts (Claudia Waddell Roberts).

Then there is the J. L. Manasus Alcove, of books donated by J. L. Manasus, Jr., of Philadelphia, son of the late Mr. and Mrs. Lacob Leonidas Manasus in memory of his parents, J. L. Manasus, Sr., for many years was a leading citizen of Clayton and known all over the county and a progressive merchant, cotton dealer and one of the financial factors of the County.

These books are circulated not only to the citizens of the city of Clayton but also to the school children and citizens of the county.

The two literary clubs of Clayton have dedicated an alcove

to the memory of the late Miss Weedie Warren, a greatly beloved Clayton woman.

The magazines of the day and popular periodicals are at hand on the stands.

This library was opened January 1, 1937. The city of Clayton furnished the lot, and the PWA money was added to by the efforts of the ladies of Clayton.

The County Welfare office is in the building. Work on beautifying the grounds in the rear of the building has been begun, with the filling in of low places with tons of red clay, on which a rose garden will be planted.

BARBOUR COUNTY LIBRARY

Mrs. J. S. Williams (Martha Crawford) and a friend of hers, Mrs. Lorraine Fletcher, of Washington, D. C., gave the honor and benefaction of a gift of an Alcove of books, as a memorial to a mutual friend, Miss Ruth Paine. The late Miss Ruth Paine was a sister-in-law of Mrs. Williams, and a schoolmate of Mrs. Fletcher's. The Alcove is now being prepared and planned. Mrs. Williams has informed the Library Association that of course they plan to get books of the highest type and interesting ones, that these books are to be used "free of charge by the children and adults of Barbour county."

The citizens of Barbour county are deeply appreciative of this honor, and of so generous and valuable a gift.

AN OLD BARBOUR COUNTY BAND

Dr. Daniel Writes Interesting Reminiscent Letter

Rushville, Nebraska, Jan. 5th, 1920.

Editor The Advertiser:

The death a few month ago of Mr. John W. Huddleston of Eufaula awakens anew some reminiscences. In this instance it is musical. His demise recalls vividly, the organization known as the Brass Band of Eufaula.

To many and probably most of your citizens this is Greek, but I know that there are a goodly number who still remember the old band, with affection. I have the honor of being a pretty regular subscriber to the Eufaula paper, since 1874, and from that time to this I recall, few, if any, references in its pages, to this once Redoubtable Musical organization.

Very soon after Appotomattox Willis and Carey Cox came to Eufaula from Lumpkin, Georgia. They opened a small grocery store on Broad street, near Dr. Thornton's office (Editor's Note: Where Spears' Shoe shop now is.) Upstairs in this building was the Band room. This was the practice room. I heard from time to time their practices, and one evening I ventured in to see, as well as hear, the personnel of the band. I was received quite cordially by Mr. Willis Cox and all the other members of the band.

The next day I called at the store and informed Willis that I would like to become a member of the Band, if there was a vacancy on any particular instrument. He said that inasmuch as either he or Carey would have to keep store, that he thought I could take Carey's horn, which was First B. flat. I said "allright," agreeing to anything that would get me into the band. So he took me into a back room and briefly introduced me, producing the instrument and its book. For some time previous to this I had been a student of the violin under Prof. Van Houten and had acquired the rudiments of solo music. This Willis knew, and in dismissing me, remarked that "as a student of the Violin, he had little doubt that my progress with the B flat would be rapid."

I took the instrument and book home and assiduously devoted my spare time to both. I was in school at the time and needed just such a diversion from my studies. Father used to say that he was glad I had become a member of the band, as that would keep me out of mischief. He told me to report at the next meeting of the band. I did so and the first piece we played was "Shepherd's Quickstep." I was warmly complimented by all members of the band on performance of the B flat part. From that time on I sustained my parts until Carey Cox left town, having taken the 2 E flat after I took his B flat. After his departure, Willis asked me if I thought I could handle the 2 E flat. I said "I don't know, but I'll try." Accordingly, he turned over to me 2nd E flat. In those days the E flats were the leading instruments. With my training on the violin, and the B flat, the E flat was not so difficult. I progressed rapidly and was soon able to take the solo parts of all pieces the band played. This was a great relief to Willis, as Carey, his brother, was gone and there was no one else to take his place.

This band was the creation of Carey and Willis Cox, brothers. They were both gallant Confederate soldiers, and were bandsmen in that service, but to what organizations they were attached I do not recall. I suppose that after the war was over they felt so imbued with martial music that they felt to continue their music in Eufaula would be to them a pleasure and a benefit to the cty. And in that supposition they were correct. At any rate the band was well received and very popular as long as it lasted. As I remember, its life was from 1866 to about 1870.

In 1868 I went off to New York to medical college, and after that I cannot follow its course. On my return to Eufaula in 1870 I did not see or hear much of the Eufaula Brass

Band, but in the hey day of our prominence we had great times. In 1966-67 we serenaded everybody that got married; we were the musical 'it" at picnics, college commencements and all public occasions called us out—firemen's parades, public holidays, etc. We were strickly amateur. In all our long service we never took a cent for our services. We wore no uniforms and we went and came as we thought we should and ought.

Our chief pleasure was in the music we made and the satisfaction it gave to others. We were actuated by a loyal spirit of public service and to that end we devoted our best endeavors. Below I append the roster of the band as I recall it from memory. This list is susceptible to probably some additions, particularly after 1868—when I was absent from its organization, but as I knew the band, it is substantially correct.

Willis E. Cox, first E flat; Z. T. Daniel, 2nd B flat; Billie Hart, 2nd B flat; L. J. Richardson, 1st tenor; Jimmie Booth, 2nd tenor; Tom Harrington, 1st alto; George McCormick, 2n dalto; Joe Singer, baritone; George Allen, Basso; John McCormick, 1st tuba; Bob Harrington, bass drum and cymbals; Will Brannon, base drum and cymbals; John W. Huddleston, Snare drum.

City council paid for our instruments, and that is one reason we never took pay for our services.

Of the pieces we used to play, in their entirety, my memory fails me, but I clearly recall "Shepherd's Quickstep," "Annie Laurie," Kathleen Mavoourneen," "There Will be a Vacant Chair," "Dixie," "The Mocking Bird," "Barry O'Brien," 'The Red, White and Blue," and "Home, Sweet Home." There were a great many other pieces, we had quite a reportoire and if I had my 2nd E. flat book I could give you all of them. I wish I had it as a keepsake and souvenir of old Eufaula. We had a macot piece; I doubt if a living soul in Eufaula remembers it; it was called by us "Sandys Mill;" the words ran thus:

> There was a man by the name of Hill
> And he wanted the loan of Sandy's Mill.
> Said he to Sandy, will you loan me your mill?
> Of course I will, said Sandy."

Now in print I cannot give you the notes of this jig, but when we were tired and wanted to relax, we used to play extempore this jingle over. This seemed to relax us and "Lusch" Richardson could Ha, Ha and out-laugh us all. We never played in church, nor for dances or funerals; we were a peculiar set and we were absolutely independent; of whatever revenue we might derive from our accomplishments as musicians, we felt at liberty to discourse our melodies where we thought it most appropriate. I wonder how many of the roster of the old band are alive. I do not know. I do know that most of them are dead. Mr. Editor, you would take some trouble to find out who besides myself are in the lands of the living, and answer the question in some future edition of your paper.

Sincerely Yours,
Z. T. DANIEL, M. D.

The Advertiser learned from Dr. George A. Beauchamp, many years a resident of Eufaula that in all probability Dr. Zadoc T. Daniel was the sole survivor of this band of over seventy years ago.

The bearers of all of these names, once familiar to Eufaula, are all dead but have descendants living in Alabama.

GOLDEN VOICED MARTIN BROS.

This history would not be complete without the story of the "Martin Brothers" whose splendid voices contributed so much to the musical life of Barbour county for many years.

They were the sons of Mr. and Mrs. J. G. L. Martin, pioneer citizens from France, whose home, corner of Eufaula and Cherry streets, known, as "Martins corner" was famous as the home of these singers. James G. H. Martin, the eldest, was, however, more of a reader, and thinker, but did possess musical talent, and often joined in with the others, as did the second brother, Charles A., who was most interested in agriculture and business, but had the fine Martin voice. The other five were the musicians, whose voices gave such delight on all occasions.

Edward T. and Eugene C., baritone, sang in the Methodist choir, and Clarence, Robert, E. L., and Victor A. sang in the Baptist choir, their fine tenor voices, vieing with each other, in timbre and melody.

The five younger of the brothers, always sang at all the social gatherings, and on the occasion of every concert, or musicale of any kind, they were always the feature of the programs.

They were French creoles and handsome men of the most courtly bearing.

One day when young Robert Martin, then about 25 years of age, met two ladies and stopped to speak with them, he held his hat in hand, until they passed on, but as they stood there another gentleman acquaintance passed by, and instead of lifting his hat, simply lifted his hand and slightly motioned it toward them—a passer-by remarked to the ladies afterwards: "You never saw a Martin brother forget the courtesies due a lady as I saw one do a few minutes ago."

They were polished "beau brummells," whose presence, socially and musically always gave joy. They were all seven fine business men, also.

They are all now dead, except Eugene C., now of Augusta, and the youngest, Victor A., of Tennessee.

Sometime in the eighties the "Cantata of Esther' was put on by the musical talent of Eufaula (which has always been notable) and Edward T. Martin took the part of King Ahaserus and Mrs. T. C. Doughtie (Carrie Malone) the part of Queen Esther. Five of the Martin brothers took parts, and it was said by the two vast audiences (The Cantata was repeated next night) that the acting of Edward Martin and the singing of the five Martin brothers was equal to any real opera company.

PRESENT DAY MUSIC TEACHERS
MRS. L. Y. DEAN, III AND MISS LUCY GLENN

Among the outstanding music teachers of today in Barbour County, one of them, belonging to the group of former years, Miss Lucy Glenn, still carrying on with the same enthusiasm and love of her work, enjoying the love of three generations of girls whose mothers were pupils through the passing years and now the past and present musical thought and power, is carried on by four—May Willie (Schaeffer) Dean, daughter of Mr. and Mrs. C. A. Schaeffer of Eufaula, and wife of Leonard Yancey Dean, III, who, although the youthful mother of two winsome children, Leonard Yancey, IV, and Helen, and is known as the perfect little home mother, and woman of brilliant triumphs, as artist, teacher and is so capable that neither her home duties, nor her artist successes have conflicted with each other. She is not only a finished pianist, but a sweet singer also. Her tact is noticeable as is her unique thought, that is shown in the programs and execution of her pupils.

Before leaving college, she took post graduate courses, one of her tutors being George Whittington, while she was at the University of Alabama and afterwards. Besides her talents, Mrs. Dean is personally very beautiful and charming at all times.

MRS. OMAR GAY

Mrs. Omar Gay is not of Barbour County, but her home is in Quitman County, Georgia, 9 miles across the Chattahoochee river from Eufaula, while her studio is in the auditorium building o fthe City High School.

She is the wife of Omar Gay, a prominent citizen of Quitman County, Ga., and daughter of the late Dan and Emma (Grant) Hammond of Coleman, Georgia. Despite living so far from her studio, she is on time to greet her large class and her ability as a musical artist is shown by the playing of her pupils at her semi-annual recitals and concerts which are always musical treats. She is a popular member of the Music Lovers Club of Eufaula, and her piano solos are gems on all occasions.

WILLIAM CAWTHORN

The latest genius to be numbered among Barbour County musicians is William Cawthorn, son of Mr. and Mrs. William Cawthorn, Sr., of Terese, Ala., who began his musical career under teachers of note in Alabama, and while yet in college took special courses in piano from several highest class instructors.

He is the only male member of the Music Lovers Club of Eufaula and is accompanist for that club. His playing has the technique of the inmate lover of rhythm, and although quite young, he is already one of Barbour County's musical artists, whose future is very bright. As organist for both Presbyterian and Baptist Churches alternately, his choir directing has been marvelous. His piano solos are brilliant executions.

His studio, where he is teaching a large class of beginners, as well as more advanced pupils, is at the Calton home near the City High School at Eufaula. He is now organist for the First Baptist Church and chairman of radio music in Barbour County.

Mrs. J. B. Bush (Mabel McRae) who is Barbour County's actress, and is a finished musician, pianist and singer, has, for many years, been giving amateur entertainments that show her to be a musical genius and a director and actor of comedy of most unusual note. She is the daughter of Thomas and Della McRae, born at Louisville, Ala., and married to John Bunyan Bush of Eufaula. Their daughter, Thelma, married Rufus Lee, and their children, Rufus, Jr., and John B., are unmarried.

Mrs. Bush is not only highly educated along musical lines, but is a finished literary scholar, and a wonderful conversational entertainer. With all her artistic talents, she is also a business woman whose energy is the marvel of the community.

JULIAN EDWARDS

The latest addition to Barbour County's list of notable musicians is Julian Edwards, the 18-year-old son of Mr. and

Mrs. J. W. Edwards. After graduating at the Eufaula High School June, 1938. He is now at the Sherwood School of Music in Chicago, where he is majoring in piano, pipe organ and voice.

Possessed of a fine tenor voice, he is taking advantage of instruction from the best teachers. Ever since he entered high school ,he has been pianist and organist for the school orchestra, and accompanist for many of splendid vocalists in the county on many occasions. He has filled the position of organist at the First Baptist Church and the Presbyterian Church, Eufaula.

He is of the most genial personality and his musical accomplishments are a great asset to his home town and friends.

Besides these God-given talents, that he is giving his very best to perfect, he is a splendid young man, greatly beloved and the star that he will place among the many brilliant ones that glow in Barbour County's Galaxy of Music will be one of the brightest.

DR. J. L. HOUSTON

For many years, one of Barbour County's most outstanding, learned and valuable citizens was Dr. J. L. Houston, of Comer, Clayton and Eufaula, Ala.

He was born in Barbour County and received his early education in the famous old Joe Espy school at Abbeville, Alabama, receiving a first grade license at the age of 17 years and immediately accepting a position as teacher, during which time he diligently pursued a line of medical study, and was later licensed to practice. In 1895 he graduated from Vanderbilt medical university at Nashville, Tenn. So fine were the examinations that he stood and the averages that he made of them that he put two years in one before graduating there. He took a post graduate course in the New York Poly clinic in New York for some time. Since 1925 he served as surgeon for the Alabama Power Company.

In 1899 he went to Texas practicing medicine, but returning to Alabama, he located at Comer, purchasing the historic old Comer home—went into farming on an extensive scale, being one of the largest land owners in the state.

In addition to his duties as a physician, he organized the bank at Comer and was its president for eight years and to him is due the fact that when the depression and financial crisis came and the bank ceased to do business, Dr. Houston liquidated the assets, paying every depositor, dollar for dollar every cent due them, plus the accumulated surplus.

He later purchased a large interest in the Advance Banking Company of Clayton, changing the name to The Bank of Commerce, and this institution paid an annual dividend at the end of the fourth year, the stock being worth $1.30.

Dr. Houston was a fine, cautious financier. He was a member of the Board of Stewards of the First Methodist Church, member of the Agricultural Committee of the Bankers Association and in 1920 was owner of plantations of several thousand acres and owner of a large herd of Whiteface cattle and gave his personal attention to his large business interests, relinquishing his large practice as a physician (which he loved) only to serve, in vital cases, and answer calls to those needing immediate attention, and so popular was he that these calls were frequent. Later he purchased the Bluff City Inn and other large buildings in Eufaula, moving his family to Eufaula, himself and his three sons personally looking after the several departments of his large business interests, making their home at the hotel.

He was deeply interested in and took active part in the politics of the state, county and city. He was a man of broad vision and of much business ability, a most substantial, progressive and useful citizen. He was a steward in the First Methodist Church, a leader in the educational factors of the County and, busy as he was, at all times he loved his profession and was a leading physician of ability. He was a member of state and county medical society.

On the 23rd day of May, 1927, while enroute to Panama City in his car to look after property interests there, his car turned over and he was thrown down a precipice, and fatally injured. He died enroute to a Dothan, Alabama, hospital. His body was badly crushed.

Dr. Houston married Belle McCarroll, daughter of the late Mr. and Mrs. Samuel McCarroll, prominent and greatly beloved pioneer citizen of Terese, Barbour County. To them were born three sons, Howard D. Gorman and J. L., Jr., splendid young business men, who with the help and advice of their mother, are carrying on his business programs and plans in handling his large estate.

The eldest son, Howard, married Carolyne Clayton, daughter of Judge and Mrs. Lee J. Clayton. J. L. married Frances McKenzie, daughter of Mr. and Mrs. K. B. McKenzie. Gorman married Mildred Vance, daughter of Mr. and Mrs. E. W. Vance. Children of Gorman, Jr. and Celese.

All live in their several homes in Eufaula, contributing to the betterment and uplift of the Community, progressive and valuable citizens like their father.

Chapter Twelve

Writers In Barbour County

CLAUDIA ROBERTS

Among the outstanding women writers of Alabama, the name of Claudia Waddell Roberts, wife of Judge Bob T. Roberts of Barbour County, shines with literary luster.

Besides her rare literary talent, her charming personality makes her always notable in any gathering and as a writer of stories, essays, editorials, and features, all bear the earmarks of that higher type of genius that is also displayed in her conversation.

Her writings have the touch of refined wit and humor that you expect to read after you have talked with her.

She is a quick interpreter of human nature and has in her makeup the ability to make the characters in her stories real.

Claudia Waddell Roberts, daughter of the late Rev. DeBerniere Waddell, D. D., archdeacon of East Mississippi, and his wife, the late Mary Elizabeth (Bellamy) Waddell, was born in Crawford, Russell County, Alabama, but has lived almost her entire life in Clayton, Barbour County, Alabama. Her father was ordained to the ministry of the Episcopal Church, his first charge being Seale, Alabama, where she attended primary school. She lived for one year at Eufaula, as the central point of her father's charges in Clayton, Union Springs and Troy when she attended school at the old Union Female College. At the end of the year, she moved with her parents to Clayton and attended the Philip Johnson School for Boys and Girls. She is a graduate of the Clayton High School; private post graduate course under Miss Eliza Bullock; graduate of the Columbia Institute, Columbia, Tennessee; graduate in short story writing under Dr. J. Berg Esenwein. Home Correspondence School, Springfield, Mass.; finished course in Palmer Institute on Authorship, Hollywood, California.

Mrs. Roberts was a four-minute speaker of the World War. A teacher of Expression, training High School boys and girls in oratorical contests, and having them win, one after the other for five years, the gold medal offered as a yearly prize for the best speaker.

CHURCH AFFILIATION

Mrs. Roberts is an Episcopalian, member of Grace Episcopal Church, Clayton, since early girlhood with only one intermission during the years 1923-1927 when she lived in Montgomery and transferred her membership to St. John's Episcopal Church—the church where her father had been ordained to the priesthood, and where her sister, Kate Waddell (Mrs. R. A.) Chapman had served as leading soprano in the choir for many years.

PATRIOTIC AFFILIATION

As a member of the Clayton Chapter U. D. C. she served as historian, recording secretary and as president for many years. It was during her administration that the Confederate monument at Clayton was erected in 1907 with every penny of the $2000 paid. She transferred her membership to the Sophie Bibb Chapter U. D. C. while living in Montgomery, 1923-1927. Returning to Clayton and finding the Clayton Chapter disbanded, she organized a new Chapter at the earnest solicitation and untiring assistance of Mr. John H. McRae, member of the 39th Alabama Regiment, with 103 members and at the state convention U. D. C., 1931, she received the U. D. C. state medal offered the U. D. C. Chapter President organizing largest Chapter 1930-31. She has served the state as second vice president for two years and as chairman of her district organized the Chapter in Clio which is still flourishing.

In 1920-1923 Mrs. Roberts was a member of the Lewis Chapter, D. A. R., Eufaula; 1923-1927 member of the Peter Forney Chapter D. A. R., Montgomery.

MEMORIAL EDUCATIONAL HALL

During the World War, a Memorial section was added to the Parent-Teachers Association with Mrs. Roberts as chairman, and the late Miss Sarah Ferrell, of Russell County, who was living here at the time, as treasurer; the late Mrs. J. L. Martin (Maggie Jones) president of the Association, and this combined organization started out to raise a lasting memorial to Barbour County boys in France. At this time Clayton was badly in need of a new school building. "Can you think of a more beautiful, a more fitting, a more useful memorial to our boys than a Memorial Educational Hall?" Mrs. Roberts asked. She wrote an appeal, it was published in pamphlet form, titled: Memorial to Barbour County Boys—World War Heroes. And it was scattered broadcast over the county.

The project went forward like magic; the time was ripe,

the need for a school building great, Barbour County boys were fighting and dying then in France. They should not be forgotten! When seventeen thousand dollars was in sight—several men subscribing one thousand dollars each—a wedge of objection was thrown into the plans from the outside and the work was halted—but only halted, for when women start out in a patriotic cause it is hard to stop them. Money already made and in the bank was counted and added to as this band of women worked.

Several years passed before a new school building was erected—erected by the Barbour County Board of Education, but with it came another opportunity for these women to have their dream come true. They went forward and made the proposition: "We'll furnish the auditorium and aid in any way we can if you will make of this building a memorial to our boys." No sooner said than done, for this educational board was in perfect sympathy with the movement. And, today, high up on Eufaula Street, stands this memorial educational hall at Clayton, the capitol of Barbour County, the city on the hills, as a memorial, not just to Clayton boys, but to all Barbour County boys who enlisted in the World War. At the entrance to this memorial educational hall, the members of that Parent-Teachers 'Association and its memorial section have placed a bronze tablet. Stop and read the inscription as you enter here, and take the message which was left by our boys for you and for me: "To you from falling hands we throw the torch, be yours to hold it high."

FACT AND FICTION

Claudia Waddell Roberts is a short story and feature writer. She has contributed short stories, feature stories, news stories, etc., to Mystery Magazine, Film Fun, Young's Magazine, Lippincotts' Magazine, Southern Miscellany Magazine, Chicago Record-Herald, Philadelphia Public Ledger, the New Orleans Times-Democrat and Picayune, Grit, Comfort, Progressive Farmer, The Sunny South, Birmingham News-Age Herald, Montgomery Advertiser, Montgomery Journal, Commercial Appeal, Mobile Press, Macon Telegraph, Eufaula Times and News, Eufaula Tribune, Barbour County Banner, Clayton Record, Writers' Monthly. A short-short story appeared in the book, Outstanding Short Fiction, 1935, The American Short-Short story.

Prize Stories

The Rusty Key—first prize May Harris contest—Mystery Magazine; In the Bridal Chamber—first prize Montgomery Journal contest; A Fair Exchange—prize winner—Progressive Farmer Contest; The Man With a Past—second prize—

Sunny South contest; Al is Standing in the Open—prize winner Grit's Third Political Symposium.

Mrs. Roberts is a member of the Eufaula Writers Club. She is a member of the Press and Authors Club, Montgomery, Alabama, serving for two years as chairman of the Prose Group, and four years as president. She is a member of the Selma-Montgomery Branch National League of American Pen Women serving two yeras as vice president, Radio Chairman for one year, broadcasting for Franklin D. Roosevelt during his first campaign, and is now holding the office as treasurer. She is a member of the Alabama Writers Conclave, and has served as publicity chairman, secretary-treasurer. Responded to the address of welcome in 1935 at the annual meeting at Montevallo. In 1931 addressed the Conclave on the subject: The Editor and I. This was sold to Writer's Monthly, and appeared in that magazine December, 1931. Addressed the Conclave at the annual meeting at Montevallo June, 1936, on the subject: What Do You Know About the Short-Shorts? This address was brought out in pamphlet form by Dr. George Lang, president of the Conclave and professor at the University of Alabama, before the combined Writers' Clubs of Selma in November, 1936; to the Study Club at Clayton January, 1937, and is booked to address the Combined Clubs of Tallassee in the fall of 1937.

WALLACE SCREWS

Wallace W. Screws, editor and publisher of the Montgomery Advertiser for many years, was born February 25th, 1839, in Barbour County. He was educated at the schools of Glenville, then Barbour County, now Russell County, where he lived until 19 years of age.

At 16 he began life's battle and worked in a store, saving money for his tuition.

June 1st, 1858, he became a law student in the office of Watts, Jacson and Judge and was admitted to the Bar in 1859, although having to take advantage of statute, as he had not yet reached the age of 21. He was succeeding fairly well when the war began and he entered the Confederate Army.

He was reared by a Whig father and naturally imbibed his political ideas. His first vote was for Bell and Everett. He was opposed to secession, but was a loyal Southerner, and went to the Confederate war and fought for the South in all the battles except Fort Pickens.

For a time he belonged to Hilliard's Legion of Infantry of 59 and 60 Regiments and was First Lieutenant of Co. E— his command—was sent to the relief of Gen. Longstreet at Knoxville, then to Virginia, where he remained until the surrender at Appomattox. After the war, he secured a position on the editorial staff of the Montgomery Advertiser.

In April, 1865, the Federal Government prohibited publication of the Advertiser and the embargo was not lifted until July 15th, the first paper appearing July 20th.

From then until his death, Major Screws was closely connected with the Advertiser as publisher, editor, owner and his courageous stands, many times in the fact of mountains of opposition, have proved him a great man.

In 1876 and 1880 he was selected secretary of state, the only public office he ever held, but throughout the years his name, his pen and his personality have been forceful influences in the state.

He declined re-election, although he could have easily secured the office without opposition.

When the Farmer's Alliance first appeared in the South, he wrote a scathing article in the Advertiser, declaring that it was a political machine and would bring about a third party, which proved to be true in Barbour County.

He was appointed by Major General Holtzclaw May of State Troops on his staff and no military man has ever been more popular.

He has, in a spectacular way, through the Advertiser, shown his force of character; courage of convictions; and always stood for his friends, under all conditions.

In April, 1867, he married Miss Emily F. Holt of Augusta, Georgia, to whom were born three sons, W. W. J., Hart and Benjamin, and one daughter, Elizabeth.

He died at Montgomery beloved, honored and deeply lamented.

WILLIE COPELAND COURIC

Willie Copeland Couric was born at the old historic Copeland home on Broad street, Eufaula, daughter of Dr. William Preston and Mary (Flewellen) Copeland. She began writing news soon after graduating from Noble Institute at Anniston, Alabama, receiving her A. B. degree. While a student at Union Female College, Eufaula, she took up art and many of her beautiful paintings and drawings have been prize winners. She finished her art studies at Corcoran Art Gallery, Washington, D. C.

For 25 years, she has been an outstanding journalist, special correspondent for Alabama and Georgia papers and society editor of the Eufaula Daily Citizen and now of the Eufaula Daily Tribune, during which time she has won special recognition as a writer.

She is a charter member of the Alabama Writers Conclave and for one year was treasurer of that organization.

She was winner of the first prize, National Contest, offered by the "Smart Set" magazine for the best essay on "Can a Married Woman Hold Two Jobs?" Her answer was in the affirmative.

She also won the first prize offered by the Birmingham Post for the Alabama Writers Conclave contest on "What Feature of the Newspaper Do You Like Best?" Mrs. Couric's answer, in a splendidly argued essay, was 'The Editorial." She knew because during all the years that she has held the position of Society Editor of the local papers, along with her correspondence and feature writing she has spent half of each day at the office of the paper, kept her own home and reared to enviable manhood, three splendid sons, who are a credit to their parents.

Her husband, Alexis A. Couric, known during the days of Barbour County (when cotton was really king) as the outstanding cottonshipper, whose sales over-reached any other cotton dealer in the Community, and his ability as a classer, was the comment of the cotton experts with whom he dealt.

Mrs. Couric is a member of the Selma-Montgomery branch of the "League of American Pen Women"—a past regent of the Lewis Chapter D. A. R.; past president of the Symposium Literary Club, Eufaula, past president of the "Guild" of St. James Episcopal church.

She served as chairman of the Committee on "Literature and Library extension" of the Federted Clubs of Alabama.

She is an enthusiastic member of the Home and Garden club and despite her much writing, she finds time to take part in all the club, civic and church life of her home town. She drives her car herself, and is a true daughter of the old South in principle, but is a strong agency for and takes active part in all the higher and better progress of the community.

Since this biography of Mrs. Couric was written she has been elected at the May meeting vice president of the Selma-Montgomery branch of the National American Pen Women's League, member of Alabama Writers Conclave and Eufaula Writers Club.

WILLIAM THOMAS SHEEHAN

William Thomas Sheehan was born in Eufaula January 1st, 1874, son of Thomas and Emma (Garrett) Sheehan, grandson of Daniel T. Sheehan, native of Cork, Ireland, and Amanda Naomi (Asherst) Crayon, who was descended from an old English family, the first of this American name, coming to this country in 1740. His father, John Adherst, was one of the first settlers of Mount Cormly, moved to Birmingham in 1873, where he was engaged in construction work, but soon died of cholera during the epidemic of that disease in Birmingham that year. His wife was the daughter of James Madison and Mary Anderson (Williams) Garrett.

He attended city schools of Eufaula, was a teacher of the grammar schools himself in 1894 to 1897. He assisted in organizing the Second Eufaula Rifles and volunteered to go to the Spanish-American war. He was made Sergeant of Company T, 2nd Alabama Regiment of Volunteers and elected Lieutenant National Guards, 1907 with rank of colonel.

In 1930 in his memory the Montgomery Spanish War Veterans named their organization Will T. Sheehan Camp. His first work was with the Eufaula Times, after William D. Jelks purchased that paper. In November, 1899, he became connected with The Montgomery Journal. He began his career in 1899 with the Montgomery Advertiser as reporter, then as special correspondent and in 1907 assistant editor. After the death of Major W. W. Screws in 1913 he was made editor-in-chief. In 1905 he and Charles H. Allen fought the Glass interest in the Advertiser, and he remained a part owner until his death.

From 1913 to 1917 he was tax collector of Montgomery County, appointed by Governor O'Neal. He was gifted, genial and wielded a most facile pen with most charming metaphor and was a feature writer of power and interest.

On the occasion of the Centennial celebration and Home Coming at Eufaula June 12, 1923, his speech was a gem that will long be remembered.

He first married in April, 1900, to Mary Crawford, daughter of Virgil and Martha Crawford. His second wife was Elizabeth Winston, daughter of Charles Henry and Irene Houston (Park) Winston. He died July 5th, 1928, at his home in Montgomery. His children were Charles Winston, Will, T. M., Jane Hopkins, Liza Janet Hill, Anne Garrett Sheehan and Irene Houston Sheehan. His widow, Elizabeth Winston Sheehan, is one of Alabama's most brilliant women of letters, having published several stories and volumes of fiction and poetry, and is one of the leading members of the Montgomery branch of Pen Women of America, a member of the Alabama Writers' Conclave, member Press and Authors Club and much beloved for personal charm.

William Thomas Sheehan was named by his grandmother, Martha (Ashurst Sheehan) William Thomas Sheehan, for William Thomas, son of John Elliott Thomas, the families living near each other and very intimate.

ERNEST DRURY CORKER

Earnest Drury Corker was born in Augusta, Georgia When quite young his father died and he came to Barbour County to make his home, his brother-in-law, Capt.

Henry C. Hart, of Eufaula being administrator of his father's estate. He began business immediately after finishing college, and throughout his career, was acclaimed one of the best accountants in all this section. He was often called on to audit, some special set of books, and was so proficient in business, that besides the regular position he held with Beringer Bros. for many years, he was able to devote his evenings to music and literature. He was a natural musician, playing several different instruments, but the cornet was his favorite and for years his instrument led the other cornets in the several orchestras that were Eufaula's pride in the long ago.

Earnest Drury Corker's facile pen was the producer, from his easthetic and forceful mind, to the newspapers of the South and Magazines, of his day of many beautiful poems that were soul stirring and will live on and on, and his feature stories and News Columns in the papers he was correspondent for, have left a most happy and lasting memory of him in the hearts of his many friends, and they were very many, for as a traveling salesman, he was known far and wide and his wonderful conversational powers, with his ready store of information on worth-while topics made him personally drawn to those with whom he came in contact.

He was a vestryman of Saint James Episcopal church, and he lived daily strictly according to the principles of his church, always the cultured, christian gentleman.

He was an enthusiastic, fraternity man, holding offices in the I. O. O. F. and Red Men Lodges, the latter was organized in Barbour County, through his influence and efforts.

He managed two Conventions of Red Men that were memorable, and was loved all over Barbour County as a valuable citizen of high toned character, business ability, and rare talents, that bring to friends the pleasures of association.

He married Kate Henry, daughter of John B. Henry, a prominent pioneer citizen of Barbour County. Their children are, viz.: Lottie, a professional nurse, who has distinguished herself in the work of her high calling; Kathleen, married H. H. Conner, one of Barbour County's leading citizens and former Mayor of Eufaula; Earnest D., Jr., United States Army, who has spent all his life after finishing school in the service of his Country. He is now located, and has been for several years, at Fort Benning, Georgia. The third daughter, Era, married George Thoma, born in Belgium, nephew of Mr. Leon Dubios of Banhoura, Belgium, and purchased the historic old Thornton Estate two miles from the city of Eufaula. Mr. and Mrs. Thoma and their little daughter reside in Philadelphia, Pa.

ANNIE KENDRICK WALKER

Annie Kendrick Walker was born in Eufaula at the old historic home at five points, marked by the famous "Walker Oak" that was recently dedicated to itself and given into the custody of the City.

She is the daughter of John Absolem and Eliza (Kendrick) Walker, prominent citizens of the old Eufaula that was so glorious in their day and time. From babyhood she was a favorite and as she grew to womanhood inherited from her brilliant mother the literary talent that has made her notable as a writer. After the death of her parents she wnt to Birmingham where her brother, Mr. Robert H. Walker, was associated with the Birmingham Age Herald, and while still very young she began writing splendid articles for that paper.

Later she went to New York and for a long time was on the staff of the New York Times, and her articles were highly praised by the most prominent literary critics.

She is also a writer of feature stories—Biographies—and has done much historical research. She is now in her old home town receiving a most cordial welcome.

LUCY WINN

Lucy Winn, daughter of the late Col. and Mrs. Winn of Clayton and granddaughter of the late Dr. and Mrs. J. J. Winn of Clayton and the late Mr. and Mrs. H. Clarence Glenn, Sr., of Eufaula, is one of the coming young writers of which Barbour County has much cause to be proud.

She graduated with honor from Agnes Scott College, Decatur, Georgia, and after taking up Journalism she spent two years in New York holding a position on the New York Sun, and since then has been devoting her time to Syndicate work and free lance correspondent for a number of papers, among them the Montgomery Advertiser, Birmingham News, Birmingham Age-Herald and other Southern papers.

Her facile pen readily weilds a solution of fact and thought, that makes her stories, real and interesting.

She also writes poetry that includes both the humorous and sublime, and she is a charming young woman with a future before her that already reveals a brilliant literary mind.

MISS LULA WALKER

Although Miss Lula Walker, daughter of the late Addison Allen and Fanny Creyon Walker, pioneer citizens of Barbour County, is now a resident of Montgomery, Barbour County and Eufaula claims her still, for it was here that she was born and spent her life until the past two years. Her maternal grandmother, Martha Asherst Creyon Sheehan, was a member of the distinguished Asherst family of Alabama, while her paternal ancestry goes direct to Revolutionary heroes that were illustrious. Her father was Captain of Hilliards Legion Grace's Brigade C. S. A.

She was educated at Union Female College at Eufaula and early showed marked literary ability, and her writings have included feature stories of note, and many verses of rarely beautiful poetry.

Her poems bear the earmarks of alert mind and visionary soul, the combination making her poetry, in many cases, sublime.

She is a student of the classics and her collection of literary gems show the trend of her scholarly thought as do her own writings, both poetry and prose.

For years she was Historian of Lewis Chapter Daughters of The American Revolution, Eufaula, and the scrap books she compiled are a credit to any organization and to her personally as a patriotic, capable and untiring researcher.

The old Walker home on Broad Street where beautiful old pictures on the walls and the handsome antique furnishings reveal the culture of the family and old lifelong friends, sadly miss the presence of the charming little woman who has gone to another home.

Capt. Walker was Cashier of the Peoples Bank, one of the pioneer institutions of Barbour County, and later years until his death, was State Agent for the Penn Mutual Life Insurance Company during which time he made for himself an enviable business and personal reputation. His handwriting was unique and very beautiful and is remembered for its peculiar style by many friends of long ago.

MRS. C. C. PUGH

Mae (Simms) Pugh, wife of Dr. C. C. Pugh, was born at West Point, Georgia, a member of the distinguished Shepherd family through her mother. This family being notable in Tenn., Texas and Washington, D. C., through a long line of Senators and Congressmen.

She was educated in the High Schools of West Point and took post graduate courses at Cox College specializing in music, afterwards teaching music until her marriage to Dr. Condy Collins Pugh, who has been pastor of the First Baptist Church at Eufaula for the past ten years. During this time Mrs. Pugh has become identified with all the literary, religious and musical interests of the County. Her own brilliant literary and poetical attainments making her outstanding and popular.

She writes short stories, and her beautiful poetry has been accepted and published in many periodicals and newspapers. Recently her Hymn "Blow Ye The Trumpet" was accepted by the Woman's Missionary Union official organ, to be used as the "Jubilee Hymn" at the Great celebration of that organization in 1938, and has been highly complimented by the Press.

Another beautiful poem, "Because Life Is So Brief," was published in the Anthology of American poets of 1936. Recently her poem, "God's Sparrows" was published in the Alabama Baptist.

Mrs. Pugh is a valuable leader in all the work of her husband's church, a past President of the "Lanier Club", a member of the Music Lover's Club, is the daughter of a Confederate Veteran, a member of the U. D. C., and a member of the Barbour County Writer's Club.

Dr. Pugh was born at Gold Hill, Alabama, graduated at the University of Alabama and the Southern Baptist Theological Seminary at Louisville, and has served as pastor at Montgomery, Ala., Hazelhurst, Miss., and other places before accepting the cal lto Eufaula where he is greatly beloved.

PAULINE COURIC

On Barbour County's scroll of fame, no name blazones forth with more luster and genuine appreciation for service done, than that of Miss Pauline Couric.

First, she is beloved as few young women are, for a personality so charming, and an inate love for children, that she is spending her life in a beautiful service for children and helpfulness to the community in so many ways that it would be impossible to enumerate them.

Her sweet nature, her great talent as a director and instructor made her notable all over the South, where she trained and put on, with local talent, dozens of "Baby Operas" that have been commented on by the Press in most flattering way. Many of these entertainments, in which tiny tots took part, being the very last word in Amateur dramatics and musical programs of type high class, proving Miss Couric a veritable artist in her line of training.

For over ten consecutive years, she has directed a "White Christmas" program at the First Baptist Church annually, that is not only the delight of every child in the community. but is the annual contribution of the community to the Christmas cheer, for the needy of the community.

These beautiful programs gotten up by Pauline Couric and the Music directed by Mrs. E. T. Long, include girls and boys from every denomination in Eufaula and every year "White Christmas" is looked forward to, with special pleasure, by the children taking part and also by those who receive the material benefit from the celebration. The great spiritual benefit goes to Pauline Couric and her helpers in this beautiful work.

From babyhood, her name has been a household word in this community because of the traits of rare christian character that began early to shine out in her daily life. Everybody loves Pauline Couric and appreciates her beautiful service she gives to the community.

She is the daughter of the late Alexis Alfred and Sarah McKleroy Couric and great great granddaughter of Reuben C. Shorter, pioneer citizen.

The Baby Opera originated in the mind of her sister, Callie Kolb, lovingly called "Lady Bird" who married W. J. Willingham, a member of the old distinguished Willingham family of Georgia, who when she married, passed on to her younger sister, Pauline, her own years of experience and her gift as a trainer of children.

Not only has she been outstanding as a director of Amateur plays, but as a writer of both prose and poetry, she has won a bright star of glory and her beautiful lines of verse, her short stories, and miscellaneous writings, place her high on Barbour County's roster of writers.

WILLIAM THORNTON COWLES

William Thornton Cowles, second son of Thomas W. and Laura (Shorter) Cowles, was born in Eufaula, the grand son of Gen. Reuben C. Shorter, pioneer financier of Barbour County.

He grew up in the city schools, received dictinction in the Junior and Senior classes of the Rusk-Hinton Boys school at Eufaula and while in his early teens was elected Librarian for Eufaula's first circulating Library.

He was a born orator, a natural poet and a scholar and thinker. He did not go to College until he attended The Southern Baptist Theological College and was in the Theological and law class with his son, William T. Cowles, Jr. His idea was to become a Minister of the Gospel, but abandoned that idea, and both father and son later graduated from Stetson Law College, Florida.

In 1885 his parents moved from Eufaula to Atlanta, Georgia, where at Atlanta and Athens, Georgia, he was associated in the cotton business with his elder brother, John Shorter Cowles. There he married Miss Edith Pope of Mobile, Alabama, who died when his two sons were quite young. After several years he married his wife's sister, Miss Annie Pope, whom the sons, only know as devoted mother. Both sons have become prominent attorneys in Jacksonville, Florida, where William T., Sr., entered politics and was prominent in all the best inteersts of the state. He was popular and but for his tragic death, would have, no doubt, some day have been Governor of the state of Florida, as his friends and supporters had already headed him for that honor.

He was a writer, whose facile pen fashioned word pictures that revealed the cultured thought and big brain of the writer. His lines of verse always revealed the romantic and sentimental thought that occupied his mind. His humor was of that dignified kind that marks the illustrious family of which he is a distinguished member.

He was big hearted, big brained, and greatly beloved in his Florida home as well as his native Eufaula home.

He was assassinated in January, 1926, on the street near his home, protecting a lady from insult. The man who killed him (Marcus Powell) was electrocuted in July, 1937, at Raiford, Florida.

His widow and two sons, William and Jack, reside at the old home in Jacksonville, Florida, where the mother is a leader in Church and social life and the sons in the legal life of the community.

R. D. SHROPSHIRE

Robert DeKalb Shropshire was born in Clarksville, Tenn., November 22, 1835, and was educated at the University of Wisconsin, expecting to be an Episcopal Minister. However he came South and entered the newspaper business.

He enlisted in the Confederate Army and at Shiloh was promoted to Major. While serving as Cannoneer, he suffered injuries that made him partially deaf. He was transferred to the Commissary Dept. and came to Barbour County and Eufaula for supplies. He was a most unusual man from every standpoint. Highly educated, a musician, and lover of Music, to the highest extent, a Democrat of the deepest dye, and he used the papers he wrote for to give emphatic emphasis to his principles. He served the Macon Telegraph as editor. Publishd the 'Bluff City Times" and the "Daily Mail" of Eufaula and the Eufaula Times and News and Daily Times

He was a scholar and a lover of classic literature. Was better versed in Shakespeare than the most enthusiastic student ever is. From printer to editor and publisher, he was familiar with the newspaper business and ran his papers on a high plane.

He was an expert chess, back-gammon player, and loved that recreation.

His marriage on November 22, to Sarah Valeria Barnett daughter of John and Mary Ann (Davis) Barnett, at St. James Episcopal church of which he was vestryman, was one of the most brilliant affairs that ever took place in Eufaula.

During President Cleveland's administration he held a

LOUISE STANDIFER HALL

position in the Government Printing Department, secured for him by his close friends, James G. H. Martin and John C. Thomas, without his knowledge, the writer of this history has most of the correspondence between Martin (who was residing in Washington at the time) and Thomas of Eufaula, relative to this appointment.)

"Shropp" as he was affectionately called, was a literary genius of a rare unique type.

His children are: Cassa Irene (Stephens) Marie Lucile (Farrington), Annie Laurie (Dolphy), Linwood and Robert deceased.

The facile pen of this literary genius, while on the Macon Telegraph and the different Eufaula papers he edited and published, was ever the production of a brain that saw and showed to others, pen pictures that were the admiration and literary delight of every reader of those days.

His humor glistened in every utterance from him, both on paper and by mouth, and every story carried an uplifting message.

LOUISE STANDIFER HALL

(Mrs. Joseph M. Hall) now of Brooklyn, New York, daughter of Mr. and Mrs. W. C. Standifer of Eufaula, Alabama, has had more honors showered upon her than any other woman born and reared in Barbour County.

She graduated with honors from the Eufaula High School, then while a student at the University of Alabama, from which she also graduated with an enviable record in scholarship, activities, honors and friendship, unanimously elected the first and only co-ed editor-in-chief of the "Corolla," the annual publication of the University of Alabama. Her election to the Presidency of the Chi Delta Phi National fraternity for authorship, which she founded, was not only a credit to herself and her many friends, but was an honor to the entire South, to claim the chief executive of this honored fraternity, whose membership is found in the best Universities of the United States. The other National officers all residing in New York and Utah.

While at the University of Alabama, she founded the Delta Chapter of Chi Delta, Pi, Alabama Chapter of the Mathematics honor fraternity, Pi Mi Epsilum, the largest social fraternity for women in the United States. She was also a member of practically all the honor societies on the Campus, a distinctive honor claimed by few. Throughout her college career, she likewise maintained a most brilliant average.

In the book entitled "Principal Women of America" published by the "Mitre Press" of London England, Louise Standifer Hall's, native of Barbour County, Alabama, name was among the 25 American women thus honored. The Birmingham News, commenting on this great honor bestowed on Mrs. Hall, carried an interesting story which said: "Great significance is attached to the publication of this book, because it represents the first ranking of American women as seen by the English. Many years were devoted to its compilation, weeding out until a finale was reached, which was, at once, enlightening and entertaining. No 'fees' nor sales of books were involved, but each name stand purely on its own resources."

Recent years Mrs. Hall has assisted her husband in his work, and after graduating from the Law department of Lawrence University, Brooklyn N. Y., she was admitted to the bar and is the first woman of Barbour County who is a full fledged lawyer. She is a member of the Seawanhaka Democratic Club of Brooklyn, N. Y., is also a gifted musician, and a woman of highest culture and personal charm, and Barbour County is very proud of her brilliant record.

Following graduation from the University of Alabama, she held the position of Instructor of Mathematics and Chemistry in Phillips High School, Birmingham, Ala., and later was elected Instructor of English, at the University of Philipines and is a member of Alabama Academy of Science; Member of the Alabama, the Memphis, Tenn., branch American Association of University women; President of Delta Chapter Chi Delta Phi.

Member of Keystone and author of Keystone Constitution; Member Pan-Hellenic Council; Member Y. W. C. A. Cabinet; Founder and Executive Secretary of Pi Alpha; Founder and Secretary and Treasurer of Newtonian Club (Freshman Mathematics Club); Associate Editor-in-Chief of the Crimson White, weekly university of Alabama newspaper On all honor rolls; Leader of Social service Dept., University of Alabama; Local Manager of Devereux Players for University of Alabama, and also local Manager of Madame Borgny manner players for Alabama; Member National Press Bureau; Junior Faculty; Fellows in Physics (first and only woman to receive fellowship in Physics.)

Following graduation from University of Alabama with first honors, she became active in the following Author Beta Pi Theta Ritual: Birmingham Branch National League American Pen women; Memphis Branch National League of American Pen Women; Was member Nineteenth Century Social and Literary Club of Memphis, Tenn.; Executive Secretary Memphis Branch of Alumni Association of University of Alabama; Councillor for Alpha Lambda Young Writers organization; Patron for Local Chapter of Delta South Eastern University, Memphis, Tenn.; Territorial Secretary for the

Philippine Islands Convention of Woman's Division of the Democratic Party, 1927-28.

In the list of Fraternities she is sole Founder of Beta Phi Theta National Collegiate French Fraternity, being Grand Executive Secretary 1927 and in 1928; Founder of Pi Alpha, now Gamma Pi Chapter Kappa Gamma; Former Vice President and President of Chi Delta Phi, the largest Authorship Sorority Founder and Member Kappa Delta Pi (Education), Pi Mu Epsilum (mathematics), Typatia (Senior Honor), New Alabama Chapter of Mortor Board-Alpha Chi Alph (Journalistic) Sorority; Seventh Woman to become an Honorary member of this man's Literary Fraternity—men only being active. She holds membership in other Forenic, Dramatic and English Professional Sororities.

In addition she has received training in Howard College, Birmingham-Southern, Peabody, Nashville, Tenn., and holds a Secretarial Diploma from Draughons Business College, Memphis, Tenn., and spent a first year at Forsman's Law school refusing nomination for class officer and is a graduate of the Brooklyn Law school of 1934, refusing nomination for class officer.

She has been nominated for Officer D'Academie, a French award to be listed in Who's Who in the New 1938 Edition.

On their return from extensive travel in Hawaii, China, Japan, Philippine Islands and the Orient in general Mr. and Mrs. Hall located in Brooklyn Heights, New York, where they are members of the Democratic and Literary, Twelfth Night and Athletic Clubs and Mrs. Hall is outstanding as a member of American Women's Associational Clubs and active as a member of the New York Branch National League American Pen Women.

Mr. Hall is also an author, a man of wide information and much learning. He was born in Elpaso, Texas, September 29, 1899, grandson of Joseph M. Hall, who was Col. in the Fifth Alabama Regiment. His grandfather was also Judge in Hill County, Texas, 24 years. His Uncle, Col. Newt Hall, was married to a Marine officer's daughter, chose the marines, although he was educated at Annapolis. He fought in the Boxer War and the grandson, Joseph, has inherited a love for energetic work and is a very busy man, being a Contract reporter with offices at 75 West Street, New York City. He is a member of the National Short hand Association and not only engaged in special reporting himself, but employs 25 to 30 other reporters. His contracts being bid on in both Washington and New York and he is Sub Contractor for the East under National Contracts. His volume of business is immense, and his ability and talent well matches that of his brilliant wife and has a personality that makes him friends.

Mr. and Mrs. Hall are both prominent and favorites in enviable business, literary, political and social circles.

ELIZABETH THORNTON COMER

The oldest and most beloved of Barbour County's women writers (while not a citizen of Barbour County, but of Midway in Bulloch, adjoining county) is Mrs. Elizabeth (Thornton) Comer, wife of John Fletcher Comer, II, of the illustrious Comer family of Barbour, which has made her Barbours own through her own married life. Although she has resided at Midway, she is known in every town and hamlet in Barbour and lover and admired as a writer who has contributed greatly to the Literary phase of uplift in Southeast Alabama. She is an ardent Confederate Daughter who is often the inspiration of the meetings of Barbour County Chapter U. D. C., and president of the Midway Chapter U. D. C. and its crown and flower.

She has written many interesting stories, made numerous speeches over Alabama at the conventions and is one of the best known Baptist Church workers in the state. She is a member of the Barbour County Writers Club. She has compiled scrap books of the Sixties and her stories of Reconstruction have been real history. On Friday, October 8th, 1937, she delivered an address on Admiral Raphael Semmes of the Confederate Navy, to large gatherings of Barbour County Chapter, U. D. C., and although she is 83 years of age, made a wonderful address, without notes, standing nearly an hour while she talked, her face beaming with enthusiasm over what she was telling. She is not only a brilliant woman of letters whose facile pen reveals her depth of character, but is sweet, gentle and dearly beloved.

LEWEY DORMAN

For a number of years Mr. Lewey Dorman, son of Mr. Alex Dorman of Clayton, gave much time to research of Alabama history, and wrote much about Barbour County, but before his manuscript was ready for the press, he was unfortunate to let it get out of his hands and was lost.

However, despite this great misfortune, he has from time to time published some very interesting pamphlets on various subjects. He is a thinker and a student of history, who sees with writer's eye, and his stories are replete with thought and expression that is most interesting to read.

All of Dorman's friends sincerely hope that his valuable manuscript may yet be recovered and published.

He now resides at Hurtsboro, Alabama.

LELLA WARREN BRECKENBRIDGE

Daughter of Dr. Benjamin Warren and Lella (Underwood) Warren. They resided at Clayton until about 15 or 20 years ago when they moved to Washington, D. C., where many members of the family now reside. Early she developed literary tastes, and recent years she has attained enviable reputation as a feature writer and newspaper correspondent.

Her husband, Mr. Brecenridge, is also a noted writer, and they spent six months or more recently at Clayton where they were at work on some Southern features.

NOTES

In the early fifties there lived at Ocheese, Florida, the distinguished Soloman family, and the young daughter of this family, Lydia, often visited relatives and friends in Barbour County, among them the family of Rev. Green Malone, presiding elder of the Eufaula district of the Alabama Conference, M. E. Church, South.

On one of these occasions she brought with her a friend, Mrs. Caroline Lee Hentz, the famous writer, whose book, "The Planter's Northern Bride," has just created a sensation.

Mrs. Hentz wrote the greater part of this book, sitting on a large Rock Island in the Chattahoochee river, near Ocheese, and for many years after steamboat passengers, passing this historic Rock Island (something like one hundred and fifty feet long and nearly the same width) would be charmed with the stories Captain B. F. Marcrum would tell of his so often passing her with his boat, and she would stop writing to wave to him. She was given an ovation in Eufaula.

It was in May, 1854, that she finished this wonderful book, and this brief account of Mrs. Hentz, a visitor to Barbour County, is just another of the many long lines of happenings over the County, that lead directly and indirectly back to "The Grand Old State of Barbour," connecting distinguished people, even if remotely, with the past. . . Barbour County has not only sent out greatness, but greatness and glory has often been brought to her.

Miss Lydia Solomon married Mr. Wellborn of the distinguished Wellborn family of Barbour County. She was a school teacher in the County many years, and after being a widow a long time, married Mr. Griffin of Pike County. She was the gifted lady of the Old South.

Chapter Thirteen

Medical Profession In Barbour County

SIX GREAT DOCTORS

> A Doctor's brain, hand and heart
> Is God's mercy gift to mankind
> And there is no earthly Art
> That can equal this gift sublime.

In these days of wonderful surgery, scientific aparatus and modern equipped hospitals there is little wonder that veritable miracles are wrought—and it is not easy to take in the many stories that could be told of some of these varitable 'miracles" that were results of the hands, brains and nerve, of some of the old family doctors of the long ago.

Barbour County has cause to be very proud of a history overflowing with stories of romance, patriotism and biography blazoned with name that glorify.

In this unique history, the names of six great men of the Medico, who have contributed their brain work in things that have made them so helpful in ministering to suffering humanity, that the world has justly accorded to them, the fame they so richly deserve.

DR. BAKER

In 1870, while practicing his profession in Eufaula, Alabama, Dr. Paul DeLacey Baker discovered and used that wonderful remedy, "Veratrium Verdi," which is universally used today by the greatest Doctors of the world in the practice of Obstetries, with success never dreamed of until its late use has shown that its discovery was one of the greatest of that of any Doctor in the country.

Dr. Baker was a man of superior attainments, both professionally and personally. More than six feet tall, keen blue eyes and long red beard reaching to his waist, he was the striking, polished gentleman of the old school.

A leader in the community, whose influence was a great asset. He died in the hey-day of his career, an honor to the town, to his profession and to Barbour County. He is buried in consecrated ground in Fairview Cemetery.

DR. MITCHELL

Dr. William A. Mitchell, in the early eighties, was the brilliant Doctor just making a record for himself in Medicine that was so phenominal that he was selected by the state Medical society of Alabama to represent that organization at a National Medical convention in New York in 1881.

DR. MITCHELL

The address that he made before that body, was so wonderful, revealing the strides made in his profession, that he was quickly chosen to represent the American National Society in Paris, France, that year.

He accepted this honor and the European and American Press commented so favorably on the address the American Doctor made before the great assembly of Doctors from all parts of the world that he was called "the most famous Doctor in America."

He was the first and only Barbour County Doctor to procure from an institutional Morgue a dead body and with his own process of acids, eradicate the flesh from the bones and again put the skeleton in form in his office. The writer saw him at work when scraping and polishing them to fit on the wires and he told some interesting things about acid process, to a group of school girls studying Anatomy.

Dr. Mitchell loved horses and his beautiful charger. "Black Charlie," with his distinguished master astride him, was the admiration of all this section.

He was a literary genius, as well as a great physician and wrote numbers of valuable articles for the leading Medical Journals of the Country, solely to give to his brothers of the Medical fraternity, the benefits of his investigation and study of many things of great import in the practice of Medicine.

He was born in Glennville, Russell County, (adjoining Barbour—when it was Barbour) April 4, 1848, and died at Eufaula July 15, 1905, and was buried in Atlanta, Georgia, the home of his only child, Mrs. Robert Ormond, 388 Capitol Ave., Atlanta.

He married Annie Dawson, daughter of W. L. Dawson, pioneer citizen of Glennville, and she also is buried in Atlanta.

DR. COPLAND

Dr. William Preston Copeland also contemporary with Drs. Baker and Mitchell, was born and reared in Eufaula and first became famous as the inventor of the "air treatment" for burns. He found that lotions and bandaging with cotton or gauze impeded, rather than hastened, healing and to his idea of washing a burn with Phenolsodique or Dalby's fluid and leaving it exposed for air healing, is practiced with great success.

Like Dr. Mitchell, Dr. Copeland wrote many interesting articles for the Medical Journals and held high office in the Medical societies of the State and County.

In 1891 his horse ran away and threw him against a telephone pole. Both legs were broken and while his fellow doctors set the shattered bones, he directed them. Unfortunately one of the Doctors insisted on setting on leg differently from the manner Dr. Copeland and Dr. Drewry directed, and Dr. Copeland, who was tall and erect, afterwards slightly limped.

Dr. Copeland was the only Eufaula Doctor ever to make a specialty of the eye, ear, nose and throat, in which he was eminently successful.

The first operation of the eye he performed was catarect. The patient, an old man who had been blind for many years. The removal of this catarect restored his sight completely. He performed this operation in his office with equipment far less scientific than that now used.

As a citizen, Dr. Copeland was one of the most valuable Eufaula ever had. His record was brilliant and enviable in the highest degree. He was born in Eufaula September 1, 1845, at the old historic home on the bluff afterwards knows as the "Austin Cargill place". He was the son of John Nelson and Caroline (Cannon) Copeland who moved from Charleston, S. C. to the ancient town of St. Joseph, Fla., on the Gulf and an epidemic of yellow fever brought them fleeing to Eufaula in 1840.

He received his education at the University of Alabama and Belview College and hospital, New York.

He was a student at the University of Alabama when it was burned and took part in the fight with the Yankees at Tuscaloosa on April 3, 1885, the day before the burning.

He began the practice of medicine in Eufaula immediately after graduation. He was one of the first Pecan enthusiasts

DR. BRITT

DR. DREWRY

DR. BAKER

DR. COPELAND

in Barbour County and was leader in all the civic and benevolent activities of the community. Interested himself and others in Bauxite industries of the County; was many years President of the Barbour County Medical Society. Was a skilled physician and an upright christian gentleman loved and honored for his long useful career, where for many years he was the oldest living native born citizen of Barbour County who had spent his life in the County. And drove his car until a month before his death at the age of 85.

He married Mary Fountaine Flewellen, daughter of Col. James T. Flewellen of Georgia, and to this beloved and brilliant lady is due the praise for Eufaula's first park and children's playground.

Dr. Copeland died after practicing continuously over 60 years, using the same office, always.

Dr. Copeland was also deeply interested in Indian Lore and wrote many articles on the Indians and their mode of living, implements of war and how they made them.

Children: Etta, married 1st, Wm. L. McCormick, 2nd, Henry A. Dent; Caroline married Lee J. Clayton; Mathilde married McNab, M. R. Reeves (both deceased); Willie married Alex A. Couric.

DR. DREWRY

The lamented Dr. John W. Drewry, whose memory is thrice blessed, not only in Barbour County, but all Southeast Alabama and Southwest Georgia, was one of the old time, small town doctors, who when an unprecedented condition arose, met it like the soldier of mankind and the King of his profession that he was and performed an operation that the surgical fraternity of that day deemed almost impossible.

The day before a municipal election in Eufaula in 1874, a crown of "around town loafers," were talking politics in the Carriage and wagon shop of James W. Faulk and when they became so boisterous that he ordered them out, one "Boots" Sheets drew a long knife and rushing on Faulk, cut him across the abdomen—he rushed after him, but fell outside—the cut severed his clothes which fell off him and as he slumped down, his intestines rolled out into the dirt.

Dr. Drewry was summoned and quickly arrived. He laid the seemingly fatally injured man on a rude work bench, called for a bucket of water and without anticeptics, other than the few inadequate things in his bag, laid every intestine in the man's body on a small towel, hurriedly procured from a neighbor, washed the dirt and grit off, stopped the flow of blood from the severed veins, placed them back in position and sewed up the gash which was from hip to hip. Mr. Faulk lived forty years after this, dying, when an old man of pneumonia.

Another great operation he performed was, picking up the ends of veins under the knee of a fifty year old man, who had been cut by a vicious hog, striking his sharp tusk into the main artery, causing a hemorage which lasted four hours leaving the man almost lifeless.

It was late at night when Dr. Drewry reached the injured man and by the light of a country lamp with a tiny curved needle, he picked up the severed artery and sewed the edges so that the blood could flow naturally through the vein—an operation, most delicate, even today, with all the modern instruments and methods and scientific rules to go by. The result showed that Dr. Drewry's hand was a master surgeon's.

Still another of his great operations was saving from amputation, the hand of a man who had five bone felons or "Whitlows" at one time. Six local physicians in consultation, said: "must cut the hand off."

The patient pleaded to save it (he was a Telegraph operator) and Dr. Drewry dipped the hand into a preparation of his own conception, then freezing the hand, while chloroform was administered to the patient he cut nine gashes in the palm of the the hand and on each finger. The treatment was so terrific that the life of the man was in great danger, but the wise old Doctor loved his patient and wanted to save his hand for him and stood firm against the opinion of the other five doctors, standing looking and assisting him, and although the patient could not lift his arm from a sling for six months the hand was eventually saved. The method persued made the old Doctor famous a third time.

Married Annie Etheridge who was the beloved physician's wife, queenly mother, as famous for her christian character and good works as her husband was great professionally. Their children were Stella, married Jason G. Guice; Carrie, married John P. Foy; John W., Jr., married, first, Annie McDonald, second, Julia McRae; Lillie and James A. were twins, Lillie married Americus A. Mitchell, Jr., and James Allen married Mamie Harrison.

He died at a ripe old age, a peer among men.

DR. SCHLOSS

When a slender, dark haired boy, played on Colby street in Eufaula fifty years ago, a representative citizen was heard to say: "That little Schloss boy will be a great man some day, I heard his playmates urging him to go fishing and he said to them, "Bah! I don't want to fish, I want to make an electric engine." Although he has not built an electric engine, other than the miniature ones he built in boyhood days, then took to pieces and rebuilt—he has built for himself a reputation as a Doctor, that places him easily, the first and most famous children's specialist, not only in America, but in the world." (I quote from a famous surgeon, who knows Who's Who in the Medical world and is always careful in his statements):

This quiet, reserved, almost timid boy, Oscar Menderson Schloss, eldest son of the late Hugo and Rachael Menderson Schloss, as a student showed early that he was taking to things that were worthwhile and it was not long after he entered the Alabama Polytechnic Institute at Auburn, Alabama, that he was recognied as a younzg man aiming high and giving the best in his makeup, to every undertaking.

Although his first ambition had been, to some extent, fixed on Electricity, the call of the Medico came to him and he responded to it with an interest and determination most unusual.

Friends of his early boyhood days recall the enthusiasm and tireless labor in the little laboratory he set up in his room at home, when a student at Auburn. How he used pieces of different kinds of meats in his microscopic experiments.

He was not robust and his father urged out of door sports, but his whole interest centered on books and experiments.

During the first years of medical courses he was under direct care of Dr. W. S. Britt (a young physician who had just begun to become famous. He is now one of the leading surgeons of the South and the thing that he is proudest of, is the fact that Dr. Oscar M. Schloss' first study and practice was under his direction).

During vacation when all the College boys at home were interested in the social pleasures of the community, young Dr. Schloss spent his time in Dr. Britt's office, buried deep in books and visiting his patients with him, using him as an example, from whom he absorbed the highest and best, which was used to help place him on the flattering and enviable plane on which he now stands commanding the admiration of the Medical world.

After graduating with honor at Auburn he went to John Hopkins; served as intern at Kings County Hospital at Mount Sinai Hospital, New York ;was Prof. of Children's diseases at Belleview Hospital. Spent three years at Harvard University, returned to New York and is now Prof. at Cornell Medical College, New York.

His fame is recorded in so wide a scope of service, that it is unnecessary to comment on any particular case, suffice it, that he is a great honor to Barbour County and to Alabama, and his home town, Eufaula.

Dr. Schloss is marired and has several children.

DR. BRITT

Over 40 years ago there came to Eufaula, Barbour County, a red headed, serious faced doctor, Walter Stratton Britt, Sr., fresh from Belleview hospital, New York, hung out his shingle in a town already famous for its several highest class physicians. The years have passed and the others have passed on—but these passing years have in many ways, too numerous to detail, made Dr. Britt easily Barbour County's first, most useful and most famous and best beloved citizen—his name a household word in large sections of two states.

While he reached the highest pinnacle of his profession, that acclaims him, one of the most skilled and most successful surgeons in the South, has made him, as it were, the idol of men, women and children, regardless of station or color. As a doctor few have ever gained the hold of affection in the hearts of the citizenship of the community.

His whole life was service to others, and his great brain, steady hand and wonderful power of endurance are marvels of everyone.

He has been known to operate four to six times, attend twenty-five patients in his infirmary—then rush ten to twenty miles in the country on emergency call and attend other patients in a day—after being up all night two nights in succession, with serious cases.

Finances were always secondary with him and the list of charty patents he has given of his best in thirty-five years will reach far into the thousands. All idea of pay was crowded out of his mind, in his love for humanity and his strong desire to relieve suffering.

Hundreds of cures he has wrought are almost miraculous and this community as a whole loves him with a reverence that is as genuine, as it is universal.

Great as he was professionally, he was also the outstanding and most valuable citizen in the community, as a man of affairs—and the city and county owe him innumerable debts, that only love and gratitude can pay.

While he was too busy ministering to the physical needs to attend church services—his interest was none the less strong and valuable—and while he was not what the world would call "pious," his heart and purse were always wide open to all religious causes. He stood for christianity in its highest phase and every act of his life was a demonstration of the true religion he lived.

He was born at Midway, Ala., September 2, 1878, the son of Mose Wiley and Mollie (Roberts) Britt, and from this distinguished ancestry he inherited the force of character that made him conspicious and honored in every walk of life.

He was of genial personality, though reserved and emphatic, and ever ready to help some one, but who had no time to waste with petty things of life. He was big and broad, and good and every day that he lived did some service to mankind that will carry his name down in history as one of the greatest and well beloved men of the Southland.

He married Kate Comer, daughter of J. Fletcher and Elizabeth (Thornton) Comer, whose lovely, noble womanhood and personal popularity has made her the ideal professional man's wife. She is equally beloved as her distinguished husband, whose "help meet" she is in all the highest and best the word implies.

Their children are Elizabeth, married to Lewis Moore, and Walter S., Jr., married to Julia Bulloch.

After a brilliant college career, Dr. Britt, Jr., became associated with his father, both in his practice and on the staff of the Britt infirmary. Dr. Britt, Sr., died May 28th, 1938, and the two young doctors, Dr. W. S. Britt, Jr., and Dr. John Ball Adams, are making the Britt Infirmary still the great institution of healing and mercy that characterized it so many years. Under Dr. W. S. Britt, Sr., whose death was one of the greatest misfortunes that ever befell Southeast Alabama and Southwest Georgia.

When Dr. Britt was buried from the First Baptist Church, the flowers that filled the altar, walls, chancel and banked in 12 windows were estimated at over two thousand dollars, sent from friends at home and other towns, and more than a thousand people from many cities were present, hundreds unable to get inside the church. A great and good man was sincerely being mourned and paid tribute.

BARBOUR COUNTY MEDICAL SOCIETY

The Southwest Alabama Medical Association was organized several years before the War Between the States. Its members included all the physicians in this section, among whom were Drs. W. L. Cowan, C. J. Pope, W. H. Thornton, E. L. Hoole, Dr. Terry, W. H. Shepherd, B. C. Flake, Eufaula; Joseph Jones, John Benson, Henry County, Dr. A. W. Barnett, Glennville, Dr. P. C. Winn, Clayton.

Medical Convention

The semi-annual meeting of the Medical Association of "Southeastern Alabama" will be held at Eufaula on Thursday the 11th of October. The physicians of this and the surrounding counties are earnestly requested to attend. P. P. McRae, Secretary.

Sept. 22, 1853

At the organization of the B. C. M. S. there was a notable

discussion as to the hypodermic syringe, and the state records show that there was much interesting discussion as to why and why not adopt it practically.

Dr. P. D. L. Baker was the first to introduce Veratrum Verdi.

Among the later years members of this Medical Society, not already mentioned, have been Drs. E. B. Johnston, noted surgeon, and his son, E. B., Jr., Dr. S. A. Holt, Dr. Albert Goodwin, Dr. T. S. Mitchell, contemporary, with Drs. Copeland, Drewry and W. A. Mitchell, H. L. Brannon, L. J. Simpson, all at the head of the Medical Society of their time. Later Dr. W. S. Britt, L. F. Tisinger, P. P. Salter, J. B. Adams and W. S. Britt, Jr., and Dr. Clarence Bennett, Eufaula, Drs. W. O. Wallace, E. M. Moore, Clayton.

In August, 1930, Dr. W. P. Copeland was the only living charter member of the original Barbour County Medical society. He died February, 1931. He practiced 67 years in Eufaula, 57 years using the same office.

At that time the following were the officers and members of this association, viz: Dr. Clarence Bennett, Eufaula, president; Dr. James Reid Clayton, vice president; Dr. E. M. Moore, Clayton, secretary and treasurer. Members: Drs. J. S. Tillman, J. F. Tomlinson, E. M. Moore, Clarence Bennett, Walter S. Britt, W. P. Copeland, Joseph L. Houston, W. R. McInnis, J. D. McLaughlin, R. N. Norton, James W. Robertson, Paul P. Salter, Louis F. Tysinger, G. O. Wallace, Huey Watson.

Membership Roll January 7th, 1896

Roll: Dr. J. K. Battle, Eufaula; Dr. B. F. Bennett, Clayton; Dr. H. L. Brannon, Eufaula; Dr. W. P. Copeland, Eufaula; Dr. J. W. Drewry, Eufaula; Dr. Albert Goodwin, Eufaula; Dr. C. L. Harris, Baker Hill; Dr. W. H. Harrison, Aften; Dr. W. A. Mitchell, Eufaula; Dr. Thomas Patterson, Louisville; Dr. W. H. Robertson, Clayton; Dr. B. S. Warren, Clayton; Dr. H. M. Weedon, Jr., Eufaula; Dr. J. J. Winn, Clayton.

Membership Roll April 7th, 1903

J. K. Battle, B. F. Bennett, R. L. Brannon, W. S. Britt, W. P. Copeland, A. J. Gilbert, J. W. Hagood, W. H. Harrison, J. L. Houston, W. G. Lewis, W. W. Mangum, W. P. McDowell, W. H. Robertson, W. A. Smart, G. O. Wallace, R. L. Hite, J. J. Winn, L. M. Winn.

Membership Roll 1911

W. P. Copeland, W. S. Britt, J. J. Winn, B. F. Bennett, B. F. Jackson, W. A. Smartt, J. L. Houston, Thomas Patterson, Robert Patterson, G. O. Wallace, C. Long, J. D. McLaughlin, J. S. Tillman, W. G. Lewis, Judson Davie, L. F.

Tisinger, L. P. Shell, W. R. Belacher, J. W. Fenn, W. R. McInnis, R. L. White, R. O. Norton, C. M. Wooley, C. H. Athey.

HOSPITALS

As early in the history of the County as 1859, Dr. C. J. Pope owned and operated a private infirmary, and notable among his nurses was "Aunt Caroline" Bouer (herself almost white) who nursed the mothers and four geenartions of the babies in Barbour County.

Later he associated with him Drs. W. H. Thornton and J. C. Terry and named the firm The Eufaula Medical and Surgical Infirmary Later Dr. B. B. Flake operated a hospital on "Thomas Hill,' later named "Flake Hill" because of Dr. Flake's hospital and home there.

During an epidemic of smallpox he cared for hundreds of negro slaves in a four-room house, assisted by the physicians of the entire County. During the war Between the States, "The Tavern" (the first house other than log cabins, built in Eufaula by Mark Williams) was used as a hospital for Confederate soldiers, Mrs. B. F. Treadwell taking the lead in all hospital service. Drs. Pope and Thornton were in charge.

Eufaula's next hospital was owned and operated by Drs. W. S. Britt and W. P. Mcdowell, the building used being the old Moulthrop home on the Bluff. It was called the "Bluff City Infirmary," opened to the public June 12, 1905. It was successfully run for a number of years and closed, Dr. McDowell going to Norfolk, Va., where he is now a renouned specialist, and Wr. W. S. Britt is owner of the Britt Infirmary, one of the best beautifully and minutely equipped hospitals in the country.

It is built on the site of the old Union Female College, and is strictly modern and complete in every in every appointment. It was opened May 1st, 1920.

It has a negro ward, and one of the most elaborate and expensive X-ray equipments to be found anywhere. Dr. Britt is sole owner, but associated with him as aids are Dr. J. B. Adams and his son, Dr. W. S. Britt, Jr., both young men who have made wonderful college records, and are capable physicians and valuable citizens.

The Salter hospital ,owned by Dr. Paul P. Salter, was opened March 20, 1923. It was formerly the old Moulthrop home, first used as a hospital by Dr. Britt and McDowell. Dr. Salter purchased the property ,added to the original (remodeled into a hospital building, recently has built another annex and now has a fine, modernly and handsomely equipped hospital. These two institutions, Britt Infirmary and

Salter hospital are by far Barbour Countys' greatest human asset. Both have fine nurses' homes adjoining and corps of capable nurses.

Young doctors who were reared in Barbour county, and have gone elsewhere to achieve and have brought honor to themselves and their home county are: Dr. Oscar M. Schloss of New York, (See "Six Great Doctors"), Dr. J. Ramser Crawford, New York; Dr. Edmonson M. Couric, Miami, Florida; Dr. John M. Edmondson, Birmingham; Dr. H. B. Dowling, Mobile, Alabama; Dr. W. P. McDowell, Norfolk, Va.; Dr. Charles Pugh Brown, Norfolk, Va.; Dr. William Stewart, Troy, Alabama, and students, Dr. Hunter Brown and Edward B. Comer, in college.

BARBOUR COUNTY'S FIRST FUNERAL HOME

Bascom Dowling was born June 15th, 1869, in Bulloch County, Ala., the son of Rev. Angus and Laura Boswell Dowling, pioneer citizens of Barbour County. He conducted his first funeral fifty years ago at Ozark, Ala. The hearse he used was a jersey wagon and a grey mule. He worked all night making the coffin. He has been in the undertaking business nearly fifty years, his first place of business being No. 2 Hart's Block, which was destroyed by fire November, 1904. His stock was wiped entirely out by the flames, leaving him about 30 damaged caskets and $28.00 in cash. From that beginning, overcoming many hinderances, he has built up his business to its present flattering status.

Although Barbour county had three other undertaking establishments, Dowling was the first embalmer and previous to his coming there had never been but three persons in the County embalmed.

The present Dowling Funeral Home is the realization of a dream of twenty or more years.

This splendid Funeral Home on Orange street is a memorial to the distinguished parents of Mr. Dowling.

The marble marker on the frontice, near the main door, tells that it is "In memory of my father and mother, Rev. Angus and Laura Boswell Dowling, who gave their life's work, that others might have eternal life.—H. B. Dowling, 1928.

Besides the main chapel offices and embalming and preparation suite on the first floor, there is the large workshops to the rear and upstairs is the large stock rooms and two bed rooms and bath, kept always in readiness for free use of the family and relatives of any bodies brought there for burial or funeral services—all modernly equipped.

This Funeral Home has proved to be one of the greatest blessings to Barbour County and its advantages were never dreamed of until the past few years have revealed them to the public.

Mr. Dowling is member of the distinguished Dowling family of Southeast Alabama, his father being a beloved Methodist minister of the Alabama Conference, whose name and life record is notable in the annals of Southern Methodism.

He married (Callie Mancill), member of a prominent Andalusia family, and their children are John W., married to Mamie Hall. They have two children, John Hall and Matthew.

Dr. Bascom, Jr., married Kathleen Pugh, of Mobile, and they have two children, Margaret and Pugh. Dr. Dowling is one of the leading physicians of Alabama.

Kathleen Dowling married L. D. Petrie and their children are Bascom Dowling Petrie and Donald Petrie.

Mancill Dowling married Laurt Stockton Malloy and holds a responsible position with the American Bell Telephone Company in New York.

Mrs. Callie Dowling is one of the brilliant literary women of the community and is a leader in The Methodist church activities. For many years she was teacher of the Adult Women's Bible Sunday school class of the First Methodist Church that bears the name "Callie Dowling Bible Class" to honor her.

After several years of poor health, she lectured today to her old class, the present teacher, Mrs. J. M. Kendall, being out of the city for a short time. She was welcomed most cordially by the entire school.

BARBOUR COUNTY WOMEN DOCTORS

Barbour County has been singularly honored in the fact that two brilliant young women who grew up in the schools of Clayton, achieved the highest in the medical profession and have practiced their profession in a rarely distinctive way.

Miss Nannie Winn, daughter of Dr. and Mrs. J. J. Winn of Clayton, following in her father's footsteps, chose the Medico. She graduated from Agnes Scott College, Decatur, Georgia, then from Goucher college, New Orleans. She then took post graduate courses in surgery and other branches of medical training at John Hopkins, Baltimore, Maryland, and practiced her profession in Alabama, Tennessee and Baltimore. For a time she practiced with her father at Clayton in Barbour County.

She was acclaimed one of the finest physicians by "Who's Who" of the Medico. Her home town, county and state were shocked when the news came that a truck had run into her car one morning, on a road in Tennessee, as she was going on a surgery call and she was instantly killed. Her brilliant career came to a tragic end.

Ruth (Robertson) Berry, wife of Dr. Ivan Berry, of Buffalo, N. Y., and daughter of Dr. and Mrs. W. H. Robertson, Sr., of Clayton, was born and reared at Clayton. After the high school terms in her home town she graduated from the University of Alabama, receiving her A. B. degree, and later graduated from Tulane receiving her full medical degrees. She maried Dr. Ivan Berry of Buffalo, N. Y., and continues a partnership practice with her distinguished husband.

She specializes in children's diseases and is on the staff of a Buffalo hospital. She is a specialist in Paedotrophy and has made an enviable reputation for herself.

Clayton and all Barbour County have just cause to be especially proud of the record of these two brilliant young women.

Chapter Fourteen
Historic Old Homes

First House Built in Eufaula

Their walls hold memories dear,
Their histories are brilliant pages,
Illumined, bright and clear
With varied stories of the ages.

Coming down Broad street, as you turn into Riverside drive along the old historic bluff, we come to the two-story English type home built by Mark Williams in 1827. He was one of the first settlers of Eufaula and of Barbour County and this was the first house built in the village, other than log cabins. It looks today just as it did when first built, and has been kept in fine repair through all, the more than a century.

It was built for a home, but for several years was used as a hotel and called "The Tavern." When the name of the village of Eufaula was temporarily (4 years) called "Irwinton," some newspaper writer erroneously called it the "Irwinton Inn,' but that was incorrect. It was never the Irwinton Inn.

FIRST HOME BUILT IN EUFAULA

During the War Between the States, it was used as a hospital for Confederate soldiers, under the management of Doctors F. C. Blake and Pope and Perry.

It was inherited by the descendants of Mark Williams. One of them (Mrs. Bathman) sold it to Mrs. T. A. Mashburn, who now owns and resides in it.

It stands on East Broad street facing the bluff drive, and from the east porch overlooks the Chattahoochee river, viewing a Georgia prospectus far up the river to Historic "St. Francis Bend.'

It has always been repainted the same light brown color, as originally, and looks exactly as it did when first built.

The banisters of the stairway, leading to the second story are hand carved and show the splendid workmanship of pioneer days, although there is some evidence of crudeness in the carving with a knife.

ELMORELAND

"Elmoreland" was built in 1842 by Americus C. Mitchell, a wealthy pioneer citizen of that portion of Barbour County, which is now Russell County, and is situated near the historic old town of Glennville, Alabama.

In those days, this town was the center of wealth, two colleges, beautiful homes, and was known far and wide for its hospitality, principally for its wealth and as the home of illustrious families.

The Mitchell lands were government grants to John Mitchell of Virginia, and were given to him in return for gallant service to his state in the Revolutionary war.

A. C. Mitchell married Mary Elizabeth Billingslea of Jones County, Georgia, and her wealth and that of her husband combined made the building of an estate so notable and progressive, possible.

Elmore remained the property of the descendants of A. C. Mitchell to 1914, when it was sold to a New England syndicate to be used for a game preserve but later, Mrs. Frank H. Elmore of Montgomery purchased it, and resided there for some years, selling it recently to B. Comer, Jr., son of the late Governor B. B. Comer.

It is one of the finest homes in the state. A. C. Mitchell, III, of Eufaula, is the grandson of Col. A. C. Mitchell, the original owner.

ROSELAND

Roseland was built in the early forties, by Col. Washington T. Toney. It is five miles from Eufaula on the River road to Columbus, and for a half century, nearly, was the most written about, talked about and visited country home in the state.

Col. and Mrs. Toney were known far and wide as the most elaborate entertainers, and this historic home has entertained more distinguished guests than any other in the state.

For years, the Toney carriages, could be seen hourly passing to and fro daily, carrying guests, and every night there was dancing and "joy and gladness" was continuous.

There were two sons and six daughters.

The eldest son, Sterling B., became a famous lawyer, married Miss Louise Burge, daughter of a wealthy Kentuckian, of Louisville, and went there to live, and died after an eventful life.

Tandy W. Toney, never married, but after his father's death was the head of the family and carried on the extensive farming and grape raising business. The large scuppernong arbor was known of all over the country. The eldest daughter, Carrie, married first Judge John Cochran, and second a wealthy citizen of Kentucky, Dr. Bradford, who spent much money, restoring "Roseland."

To Judge and Mrs. Cochran was born a daughter, Carrie, who married Bishop Jackson of Alabama and to her was born a daughter, Caroline, and a son, Mellville. Caroline Jackson married Dawson McGough of Glennville, Ala. Caroline Cochran's second marriage was to Robert L. Love. To them was born a son, Robert, Jr.

The next daughter, Pet Toney, married Joseph W. Flournoy, and to them was born a son, Washington Toney Flournoy. After her death Mr. Flournoy married her sister, Janie Toney, and to them were born Sallie Flournoy, who married Thomas Irby of Buffalo, N. Y., and Rosser Flournoy, who married Mr. Johnson, of Meridian, Miss.

The next daughter, Ida, married Dr. S. A. Holt of Eufaula —no children. Clara Toney married George Houston of Mobile and the youngest daughter, Sarah, married Governor W. C. Oates of Henry County, and later of Montgomery. Just before he was elected governor of Alabama. He purchased "Roseland' and it was his home, thereby making the third Barbour County citizen governor of Alabama. B. B. Comer was the fourth.

To Governor and Sallie Toney Oates was born a son, William C. Oates, of Montgomery. He maried Mildred Saffold and to them was born a daughter, Marion Oates.

All of this family, except a few of the third generation have passed on and "Roseland" has for many years belonged to Mrs. Fannie Shorter Upshaw, who has a farm agent who runs the plantation and is still of great interest in Barbour county.

SHORTER HOME

Shorter Home on Eufaula street is owned by Mrs. H. L. Upshaw, daughter of Eli S. Shorter, II, who built it originally, is one of the most elegant homes in Alabama. (See other references to these homes in different biographies in this history).

THE GABLES

The elegant Old English home of Mrs. Eli S. Shorter, III, on Eufaula street, built just a few years since. The fine old colonial home of the distinguished Couric family, built by Manturan Couric in pioneer days, now occupied by Misses Mollie and Pauline Couric.

BUENA VISTA

Buena Vista—The grand old colonial home of Mrs. William D. Jelks, daughter of Mr. and Mrs. Henry R. Shorter, which was built by Mrs. Shorter's mother, Mrs. Addie Keitc Treadwell, which has a long romantic history of sweetest sentiment, and just across on the same Hill, is the Cato home, built by Col. Lewellen Cato, which also has an unique history, having been sold years ago to Mr. Edward B. Young, Jr., and then purchased back by Dr. J. C. Cato, son of the original owner, whose wife and children now own and occupy it.

Adjoining this fine old home is the elegant historic old Young-Dent-Hurt home on the Hill, built in the late fifties by Edward B. Young, Sr., wealthy, pioneer banker of Barbour County. It was the home where the large Young family was reared, and then for many years owned by Captain S. H. Dent, son-in-law of Mr. Young, and all the Dent Children were reared there. It is now the home of Captain Dent's daughter, Mrs. George N. Hurt.

OLD LANEY HOME

Just across the street, to the west, is the artistic home of the old Laney family, one of the wealthiest in all this section in pioneer days. The china and silver owned by this family is possibly the largest collection ever owned in Barbour county.

It was built in the fifties by Charles Laney, and sold in the late seventies to Robert Joyce Woods, and his wife, Cordie (Jennings) Woods, son of William Henry Woods, pioneer financier of Barbour County, who employed Prof. Frederick Tufferd, a French landscape gardener, to lay out the plots, beds and driveway through the grounds and planted great circles of Old English boxwood, which today is the admiration of all gardeners.

The house is a French Chatteau, with most artistic mouldings, for stairways, windows, doors and the iron rail that circles the roof of house and veranda and sunporch is typical French style.

When Mr. Woods moved away from Eufaula to Memphis, Tenn., he sold the place to Mr. M. M. Beringer, who with his wife and three sons, made it their home for many years, after which they sold it to Mr. and Mrs. J. W. Marshall, building a smaller brick Bungalow on College Hill on Broad street, where they resided until their death.

Because of the many beautiful Photinia bushes, that adorn these grounds, Mrs. Marshall named her home "Photinia Gardens" and while she holds to the old setting of shrubbery, she annually grows the modern perennials and annuals. This house is one of the most attractive in Barbour County.

McRAE HOME

The most historic home in the County, possibly, is the McRae home on Broad street, now owned by Miss Jennie McRae, daughter of Mr. J. C. McRae, who purchased it from the heirs of Dr. A. J. Pope, who built it in pinoeer days. In the front yard is a century old oak tree, under which General Alphesus Baker of the Confederate Army stood, when Miss Ella Pope (Mrs. Dozier Thornton) presented to him the Confederate flag, which he carried when he left Barbour County, with the First Volunteer Company, the Eufaula Rifles, when they answered the call to arms in 1860. Barbour County Chapter U. D. C. selected this spot as the suitable one to mark as the most historic spot in the County.

It was at this home that Dr. Pope, then Mayor, entertained at dinner, General Grierson and his staff, of the Union Army, when they marched through Eufaula on that memorable April day in 1865.

WINN HOME

Nestling in the shade of historic trees on Eufaula street in Clayton is the Wynn home, famous as the dwelling place for three fourths of a century of the distinguished Winn family.

Dr. and Mrs. J. J. Winn reared a large family and within these walls there lingers down the years the atmosphere of higher education, Religious culture, literary attainment and professional achievement, that has made this family one of the most illustrious, not only in Barbour County, but in the state of Alabama.

Today it is the home of the eldest daughter, Mrs. Mamie Fryer, Col. Jamie J. Winn and Misses Pauline and Hattie Winn, the others remaining members of the family residing in other homes.

This home reflects the Old South and its inmates have lived by that strict old Presbyterian code that exalts those who make it their daily guide.

HAWKINSVILLE

Fourteen miles from Eufaula on the Glennville road is Hawkinsville, the lovely ante-bellum home built by the late Col. Hiram H. Hawkins in the seventies, when he was the leading agricultural, educational and political power in Barbour county.

It was at Hawkinsville where all the Grange and Alliance barbecues, were held and it was known far and wide for cordial and elaborate hospitality. Many of the most famous speeches have been delivered from the front veranda of "Historic Hawkinsville." The inside furnishings of this home were handsome and in keeping with the cultured taste of Mrs. Hawkins, who was the typical southern home maker and artist and a woman of high literary attainment.

Two years ago "Hawkinsville" was purchased by Mr. Donald Comer of Birmingham, who has added modern conveniences and with his family are spending much of the time each year at this fine old country place.

OLD COMER HOME AT OLD SPRING HILL

The old home of the late John Fletcher Comer, Sr., who was the builder when he came to Barbour County in pioneer days from Jones County, Georgia, to Barbour County, and with the Drewrys and Etheridges settled at Old Spring Hill 18 miles from Eufaula. It was for a long time used by ex-Governor B. B. Comer as a hunting lodge, but has recently been sold to his daughter, Mrs. Herbert Rider, and another tract, where a new home will be built has been sold to another daughter, Mrs. Frank Lathrop.

A new school will be built by the Comer family at Old Spring Hill. This with another son, J. F. Comer, owning "Elmoreland" makes four old historic homes in Barbour County belonging to the illustrious Comer family—all on the highway leading to Montgomery.

KENDALL HOME

KENDALL HOME

"Homewood," the beautiful Kendall home on College Hill, was built by Mr. James Kendall in 1873-74 and has through all the years been one of the most attractive and best kept, elegant homes in Barbour County.

Its terraces, beds of rare flowers, bordered walks, Pergola, and lily pond, added in recent years by his granddaughter, Mrs. L. Y. Dean, II, and its rare furnishings, and the view of the country around, far over into the Georgia hills, from the upstairs balconies and third story Cupalo, make it especially notable. It is now the home of Mrs. Dean, her mother, Mrs. J. M. Kendall, and her brother, Joseph J. Kendall.

MAGNOLIA VALE

Two lovely women of the old Regime, each the mother of two equally lovely daughters, reigned as queen mothers at Magnolia Vale, the Old Woods-Sylvester-Bloodworth home on Eufaula street.

This was the social center of the society of young people of two crowds, the young ladies and the debutantes, and the four daughters who were the attraction of this historic home were Anna Sylvester, later Mrs. E. M. Edmunds; Laura Sylvester, later Mrs. W. A. Davis (still living at Anniston, Ala.); Ida Bloodworth, later Mrs. Frank Woodruff, and Ola Bloodworth, later Mrs. J. E. Sapp. During the eighties, every Sunday afternoon the young men of the city called in groups at "Magnolia Vale," and there was always a bevy of young girls there to help the four hostesses entertain them.

As the years passed on and these belles went to new homes, and death came in to take away Mrs. Sylvester and Mrs. Bloodworth, the old home was sold to Mr. and Mrs. H. Lampley, who modernized the old colonial building and today it is owned and occupied by Mrs. Harmon Lampley, II, and her family, two sons, Harmon, III, and Hinton Lampley, and Mrs. Lampley's father, Henry C. Holleman. There are today only five women of those of other days now living to recall with joy those joyous scenes of the old days, and the memories that cluster around Magnolia Vale, and only one young man.

HIGHLAND VIEW

Further out on the hill is Highland View, built by Col. Eli S. Shorter in the seventies adjoining his own home and presented to his daughter, Annie Shorter, wife of Col. J. H. Leftwich of Virginia. It is now the home of Mrs. Clarence P. Roberts, who many years ago named it Highland View.

LONGVIEW

Longview is the elegant brick home on the bluff that Mr. Robert Moulthrop built in a picturesque spot, where the old historic Shorter mansion was built by Col. Reuben C. Reuben C. Shorter, but which was torn down in later years. The Moulthrop family have made it one of "the homiest of homes," surrounded by magnificent pecan orchards, and is the home of one of the largest and finest chicken farms in Alabama. Mrs. Robert Moulthrop and her youngest son, Moss, and family make it one of the happiest and most beautiful places in the County.

TRAMMELL HOME

BEAUTIFUL AND UNIQUE BARBOUR HOME

Perhaps nowhere in Alabama is there a more beautiful and unique in all its appointments than the notable Trammell home twenty miles from Eufaula on the Old Spring Hill road in the Cowikee settlement in Barbour County.

The Trammell farm, owned and operated by Mr. Byron Trammell and his son is one of the outstanding farms of Southeast Alabama. It consists of 2860 acres operating about fifty plows, and besides the large cotton crop every year, the Trammell plan is diversification, and is run strictly scientifically; modern methods, supplanting the old-time ones, although the Trammell success is largely due to personally thoughout and used specific programs, arrived at by yearly experience. The commodious farm house, built of selected logs, is finished inside and equipped with every modern convenience and the handsome furnishings were selected and matched to location achitecture, and carried out according to the artistic taste of the inmates of the home.

Mr. Trammell has been one of the leading citizens of Barbour County, since 1916, and takes great interest in all the programs of the Community. Mr. Trammell was born in LaFayette, Chambers County. He has one son, Raymond Trammell, who married Miss Annabel Dismukes of Comer, Ala., and they have two children, Mary Ann and Leita. Mr. Byron Trammell died October, 1938.

"WEELAWNEE"

The Hunters and Williams and Hayes families, as far as research shows were large land owners in Barbour County, their holdings being near "Weelawnee' creek, about 8 miles from Eufaula—and When Mr. John R. Hayes married into these families he purchased much of both Hunter and Williams lands, adding to his already large plantation.

He was not only one of the largest and most successful farmers in Barbour County, but was for many years engaged in business in Eufaula, a member of the warehouse and cotton buying firm of Kolb, Couric and Hayes, who built the old historiq Shorter Opera House at Eufaula.

His first wife was Miss Mary Williams, and his second wife, her sister, Miss Eddie Williams, who after his death, managed the large farmng interests with ability that was the admiration of all this section. She personally looked after all the details, spending most of every day on her horse riding over the vast fields and her success as a farmer was unprecedented.

Her flower and vegetable gardens were rarely beautiful and the home "Weelawnee" was one of the most picturesque and beautiful anywhere to be found. The large house, with its profusion of costly and rare antique furniture, was known and commented on far and wide

Several years since Mrs. Hayes' death, the family have scattered, and the large plantations have been sold to different parties, cut up into smaller farms.

Edwin Hayes married a French lady and they live in Ohio; John R., Jr., married Claire Lynch of Columbus, Ga., and they now reside in South Carolina; Moselle Hayes married a Mr. Guinn; while Corine Hayes married a Mr. Gunn and resides in Huntsville, Ala.

Weelawnee, like Roseland, was for many years notable for its hospitality, wealth and culture and is a bright page in the social history of the County.

After the burning of the old historic home Weelawnee, the

younger daughter, Mrs. Gunn, built a beautiful new modern home on the plantation, several miles nearer Eufaula than the former one. This was also a handsome home, but like the former one was destroyed by fire and was not rebuilt.

On the Hayes plantation a negro, Marshall Rhodes, was foreman for Mr. Hayes for years. He grew up on the place from boyhood and remained in the service of them until they left for other homes, and he is still in the home built for him, and still carrying on on the "Hayes place" as his cottage is calld.

COURIC HOME

The fine old colonial home of the distinguished old Couric family, was built in the forties by Charles Mauturon Couric, grandfather of Misses Mollie and Pauline Couric, who were born and spent their lives there. It is on Eufaula street, and has housed five generations of Courics.

MONT McNAB

Mont McNab was built in 1885, by Dr. W. N. Reeves on was was originally "Thomas Hill," Elliott Thomas being the original owner of the land, which is the highest point for miles around, overlooking Chewalla creek reaching west 150 acres. It was also called "Blakes' Hill," because of the fact that during the War Between the States, Dr. F. B. Blake established a smallpox hospital on the summit of this hill.

When Dr. Reeves built the beautiful mansion his father-in-law, Mr. McNab, was still living, the head of the family, and the new home was named "Mont McNab."

The driveway that climbed the hill led from "Garden Lane," Sanford street and Cowikee street. At that time Mr. P. B. McKenzie was mayor of Eufaula and resided on Garden Lane and one day he said, "This street leads up to Mont McNab, a real highland spot, and should be called "Highland Avenue," and he forthwith began calling it Highland Avenue. Others followed his example, hence the name of this street is generally, but erroneously called Highland Avenue; for as a matter fact the name of the street was never (and research has been made of records to be correct in the statement(legally changed and is still "Garden Lane" as originally named.

Mont McNab was the scene of many elaborate and historic gatherings. When Jefferson Davis visited Barbour County in 1886, Dr. and Mrs. W. N. Reeves gave an elegant reception to the Confederate Chieftain at Mont McNab, which was a never to be forgotten occasion.

It was for several years the regular meeting place of the Monday night club of young people, and the musical programs of that club were delightful affairs.

The fine bowling alley was also where the young people enjoyed many evenings.

The wedding reception that followed the marriage at the First Baptist Church on the evening of February 22, 1887, of the only daughter of Dr. and Mrs. Reeves Islay to Mr. Harmon Lampley at Mont McNab was one of the most brilliant wedding receptions ever given in Barbour County.

After the death of Dr. and Mrs. Reeves, Mont McNab was temporarily occupied by Mr. J. H. Reeves and family, while their home was being rebuilt and one summer afternoon in 1904 beautiful Mont McNab was burned to the ground. With all its handsome furnishings, and rare old family heirlooms belonging to both W. N. and J. H. Reeves, among them two practically new Steinway pianos worth several thousand dollars, one belonging to each family.

It has never been rebuilt, but the old carriage house has been turned into a residence on the Cowikee street entrance.

MITCHELL HOME

The historic home of A. C. Mitchell in Eufaula. Built in the sixties by his grandfather, Dr. J. W. Drewry and later, was the home of his daughters, Mrs. J. G. Guice (Stella Drewry) and Mrs. Americus C. Mitchell III Lillie (Drewry) Mitchell.

It is notable through 4 generations of most distinguished —now the home of Americus C. Mitchell III, who married Catherine Lewis, daughter of Mr. and Mrs. G. N. Lewis, originally from Virginia. Children are Lillie Mitchell II, and Lewis Mitchell.

HOME OF THE AUTHOR
334 Sanford Street, Eufaula, Alabama

Every single one of the more than ten thousand flowering bulbs, over three hundred roses and hundreds of Annuals, Perenials and miscellaneous shrubbery and plants growing in these gardens were planted by the author's own hands during a period of 39 years.

Chapter Fifteen
Faithful Old Servants In Barbour County

> There's not many of them left,
> These faithful servants of long ago,
> But they hold places in memory's cleft
> As the years pass, both swift and slow.

Among the faithful old servants of Barbour County comes first, the large family owned by James Linguard Hunter. The head of this colored family, "Uncle June," less than five feet high, dark complexion (but not black nor mullato) kinky hair and beard—and his wife, "Aunt Dina" almost white and a queenly old woman. Both were devoted to their master's family.

"Uncle June" was foreman on the Hunter farm out about two miles from Eufaula, and she was the family nurse. Later years, she was "monthly nurse" for many other leading families, caring for the mother and infant one month. Their only son, Bowman Glascow, grew up and was the leading tailor in this section for many years, being employed by the largest clothing establishment in Southeast Alabama, from young manhood until his death.

He had a fine home on Western Heights, reared a family that was a credit to him. His daughter, Elizabeth, married Prof. J. W. Murphee, Superintendent of the colored schools of Eufaula, and his two sons, John and Alex, went to Washington, D. C., when Senator Pugh (whose wife was John Liguard Hunter's daughter) went to Washington to live, and were his butlers and coachmen during all the years of his United States Senatorship at Washington.

The eldest daughter, Laura Hunter, married Thomas Lamson, butler for the McNab Reeves family, his lifetime, and Laura was the devoted nurse and maid in this distinguished family.

Maria Hunter married Stephen McGough, a well known Carpenter. They were the servants of the Reeves-Lampley family and their daughter, Elizabeth McGowan, married first Lovie Love, a well-known Carpenter, and her second marriage was to Fred Poscott. Her daughter married Albert Jackson.

"Aunt Maria" was the nurse for all the children of Captain

and Mrs. L. Y. Dean and the children of Mr. and Mrs. H. Lampley, while her daughter, Eliazbeth McGowan Poscott, has spent her life in the service of the Lampley family, being the most devoted "mother nurse" nurse as well as faithful servant to this family and children, and she is still serving Mrs. Harmon Lampley, II, and children, as her daughter, Lillian Jackson is still serving Mrs. T. L. Moore, daughter of Captain and Mrs. L. Y. Dean.

The other daughter of Uncle June and "Aunt Dina" Hunter, was "Aunt Eve," who married Charles Callaway, and she served the Couric, and McKleroy families, many years, nursing three generations.

When the mother of these, "Aunt Dina," died, her funeral was held in the Presbyterian church of which she had long been a member, always attending the services on Sunday morning and other times, attired with a beautiful plaid Bandana, turban folded neatly around her head, and in winter, across her shoulders, a fine plaid shawl. Every sacrament of the church was given her in warm fellowship by every member, as if she had been white as the membership was.

Edward Springer, came to Barbour County from Georgia, with the Mercer family, whose Coachman he had been for a lifetime.

After the death of Dr. and Mrs. J. W. Mercer and moving of the others of the family from this section, "Springer,' as he is called, took up painting for a livelihood, but is now blind and too feeble to get about, but a wife he married late years cares for him, and he is on the Barbour County relief rolls. He has been a deserving citiezn. Springer died February 16, 1937.

The Peterson family (colored) was a large one; Peter and Anne Peterson were servants for the McRae and Kendall families for a half century and their children have followed them in serving the third and now the fourth generation of these two prominent families.

Then later there was Gene Perry, who as a lad was buggy boy for Dr. J. W. Drewry. He served the family through his youth and manhood, until after Dr. Drewry died in the Nineties, he studied for the ministry and for many years has been a respected and faithful Baptist preacher. He and his wife, Willie Perry, have been valuable colored citizens, and their children have been an honor to them. A daughter, Rachael, married a respectable negro, who died in a few years, and she has been a school teacher of note in the Barbour County Schools, and now holds a position on one of the notable training schools for teachers and nurses in Detroit, Michigan. She holds several diplomas.

The son, George Perry, has for many years been employed in the U. S. Post Office in Brooklyn, N. Y., as janitor, after serving as Western Union messenger at Eufaula, until after manhood.

John Bouer (like "Uncle June") a little black man, with heavy beard, who spent his life, a skilled carpenter in Barbour County,) and his wife, "Aunt Caroline," reared a large family, and like "Aunt Dina," was also a nurse. As a young girl, Dr. J. C. Pope, mayor of Eufaula and the head of the first Infirmary, Barbour County, owned this couple, during slavery days, and 'Aunt Caroline" had the advantage of learning professional nursing by experience, in this infirmary, and as she grew to womanhood Dr. Pope considered her most proficient. During the War Between the States, she was Dr. Pope's chief assistant in his hospital and professional work. Her six daughters, all followed her as nurses, trained by her, and have left an enviable record in Barbour County and elsewhere, as nurses.

Easter, the eldest, married Nathan Fryar, lifelong driver of the Southern Express Company at Eufaula. Amanda married Prince Williams, porter for the largest grocery company in Southeast Alabama. He died while employed by Schloss and Kahn of Montgomery, as head porter.

Cora Belle married Ben Johnson, lifelong porter of H. Schloss, of Eufaula, largest clothing establishment in Southeast Alabama.

Flora married first James Collins, owner of the Eufaula Transfer and Hack Company. She married second Dubb McCree, who was assistant to the city weigher of Eufaula's warehouses for a life time.

Eugenia married Dan Johnson, head bartender for Pat Morris Wholesale and Retail Liquors, in the days of barrooms.

Minnie married Robert Jackson Farmer. Laura died unmarried.

Their sons wer: John, many years brick mason deceased; Charles, carpenter; William, Carpenter. The children of all these are respected citizns of this community.

Perhaps the two best known in later years were twin sisters, Belsie and Elsie Long, who grew up, their parents well to do, and sent them to the Booker Washington Schools at Tuskegee. Elsie married Jake Jackson, a porter, who after twenty years 'service in Eufaula, went to Albany, Ga. Belsie married Thomas Barclay, a well to do farmer, living near Eufault. She spent her life as Eufaula's caterer, helper and friend of every club woman. She had charge of all the weddings, all the parties, and was also always on hand at all the funerals. She was also well educated, the finest cook known in the community, and the most excellent all round servant to be had.

She was capable, tactful and discreet, and it has often

been said: "Belsie Barclays' going from Eufaula was its greatest loss."

When her husband, who was also a valuable butler and house and yard man, died, her daughter, Genie, living in Ohio, carried her home with her, and recently she died there.

Maria Holiday has been the faithful servant for Mrs. Geo. W. Peach at Clayton over fifty years, and is still with her, giving the best services she can at her advanced age. Mrs. Peach thoroughly appreciates her long years of faithfulness, and is caring for her old age needs.

Joe Drewry and his son, John, served the McGee and Thompson families at "Oaklawn," near Eufaula more than forty years and this service warrants recognition. In the eighties Jerry Daniel's Band was the pride of Barbour County and for music at all times, the Grange, Alliance, and political meetings it was depended upon, and Jerry, as he strutted in front of his marching musicians, was a very important personage.

Cato Gardner was his drum major and little dwarfted Bill Thompson was traps and drum player.

Cato Gardner, was also a valet to the young men of the society, dancing sets and felt his importance.

Jerry Brooks owned the city bus at Eufaula in the seventies, and carried the little girls to school.

Three interesting negroes of the old regime, who came to Barbour County from Lumpkin, Georgia, following their old mistress, Mrs. Mary Crocker Aldee, who had moved to Eufaula, were Banks and Ruffin Ellis, two of twelve children, who had been born to Douglass and Viney, slaves of Mrs. Aldee. The other was Alex Hamilton, also born on the Crocker-Aldee plantations near Lumpkin, Ga.

Alex Hamilton was also a carpenter, built many fine houses in Barbour County, and in 1880 went to Atlanta, Ga., where he amassed a fortune, after securing the eternal gratitude of the citizenship of Barbour County, by preventing a great riot and loss of life, during reconstruction days.

Banks worked for the children and grand children of Mrs. Aldee, over 20 years, until his death; and Ruffin was baggage man at the Central of Georgia Depot at Eufaula for nearly 50 years.

When he was near death, and was asked how old he was, he said to Mr. Seth Mabry, railroad agent, by whom he was employed, many years before: "Phone Missie Mattie and tell her to look in the family Bible and tell you my age. I know "Ole Missie put it dare, when I was born." (The Missie Mattie he referred to is the writer, Mrs. Aldee's granddaughter. Ruffin felt himself so much one of the family, that he believed his name was there. It was not, but the third generation knew all about him and his faithfulness.

Perhaps the most notable negro ever in the county was Lewis Jones, who was brought from Apalachicola, Florida, where as a boy he worked in a salt factory. Mr. Elliott Thomas brought him to work on his cattle farms, after which he was messenger for the western Union Telegraph company at Eufaula for over 20 years. He was first employed by LaFayette Howe, owner of the Columbus and Apalachicola Telegraph Company, which was seized and appropriated by the U. S. government during the War Between the States, and afterwards absorbed by the Western Union). He was the special messenger sent on horseback from Eufaula to Clayton, Ala., carrying the official news of the Secession of South Carolina (see Grierson's March Through Barbour County, page—)

He had suffered a sunstroke, and wore, always a broad brimmed felt hat and carried an umbrella. He was short and dumpy, with a monkey like face and was always smiling.

On one occasion a Democratic Convention was being held in Shorter Opera House at Eufaula in the early eighties. Lewis had a telegram for one of the distinguished speakers on the stage, and refused to deliver it to an usher, but seeing the gentleman it was for, he walked down the aisle, around to an opera boxdoor and passed on through and out on the stage.

At this juncture the speaker on the floor stopped, saying: "Let's see what Senator Jones has to say to this body," and as he handed the message over a roar of applause and cries of "Senator Jones" rang through the building. After that Lewis was always called "Senator Jones" and he delighted in telling the small children of the family he worked for who would stand around him at his mealtime how the "Democrats that day at the opera house elected him a 'Senator.'" He was devoted to this family of children and a faithful old man, who felt that the Western Union Telegraph Company belonged to him and depended on him. He lived to a ripe old age, dying in 1902.

The character, so familiar today, to be included in this number of faithful servants, is "Pap Speight," whose story under "Features" appears in another part of this book.

Abe Brown, the coachman and butler for Dr. and Mrs. W. H. Thornton, and later for Col. and Mrs. G. L. Comer, was one of the very best.

It was a notable fact that Abe carried the Thornton carriage to every funeral that took place in Eufaula for a half Century, and after he died, Eugene Barry took his place in the Thornton-Comer family, and both were well known for faithfulness to duty.

The finest and most notable cook ever in Barbour County

was Hulda Winbush, who was head cook at the Freeman hotels — Arlington, National, St. Julian and Bluff City Inn— consecutively. Of bulky build, she was, nevertheless, active, capable and felt that she owned the Freeman children, making them a most valuable servant as the years passed. She was a culinary artist.

When the First Baptist Church was built on the bluff in pioneer days, the Sexton (now called Janitor) was Isam Cooley, a most worthy negro, whose large family was highly respected. He served for many years, until in the late seventies, Daniel Walker was elected as his successor, he being too feeble to continue. Daniel served the new church, built in 1867, faithfully and when he died in 1904 his funeral was held in the First Baptist Church which he had served so long, and was a full fellowship communicant of; and the Deacons of the Church acted as pallbearers.

Dr. Wharton, who was the pastor for many years, told an amusing incident that showed the humor and human nature evident in "Dan's" (as he was called) make-up. It was a rainy Wednesday night, and at the prayer meeting hour only the pastor and the Janitor were present. They waited long after the opening service time, when Dr. Wharten said: "Well, Dan, it looks as if you and I are the only ones to be here tonight" when Dan very solemnly replied: "Yes Sir, and you and me wouldn't be here if we weren't getting pay for being here."

Rev. A. J. Dickinson was the pastor at the time of "Dan's" death and conducted the impressive services. The choir of the church with Mrs. E. T. Long, organist, rendered special music. It had bee nthe custom for Dan to always be served the communion with the members of the church he served, although his membership was in the colored Baptist Church.

William Spotswood, known to several generations as "Uncle William," but for his kinky hair and yellow skin, could easily have passed for the cultured gentleman of the old South. He came to Barbour County before the War Between the States, given as a wedding present to a member of the distinguished Spotswood family of Virginia, a daughter who married and went to South Carolina, and was sold in a lot of slaves at Charleston after the death of his young mistress.

He was eventually sold to a member of the Courtney family and brought to Barbour County, and when he was set free, went to work and built him a neat cottage on Flake Hill at Eufaula, where he and his wife, Susan, became famous, she as a cook for Eufaula families, and he as an expert gardener.

His hands trembled always with some kind of Palsy, but he was intelligent, a deacon in the African Baptist Church, and a loyal Democrat. He had imbibed all the traditions of the Spotswood family, and was very proud of being "a Spotswood."

In 1874, when Barbour County was under Republican domination," "Uncle William" and "Aunt Susan" had rented their home, and were living in the servants' quarters of the writer's home, he the gardener and yard man, and she the cook. It was November 3, the memorable election day, when at ten a. m. shooting began, that sounded like millions of firecrackers—Uncle William sawing limbs off Chinaberry trees i nthe back yard, and was so frightened that he dropped the saw and fell to the ground and ran first into his house near by, got his coat and hurried down a steep bank that overlooked a branch that ran not far off and hid under projections that potato vines covered.

As a boy in Virginia, he had heard politics discussed and having been used as a Western Union Telegraph Messenger, on many occasions, he was urged to come out from his hiding place to get his dinner he said "I am a Virginian, a Democrat, and I am afraid to get too near these Carpetbaggers that's causing all this trouble."

That evening he voted under the protection of Mr. Thomas Cargill, a prominent citizen.

William and Susan were the parents of one child, a son, who in 1883 was barely grown and was a stevadore on the steamer Geo. W. Wiley, which in April of that year sank at the wharf at Fort Gaines, Georgia, during a freshet that carried the river far above danger mark.

His body was never found, and his parents collected an insurance policy that had been written only a week before the accident, and in 1920-'30 Charles Spotswood turned up at Eufaula, came to the home of the family they were living with when he went away. He told them, "That his almost lifeless body was picked up by a fishing schooner in Apalachicola, Florida. He went to New Zeland where he had lived for years, coming back to Apalachicola, Florida, and back to Eufaula to find his parents dead. He said he wrote several times, but it seems his letters were not received, and he went back to Apalachicola, Florida. I was sure that he was the boy, Charles, for all he told "fit in" to prove he was telling the truth.

The singular thing is that he was picked up two hundred miles away from the wreck, two days after, and was still alive to tell the tale.

PART III

Chapter Sixteen
Past and Present County Officials

County Judges

Alexander McCall, 1834-40; George L. Barry, 1840-45; Patrick H. Mitchell, 1845-48; George L. Barry, 1848-50; John Jackson, 1850; William R. Cowan, 1850-56.

Probate Judges

Judge S. Williams, 1856-1865; Henry L. Tompkins, 1865-68; Henry C. Russell, 1868-74; A. J. Laird, 1874; Wiley E. Jones, 1874-82, impeached; A. H. Alton, 1882-98; W. H. Pruett, 1898-1904; T. D. Grubbs, 1904-16; B. T. Roberts, 1916-22; H. R. Lee, 1922-28; Dr. G. O. Wallace, 1928-34; J. F. Laster, 1935.

Sheriffs

Harlee Hobdy, 1832; Hartwell Ball, 1834-37; Duncan McRae, 1837-41; John McRae, 1841-46; Buckner Williams, 1846-58; John McRae, 1858-61.

Buckner Williams, 1861-64; John W. Johnson, 1864-65; F. M. Moseley, 1865-68; William S. Russell, 1868-71; James C. Flournoy, 1871-74; B. Frank Hart, 1874-76; Walter S. White, 1876-80; Sandy Martin, 1880-84; G. T. Long, 1884-88; M. L. Passmore, 1888-92; William J. White, 1892-96; John B. Laseter, 1896-1900; S. J. Caraway, 1900-1907; W. M. M. Teal, 1907-1911; Robert Teal, 191-95; W. M. Teal, 1915-1919; John B. Laseter, 1919-1923; Oscar Teal, 1937-31; R. P. Williams, 1931-1935; J. P. Williams, 1935.

Circuit Judges

James Coleman, 1833; John Ledbetter, 1840; N. McDonald, 1840-44; B. F. Petty, Sr., 1844-1856; J. C. McNab, 1856-58; William H. Locke, 1858-62; George W. Coleman, 1862-68; Aron T. Spence, 1868-74; J. C. McNab, 1874-80; Henry Bradley, 1880-86; John C. McNab, 1887-98; M. McCraney, 1898-1904; B. C. Cox, 1905-1920; B. F. Petty, Jr., 1920-23; Ben H. Baker, 1923.

Tax Collectors

H. A. Davis, 1865-68; George W. Williams, 1868-71; T. R. Sylvester, 1874-84; B. C. Bennett, 1884-88; Charles F. Massey, 1888-92; J. J. S. Willis, 1892-98; B. T. Roberts, 1898-1916; J. S. Grubbs, 1916-27; J. T. Searcy, 1927; 35; J. L. Reynolds, 1935.

Tax Assessors

L. A. Adams, 1868-71; David Lore, 1871-74; W. B. Stewart, 1874-80; W. S. White, 1885-1906; R. M. McEachern, 1906-1936; Clarence Norton, 1935.

County Superintendents of Education

Frank W. Eidson; Geo. H. Dent; C. S. McDowell, Jr., 1896-1900; B. Davie, J. T. Learcy, A. C. Anderson, L. P. Laird, P. A. McDaniel.

W. R. COWAN

W. R. Cowan was the first Judge of Probate of Barbour County to serve as a Probate judge. The previous title was County Court Judge.

A number of others, as seen by the list, had served in that capacity before him.

Previous to being elected Judge, he had been engaged in the Drug Business at Eufaula with W. Eugene Besson.

He was a pioneer citizen of the County, who lost his arm in a fight with Indians, during their outbreaks in Barbour County.

PROBATE JUDGE J. S. WILLIAMS

JUDGE J. S. WILLIAMS

Previous to 1856, the Probate Judge had been styled as "County Judge" and the 2nd Judge to be styled Probate Judge of the County, was Judge J. S. Williams, who served until 1865. The following is the slate of the County Officials of that time, clipped from the "Spirit of the South," of 1859:

County Officers

Judge J. S. Williams, Judge of Probate; Wm. H. Locke, Clerk Circuit Court; Thomas Robinson, Sheriff; F. M. Wood, Sec.; R. J. Yarington, School superintendent; Wesley Bishop, Louis Christian, Robert Dill, Henry Faulk, Commissioners; W. K. P. Russell, Tax

Assessor; Hart McCall, Tax Collector; M. M. Laseter, Coroner; Whit Clark, Treasurer.

Judge Williams imigrated to Barbour County from Virginia and Georgia, with older brothers, when he was a very young child, and settled in the Louisville section. He was of English descent and a man of integrity and force of character. His mother was from North Carolina Scotch ancestry, and the descendants have, on down through the generations, been leaders in making Barbour County famous for great men.

His son, Judge Jere N. Williams, was one of the heroes of reconstruction times and his grandson, Judge J. S. Williams, now judge of the Third Judicial Circuit of Alabama, illimine, not only Barbour County, but Alabama history.

He married Effie McNeill, whose ancestors also were the earliest settlers of the Louisville section of Barbour County.

As Judge of Probate during the period of the War Between the States, his position was not an easy one to fill, and even later, on the reconstruction period, when a Republican was holding the office of Judge of Probate, Judge Williams' influence was strong and his efforts to readjust things had great weight in downing the raga muffin misdemeanors, and finally obliterating Republican rule in Barbour County. In the record files at the Court House at Clayton and also at Eufaula, are to be found many old documents that reveal the power and might of Judge J. S. Williams as an executive, as a man and a citizen. He was made of that unyielding metal of honesty of purpose, personal ability, and genuine Southern patriotism.

HENRY CLINTON RUSSELL

It is a very noteworthy fact that, amid all the Republican trouble in Barbour County, brought about by the actions of Elias M. Keils and the coming into the County of money-seeking Carpet-Baggers and scalawags there was in the County serving as Probate Judge from 1868 to 1874 a Republican who was a gentleman and a clean politician, Judge Henry Clinton Russell. He came to Barbour County and from North Carolina and was a large land owner and farmer, and his entrance into politics, was largely due to the fact that his interest in the Republican party centered most on National Republicanism, rather than state and county Republicans. He was personally a man of honor and integrity, therefore, above the things that cropped out in Barbour County during his administration as Probate Judge. He was honest and loyal to his party, deploring the diabolical acts of the carpet-baggers and scalags that flocked into the County.

A careful search of Judge Russell's official record, as

Judge, despite the fact that he was a staunch Republican, does not show a single act of his that was other than honest of purpose.

His position was a hard one to fill. A Republican in a Democratic County at a time when chaos reigned and criminal acts were committed by men calling themselves members of the part yhe represented. On November 6th, 1874, he wired the following message:

To Governor David P. Lewis, Montgomery, Alabama:

The situation in Barbour County is a disgrace to the Republican party. I am powerless to act on my own convictions. Fearful much more trouble here. Signed: H. C. Russell.

The original copy of this message is preserved among many Western Union telegrams of that time.

At the close of Judge Russell's term of office as Judge of Probate, he again devoted his time to his extensive farms, until appointed Postmaster at Eufaula by President Arthur.

Judge Russell was broadminded, fair and courageous, and although he differed politically, as to national politics, he was a valuable citizen and held in high esteem by many friends in Barbour County. When the family sold the historic old home six miles from Eufaula, with its several thousand acres of land, to the Alabama Pecan Company, they moved to town, to the handsome home on Eufaula street (one of the most elegant homes in the County) built by the elder son, Mr. David Lore Russell, deceased. The old country home was burned recently.

Judge Russell married Miss Arra Ella Lore, daughter of David Lore, pioneer citizen of Barbour County, the letters of whose name were chosen to name four streets in Eufaula,. viz: Livingston, Orange, Randolph and Eufaula.

Their children are: David Lore, deceased; Harry C. Farmer, now of historic "Ashland," the notable old "Ricks Place" in Clay County, Georgia, which has been named Russmore; William, who also served as Postmaster many years at Eufaula, appointed by President Theodore Roosevelt in 1904); Joseph Brantley; Irving Warner; Miss Atalene, all outstanding citizens in their several communities. The historic old Russell home, six miles from Eufaula, was built by Mrs. Russell's father, David Lore. She was born and spent her life there until moving to the city.

NOTE: Joseph Brantley died Nov. 16, '38, Harry C. Brantley died July 26, '38. (Since biographies were written.)

AUGUSTUS HOLMES ALSTON

Augustus Holmer Alston, lawyer, supernumeray Circuit Judge, man of letters and educational philantropist, was born in Bibb County, Georgia, November 17th, 1847, and died at Clayton, Alabama, October 25th, 1918.

He was the son of William and Elizabeth Howard Alston; the former born in Hancock County, Georgia, in 1806—married at Georgetown, S. C. and died in Texas in 1849—and the latter, a native of South Carolina, who died near Decatur, Georgia in 1866. He was the grandson of Robert West and Henrietta Green Alston. The former removed, at an early date from Halifax, N. C., to Hancock, Georgia, and thence to Florida, and subsequently returned to Georgia, dying at Thomasville, Georgia.

AUGUSTUS HOLMES ALSTON

Judge Alston, while a native of Georgia, with an enviable Georgia background, came to Alabama, after the War Between the States, where he served as a member of Company C. Ninth Tennessee Cavalry Regiment, Basil Duke's Brigade, General John M. Morgan's Command.

He was captured at Mount Sterling, Kentucky, and remained prisoner at Rock Island, Illinois, until the close of the war.

He read law under General Alpheus Baker and Colonel S. C. Cato at Eufaula and served two terms as Judge of Probate in the seventies and early eighties.

The first time he was appointed by Governor Thomas Watts to succeed Wiley Jones, who had been impeached, and because of his popularity, high character and his ability to handle the serious matters that reconstruction troubles had brought into existence, the second time he was elected by an overwhelming majority.

In 1889 when the office of Supernumerary Judge was created he was chosen and elected by the Alabama legislature to fill that position.

In 1904, he was elected by the people and again, reelected in 1910 by the people of the state at large.

He served as chairman of the third Democratic Executive Committe of Barbour County and was known and relied on, as the wise and clean official, whose program was readjusting a chaos that had prevailed in the County throughout the early reconstruction period.

December 7th, 1867, he married Anne Maria (daughter of Colonel Edward S. Ott and Amanda Alston Ott), the former a member of the Provincial Congress, and who commanded a South Carolina regiment during the War Between the States —granddaughter of William and Charity, great granddaughter of James and Christian (Lillington) Alston.

Judge Alston, was tall and erect and personally bore all the earmarks of the aristocratic born, that he was; A high toned gentleman of the old school, but who was broad enough to adapt himself to all the conditions that touched him.

As a politician he was just, fair and open, and commanded the highest respect of even those with whom he differed.

He was a Methodist churchman, in all that membership in that great organization means. His rare intellectual attainments, his ability as a lawyer, and his interests in the Educational developments of the state made him at all times a most valued and honored citizen.

A handsome painting of him hangs on the wall of the Library of the State College for Women at Montevallo, Alabama. It was placed there by the late Dr. Palmer, president of this institution of which Judge Alston was the first trustee and one of the first and strongest forces to bring about the great success of this college.

As a Judge, he was just and humane, but strict to the letter of the law, in all his rulings, and the Alabama Bar, recognized him as one of the ablest judges in the state, as well as a keen, capable attorney, and his unique charges to the juries serving his court have called forth well derserved comment.

At the funerals of Judge and Mrs. Alston, the former, 1918, and the latter, 1931, the Methodist Church at Clayton was overflowing with friends of this beloved and distinguished family, and hundreds that could not get inside the church, stood beside the graves of both of them, paying tribute of love and esteem, to a couple, whose lives had been an inspiration and helpful to the extent that their names will live in memory, thrice blessed for all, friendship and example of citizenship meant to the community and to each individual who had lived in the community with them.

Children:—Four sons who left flattering fields of endeavor

in Alabama, to cast their lots in Atlanta, Georgia, have reached enviable heights in their careers in that city, Barbour County giving to Atlanta four sons, for one father that Georgia gave to Alabama long ago.

Robert Cotton Alston and Philip H. Alston are members of one of the leading law firms of the South. Alston, Alston, Foster and Moies.

William Ott Alston is at the head of one of the largest and most successful Loan and Real Estate businesses in Atlanta.

The last of the four to locate in Atlanta was Augustus H., Jr., who for many years was with the Federal Reserve Bank of Atlanta. Two or more years ago he was sent by this bank to Havana, Cuba, to manage the Federal Reserve Banking Business there, and just a few months ago succumbed to an illness that caused his death, and he was brought home to Atlanta for burial.

Edward Ott Alston is a prominent business man of Denver, Colorado.

Robert C. Alston married Caroline Dubignon, of Savannah, Georgia.

Philip H. Alston married May Lewis, of Greenville, S. C.

William Ott Alston married Margaret Wright, of Texas.

Augustus H., Jr., married Marian Wooly, of Atlanta.

Annie Louise Alston married Carl Adams, of Prattville, Ala.

Augusta married Lawrence Haywood Lee, of Montgomery, Ala.

Elizabeth Drake Alston married Derrell J. Grubbs, Clayton, Alabama. the latter now owning and occupying the beautiful, historic old home of her parents at Clayton, where she dispenses the same charming hospitality that her lovely mother did, and where this family of brothers and sisters often come to visit the old ancestral home—so full of history, romance and sweet sentiment.

On December 5th, 1928, Col. Robert Cotton Alston, of Atlanta, formerly of Clayton, Barbour County, Ala., delivered an address on the Constitutional Convention of 1787, before the Jacksonville, Fla. Bar Association, and so wonderful was this address by this distinguished Atlanta attorney that on December 10th Senator Duncan U. Fletcher asked and was granted permission to have it printed in the Congressional record. This brought forth the introduction of a resolution providing for the preparation and distribution of pamphlets containing the Constitution printed in foreign languages and in English.

In his speech, Colonel Alston showed that he regards the constitution the greatest document in the history of the

American people, and thinks that every citizen, or applicant for citizenship should familiarize himself with the events leading up to its making.

Like his lamented father, Judge A. H. Alston of Barbour County, Colonel Robert Alston is one of the leading legal lights in the South today. He died March, 1938, greatly mourned.

JUDGE WILLIAM H. PRUETT

Judge William H. Pruett was born near Midway, Ala., in Bullock County, but moved into Barbour (adjoining) when a young man and was one of the largest and most successful farmers in that section of the County for many years. His country home "Oakland," and fine dairy, near Hoboken, a suburb of Eufaula, was for many years one of the best all-round country homes. During the years of his terms of office, as Judge of Probate of Barbour County, 1898 to 1904, he resided at Clayton and coming back to Eufaula after he retired from politics he resided at his wife's ancestral home on Randolph street.

He married first Miss Anne Browder, daughter of Major M. S. Browder, for whom Browder street in Eufaula is named. The fine old Browder home stood where the S. A. Bullock home now is, and was one of the most historic in the county. To them was born a daughter, Willannie, who married H. Fitzhugh Lee, son of Alto Vela Lee, and is Public Service Commissioner of Alabama. Judge Pruett's eldest sons, O. Browder, married Ella Parish, issue, daughter, Grace, married Walker and Garret Pruett married a Georgia girl. Browder was drowned while swimming with some school boy friends when a lad, and H. F. Lee, Jr., now a college student.

Judge Pruett married second Miss Anna Roberts, only daughter of G. A. Roberts. One son was born to them, Albert Roberts Pruett.

His third wife was Janie McKay-McDowell, and it was said by his many friends that "the three women Judge Pruett married were of exactly the same type, brilliantly educated, each one 'to the Manor born,' cultured, of gentle, sweet disposition and most charming personality."

Each one was a lovely Christian and southern woman, greatly beloved. Judge Pruett was a distinguished man, who was strong in his convictions, of strict integrity. It was often said of him that he was an honest official with high principles, and while not a proverbial politician, he was notable for justice to his fellow man.

Judge Pruett was a brave and loyal Confederate soldier. He enlisted as a volunteer in the first Alabama regiment, Captain, I company, and was discharged as a Major.

THOMAS D. GRUBBS

Thomas D. Grubbs was born at the old Grubbs home in Abbeville, Alabama, the son of J. W. and Elizabeth Blair Grubbs. He attended the Abbeville Agricultural schools and graduated, specializing in civil engineering.

He was in the mercantile business and for many years has been president of the Clayton Banking Company.

Served as Judge of Probate of Barbour County from 1904 to 1917, during which time he made political and personal friends that were drawn to him by his principles of high toned integrity, and his methods as an office holder, that stamped him a man of keen insight into business problems and broad minded and just in all his dealings.

His popularity as a man and leader in the County has been manifested in many ways.

He also served as Mayor of Clayton and personally is the genial, cultured gentleman who is an asset to his town and county, as well as valuable as a citizen.

He married Nettie Passmore Lee, daughter of Mr. and Mrs. M. L. Passmore, and their children are Thomas, Jr., and Jack, both married. He is still in the banking business.

JUDGE BOB THOMAS ROBERTS

Bob Thomas Roberts was born in Eufaula, Barbour County, Alabama. His father, Thomas Hill Roberts, of Virginia, came to Eufaula in his early manhood, and was married to Ann Elizabeth White, of Clayton, Alabama. They lived in Eufaula until war was declared between the states when he moved to Clayton to enlist and to leave his wife and two small children, Mary Hill and Bob Thomas, among her people. He enlisted in the fifth Alabama regiment with Dr. James J. Winn, W. H. Thomas, and many other Barbour County men. He was made first lieutenant of his company, and was acting captain when fatally wounded at the battle of Malvern Hill. He died, with Dr. Winn in attendance, and was buried in Virginia. His family remained in Clayton where his son has been ever since.

Bob Roberts was educated in the old "Clayton Academy" but having to help in the struggle to live, he had to quit school at the age of fourteen and finish this education by the help of his aunt, Miss Atlanta White—whose culture and learning is a part of the history of Barbour County—and by continuous reading of history, in which pastime he still indulges. Starting out in life, he did such work as boys of his age usually do. He clerked in stores, and then did writing at the Court House in the offices of the following good men who now have gone to their reward, viz.: Hon. John A. Foster,

Registrar in Chancery; Hon. John C. McNab, Clerk of Circuit ourt; and Hon. Wiley E. Jones, Judge of Probate. For fifteen consecutive years after this, Mr. Roberts held the office of Clerk and Treasurer of the town of Clayton, and for a few years following was in the mercantile business.

After the death of the lamented W. J. White, Tax Collector of Barbour County, Mr. Roberts was appointed his successor by Gov. Joe Johnson, and was elected to this office for four consecutive terms, being Tax Collector of Barbour County from 1898-1916 at which time he resigned this office to enter the race for the Probate Judgeship. He was elected and served as Probate Judge for six years, 1917-1923, and being defeated for re-election was thereupon appointed an Associate member of the State Tax Commission by Gov. W. W. Brandon, which appointment Judge Roberts held for the four years of the Brandon Administration, living in Montgomery with his family from 1923 until 1927.

Judge Roberts says that, "the cause of his success was the fact that he did the job right, and that his books prove the fact."

Judge Roberts has never given up his citizenship in Barbour County, but has always voted here. Returning to Clayton after four years in Montgomery he was elected mayor of Clayton for two successive terms, at the end of which time he retired, and now devotes the most of his time to his own private business, but is still active in political interest in the county.

He was married in his young manhood to Claudia Waddell, daughter of Rev. DeBerniere Waddell, D. D., and his wife, Mary Elizabeth, Bellamy Waddell. They were married in Grace Episcopal Church, Clayton, Mr. Waddell performing the ceremony. From this union there are four children:

Hugh Waddell Roberts, graduate of the University of Alabama, Sigma Nu Fraternity, editor-in-chief of the Crimson-White, the college paper; sports editor Birmingham Age-Herald, Birmingham national political writer, Washington, D. C.; executive manager Georgia Branch Associated General Contractors of America, Inc., Atlanta, Georgia. He married Eddimae Hester, daughter of Dr. and Mrs. William Hester, of Tuscaloosa.

DeBerniere Roberts, Alumnus University of Alabama, Phi Kamma Delta Fraternity; graduate Poughkeepsie Business College, Poughkeepsie, New York; bookkeeper, real esate, insurance, Birmingham and Mobile, Alabama, and Florida. Married Sarah Bishop, Birmingham.

Bessie Roberts, wife of John H. Peach, who is a graduate of the University of Alabama, Sigma Nu Fraternity. Lawyer. Member of the law firm of Andrews Peach and Almon, Sheffield, Alabama; legal advisor to Gov. B. M. Miller; member of the law firm of Peach and Caddell, Decatur, Alabama.

Mary Roberts, wife of W. C. Beatty, who holds an important position with the State Department of Agriculture, which position he has held for seven years under the administrations of Gov. B. M. Miller and Gov. Bibb Graves. Mr. Beatty has extensive farming and livestock interests at Clayton.

The Roberts' homes, both in Clayton and Montgomery, have been notable because of the popularity of the family.

The Clayton home is especially notable. Years ago it was built by the Petty family and is most unique and attractive. The site is the center of the town, is octagon in shape, two-storied and is surmounted by a cupalo. Since Judge and Mrs. Roberts have owned it, these many years they have added all modern improvements and beautified the grounds with finest shrubbery. Some rare and beautiful Murals adorn the walls of the parlors and the library is stocked with well filled book cases.

Judge Roberts is modest and given to overlooking the fact that in Barbour County he is today counted one of its very strongest forces in all the interests of the Community. Judge Roberts died September 1938.

HUEY R. LEE

Huey Reynolds Lee was born at Clayton September 22nd, 1886, son of Robert M. and Annie Reynolds Lee, and grandson of Needham Lee, who came to Barbour County in his young manhood. He was educated in the public schools of Louisville and Clio and then attended the Southern Agricultural school at Abbeville, Ala: he then entered the Southern University at Greensboro, completing his education at the University of Alabama. After graduating he spent another year, a law student at the University, after which he gave all his time to assisting his father in his extensive farming and mercantile business.

In October, 1907, he assumed the managership of the Eufaula Times and News, leasing the paper and plant; changing its name to the Eufaula Citizen.

During this time he was appointed clerk of the Jury Commission of Barbour County and returned to Clio, transferring his newspaper lease in 1915 he was candidate for Circuit Clerk and was defeated by only 19 votes, showing his popularity.

While in the Cotton business, he was appointed tax adjustor for Bullock County by Gov. Kilby, retiring from that office in 1923.

During his term of office taxes of the County were raised

from about thirty-three and one-third per cent, and, while this was a necessary increase when he ran for Probate Judge, it was against this handicap of tax raise dissatisfaction against him that he had to combat in the election. He succeeded, however, in winning by a flattering majority.

He is a loyal democrat, a broad-minded, clean politician.

During the World War he led the drives for all the attendant purposes, notably Liberty Loan Bonds and war saving stamps, and contributed liberally to all patriotic movements.

He is enthusiastic along all civic, local and patriotic lines, and one of Barbour County's best citizens, untiring in all his undertakings and a capable official.

Personally he is genial, always ready to do a service for a friend, and possesses that world of information always on the tongue's end of the student that he is of humanity, as well as of books.

He married Janet McDowell, daughter of the late Charles S. and Margaret McKay McDowell. Children: Huey, Jr., student at college; Margaret, deceased, and Charles McDowell Lee, high school boy.

He resides at Eufaula, but spends much time looking after his interests on the Lee farms near Louisville and Clio.

JUDGE OF PROBATE

Judge G. O. Wallace was born in Pike County and educated in the schools of that county. He studied medicine at the state university, at that time located at Mobile, Alabama. where he graduated with high honors. He practiced medicine at Clio 27 years, then at Baker Hill ten years.

For three years in succession he served as president of the Barbour County Medical Society. During the World War he was a member of the draft board; was county health officer of Barbour County three years; a member of the Alabama Medical Association; member of the Barbour County Medical Society and member of the Barbour County Medical Board of Censors.

He was elected to the County Board of Education in 1924, serving until he resigned to run for the office of Judge of Probate of Barbour County at the urgent solicitation of his friends.

While a citizen of Clio, he served on the Clio City Council and was trustee of the city schools of Clio.

Dr. Wallace was elected Judge of Probate of Barbour County, serving from 1929 until 1934. He is a scholar, a physician of ability and a man of clean character; a genial, genuine man of highest principles. He is widely known and esteemed as one of the County's most valuable citizens. Since his term of office expired, he has resumed his practice of medicine at Clayton, where he now resides. He is a consecrated churchman of the Methodist church, a Mason and a steward on the district board of the M. E. Church; A W. O. W., and a member of the Clayton Commercial Club.

Dr. Wallace was married first to Miss Mary McEachern of Brundidge.

He married second Miss Mae Wyatt, of Drakesboro, Ky., a charming lady who is a leader in all the church, club and civic life of her community.

She was appointed postmaster at Clayton in 1934 by President Roosevelt, and is filling the office with marked ability, being assisted by Mrs. S. J. Wright.

JOHN FOY LASETER

John Foy Laseter was born at Clayton, Alabama, the son of John B. and Lucinda (Bennett) Laseter. He attended the local schools at Clayton and his first business years were devoted to the grocery trade, after which he was traveling salesman for a large shoe house, when his many friends prevailed on him to enter the race for Probate Judge of Barbour County. He was elected by a flattering vote and entered upon his duties as Judge of Probate, January, 1935.

His ability to hold this high office, with dignity, justice and honor to the County and to himself, has already been manifested in the short time since his election, and that this selection was a wise one is very evident.

He is young, has the benefit of experience into County affairs, gathered from association with his father and the knowledge that observance of political life, at the County seat daily has given him. No man better fitted to hold the office of Judge of Probate could have been found.

His integrity of character added to his efficiency make him an office holder of benefit in many ways to the county and its citizenship. He married Lola Hillburn and they have three interesting children, Foy, Jr., Lucinda, and Thomas, and their home in Clayton is a place where joy lingers and the old traditions of the Laseter family are maintained.

Chapter Seventeen

Reconstruction Days
K. K. K.

Richard Busteed had been appointed by President Lincoln on November 17, 1863, as district judge of Alabama. He took the oath of office in 1863 and for ten years he led the indignities and horrows of Reconstruction, but was personally so obnoxious, everyway, that he was eventually removed from office.

The equality of the blacks and whites was forced in schools and churches by federal militia and some contemptable Congressmen attempted to get Congress to take lands from the whites and give it to the blacks. No law was sacred, because it could be set aside, whenever it interferred with the wishes of Republican agents, that were stationed all over the South.

Negroes were even allowed to vote in some instances when the white man's vote was denied him, and for a long time Barbour County was literally in the hands of carpet-baggers and unscrupulous scalawags.

Office seekers from the North poured into Alabama and secured a hold on state and county government. These adventurers, known as Carpet-bagger and scalawags, were busy turning weak-kneed Barbour men into scalawags, and when President Johnson vetoed Congress' bill establishing the "Freedmen's Bureau," exasperation over the County's political condition had reached a limit that called for action.

The object of these carpet-baggers was, chiefly "The Spoils of Office," as personally they cared nothing for the negro. But, he had been a slave and set free, and some were fooled into a "Black Man's Party," as they termed it, frightening the negroes into believing that to oppose their former masters' politics, they were made members of this Freeman's Bureau," which reached a point of control of both the negro vote and labor.

In Barbour County, these rascal agents bought land with government money, they were handling fraudulantly, and put negroes on these lands. The conditions were so terrible that the honest, loyal men of Barbour County could no longer submit and with a courage and determination that has been the pride of the County, since some of the bravest and noblest men of the South, in effort to combat these forces of evil, operating politically and otherwise, organized themselves into the "Ku Klux Klan" in 1870 in Pulaski, Tenn., and gradually spread through the South. The object of this organization, operating secretly, was to keep advised of the treachery of the radicals and to overcome their efforts to annihilate the white Democrats in all their efforts to control.

At first, this organization had no political objective, and its purposes were purely "safety" for all citizens.

The mysterious actions of the Ku Klux Klan, night riding, created fear among the negroes and really had great weight in righting many wrongs and preventing others.

It may seem a far cry, back to the days in Barbour County, when efforts put forth to reelect Republicans, simply to defeat Democratic nominees, because they were Democrats, when Red Radicalism had brought with its reign in the County, death, destruction and desolation. Was it not to be expected that the ghosts of the men who lost their lives in the patriotic struggle for justice, should rise up "Bancho" like and "Will Not Down," in the face of what confronted the Southland after their noble sacrifice for home and country?

Personally, I loathe the "waving of the bloody shirt" in a reunited country, all loyal to the stars and stripes, but I also loathe the disloyalty to a principle of justice and right that was bred into Southern Democrats and nurtured by the sacrifice and efforts of heroes; and today writing this history, 70 years after a conflict in which the years and their trend, have proved that those who lost were more glorious in their defeat than those who won were in their victory. I am impelled to emphasize the statement that "The bravery and valor of the Southern Soldiers; those who went forth from Barbour to fight on the battlefield, and those who came back and fought (just as dastardly and dealy) a foe, face to face, throughout Reconstruction Period, will live forever in the hearts of all loyal Southereners.

In 1869 this Klan was dissolved by the Grand Wizard. It had been known as "Konfounded Krooked Konondrum."

The Klan had nothing to do with dogma, creed, or ritual, but insisted on every member carrying himself by the code of conduct, promulgated by Jesus Christ," and its tenits were the highest standard of morals and living.

When the K. K. K. was organized in Barbour County, the County was on trial, and was being weighed and valued and the coming on the scene of this mystic band pulled the scale of political favor to a balance that was of benefit, that helped right much of existing wrong and also helped bring about the high degree of unity in the thoughts and feelings of the peo-

people, establishing a regard for the observance of he rules of common decency and honesty.

The Klan was organized to help in the accomplishment of a task of great magnitude and vital importance.

The citizenship of the South was in dispair, something had to be done and in desperation, with no time for deliberation as to methods, but with procedure, based absolutely upon the Constitution and laws of our country; and not unmindful of the fact, that both the federal and State Constitutions guaranteed, freedom of belief, and practice, the K. K. was organized, and its activities conducted, entirely within the law. As regards the organization, but as is nearly always the case, there were some few, "stragglers on" of the same type as the Carpet baggers and scalawags, that at times committed depredations, that gave untrue and unjust, suspicions to the aims and intents of the organization.

Negroes had been, everywhere, organized, and taught to hate the white people of the South and until Martial law was established in Barbour County, they had controlled the elections, (doing this to an extent, even while martial law prevailed) being the tool of the scalawag politicians even to being allowed to hold office, despite their ignorance and illiteracy.

The white men of the Southland, who had fought for the Confederacy, their homes, and their all, were the direct objects of the so-called "Union League," directed upon and used against them, their property invaded, their homes menaced, and in many instances the white women of the South became the victims of negroes, inflamed by the teachings of these Carpet-Baggers and scalawags.

To meet this terrible condition, the Southern manhood, seeing the peril of what, not only threatened, but had already taken place, was exasperated to blood boiling resentment, and like a great wave this resentment leaped through the South and after one hour of consideration after the project was launched, two million men were mobilized, in less than 24 hours —against the rise and assault of misguided and inflamed negroes, and infamous white trouble makers.

The formation of the K. K. K. was the Clarion note, the soldiers of the "Invisible Empire" sounded over the Southland

The superstitution of the negroes responded to the mystic actions of white robed Klansmen, and the story (never fully told) of how those mysterious actions did affect on the superstitions of the negro, and showed to their false friends the scalawags, their power, in a way, that is one of the most remarkable records on the pages of Southern history.

The supremacy of the white man was established and the purity of the Anglo-Saxon race was maintained, and both races, black and white, settled down, side by side, in peace and contentment to work out their differences.

In those trying times, it was a flaming torch of genius and missions that the K. K. K. held a loft, a challenge to every 'native born American, to face the crisis to serve our Democracy for generations to come. Had the principles of the original K. K. K. been adhered to, as it was in Reconstruction days, and used only when necessary to "right political and other wrongs," that were illegal and had the organization kept clean all its tenits the great harm done late years, in political circles by the present so called K. K. K. would have lived in the minds of the populace, credited with what it accomplished for the South in those dark days. But, unfortunately, the modern KKK, 75 years later, is not what the old K. K. K. was. Instead of this organization today operating to "clean out" it has allowed the "injection" of shrewd and unlawful political practices, to buy the votes of weak-kneed voters, who succumbed to the artifices used by members of the Klan, in right recent campaigns, to elect the candidates, they had been won over to.

In several elections the old K. K. K. methods were used and there was much mysterious talk of "dark rainy nights and Bloody Moons." "The Barbour County Fever" was prevalent for many years. Young men would serenade the Radicals of the community, and notify them in every way possible and their famliies would refuse to recognize socially the families of carper-baggers and scalawags. They would not sit by them in church and the children initated their elders.

In a table of alleged outrages, compiled from K. K. K. Testimony of 30 counties in Alabama, Barbour County does not appear.

K. K. K. methods of regulating Society were not new; but old as history. It was not used in these troublesome days to advantage; in these latter days there were evidences that the high plane of principles carried out to the letter, during reconstruction has not been adhered to in politics and the K. K. K. has been used for other than honorable purposes by the injection into its (modern fraternity) unlawful and unworthy political practices that are nefareous.

When the people of Barbour ounty themselves persecuted by aliens and by an unjust law, unjustly administered, they naturally sought some means, outside the law to protect themselves.

However, it is a certain fact that such experiences as these could only result in a weakening of respect for law and the inefficiency of the old K. K. K. plans, used today, which hinder, rather than help, politically as they did in 1874.

Chapter Eighteen

Organization of Democratic and Conservative Party

In Barbour County, the best men took hand in the Ku Klux Klan activities—even mystic as they were—and to these activities is due much of the clearing out of the County of the obnoxious and criminal invaders. They were using the negro to keep control of the County, and in January, 1865, Barbour County leaders were presented at Montgomery a number of spirited leaders, when an appeal was made to the negroes, "not to longer be misled by the white men making them false promises."

Following this meeting was the organization of the Democratic and Conservative party, which in 1874 elected Governor Houston and a majority of Democrats in the legislature, and the terrible reconstruction period came to its end, with the removal of Federal troops.

Barbour County took active part in the restoration of law and order. At that time, there were six negroes to every white in the County and the task of undoing of the tear down was a gigantic one.

For a long time, about all the government, the people of Alabama had was that furnished by the Commanders of Military Posts.

In the late summer, after April 29th, 1865, there was practically no governor, and this was due to the lawlessness of the soldiers in some of the Garrison towns. The so-called military government was even worse than no government at all. Most of the best soldiers had been mustered out, and while no negro soldiers were left in Barbour County, those stationed in other counties that were strong in Confederate patriotism became unruly and disorderly.

When the Radical Civil Rights bill was forced through (See notes) also the bill for continuing the Freedman's Bureau and in 1866 an amendment claiming it was a test of honesty and faith in the South—and Alabama rejected this amendment, the voice of indignation from Barbour County spoke loudly and it was voted down. Later in 1867, ten states were divided into military districts and a military officer put in charge of each district. This officer controlled reconstructions, the negro being the center around which Reconstruction wheels were revolving and the Congressional Reconstruction plan was the feature in the reconstruction of the state and of the social, as well as economic, activities.

In Barbour County, be it said along with many other statements proving the honesty, loyalty and justice, that has so glorified this County, that a great number of the slaves of these citizens (who made the County) suffered similar and even worse indignities, before the light broke through the little rift, begun by the loyal efforts that finally were successful, in driving out the carpet-baggers and scalawag offenders, who had feasted on and reveled in the tearing down of the ruling of those corrup actions, in which many unprincipaled whites were more corrupt than the negroes—in the practices suggested by the influence of Elias Keils, of whom the most charitable construction that can be put on his acts is the belief that his dominating, egotistic nature and bravado, daring and his greed for money (which he accumulated by receiving unlawful perquesites and fees from ignorant negroes and whites, at his mercy—and many personal ways of getting money and other acts, revealed to this writer, obtained from the old Western Union files, stored for years in the cellar of the John McNab Bank, and brought to light in 1891, when that cellar was used as a store room by the Southern Bell Telephone and Telegraph Company broke loose those old boxes stored there and as trash was destroyed by the manager of the Telephone Exchange.

From these telegrams it was learned that Keils was, with fear, being backed by Republican leaders in Alabama and cared more for holding office, that he might secure money by any means, secured through his office, but was without an atom of patriotism in his make-up.

To him the Republican party was simply "a means to an end" for him to carry his point quickly, with an uneducated person. During his term of office, he acquired a fortune, speculated and left Barbour County a rich man.

His egotism, shrewdness, bravo and selfishness—when it could no longer serve his purposes—brought him to a grief that really overtook him (and who knows, possibly repentance,) when in effort to steal votes at Old Spring Hill voting precinct in the riot his 16-year-old son was fatally shot down beside him. It was rumored that he held his boy up before him, not dreaming but what that act would stop the shooting. No one who knew Keils believes that he was dastardly enough to do this. The facts as seen in the report of that riot shows that it was dark and it was random shooting that killed Willie Keils. Eye witnesses say it was black dark and Keils was under the table when the hastily extinguished lamps were relighted and showed the boy on the floor dying.

Mrs. Keils did, however, claim that she "begged her husband not to carry her boy with him to this voting precinct "and her grief was pitiful to witness. She was a most excellent Christian woman. Then Judge Keils was practically forced to leave Eufaula. He went to Washington, D. C., and later to Yankton, Dakota, after selling his palatial home on Barbour street, and all his farms and other property.

After his death Mrs. Keils came back to Eufaula to reside with her sister, Mrs. Fanny Sylvester Thornton. She was 90 years old when she died and is buried beside her martyred son in Fairview Cemetery. In her later life, she gave the same interest and devotion to the First Baptist church that she did in early life and was beloved by many friends who appreciated and sympathized with her during the years of sorrow and embarrassment over the attitude of her husband politically in Barbour County.

One of the greatest problems Barbour County had to face was when these soldiers, who were the County's best citizens, came back from the war to face the devastation, ruin of their homes, their confiscated property, worthless money, and to a demolished civilization their slaves, in whom was invested their capital, was the newly freed negro who had been their property.

The negro had become the ignorant tool of unscrupulous Republicans, who, because the Republicans were controlling the National Government, by selfish, and fanatical programs, and were determined to crush the South every way possible.

The situation called for men of courage and determination to meet it, and by bravery they took up the struggle to rebuild the South.

The negro race, freed, was too ignorant to adjust themselves to the new state of things, and did not know how to use their freedom, but the history of the years since that troublesome time shows that the negro did not receive from the Republican party, whose cause he was induced to espouce, the full justice due him, from them and his wonderful rise to the present position he occupies as a citizen is the fact that he has been humanely treated by the white race of the South, whose kindness and consideration and principles of Justice to all, has made possible the advancement of the negro race.

The biographies of old slaves of Barbour County, in this history reveal the attitude and acts of the former owners of these slaves.

The election upon the Constitution and for officers occurred early in February, candidates nominated by carpet-baggers and extreme scalawags, many of whom were members of the

Conventional Party and were supportey, of course, by the Union League. This was opposed by the whites, who quickly registered. It was to defeat the Constitution and the candidates by voting for it. This project of a negro vote to keep to Radicals failed by 13,550 votes, lacking in that much of a majority of all registered votes, required by the Reconstruction act.

The fact of scalwags and carpet-baggers failing to keep their promise to the negroes caused their vote to fall and it was largely due to this disappointment on the parts of these carpet-baggers in Barbour county that they began to 'fold their tents and silently steal away."

By 1874, the Republican party had begun to rapidly weaken in Alabama. Failure to meet the promises made by the scalawags had caused the negro to revolt, and desert.

Democrats were determined to clean out the Republican domination.

Barbour County was opposed to a race issue, and "White vs. Black" was the way the leaders, who called themselves "White Man's Party," characterized it.

Notwithstanding the fact that the war and its Reconstruction period has put Barbour County, literally, "in the depths,, no other County in any Southern state has had such conditions to combat as those brought about through an office holder such as Keils. Despite her losses and the attendant inconveniences, her citizens, with courage, born of the principles that make men great, and despite all that had been done to influence and incite the negro against his white former master, by leaving in their minds false accusations to prejudice them, there were many, many cases, where faithful old family servants refused to leave and remained in the families of their former owners.

In Barbour County there are today dozens of descendents of these old slaves, still serving the third and fourth generations of their ancestors' owners, and they constitute the best element of the colored citizenry of the county. Among the more skilled laborers, faithful servants, whose conduct and daily life has commanded the respect of their employers. When the Barbour County negro began to find himself, after being lost so long in the tumult and haze of Republican influence, he began to realize the folly of the stand he had taken and realized that his "old master" had been his best friend.

Mrs. Victoria Hunter Clayton, wife of General Henry D. Clayton, in her book, "White and Black of the Old Regime," tells that, "whether husband returned from the war, he called up his slaves and told them that they were free, and advised them to stay on for a share of the crop. To them who might want to leave, he offered conveyance and provisions for the remainder of the year. "The response was, "Master, we don't want to leave, we want to stay right here with you." Most of them who left the farms of their former owners were those lured by the belief that they were to be .iven "forty acres and a mule." The Yankees had left in their minds the idea that they would be fed by them.

Although some of the white leaders of Barbour County were opposed to race issues, the campaign did become so, "White vs. Black" was the way the Montgomery Advertiser characterized the "White Man's Party," in Barbour County, and it was observed that the race struggle in the South was the result of white against black for political suffrage." The Democratic papers and organizations exercised themselves to whip all the whites into line. One writer said: "All the good men of Alabama are for the white man's party; libelers, liars, hand-afters and traitors are for the negro party."

Federal officials, before the end of the war, had established organizations in many North Alabama towns. There was the "Union or Loyal League," with a grand council, with headquarters at New York and a Grand National Council at New York called the "Union League of America.

Representatives of this organization came into Barbour County and were detected through telegrams that came to them through the telegraph office at Eufaula, which was under Federal domination and control. It so happened that a Democrat could read one of these telegrams over the shoulder of a scalawag he had in custody. He had been watched, holding conferences with negroes on the Hunter ulantation near Eufaula and in effort of several men to learn the full meaning of the message that arroused suspicion, he stuffed it in his mouth in the scramble and it was torn so only half of it was readable; but that revealed the true situation and he was secretly gotten away by Barbour County men, locked and barred in a house on the Hunter plantation until a meeting of Barbour County men could be held, some hours later, to decide what steps to take to stop what he was trying to do to incite the negroes.

He escaped, was captured several miles away and turned over to federal guards at Eufaula, who claimed that they had no knowledge of him and no right to, or intention of holding him.

The telegram was from Cleveland Ohio, told of money being sent him and a few days and was signed—Frank Carefull (evidently a fictious name). Four hundred dollars did come to a Frank Carefull at Eufaula, but this man denied the name. He claimed he was Joe Allen and the Telegraph Company returned the money, reporting in a service message, "Impossible to find any one who admits he is Frank Carefull." The manager of the Telegraph Company ws satisfied he was the man, working for this organization, but, trapped, feared to take the money.

In 1865 40 per cent of the voting population of North Alabama joined a half dozen lodges, called Chapters, and in 1887 took negroes into membership, showing that corrupt financing was not the worst part of a Reconstruction.

In the upper part of Barbour County (now Russell) the Union Army invasion, wrought possibly the most terrible havoc of any place in Alabama. At the beautoful old Evans home in Glennville, Mrs. W. A. Dutton, whose first husband was Mr. Wiley Goolsbee, father of Mr. Warren S. Woolsbee, of Eufaula, as Miss Cynthia Evans, was the charming daughter of this home which was beautifully adorned with every luxury, wealth and culture could give—many years ago told the writer this story. "I was walking across the garden when two Yankee soldiers walked up to me and followed me into the house where my mother sat. They asked for food and she gave it to them and as they sat at her dining table a company of soldiers drove up. There was no attempt at physically harming us, but an officer walked around and ordered his men to mutilate all our beautiful pictures, took our silver and with a big iron (looked like a block) with a wooden handle struck the tea pots, broke knives, forks and spoons into pieces and when every piece of china had been broken, ordered his men to throw the "litter" into the well, which they did. As if this were not enough, they then took all our bedding, made a bonfire, and after emptying the smoke house of all our food, which they carried with them, they rode away. I don't recall whether or not Mrs. Dutton told me the Company. She probably did not know, but her story was so vivid and so heart rending that I shall never forget it. I never see a lovely silver service that I do not recall the expression that was on her face, as she told of the horrors of that raid on her home.

Another place in Barbour County, where personal property was destroyed was near Batesville, Alabama, where on the Williams farm the meat for six families had been stored in the Williams' smokehouse, because the owners had no suitable place to keep it safely through the winter.

Yankee soldiers, belonging to an outfit that was going from Georgia through to the Batesville section, stole a wagon and two horses and carried away with them every piece of meat in this smokehouse, several hundred hams and bacon. They were fired on from under cover by two farmers, who were afraid to come out under cover of four guns, and several miles away. Nex,t day the wagon was found, but the horses and meat had been carried on, showing that other soldiers had not been far away to help in this stealing.

Chapter Nineteen
Sons of The South

They were the soldiers brave,
Thoughtful, daring and of steady nerve
Who sought the South to save,
And knew no command, but serve.

When the heroes who fought through the four years' struggle of the War Between the States—a struggle of cold, hunger, physical and mental pains and privations—returned to Barbour County, the victims of a defeat, in which they figured more gloriously than their opponents ever did in their victory, and with a determination that has been the admiration of the whole world, they began over again, and in all the annals of history these Barbour County veterans of the War Between the States have been acclaimed heroes of a type the world should honor.

On Armistice day, 1936, when little interest was manifested in a school celebration, in which the American Legion was to feature, Veterans attending, but they failed to appear—a "Gold Star" mother of the World War, grieved at the lack of interest shown, said, "Why is it that through all the years, at any Confederate, Memorial or celebration, the interest is always at fever heat and the spirit of Confederate patriotism kept alive, and we mothers and widows of the World War get so little co-operation in demonstrating our patriotism and feelings. "A woman standing nearby replied to her, saying: "This is the reason: The sufferers from the War Between the States have grievances and heart hurts far greater than those of the World War."

The World War took nothing from the family of the soldier, but his life (granting that was the greatest) but practically all of their families (there are some few unjust exceptions) of those who gave their lives in this noble sacrifice, have been paid, in money, death compensations, insurance, compensations, bonuses and pensions, and not a single American home was burned, pillaged or property destroyed.

While in service the American World War soldier was fed, clothed, and even entertained by paid entertainers, when not at the front, and salaries paid them for their service—while on the other hand the Confederate soldier volunteered (but few were conscripted).

What did he and the South suffer and lose? He left home, family, many coming back to find thir homes ruthlessly destroyed, everything gone, this destruction going on while they suffered all the pangs of war, and languished in prison, while their property was being destroyed.

The blackest page on American history is the story of the deliberate desecration of the Southern homes by the Yankee soldiers, at the command of "Yankee" officers.

Here in Barbour County, when the conflict was over, and the maimed and wounded and starving Confederate soldiers limped through the long miles, weary and health gone, there had already sprung up, backed by the followers of one bad leader, stumbling blocks to impede every constructive effort put forth for making over things.

Robert C. Alston, son of Judge A. H. Alston, judge of probate of Barbour County during Reconstruction days— and probably the most forceful and effective instrument of Barbour County's readjustment—after traveling through the regions of France, which were the most devastated in the World War, said—"I have seen their recoupment, and I note that the Southern States suffered more than the most devastated of all the regions, for when our people returned they came back to a country without laws, without government, without currency, without friends. The United States Government was in intense enmity to it and to the Southern people. The outside world was obliged to accept the view of the government. It is only within the past 35 or 40 years that there has been any great change. The two fundamental basis of this change was the marvelous eloquence of Henry Grady and the Spanish American war. I have the most profound respect for those who through a changing civilization in such a community as Barbour County, stood firm to those things which we regard as essential and still through the years have shown enough change to keep pace with the world."

In Barbour County, some of those who passed through and were very close to this reconstruction era and felt and knew its importance were S. H. Dent, C. F. Massey, A. H. Alston, J. S. Williams, G. L. Comer; J. F. Foy, R. S. Jones, R. M. Lee, J. L. Pugh, J. M. Buford, Alpheus Baker, W. N. Reeves, R. F. Kolb, H. R. Shorter, Eli S. Shorter, J. C. Cochran, E. C. Bullock, M. A. Brunson, H. D. Clayton, Alto V. Lee, A. S. Borders, W. H. Pruett, J. W. Brannon, Austin Cargill.

Among those who came back maimed, leaving a limb in the battlefield were: Eben Priest, leg; J. G. Guice, arm; L. Y. Dean, arm; J. W. Tullis, leg; P. W. Brannon, foot; J. H. Evans, an arm.

TO THE PEOPLE OF BARBOUR COUNTY

The abolitionists have triumphed. Shall we submit? Will Alabamians permit Abolitionists to rule them? Shall we yield like slaves or resist like freedom? The great counsel of her citizens and we call upon the people of Barbour County to assemble at Clayton, Nov. 19th, to deliberate and act.

Come Southern men of all parties. Shut up the doors of your business houses and leave your plows in the furrows and let us take counsel together. The South demands union of her sons. Let us bury the past divisions and come together at the appointed hour and like brothers prepare for safety and resistance.

Signers in Order

John Gill Shorter, Alpheus Baker, Henry DeLamar Clayton, C. A. Parker, G. M. Bates, T. R. Coleman, T. H. B. Rivers, Eli S. Shorter, John A. Foster, Coridon Wilson, S. Bradley, Thomas Robinson, William Smith, B. F. Petty, Jefferson Buford, W. C. Espy, W. W. Mills, W. L. Blair, S. Fleresheim, James L. Pugh, William H. Chambers, William A. McTyer, J. M. Buford, J. C. Clayton, H. M. Tompkins, H. M. Hunter, W. R. Cowan, J. M. Cary, E. C. Bullock, Jere N. Williams, Fern M. Wood, Henry R. Shorter, D. M. Seals, H. M. Barksdale, J. . Russell, John J. Norton, H. O. Screws, W. S. Kennedy, John C. McNab, E. McNeese, J. L. Carruthers, John W. L. Daniel, W. B. Boen, H. R. Fryer, B. M. Hendrix, W. D. Wood, M. Lightner, George Coleman.

Volunteers were so numerous in Barbour County and enthusiasm such that although there were no arms, there was daily drilling.

So interested was Mrs. Roxanna Bethune Wellborn that she went to Richmond, saw the Secretary of War and secured a complete equipment, telling her that arms would be sent at once, but she waited and carried them with her with great dispatch.

In February, 1860, a volunteer company, "The Pioneer Guards," met at the Market House at Eufaula and organized with the following officers: William H. Chambers, Captain; John W. Clark, First Lieutenant; Henry C. Hart, second Lieutenant; Weeks Pippin, Third Lieutenant; John B. Hart, Orderly Sergeant Sergeant; A. J. Locke, Second Sergeant; G. F. Boatright, Third Sergeant; E. H. Hunter, Fourth Sergeant; R. Cherry, Fifth Sergeant.

Corporals:—William H. Betts, F. Rountree, William M. McLeod, John Raleigh; Dr. C. Terry, surgeon, and C. W. Snow, secretary. Sixty men enrolled.

The Company made its first appearance in full uniform o nthe streets of Eufaula, Oct. 11th, 1860. July 4th, 1860, the Volunteer Companies of Barbour met in Glennville, Alabama, for the purpose of organizing a regiment and electing commissioned officers. following companies met: The Eufaula Rifle; Clayton Guards; Glennville Volunteers; Silver Run Guards; Pioneer Guards; Military Guards; Perote Guards; and Louisville Blues.

Resolutions were adopted that the above companies be organized into a regiment called the "Third Volunteer Regiment of Alabama."

On motion of Captain Chambers of the Pioneer Guards, Captain Henry D. Clayton was elected Colonel of the Regiment with apt. Gary of Glennville as Lieutenant colonel, and Capt. Lewis, of Silver Run, as Major.

Mrs. B. F. Treadwell mother of Mrs. Henry R. Shorter, floated from the cupolo of her home on College Hill, a Confederate flag, and Captain Alpheus Baker, on one occasion, marched his company, "The Eufaula Rifles," to the front of the residence and fired fifteen rounds of salute to the flag, and to honor this loyal Southern woman, who gave such noble self sacrificing help to the Confederate cause.

A detachment of Pioneer Guards also carried up a new cannon and fired 15 rounds. This cannon was called the little "Fire Eater.' Many years after from the bluff where this election of President Cleveland. It was reloaded to fire 21 rounds and when it "went off" Mr. Edward Stevens of Eufaula was accidentally killed.

Chapter Twenty
Reconstruction Facts

Controversies between state and nation, clashes between the Federal troops and the whites who had settled on lands ceded by the Indians, over whom the state, established jurisdiction, had provoked a state of political unrest in Barbour County—and this was aggravated by the arrest of Governor John Gill Shorter, Barbour County's own and Alabama's first War Governor, with him was also arrested his predecessor. Governor Moore, and his successor, Governor Thomas H. Watts. The entire state was defiant, and Historian Walter S. Fleming states for six months after the surrender, there was practically no law in Alabama, except in the immediate vicinity of the military posts, where the Commander exercised a certain authority over the people of the community."

These troops were even more troublesome than the robbers and outlaws, from which they were supposed to protect the people."

This was also a time of financial chaos; there was no value to stocks, bonds or any kind of securities. The Confederate money was not acceptable. The ruthless destruction of homes and property was in terrifying evidence.

The cotton business was paralized, guns, horses and mules were stolen and confiscated. There were no farm laws, no taxes, really no foundation to begin to build over with; and when the soldiers returned to their Barbour County homes with only heart break, their determination to carry on has been the wonder of the century.

In Barbour County, for months Federal troops, at intervals, came through the County, and several times arrested white men, on charges preferred by negroes and carpet-baggers. The Union League and Freedman's Bureau were used by these Red Radicals to control the election of delegates to the Constitutional Convention of October, 1867 when slaves were first allowed to vote and Barbour County was one of the 22 counties having negro majorities.

They were marched to the voting polls in great droves, armed with guns, pistols, knives, and they would vote at one precinct, and go to another voting a different name. No whites were allowed to vote.

In Barbour County, the white man's party had declared

the issue to be white vs. black, declaring that if the whites were defeated the county was to be turned over to the blacks and when the Republicans kept on with their charges of "outrages by the whites on the negroes," General J. T. Morgan was arrested for violation of the Enforcement acts in Barbour County. J. M. Buford, the fearless editor of the Spirit of the South, General Alpheus Baker, of military fame, W. H. Courtney, county official and E. J. Black, also of the Spirit of the South staff, were also arrested. The situation was tense, the Democrats were desperate.

Democratic gatherings were held and a campaign fund was raised.

It was evident that the Democrats were no longer going to allow the Republicans to control the elections.

The riots at Eufaula and Old Spring Hill were the outcome of the terrible situation, which it developed was worse at these two places than at any other points in the state, and the trouble at Eufaula came to a climax, when a negro tried to vote a Democratic ticket and in the great mob of instructed negroes the riot began.

Although some of the white leaders of Barbour County were opposed to race issue, the campaign did become so. "White vs. Black" was the way the Montgomery Advertiser characterized the "White Man's party in Barbour County," and it was observed that "the great struggle in the South was the race struggle of white against black for political suffrage."

The Democratic papers and organizations exercised themselves to whip all the whites into line—one writer said, "All the good men of Alabama are for the White Man's Party; outcasts, libelers, liars, and traitors are for the negro party."

Federal officials, before the end of the war had established organizations in many North Alabama towns. There was "The Union or Loyal League," with a grand council with headquarters at New York, and Grand National Council at New York called the "Union League of America."

Representatives of this organization came into Barbour County, and were detected, through telegrams that came to them through the telegraph office at Eufaula, which was under federal domination and control. It so happened that a Barbour County Democrat could read one of these telegrams over the shoulder of a scalawag he had in custody.

He had been watched, holding conferences on the Hunter plantation, near Eufaula, and in effort of several men to learn the full meaning of the message that aroused suspicion, he stuffed it in his mouth. In the scramble, it was torn, so only half of it was readable, but that revealed the true situation, and he was secretly gotten away by Barbour County men, locked and barred in a house on the Hunter place until a meeting of Barbour men could be held some hours later to decide what steps to take to stop what he was trying to do to incite the negroes.

He escaped, was captured several miles away, and was turned over to the Federal Guards at Eufaula, who claimed they had no knowledge of him, and no right to, or intention of, holding him.

The telegram was from Cleveland, Ohio, told of money being sent him in a few days, and was signed "Frank Carefull" (evidently fictitious name). Four hundred dollars did come to a Frank Carefull at Eufaula, but this man denied the name, claiming he was Joe Allen, and the Telegraph Company returned the money, reporting "impossible to find any one who admits he is 'Frank Carefull.'" The manager of the company here was satisfied he was the man working for this organization, but trapped, feared to take the money.

In 1865, 40 per cent of the voting population of north Alabama joined a half dozen lodges, called chapters, and in 1867 took negroes into membership, showing that corrupt financeering was not the worst part of Reconstruction.

In the upper part of Barbour County (now Russell) the Union Army invasion wrought possibly the most terrible havoc of any place in Alabama. At the beautiful old Evans home in Glennville, Mrs. M. A. Dutton, whose first husband was Mr. Warren Goolsbee, father of Mrs. W. S. Goolsbee, of Eufaula, as Miss Cynthia Evans, was the charming daughter of this home, which was beautifully adorned with every luxury that wealth and culture could give. She told the writer this story many years ago.

"I was walking across the garden, when two Yankee soldiers walked up to me, and followed me into the house, where my mother sat. They asked for food, and she gave it to them, and as they sat at her dining table a company of soldiers drove up. There was no attempt at physically harming us, but an officer walked around and ordered his men to mutilate all our beautiful pictures, took our silver and with a big iron (looked like a block) with a wooden handle, struck the silver pitchers and tea pots, broke the knives, forks and spoons into pieces, and when every piece of china had been broken, ordered his men to throw the litter into the well which they did. As if this was not enough, they then took all our bedding, made a bonfire, and after emptying the smoke houses of all our food, which they carried with them, rode away. "I don't recall whether or not Mrs. Dutton knew and told me the company. I presume she did not know, but her story was so vivid and so heart rending that I shall never forget it. I never see a lovely silver service, that I do not recall the expression that was on her face as she told of the horror of that raid on her home.

Another place in Barbour County where personal property was destroyed was near Batesville, Alabama, where on the Williams farm the meat for six families had been stored in the Williams' smokehouse because the owners had not suitable place to keep it safely through the winter, and one night four Yankee soldiers, belonging to an outfit that was going from Georgia through this section, stole a wagon and two horses and carried away with them every piece of meat in this smokehouse, several hundred hams, bacon, etc. They were fired on, from cover by two farmers, who were afraid to come out under fire of four guns, and several miles away next day the wagon was found, but the horses and meat had been carried on, showing that other soldiers had not been far away, to help in the stealing.

It is highly probable, however, that the officers of their company never knew of this act, or, on the other hand, they may have planned it. In either case, the Barbour County people were the sufferers.

In a table of alleged outrages, compiled from K. K. K. testimony of 30 counties, Barbour County does not appear.

K. K. K. methods of regulating society were not new; but as old as history. It was used in those troublesome days to advantage; in these later days there are evidences that the high plane of prnciples carried out to the letter during reconstruction has not been adhered to in politics, and the K. K. K. has been used for other than honorable purposes, by the injection into its (modern fraternity) unlawful and unworthy political practices that are nefareous. When the people of Barbour County found themselves persecuted by aliens and by an unjust law, administered unjustly, they naturally sought some means, outside of the law, to protect themselves.

However, it is a certain fact that such experiences as these could only result in a weakening of respect for the law, and the inefficiency of the old K. K. K. plans used today, which will hinder, rather than help politically, as they did in 1874.

In 1872, one David P. Lewis, deserted from the Confederate cause and a "political turncoat," was the Republican candidate for governor of Alabama, nominated over Thomas H. Handley of Mobile. There was some discontent with Lindsey formented by Republican promoters and Hendey was unable to arouse in votes in the northern counties. With Democrats in control of both the house and senate, the Republicans were in a predicament—but only one carpet bagger was elected to the House of Representatives, the first negro sent up by Alabama negro farmers. The Republican party was overthrown in 1874 and the scalawag reign in Barbour County was over.

Democrats were more harmonious and united than ever before, and were determined to put Republicans out from office, even if force was necessary to do so.

THE RIOT AT OLD SPRING HILL

On the Central of Georgia Railroad, twenty miles from Eufaula and the Chattahoochee river, is the station now called Comer. Five miles from this station is "Old Spring Hill."

Fifty years ago this was a thriving village, the people still living on their plantations in the country. Those who read of "reconstruction," still going on in the old world, can hardly realize what our Southland endured during our "Reconstruction" after the War Between the States.

Federal soldiers were stationed in all the principal cities in the South. Scalawags, Carpet baggers and the newly freed negroes lorded it over the people.

Busteed, the infamous federal judge, located in Montgomery—Lewis the Republican governor. For nearly ten years the South had borne indignities, bankruptcy and humiliation. They could endure no more. The determination had come to every state, to throw off this infamous yoke. Such was the situation when the general elections were to be held on the first Tuesday after the first Monday in 1874.

One of the voting places was at Old Spring Hill in Barbour County in a vacant store next to an unoccupied one on a corner.

Elua M. Keils, a southern white man, who had sold his birthright for the meager pottage of a county judgeship, was a candidate for re-election. He sensed the brewing storm and had petitioned General Swayne to send down a company of soldiers from Montgomery.

Then, a man could vote anywhere he chose in his own county.

This place and Eufaula had been selected for the Republicans to 'carry," so the word had been sent ' Sont" for the negroes (they could vote then) to gather in those two places. For weeks the men had been meeting and planning for this election.

Each one subscribed ten dollars for what purpose "deponent sayeth not." However, it was not long until big boxes, filled with pint bottles (easy to put in the pocket) of whiskey arrived, and were placed in the store on the corner. On the day that the soldiers were to arrive at the station the negroes went to meet them, in buggies or any vehicle they could get—

[198]

no matter how shabby. The white men were there, too, in the nicest conveyances that could be obtained.

Of course, the soldiers chose to go with the latter. They were quartered in the school house, that building and the church, only a few hundred yards from the polling place.

The ladies were there to greet these soldiers, with smiling faces and well filled baskets of pies, cakes, custards, in fact, with all the dainties and substantials that a Southern kitchen could produce. These courtesies were kept up for the soldiers were there a week or more before the election, often joining in the hunting parties, a new sport to them. A young sergeant was made very nervous in one of these hunts, when his companion's gun went off several times by accident during the day.

On the day of the election, that day one of the most tragic and most comical in the history of the state, you could see people coming in—some riding, some walking, until the whole place was alive with humanity. Every white man was armed with a pistol or gun and a pint bottle.

Keils was one of the first to arrive. He had with him his only son, Willie, just sixteen years old. The leaders in this day's doings knew they were taking their lives in their hands. Never once did they fear or falter for the result, even Dr. Barr, of staid Presbyterian belief, by his courtly demeanor showing his F. F. V. ancestry, would slap his breast and exclaim, "Go it boys, Old Barr is with you."

One mother pleaded with an older son, "Do take care of your brother." His reply was, "Mother, that boy ain't afraid of the devil."

The men would take out their bottles, take a drink, throw them down, instantly they were grabbed and emptied by the negroes, causing many of them to get too drunk to vote (just what they wanted) or do anything but drop down in a drunken stupor.

Soon after the polls were opened, there were several shots fired. Keils sent post haste for the soldiers to come, telling them that the white men were killing all the negroes." This same sergeant who was so nervous on the hunting trip sent word that if there were not enough white men to kill them all that he and his company would come down and finish the job, thus showing their sympathy for the people, and putting a quietus on the negroes. Ever and anon the suppressed excitement would be shown by brawling and pistol shots. Keils had already begged Dr. Barr to get him out of the house and away from the place, saying he would leave the country and never give any more trouble.

Dr. Barr told him that it would be death for both of them to attempt it.

Several times the back door had been broken open, regardless of the men guarding it. At one of these times, Joe Simon, overcome by drowsiness, having kissed his pint bottle, too often had gone inside, crawled under the counter and had fallen asleep.

Night came. The lamps were lighted. Counting the votes had begun. Suddenly a fusilade of shots, the crashing of doors and windows were heard almost at the same time. The lamps were shot out, the house in darkness, cries from within were heard "help help, I'm shot all to pieces." These from Joe Simon, who hadn't been touched. A lamp brought from a distant house revealed Keils on his knees before J. W. Comer, to whom he had given the Masonic sign of distress. The latter was shot in the leg by Walter White, who in the darkness thought he was shooting Keils in the head. Mr. Comer had several times knocked aside the pistol of a younger brother, trying to shoot this same Keils, thinking he was the one who had shot his brother. This arch traitor was not hurt. Alas, there lay young Willie Keils, shot fatally. Five bullets were in his body, the victim of his father's greed, whose pistol did the deadly work no one knows.

Guarded by Wallace Comer and Joe Alston, one on each side, as some of the men still wanted to kill him, Keils was escorted to the home of Grandma Drewry. To this place also was taken the body of the dying boy. During the riot Bill Herritt's coat tail was shot off by Jim Long. The former said that "he flew on the wings of the wind, never stopping for breath until he splashed through the waters of Red River, four miles away."

By this time there was not a negro to be seen. One, a manager of the election, named Battle, said afterwards that he crawled on his hands and knees until he fell into Cowikee creek, two and one-half miles away.

Another negro crawled as far as he could under a store at the corner, then being caught by a nail, stayed there for hours before he was rescued.

In the meantime the ballot box had been carried off and buried in the woods.

Who can imagine the agony of that poor mother's waiting? Waiting all that dreadful day, in her Eufaula home, fearing she knew not what—till at last the message came: "your son is mortally wounded."

An eye witness told me that when she reached there, in the gray dawn of the morning, her eyes wild with grief, her hair streaming over her face and shoulder, she was the very picture of tragedy itself. Her reproaches were heart rending. "Oh, Mr. Keils, I begged you not to bring my child here. You did it to shield yourself, regardless of him."

When this boy was buried the next Sunday in Eufaula, there was a stream of negroes over a mile long on one sidewalk, and only two carriages to follow the victim to the grave

The principal actors in this life's drama, were all indicted: J. W., B. B., and J. F. Comer, Tobe and Joe Alston. Walter White and others were summoned to the station to make bond.

The three former made bonds for eleven thousand dollars each, and the others for ten thousand.

Hardly a man in the county, but went to the station to go their bonds. When the mother of the Comer boys was asked if she were worth thirty thousand dollars, she replied: "Before Tuesday's election I was poor, but now I feel rich."

When one lady was informed of the results of the election, she exclaimed, "Thank God red blood is still flowing in the veins of our Alabama men." Thus were the shackles broken from our fair state and from all the southern states, for scenes similar to these were being enacted in them all.

Let us hope, let us pray, that never again will the tryant's horde invade our Southland, and that it will ever be THE LAND OF THE FREE AND THE HOME OF THE BRAVE.

(Signed) MRS. J. F. COMER, Midway, Alabama

RIOT AT EUFAULA NOV. THIRD, 1874

The smoke of the fires of War Between the States had not entirely disappeared, for the smouldering embers were being constantly kept stirred, for a re-fing of political graft, by the red radicalism kept at fever heat by the office seekers and their henchmen.

When the morning of Nov. 3rd, 1874, dawned at Eufaula, where lived Elias M. Kells, the Republican judge of the City Court, Democratic citizens felt that the graveness of the situation called for special precaution at the polls and to this end a number of citizens headed by James Buford, had arranged for extra watch guards, and deputy sheriffs all over the County, at each polling place, for there was every indication that there would be an effort made to control the voting and stuff the boxes.

For a long period, federal military rule had created minor misdemeanors and daily rendevous of the negroes and their scalawag leaders had brought about a state of unrest that grew into anxious fear. The whole County was almost entirely under Republican rule and domination.

Many of the best citizens had, years before, been forced to sign an oath of allegiance to the federal government, during the four years of the war, and the personal feelings of the majority of Southerners against those so unfortunate as to be forced to sign this oath of allegiance was not the kindest in some instances. Therefore, the unrest, fear and dissatisfaction in many homes was very tense.

Once before, since the date of negro emancipation, a great riot at Eufaula had been threatened, but was providentially averted, but grim, gaunt suspicion stalked everywhere. The election and its always attendant anxiety was on the heart and mind and in the face of every loyal citizen.

James M. Buford, as far back as 1854, before the War Between the States loomed, had with his patriotic, but red hot editorials in the "Spirit of the South," Barbour County's leading newspaper, kindled a flame in the Democratic heart and soul—that by the time these reconstruction troubles had begun to undermine the Democratic structure, the citizenship was incensed to a readiness to act, when a crisis arose.

This crisis did come. By ten o'clock the streets were thronged with negroes (population has always been 6 negroes to 1 white, in Barbour County). Lunch stands were set all over Broad street, from Eufaula to Livingston streets. These stands were all run by negro women. The Western Union Telegraph office was upstairs, over the now Thomas Drug store. A Republican henchman was making a speech to negroes gathered as thick as they could stand in the street. Mr. Buford and several other citizens came down the stairs from the telegraph office, and as he struck the sidewalk, guns and pistols began firing, the sound that reached far and wide continuing for over ten minutes) resembled the setting off of millions of firecrackers.

No one ever knew who fired the first shot, but the quick firing, after ceasing for several minutes, began again and soon there were several negroes lying on the streets wounded and several dead.

Mr. Buford's gun struck one of the women at the lunch stand, killing her, and a young boy standing near her, about ten years old. When he saw them lying dead, he cried out "My God, that I should have done this."

Despite the fact that he was shooting as a patriotic citizen, in effort to quell a riot, in which hundreds of negroes were shooting at random—at the instigation of cowardly scallawags and infamous Republican henchmen— the fact that he had killed a woman and child threw a shadow of personal regret and sorrow over a very useful and brilliant career.

That night the buildings of the East Alabama Fair Association were burned to the ground, lighted by incendiaries, who were not in sympathy with the policies of the "Grange," an organization sponsored by the best Democracy of the County.

Suspects were arrested, tried and sentenced, and many threats were made for months against many citizens.

It was at a riot at Old Spring Hill this same night that the sixteen-year-old son of Republican Judge Keils met his death from an unknown hand that shot him.

It was said that Keils held his son up before him, thinking no guns would be fired against the boy, and this would no doubt have been the case had the light not been knocked out, and in the darkness there was no way of knowing the boy was in front of the father. Bad a man as Keils was considered, few there were to believe that he was coward enough to push his son into danger to save himself. There was no pity for him and deep sympathy for his wife, who was a fine Christian woman, a member of one of the prominent old families of this section, her life ruined by the politics of her husband.

He had amassed a fortune, from the office he held, built one of the finest homes in Alabama (still standing—now the home of Mr. George Dent, II, and George Dent, III, and little George Dent, IV, on Barbour street, Eufaula), but when citizens of the County, resenting all that he had been the direct cause of, masterfully took hold of the situation they made it imperative that he leave.

He went to Yankton, Dakota, and Washington, D. C., where he could be at home among Republicans.

The following letter written back to a friend who had befriended his wife in her trouble the night he was arrested and put in jail at Eufaula shows his attitude toward Eufaula. We wrote back his delight to see certain Eufaula candidates defeated for office.

At the Keil boy's funeral the father invited negroes into the parlors and it is said that it was one of the most disgusting, as well as heart rending spectacles ever witnessed here.

But even before 1874 there had been another riot (the worst of it being squelched) in Eufaula, the outcome of Republican office holding and Republican domination in the County.

There was a group of eight negroes—four brothers named Thomas, others named Cowan, who had been owned by leading citizens and who after the emancipation of the negro felt that they had the right to stand on equal footing with white citizens.

Bray Brothers—John W., William H., Nathan M., and Wells J.—owned a large wholesale and retail hardware store, carrying a heavy stock of guns, ammunitions and firearms. These negroes conceived the idea of and planned to break into this store, arm themselves, set fire to the store, and when the male citizenship left their homes to fight the fire, they would rob the homes and set fire to them, thus destroying the town. They confided in and tried to get cooperation from one Alex Hamilton, a mulatto contractor and builder, who as a slave had belonged to the distinguished Crocker family of Lumpkin, Georgia, and he, having come to Eufaula as a slave of a member of this family living here had remained in the service of this family for a long time after being freed. He was a negro of superior intelligence and proved to be of good, honest character.

In sympathy with the white element, he confided to Officials and for weeks this band of plotters gathered nightly on the Iron steps of the John McNab Bank, discussing their plans. Alex Hamilton was always present, attending these meetings as one of them.

Mr. Elliott Thomas, of Eufaula, was secreted in the cellar of the bank each night, where he could hear all each man said. He was a rapid scribe and took down the details of all they planned. Their signal to enter the store was to be "Keno," and when it was given on the fatal night, 50 or more citizens, headed by the mayor, Dr. C. J. Pope, Capt. S. H. Dent and others, fully armed, rushed in, arrested the negroes, tried and convicted them all. They served terms in the penitentiary.

The city of Eufaula presented to Hamilton a gold watch and chain and a lot to build him a house, on which he did, living in it until some time in the late eighties. He moved later to Atlanta, taking contract to build one of Atlanta's largest and finest buildings. He remained there. He had built many of the finest old homes in Barbour County.

When Col. A. H. Alston was appointed Judge of Probate, following the impeachment of Wiley E. Jones, the chaotic conditions in the County were due to the long period of reconstruction and its resultant evils. He had a gigantic task before him, but his keen insight, knowledge of the law and the obligations of the office holder were so serious that only a strong will and determination could have brought order out of chaos as he did.

He cleaned out the political pot thoroughly and so splendidly did he succeed against almost insurmountable odds that he was re-elected twice and was the first to break the Republican shackles that had crippled and disgraced the county for so long.

DEMOCRATIC AND CONSERVATIVE TICKET FOR 1874

For Governor—George H. Houston of Limestone County.
For Lieut.-Governor—R. F. Ligan of Macon County.

For Justices of the Supreme Court—Thomas J. Judge of Butler County, R. C. Bricknell of Madison County and A. R. Manning of Mobile County.

For Attorney General—J. W. A. Sanford of Montgomery County.

For Treasurer—Daniel Crawford of Coosa County.

For Supt. of Public Instruction—John M. McKleroy of Barbour County.

For Congressman at Large—B. B. Lewis of Tuscaloosa; W. H. Forney of Calhoun.

For Chancellor—Eastern Division—Neil S. Graham of Macon County.

For Congressman from Second Division—Jere N. Williams of Barbour County.

For Judge Eighth Judicial Circuit—Henry D. Clayton of Barbour County.

For member of the Board of Education—Second District—J. D. Padgett of Crenshaw County.

WHITE MAN'S TICKET OF BARBOUR COUNTY

For Judge of Eufaula City Court—Alpheus Baker of Barbour County.

For the Legislature—Dr. J. E. Crews; Winston Andrews.

For Judge of Probate—Wiley E. Jones.

For Clerk of the Circuit Court—John C. McNab.

For Sheriff—B. Frank Hart.

For Treasurer—R. A. Solomon.

For Tax Collector—T. R. Sylvester.

For Tax Assessor—W. B. Stewart.

For Clerk of Eufaula City Court—George H. Estes.

For County Commissioners—Frank M. Cordeman; John C. McRae; A. Reeder; B. B. Comer.

For Coroner—Theo Pruden.

LIST OF LAW FIRMS IN BARBOUR COUNTY FROM 1850 TO TODAY

Cochran and Bullock—John Cochran and E. E. Bullock, Eufaula, 1853; Pugh and Buford—J. L. Pugh and J. M. Buford, Eufaula, 1853; Cato and Cato, Eufaula, 1946; Alpheus

Baker, Jr., Eufaula, 1851; Eli S. Shorter, Eufaula 1852; M. B. Wellborn, Clayton, 1854; D. M. Seals, Eufaula and Clayton, 1854; H. D. Clayton, John M. McLeroy, A. M. McLendon, Clayton, 1854.

Since the War Between the States—At Clayton:

A. H. Alston, Joe White, Alto V. Lee, George H. Peach, deceased, Alex H. Thomas deceased, E. Perry Thomas, de-deceased, James J. Winn, J. S. Williams, T. M. Patterson, Millard Jackson, George Andrews, Sr., Guy Winn, deceased, Crews Johnson, Preston G. Clayton.

At Eufaula—C. S. McDowell, A. M. McDowell, G. L. Comer, A. H. Merrill, C. P. S. Daniel, L. . Brassel, A. H. Merrill, W. H. and A. K. Merrill, John D. Roquemore, J. Long, W. C. Swanson, S. H. Dent, Jr., deceased, Lee J. Clayton and Lee J. Clayton, Jr., Chauncey Sparks.

Chapter Twenty-one

The Granger-Farmers' Alliance and Silver Question

The National Grange was organized in 1872, and a few months later there were local Granges all over the state. It promised social and economic redemption for farmers and made strong appeals because farmers were in need of any kind of salvation. By 1875 there were 650 in the state and members numbered 17,440. Picnics, barbecues, rallys and speech making. The main object was to improve agriculturally, by the mind, as well as by the hand. Soil improvements and diversification were stressed.

The Grange finally developed into a business enterprise, and nothing but lack of money to operate prevented the experiment of opening up banks and the establishment and maintenance of general trade in merchandise, farm products, etc., for the benefit of stockholders. The Grange did establish a system over the state to act as agents and a Granger's Life and Health Insurance Company of the United States at Mobile in 1875.

By co-operative buying and selling Grangers in Barbour County, headed by Col. Hiram Hawkins, undertook to reduce the cost of cotton, corn and feeds, storage, insurance, bagging and ties and fertilizers. Although operating on a non-political basis, the Grange did get into politics and took active part in the overthrow of the carpet baggers. It was so strong in the legislature of 1876 that it was called "the Grange Legislature."

The Grange element was entirely progressive in the Democratic party and had much influence in all the objectives at that time.

Grange influence was felt in the R. R. Commission, State Department of Agriculture laws, Immigration laws, and all reforms in the state. But, unfortunately, the Grange did not solve the farmers' problems, and the organization failed, because of forces, exercised by its opponents and also by its own mistakes.

In Barbour County, the Grange lasted until late in the eighties, longer than in some other counties. However, the death of the Grange was not evidence that the farmers in

Barbour County were through with organized effort, and from that time until now there have been found now and then (left as echo from those days) some of the same spirit that had its birth in the Grange movement.

ALLIANCE

Later the Farmers' Alliance was created and organized, following the example of Madison County in 1887. It had all the advantages of the Grange, bending more to politics and at first it was favored by the newspapers, but finally had only the good will of its own publication, "The Southern Agriculturist" and Farmers' "Alliance Advocate."

Its endeavor was to promote better farming and to save the farmers from the harms of mortgages and crop lien system and to protect them from the evil grips of the monopolies, trusts, usurers, and extortionists.

Incorporated in 1889, it functioned until the agricultural forces began to fret.

Reuben F. Kolb, Agricultural Commissioner of Alabama, and an enthusiastic Alliance leader, published some hand bills, that were persausive and in 1886 he exhibited "Alabama On Wheels," through the North and West. During the eighties the legislature was friendly to the farmers, but the growth of the farmers' movement in 1886 alarmed politicians and many of them quickly joined these farmers' organizations.

"Alabama On Wheels" was a Louisville and Nashville Railroad Company's car exhibiting the resources of the state of Alabama, with Capt. Kolb and other prominent citizens of Barbour County in charge.

There began to be talk about "Rings," "Tax Burden," "Honest Count" and "Discontent Between County Sections." sprang up. The Alliance, under Capt. Kolb of Barbour and Rev. S. M. Adams of Blount County were drifting too deep into politics, it was claimed, when the Birmingham Age-Herold (then friendly to the Alliance) on July 3rd, 1889, said "the forces are organizing and several classes of the people who have ills to cure and complaints are getting together" and soon the state was about to get into a grave political upset. Some members contended that the Alliance should "make its own politics." Later farmers recognized to some extent their own mistakes, but blamed others for most of their troubles, assailing the "Tariff" and "Trusts" and demanding a "larger and more elastic currency," more "adequate transportation."

They felt the low price of farm products was the cause of the scarcity of money. They favored expanding the volume of currency, some were so strong in their convictions that they bolted the Democratic party and when silver became the chief hope of currency expansion, the farmer clamored for its free and unlimited coinage, not doubting that they could succeed, if there were ample currency in the county, and if railroad freights were reduced.

Their lack of knowledge on all these problems made agricultural reform slow and after a short period of seeming success, the co-operative business enterprises failed completely, suffering from lack of capital, credit and experience.

The leaders of this movement in Barbour County, R. F. Kolb and Col. Hiram Hawkins, Master of the State Grange. Both, having large farming interests in the County, made valiant efforts to hold both organizations together, but the political phase was taking on varied shape, and both died for want of sufficient and proper nourishment and application.

The war and reconstruction conditions had impoverished and demoralized the farmers, whose continued poverty became harder to bear in the face of industrial activities around them. When gaunt poverty stalked among them and success was plainly to be seen in the mercantile, banking, professional classes, the comparison that was the outcome of the distressing situation caused the farmers of Barbour County to attempt to reestablish themselves but, being without money, or credit this work of restoration was slow with nothing but land (and most of it rented) as security for loans. The situation narrowed back to only the "crop lien." It had been tried before the War Between the States to some extent but the exegencies of "after the war" and reconstruction made this almost impossible until in 1877 a law was passed which made this 'crop lien" law permissible, and later it was modified to allow the tenant with his landlord's permission to open store accounts. But (especially in the case of negro land tenants, this law proved, by its abuse, unwise, and the cry for help was back to banks and money lenders, but even this was not practical for banks felt that prospective crops were not good bank security.

The cotton market, because of his mortgaged crop, was not a competitive market for the tenant farmer and he neither had much opportunity. His mostly merchant creditor owned the crop and he was rarely ever able to pay off this indebtedness.

With most of the farmers in debt, and crops not sufficient to pay out, it naturally followed there was little competition among the merchants for trade, and with banks not giving direct aid to farmers, many of the farms passed into the hands of the merchants, loan agents and a few, very few, of the more successful farmers between 1880 and 1890.

In Barbour County, many farmers were in grave condition, debts piled up, taxes became a great burden, high protective tariff made living commodities almost out of reach, and it seemed to the farmer that the commercial world had conspired against him and his efforts to solve his problems by a co-operative plan which had failed because there were so many obstacles fighting success.

The farmers sought remedies for their peony and poverty and there were many claims that the farmers themselves were responsible for their condition and that their move was agitation begun by them in the eighties that first gave rise to a scientific agriculture in Barbour County.

It was claimed that Cotton was consuming too much of the substance of the people and an Alabama paper attempted a revolt against cotton ruling and after much pro and con, Commissioner Betts and Prof. J. S. Newman of the State Agricultural experiment station at Auburn, suggested and urged crop diversification and the reducing of agriculture to a scientific basis. He told the farmers that "it was certain Agriculture would have to come to the same basis on which other industries of the country succeeds; and that they would have to "be a definite reduction in cotton acreage in favor of food and feed crops, use of proper fertilizers and strong and rigid economy."

In Barbour County, there were Alliance men who were ready to lead in the work of reforming the state and nation, and the man who took upon himself the greatest of this effort was this same Reuben Kolb. He had been "to the manor born," a lineal descendant of Lords and Kings of England, but with all a heart throb for the oppressed, as had his friend and neighbor, Hiram Hawkins.

Democrats in Barbour County had felt the strike of Republican dominations through reconstruction days, but that was over now, and there was now grave fear of greenbackers or Republicans, but in the election of 1890 the Farmers' Alliance struck a blow that was a veritable jolt. The farmers did have grievances and the Alliance concluded that "these grievances could be redressed, only by political action" and being aware of their might, because they were strong in numbers, they attempted to control the Democratic party, the newspapers and politicians and succeeded in making them tody to them. Kolb had gathered about himself for years some strong friendships. He was Agricultural Commissioner of the state in 1887; president of the Farmers National Congress, and unlimited authority was given him. He attended every agricultural institute, meeting or gathering and won thousands of personal friends by his genial personality, and persuavive power. He was also ambitious and long before time for the election of 1890, he saw political possibilities for himself and although the Alliance did not (they claimed) include politics in it, stenets, former political teaching to them, unaware, had begun to bear fruit in the Alliance. In the Convention of August, 1889, Kolb was endorsed for Governor.

He went to St. Louis to attend a National Congress of Farmers that had been called to work out assisted by the Knights of Labor a charter of "Liberties for Toilers of the Fields and Factories," chief of which were: Abolition of National banks and substitution of legal tender—treasury notes—for National Bank notes. Free and unlimited coinage of silver, a fair tax system and economy in public expenditures, laws dealing in futures of agriculture and mechanical production, laws pertaining to ownership of land and the reclaiming of all lands owned by railroads and other corporations in excess of their actual needs, to be held for actual settling and the public ownership of communications and transportation." To these demands the Southern Alliance added a sub-treasury plan."

The delegates agreed that only such candidates for office as could be depended upon to enact these principles into the statute law, uninfluenced by party caucus, should receive the votes of their respective organizations and this caused great discussion in Alabama. In Barbour County it created varied opinion before the meeting of the state convention June, 1890.

These principles were objectionable to Conservative Democrats and the Montgomery Advertiser said, "Never had certain of its doctrines found place in the Democratic Caleans." The wine proposed was too new for old bottles and the rock-ribbed party organs like the Advertiser and the Register deplored the proclamation of such heresies, and they made a strong attack on most of the program, particularly those parts advocating the abolition of National banks, public ownership of railroads and the sub-treasury scheme.

The Mobile Register pointed out that the sub-treasury plan could furnish no relief to farmers who mostly needed assistance unless they possessed unmortgaged cotton and corn. They could not use the credit system proposed, asserting that the sub-treasury bill was a rich man's scheme and would benefit non-Alliance men and ruin those belonging to the Alliance. This great doubt in the minds of even Alliance men made Kolb's plan doubtful.

The opposition to Kolb was led by the Montgomery Advertiser, which paper was most vitriolic in its denunciations. The Birmingham Age Herald was friendly to Kolb at first, but viewed the political situation from both angles and "watched" its editorial statements with caution. It said "This white man's party of ours in Alabama is broad enough to take in all who vote the ticket that stands by the nominees and is true to the cause of a white man's government when different standards are set up; when all men shall be read out of the party who have any notion different from other people—then Democracy's date has come."

The campaign was a spectacular one. The Alliance Advocate replied to the Advertiser and the contest was hot and fierce and not before the records of participants were brought to light and old stories given new wings. Many were most ludricous. The Alliance was in the limelight and much in the politics of the time. In Barbour County the Alliance men were loyal to their leader, although many differed with him. However, while the Advertiser was denouncing Kolb as party rebel, his home town paper, the Eufaula Times, claimed that he was as good a Democrat as Thomas Jefferson, nay, he is a better Democrat than was the great Virginian," it asserted, and has done more for the party in Alabama than any other man.

The real cause of Kolb's defeat was, viz: At a caucus of his opponents, the night before the election, it was found that neither Johnson, nor Crook could beat Kolb, but that Judge Richardson could beat him by four votes and Jones by thirteen.

Whereupon, it was decided to combine on Jones, the strongest of the Conservatives in the Convention. It was said, too, that if Jones had not been nominated the Montgomery delegation would have supported Kolb.

FROM LODI, ALABAMA, JULY 1ST, 1889

To the Alliance of Barbour and Henry Counties, Alabama: How would this suggestion for a warehouse in Eufaula meet with your approval?

For each sub-Alliance to decide how much stock it would take in a warehouse after consultation with its members, appoint delegates to meet in Eufaula on the 19th day of July, to make the report of the subscription from their respective Alliances so that the meeting will be able to act intelligently without calling other meetings. I think the president of each County Alliance might make a request of the Sub-Alliances in keeping wtih the proposition, provided it is not inconsistent with the object of the meeting on July 19th.

If we intend business, let us go in business form and let those parties who have property to dispose of know that we come with the money and that we want to buy.

MASONS IN BARBOUR COUNTY

Harmony Lodge No. 46 Free and Accepted Masons was organized in what was then Irwinton in 1838 with tthe following charter members, viz: John P. Boothe, Isaac Nathans, Reuben C. Shorter, Levi T. Wellborn, A. Treadwell, L. N. Broughton, James Young, D. T. Driggers, Isaac Daniels, D. S. Taylor, C. C. Mills, Eley C. Holleman.

The following have served as "Worshipful Master:" Thomas Cargill, Zadoc C. Daniel, G. A. Roberts, James Milton, George A. Beauchamp, G. L. Comer, D. Seth Mabry, H. B. Dowling, George M. Dent, J. T. Mainor and a Mr. Halsted.

The Lodge purchased a handsome building on Broad street many years ago from Woods and Raney, and for more than 60 years have used the same Lodge Room in this building.

The names of E. Stow, Robert Moulthrop, Sr., and R. Moulthrop, Jr., John C. Thomas, James Milton and G. L. Comer stand out notably as leading members of this Lodge in the long ago. John C. Thomas was keeper of Records and Seal 30 years.

CLAYTON LODGE

The Royal White Heart Lodge No. 10 A. F. and A. M. at Clayton has a long honorable record.

The present W. M .is J. D. Vinson and Secretary, C. C. Scheffer.

CLIO LODGE NO. 566 A. F. F. & A. M.

One of the oldest Masonic Lodges in Alabama was the Holsey Lodge No. 68 of Glennville, Barbour County, then—now Russell County. William L. Johnson was W. M.

WOODMEN OF THE WORLD IN BARBOUR COUNTY

Chewalla Camp No. 16 W. O. W. at Eufaula was organized in 1897, with 20 charter members. J. D. Schaub has been clerk since its organization.

ODD FELLOWS

I. O. O. F. Lodge No. II was organized in May, 1857, at Eufaula. The annual celebration was held May 16, 1854, with C. A. Battle, of Tuskegee, speaker.

The annual celebration of Eufaula Lodge No. 11 will take place on Wednesday, May 10, 1854, an address will be delivered at the Methodist church by Brother C. A. Battle, of Tuskegee. Brothers of the order and the public generally are invited to attend.

—E. S. Shorter, C. Rhodes, J. Hardman, W. H. McIntosh, H. Black, H. P. Pratt, Committe.

B. P. O. E., Eufaula No. 12, functioned for many years in Barbour County, but for the past ten years has been non existent.

Chapter Twenty-two

Military

These men wore the banner of the South that was unalloyed
Its tenets flying to the breeze,
And the echo of its song of joy
Is the opportunity we seize,
To reveal in its pride and glory
Of Home and Country so dear—
That is an old, old story
That each generation loves to hear.

The old Eufaula Rifles was organized June 23rd, 1857. Capt. B. F. Treadwell was first captain and there were 41 members. During the struggle there were the "Shorter Volunteers," "Barbour Greys," "Clayton Guards." In 1853, "The Eufaula Huzzars" was organized and a year later, the Eufaula Militia. March 17, 1860, Alpheus Baker was made captain of the "Eufaula Rifles."

On Nov. 3rd, 1861, the Eufaula Rifles saluted the first secession flag hoisted in Eufaula. In 1880 the Eufaula light Infantry was organized with Clement Clay Shorter, captain. Many of the officers and members of this Company—which during the eighties, was responsible for some of the most brilliant social history of any city ever recorded—have gone to answer the eternal roll call, cut off in their young manhood, but passing away at home, not like these of the first Eufaula Companies dying on the battle fields.

Charles R. Ross, Will Ross, Jacob Ramser, Will M. Bray, Alexes Besson, Ernest K. Brannon, all died in the eighties.

Only recently James E. Sapp, George W. Whitlock and others. Jere Danile, the Colored Drum Major of the Company, and little old Bill Thompson, Armory Janitor, were always loyal to the soldier boys, thinking them the greatest soldiers that ever donned a uniform. Both of them wore this uniform on all occasions.

In 1897, the Light Infantry having long before disbanded, when the Spanish-American war sounded reveille a company was organized, with J. R. Barr, Captain, and the Company went to Miami, Fla., until Cevera's defeat. The following were officers of this New Eufaula Rifles:" J. R. Barr, Capt.; R. A. Ballowe, Robert Stephens, Dan B. McKenzie and Ray Irby all served as captains.

Hart's Hall was used as an Armory, until it was burned November, 1904. Then a hall in the Irby building was used.

EUFAULA LIGHT ARTILLERY

Organized February 26th, 1862. Composed of men from Barbour and adjoining counties—two hundred and sixty two, rank and file This company was equipped with guns and ammunition, this battery joining the Army of Tennessee and was in all its operations throughout the war. Forty-eight men were killed and wounded and 36 lost their lives by disease. J. W. Clark was captain and they surrendered at Meridian, Miss.

Roll

Officers were John W. Clark, M. D. Oliver, W. J. McKenzie, J. H. G. Martin, John D. Snipes, Nathan H. Thornton, John O. Martin, W. S. Danforth, A. W. McKenzie, M. W. King, James H. Russell, W. M. Brannon, Jr., William A. McTyer, W. A. McDuffee, William Henry Woods, Charles C. Robinson, Charles A. Wallace, Thomas R. McTyer, A. A. Couric, Osburn R. Flournoy, William E. Moore, James M. Espy, H. Clarence Jordan, Ben F. Barksdale.

Privates

Charles W. Askew, A. W. Brannon, W. E. Besson, F. L. Barrett, W. J. Bray, William M. Bostick, J. D. Brown, P. Bernstein, J. D. Bush, J. A. Chambers, J. Chandler, R. V. Cadenhead, John Courtney, J. C. Carroll, J. C. H. Cunningham, W. H. Craig, A. K. Dickinson, M. Daniel, J. W. Dearing, J. S. Espy, Jas. I. Etheridge, P. Follmer, J. Ford, J. Foreman, S. J. Flournoy, J. Farley, J. H. Green, Moses Griffin, H. P. Gunnels, J. H. Hardwick, . M. Hayler, J. S. Hunter, John C. Holder, J. C. Iverson, J. Johnson, P. W. Jones, T. J. Jones, K. Kilpatrick, W. C. Kelly, William Loftin, S. A. Loman, L. Pippin, J. M. Ryals, E. F. Loman, J. H. Lunsford, G. B. Lunsford, J. L. Lawhorn, W. H. Magruder, J. R. May, H. K. Nixon, William Pippin, T. W. Jarsons, H. P. Pratt, Frank M. Prigdeon, J. E. Poster, Matthew Prince, C. Paramour, Sanders Quick, T. J. Saulsberry, D. G. Sullivan, A. Stevens, T. D. Tindal, George Foy, F. Villeret, A. Whittington, H. D. Williams, J. C. Barnett, B. E. Nance, H. R. Young, J. C. McRae, G. P. Pernal, Chambless, O. S. Wells, B. Jones, J. Hamilton, William Cobb, B. F. Hart, J. C. McDuffee, S. A. Elyea, E. S. E. Bryan, C. Baker, M. Bennett, H. D. Botsford, J. H. Borrow, J. C. Bowden, R. H. Wright, C. Browning, F. M. Caldwell, Patrick Corbitt, H. C. Clephorn, M. W. Clements, A. Cunningham, R. Cunningham, J. W. Clark, M. Darkin.

EUFAULA LIGHT ARTILLERY

W. D. Danforth, J. H. Dent, J. B. Daniel, R. Elliott, A. D. Fuqua, E. N. Fountain, P. Faulkner, Thomas J. Flournoy, J. D. Glass, T. Grier, A. McHenslie, Harrison Hart, C. B. Hart, J. Holder, R. W. Hunter, F. M. Johnson, F. A. Jackson, C. J. Jones, C. Kliffmiller, J. C. Kelly, Frank Lowman, L. Y. Lowman, W. Mangum, J. C. Ricks, A. B. Lawson, A. F. Laarie, W. H. Lawhorn, C. A. Mallory, C. F. Massey, William M. McLeod, George W. Martin, G. W. Pippen, J. L. Perkins, L. B. Patterson, E. E. Royal, Sam Stern, E. H. Shields, J. R. Sawyers, J. B. Sasser, A. G. Smith, R. J. Thornton, C. B. Talbert, P. Turage, J. F. Wellborn, G. W. Williams, R. J. Woods, J. L. Wilson, J. M. Williams, L. Windham, A. H. Young, J. S. Doughtie, E. Austin, P. Lunsford, J. McRae, G. H. Sporman, A. M. Benton, H. R. Stephens, J. Capel, George Dubose, J. Arrington, William A. Gaston, J. H. Poston, A. H. Merrill, C. R .Fields, J. W. Glass.

Copied from Eufaula Paper—

Copy Eufaula Rifles Parade Ground Barrancas Barracks, Pensacola, Florida, April 8th, 1861.

At a meeting of the Eufaula Rifles, the following resolutions were adopted: Resolved that thanks of this company be tendered to our kind friends at Eufaula for their continued interest in our welfare, manifested by sending us presents of good things. Please kindly publish for us.—Signed J. W. Howard.

Following is a list of contributions:

Mrs. J. G. Shorter, 2 pair blankets and two pair socks.
Mrs. J. G. Hunter, 3 pairs socks.
Mrs. Battle, 1 pair socks.
Mrs. Reuben Shorter, 3 pairs socks.
Mrs. J. W. Howard, 2 pair blankets.
Mrs. Ott, 2 pair blankets.
Mrs. H. R. Shorter, 1 pair blankets.
Mr. Hall, 1 overcoat.
Mrs. R. R. Howard, 24 blankets.
Mr. Bernstein, 1 blanket.
Mr. J. Hardy, 3 blankets.
Miss Kate Stow, 2 pair socks.
Mrs. A. Stow, 1 pair blankets.
Mrs. R. R. Howard, 1 blanket, 1 shirt, 1 cot.
Mrs. McKenna, 1 pair blankets.
J. A. Ramer, 1 pair blankets.

KOLB'S BATTERY

The original Barbour Light Artillery, known as "Kolb's Battery" — William Beáuchamp, standard bearer — was organized in Eufaula and entered into service on May 27th, 1862, One hundred and twenty strong. Only sixty of the number returned after three years service in the battles of the Western Army.

OFFICERS

R. F. Kolb,—Captain.
Robert Cherry—First Lieutenant.
B. F. Powers—Junior Second Lieutenant.
Robert Flournoy—Senior Second Lieutenant.
William Young Johnston—Junior Second Lieutenant.
John R. Buford—First Sergeant.
H. C. Billings—Second Sergeant.
W. M. Flournoy—Third Sergeant.
George H. McGruder—Fourth Sergeant.
W. T. Lester—Fifth Sergeant.
W. W. Booth, Sixth Sergeant.
T. A. Russell—Seventh Sergeant.
W. H. Carlisle—Eighth Sergeant.
C. R. Wellborn—First Corporal.
George Boyer—Second Corporal.
F. C. McGruder—Third Corporal.
R. M. Head—Fourth Corporal.
J. J. Grayson—Fifth Corporal.
W. M. Campbell—Sixth Corporal.
E. M. Sanders—Seventh Corporal.
J. T. Fuller—Eighth Corporal.
J. S. Jordan—Ninth Corporal.
Thomas Cobb—10th Corporal.
J. A. Cawthorn—11th Corporal.
H. A. Thomas—12th Corporal.

PRIVATES

William Adcock, Moses Alexander, G. F. Allen, Thomas Bonner, B. B. Bailey, J. H. Bowden, J. W. Bird, John B. Burke, Silas Burke, J. T. Brown, J. W. Brown, Steven Bedsole, Benjamin Bessant, J. C. Boggers, M. T. Britt, W. M. Bryan, John T. Coleman, J. H. Carraway, J. G. Cobb, J. N. Cawthorn, C. H. Couric, J. M. Craig, William Childers, J. F. Corbitt, B. L. Cochran, S. R. Cotton, Warren J. Clark, T. M. oker, G. F. Corbitt, B. L. Cochran, S. R. Cotton, Warren J. Clark, T. M. Coker, G. F. Courson, E. T. Colley, John H. Boswell, W. H. Doughtie, John R. Davis, Isiah Davis, C. L. Driggers, G. W. Dunaway, M. W. Deshazo, S. C. Echols, W.

H. Everett, Young R. Folsom, John Forehand, William Fuqua, John W. Fields, William Glass, T. M. Glass, J. G. Grantham, J. A. Garland, T. J. Garlond, A. J. Glover, W. A. Hughes, S. Herring, H. B. Hill, J. J. Highsmith, H. M. Hendrix, R. D. Hendrix, Jesse Harkell, J. B. Hunter, Lewis Hunt, H. H. Hodges, Chapell Hall, H. H. Harper, R. M. Head, B. V. Iverson, J. H. Inman, Parren James, J. H. Johns, J. A. Johns, J. W. Johns, W. Y. Johnston, A. S. Kennedy, George Kenny, John J. Kaigler, T. C. King, S. Lunsford, John S. Lunsford, James A. Lynn, William Long, F. A. McAlpin, James R. Martin, Sylvester Martin, John E. Moore, James T. McBride, A. M. McCrackin, H. C. Norwood, John L. Nix, S. F. Morton, H. A. Nixon, A. A. OHara', Dempsey Odum, W. L. Pinnis, F. M. Pittman, John Peak, T. W. Patterson, John Pippin, Asa Rabun, Charles Redmond, James T. Robinson, J. T. Robinson, W. H. Stephenson, Turner Smith, P. W. Smith, L. M. Smith, L. O. Shepherd, J. D. Shepherd, Angus A. Stewart, C. F. Stewart, W. M. Spirlin, A. J. Spurlin, L. A. Simms, E. B. Sims, C. M. Sanders, B. F. A. Thomas, W. M. Thomas, G. W. Burke, G. M. Taylor, J. M. Vickers, J. L. Wells, M. M. Watson, John Wright, T. C. Wright, G. W. Washington, Green Williams, E. C. Wall, W. M. Williamson, Rollin Wellborn, Bennett Ryan, John Winn.

RECRUITS WHO JOINED DURING THE WAR

Macy Davis, Frank Bassett, Anderson Dobbins, Frank Dobbins, Frank Butts, Joe Bennett, William Bennett, Jeter Ross, Gary Burke, W. Thomas, William Danforth, Lee Irby, J. C. Spurlock, William Bledsoe, S. N. Wellborn, William Beverly, J. F. McTyer, Henry Brown, B. W. Clark, William Bearsherl, Clee Johnson, Gib Long, B. W. Smith.

October 13, 1862, the Confederate Congress passed an act authorizing the President to present "Badges of Distinction to soldiers for individual acts of bravery in battle—among the first of these was a medal to Ebenezer Priest of Eufaula. Companies A and E were Eufaula men and on the Honor Roll Barbour County was well represented.

HONOR ROLL BATTLE MURPHREESBORO
39TH ALABAMA REGIMENT

Adjutant J. M. Macon; Second Lieutenant E. J. Thornton, Company K; Second Lieutenant E. C. Petty, Company K; Sergeant C. K. Hall, Company H; Sergeant J. W. White, Company H; Sergeant Ebenezer Priest, Company K.; Private W. C. Menifee, Company A; Sergeant A. L. J. Talbot, Company A; Privates S M. Martin, Company B; John Dassby, Company C.; E. Burkees, Company D; Frank Jones, Company C; William Meadows, Company F.; Sergeant John H. Poyer, Company G; Sergeant F. H. Espy, Company G; Sergeant Flowers, Company I; Sergeant J. S. Wilson, Company K; 7th Battalion Sharpshooters; Private J. A. Rutherford Company A; Private W. S. White, Company B. The 39th Alabama Regiment was organized by Col. H. D. Clayton.

Ebeneezer Priest lost a leg when color bearer at the battle of Atlanta, having been transferred from the Eufaula Rifles to 39th Alabama Regiment.

Prest while at the head of his regiment, was shot in the leg as he fixed his colors to the works, saying ' Follow the flag boys.'

Miss Alice Priest, his daughter, now living at the old Priest home on the bluff, in the section where Eufaula was first settled, has a piece of this flag and also a medal her father received for other deeds of bravery, during his service for the Confederacy.

Other Barbour County wounded were viz: Ebeneezer Priest lost leg; Dr. Carter a leg; Captain J. W. Tullis his foot; W. Judson Brannon, part of his foot; John Sauls, face twisted from a minute ball; Charlie Hart, injured Spine; Bryan James, J. C. Guice, James Hancock and James Evans lost an arm each. Osborn Wells, wounded in the leg; J. E. Spann, seriously injured and afterward recovered in hospital, located temporarily on Broad at Eufaula; James H. Baker was shot in the eye and blinded; R. Q. Edmondson, wounded in the face and later in the shoulder; Captain S. H. Dent was wounded three times, but remained on the battlefield until the year ended.

Those of Barbour County slightly wounded were: G. W. Barefield, R. Samuel Jones, Allen H. Merrill, Dozier Thornton, Joe Flournoy, John Poston, Henry H. Davis, Hol Harrell, William Bray, Nathan Bray, Junius Montgomery Macon, Charles A. Massey, W. E. McCormick.

Dr. John W. Drewry served with great distinction as surgeon of the 35th Regiment.

Captain Leonard Yancey Dean, who came to Eufaula in 1869, brought with him the empty sleeve, and arm left on the battle fields, going when a young man from his home in South Carolina to the war, and coming out of many battles, a hero.

In every cemetery in Barbour County, there are monuments, and unmarked mounds that silently tell of the bravery and loyalty of those who fought, bled and gloriously died for "Dixie Land."

Note: Since this was written all the graves have been marked.

LIST OF BARBOUR COUNTY VOLUNTEERS
C. S. A.

Barbour Volunteers—1860—Organized at Market House at Eufaula.

Eufaula Rifles—1861—Alpheus Baker, Captain.

Eufaula Light Artillery, 1862—February, 1862—Captain Clark.

Kolbs Battery—1862—Kolb Captain—Original Barbour L. A.

Honor Roll Murphysboro 39th Alabama Regiment.

Seventh Battalion Sharpshooters.

Eufaula Huzzars, August 11, 1853—W. B. Brannon, Captain.

Chapter Twenty-three

Veterans Who Received Crosses of Honor

The story of how General Lee,
At Appomattox, that eventful day
Made the whole world see
The glory of the boys in gray.

The list was compiled by Miss Mary Clayton, founder of the chapter, and completed by Mrs. Erin McCormick Jones. Registrar Barbour County Chapter.
The list begins in 1902:

1. J. L. Adams, P. Company, H. 5th Georgia Regiment.
2. Moses Alexander, P. Kolb's Battery.
3. E. L. Brown, Sergeant Co. B., 5th Regiment, S. C. Volunteers.
4. M. D. Britt, 2nd Sergeant Regular Co. K. 10th Regular Confederate Volunteers.
5. G. W. Barefield, P. Co. K, 39th Alabama Volunteers. Imprisoned at close of war and discharged by special act of Congress.
6. William Henry Brown, P. Co. B., 57th Alabama Volunteers.
7. J. A. Barnes, P. Company Independent of Scouts.
8. P. T. Brown, P. In Kolb's Battery.
9. E. B. Beasley, P. Co. B., 2nd. Regiment Alabama Volunteers.
10. J. T. Blassingame, 2nd Sergt. Co., E. 39th Regiment Alabama Volunteers.
11. T. J. Brown, P., Kolb's Battery.
12. W. N. Beverly, P. Co., H. 39th. Alabama Regiment Volunteers.
13.—J. J. Creyon, P. Co. A, 1st. Regiment Alabama Volunteers.
14. A. A. Couric, discharged as corporal; entered P. in Co. D., 1st. Alabama Volunteers.
15. Henry C. Compton, entered P. Co. A 37th Alabama Regiment Volunteers, dsicharged as corporal.
17. Jason Cleghorn, P. Co. K., 39th Alabama Regiment Volunteers.
18. S. H. Dent, entered B. Co. 1st. Regiment Alabama Volunteers; discharged with rank of Captain of Artillery, "Dent's Battery."

19. G. H. Dent, P. 1st. Regiment Maryland Volunteers. Reinlisted in Dent's Battery August, 1852.
20. L. Y. Dean, P. Co. B., South Carolina Volunteers; rank of Sergeant. Afterwards Captain of Co. E. South arolina Infantry.
21. J. H. Evans, 4th Sergeant Co. G., 13th Regiment Georgia Volunteers.
22. S. J. Flournoy, P. Eufaula Light Infantry (Eufaula Battery).
23. J. G. Guice, P. Co. K., 31st Regular Georgia Volunteers, Army of Northern Virginia; when discharged was special scout and sharpshooter. Lost an arm.
24. T. A. Griffin, P. Co. K., 39th Regiment Alabama Volunteers.
25. John Engram, P., Eufaula Light Artillery.
26. Thomas H. Adams, P., Co. G., 1st Regiment, discharged at Greensborough, N C.; rank of Corporal.
27. J. T. Bolt, Corporal Co. G., 22nd Alabama Regiment (Clayton).
28. Andrew H. Beauchamp, P. Co. F., 1st Alabama Regiment Volunteers
29. J. W. Brown, P. Kolb's Battery Artillery Volunteers.
30.—A. B. Bush Lieutenant Co. D., 63rd Alabama Regiment.
31. Willis Butts, Butt. Co., D., 63rd Alabama Regiment.
32. J. W. Comer, P. Co., H. 57th Alabama Regiment Barbour County.
33. Barbour Cherry, First Lieutenant Kolb's Battery, 4th Battalion; discharged rank captain.
34. Henry D. Clayton, P., Clayton Guards, discharged with rank of Major General.
35. W. P. Copeland, P.Co.,Clayton Corp Cadets; rank Sergeant.
36. G. L. Comer, P., Alabama Corps Cadets.
37. J. J. Carr, P. Co., H. 57th Alabama Regiment.
38. Alfred Dickinson, P. Eufaula Light Artillery.
39. W. D. Danforth, P., Eufaula Light Artillery.
40. M. D. Deshazo, P., Kolb's Battery.
41. J A. Dobbins, P. Kolb's Battery.
42. R. Q. Edmonson, P. Co. 45th Regiment, Alabama Volunteers.
43. J. W. Folsom, P. Co. A., 1st Regiment Alabama Volunteers.
44. James T. Flewellen, Captain 39th Regiment Volunteers A. V. C., the Mitchell Volunteers.
45. Timothy Green, Company K., 37th Volunteers (Pike County.)
46. T. P. Graves, P., "Sweet's Battery," Glenville.

47. Freeman Griffin, P. Co., F., 39th Regiment.

48. Joe Hartung, P. Co., 46th Regiment Georgia Volunteers.

49. John Hartung, P. Co. B, Eufaula Rifles 1st. Regular Alabama Volunteers.

50. Geo. N. Hancock, P. A. 5th Regiment Alabama Volunteers.

51. W. H. Hall, P. Co., K. 15th Regiment Alabama Volunteers.

52. John J. T. Hatfield, P., Co. E., 57th Regiment Alabama Volunteers.

53. Hiram Hawkins, Captain Co. C., 5th Regiment, Kentucky Volunteers; discharged with rank of Colonel.

54. Joseph Bertram Hoole, P., Eufaula Rifles, 1st Regiment, Alabama Volunteers.

55. Jas A. Hogg, Member Dick Dowling's Camo U. C. V., Houston, Texas; 1st Lieut. Company A, Cook's Regiment; discharged ranking Major Drill Master.

56. Lee E. Irby, P., Kolb's Battery.

57. R. L. Jones, P. Co. R., 15th Regiment Alabama Volunteers, Woods division, Longstreet's Corps.

58. Joseph Jones, Eufaula Light Artillery.

59. Joe Jones, P. Co., E. Alabama Regiment Volunteers, Louisville.

60. William Young Johnson, P., Eufaula Rifles, Inf., 1st. Alabama Regiment Volunteers.

61. C. B. Kellar, 2nd Sergeant, C. C., 1st Florida Regiment Volunteers.

62.—E. N. King, Member Camp No. 1108 N. C. V. P., Co. H., 13th Regiment Georgia Volunteers.

63. L. W. McLaughlin, P. Co K, 1st Regiment Louisiana Volunteers, N. O.

64. A. J. Locke, P. Co., 1st Regiment Alabama Volunteers.

65. Harmon Lampley, P. Co., A., Alabama Cadets Regiment, Alabama Cadets Volunteers.

66. John Lunsford, P., Eufaula Light Artillery.

67. C. F. Massey, P., Eufaula Light Artillery.

68. Allen H. Merrill, P., Eufaula Light Artillery (Eufaula Battery).

69. Franklin S. Margart, P. Co. D., Regiment 13th, South Carolina.

70. T. S. Mashburn, Co. B., Battalion (Walkers) Sumter County, Georgia.

71. William Hoadley Bray, 1st Lieutenant Co. K., Jeff Davis Legion Young's Brigade;; promoted to Captain.

72. W. J. Moore P. Co. E., 23rd Regiment Alabama Volunteers; discharged Orderly Sergeant.

73. Thomas S. Mitchell, M. D., P. Co. H., 54th Regiment Georgia Volunteers Surgeon.

74. J. H. G. Martin, P. Co. 8., 1st Regiment Alabama Volunteers.

75. Daniel B. Methvin, P. Co. F., 61st Georgia Regiment Volunteers, Infantry.

76. D. D. McDonald, Company 1, 6th Regiment Florida Volunteers (Clayton).

77. Thos. R. McTyer, P. 1st Regiment Alabama Volunteers.

78. William Emmett McCormick, P. Co. D. 59th Georgetown, Alabama Volunteers.

79. George C. McCormick, P., 7th Regiment, Alabama Volunteers.

80. James E. McComick, P., Co. D., 53rd Alabama Regiment Volunteers, Calvary.

81. Charles S. McDowell; enlisted P. Co. Lynch's Battery Regiment, Tennessee Volunteers; afterwards Co. A. Pages Battalion, Artillery; promoted to 1st Lieutenant with colors, Pages Battalion, Echols Division, Army West Virginia.

82. John M. L. McRae, P. Co. B. 1st Alabama Regiment Volunteers; promoted to Quartermaster Sergeant.

83. D. L. McKinnon, P. Co. C., 1st Alabama Regiment, Volunteers. Afterwards Company C., 39th Regiment Alabama Volunteers (Louisville).

84. J. F. McTyer, P. Kolb's Battery, Stors' Battalion.

85. John C. McNab, Captain Co. K., 29th Alabama Regiment, Alabama Volunteers.

8. John C. McEachern, Corporal Co. F., 1st Alabama Regiment Volunteers; promoted to 2nd Lieutenant Company F., 1st Regiment Alabama Volunteers.

87. John Nary, P. Co., 6th Regiment, Kentucky Volunteers; resident of Kentucky; moved to Hoboken, Eufaula suburb.

88. W. H. Pruett, Captain "I" Company, 1st Regiment, Alabama Volunteers; discharged Major.

89. John H. Poston, P. Co., Eufaula Light Artillery.

90. E. B. Priest, P. Co. K., 9th Regiment, Alabama Volunteers, color bearer, lost a leg in the Battle of Atlanta. lanta.

91. W. J. Robinson, P. Co. L., 34th Regiment Alabama Volunteers. Mustered out as 2nd Sergeant.

92. James Ryak, P., Co. A., 1st Reg., Alabama Volunteers; afterwards "Eufaula Battery."

93. George Albert Roberts, Captain Co. K., Davis Legion Young's Brigade, Butler's Division, Hampton's Corps, Army of North Virginia.

94. J. H. Reeves, P. Co. C., Corps Cadets (Dallas County).

95. B. W. Smith, Sr., P. ompany, Kolb's Battery, Colonel Williams Artillery, French's Division, Army of Tennessee.

96. John Sank, P. Co. F., 15th Regular Alabama Volunteers.

97. C. C. Skillman, P. Co. C., 9th Regiment, Kentucky Volunteers.

98. Simon R. Smith, P. Co., Kolb's Battery.

99. John W. Sheally, P. Co., G., 45th Regiment Alabama Volunteers.

100. R. G. Smith, P. Co., 1st Regiment Alabama Volunteers.

101. J. C. Cobb, Co. Eufaula light Artillery.

102. John G. Smith, P. Co., F., the Regular Alabama Volunteers.

103. John W. Tullis, Lieutenant Hardaway's Battery Alabama Volunteers; promoted to Captain.

104. J. E. Tucker, P. Co., K., 29th Regiment Alabama Volunteers.

105. Geo. W. Thompson, P. Co. D., 46th Regiment, Alabama Volunteers.

106. Dr. H. M. Weedon, Medical Officer 4th Regiment Florida Volunteers, Surgeon.

107. Edward B. West P., Co. H., 4th Regiment Georgia Volunteers; discharged rank 2nd lieutenant, in charge of ambulance corps.

108. Dr. James J. Winn, P. Co. A., 5th Regiment Alabama Volunteers.

109. Additional names—Copies of their certificates of eligibility have been lost.

Capt. E. L. Graves (Harris Station, Georgia).
H. C. Compton
Lain McCarrell, Terese, Alabama.
R. C. Patrick.
Isaac Wells.
J. G. McIntosh.

ROSTER OF LOUISVILLE BLUES

P. Bloodworth, Captain; W. J. Grubbs, 1st Lieut.; J. R. A. Passmore, 2nd Lieut.; E. B. Harrison, 1st Sergt.; B. B. McKenzie, 2nd Sergt.; James Lang, 3rd Sergt.; J. D. McLendon, 4th Sergt.; H. Washburn, Fifer; W. W. Herring, K-Drummer; G. C. McCune, B-Drummer.

Privates F. M. Armstrong, J. W. Beasley, A. W. Cane, William Dorman, R. JP. Daniel, J. Danforth, Joe Daniel, R. W. Elmore, H. Freeman, W. V. Grubbs, A. Guice, E. Herring, Fred Helms, J. Jurst, J. Hunter, R. L. Hobdy, Ras

Jackson, J. Jones, A. Johnson, W. James, S. Kirkland, William Lunsford, W. Ludlums, J. L. McRae, Phil McKay, Phil McLendon, John McCormick, G. McEachern, W. B. Moseley, V. Minchen, J. Morris, Lee Phenix, Charles Reeding, S. D. Smith, S. Sanders, N. K. Stephens, J. S. Stokes, J. Turner, W. J. White, S. Benton, William Beverly, R. M. Barksdale, William Burton, Alex Baker, J. J. Capel, M. Cumbie, Bone Cawthorn, T. Dorman, J. Dous, James Daniels, S. Deshazo, N. Hudson, E. Emerson, H. L. Faulk, F. Grubbs, Bill Grubbs, R. Herring, G. L. Herring, L. G. Herring, Bob Hyatt, Dan Hunter, A. W. Hays, J. W. Jackson, Ben Jones, J. D. Joy, D. Johnson, R. Knight, L. Lampley, L. L. Lee, W. A. Lewis, D. L. McNoll, L. L. Lee, W. A. Lewis, D. McNab, D. M. Kinnon, Rev. A. McLendon, P. M. McKinnis, J. L. McNair, B. Murphrey, F. Martin, H. H. Moreland, William Price, J. J. Quick, S. Sasser, Hardy Smith, P. Sheppard, W. P. Stephens, Dr. J. K. Turner, G. V. Utsey, A. Wilkins, S. Williamson.

MILITARY MEETING

Pursuant to previous notice a meeting was held in the Market House this evening, August 11, by those favorable to the formation of a cavalry company in this place. On motion A. H. Dickerson was called to the chair, and M. C. Westmoreland requested to act as secretary.

The meeting was organized, the object explained by the chairman, and the names of a sufficient number being obtained to organize a company, they proceeded to elect officers when the following gentlemen were chosen:

W. B. Brannon, Capt.; G. W. Brannon, 1st Lieut.; W. H. Roberts, 2nd Lieut.; William Smith, 3rd Lieut.; R. T. Ranson, 1st Orderly Sergeant; J. F. Treutlen, 2nd; D. McCall, 3rd; L. H. Brown, 4th; William Beeman, 1st Corporal; T. K. Appling, 2nd; M. Sinquefield, 3rd; G. W. Rice, 4th.

The following gentlemen were appointed a committee to draft by-laws for the government of the company: D. McLean, M. Sinquefield, D. McCall, G. W. Brannon and W. H. Roberts.

The following were appointed a committee on uniform: W. M. C. Westmoreland, G. W. Rice, William Smith, T. K. Appling and W. D. Brannon.

There being no other business to transact in motion the meeting adjourned sine die

A. M. DICKERSON, Chairman.

W. M. C. Westmoreland, Secretary.

—Clipped from the Spirit of the South September, 1853.

Most Perfect Body of Soldiers

The First Alabama Battalion of Artillery, organized at Fort Morgan February, 1860, attained such high degree of discipline, that the Federal General Granor pronounced it "The Most Perfect Body of Either Army."

Eufaula Rifles Took Part in Inauguration on Their Way to Pensacola

Jefferson Davis, senator from Mississippi before secession, was chosen president of the Confederate States of America, Feb. 9, 1861. He was chosen by the Congress of the provisional government, convened in Montgomery.

The day before the constitution had been drafted, patterned in part after that of the United States, though embodying articles for which the South had seceded.

It was a gala occasion in Montgomery—the new capital for a new nation. Flags, banners and bunting floats over the streets and from the tops of buildings. Enthusiastic youth paraded while the more mature gathered in excited groups at the street corners.

It was the birthday of the Confederacy. The day before, a government had been formed, but Saturday, Feb. 9. Jefferson Davis was its head. Alexander H. Stephens, of Georgia, was vice president.

The Eufaula Rifles, which took a leading part in the affairs of the Confederate States, attended the inauguration of Jefferson Davis. The Rifles were on their way to Pensacola under command of Col. Alpheus Baker who was afterwards promoted to Brigadier General. They went to Pensacola to take command of the fortifications there.

After a year they returned to Eufaula and were organized into the Eufaula Light Artillery.

After the war military organizations were maintained at Eufaula and in every war the United States has been well represented.

During the Spanish-American war, Capt. J. R. Barr, so we are informed, was in command of the Eufaula Company.

After the resignation of Capt. John Barr just at the close of the Spanish-American War, Capt. E. H. Graves (now colonel) was elected Captain of the Eufaula Rifles and subsequent captains were Capt. George Whitlock, Capt. C. S. McDowell, Capt. R. A. Mallowe, Capt. D. B. McKenzie, Capt. K. B. McKenzie, Capt. R. G. Irby, Capt. Bob Stevens, Capt. Henry Perkins.

Headquarters 85th Regiment Alabama Militia
Eufaula, Ala., Oct. 21, 1853, Special Order No. 1,

The Commissioned, non-commissioned officers, musicians and privates of 85th regiment, Alabama Militia, are hereby ordered to be and appear at Eufaula, Alabama, on the 15th of November, next, for review and inspection—The commissioned and non-commissioned officers will attend at Parade ground on previous day for drill. By order of:
COLONEL G. A. ROBERTS,
R. L. Moore, Regimental Adjutant, Eufaula, Oct. 22, 1853. 18-tf

Military Notice

On Saturday, the 10th day of September, next, there will be an Election held at the various places of holding Company Musters, in the Eighty-fifth (85) Regiment, 11th Brigade, 5th Division, A. M., for the purpose of the same. By order of Brigadier General.
T. FLOURNOY.
B. F. Treadwell, Adj., Gen.
Aug. 10, 1853.   8-tf.

EUFAULA HUSSARS

The "Eufaula Hussars" were organized at the Market House Eufaula, August 11th, 1853, A Calvary Co.
W. B. Brannon, Capt.; G. W. Brannon, 1st Lieut.; W. H. Rolens, 2nd Lieut.; William Smith, 3rd Lieut.; T. R. Kansom, 1st Orderly Sergt.; J. H. Treant, 2nd Orderly Sgt.; B. McCall, 3rd Orderly Sergeant; L. H. Brown, 4th Orderly Sergeant;; William Beeman, 1st Corporal; T. R. Appling, 2nd Corporal; M. Sinquefield, 3rd Corporal; G. W. Rice, 4th Corporal
Made its first public appearance October, 1853. Regularly Recd.—From "Spirit of the South."

NOTES:

TIMES OF THE SOUTHERN CONFEDERACY

Written by Ada Young Martin, Daughter of Edward B. Young, Pioneer Citizen of Barbour County and Wife of James G. Martin, Prominent Politician Of Reconstruction Days

The war clouds were gathered in 1860. Our people of the South, enthusiastic and full of joyous hope, looking for a bright day coming, felt little fear. Carolina, on December 20th, 1860, seceded from the Union; Mississippi, January 9th; Florida, January 10th; Alabama, January 11th; then on as their legislatures met, until October 31st, 1861, 13 stars graced our glorious flag. Companies in Barbour County began vigorously making ready Clayton Guards and Pioneer Guards of Eufaula, were in camp. Those with the Eufaula Rifles, were all local companies of the states. The Eufaula Rifles, under Captain Alphues Baker, were fortunate in reaching Montgomery in time to become part of the Confederate States.

All our Barbour County Companies were members of the 1st Alabama Regiment Colonel Henry D. Clayton, ommandei. All served their time of enlistment.

After their return the Eufaula Light Artillery, was organized and left March 26th, 1861, for Tennessee. John W. Clark, captain. Other companies quickly followed. The war was seriously on us; depressed, when our troops failed; bright and bouyant at their successes.

Many can remember the trying and troublesome times, our noble boys fighting valiantly until outnumbered. They came home paroled on May 10th, 1865. What a home coming? Wounded and worn, feeling all lost, still gallant in spirit, they went to work to build up their own beloved country. Eufaula and Barbour County were fortunate in escaping some of the horrors of the after war period and the Reconstruction days.

The Armistice was declared before Grierson reached Barbour County. Then came the reconstruction days, full of horrors and troubles.

The fearful riots, which were controlled only by the indomitable spirit of our brave men. There were many trials in those days, but a good God brought us safely through.

UNVEILING OF CONFEDERATE MONUMENT AT EUFAULA, NOV. 24TH, 1904

The Confederate Monument that was built under the auspices of Barbour County Chapter, United Daughters of the Confederacy, was unveiled today, with interesting ceremony. It stands at the intersection of Broad and Eufaula streets, and is not only a monument to the Confederate heroes whose bravery it commemorates, but is also a lasting monument to Mrs. Stella Drewry Guice, wife of Jason G. Guice, one of the brave Confederate soldiers, from Barbour County, who lost an arm in the war between the states, fighting for the Southern Confederacy, and daughter of Dr. John W. Drewry, a famous physician, whose wonderful surgical skill was so helpful and was so generously given to the wounded soldiers.

Mrs. Guice spent several years of hard work, the leader in the labor of love and patriotism, that raised the money to pay for this monument. She had good help, but her personal work was the largest factor in erecting this beautiful memorial.

The following is the program of the unveiling exercises:

The line of march began at 12 o'clock at the courthouse. up Broad street to the monument, in the following order: 1. Band playing "The Bonnie Blue Flag." 2. Military Company Eufaula Rifles, members who were sons of Veterans, wearing badges of white and red. 3. Float, girls representing the Confederate states: Misses Lila Merrill, Addie Skillman, Lucy Kellar, Mary Ross, Carrie Spurlock, Eloise Foy, Serana Brown, Bessie Seligman, Janet McDowell, Mary Comer, Cerrelee Irby, Pauline Couric. 4. Veterans wearing crosses of honor. 5. Floats: U. D. C. Barbour County Chapter and visitors. 6. Carriages, Speaker and Ministers. 8. Carriage, City Council. 9. Citizens and school children. Program announced by the Mayor.

1. Prayer by Dr. W. B. Wharton. Reading of list of troops by companies from Barbour county, 1861-1865 and roll call of Eufaula Companies—Capt. S. H. Dent, commander of Camp 3.

3. Veterans surrounding base of monument respond to name as called; salute from military.

4. Cords drawn, unveiled monument—Misses Ida Prudent and Mary Merrill; band playing "Dixie Rebel Yell."—Everybody.

5.—Presentation of monument from Barbour County Chapter U. D. C., to City of Eufaula, by Miss Mary Clayton (she having been organizer of Barbour County Chapter and daughter of the late Colonel Commanding the first regiment of Alabama mustered into Confederate service, composed largely of Barbour Troops.) Response from the Mayor for the city.—Mayor H. H. Connor.

6. Introduction of speaker by Mayor.

7. Address—Captain Ben Screws.

Benediction—Rev. E. L. Hill.

Chapter Twenty-four

Memorable March of Grierson's Army Across Chattahoochee River

It was noontime of a glorious last of April day, 1865—the smoke of battle had not entirely cleared away and the echo of the roar of guns was still in the Southern air—when a messenger galloped over the Western hill, reporting that a Regiment of Union Calvary was coming."

There was consternation over all of Barbour County, the little town of Eufaula, Alabama, was astir. Soon men and women were busy hiding their valuables, for it was feared that the "Yankees" would pilfer and burn the town, as General Benjamin H. Grierson (it was rumored) had not yet heard of General Lee's surrender at Appamattox and no report had been received from Capt. James Hobby, of Louisville, who had gone out with two boys just grown, Edward Young and Edward Stern, who were his emmisary of "Truce." It was a fact, however, that they had met General Grierson before he reached Troy, Ala., and were the means of saving both Troy and Eufaula from being burned

After accepting the "Truce," General Grierson sent a messenger ahead, demanding further "Truce" at Eufaula, and Dr. C. J. Pope, then mayor of Eufaula, and several prominent citizens rushed over the hill to meet General Grierson beyond College Hill.

The men and horses of the Regiment were tired and jaded and the march over the hill, down Broad street and across the Chattahoochee river to the Harrison fields on "Tobenai" creek in Quitman County, Georgia, was slow—for twelve hours a steady phalanx passed along.

It had been their intention to camp on the Alabama side of the river, but the Mayor and committee, urged against it and the Georgia site was selected because of the fine spring and supply of water from the creek for the horses and camp use. Provost guards were stationed about the streets of Eufaula during the several months that the Regiment remained in camp and all this section was under Federal Military restriction.

Dr. Pope escorted General Grierson and his staff to his home, where he entertained them at dinner and Mrs. Pope (who was a most loyal, heart and soul, woman of the South (sister of General Henry D. Lamar Clayton of the Confederate Army and father of the late Henry D. Clayton, Federal Judge, and Mayor Lee J. Clayton, Eufaula, and Colonel Bertram Clayton, U. S. Regulars, who was killed in France during the World War—while a most gracious hostess to these Union army officers—drove home to them some pointed facts, relative to heart-breaking conditions, brought about in the South by this War Between the States."

General Grierson paid a high tribute to her loyalty and to her tact, in speaking of the courteous way she received him and his staff in her home.

My grandmother (a staunch Southerner) told me the story of this march through Eufaula and how, as the soldiers came over College Hill, playing "Yankee Doodle," Prof. J. C. Van Houten, the great blind musician (who born in New Jersey, had cast his lot in the South, living in Eufaula until his death in 1889—sat on Mrs. Sarah Shorter (Hunter's) front porch, immediately across the street from Dr. Pope's home—for hours as the Calvary passed, playing "Dixie" on his violin. Though he came from "Yankeeland" only a few years before the war, in after years he loved to tell to his Southern girl music pupils, how that day "his bow refused to bring forth for him any note of melody, but that of "Dixie."

Files of old Telegraph messages (all offices between Columbus, Georgia, and Apalachicola, Florida, had been seized and appropriated to the United States Government Service) show that General Grierson had orders to seize no personal property, other than horses, and it later developed that the only horse he took that day was the one belonging to LaFayette Howe, owner of the Columbus and Apalachicola Telegraph Company, and used by G. W. Barefield, linesman for the Howe Telegraph lines, operating between Silver Run (Seale, Ala.) and Mrs. Mary Barnett, pioneer citizens of Eufaula, who lived next door to where the First Baptist Church now stands, corner of Randolph and Barbour streets—told me when I was a young girl a story of how she had "hidden between the ceiling and roof of her house, more than one hundred pounds of sugar, a quantity of cured hams and her silverware—fearing her house would be searched and property seized by pilferers belonging to Grierson's army." She kept boarders and two or three soldiers did ask for supper at her table, but no search of her premises was attempted.

The Confederacy Commissary was less than a block away away from the Northwest corner of Broad and Randolph streets and she told me that she "saw the doors opened and the U. S. officers helped themselves. Numbers of barrels of whiskey stored in the cellar were brought up, the heads broken in with an axe, the contents poured out in streams that flowed down the ditch that paralleled the sidewalk in front of her house.' She "saw men, both white and negroes, down on their knees, sipping and lapping up the whiskey as it flowed along in the ditch." She also saw numbers of pigs (the four foot species) lying about the streets drunk from drinking it out of the gutter.

There was great relief to the hearts of many who were terror stricken, at the marching through the streets of so many "blue coats," when night came and there had been no rioting. The soldiers were peacefully sleeping in camp across the river.

During the four or five months that they remained on 'Tobenani" creek they did some hunting and fishing and daily visited Eufaula and Cuthbert, Georgia, and Fort Gaines, Ga.

Mr. J. E. Lanier, of Cuthbert, Ga., then a resident of Quitman County, Georgia, told me some very interesting stories of the sport these soldiers made of many of the negroes in the neighborhood of the camp, making them drill for their amusement—telling them they were to be made soldiers.

The first impression that Emancipation had put into the minds of many of the old slaves, who were farm hands, was that "the object of the war was, not only to free them, but that each Master would have to give to each male slave (when set free) "forty acres and a mule." One day a "Smart Alec" soldier said to an inquisitive negro, "Bring me $2.50 and I'll write you an order for your ' forty acres and a mule." Sam raised the money and in return, received a slip of paper, which he forthwith hurried to present to his old "Marster." On the paper was written; "Lift this black rascal out of his boots, I have just lifted him of $2.50."

Many similar advantages were taken of the ignorant negroes, who looked up to these soldiers as veritable gods of deliverance, until they suffered in many ways at their hands.

The home of Dr. Pope, (now the McRae home) was notable also, as the place where his daughter, Miss Ella Pope (later Mrs. Dozier Thornton) presented a Confederate flag to the Eufaula Rifles, the day this Company of Barbour County Volunteers left Eufaula for the War Between the States. Barbour County chapter U. D. C. will mark this spot and two other historic places here this fall. Barbour County U. D. C. contemplates placing a marker on the great oak tree in the front yard of this home, under which General Alpheus Baker, distinguished Confederate officer, who carried this Company to the front, received this flag. General Baker was one of the most distinguished generals of the Confederate Army, and became one of Alabama's most illustrious sons. He was famous as one of the "South's silver tongued "orators and was a notable lawyer and politician.

The word Telegram always, perhaps more than any word in the English language, arouses curiosity, stirs varied emotions in human beings, "stop" and "go on." On another memorable day in Barbour County, December 20th, 1860 a telegram from Washington had been received at Eufaula that aroused the people to an undesirable tensity of feeling.

This telegram stated that "the people of South Carolina had seceeded." The messenger at the telegraph office was a unique character, a negro named Lewis Jones, less than five feet high, stout, with features very monkey-like. He had received a hurt on the head working in the salt making houses at Apalachicola, Florida, and to protect his head from heat and cold he always wore a broad brimmed felt hat and always carried an umbrella. Immediately on receipt of this important telegram, the same old telegraph horse that was later stolen by soldiers of Grierson's army—was saddled and Lewis with the news of the secession of South Carolina, secure in his pocket, was started on the 21-mile trip to Clayton, Ala., the county site of Barbour County.

Lewis was alert to the expectancies of prevailing war conditions and realized the importance of the document he was carrying. As he galloped over the hill near "Rockland," the surburban home of Major M. A. Brunson, a prominent citizen to whom Lewis was accustomed to deliver many business telegrams, met him. Expecting him to stop and hand one to him, Major Brunson attempted to stop him, but Lewis replied: "No, Mars Brunson, I can't stop—I'se in a big hurry. Carolini done seed sumthin and I'se got the news in here," tapping his breast pocket. Lewis was on hand when General Grierson filed many telegrams at the Eufaula office and was heard to proudly tell him, "I was de one dat carried the news to Clayton about what dem Calini niggers and poor white trash seed over dare." General Grierson was greatly amused and interested in the story Lewis told him. He lived to feeble old age in Eufaula, a familiar figure who always felt, and made everybody else see, what an important feature he was in the telegraph business of the community.

General Grierson was described to me by my father (John C. Thomas) who was manager of the Eufaula Telegraph Office and had much business with him during the time his regiment was encamped across the river from Eufaula)—as a man of most pleasing personality—who many times sat in his office and chatted cordially with him, never once referring to their differences regarding the war, but always eager for every item of news from headquarters.

He was quite indisposed for several days, at one time, but despite signs of suffering in his face, he came regularly, each day, to send his replies to messages delivered to him by messenger at his headquarters. His writing was regular and plain. The following is a copy of one of the large number, now in possession of the writer.

> Headquarters Quitman County, Georgia
> U. S. Army, Division No. Six,
> June 7th, 1865.
>
> To Lieutenant C. S. Crosby,
> U. S. A. Relief Corporation,
> Pensacola, Florida.
>
> Lieut. Pace enroute to you with instructions and map. Detachment should reach you June 9th.
>
> Signed—Grierson, C. T. C.

During the months that General Grierson's regiment camped in Quitman County, Georgia, he formed a personal friendship with Dr. Mark Shivers of the little town of Cotton Hill, Ga., who assisted the regiment Medico in several major operations at his office. The Quitman and Clay counties line was within the camps and the famous old Baptist church at Cotton Hill (Shiloh) still standing, was thronged with Union soldiers every Sunday.

The C. C. C. camp that was at Cotton Hill the past three years has recalled this fact by again being the place of worship for men in government military service.

In 1872, one David P. Lewis, a deserter from the Confederate cause and a political "turncoat," was the Republican candidate for governor of Alabama, nominated over Thomas H. Hendley, of Mobile.

There was some discontent, formented by Republican promoters, and Hendley was unable to arouse interest in the northern counties. With Democrats in control of both houses, the Republicans were in a predicament—but only one carpetbagger was elected to the House of Representatives, the first negro sent up by Alabama negro farmers.

The Republican party was overthrown in 1874 and the Scalawag reign in Barbour County was over.

Democrats were more harmonious and united than ever before and were determined to put Republicans out of office, even if force were necessary to do so.

NORTHERN MEN COME SOUTH AND ESPOUSE SOUTHERN CAUSE

Among the pioneer citizens of Barbour County, there were some notable men who espoused, heart and soul, Southern principles, and they (and their descendents) have been an honor to Barbour County.

In the thirties came Edward B. Young from New York. He was the moneyed man of those pioneer days and his bank, the "Bridge Bank," was the first bank established in the County.

Later came Chauncey Rhodes from Weathersford, Connecticut—spent his life cashier of the John McNab Bank. Volunteered for the Confederate Army enlisted and started to the front, but has called back from Fort Gaines, Georgia, because he was so badly needed in the bank's business, and no one capable of filling his place could be had. Like Mr. Young he was loyal to the South.

Then four Bray brothers, from New Haven, Connecticut. Two William H. and John W., went to the front and fought for the Confederacy. The third brother, Nathan M., was Mgr. of the arsenal that furnished the arms and ammunition for the Southern soldiers. His daughters, Misses Katie and Ethel Bray have in their possession the honorable discharge, with special remarks of appreciation of his services, thereon, of which they are very proud.

The fourth and youngest brother, Wells, J., was also in the store and offices of the firm and later was mayor of the City of Eufaula for several terms.

Robert Moulthrop came from New Haven, Connecticut, coming to superintend the building of the railroad bridge across the Chattahoochee river at Eufaula. When that job was completed, he remained, and became the largest manufacturer of brick in southeast Alabama or southwest Georgia. He was a broad-minded, loyal citizen, amassed a fortune, was trueot to Southern principles and was one of the most honored and valuable citizens who ever lived in the County. He was an enthusiastic Mason and Knights Templar.

James Milton came to Barbour County as watchmaker for N. M. Hyatt. He was a native of London, England. Soon he established a business of his own and became thoroughly Southern, possibly the best beloved citizen in the city of Eufaula from many standpoints out of the ordinary. Mr. Hyatt came from New York, spent his life here and left in the hearts of his descendants an inate love for his adopted home.

John H. Whitlock came from Perry, Georgia, soon after the War Between the States, from which place he enlisted in the Confederate Army. His record for loyalty and bravery is an enviable one. He came South to Perry from his native New Jersey home; later his brother, George, followed him and they spent their lives in Eufaula, leaders in everything except politics in which they took no part but in later years they were loyal to the South.

James Baker, a musician, who was the finished artist and violin teacher, came from his northern home at Boston, entered the Army of the Confederacy, and while a member of his company's band, was so badly wounded that he lost his eyesight.

He was brought from the front to a hospital at Eufaula, and when all was over he married a Barbour County girl, Mary Ann Barefield, whose mother had been one of the Barbour County women to nobly care for the Southern soldiers in the hospital here.

Many years he kept a store (although almost totally blind) and with her assistance he made a success that was most unusual for a blind man.

He was also a composer of music. He was at New Orleans, La., when he enlisted. His daughter, Mrs. Thomas H. Wats, resides in Chipley, Florida, and his son, Graddy Baker, at Verbena, Alabama.

CAPTAIN BENJAMIN H. SCREWS

General Grant and Captain Benjamin H. Screws
(New York Herald, June 29th, 1876)

Impudence at the White House. Bold Expression of a Defiant "Reb"

"When the personal introductions were concluded, Captain Ben H. Screws, of the Montgomery (Ala.) Advertiser, spoke as follows:"

Mr. President:

I have the pleasure of introducing to your excellency my companions of the Press of Alabama, who have visited the National Capitol for the purpose of obtaining a nearer and more perfect view of the traditional animal—the elephant—than the Telegraph could give them in the dusty recesses of their fa roff sanctums. We have come, Sir, from the land of th South, the land of fair and noble women and brave men, of the magnolia and the vine, the land of the far famed Ku Klux, on whose back, Mr. President you have twice ridden into the realms of almost Imperial power. The down trodden and oppressed poor South—poor and despised today, but once rich in every element of national grandure and glory. The voice of her dead sons echo yet in the Halls of your stately Capitol, built with treasure contributed by the cotton fields of Alabama, in brighter and better days.

And while on this subject, Sir, you will pardon me for saying that the rich tapestry of your own mansion and heavy damask which curtains these lofty windows were also contributed in past by that same South. But that was in the day of her pride and power, when like our symbolic Eagle, she dared to gaze in the eyes of the sun and flinched not from the fiercest of his rays.

But, Sir, I will desist, the South needs no eulogy. A truthful record of her achievements, in peace as well as in war, will encircle her brow with a glory as bright and enduring as the diadem that sparkles in the night of her cloudless skies. Oppressed, she may be, and is today, but like Anteus of Old, she will gather fresh strength from her fall and spring up again with the light of her rising greatness, gilding and glorifying every page of her history, past, present and to come. There is today a corn field in Alabama, unmarked upon the map, but beneath whose fruitful soil there is a mine of wealth which will develop Birmingham into one of the mightest cities of the world.

Heaven will bless Alabama, the Philosophic Poet informs us, Mr. President, that the pen is mightier than the sword. On the truth of this apothegem it does not become us to speak, nor you hear. You have tested the power of the one we have endeavored to exemplify the might of the other.

Your victorious sword, twined though it may be from hilt to point, can never be so completely covered with evergreens and flowers that blood will not show in its polished blade. Your triumphs left the blackness of ashes—the mournful tears of the widow, and the piteous cry of orphans, to testify of their cruelty. For your victories, you are hailed as the savior of the Nation.

We for ours, claim no higher honor than to be called the saviors of freedom and the champions of Liberty. The vanquished, who fell beneath your Legions were but mortals. Mr. Morse, the printer, encountered the very lightnings in midheaven, and yoked them to the vehicles of thought. It is related, Mr. President, of Scotland's favorite Monarch, King James VI, that on one occasion he encountered a bold mountaineer, who demanded homage of his Sovereign, on the ground that James, although King of Scotland, when at Stirling, was but a subject when at Kipping.

You may be King in Stirling, said he, but I am King in Kipping; and the good natured King admitted the justice of the bold claim, and paid the required tribute. In like manner do I, Sir, even in this august presence claim your respect, for although you may be President of the United States, I am President of Lomax Fire Company No. 4, of Montgomery, Alabama, and am entitled to all the dignities of that exalted station.

We sympathize with you, Mr. President, in the discharge of your arduous labors and as much as men may, who can show no bright record for loyalty, extend to you the assurance of our respect and esteem.

As I said before, we may have come to Washington to see the elephant, and have now viewed the animal in all his entirety, and are ready to hear him speak."

Note: The above account appeared in the New York Herald, the morning following the visit of the Alabama Press Association to General Grant, and created a Nation-wide sensation.

This speech constituted a Bible of Southern Democracy, in Reconstruction days, and in its viewpoints is vital today.

Captain Screws, who as a boy captain in the Confederacy died early, largely due to a wound received at the Battle of Atlanta.

His speeches, with their fire and literary finish, rank with those of Yancy Toombs and Hill.

NOTES:

MURMURS OF WAR

While this article has no direct bearing on, or in, Barbour County History, it is injected herein because of the fact that the author of this history wrote it one fearfully hot day in August, 1900, and it was published that day as an editorial in the Eufaula Daily Times. News was scarce that day, and it was written merely as a "filler."

In Dec., 1915, when the prophesy of this editorial had come so literally true, it was published a second time in the Daily Citizen.

It is reproduced here simply as a matter of history.

If ever the adage was true that "Kings and Monarchs sit upon precarious thrones," it is certainly applicable at the present time, when the fires of war are blazing in some far away countries and smouldering in others.

England has much to fear; her Irish subjects are everywhere plotting and planning. The manacles they have long worn are clanking with omnious sound and the "sons of the Shamrock," both there and in this country are awaiting to make England's necessity Ireland's opportunity.

Queen Victoria, good woman that she is, will have much more on her hands than she has now, in trying to preserve her possession and dominions abroad.

The red flag of the Anarchist waves in LaBelle, France, and the restless, excitable Frenchman paints for the bloody field of battle.

Germany, with her varient, contentious confederates,

is moving like the troubled sea and casting up from her depths "the mire and dirt" of past, but not forgotten quarrels.

The down trodden, the idle and starving Myriads of Spain and Italy will hail any move with joy that promises relief from oppression and when the match is set and the fire rages the crowned heads, innocent though they may be, will ache with the roar and din of war.

From the far Orient, the echo of the guns of the allied armies is sounding across the sea, into the ears of rulers of the great nations and the sound is a jar that stirs the already troubled breasts.

These undercurrent waves of war and disaster may be submurged by the "dogs of war" restlessly sleeping on the shores of each country, while the whole world watches them with curious anxiety, waiting to see which one will be the first to thrust his sharp fangs into the heart of peace, sleeping beside him.

The historical student, ever on the alert, methinks has, his far seeing eye lifted to skies that ever seem blue over the 'Fatherland," and in the future, yea, the near future, sees the reflection of the marching hosts of Germany, carrying out and obeying the teachings of Frederick's ambition, instilled into them and his descendants, by holding up the hands of his beloved grandson, Wilhelm II.

Whether the future carries them down in defeat or raises them to the highest glory, the World will, before a half century, recognize the Hohenzollen rulers as the most fearless, intellectual and the scheming the world has ever known and every nation on the globe will have left the strong hand of their power.

Wilhelm's arm, though withered, will be able to execute the cunning of his brain.

Our modern world has defined religion, God, and the Christian Church as so complex that the shrewd ruling classes have laughed at the Ten Commandments as old fashioned and have left God's laws out of the struggle of the nations for political liberty.

In every country, where the Church rules the state, there smoulders the embers of the fire-kindled by the German Democracy of 1891, that adopted a program that will yet stir the world.

BARBOUR COUNTY SOLDIERS WHO DIED IN FRANCE DURING WORLD WAR

Colonel Bertram T. Clayton

Colonel Bertram Tracy Clayton was the highest ranking officer of the World War to be killed in France. He was the son of General Henry D. Lamar Clayton, a graduate of West

Point of 1886. Resigning, he located at Brooklyn, New York, and became an engineer. He served in the Spanish-American war, organizing the troop that he commanded. From 1899 until 1901 he was Colonel of the 14th Regiment, National Guard, of the State of N. Y., later being appointed Captain and Quartermaster. He also served as chief Quartermaster of U. S. troops in the Canal Zone in 1911, and during the World War he was chief Quartermaster of First Army Corps A. E. F. in France and was in service when killed by an air raid. He is buried in Arlington National Cemetery. General Pershing, who was his classmate at West Point, acted as pallbearer at his military funeral. His cousins, Rev. Bertram and Rev. Wyatt Brown, Episcopal clergymen, officiated at this funeral.

Daniel Thomas Tully—Sergeant First Class, 35th Service Company, Signal Corps, First Division U. S. Army. Born in Eufaula September 15th, 1892. Served as O. M. I. Cadet 1903 to 1905, Buffalo, N. Y., with Alabama National Guard, crack Co. G., Second Infantry, 1908 to 1914. Joined U. S. Army 1914 and served Radio Co. A, Canal Zone, December 1915 to April 1916; Mexican border Radio Company A, April 1916 to June 1917. Left U. S. for France on June 12th, 1917, with General Pershing's first detail, called "Pershing's Pathfinders." He arrived in France on June 28th, 1917. After being engaged in nine battles on French soil, he was a member of the Army of Occupation, Germany, in Nov. 1918. He was transferred to 35th Service Co., Signal Corps, Paris France. Killed at Toury, France, Sept. 4th, 1919. Interment in A. E. F. cemetery 34 at Surenes—on Seine, Paris, France, Sept. 6th, 1919, with full military honors. Reinterment, National Cemetery, Arlington, Virginia, September 6th, 1912. Wound Chevron authorized August 9th, 1919. War Service Chevrons, Dec. 12th, 1917, June 12, 1918 and June 12, 1919.

James Asbury Boswell went into service as first lieutenant of infantry in the Officers Reserve Corps on November 27, 1917, and lost his life on September 30, 1919, in France. He died of wounds received in action while serving as first lieutenant of the 371st infantry. He is buried at Elmore, Alabama. He enlisted from Eufaula, where he was principal of the Eufaula High school.

Hinton Watson Hollemon, Army serial No. 8,421, enlisted in the National Guard on July 23, 1915, at Montgomery, Ala. He was killed in action at the Battle of Chateau Thierry, France, July 26th, 1918, while serving as a private first class, in Arlington National Cemetery, Arlington, Virginia, with Company, July 26th, 1918, while serving as a private first class, military honors.

Robert Warren Brannon, Army serial No. 995,956, enlisted in the National Guard July 1, 1916, at Montgomery, Alabama. He was killed in action on October 17, 1918, while serving as Sergeant with Company B, 167th infantry, Rainbow division. After having been allowed to select sixteen of the bravest men of the Company, he was sent on patrol duty at four o'clock in the morning through the Argonne Forest. On this mission he and seven of his companions were killed. Just before going on this trip he told one of his companions to tell "the women of his home town Eufaula, that it was for them that he was gladly giving this risk to his life."

When the death angel was hastily and ruthlessly spotting victims on the battlefields in France, his eyes fastened on "Jeff" Quillen, a mere lad of 16, who with his elder brother, insisted against pleadings of his parents, Jefferson and Belle McRae Quillen, who finally consented, despite the youth of both of these fine boys, and they went forth.

They enlisted in the 42nd division of the 167th Infantry (Rainbow Division) and when on July 26th, 1918, in the fierce battle that reaped down the "crown and flower" of America "Jeff" was a victim. His brother, B. D., came back, a victim of shell shock.

"Jeff rests in a grave in "Orse-Aisne" cemetery in sunny France where the poppies bloom.

A memorial was dedicated to him at his home town, Clayton.

BARBOUR COUNTY U. D. C.

The Alabam Division United Daughter of the Confederacy was organized at Montgomery, April 8th, 1897.

Barbour County Chapter No. 143 was founded by Miss Mary Clayton the same year, at which time the meeting was held at her home and the Chapter also named by her. She presented as a gift to each member their certificate of membership on Lee's birthday January 19th.

The officers were: President, Miss Mary Clayton; first vice president, Mrs. J. C. Guice; second vice president, Mrs. R. F. Nance; historian, Mrs. E. L. Brown; treasurer, Miss Victoria McEachern.

The fifth annual state convention was held in Eufaula May 14-15, 1901, and the thirteenth annual convention on May 4, 1926.

The U. D. C. Monument costing thirty-two hundred dollars was built during the administration of Mrs. J. G. Guice as president.

The boulder on the Jefferson Davis Memorial Park was placed during the presidency of Mrs. O. R. Spurlock at a cost of two hundred dollars.

Thirty-eight dollars worth of shrubbery was planted in this park, which is directly on the Jefferson Davis highway.
—From the records of Mrs. Erin McCormick Jones
—Barbour County U. D. C.

JEFFERSON DAVIS VISITS BARBOUR COUNTY

In April, 1886, Jefferson Davis and his daughter, "Winnie," Daughter of the Confederacy, as she was called, visited Eufaula, and the occasion was a memorable one. The party was entertained at the old St. Julien hotel, and the President of the Confederacy made a speech from the gallery of the hotel to more than two thousand people who had come from all parts of southeast Alabama and southwest Georgia to hear the beloved "Chieftain of the South."

The County had many veterans of the War Between the States, living then, and they stood with heads bared as they listened to him, and at each round of applause, some patriotic old soldier gave vent to the "rebel yell," which every voice caught up.

That night Dr. and Mrs. W. N. Reeves (Dr. Reeves had been a major in the Confederate army) gave a brilliant reception at "Mont McNab," their palatial home. This was possibly the most notable occasion ever given in Barbour County. Present on this occasion were six Martin brothers, sons of Mr. and Mrs. J. G. L. Martin, pioneer settlers of Eufaula.

On the program prepared for the evening were several southern songs which these brothers, Edward, Eugene, Clarence, Robert, E. L. and Victor sang, and then at the request of Mr. Davis they sang "Come Where My Love Lies Dreaming" and responded to encore with a beautiful rendition of "Dixie." At this reception, the late Mrs. L. Y. Dean presented Winnie Davis with an armful of red and white roses, which she held during the evening. Mrs. Charles S. McDowell, Jr., Past State President of the Alabama Division United Daughters of the Confederacy, who has probably done more than any other woman in the County to keep alive the spirit of the justice of the Condeferacy, and the work to hand down to coming generations, just what it meant to the South, and is a loyal, genuine daughter of the South, recalls with great pride, that as a little girl, Caroline Dent. Her brother, Edward Young Dent, held her high upon his shoulders that she might see and hear Jefferson Davis speak.

The Jefferson Davis highway crosses the Chattahoochee river, passing through Eufaula, a portion of Barbour County, and the Boulder that marks this highway, erected by Barbour County Chapter U. D. C., was dedicated some years ago when Congressman Henry B. Steagall made a speech that rang with the greatness of the only president of the onfederacy and the beloved martyr of the South.

This highway, passing through Alabama and Georgia, goes nearly to points that Mr. Davis traversed in his painful forced flight from oppression and injustice.

Chapter Twenty-five

"Address of the Fifty"

Eufaula, Barbour County, Alabama, April 9, 1874
To our fellow citizens:
The undersigned committee of fifty, among the oldest citizens of this community, was appointed by the desire and unanimous vote of a large assembly of the people, held irrespective of party, at the city hall in Eufaula on the evening of the 28th ultimo.

Anonymous correspondents, whose communications have been vented upon the public through the channels of the State Journal at Montgomery, have recently assailed our people as enemies of peace and order and charged them with the authorship of riot in this city on the 23rd day of February, last.

Then at the opening of last December term of the City Court at Eufaula they were called upon to listen in patience to a tirade of mendations and offensive accusations uttered from the bench, in the shape of a charge to the grand jury by a person occupying that high station, who prostituted it, to the purposes of injustice and availed himself of this unusual chance to force a respectable audience to listen to his mailing the community in which he lived and utter slanders upon it, which could not there be replied to.

It is remembered that speaking of the white people here generally, he contrasted them unfavorably, with those of other sections of the state that he characterized as a mob, stating that we prescribed and endeavored, maliciously to injure those who differed with us in political opinions; denounced us as law breakers and law- defyers; charged that we were unfriendly to the interests of the colored man and that, with evil intentions we had introduced and favored the order of Patrons of Husbandry, which he stigmatized as nothing less than a second edition of the Ku Klux Klan, claimed that we sympathized with criminals and habitually strove to screen them from punishment; declared that some of the most prudent and respectable lawyers at his bar deserved to be—and but for his mercy would be, stricken from the rolls for giving certain legal advice to parties whom he desired to punish, and foully aspersed the City Council of Eufaula, by the assertion that they were enemies of law and order, and the abettors and apologists of murder.

The duty with which this committee has been charged by the authority of the public meeting which appointed it was to prepare for the consideration of our fellow citizens an address whose faithful statement of the real facts should repel these islanders and fix the blame of the increasing lawlessness and crime in our midst, where it justly belongs.

In coming forward to bear testimony to the existence of some things calculated to mortify the minds of the community and of lamentable occurrences which threaten its peace and and best interests, we are free to acknowledge that we have no pleasant task to perform.

We feel ourselves commanded by a reluctant sense of duty to ourselves and our community—and coveting, as we do the good opinion of our fellow citizens throughout the state, we shall endeavor to discharge the duty of our vindication from false accusation, in the spirit of fairness and justice.

We shall not descend into every fact and particular which justify the statements we shall make, since that would fill a volume; but we hold ourselves ready, wherever it is properly demanded, to produce irrefutable evidence of the truths we assert, and we pledge our honor and veracity for the accuracy of all the matters and things contained in this address, in which we respectfully invite the consideration of a candid public.

In the first place, we assert that the white population of this community has been slandered by the accusation that they were the authors of the riot, which occurred in this city at the Municipal election of February last.

A large majority of the people here composing, as it does, the bulk of the intelligence and substance of our inhabitants, claimed the right to elect a council of citizens to whom a prudent constituency would be willing to entrust the important duties of the city government, and with a marshal and clerk who had been tried in the balance and found not wanting, and a mayor whose prudence, honesty of purpose, capacity and established character, fully justified the public confidence.

In opposition to the right, thus claimed by that majority, a ticket with an incompetent black candidate for marshal and a black pauper who signs his name with an X mark, for alderman, in one of the most important wards of the city was started by a few designing leaders backed mainly by the ignorant and irresponsible negroes, many of them the loungers and vagrants who infest our streets and most of them even if correctly inclined, without the capacity to understand their own interests or comprehend the consideration due to those who bear the burden of taxation.

The colored people influenced by this opposition and with their prejudices, aroused to outrageousism against the whites, appeared at the polls on the day of the election in temper which manifested their desire to generate disturbance. The influence of mean whiskey was plainly visible and green hickory sticks, freshly cut as if for the occasion were noticed in the hands of some of them, not notorious as observers of the peace.

Yet such were the precautions adopted by the city authorities and the managers that order was presented and the voting went on quietly for several hours, until, at length, an overbearing negro, with a drawn knife in his hand, unlawfully entered into the voting enclosure and undertook to enforce by violence, the reception of a ballot of a black man well known to be an idiot. This unlawful conduct met proper opposition from the Democratic challenger and the intruder was promptly ejected from the enclosure by him. A negro under the influence of whiskey and armed with his green hickory stick immediately took up the intruders' quarrel and a difficulty ensued; blows were exchanged and the pistol firing commenced, the first shot being fired by a negro. This shot provoked firing in reply. Is there any cause for wonder that under provocation a riot should have taken place? The same provocation would have brought it about in the most quiet city in the Union.

Intelligent citizens, however peacefully inclined, would nowhere have remained passive, under such insult and aggression. The riot occurred not, as we believe, by accident, but as the natural result of causes which have lately developed themselves in a greatly increased bitterness of feeling on the part of the blacks toward the whites and a greatly increased boldness and frequency of crime committed mainly by the former.

This unhappy state of affairs, we are reluctantly forced to declare, is mainly due to the wicked influence of one individual in our midst, Elias M. Keils, judge of the City court of Eufaula. This man, who occupied the bench without ever having been a lawyer, without ever having made the slightest preparation for the discharge of his judicial duties, by the practice or even study of that profession, which is every well regulated government finds its most honorable and as it were, its closing and crowning reward in the high position which he so rashly and recklessly ventured to begin with, obtained that position in the first place by false pretense practiced by him upon the bar and the people, that so soon as he received from them the compliment of an election he would resign the office in favor of a certain gentleman of the Bar who was competent to fill it. This was the distant understanding by which he imposed upon a large number of people whom he thus defrauded out of their votes.

As soon as it was ascertained that this agreement was not to be carried into effect, but that Elias Keils would attempt to execute the functions of a judge the entire Bar with but one single exception addressed and presented to him a respectful request in writing that he would resign this office, and the reason assigned by the solitary lawyer was as he stated, that "he knew the judge would come to him as his best friend for counsel on the subject when he, too, would advise him to resign. Such action as this by an entire Bar has probably never before in the history of American courts been forced upon the progression; proverbial as it is for deference to the bench.

The incumbent, determined, however, to disregard this united remonstration of the bar, he retained his seat upon the bench and there is no unprejudiced man of any party who dare deny that he has so administered the law in the Court where he presides that he has long since become an admitted burlesque and a public mockery. He has lowered his tribunal to that degree that no inhabitant who feels any pride in the country where he dwells and possesses intelligence sufficient to have an idea of what a court should be can think of it without humiliation.

Let any disinterested stranger enter the "place where justice is judicially administered" by this office. He will catch no glimpse here of justice or its majesty of punishment, with its terrors for evil doers; of the impartial, righteous law speaking its thunders to the guilty, and its assuring judgments to those who abide by and regard it.

He will witness there—what we have to look upon day by day and term after term—only the learnings and blunderings of a magistrate, destitute of the information indispensible to the decent discharge of its simplest duties and at the same time without the conscience to feel self-reproach for his gross delinquencies in one respect, or the pride to be ashamed of his gross deficiencies in the other.

Since he has officiated as the presiding officer of that court, he has alarmingly demonstrated how injurious he can be, influence upon good order and public morality of an otherwise insignificant person who happens to be an ignorant and unscrupulous judge. Of this evil influence we propose to instance some examples.

The Grand Jury, being the indispensible and initial agency in the punishment of all crime, it is especially desirable that in the punishment of all crime, it is especially desirable that its members should not be criminals themselves. "The law, as well as the immemorial customs of our country have always demanded that this important body should be composed of the best and most reliable of its citizens; of men of honesty, impartiality and intelligence and who are esteemed in the community for integrity, character and judgment. Yet this judge has permitted black members of his party, fresh from the cells of the penitentiary, criminals themselves, with the stench of the City jail still hanging around them and malefactors under indictment for larceny (for which they subsequently pleaded guilty) with their names staring at him from his state docket to sit and serve as grand jurors in his court.

Nor can he claim for this outrage the palliation that he was ignorant of his power to prevent this degradation of his court and purge the panel of such villians. For which he complacently suffered these unmolested upon his own motion he dismissed a number of respectable intelligent white citizens belonging to the opposite party to his own. Among them were gentlemen who had worthily represented the state in the legislature in its better days, for reasons, at one term best known to himself; at another because, as he he alleged, these distasteful jurors at a time when it was difficult, if not impossible, to obtain any other currency had expressed their willingness to receive and pay out Eagle and Phoenix money notwithstanding his aversion to its circulation here.

He has further disgraced his court room by allowing a black member of his party, accused of burglary and then under bond to answer any indictment that might be found against him, for that crime to officiate in his court, and be stationed at the entrance to the Bar so that gentlemen of the professional parties obliged to enter there would only do so by permission of a negro whom, they had probable cause to believe to be a felon.

The employment of such characters in the execution of the laws cannot fail to diminish that respect for them which is the cherished object of wise government to increase and to preserve.

Among other outrages upon the law, which he has perpetrated and which has had a direct tendency to increase crime in our midst, we call the special attention of the public to that remarkable one whereby he undertook to destroy the power of the city government of Eufaula to punish violators of its municipal regulations by guaranteeing an acquittal to every offender who would appeal to the City court for any judgment rendered in the Mayor's court against him.

In the case of every black convict who came there by certiorari or appeal at the last term of court he ordered and entered up the false judgment of "jury and verdict not guilty." Thus with a dash of his pen, making the record, which we are taught to believe "Imports, absolute veracity," speak a lie; and turning loose unpunished all those convicted defendants against the remonstrations of the City Attorney, and in one case at least against that of the defendant's counsel himself. The thieves and violators of public decency, the brawlers and drunkards and vagrants in a city of five thousand inhabitants, the nightly prowlers and disorderly men and women whom the firm hand of punishment in the mayor's court had heretofore been keeping down have thus been taught by this judge that his court was not the asylum to which they might always confidently fly for protection and acquital.

Of course such characters have not been slow to learn the gratifying lesson of and profit by its instruction, and it would indeed be difficult to estimate on the one hand the encouragement to the evil and disorderly afforded by this amazing grant of judicial license issued to them from the bench, or upon the demoralizing influence which it has exercised upon those who have henceforth been prudent enough to fear the law and keep within its bounds.

And while thus alert to effect the release of those black criminals seeking refuge in his courts his indecent eagerness to force the conviction of a respectable white citizen for an alleged failure as a commission merchant to take out his license prompted him to an invasion of the province of the jury which the Supreme Court that set aside his judgment, in perhaps the severest language of rebuke ever applied by that tribunal to a judge in Alabama—characterized as "unprecedented."

This demonstates at least that he could not act against offenders if he would.

In his charge to the grand jury at the opening of the last December term, he showed himself the undisguised apologist for larceny, by saying in substance with a tone of voice and expression of countenance and shake of the head—which reported language cannot translate—but which was none the less significant and intelligible, especially to the negroes of his audience for whom it was intended and who received it with scarcely suppressed applause, "Gentlemen it is true that there is a good deal of stealing going on, but you know, gentlemen, that the farmers in the country don't pay their hands and they are obliged to live—they can't starve, and if you should find any bills against persons who have been stealing, you ought to examine and find out whether such persons have been paid by their employers also." Such language might have been expected on the stump from some pestiferous demagogue who, to serve his purpose, was willing at any risk to stir up strife between the races. But coming from a judge upon the bench it was simply infamous. It was at once a slanderous accusation against the whites in this county of a general dishonesty practiced upon their employees, and insidious intimidation to the blacks that there was a prima facie presumption in their favor that they had not been paid by their employers and a sympathetic admission that the wronged laborers had a right to make up their losses by becoming thieves. In the relations which the two races occupy to each other in this County and in the present state of affairs around us, then the frequent immunity of stealing is the great disheartening curse of the whole country, a more mischevious utterance could hardly fall from a judge's lips. It is not surprising that negroes have since been heard to say that "the poor colored people" should not be punished for stealing and refer to this charge as good authority for the opinion.

Who wonders with such loose talk from the bench, listened to by an ignorant, unreflecting and needy set of misguided people, that the crime of larceny should flourish in this community and increase as it has done of late until every species of property has become a prey and every honest man, white and black is shocked at its universality and all but ready to despair of any peaceful remedy for its repression.

Among other improprieties committed by this official on the bench happily unexemplified in the judicial annals of the state we shall content ourselves by referring only to that one in which his effort to screen a party charged with forgery, he performed the rare maneuver of pocketing the indictment, and when detected in this act and forced to have the paper filed he suspended from office the sheriff of the County for telegraphing to Montgomery for the arrest of the accused, appointed a negro to succeed him and afterwards possessing himself again of the indictment, sent it by a negro member of the grand jury back to that body, with the verbal message of recomendation petition or command—we scarcely know which—that they should consider it.

The only excuse that can be offered for these persistent efforts of the judge in behalf of the accused is that the latter happened to be his son-in-law.

At chambers, his general line of conduct has been the same as that upon the bench. His constant effort seems to have been to make "the way of the transgressor (provided he were a black man)easy instead of hard.

He has been known to release without trial or legal investigation whatever, upon the prisoner's own worthless recognizance, a black ruffian in arrest upon a warrant lawfully issued by a Justice of the Peace here, for the attempted murder of an estimable white farmer of this County—the criminal instantly availing himself of the "escape perpetrated by Judge Keils in his behalf—to flee from justice to another state.

He has habitually employed habeus corpus as a mere contrivance to effect the release of criminals, fugitives from Georgia, vagrants, thieves, perjurers, burglars and has constantly perverted that great writ of Liberty to purposes which only the felon and malafactor could approve. In fact, such has been the general luck of black criminals before this judge that it has come to be a notorious fact that whenever any of them get into trouble for violations of the law, it is their habit to make at once for him as the best adviser they could possibly obtain to manage them out of their difficulties. We solemnly believe, fellow citizens, that these acts of this inefficient administration of the law by the judge presiding here have had disastrous effect to increase and encourage crime in this community. The peace-loving citizen is comparatively powerless against the criminal without the assistance of the law and that assistance has not been afforded by the judge.

All crime is probably on the increase and thrives under his worthless administration. No such state of things has heretofore existed in this county since its settlement. No man can shut his eyes against it.

Stealing, forgery, perjury, attempts at assassination, burglary, robbery, murder flourishes over us, and yet we hear of few punishments inflicted by his court.

The gallows has gone, out of fashion, the penitentiary is but little used—the chain gang has become a sort of myth. Thieves roam at large unpunished and offenders, admitted to be guilty, walk our streets unhampered.

In the meantime our community suffers in its comforts, its reputation and its material interests.

The people who trade with us from below complain that they are afraid to come to Eufaula, except in companies, for fear of being robbed by the negroes who infest the suburbs.

Property is stolen almost every night. Men supposed to keep their money about their premises live in constant and well grounded fear of midnight murderers.

Our wives and children feel an unusual sense of security in their homes and no man can leave his family for a night without being tortured by fears and apprehensions for their repose and safety.

Notwithstanding, fellow citizens, the slanders that have been uttered against us as a community, notwithstanding what we have to endure in the present and have borne in the past, we assert our just claim to your regard as a prudent and law abiding people.

We repel the foul aspersions attempted to be cast upon our good name as citizens and point to our history for the past eight years, in vindication of our right, to be regarded as eminently peaceful and patient community.

We address you now, only in the spirit of self defense and the interest of future self protection. We have non political purpose to subserve, no political design to accomplish hereby, and we solemnly declare that in what we have said of Judge Keils, we are moved by no desire to wrong or defame him. It is in vain to say that we have spoken of him as we have done herein from any political prejudice that sways us.

The postmaster at Eufaula, the justice of the peace, the tax collector, the sheriff and the other officers of this county all belong to the same party as Judge Keils and yet we regard these gentlemen with far different feelings from those which we are constrained to entertain for him. We have spoken of the past administration of justice in this city, as we believe its truthful history warrants, and during present evils and seriously apprehending greater ones that must result from the same causes which have produced those that now affect us; we appeal to all good men without regard to party, to make an effort to arrest these evils by securing a just, impartial and firm administration of the law in this community; and to this end we invite all fair-minded Republicans, white or black, to come forward and cooperate with us in the accomplishment of a purpose so devoutly to be wished.

Signed—John McNab, chairman; E. B. Young, J. G. L. Martin, W. H. Bray, M. Bernstein, S. H. Dent, Alpheus Baker, D. G. Stern, R. A. McTyer, M. C. Williford, M. B. Wellborn, A. Archer, W. T. Simpson, H. R. Shorter, Eli S. Shorter, Thomas Cargill, James L. Daniel, G. A. Roberts. J. P. McDowell, Jacob Ramser, J. M. Bloodworth, B. B. Fields, H. E. Williamson, S. W. Goode, A. A. Walker, W. H. Thornton, H. C. Hart, A. W. Barnett, C. Rhodes, N. M. Hyatt, E. Plant, W. H. Foy, V. D. Tharp, Z. J. Daniel, J. T. Kendall, A. McKenzie, J. L. Pugh, F. M. Wood, F. Shepherd, D. M. Seals, J. A. Walker, J. S. Dobbins, J. W. Drery, Henry Baker, James Tansey, J. G. Smith, W. N. Reeves, Edward Stow.

PART FOUR

Chapter Twenty-six

Newspapers

The first newspaper published in Barbour County was the Irwinton Herald, published by J. M. Davis and printed by Jack Hardeman in 1837. It lasted only one year as it advocated the Union party. It was to become the property of John Curry and J. P. Boothe, who published it as a morning paper, printed by John Bosworth. It was succeeded by the "Nepenthus," but was soon sold out.

In 1841 The 'Champion of Democracy" was started up, was afterwards moved from Eufaula.

In 1841, the Southern Shield, a Whig paper was launched by Benjamin Gardner in 1841. Its motto was "The Cradle of Science, the Nursery of Genius," and the Shield of Liberty." Southerners were not in sympathy with its policies and it died, after only four years.

On June 25, 1845, The "Eufaula Democrat" began publication by John Black and Edward C. Bullock, and was successful. It had already been shown that the newspaper is the driving wheel that moves more than anything else could, the machinery of progress, and though we may weep over its pages, cry over them, argue over it, swear over it and disagree with all its policies, we cannot do without it, for it gives the NEWS and the NEWS is the life of everything.

So when the publication of the Democrat began, its news, voicing the sentiments of the people and its editor and publisher, were to succeed by their popularity.

In 1850 the political agitation foretold the War Between the States, even ten years in advance and the name of the Democrat was changed to "The Spirit of the South" and during the years of the great struggle it was strong in its convictions and held firmly to its principles and advocacy of states' rights.

During the fifties Major J. M. Buford, whose pen stories glistened with the light of genius and whose editorials in those days helped to sound Alabama secession decree, was editor.

The Spirit of the South's motto was "Equality in the Union or Independence Out of it."

During 1855-56 H. H. Goode and John Wagnon established a paper called "Native" which was ably conducted, supporting Filmore for President. Another paper published at Eufaula was the Eufaula Dispatch, published by M. H. Butt. It was established January 12, 1866, but only existed six months.

Before 1860 the name was changed to the Tri-Weekly News, which Mr. Jno. Black published until he died early in the seventies. Capt. A. A. Walker and M. A. Merrill Sheehan had for some time, published another newspaper contemporary with Mr. Blacks News, it being the "Bluff City Times," and when Messrs. Walker and Sheehan bought the News they called it "The Times and News" in 1876.

On April 1st, 1869, The Bluff City Times, a weekly, was established by Post and Williams and continued until April 23rd, 1872, when Captain J. M. Macon bought it and changed it to a daily. It suspended publication in 1874 and finally Richard Williams and Company became owners of and conducted it until 1879 when they were succeeded by the Eufaula Publishing Company, which operated for a short while.

In 1880 Mr. William D. Jelks came to Eufaula, purchased the paper and plant and was so successful in publishing the Times and News, making it one of the greatest papers in the state. During the 20 years that he published it, he had associated with him Lucien Walker, whose pen sketches rose hued and golden lined are recalled tenderly. He died in Birmingham years ago. Edward J. Black, son of the founder of the paper, patriotic son of the old Eufaula, a lover of the new, died a few years ago in Thayer, Missouri, where he was publishing the "Thayer News."

Robert D. Shropshire (familiarly called Shropp) the quick news gatherer, and glowing story teller, was laid to rest in Fairview cemetery some years ago, brought home from Birmingham, and laid away at the twilight hour.

Mike Brannon, the inimitable and only one Mike, of Cleveland Fabbit Foot fame, who not only wrote beautiful lines a long time for the Times, but published here at one time in the eighties a paper of his own, the "Daily Mail," and was identified also with the Daily Bulletin, a small paper owned and published by Dr. J. B. Hoyle, of Hoyle's "Rheumatism Cure" fame.

Mr. Brannon was forced to give up newspaper work on account of his eyesight, and he too, long years ago passed on to the mystic beyond.

Two younger men, who began life with Mr. Jelk's paper, and remained with him until he sold out are J. D. Schaub, now the proprietor of the "Times Book Store," the oldest book store in Barbour County, and the largest business of that kind between Macon, Georgia, and Montgomery, Alabama. Mr.

MRS. A. A. COURIC   H. L. UPSHAW

J. D. SCHAUB   MALCOLM McEACHERN

Schaub, immediately after finishing school, came from LaGrange, Ga., to accept a position in Mr. Jelk's book store, and today is one of Eufaula's most prominent business men and best beloved and valuable citizens.

Mr. Schaub is also president of the City Council.

The other young man was R. Malcolm McEachern, son of J. C. and Victoria Williams McEachern, first families of Barbour County, who began his career carrying the Times, and has since been an honored and outstanding citizen. He was elected to the office of tax assessor of Barbour County in 1900, and has held the office 35 years, being successively reelected at each election until 1935, when he was defeated by a conspiracy of sold votes, a few hours before the polls closed. Mr. McEachern refused to put up money to secure votes. The fight against his reelection was made to get the office moved from Eufaula to Clayton.

One of the most important personages ever connected with the Times was Mr. G. W. Barefield, "Wash," as he was familiarly known. He served the paper in every capacity, editor, reporter, printer, foreman of printing department, solicitor, collector and advertising agent, and was identified with all its interests from 1860 to 1903. He was personally known to every subscriber of the weekly as well as the daily, and was as enthusiastic over the paper's success as if he had been the proprieor.

He was a man of superior intelligence and was called by his close friends "Eufaula's Bureau of Information." His grandfather and great grandfather were among the first settlers of Eufaula and he loved the place patriotically. No tribute to his life could be too high.

Mr. Charles A. McKinnon, now one of the publishers of the Troy Messenger, was foreman of the Times and manager of the composing room for over 20 years, and one of the most thorough and all-round newspaper men of the South. He is of high integrity and superior literary knowledge.

In 1890 Mr. Jelks sold the Times and News to Moore and Muir of Bowling Green, Ohio, and in 1901 Mr. Moore sold his interest to A. G. Muir.

In 1880 Dr. J. D. Hoyle published the daily and weekly Bulletin, and after three years the Daily Mail was born of the Bulletin's parentage, with W. R. McKenzie manager and Mike M. Brannon, editor.

Mike Brannon, the inimitable and only one Mike, of Cleve- the Daily Mail and Rabbit Foot and Satin Issue fame, wrote beautiful lines a long time for the Times. While editing the Daily Mail in the eighties he was forced to give up his newspaper work on account of his eyesight .

A paper established at Clayton by Captain Benjamin H. Kieser was the "Banner." It was a spicy Democratic paper by H. D. Clayton and was edited by H. D. Clayton. It was sold to John Post. He also published "The Primitive Baptist," a religious paper.

In 1870, E. R. Quillian commenced publishing the "Clayton Courier."

In 1908 Mr. R. M. Lee of Clio leased the paper and in 1909 Hyatt and Berry leased the plant. Later they sold their lease to Beahrs and Cory, who changed the name to "The Citizen."

Mr. Muir sold the plant and paper to T. G. Wilkinson, who published it for several years. He leased the paper to J. K. Simmons, who published it only a short time, after which Mr. Wilkinson sold it to the Eufaula Daily Tribune, published by H. L. Upshaw, who is now giving a most excellent newspaper service to the County and public generally.

Mr. W. C. Croker is managing editor, Mrs. A. A. Couric (Willie Couric) society and feature editor.

CLAYTON NEWSPAPERS

In the early sixties the Clayton Banner, published at Clayton by Post and Colson, was a weekly paper, and Jefferson was the political editor. James E. Colson was the editor in chief. It was a patriotic sheet and voiced the sentiment of the Citizenry as to the state of affairs in Barbour County.

Later came the Clayton Courier, published by E. R. Quillen, who from 1880 to 1896 assisted principally by his sons, published the Courier.

Then Lawrence H. Lee became publisher for a time, but E. R. Quillen remained with the paper, and in 1901 Peach and Williams became publishers with J. S. Williams editor. Following, B. L. Bland and A. L. Bland were publishers and in 1906 A. C. Bishop became publisher.

Another change in 1906 made W. E. Floyd publisher, and in 1910 G. Ernest Jones took charge. In 1907 the name was changed to The Record Publishing Company and in connection with the Louisville News was published.

E. R. Quillen and sons published the Courier from the late Seventies for many years, and the family was notable in newspaper publication at Clayton for several generations. In 1913 Robert Davis was publisher and in 1915 W. L. Gammell bought the Record and since then has been the A-No. 1 newspaper man, whose splendid, spicy weekly sheet is a loud voice in the uplift of, not only Barbour County, but the adjacent Counties of Dale, Henry and Pike. The job printing department of the Record is worthy of special note, and Mr. Gammell is one of the most enthusiastic, alert and outstanding editors of the state.

CLIO FREE PRESS

In 1906 G. Ernest Jones published the Clio Free Press. In 1915, Allen Newberg was publisher and in 1917 G. Ernest Jones was again publisher, later going to Birmingham, the Free Press being published for a time by A. D. Teal and O. G. Easterling.

Chapter Twenty-seven

Barbour County Schools

The schools of Barbour County come first.
They have long been Charlie McDowell's hobby
And the boys and girls thirst
Always for him to lobby.

PROFESSOR P. A. McDANIEL

One of the best informed and most scholarly men of letters in Barbour County is Professor P. A. McDaniel, Jr., superintendent of education of Barbour County.

He received his high school education in the Schools of Abbeville, Ala., which are among the best in the state of Alabama. He graduated from the University of Alabama and took special post graduate courses at the University of Virginia and from Peabody College, Nashville, and the University of Tennessee.

THOMAS GREGG WILKINSON   PROFESSOR P. A. McDANIEL

Prior to coming to Barbour County in 1919 to accept a position he now holds, he held the same position in Henry County, Alabama.

He has held this position now for twelve years or more and under his superintendency, the County schools have progressed. Many consolidated schools have been established and are progressing splendidly.

Personally Prof. McDaniel is a man of most pleasing address, genial, and bears all the ear marks of the cultured educated gentleman that he is, capable, painstaking and a valuable leader in educationl lines in the County. He is vice president of the Commercial Club of Clayton; a Mason ; a Woodman of the World, and an active member of the Methodist church of Clayton.

The family home in the suburbs of Clayton is one of the most attractive in the County.

THOMAS GREGG WILKINSON

Thomas Gregg Wilkinson was born in Florence, S. C., He had his early education in that city and is a graduate of the University of South Carolina, Cornell College, New York, and Peabody Institute in Nashville, Tennessee.

He came to Barbour County in 1908 from Washington, Georgia, where he was superintendent of the schools. As president of Alabama Brenau College (formerly Union Female College, Eufaula) he soon established himself as an educational leader and is a most capable school executive. After publishing the Eufaula Daily Citizen nine years, he was elected superintendent of the city schools of Eufaula, which position he still holds, with a splendid record, of achievement. Under his charge, the school has progressed along every educational, moral, mental and physical line for the betterment of the pupils and teachers. The faculty numbers 20 teachers.

Prof. Wilkinson was president of the Commercial Club for a while, after being its secretary for twelve years. He is a Rotarian, an Elk, and a K. of P. He is alert to all the educational interests of the entire County, and is one of the most highly esteemed and valuable citizens of Eufaula. He married Agnes Ezell, of Pulaski, Tenn., who is one of the most brilliant musicians of the state, and who is the director of Public School music in the city schools. Her school orchestra and Glee Club is the pride of the city and the school.

Their children are a daughter, Edith Wilkinson Bell and James Wilkinson.

FIRST BARBOUR COUNTY SCHOOL

In 1837, despite the fact that it was a year of misfortunes, a schoolhouse (the first in Barbour County) was built and called the Irwinton Institute.

Mr. A. K. Merrill and a Mr. Goldwaithe were the teachers. Previous to this a Miss Perry had taught a small school. In the early fifties Capt. S. H. Dent taught a school on Broad street in Eufaula and in 1853 Misses McDowell and Storey opened the Eufaula Female high school, with Mrs. M. Sandiford in charge of the Music Department. On January 2nd, 1854, The Eufaula Male Academy opened in the Hall just below the Temperance Hall in the City market house. A. D. Bates was principal.

In 1853, John McNab, then intendent of the town of Eufaula, called a meeting of members of Harmony Lodge 46 F. A. A. M., I. O. F. F. Lodge Number 3 and the Lodge of Independent Order Sons of Temperance, and a Board of Trustees for Union Female College was organized.

The contract for building was let to George W. Whipple, and in January, 1854, the handsome large building was opened for service, with William H. McIntosh, the first president, assisted by Charles M. Mallory. They were succeeded by the following as the years passed on: From 1870 to 1873, Col. Hiram Hawkins, W. H. Patterson, E. B. Armstead and B. F. Moody, associate president from 1879 to 1883. Then from 1883 to 1886 E. G. Brownlee was followed by T. E. Jones and T. G. Lamar, with Misses Corine and Eliza Janes, leading teacher of the faculty.

In the early nineties, Prof. Thomas G. Simons accepted the presidency and the musical record of his talented wife, and her Choral Society are among the most notable historical features of this Old College.

Following Prof. Simmons, Messers Asa Van Hoose and Dr. H. C. Pearce, from Brenau College, Gainesville, Ga., leased the college, and named it Alabama Brenau. They sold their lease to President Thomas G. Wilkinson, but the opening of the Woman's College at Tallahassee, Florida, took so many of the boarding students from Alabama Brenau, that its abandonment as a college was inevitable.

During the years of the building of a new public school building on Sanford street, the Public school was housed in the old U. F. College.

U. F. College was built by the cooperation of Harmony Lodge Number 46, F. A. M., I. O. O. F. and Lodge Number 3. When the Old Lodge of Independent Order of Sons of Temperance" went out of existence that organization, transferred their interest in the college to the City of Eufaula. Just prior to the taking over of the College by Messrs. Van-Hoose and Pearce, the Masonic and Odd Fellows' lodges relinquished their claims in favor of the City also.

This college was a magnificent building, and the history of the institution, most colorful and romantic. It was built of lumber from trees that grew in Barbour County, and the lumber sawed at The Mill of the Thomas and Girky, eight miles from Eufaula.

The nine year old boy, John C. Thomas, who measured and recorded every foot hauled, to use in this building, when he grew to manhood, was secretary of the Board of Trustees of this college from 1863 until his death in 1891. The handsome image of Minerva that stood on the highest pinnacle of the roof of the chapel was carved from a solid pine tree four feet in diameter, that grew near the mill that sawed the lumber. The statue was carved by an artist whom Mr. Whipple knew in Pennsylvania. He came to Eufaula for the express purpose of carving it. When the City of Eufaula sold the lot on which the College stood to Dr. W. S. Britt, this unique statue was hauled to the court house yard in Eufaula among lumber that was a part of the torn away building.

Mrs. Thad C. Doughtie, wife of the City Clerk of Eufaula, asked that it be given to her, and when her request was granted by the Council, she shipped it to the Department of Archieves and History at Montgomery, where it is being preserved as one of the historic relics of the County of Barbour.

On the site of the historic old college, now stands the Britt Infirmary.

The first public school in Eufaula was in the early fifties, taught by Capt. S. H. Dent, then a young man, who had come to Eufaula from Charles County, Maryland, on Broad street. The first city free school was taught by Miss Victoria Hoole in a two-room building on Garden Lane sometime in the early eighties. The school grew and soon a principal was elected —the first being Mr. Kilpatrick.

In 1889, the first city school was built on Sanford street, the contractor being Charles A. Stevens. The history of this school is such, that the County and State may well be proud of it. The wonderful building, fine system of education, and all the departments are the fruition of the dreams of James Milton, S. H. Dent, John C. Thomas and J. W. Tullis, who held a meeting in Milton's store in the summer of 1882, after there had been some serious consideration, by the Board of Trustees of Union Female College over conditions arising during the year, that showed a city governed school for the city might not be a bad idea. At this meeting was formed a city board of education, trustees were elected and each year since then the school has progressed.

The superintendents have been Kilpatrick, J. R. Hankins, F. L. McCoy, H. L. Upshaw and T. G. Wilkinson, who brought with him to the city schools years of experience as college professor. During the years he has been superintendent the school has gone steadily up the line of progress in every grade and school feature.

The buildings are among the finest in the state, with every equipment, and unexcelled faculty of twenty teachers.

One of the finest features is the Public School Music Department, under the direction of Mrs. T. G. Wilkinson, who directs a splendid orchestra of 50 pieces and teaches a Glee club of over fifty.

Before the days of the City Public Schools, the Male Academys and private schools for boys were noteworthy features of the Educational facilities of the County and Town.

In 1862, the Male School, under the direction of W. H. Patterson was taught on College Hill. Then there was the Dobbins School on the corner of Eufaula and Browder streets which was taught by Prof. Dobbins and wife, and Mr. Mallory.

During the late seventies and early eighties, the Rusk-Hinton school for boys, taught by Profs' Thomas R. Rusk and James Hinton on Garden Lane, was where the larger and more advanced boys were fitted for college. For many years Prof. T. A. Craven, and Prof. W. H. Patterson taught the older boys, and during the eighties Prof. Arnold taught, following Craven and Patterson on College Hill.

During the War Between the States there were several private schools for little girls, and during reconstruction days the girls were carried to the college in Jerry Brooks' bus, because it was not deemed safe for children to be on the streets going to and from school.

Twelve years of elementary and high school education, without leaving home. This is made possible by a system of buses over the county (practically 50) to transport the children to and from school.

There are six consolidated schools in the county—each one furnishing 6 years of elementary—3 of junior and 3 of senior high school training. At Blue Springs, Alabama, agriculture and home economics are taught and agriculture is taught at Baker Hill and Clio.

This fine school system in the County has been brought about by the efforts of the County Board of Education.

GLENNVILLE SCHOOLS

On October 3rd, 1853, the following notice appeared in the columns of the "Spirit of the South:"

Notice to contractors for building:

"The trustees invite the attention of contractors to their proposition for the building of an edifice for their collegiate Female Institute, Glennville, Barbour County, to be 60 x 80 feet, two stories, 30 feet high, with Cupolo, Colunade balcony and necessary for fashionable exterior finish, and the interior to be divided and arranged commodiously for the uses designed— according to the draft, minute plan and specifications, which may be seen in the hands of Dr. E. P. DuBose, president of the Board; or any information as to the above together with the forms and conditions of payment, that may be desired, by letter postpaid to him will be furnished. Sealed proposals for the completion of same, directed to him, will be received until Tuesday, Nov. 1st, when the contract will be let to the lowest bidder, competent, who will be required to furnish bond and ample security for the prompt and faithful performance of his contract. By order of the Board signed M. M. Glenn Sec. pro tem.

The above college was built and served for years as one of the finest in the state. The Board of trustees were:

E. E. DuBose, president; A. M. Sanford, William Freeman; A. C. Mitchell; R. Mitchell; J. M. Raiford.

M. M. Glenn was secretary and treasurer.

CLAYTON SCHOOLS

At Clayton the earlier schools were taught by teachers of private schools, but in later years a fine school house has been built and a public school maintained.

Limited consolidation of schools was undertaken in Clayton, about 1918, and the school made an accredited one. So marked has been the progress of this school that it now ranks among the largest of the county.

The first private school on record in Clayton was taught by Miss Nannie Valentine. Another excellent teacher recalled (still living at Clayton) is Miss India McRae.

The present superintendent of the Clayton High school is Prof. W. E. Calhoun, who ranks high as an educator and his faculty is voted the very best. The handsome school building is a credit to the county.

At Louisville the schools have always been the very best and that best was made even better by the consolidation of the schools of the county. The High school is making a fine record under Prof. R. O. Dykes. The excellent principal of the grammar school is Mrs. B. Tillman. At Old Spring Hill (a historic community) a four room, state-type building was erected some years ago, through the liberality of Gov. B. B. Comer, whose brother with him had endowed this school with funds to meet those subscribed by Donald Comer in late years. And other members of the Comer family have helped. At Comer the building of three rooms was by private subscription and is now a finely equipped school.

At Baker Hill (where the school building is commodious and handsome) there have been yearly all the advantages of a City school and the movement has spread to Clayton, Richards Cross Roads, Elamville, Mount Zion and Louisville.

Lately a large consolidated elementary school building has been built at Clio, with seven class and grade rooms and a large auditorium.

Texasville and Pimple Hill, although in the additional territory, responded to the movement for better schools and at a considerable cost Texasville built a fine building. Mt. Zion has a nice brick building.

Baker Hill territory embraces Rocky Mount, and Richards Cross Roads, and like Blue Springs, Baker Hill is one of the five accredited schools, with vocational departments.

From pioneer days, Barbour County has stressed the importance of educational qualifications, until the teachers of today (not a single third grade teacher is employed in the County). In 1915 there were 97 high school students enrolled in the County schools. The enrollment of 1936 is between 835 and 900.

In the Barbour County schools, health is stressed and every school is regularly visited by county health officers and health nurse.

Chapter Twenty-eight
Churches In Barbour County

> The Churches are Sanctuaries Holy,
> Where we personally commune with God
> And hear, over and over, the story
> Of the life paths the Savior trod.

As early as 1822, the devout old Scotch Presbyterians who settled the lower part of the County near Louisville worshipped under bush arbors, but by 1823 a Methodist church had been organized by a "circuit rider" preacher, and was called "New Hope," but it was not until 1896 that the Louisville Presbyterian church was organized.

The Pea River Presbyterian church was organized in 1823 some of its members being among the settlers that landed at Eufaula and later made their way further westward through the County. Therefore, it is a fact that the church at Pea river, with an ancient cemetery (a most beautiful spot) is the oldest church in the county. In 1935, D. C. Turrentine, circuit preacher, organized the first church at the Eufaula settlement, and the building erected for the purpose of both schoolhouse and church, was adjoining the plot on which the courthouse stands. The land was owned by Floyd Lee, settler who willed it to his daughter, Mary Lee McLean, who lived to be over 90 years of age. The building still stands and is today the storehouse of James Faulk, general merchandise store on Broad street. The first pastor was Zaccheus Dowling (great great uncle of H. B. Dowling, prominent citizen of Eufaula today). Rev. Zacheus Dowling was presiding elder of the district reaching (in those days) Macon, Ga. to Montgomery and Greenville, Ala., and to Pensacola, Florida ,and he made the circuit on horseback. Following his charge here, were J. Boswell, 1836, and W. B. Neal, 1837 and 1838.

FIRST WOMAN'S MISSIONARY SOCIETY WAS ORGANIZED IN BARBOUR COUNTY

The first Woman's Missionary Society ever organized in the Methodist Church, South, was in Barbour County, at Eufaula First Methodist Church. In 1877, Dr. Henry D. Moore was pastor of this church.

There was a Council of Bishops, a General Conference, held at Atlanta, Ga., and Dr. Moore was in attendance.

At this Conference, Bishop Chandler presided, and the question of permitting Women's organizations came up. There was prolonged and heated discussion, pro and con, but the decision of the Conference was in favor of granting this privilege to women. Dr. Moore came home and reported the decision to his congregation, and immediately the women of the church organized "the First Women's Missionary Society in the Methodist Church, South." Mrs. Henry A. Young (Maria McRae) was elected president.

Among the charter members were Mrs. J. T. Kendall, Mrs. J. W. Drewry, Mrs. Thirza Malone, Mrs. S. H. Dent, Mrs. H. M. Weedon, Mrs. J. G. Guice, Mrs. N. W. Roberts, Mrs. R. Q. Edmondson and others.

This first Woman's Missionary Society ever organized within the ranks of the Great Methodist Denomination, added another very important fact to the already long list of "Firsts" in Barbour County.

This organization is functioning today under the name of Woman's Missionary Auxiliary of the First Methodist Church. Mrs. Charles S. McDowell has been the president for many years, and was succeeded on January 1st by her niece, Mrs. John R. Barr, an enthusiastic young woman, who is carrying along the record of consecrated women of her distinguished Young-Dent-Hurt family, who have figured so notably in the history of the Church.

Following Mrs. Barr was Mrs. E. P. Clark, who served in 1937-38. Mrs. W. C. Flewellen, daughter of the late Dr. P. P. Hurt, notable minister, is now President.

METHODIST CHURCH OF EUFAULA BEGAN 100 YEARS AGO

(Author's note—We are indebted to the late Capt. S. H. Dent for the history of the Methodist church in Eufaula).

In the year 1834 two missionaries were assigned to the section of East Alabama, and it is supposed that the first Methodist sermon was preached in the village located on the Chattahoochee, known at that time as Irwinton, during that year. For three years these missionaries of the Alabama conference served through this section, establishing churches and organizing circuits. In 1838 the name of Irwinton charge appears for the first time in the Minutes of the Conference. It is supposed that the First Methodist church was built in Eufaula in 1837 (the name being changed from Irwinton back to its original name, Eufaula, by act of the legislature in

1844) as we find a record in the history of the Presbyterian church of that year that they were uniting in a revival service at the Methodist church.

The Methodist policy in those olden days required a rapid change in pastors and for thirty years the Eufaula church had almost that many pastors. Among those who served as pastors and presiding elders, we mention a few who were men of ability and leadership: Ebenezer Hearn, J. Boswell, W. B. Neal, Zaccheus Dowling, Green Malone, Stephen Pilley, O. R. Blue, M. S. Andrews, J. L. Cotton, A. S. Andrews, A .J. Briggs, E. M. Bounds, H. Urquehart, W. M. Motley, J. R. Crawford, J. B. Cottrell and J. M. Mason.

In the years 1874-75 the second church building was erected on the spot where the Methodist property is now located. Dr. Bounds was the loved pastor during that period. It was through his fidelity and the liberality of the Eufaula people that a brick building was erected at a cost of $13,000. This building stood as a temple of worship and a thing of beauty for forty years. During the pastorate of Rev. H. C. Threadgill the present building was erected at a cost of about $50,000, and will meet the needs of the church for years to come.

The Alabama conference has held five sessions of its annual meetings in the Eufaula church, 1859, 1875, 1883, 1892 and 1906. Eight bishops have preached in the Eufaula church, Kavanaugh, Doggett, Marwin, Keener, Pearce, Duncan, Fitzgerald and Candler.

In recent years the church has been under the leadership of great preachers. Men like J. S. Frazer J. A. Peterson H. T. Johnson, O. S. Welch, W. P. Dickinson, H. C. Threadgill, J. E. McCann, I. W. Chalker, W. R. Bickerstaff, P. S. Hudson, and E. A. Dannelly. Two pastors have died while engaged in the duties of the church in recent years. Dr. Dickinson was killed in the tornado of 1919 and Dr. Dannelly died in the close of his first year in 1928.

The church is proud of its long history of Christian service. Many of the state's leading men and women are recorded upon its registers. To look back over the names of those who have worshipped about the sacred altars of Methodism in Eufaula is to have the soul filled with sacred memories.

J. W. Moody followed Dr. Dannelly, and Dr. O. S. Welch followed him; then Rev. J. L. Daniel; and Dr. W. H. McNeal is the present pastor.

FIRST METHODIST PASTORS AND PRESIDING ELDERS

In 1834 when the village was served by mission ministers, it was under the control of the Chattahoochee Mission.

1835—H. M. Findly and Sidney Squires included in that mission.

J. E. Boswell, P. E.; Zacceous Dowling, P. C.

1836—J. Boswell, P. E.; W. B. McNeal, P. C.

1837—Ebenezer Herndon, P. E.; J. Boswell, P. C.

1938—Now Irwinton Charge. W. B. Neal, P. E., Ebenezer Herndon, P. E.

1839—Green Malone, P. E.; 1839-1940, John W. Star, P. C.

1841—Noah Laney, P. E.; C. D. Eastman, P. C.

1842—Thomas Lynch, P. E.; Stephen C. Piley, P. C.

1843—Thomas Lynch, P. E.; Stephen C. Pilley, P. E.

1844—Thomas Lynch, . E.; T. H. P. Scales, P. C. Eufaula and Glennville.

1845—Thomas Lynch, P. E.; Samuel Armstrong, P. C.

1846—First year Eufaula a station—John C. Carter, P. E.; James A. Heard, P. C..

1847—John C. Carter, P. E.; O. R. Blue, P. C.

1847—T. H. Foster, P. C., part time.

1848—T. H .Foster, P. C.

1849—Samuel Armstrong, P. E.; Walter H. M. Daniel, P. C.

1850—Samuel Armstrong, P. E.; C. C. Gillespie, P. C,

1851—Samuel Armstrong, P. E.; C. C. Gillespie, P. C.

1852—Samuel Armstrong, P. E.; C. C. Gillespie, P. C.

1753—Stephen F. Pilley, P. E. Pilley, P. E. Mark S. Andrews, P. C.

First year conference held at Eufaula:

1854—Stephen F. Pilley, P. E.; F. M. Grace, P. C.

1855—Stephen F. Pilley, P. E.; James L. Cotten, P. C.

1856—Stephen F. Pilley, P. E.; James L. Cotton, P. C.

1857—F. G. Ferguson, P. E.; W. A. McCarty, P. C.

A. S. Andrews replaced Mr. McCarty for a short time on account of bad health.

1858—F. G. Ferguson, P. E.; W. M. Motley, P. C.

Conference met in Eufaula in Dec., 1859.

1859—John W. Laney, P. E.; W. M. Motley, P. C.

1860—John W. Laney, P. E.; Allen S. Andrews, P. C.

1861—John W. Laney, P. E.; James L. Cotten, P. C.

1862—John W. Laney, P. E.; James L. Cotten, P. C.

1863—W. H .Ellison, P. E.; Joseph B. Cottrell, P. C.

1864—W. H. Ellison, P. E.; Joseph B. Cottrell, P. C.

1865—W. H. Ellison, P. E.; William Shepherd, P. C.
1866—W. H. Ellison, P. E.; William Shepherd, P. C.
1867—W. A. McCarty, P. E.; William Shepherd, P. C.
1868—W. A. McCarty, P. E.; William Shepherd, P. C.
1869—W. A. McCarty, P. E.; A. J. Briggs, P. C.
1870—W. A. McCarty, P. E.; A. J. Brigfis, P. C.
1870—W. A. McCarty, P. E.; A. J. Briggs, P. C.
1871—J. L. Cotten, P. E.; A. J. Briggs, P. C.
1872—J. L. Cotten, P. E.; E. M. Bounds, P. C.
1873—W. H. Ellison, P. E.; E. W. Bounds, P. C.. Bounds begged to remain by all.
1874—W. H. Ellison, P. E.; P. E. Bounds, P. C.
1875—W. H. Ellison, P. E.; E. M. Bounds P. C.
1876— W. H. Ellison, P. E.; J. Bancroft, P. C.
1877—H. D. Moore, P. E.; J. Bancroft, P. C.
1876—H. D. Moore, P. E.; J. Bancroft, P. C.
1879—R. B. Crawford, P. E.; R. H. Rivers, P. C.
1880—R. B. Crawford, P. E.; R. H. Rivers, P. C.
1882—R. B. Crawford, P. E.; R. H. Rivers, P. C.
1883—H. Urquehart, P. E.; M. S. Andrews, P. C.
Conference this year at Eufaula.
1884—H. Urquehart, P. E.; M. S. Andrews, P. C.
1885—H. Urquehart, P. E.; M. S. Andrews, P. C.
1886—H. Urquehart, P. E.; E. L. Lovelace, P. C.
1887—J. M. Mason, P. E.; R. B. Crawford, P. C.
1888—J. M. Mason, P. E.; R. B. Crawford, P. C
1889—J. M. Mason, P. E.; R. B. Crawford, P. C.
1890—J. M. Mason, P. E.; W. M. Motley, P. C.
1891—W. H. Wilde, P. E.; W. M. Motley, P. C.
1892—W. H. Wilde, P. E.; W. M. Motley, P. C.
1893—W .H. Wilde, P. E.; W. P. Dickinson, P. C.
Conference in Eufaula that year.
1894—W. H. Wilde, P. E.; W. P. Dickinson, P. C.
1895—W. S. Wade, P. E.; M. S. Andrews, P. C.
1896—W. S. Wade, P. E.; M. S. Andrews, P. C.
1896—W. S. Wade, P. E.; M. S. Andrews, P. C.
1897—W. S. Wade, P. E.; M. S. Andrews, P. C.
1898—W .S. Wade, P. E.; John S. Frazier, P. C.
1899—John R. Peavy, P. E.; H. D. Moore, P. C.
1900—John R. Peavy, P. E.; H. D. Moore, P. C.
1901—T. F. Mangum, P. E.; John A. Peterson, P. C.
1902—T. F. Mangum, P. E.; John A. Peterson, P. C.
1903—T. F. Manghum, P. E.; John A. Patterson, P. C.
1904—T. F. Manghum, P. E.; John A. Patterson, P. C.
1905—J. M. Mason, . E.; B. C. Glenn, P. C.
1906—J. M. Mason, P. E.; H. T. Johnson, P. C.
1907—B. C. Glenn, P. E.; O. S. Welsh, P. C.
1908—B. C. Glenn, P. E.; O. S. Welsh, P. C.

1909—J. E. McCann, P. E.; H. C. Threadgill, P. C.
1910—J. E. McCann, P. E.; H. C. Threadgill, P. C.
1911—J. E. McCann, P. E.; H. C. Threadgill, P. C.
1912—J. E. McCann, P. E.; H. C. Threadgill, P. C.
1913—W. P. Hurt, P. E.; H. C. Threadgill, P. C.
1914—W. P. Hurt, P. E.; H. C. Threadgill, P. C.
1915—W. P. Hurt, P. E.; W. P. Dickinson.
1916—W. P. Hurt, P. E.; W. P. Dickinson, P. C.
1917—W. P. Hurt, P. E.; W. P. Dickinson, P. C.
1918—W. P. Hurt, P. E.; W. P. Dickinson, P. C.
1919—W. P. Hurt, P. E.; W. P. Dickinson, P. C.
1920—C. A. Cornell, P. E.; F. A. Rogers, P. C.
1921—C. A. Cornell, P. E.; F. A. Rogers, P. C.
1922—B. F. Marshall, P. E.; I. W. Chaulker, P. C.
1923—B. F. Marshall, P. E.; I. W. Chaulker, P. C.
1924—B. F. Marshall, P. E.; I. W. Chaulker, P. C.
1925—D. P. Slaughter, P. E.; R. S. Hudson, P. C.
1926—D .P. Slaughter, P. E.; R. S. Hudson, P. C.
1927—D. P. Slaughter, P. E.; R. S. Hudson, P. C.
1928—D. P. Slaughter, P. E.; E. A. Dannelley, P. C.
1929—C. S. Talley, P. E.; D. W. Haskew, P. C.
1930—C. S. Talley, P. E.; D. W. Haskew, P. C.
1931—C. S. Talley, P. E.; D. W. Haskew, P. C
1932—C. S. Talley, P. E.; D. W. Haskew, P. C.
1933—R. A. Moody, P. S.
1934—R. A. Moody, P. E.; O. S. Welsh, P. C.
1935—R. A. Moody, P. E.; O. S. Welsh, P. C
1937—R A. Moody, P. E.; J. L. Daniel, P. C.
1938-39—Dr. Schafer, P. C.; Dr. W. H. McNeal, P. C.

PRESBYTERIAN CHURCH

It was in 1836 that the First Presbyterian church was organized in Eufaula, with sixteen members, eight of whom were members of the Morrison family. It was during the time that the village of Eufaula was temporarily called "Irwinton" to enable some commercial arrangement with one William Irwin, to be put over.

The first pastor was Rev. James Stratton.

During a protracted meeting held in 1838, in which Methodists, Baptists and Presbyterians worshipped together at the Methodist church, there was much religious interest and soon thereafter the Presbyterian congregation occupied the new church they had built on the corner of Forsyth and Washington streets on the Bluff. This building was afterwards made into a fine residence and owned and occupied by Mr. John Hartung; later by his widow, Mrs. William Link and daughter, and finally it was sold by Mrs. Link's daughter, Mrs. George Ferrell, to a colored Lodge for a club house.

Many historic weddings and funerals took place in this old church, which was one of the finest in its day.

The pastor of this church from 1840 to 1848 was Rev. R. C. Smith, who resigned to accept a professorship in Oglethorpe college. He was followed by Evan McNair who served from 1857 to 1864. The War Between the States ended his pastorate, and he was appointed Chaplain of the First Alabama Regiment by President Jefferson Davis.

From 1867 to 1880, Rev. J. C. Robinson was pastor. During his ministry, 90 members were added to the church roll and the present fine church edifice was built at a cost of $26,000. In a history of this church, written by the late C. S. McDowell, Sr., that able critic and fine writer and thinker, says of Dr. Robinson, "He was as venerable as Moses, had the learning of Confucius, and the piety of the Apostle John. His daily walk and conversation was a benediction to his people."

From 1898 to 1891, Rev. S. Addison McLeroy was pastor. He married Miss Ellie Richter, of Eufaula, at one of the most notable weddings that ever took place in this church, and he was one of the most consecrated preachers.

In the early eighties, Rev. J. M. Lowry served the church, and was most popular and consecrated.

Mr. McLeroy was followed by Rev. D. N. Yarbrough, pastor from 1895 to 1900, when Rev. E. L. Hill served from 1901 to 1906. Under his care, the church prospered as never before. 76 members were added, a fine pipe organ was purchased. Dr. Hill resigned to accept a call to the Presbyterian church at Athens, Georgia, which he is still serving, greatly beloved, and has been called to this pastorate for life, after already having served over 25 years, a great compliment to a man. . In Barbour County he was and is much beloved and admired for rare Christian traits.

He was succeeded by Rev. D. J. Blackwell, who served from 1907 to 1916, going to Quincy, Florida. Recently he has been called to the pastorate of the Presbyterian Church at Leaksville, N. C. Mr. Blackwell also carried with him the admiration of this section.

In 1917, Rev. D. J. J. McPhail came to The Eufaula Presbyterian Church, and until 1924, was the "Good Samaritan of this community, as well as the beloved and learned pastor. We went about daily doing good, and his name was a house hold word among the poor and needy.

During the influenza epidemic of 1918, Mr. McPhail, daily and nightly, worked in many ways to help the situation. The physicians of this section said, "They could not have handled the situation as they did, but for the wonderful personal aid of "Parson" McPhail." He went to his charge at Demopolis, Alabama, carrying the love and gratitude of the citizenship. Many times he has, in recent years, come back to officiate at the funerals of intimate old friends, and each time a heartfelt loving greeting has been his.

After Dr. McPhail, came, Rev. J. Leighton Scott in June, 1925. During his splendid ministry 83 members were added to the roll, the church grounds were beautified, and the church grew in many ways.

Following Mr. Scott, came Dr. J. E. Hobson, who was a wonderful preacher and a man whose eloquence and personality made him an asset to the community, not only as a religious leader, but as a citizen. He and his charming wife took active part in all the interests of the community, and their going away, following his resignation a few months ago, was a source of deep regret. He resigned because of the state of his health, and went to his old home in Mississippi.

Just last Sunday, July 11th, Rev. C. Walker Session was installed as the pastor of the church. The ministers of the Alabama Presbytery, taking part in the exercises were Rev. Stanford Purnell, of Union Springs, Rev. W. B. Clemmons of Prattville, Ala., Rev. Claud Gillespie Pepper of Greenville, Ala. Rev. Sessions came here from the Demopolis, Alabama, church.

The Women's work of this church has been outstanding. It was first organized in 1866 and among the ladies interested were Mrs. W. T. Simpson and Mrs. Nathan Bray.

Mrs. E. Y. Dent (Annie McCormick) organized the Annie Dent Circle and the Young Ladies Improvement Society, organized by Mrs. L. Y. Dean (Caroline Simpson) in 1901, is today carrying on as the enthusiastic woman who organized them would have them do. Miss Katie Bray has been the treasurer since its organization.

The Junior Christian Endeavor is directed by Misses Georgia Ferrell and Miss Natalie Stewart.

The 85 year record of this church is especially historic.

FIRST BAPTIST CHURCH AT EUFAULA

The First Baptist church at Eufaula was constituted June 24th, 1837, in what was then known as the town of Irwinton— the name having been changed in 1835 from its original name Eufaula—and was called "The Irwinton Baptist Church." This name it retained until 1843, when by Act of the Legislature the name of the town was changed back to its original name Eufaula. The church by unanimous vote, adopted the name of "The Eufaula Baptist Church." This name it bore until April 12th, 1869, when, for proper considerations, it was changed to that of The First Baptist Church of Eufaula, Alabama, and so incorporated.

The council officiating at its constitution was composed of Rev. Peter Eldridge, Rev. Joel Sims, and Rev. Stephen Rowe. The following members constituted the original organization: Cullen Battle and wife, Mrs. Jane Battle, Samuel Brown and wife, Ann Brown, Seth N. Broughton, Maria Betts, Olivia Barefield, Mary Bailey, Thomas Cargill and wife, Lucinda Cargill, Mary Ann Dennis, Josiah Jackson, Charlotte Martin, Lucy Moore, Seth Piland, Reuben C. Shorter, Mary Shorter, Col. E. S. Shorter, Mrs. Sarah Shorter Hunter (Bates), and Mary B. Shorter Thornton, Archibald Seals and wife, Nancy Seals, parents of Col. D. M. Seals, Miss Emily F. Shorter and Elizabeth Wharton.

The church was constituted in the Male Academy, which stood on the northwest corner of Union and Livingstone streets, in which they, for some time worshipped, using for a Baptistry, a pool on Union streets, fed from a spring from the town branch, between Randolph and Orange streets, where the Standard Oil plant is now located.

The spacious wooden building on the bluff was used for worship for over thirty years and was dedicated May 23rd, 1841. The service was conducted by Rev. Thomas Cartis; Rev. Joseph S. Baker; Rev. Charles D. Mallory; Rev. Thomas Muse and Rev. James Matthews.

The present house of worship was erected at a cost of $35,000 and began in 1869 and dedicated on November 5th, 1871. Dedicatory services were conducted by Rev. J. L. Burrows, A. J. Battle, W. H. McIntosh and M. B. Wharton. Since its organization the church has had the following officers:

PASTORS

William M. Tryon, 1827-39; James Matthews, 1840;; William P. Patterson, 1841-43; James Matthews, 1844-45; Jonathan Davis, 1846-47; S. Henderson, 1848; W. H. McIntosh, 1849-59; W. N. Reeves, 1860-61(pastor absent in the Army until close of the war, then resumed pastorate 1864-66).

M. B. Wharton, 1867-71; J. H. Kinnebrew, 1872; P. T. Warren, 1873 (part of year); H. M. Wharton, 1874; W. N. Reeves, 1874-76; O. F. Gregory, 1877-78; M. M. Wamboldt, 1879-81; J. E. Chambliss, 1882-84; G. A. Nunnally, 1885-87; W. L. Pickard, 1889-1890; J. C. Hiden, 1890-93; E. P. Lipscomb, 1882; J. G. Bow, 1893; W. H. Hubbard, 1899-1901; M. B. Wharton, 1907-1908; J. A. French, 1908-1915; A. J. Dickinson, 1915-1817; W. H. Tew, 1918-1921; R. E. L. Harris, 1922-1925; C. C. Pugh, 1926.

DEACONS

Cullen Battle, Reuben C. Shorter, Seth N. Broughton, William Archer, P. M. Callaway, John Gill Shorter, D. Mims, Chauncey Rhodes, J. A. B. Besson, R. D. Mallory, Z. F. Nance, John A. Walker, C. W. Wells, Dr. S. A. Holt, Dr. W. H. Thornton, D. M. Seals, A. A. Couric, B. B. Davis, F. B. Moodie, Sr., S. G. Robertson, W. A. Davis, Jere H. Reeves.

CLERKS

Thomas Cargill, J. G. Shorter, William H. Thornton, P. M. Callaway, B. B. Davis, C. Rhodes, W. S. Paulin, A. L. Gaston, J. S. Paullin, J. A. Grady, Henry Davis, J. F. Cargill, W. H. Locke, J. A. Hunter, J. A. Hunter, J. D. Billings, J. H. Reeves, R. F. Nance, George B. Davis, O. T. Moore, C. M. Gammage, A. B. Roberts, Mrs. Julia McKay.

Treasurers—J. G. Shorter, C. Rhodes, J. A. B. Besson, G. L. Comer, John G. Smith, W.A. Davis, Jere H. Reeves, B. B. Davis.

The following have been licensed to preach by the church: A. J. Chaplin, 1840; W. H. Patterson, 1845; J. Battle, 1851; M. Callaway, 1854; C. J. Stephens, 1875; H. K. Battle, 1857; H. R. Schramm, 1888; J. S. Paulin, 1857.

Ordained—James K. Kramer, 1891; Henry R. Schramm; Charles Clark, 1920; Grady Ketchum, 1922.

Among those who have served as pastors during this long period are to be found the names of some of the most cultured, useful and emminent men in the denomination. It was during the first pastorate of Dr. M. B. Wharton, 1867-1871, when the church's location was changed and a handsome building erected on the corner of Randolph and Barbour streets, which location is still occupied by the church. After an absence of thirty years Dr. Wharton returned to the church's pastorate in 1901, remaining until his death in 1908. It was during this later pastorate of Dr. Wharton that the church building was destroyed by lightning and the present noble structure erected on the same spot. To him was thus given the unique distinction of supervising the erection of two edifices for the congregation at an interval of nearly forty years. It is a pathetic fact that he was never permitted to preach in the latest structure on account of declining health, but his body lay in state there on the day of his funeral with a military guard of honor. A handsome marble statue of Dr. Wharton now stands by the church, at the intersection of Barbour and Randolph streets as a token of the high esteem in which he was held by all the people of Eufaula.

The first money raised for the building fund for the present church was made by Mrs. M. B. Wharton and Mrs. J. C.

Thomas, who crocheted children's sacques and baked old fashioned milk yeast bread and sold it, raising the first $50.00 placed to the credit of the building fund.

Dr. Wharton, pastor, traveled all over the country, soliciting donations, and in three months, several bales of cotton, three carloads of corn, meat, lard and grain had been shipped to Eufaula by western wholesale merchants. Fancy work was done on a large scale, by the women of the congregation, and in December of 1875 a great bazaar was held in Hart's Block, lasting a week, when articles were auctioned off, and the venture netted over six thousand dollars for the building fund.

The church was built, partly on borrowed money, and ten years after Dr. Wharton had long gone to other fields of labor, one bitter cold January Sunday he came back to the old church, preached a sermon and held a church conference lasting from 12 to 3 p. m. during which time every note held against the church was delivered up and burned, thereby relieving the church of the debt.

In 1900, Dr. Wharton was prevailed upon to accept the pastorate of the church again, and he came back after thirty years.

In July, 1907, the church was struck by lightning and burned, all being destroyed except the brick walls, the pulpit chairs and clock.

It was rebuilt at a cost of $20,000 under the direction of the pastor, but before the seats had been placed Dr. Wharton died in Atlanta, Georgia. His body lay in state in the beloved church he had twice builded, with military guard of honor, but the funeral was held in the First Methodist church because of no seats in his own church. Dr. J. A. French succeeded Dr. Wharton as pastor.

The first handsome organ in this church was a Mason and Hamlin Reed three-tier keyboard, presented to the church by Prof. J. C. Van Houten, who was the blind organist from 1856 until his death Dec. 25th, 1890.

A handsome John Brown pipe organ was purchased for the new church, which was in use until a few months ago. Mrs. Eli S. Shorter, in loving memory of her husband, the late lamented Eli S. Shorter, a deacon and most valuable leading member of the church, presented to the church a handsome new high grade $5,000 Moeuller pipe organ which has just been installed. Mrs. Edgar T. Long (Mamie Rhodes) is the organist who has been the beloved musical leader of this community nearly sixty years, and is still the brilliant musician. She followed Prof. Van Houten, who was her teacher, and except for the 14 years she resided away from Eufaula, has been the church organist. During those 14 years, Miss Islay Reeves (Mrs. H. Lampley) and Miss Mattie Thomas (Mrs. C. M. Thompson) filled her place as organist of this church, assisted a short time by Mrs. J. C. Bow, Mrs. Fanny Raleigh and Miss Emma Brooks (Mrs. O. Worthy).

The Sunday school for many years, under the superintendency of the late W. N. Reeves and G. L. Comer, was recorded as the largest and most flourshing Sunday schools in the state. Today its Men's Bible class is notable. A few years ago the late Mrs. Wylena Lamar Shorter, wife of the late Eli S. Shorter, II, donated to the Sunday school a lot adjoining the church, and the late Marion Gay, Deacon of the church, left in his will a donation of $1,000 to be used to begin a Sunday school annex. This has been completed for the present, but it is planned to later build an additional upper story to this fine building.

On June 24th, 1937, the church celebrated its one hundredth birthday when the pastor, Rev. C. C. Pugh was in charge of the splendid program offered. It was greatly enjoyed and it was a happy season of memories and rejoicing. The only two living pastors who had previously served this church, besides the present pastor, Dr. Pugh, are Rev. R. E. L. Harris of Hogansville, Georgia, and Dr. A. J. Dickinson of Mobile, Ala. They were present and took active part in every service. Dr. Harris preached at the opening servi and on Friday evening there was an address by Dr. Dickin son. The history of the church was given by Mrs. Clifford A. Locke (Retta Thornton) whose mother, Mary Shorter Thornton, and grandparents, General and Mrs. Reuben Shorter, were founders of the church. On Saturday morning Mrs.. R. R. Moorer, superintendent of the Young People's Department, and Mrs. C. P. Roberts of the W. M. U. made beautiful talks on 'Love," which was singularly appropriate. Mrs. Mattie Wharton Moore, daughter of Dr. M. B. Wharton, of blessed memory, gave the history of the Women's work of the church from its organization until today.

The feature of the celebration was the informal reception and garden party, given by Mr. and Mrs. H. L. Upshaw to the entire membership at their beautiful home on Eufaula street.

It was a very happy occasion with beautiful flowers on the lawn and in the flower garden in the rear of the home, brilliantly lighted and a bevy of young girls serving the guests delicious punch, sandwiches and accessories. It was an occasion that will be long remembered. Mrs. F. W. Jennings and Mrs. Mattie Wharton presided over the book in which every one present registered as they did fifty years ago when Mrs. Upshaw's parents, Col. and Mrs. Eli S. Shorter, II, celebrated the fiftieth birthday of the church at the same home in a similar way.

The Southside Baptist Church was organized in the early nineties and was the outcome of a Mission Sunday School, which had its beginning in a S. S. organized by a band of women First Baptist Church who taught children and grown-ups for several years every Sunday in the parlors of Mrs. J. C. Thomas and who sponsored a school for children in a school house rented, near by, where the Southwest Baptist Church now stands, and taught by Miss Sarah King.

These ladies were Mrs. J. C. Thomas, Mrs. C. Rhodes, Mrs. J. D. Godwin, Mrs. S. G. Robertson, Mrs. A. A. Couric and Mrs. W. J. Brannon. They were assisted by the pastor, Rev. J. Bow of the First Baptist church.

Deacon Cliff A. Locke and wife, Retta Thornto Locke, gave the lot on which the Southside Baptist church was built.

The Washington Street Methodist church was also the outcome of this Sunday school movement by these women and so interested was Mr. G. T. Marsh, superintendent of the Cowikee Cotton Mills, that he took the initiative and the Washington street Methodist church was built and dedicated before the Baptist church was. This church is now on the Eufaula circuit and has had the following pastors: W. R. Green, W. Y. Vreeland, A. B. Carlton.

Malone's Chapel, known as the "White Church," was on the Eufaula circuit, but in 1895 the membership was moved to the Washington Street church, Eufaula. This church was four miles from Eufaula.

CLAYTON BAPTIST CHURCH

By Dr. C. H. Turner

The Clayton Baptist church is said to be the oldest church as to its organization ,which is now in existence in the town of Clayton. Mrs. Mary Foster Roberson says she has heard her father say when he first moved to Clayton that the Baptist church was the only church in the town and other denominations worshipped and worked with the Baptists in the old building. At that time prior to the War between the States, the house was a two-story building and the upper story was owned and had been used by the Masonic Lodge. That arrangement lasted until the Masons sold their interests in the building to the Baptist organization. He said at the time Judge Henry D. Clayton, an Episcopalean, was acting as superintendent of the Sunday School held in the Baptist Church. Later the main auditorium of the Church was dedicated to the worship of God by the church and the Eufaula Association of 1890. The writer of this article has been unable to find any data as to the original organization or Constitution of the Baptist Church.

The longest pastorate was held by Rev. James Stratton Paullin, who was called to serve the Clayton Baptist Church, about the year 1857 or 1858 and preached for the church for a period of 23 years, with the exception of a short interval, until his death in 1882. Missing records forbid mention of pastors until 1907 when Rev. J. S. Yarbrough was called to the pastorate. Other pastors, Rev. B. S. Bailey, C. J. Crawford, E. H. Crawley, E. S. Atkinson, W. E. Fendley, J. H. Wyatt served the church to 1929.

The present pastor, Charles S. Turner, has served for several years. The membership of the church is over 2 with an average attendance of over 85. The church possesses two large pulpit Bibles, one bound in sheepskin, which was evidently purchased or presented to the church from the following writing on the fly leaf about the year 1873: "Holy Bible of the Baptist Church, April 27th, 1873." The other was a memorial gift to the Clayton Church from Mary L. Borders in memory of her husband, Q. H. Borders, Oct. 21st, 1894.

EPISCOPALIAN CHURCH
Organized 1845

Although the foundations for St. James Episcopal Church were laid as early as 1838, when services were held in "The Tavern," a devout band was planning for a future house of worship, while yet the settlement was a small Indian village.

The record of the church proper began with a petition asking for the Bishop of the Diocesean Council of Alabama to recognize a group of persons forming themselves into a vestry as a church on April 22nd, 1845.

It is a fact, however, that the foundation of the Parish was laid as early as 1838 and occasional services were held in such places as were available. The following composed the vestry: John L. Gay, John L. Hunter, J. W. Smith, W. T. Dewit, James Beatish and Irwin Miller.

In 1844, Rev. John L. Gay held services three months in the old building built by Mark Williams as a residence, but used for several years as "The Tavern" (now owned and occupied by Mrs. T. A. Mashburn. In May, 1850, steps were taken to erect a church edifice and a finance committee was appointed to buy a lot. A lot on Barbour street, next to the home of Humphrey Foy, was donated by Mr. H. P. Adams for the purpose of building a church. The subscription list was headed by Nelson Clayton and Mrs. C. J. Pope, —a donation of $500. In August of the same year the building was completed and in 1852 a fine toned bell was purchased which is being used today to ring out the call to worship.

William Kimmerman followed John L. Gay who was the first Episcopal missionary and in 1800 George T. Cushman visited the parish monthly, meetings being held in the upper room of the market house on Broad street. In 1850 Bishop Cobb visited the parish and baptized and confirmed quite a number. Then steps were taken to complete the erection of the church in 1851. William Ellis was given charge as rector. He was followed by Rev. Mr. Steele in January of 1860. Then came Thomas Beards, serving until 1862, when the church was again without a rector. W. I. Boone came for a short time, but resigned to go to China as a missionary. He went to China and became the first Episcopal Bishop of China. Rev. J. C. Davis became rector serving until 1881. Under his pastorate the record of the first representation of the Parish in the Diocesan Council was made, and at a session in 1870 the Rector was present and the following vestrymen were delegates:

William H. Bray, I. H. Hobdy, P. D. Moultrop, Earnest Catterville and James Ross.

At this time a handsome Reed organ was purchased and Mr. J. H. Whitlock was the organist of the church for many years.

During the pastorate of Rev. Theodore Reed, a new lot was procured and the plans for moving the church were made.

Rev. Reed resigned and under the pastorate of Dr. E. W. Spaulding the church was moved and improved, on the lot facing St. James street in the rear of where the present church stands.

A handsome rectory was built and a fine organ purchased. Dr. Sualding did much for the church, but in 1892 he resigned and was succeeded by Rev. I. O. Adams from Pine Bluff, Ark.

During Dr. Adams' rectorship, Mrs. Margaret Tansey presented the church, in memory of her husband, James Tansey, a vestryman, a marble Baptismal fount. Miss Eliza Merrill organized the "Little Gleaners," a children's missionary band, and Mrs. Henry D. Clayton organized the "St. James Guild" in 1892.

In September, 1904, Rev. Bertram Brown was Rector and the building of a new brick and cement church on the corner of Eufaula and St. James streets was begun. In 1909, Rev. Brown resigned to go to Tarboro, North Carolina. Both Rev. Bertram E. Brown and his brother, Bishop Wyatt Brown, are natives of Barbour County, descendants of the Hunter-Hoole—pioneer families of Barbour County.

Rev. T. Henry Johnston came in 1909 and carried on the work and the beautiful church was completed. Dr. J. B. Whitlock drew the plans for this church and gave his time, thought and money to hasten its completion.

Rev. C. M. Murray succeeded Mr. Johnson and following him came Rev. J .C. Heyes of England followed him and served several years. The present Rector is Rev. Scott Smith who comes twice monthly from Bainbridge, Ga., to hold services.

Note: Since this was written Rev. Scott has returned to England and Rev. Crenshaw of Dothan is Rector of St. James.

PEA RIVER PRESBYTERIAN CHURCH

The Pea River Presbyterian Church, seven miles from Louisville, was organized in 1823 and for a long time services were held under bush arbors. The membership was composed of the Scotch settlers, among whom were: Murdock Martin, W. H. McEachern, Elders Jim McDonald, Kate Wilkinson, John McNeil McLendon.

It is the oldest church in the county. The beautiful cemeter adjoining is still kept in beautiful order, and services have been held in this church continuously since its organization in those early days. It is said that Indians often attended the services.

OTHER CHURCHES

Other churches in the County are:

Palmyra, (Presbyterian) 11 miles from Eufaula on the Clayton road.

Mount Pleasant Methodist—four miles from Louisville.

Mount Zion Baptist—7 miles from Louisville.

Prospect Baptist—10 miles west of Louisville.

Pleasant Grove Baptist — northwest three miles from Clayton.

Bethlehem—oldest Baptist church in the county—near Louisville.

White Oak Methodist between Eufaula and Clayton.

Epworth Methodist—5 miles from Eufaula.

Batesville Methodist—14 miles from Eufaula.

Rocky Mount—Clayton road.

Basom Methodist—5 miles on Clayton road.

Mount Zion near Clayton.

Old Spring Hill.

Comer.

White Oak Springs—11 miles from Eufaula.

CHURCH OF THE HOLY REDEEMER

Early in October, 1860, Right Rev. Bishop of the Catholic Diocese of Alabama arrived in Eufaula and began the formation of a society to plan for the organization and building of a Catholic Church at Eufaula, which was the first established, and is still the only Catholic Church in Barbour County.

The lands, something over three acres, was donated by Thomas St. Ledger, a communicant of the Catholic faith.

Years later, 1880-1881, his daughter, Miss Sue St. Ledger, (the family having moved to California) visited the Colby family here, then living in the Church Rectory. While here she made a generous donation to the annual budget of the church.

The church was dedicated December 1, 1861, and for several years was a mission church, and the only Catholic church in southeast Albama or Southwest Georgia for many years. The first priest to serve the church was Rev. Cornelius T. O'Callaghan.

A bell tower on the church was built in 1899 at a cost of $600 during the pastorate of Rev. Robert G. McQuillan.

On March 5th, 1919, a terrible cyclone destroyed this historic old church and work of rebuilding was under the direction of Rev. J. A. Tomerlin.

Misses Evelyn and Dorothy Sapp mailed out thousands of appeals all over the country for donations for the rebuilding fund for this church, and the response was most generous.

The new church was built on the lower end of the church lot, corner of Broad and Macon streets. The new Rectory was built adjoining the new church.

It was dedicated May 19th, 1921.

The beautiful Marble altar was donated by Mrs. Robert Cherry of Eufaula and her daughter, Mrs. John M. Little, of Baltimore.

The altar railing was donated by the family of Mr. J. E. Sapp and the Stations of the Cross were donated by special effort of Father Tomberlin and others, Mrs. W. K. Hamilton and Mrs. Walter Jones heading the list.

Mr. Richard Ryan of Montgomery, Ala., was the architect and builder and during his stay here was the guest of his warm friend, Father Tomberlin. Many of the priests who have served this church were outstanding in the world of Theology and Religion.

Both Father A. J. Ryan, "Poet Priest of the South," and Father Savage, later Monsigner, and Father Robert McQuillan were greatly beloved citizens of every denomination.

Father Ryan served the Church in 1867, but came back

many times during later years to visit the many friends he made. Father Savage also often came over from Montgomery to visit his many friends. Many of Father Ryan's most beautiful poems were written during his stay in Eufaula.

This writer knew him when a young girl, and often sat at his feet to hear him read his poems and tell, with tears streaming down his cheeks, that the poem, "Their Story Runneth Thus," was his own life's romance.

His memory is blessed in this community.

Father McQuillan was notable for his broad mindedness and genial, happy personality and was greatly beloved.

The present pastor, Rev. George Royer, is popular and his many friends hold him in highest esteem. He is an ideal Christian leader in the community and active in all the progressive efforts of the County.

The following is a list of the pastors who have served this Parish:

Rev. Cornelius T. O. Callaghan, Rev. G. G. Brown, Rev. John B. Basden, Rev. Edward G. Taylor, Rev. A. J. Ryan, Rev. Denys Savage-Monsignor, Rev. W. John Hamilton, Rev. John B. Baason, Rev. R. Fullerton, Rev. John W. Shaw, Archbishop of Louisiana; Rev. Robert G. McQuillan, Rev. D. P. Hogan, Rev. A. S. Sweeney, Rev. Cyrin Thomas, Rev. John C. McEvoy, Rev. Michael Genet, Rev. Michael Hourrican, Rev. Walter J. Tobin, Rev. J. A. Tomerlin, Rev. Philip McCormick, Rev. Bernard L. Platte, Rev. Earle LeBaron, Rev. George C. Royer.

CLAYTON CHURCHES

The following history of the M. E. Church at Clayton was written by Martha Crawford Williams, wife of Judge J. S. Williams of Clayton and daughter of the late Dr. R. B. Crawford, of the Alabama Conference, and who was greatly beloved in Barbour County, where he served churches, both as pastor and presiding Elder.

"Beyond the dates of the oldest blackened stone, in our sacred cemetery rises the ghosts of the past. Perhaps "spirits" would be a better word, for the same exalted word, for the same exalted purpose that placed the Methodist and Baptist churches of Clayton, Alabama, side by side and required that the cemetery lie between, guides the conscience of the people still.

So, whether "Spirit" or "Ghost,' we prove true to the request made when Mr. Clark gave to us the property on which both churches were to stand

Never can cooperation and sympathy be lacking, never can interest grow indifferent as long as memory lasts and gratitude abides. The tie that unites our hands over the graves of our dead, binds our hearts in holy zeal for all denominations.

Below this soil lies the bones of unmarked dead, and when, as happened recently, a new grave is dug and by chance bones and coffin handles are brought to light, every one shudders in the thought that unknowingly a desecration had been committed and, reverently, the wrong is made right.

Years and years ago there was no thought that space would be sought beyond the great gift Mr. Clark had made, and those who needed a place to bury their dead were free to make their choice.

With the growth of the "City of the Dead," there is a need that ground be carefully charted and before those in our midst who remember, answer the call, effort should be made to identify and mark all graves. Close to the Methodist church lies a black and lichened stone simply marked "Euphenmia McNeil," and the years are 1808-1878.

In the grey dawn of a morning, 1822, this little girl left her home in Richmond County, N. C., to journey with a band of Scotch immigrants to Louisville, Ala. There the Presbyterian church knew its first stronghold in this section. Later she joined the Methodist church with her "preaching' husband and became one of its most devout and consecrated members.

On through time we have followed with interest those who intermarry into other churches and on Sunday, when the pews begin to fill, we feel that the Winns, the Alstons, the Claytons, the Lees, the Crews, the Williams, the Ventresses, the Coxs, the Andrews, the Davies, the Lloyds, the Martins, the McCraes, the Jennings, the Grubbs, the Meadows, the Dents, the Pettys, the Herlongs, the Peachs, the Whites, the Robertsons, the Clarks, the Lighteners, the Fryars, the Warrens, the Stewarts and that great number of others not familiar to one who came recently into this community to join that vast "Celestial Church who hold their interest still in the earthly thought of beloved association; bow their heads in benediction and through the endless ether pray for greater unity, for more understanding love, one church for another.

The very roots of our success, of our future, of our spirituality are buried in this tradition of our elders, this tradition of our elders, this heritage of united brotherhood.

As far as I have been able to trace, in the very limited time allotted to me, I find the dominant figure of the Rev.

W. H. Ellison, typical of the finest Methodist principles, noble heir to a noble line of consecrated members. Many remember still and his descendants are among our valued citizens.

Rev. Sharer served Clayton during this early period and the time given is before 1871. In that year we discover that Rev. J. W. Glenn was in charge of the Clayton Methodist church during the time from about 1865 to 1894. Rev. Bascom Glenn was pastor and his wife, who died during this pastorate, is buried in the first section of the cemetery west of the church; succeeded by Rev. Scott Wade and was followed by the unforgettable and charming Irish minister, J. S. James. Revs. S. C. Bird, H. H. Bird, H. H. McNeill and C. B. Pilley bring this record to a close.

The following pastors are largely from memory and were furnished by R. L. Petty, Senior Steward, who for 40 years has served his church without failure, and who has been looked to, in all matters of importance, during his term of office. He has taken responsibility unflinchingly and at all times placed the church and her good above all else. He is regarded with respect by all and with veneration by those who serve with him.

From Dr. Ellison to Rev. C. B. Pilley, we cover the years about 1865 to 1900. In this latter Rev. Walter Bancroft came —followed by Rev. George Sellars in 1901.

Rev. Sellars was the builder of the present church, a frame structure, much larger than the old building which it replaced and which stood just behind the present structure. In 1904, Rev. R. H. Lewis was pastor, succeeded by Rev. R. A. Moody in 1905; Rev. S. G. Boyd in 1903, and Rev. J. P. Roberts in 1910; Rev. W. S. Street in 1911; Rev. H. M. Andrews in 1913; Rev. J. F. Feagan in 1917; Rev. B. C. Glenn in 1919; Rev. P. S. Hudson in 1921; Rev. T. J. Cross in 1922; Rev. A. L. Sellars in 1923; Rev. O. C. Lloyd in 1926; Rev. J. E. Tatein in 1928, and the magnificent logician, intellectual giant and deep student, Rev. W. P. Hurt in 1929; Rev. F. M. Atchinson in 1932 and Rev. H. M. Williamson in 1934.

With the last named we come to the period in our church history that marks the almost unbelievable, the remodeling of the church with practically no outstanding debts. Rev. Williamson, a contractor of decided talent, gave to the community his services, using skill in such a way that at the expiration of a few months the frame structure was transformed into one of brick. The steps leading to the main entrance were given by Miss Ida Robinson in loving memory of her brother, James, a former student of the Southern University at Greensboro and a devout and loyal Methodist. Near this entrance, the Margie Parish Circle has placed a cornerstone of white marble commemorating the splendid services of Rev. George Sellars and Rev. H. W. Williamson.

The entire population is conscious of a debt of gratitude for Rev. Williamson's remarkable management, skillful work and useful thought.

Mr. Clark, who gave the land for the church and cemetery, was the father of Captain Whit Clark, father of the wife of Governor Kilby.

The records of the church prior to 1900 were not procurable and information given before that date is subject to correction. The date from then on is taken from the register now in the hands of the minister in charge. Many figures prominent in Alabama Methodism have served this church. Bishop Hoss, of blessed memory, dedicated the present structure on its complettiton.

We regret that we cannot furnish a complete history of the Methodist church here, but this church is contemporary with Clayton and began to function as soon as the town was organized, one hundred years ago.

—Martha Crawford Williams.

GRACE EPISCOPAL CHURCH

General Henry D. Clayton gave the ground for the Episcopal church in Clayton, Mrs. Clayton raising the building fund.

The first trip that the Vicksburg and Brunswick Railroad made from Eufaula to Clayton, carrying passengers, the tickets were given to Mrs. Clayton and on that night a supper was given and a Bazaar held in the court house at Clayton.

Almost everybody in town gave a nice gift for the Bazaar and the proceeds from this, and the supper and the fares for the Railroad trip of the train amounted to $550.00.

The church was built, and throughout the years has been served by the same rectors that have served St. James at Eufaula.

Among the first of the distinguished divines who ministered to this parish was the late Rev. DeBerniere Waddell, D. D., who later was the greatly beloved Archdeacon of Mississippi. His wife, the late Mary Elizabeth (Bellamy) Waddell, was his helper and inspiration in all labors in both Barbour and Russell Counties.

This church, like St. Stephens Mission at Glennville, Alabama, and the "Morningside" Mission at Eufaula (served by lay members of St. James Church at Eufaula) are evidences of the influence of the Episcopal denomination in Barbour County.

Members of the Clayton family are the same force in

Grace Church today that they were in the long ago. Miss Mary Clayton, taking her mother's place in the Church, is still carrying on as she did.

Mrs. B. T. Roberts, daughter of Rev. DeBerniere Waddell, D. D., is one of the strong forces in this church.

PRESBYTERIAN CHURCH IN CLAYTON

For a number of years the Presbyterian congregation at Clayton worshipped in the Methodist Church building until through the influence and personal efforts of Dr. J. J. Winn, Mr. W. H. Thomas and others, a Presbyterian Church was built.

The record of the ministers who have served this church, as kept by the clerk of the Sessions, Mr. C. A. Morrison, have been as follows: Malcolm M. McKay, B. D. D. Greer, J. T. Bruce, P. P. Winn, E. H. Gregory, J. P. McAlpine, Malcolm McGilvary, J. S. Shaw, S. H. Rogers, J. W. Stork, Reverend Comfort, J. D. McPhail, J. Leighton Scott, J. E. Hobson.

The church is a neat, artistic building on Eufaula street, and has been the scene of many beautiful weddings of members of old distinguished families, and within its walls have been said the funeral rites of some of the most illustrious men of Alabama.

Through all the years, the Winn family and the Thomas family have been foremost and unceasing in their love for, and interest in, this church—giving it of their best always.

GOOD HOPE BAPTIST CHURCH

Founded in Barbour County—New Russell County

On July 29, 1837, Good Hope Baptist church in (then Barbour, now Russell County) was organized, and has been active ever since.

It was organized with 14 members and as the years the membership increased—but during these latter years has dropped to only a few.

The changes of the times, places and people, carrying the population of the section elsewhere.

Rev. Obediah Echols was the first pastor and Reverend Charles Brewer is the present pastor.

At the celebration of the one hundredth birthday of this church on August 8, 1937, there were present descendants of former members from Virginia, North Carolina, Georgia and even from Pennsylvania.

Some of the pastors of this church were W. E. Long, 1846, and at this meeting in August his granddaughter, Mrs. Minnie Long Flournoy and children were present. In 1847

B. M. Ware was pastor. From 1857 to 1871 J. W. P. Brown was pastor, and in 1861 J. T. Cloud was pastor.

In 1893 a great revival was held (long after it was made Russell County) and among those who united with the church were: James Thigpen, James Tolbert, J. D. Williams, Monroe Bush and many others.

C. K. Henderson was pastor in 1872 and he was notable as a writer of a book that created great interest at that time.

C. D. Benton organized churches at Oswichee, Hatchechubbee and Hyram, from some of the members of old Good Hope Church.

WHITE OAK CHAPEL

White Oak Chapel was dedicated by Rev. I. I. Laturn of the Alabama Conference on the Third Sabbath in October, 1859, and the Society was organized by Rev. I. I. Cassidy, mostly from members of the disbanded "Mount Pleasant Church." This statement was found in the old White Oak Register.

The land for the church lot and cemetery was given by Ezekiel Alexander in 1879. The oldest marked grave was that of his son, Asa Alexander, who died in 1861, just two years after the church was dedicated. Many negro slaves were buried in White Oak Cemetery, but the graves are not kept up, and there are no markers for any of the graves, the back section having been used for the negro part. According to Miss Mollie Sanders, the oldest living member in years of membership, the first person buried here was a man, murdered not far from the church.

The first building used for a church was an old log school house here long before 1859. A few years later a small church was built of undressed lumber and not ceiled. This was erected in front of the log school house.

As accurately as can be found in 1888, about fifty years ago, the community, having grown, needed a larger and better church, and the present building was erected. Mr. Mose Alexander and Mr. Seab Espy obligated themselves to furnish the lumber and it was sawed at the mill of Moses Alexander and Samuel McCarroll. The benches made at that time were hand planed. The old church building was moved to the rear of the present building. There were present Sunday at the "Home Coming celebration in 1938 several who remember playing around this old church when it was being built. The school house was later moved to the E. K. Lamar place. White Oak Church was given its name from "White Oak Creek." Among those present were members of the fifth and sixth generations, who are direct descendants of Ezekiel Alexander.

Chapter Twenty-nine

Cemeteries In Barbour County

>God's acres, where rest secure
>All who life's tasks ended
>From all pain or allure
>Are, forever and forever defended.

Nearly one hundred and fifty years old, the Cemetery at Pea River Church is of course the oldest burying ground in the County. It is kept in perfect order, cleaned and beautified every year by descendants of the old families who lie buried there. It is one of the most beautiful historic spots in the County.

The old church is still used, weekly, its members coming from all directions of the community to worship. It is directly on the Pea river, seven miles from Louisville—Presbyterian.

Then there are:

The Cemetery at Louisville.

Mount Pleasant Cemetery, 4 miles from Louisville—Methodist.

Grubbs family Cemetery, 7 miles below Louisville—Baptist.

Mount Zion Cemetery, 7 miles west of Louisville—Baptist.

Prospect Cemetery, 10 miles from Louisville—Baptist.

Pleasant Grove Cemetery—Northwest from Clayton, 3 miles—Baptist.

Pea Creek Cemetery—Baptist.

White Oak and Batesville Cemetery—Methodist.

Epworth Cemetery, five miles from Eufaula Church and Cemetery—Methodist.

Rocky Mount Cemetery—Methodist.

Palmyra Cemetery, 8 miles from Eufaula and Clayton—Presbyterian.

Bascom Cemetery, 8 miles from Eufaula on Clayton road.

Mount Zion Cemetery, Fenn neighborhood, near Clayton,

Pine Grove Cemetery, near Eufaula—Baptist.

Malone Chapel Cemetery, 4 miles from Eufaula—Methodist—Called the "White Church and Cemetery," but long ago torn away.

EUFAULA

Beautiful Fairview Cemetery is Eufaula's pride.

The first Superintendent and Sexton of the Eufaula Cemetery that the records show was John Vaughn who held the position nearly half a century. When he died Mr. C. B. Kellar was appointed and served many years.

Following him was Mr. A. J. Chambliss, whose administration was notable for the beautiful flowers he planted over the Cemetery annually for a number of years. After he died, Mr. F. W. Carrol was appointed Superintendent and is the present efficient and untiring Superintendent who gives a most excellent service to this most important city office.

When Charles S. McDowell was mayor he managed the finances of the city in such an excellent manner that he was able to purchase additional land to enlarge the Cemetery and beautify it by enclosing both, the land for additional lots and for an entrance park, which he enclosed with the iron fence obtained from the court house warerooms, where it had been placed when taken down from around Union Female College, when that institution ceased to exist.

Originally Eufaula (in pioneer days) had a public Cemetery, now known as the "Old Cemetery," but in the late forties, Masonic Lodge No. 46 F. A. A. M. purchased a plot of land over the hill from this old cemetery, each Mason purchasing a lot. Soon I. O. F. Lodge No. 3 purchased a section and the Presbyterian Church purchased the section between the Masons and Odd Fellows section. The Jewish Synagogue purchased the "Last Resting Place, adjoining the Odd Fellows section and loverlooking the high precipice next to the railroad.

During the Eighties, the Masonic Lodge purchased from Dr. A. Ogletree the beautiful site adjoining the "Old Cemetery" and overlooking the railroad. This was known as the Ogletree plot, new Masonic Cemetery.

The land purchased by the city (the plot map measured and made by Mayor McDowell) included the lands purchased from the Milton and McCormick estates, reaching from Randolph street to the original Masonic entrance line to the Cemetery.

In later years the city purchased from Captain L. Y. Dean the South annex to the Cemetery, reaching from the Whitlock Memorial Gate Entrance, to the original line of the Odd Fellows section now known as the "Dean annex." The pavillion in Cemetery Park was originally the Bandstand on Broad street, and was moved to the cemetery at the suggestion of Mrs. T. L. Moore, to be used as orator's stand, Confederate Memorial days, or other public occasions.

There are two entrances to Fairview, one on Randolph street leading into the Park with a circling driveway.

The other entrance is the imposing gateway to the Orange street entrance erected by Dr. J. B. Whitlock as a memorial to his parents, Mr. and Mrs. J. H. Whitlock, beloved citizens.

The oldest cemeteries in Eufaula are the old private burying places on the Bluff of the Shepherd family, brick enclosed, and the Wellborn family, the latter the ancestors of Col. Max B. Wellborn, former governor of the Federal Reserve Bank of Atlanta, now of Anniston, Alabama.

Not very far away, further along where the Bluff also overlooks the Chattahoochee river, is the old, historic Shorter family cemetery, where rest so many of Barbour County's illustrious dead, who were shining representatives of this distinguished pioneer family.

COLORED CEMETERY

The colored cemetery at Eufaula, "Pine Grove," on the Southeastern outskirts of the city, has been the burying grounds of the colored dead of this community for over 60 years, and for the last 40 years Sam Reynolds has been the Sexton.

SPRING HILL CEMETERY

At "Old Spring Hill" near Comer in Barbour County is one of the most historic Cemeteries, anywhere to be found.

There rests in a handsome mausoleum the bodies of members of the illustrious Comer family and nearby is the historic church where this family worshipped.

Chapter Thirty
Barbour County Politics In 1884

BEAT MEETING MAY 27TH, 1884

A few minutes after 12 o'clock, Mayor Comer called the meeting to order and called A. H. Merrill to the chair. R. B. Kolb then made a motion that J. H. G. Martin be made permanent chairman. Mr. Martin stated the object of the meeting briefly. H. D. Clayton made a motion that delegates to the County Convention be elected by ballot.

The 41 names receiving the highest number of votes to be the delegates was decided upon. These motions prevailed.

The chair appointed Messrs. E. B. Young and John O. Martin as tellers. On motion the polls were to kept open until 11:30 o'clock P. M. In the meantime the Convention took an informal recess convening again at 1:30.

A motion was made that a committee be appointed to suggest a "Beat Executive Committee." The following names were then nominated by the nominating committee and approved: R. F. Kolb, chairman, A. H. Merrill, Ambrose Wellborn, T. R. McTyer, H. C. Glenn.

Capt. Kolb offered a resolution instructing the delegates to vote as a unit. Col. Irby offered a substitute to the effect that each member vote as he pleased. The resolution and substitute, elicited a warm debate. Capt. Kolb, Colonel Irby and J. H. G. Martin took a prominent part in it.

The resolution of Captain Kolb was tabled and the substitute was dropped. This leaves each member of the delegation to vote just as it pleased him. Capt. Martin's eloquence and remarks were received with rounds of applause, but Col. Irby's elicited the "Rebel yell," from several enthusiastic members of the meeting.

Several motions, providing for alternates were voted down, which leaves the elected delegation who are present at the Convention the privilege of voting the entire strength. The Convention adjourned in the jolliest humor.

On June 17th, 1884, Capt. Kolb, member of the Democratic Executive Committee for Barbour County, had printed ten thousand copies of his minority report and had them distributed over the District. He had much faith in the document, which was the fruit of his own pen and his enthusiasm, and he hopes and believes, that it will make an impression on the people of the District. He tells us that in case Russell and Lee elect Roquemore or Williams delegates to the convention, 41 being a majority, and they decide to seat the increased delegaton from the five counties, Barbour, Russell, Lee and a part of Bullock, he will withdraw from the Convention.

The Captain says his name is O. K. before the people and he is willing to have his cause adjudged there.

Such a course will make things lively in the district and give us something to talk about during the dull summer days, if to no other purpose.
—From the Eufaula Daily Times, June, 1884.

The Nominating Question

One of the questions that came up for considerable discussion in Barbour political considerations in the year 1884 was that of "Shall We Nominate?" and from the proceedings of the different Beat meetings it showed May 27, 1884, that there would be about 36 votes giving the Beats only such strength as the Executive Committee gave them in an apportionment previously published by the Eufaula Times and News; who go to the Convention pledged to oppose nominations by that body.

The beats that send the selected delegates will be entitled to more votes than they get by apportionment mentioned.

We may conclude, however, for over it may be, and we hope is, only a fight by these disaffected—or a larger representation.

But, if it be true that they are really opposed to nominations personally, the question arises: will the convention press the objectionable feature over them? We invoke the wisdom of the Democracy in healing any breach that may occur. A compromise to every difference. Let us be united.—Times and News.

Kolb Making Good

It is gratifying to the many friends of Captain Reuben F. Kolb of Barbour to know that he is making good as Commissioner, although it is nothing more than they expected. Capt. Kolb has gone at the work, in the right spirit, and is doing all he can to help the farmer and from all reports he is doing it splendidly.

The office of Commissioner of Agriculture is a most important one as the farming interests is one of Alabama's chief assets. The Farmers' Guide says: "It goes without saying that Capt. Kolb is the farmer's friend and will at all times

be found laboring for the upbuilding of the agricultural interests of the state.
—Montgomery Journay, June 29, 1911.

The Convention met in Montgomery May 28—all factions in fighting spirits. On the first ballot Kolb led by a large majority and held it for a 33 lead; but, on the 34th, his opponents combined and Jones was nominated—Jones 269; Kolb 256. He accepted the verdict, but his friends claimed that he was cheated.

According to the Eufaula Times of June 1st, the vote stood: Kolb 23,548; Johnson 10,425; Richardson 8,856; Jones 4,523. Crook's vote was said to be about the same as that of Jones. Kolb's defeat did not weaken his prestige with the Alliance friends; they strongly believed that he had been defeated by "machine politics" and were more determined than ever to put him in high office and in November the Farmers National Congress unanimously elected Kolb their president.

Kolb-Pugh

The Alliance in the Legislature urged Kolb to enter the race against Pugh, but there were complications caused by the entry of two former governors, Seay and Watts.

"Kolb only controlled 48 votes and after several days' hard political work he and Watts withdrew in favor of Pugh —and Seay was defeated. He had supported the free coinage of silver, reduction of tariff, restoring of bank privileges and an aggressive record and he was from Kolb's own County of Barbour, made it expedient that Kolb support him when it was clear he himself could not secure Pugh's place—Montgomery Advertiser.

"The Ocala platform was a potent factor in this great quarrel in the Democratic family. In December, 1890, the Farmers' Alliance met at Ocala, Florida, and formed a Union with the Mutual Benefit Association."

The Colored Alliance and the Knights of Labor adopted a new confession of faith. It was a reversion of the St. Louis platform, the new feature being the extension of the subtreasury to cover the loans upon real estate and a more rigid, honest and just control, instead of public ownership.

The consolidated body was to be governed by a supreme council, in which each component organization was to have as many votes as it had legal voters.

The Alabama Alliance approved the Ocala platform and Kolb as Alliance candidate for Governor, was made to stand on it, though he claimed that the principles of the platform were matters to be acted upon by the National Party Convention, and that the state campaign should have nothing to do with them.

The conservative papers flouted this vote and carried the fight to Kolb on the "Ocala lunacy," the Mobile Register leading the way. It's editor, Joseph Hodgson, was probably the only journalist in the Jones ranks, who did not praise Kolb for his magnamity towards Jones after the latter's nomination.

The Ocala platform brought forth the danger of return to negro rule, since there were more negro Alliance men, than white and could vote any measure they saw fit or were co-erced into voting on. The fear of "rotten doctrines," using the negro, troubled the hearts of the old leaders, and there was warning against negro domination.

The entire Alliance program was attacked. It began to be whispered that there was Republican conspiracy to break up the the South by joining the Alliance and thought of seizing the Democratic party. They claimed the Alliance was composed of "old reconstruction soreheads and single tax cranks and greenback advocates"—all who had persistently fought the Democratic party at every step. All of this was "bunk."

"Some of the Jones papers claimed that the Alliance was controlled by a secret inner organization, known as 'Gideons'."
—Alabama History.

"The Kilbites styled themselves as the 'Simon pure Jeffersonian Democrats and their enemies as 'Machine Democrats'."—Alabama History.

On August 1st, 243,303 persons voted for Jones a majority of 11,425 more votes than Kolb. Kolb carried 8 more counties than Jones.

Kolb would not accept the official returns, claiming that he carried the state by 40,000 votes. He claimed 'dead negroes" and "faithful hounds" had been voted. His followers talked of NOT SUBMITTING. The Birmingham News said, "It was a frightfully hard fight, between brethren of the same household—let us wipe out and begin anew"—and suggested "a reorganization of the party, so as to give the Jeffersonians equal representation and a new electoral ticket acceptable to both factions.

The Jeffersonians wanted no compromise and they and the Populists fussed and put out a candidate for Congress and each district.

Oats Election—According to the returns Kolb received 32,130 votes less than in 1892. It was said the Black Belt held their returns until the white counties reported—Alabama History.

The Barbour County Kolb drama ended with its records showing that Kolb was the victim of the manipulations of election returns in the Black Belt, but when his political sun went down, the principles he and his friends championed continue to live and have even today influence in the state's politics. Whatever may be said of Kolb's motives, he represented at that time the mass of suffering humanity. He was an exponent of those new forces that began to shape the nation's life at the turn of the Century.

TO THE PEOPLE OF BARBOUR COUNTY
May 18th, 1884

In regard to the recent challenge of Mr. D. H. Bishop; having seen Mr. Swanson, Mr. Davie Alston, C. H. Comer, Dowling, R. E. Wright, the Gay brothers, W. H. Thornton, J. M. Bishop, J. A. J. Gibson, H. B. Florence, J. F. Marshall, Z. T. Weaver, A. M. Gray N. N. Vaughn, R. F. Epperson, H. J. Williamson, J. M. Alston, N. B. Coles, J. R. Stewart and others—they advised me that candidacy is not a personal fight, in which our neighbors are to be involved, but that we are seeking a nomination by the County and the preferment we seek and should be left to their desires.

Signed—B. F. Long.

This is published in this history just to show the state of political agitation in the county at this time, 1884—M. T. T.

Proceedings of agricultural meeting February 9th, 1884, at Hawkinsville by the Barbour ounty Agricultural Association with Col. H. J. Irby calling the meeting to order. Important routine work was discussed, and plans adopted for the year's work adopted. Members present were: John E. Ingram, William Jernigan, Thomas R. McTyer, J. D. Bryan, D. Thornton, M. D. Carden, S. C. Daniel, W. H. Pruitt, E. M. Searcy, J. H. G. Martin, W. A. Doughtie.

The Farmers Grange was also discussed.—H. Hawkins, Pres.; R. F. Kolb, Secy.

THE REPUBLICANS, MAY 27th, 1884

The Times and News Reporter Interviews Judge Russell

Yesterday afternoon the reporter had a talk with Judge H. C. Russell the most important Republican in this district, on the subject of county and District politics. In answer to a question, the Judge told a Times man that "he would prefer that the Democrats next Wednesday nominate candidates for county offices. He wanted, he said to whip the Democrats, while organized, or else he would like to see the Democrats wear themselves out by Conventions, which so frequently produce disorder in the ranks." Personally "he did not favor nominations by his own party but he thought it likely that nominations would be made by the Republicans in every county in the state."

We told the Judge frankly that we were talking as a newspaper man, so that he might make his utterances, as guarded as he liked."

On the subject of Congressional politics he said "he was sure that with a good live, energetic man on a political platform—and he could place his hands on a man who had the requisite, qualifications his party could carry the district over 3,000 majority."

The Judge talked as if he were much enthused over the present success of his party" while he admired Arthur and thought it proper to let well enough alone. At the same time, the nomination of Blaine would meet with his heartiest endorsement."

Blaine, he said had quite a large following in this district and he thought it possible, as candidate for Congress, on Blaine's tariff platform would win a larger majority than if some other man was placed on a ticket with Arthur as the Republican candidate.

We regard Judge Russell as the head of the party and look upon his judgment as being excathedra.

It is very plain that the Republicans propose to have a a candidate before the people for Congress next fall and, too, that the party will present the usual front.

For all that, however, the candidate which they bring out will be badly left.—Times and News.

Judge Russell June 10th, 1884

Judge Russell has been a Blaine man. He explained to us some weeks ago that 'he favored rewarding good actions and for this reason desired a vindication of Arthur, by a nomination of Arthur. He was always a half Blaine man, however, he added and would not be satisfied with his nomination. The reporter met him Saturday and the Judge was wreathed in smiles. "I am delighted with the news,' said he. The Judge was quite voluble with the latest from Chicago'.—Times and News.

COUNTY NEWS OF INTEREST

In December, 1885, Barbour County had in its bounds 12,000 slaves valued at $8,000,000.

525,000 acres of land valued at $4,000,000.

Town lots, $500,000. Total, $12,750,000.

Court house at Clayton built May, 1854, at a cost of $9,695.

Barbours Voting' Strength

Barbour's Voting strength in 1900 was viz:

Whites, 2,889; Blacks, 4,201. Registered voters, Whites, 2846; Blacks, 42.

In 1872, one David P. Lewis, a deserter from the Confederate cause and a political "turncoat," was the Republican candidate for Governor of Alabama nominated over Thomas H. Handley of Mobile. There was some discontent with Lindsay fomented by Republican promoters and Handley was unable to arouse interest in votes in the northern counties, with Democrats in control of both houses. The Republicans were in a predicament—but only one carpetbagger was elected to the House of Representatives, the first negro sent by Alabama negro farmers.

The Republican party was overthrown in 1874 and the scalawag reign in Barbour County was over.

Democrats were more harmonious and united than ever before and were determined to put Republicans out of office even if force were necessary to do so.

In 1860 in Barbour County 88,000 oxen ploughed the fields and drew wagons.

The Montgomery and Eufaula railroad received a loan from the Federal fund of $116,782.64.

In 1857 the Mobile and Girard railroad with mail pouches to Troy and Eufaula began to link up with the great roads and from 1840 to 1850 the railroad spirit was aflame. Twenty-five companies in the county were chartered.

When the dirt road from Eufaula to Clayton was changed in 1922, human skulls were unearthed, showing that bodies killed in the Indian war had been shallowly buried in that section.

Martin McNeil, a prominent citizen of Louisville, moved further westward several times to escape the Indians.

Walter Dent Wellborn, some years ago, told of Dr. Levi Thomas Wellborn of Jefferson Medical College, Philadelphia, Pa., chief surgeon under General Wellborn at Pea River having raised an Indian boy, who later went to Indian Territory (now Oklahoma) to join his ancestors. He became an Indian chief, built a town and named it Eufaula (now a principal city of Oklahoma.)

In 1826 Carson Winslett, F. W. Pugh, John D. Thomas, W. Durham Lee, Lochlan McLean, James Gorman. Mark Williams and Josiah Flournoy, built houses entirely out of logs, and it was not until 1835 that a house of planks and planed lumber was built. Mark Williams built the residence, afterwards used as a tavern, then a hospital.

General William Wellborn, 1937-1840, represented Barbour County in the Senate, commanded two hundred men fighting Indians at Pea River (last fight) with great valor.

Ezekiel Alexander bought of Jim Henry (Indian Chief) in 1934 a plantation in Dale County.

Two daughters of Judge Cochran are buried in the old cemetery (private) on Riverside Drive, on the Bluff at Eufaula.

W. Eugene Besson was born in a Fort at Fort Gaines, Ga. For many years he was druggist at Eufaula, brother of J. A. B. Besson and of Mrs. J. G. L. Martin, all from France.

W. R. Cowan, Judge of Probate of Barbour County, living at Clayton, lost an arm in the fight with Indians at Eufaula.

Jim Henry, Indian Chief, was captured by officers and jailed at Girard, Ala., and then carried to Chambers County and tried, was not convicted, and escaped and at the Creek Indian Reservation Bishop George R. Pierce accepted him as minister under the name of Rev. James McHenry. He was notorious.

Three hundred Indians in 1834 with Jim Henry as chief wanted to burn Eufaula, but General Gordon of Henry County brought a Company of Volunteers from Abbeville. Henry escaped and burned Roanoke, Alabama.

Indians assembled between Big and Little Uchee Creeks, led by Jim Henry.

Maj. Perry of Barbour County and his Rag-a-Muffin Band were popular over the county at all the political meetings.

James L. Pugh, who was the Coleague of Senator John T. Morgan from 1880 to 1897 was the man from Barbour, whose career from mail rider along Indian trails and pioneer roads, to a seat in the United States Senate, succeeding Senator Morgan was one of the greatest feats in Barbour history.

Lee A. Jennings, Captain Company D., 39th Infantry, Alabama Volunteers, offers a reward of $30 for apprension of Ely J. Strickland, aged 42, a deserter from his Company. Strickland was from Dale County.—From the Spirit of the South September 23rd, 1862.

Capt. A. S. Daggett was born in Washington, D. C., in 1835. At the time of his death he was said to be the oldest Army officer Veteran of the War Between the States. He was in command of Company U, Soldiers, stationed in Barbour County at the time of the Reconstruction troubles of 1874.

Brigadier General A. S. Daggett owes his office of Brigadier General to Dr. Zadoc Daniel, a Barbour County boy, in the sixties.

Capt. Daggett contemplated quitting the service. "You are a born soldier, stand by the Army and you'll come out as a Brigadier General," he said to the young captain one day. The prediction came true.

THE INJUNCTION, JUNE 17, 1884

Kolb makes minority report to the recommendation of the Executive Committee.

To the Democratic voters of 3rd Congressional District of Alabama which includes Barbour County.

A meeting of the Executive Committee of the Democratic party of the 3rd Congressional District was held at Montgomery on the 5th for the purpose of arranging a Convention of the Democratic party of the District, to nominate a candidate for representative in the 49th Congress.

It was the duty of this committee to fix time and place for holding this Convention and recommended a basis of representation upon which the vote in that Convention should be primarily fixed. That committee was: General A. C. Gordon, Henry; W. E. Mauldin, Dale; J. J. Hammond, Coffee; A. H. Laney, Geneva; J. W. Wright, Russell; John A. Kilpatrick, Lee; R. F. Kolb, Barbour.

Every member was present August 27th and Union Springs was chosen as a place for holding the Convention. To this action of the Committee I offer no objection, but I do object to the vote allowed the various Counties in the District and earnestly protest against the action of the Committee in that respect The Counties were allowed votes as follows: Barbour 16; Lee 3; Russell 9; Bulloch 13; Henry 11; Dale 8; Coffee 6; Geneva 4. In all there were 80 votes.

Since 1870 the State Executive Committee has always adopted the last gubernatorial vote, as is the basis of representation in the state and Congressional Conventions and precinct, sub divisions have always followed in their lead and fixed the same vote as a basis. A change has been attempted in some instances, but never with satisfaction or without injustice.

In this District, in 1872, the vote was based on the vote for Governor in 1870. In 1874 it was based on the vote of 1872; in 1876 on the vote for Governor in 1874. In 1870 the Executive Committee, in making the call for the Convention reduced the vote of Bullock County on complaint of the Southern Counties of the District, but the Convention upon assembling restored Bullock's vote to 15—the number it was entitled to—on its vote for Governor and this Convention of 1878 at the instance, it is said, of the County of Henry recommended that the vote of the Congressional Convention of 1880 be based upon the vote for Governor in 1878. This vote had already been taken and in 1880 the Congressional Convention was so held.

In 1882, the Elba Convention was held upon the vote for Governor in 1880 as a basis of representation.

Since the organization of the District in 1875, the vote of Counties stood in the Convention as follows: In 1878, Barbour, 15; Dale, 7; Henry, 8; Russell, 10; Total 72, of which Lee, Barbour and Russell had 55.

It will be seen that the gubernatorial vote has always been the basis of representation. The rule is long and well established and it can be easily understood that when there is a departure from this settled rule the door for intrigue and manipulation is opened and partnership is invited to enter. Once departure from the rule and suspicion is aroused and perhaps justified of some particular favorite.

In the case in hand it will certainly require explanation to understand why the votes of Henry, Dale and Coffee were placed on the basis of the vote of 1882 for Congressman and thus increased from 18 to 29, and why the vote for Governor in 1880 or solely on the claim that there were Democratic votes enough in the County to justify it and was thus increased from 5 to 13 and why the vote in Barbour County polling 3,183 votes in 1880 (both in the same year, Bullock cast its vote on which it was allowed 13 delegates) should not have had their vote increased at all.

When the matter was under consideration, I moved the committee to have representation of counties on the Governor's vote, to have the representation of the counties on the Governor's vote in 1882, in accordance with the established rule and following the convention, then in session, in this particular, as it had just taken this action, but the motion failed. Then that the vote be based on the Gubernatorial vote of 1884, which is yet to be taken and which, of course, none of us could know, and this motion was lost. Then that each county be allowed the highest vote it ever cast, and this was rejected. And then, in the earnest desire to agree with the other members of the Commttee upon a plan that I might recommend the party, I went to the extent of offering to concede the large increase in the vote of the Counties of Henry, Dale, Coffee, Geneva, Bullock, if the County of Barbour, Lee or Bullock, or all of them together, were conceded an increase of 4 votes, but by a vote of 5 to 3 this proposition was also rejected and the committee then increased the votes of Henry, Dale, Geneva, Coffee and Bullock 19 votes, so as to give them a majority vote in the Convention, upon organization, and RIGHT HERE I want the Democratic voters of Russell County to know that the member of the Executive Committee from Russell, Hon. J. W. Wright, voted against each and all of my motions and thus refusing his own county an increase of representation—while voting such increase to the others.

The members from Bullock and Lee, Messers McCall and Kirkpatrick, seeing the justice of my demands, voted with me on all my motions.

There was a departure from all precedent, in fixing this basis of representation, and the action of the committee in determining the vote each county should cast, on organization, is purely arbitrary and places the Convention absolutely under the control of the friends of a particular candidate for Congress. If this result had come from an adherence to the rules that have heretofore governed the action of Executive Committees, no one could complain, but when in conflict with all precedent and by raising the vote of some counties and refusing to raise others who had the same claim for an increase of its vote it cannot be expected to give satisfaction.

It is well known that five counties whose votes were so largely increased are all supporting one of the candidates for Congress, and to these five Counties the absolute control of the Convention has been given, regardless of how the Counties may vote.

These five Counties possessing, as they do, a majority of one on the Convention by a vote of this Committee can vote to keep their favor in the Convention and nominate their favorite by a majority vote, as the address of that of the Committee indicates may be done.

It simply amounts to this Executive Committee of eight men, forming themselves into a Congressional Convention, nominating a candidate for congress. If such practice as this is tolerated by the party, it is easy to see how an incumbent of office may perpetuate himself in office, indefinitely by arranging the executive committee in his interest. The inevitable result of a departure from well established rules is to excite distrust and give real and fancied cause of complaint, destroying confidence in the party management and in the fairness of party associates.

Barbour County sat in the Convention of 1880 with 26 votes while Bullock had 13. Since then neither County has cast votes on any election, to entitle it to a higher vote, yet the majority of this Committee go back to the Governor's election of 1880 to find a basis for Bullock's vote of 13, refuses to do the same for Lee, Russell and Barbour. These causes will lead to consequences in every way undesirable for reasons pressed.

I withheld my name from the call of the Committee and while I endorse the call of the Convention and the time and place, for holding it, I could not, by placing my name to the paper under protest, give even that sort of an implied assent to the injustice done Barbour, Lee, and Russell Counties in fixing these votes. I endorse the call for a Convention at Union Springs on the 27th day of August, 1884, and recommend that each County be allowed, on organization, one vote for every two hundred Democratic votes cast for Governor in 1882 and one additional vote for every fraction of such a vote over one hundred, giving Counties the following representation: Barbour, 16; Bullock, 5; Coffee, 5; Dale, 5; Geneva, 3; Henry, 5; Lee, 13; Russell, 9.

R. F. KOLB, Member Executive Committee 3rd Congressional District of Alabama, Eufaula, June 10, 1884.

Chapter Thirty-one
Disasters In Barbour County

For long years, it was an often referred to fact that Barbour County had been most fortunate in being free from disasters.

There had never been any epidemics or great storms or terrible accidents on record, until in 1882 a gale blowing from the Gulf was reported from Pensacola. It was Saturday, the 9th of September, 1882, and the wire received stated that it was the worst ever known and would possibly reach Eufaula and this section by nightfall.

It had been drizzling rain all day and by 8 p. m. the wind reached gale proportions. It was a hurricane that lasted throughout the night and when day dawned hundreds of trees were uprooted houses unroofed, others blown down. At nine o'clock two citizens closed their places of business in the downtown section and started to their homes on Sanford street and College Hill. It was blowing and raining, and so dark (no electric lights then) and all the kerosene street lamps put out. The streets were a network of fallen trees and debris, that impeded their progress and these men did not reach Sanford street until twelve o'clock, drenched and exhausted.

They stopped at the Sanford street residence, but the College Hill resident insisted on getting to his family and went on, stopped at the Kendall home, got a fresh lantern and dry coat, and reached his home, just beyond the College, after two o'clock, almost fainting upon arrival.

The next day his hat which had his name on the inside band was picked up on the bluff, three fourths of a mile away, There were no lives lost, but thousands of dollars worth of damage to homes.

Barbour County's next disaster was two years later, when on the 15th day of September, 1884, the Compress, owned by the Compress Companies of the Central of Georgia Railway Company and which had only been completed 15 days and was just beginning operation that day, was blown up at three o'clock in the afternoon and the burning cotton and other burning fragments that flew more than a half mile in the blast set fire to a dozen other places in the city of Eufaula.

The engineer was hurt and the negro fireman, John Wimbush, was killed. The manager, Mike Pickett, a young man from Georgia, was instantly killed. Mr. William Holleman, one of the members of the office force, was seriously hurt, both his ears being burned almost off.

It was a time of panic. A hard wind was blowing, and carried the flames nearly a mile. The fire department was rushing for hours to check small fires all over the business section of the city.

The Compress was rebuilt immediately, and the first Superintendent it ever had, Mr. Dan Mabry, is still holding his position with the present owners. The railroad sold this Compress to a Syndicate of Compresses and then in 1899 Dean and Moore, warehousemen of Eufaula, bought it and their estates are the present owners. Mr. Mabry is still holding forth, despite his advancing age, while Mr. T. L. Moore's son, Lewis M. Moore, is the manager.

Mr. W. W. Robinson and E. A. Hudson, deceased, were associated with the Compress for many years. Mr. C. C. Hanson was manager for a long time.

Many laborers at the Compress were slightly hurt.

Wreck of Central of Georgia Train

The next great disaster was the Wreck of the Central of Georgia passenger train on the E. and O. railroad five miles from Eufaula on the morning of October 13th, 1913.

The train was loaded with several hundred passengers from the lower part of the County, all coming to Eufaula to attend the State Fair, holding that wek.

A split rail was deemed the cause of the cars leaving the track and being dumped down an embankment.

About 550 were badly hurt, many seriously.

Among the killed were a Mr. Peak and a Mr. McRae.

But the most terrible of all was the Cyclone that struck the County on March 5th, 1919. It lasted only a few minutes, but left death and ruin in its path, which crossed Barbour County

It came from the Southwest, dipping here and there, and carried with it as it flew along destruction most terrible. Thousands of trees were uprooted and broken off, houses blown down and unroofed and the rain pouring in. It took part of the roof off the St. Julain Hotel, Ross Hardware Company, blew the top stories off the Beringer Brothers and Schloss Clothing stores, the brick and mortar falling on the Whitlock and McRae stores and burying beneath the great piles of masonry the bodies of Rev. W. P. Dickinson, pastor of the First Methodist Church; Dr. J. L. Adams, whose office was in the McRae store; and Mr. E. J. Seacy, who with

Dr. Dickinson, was in the office with Dr Adams conferring together on some Church matters

The fourth victim was Mr. S. F. Lawton, a traveling salesman who was standing in the door of Whitlock's store when the storm struck it. He lived in a Western city, and his remains were shipped to his family the night after the cyclone. Dr. J. B. Whitlock, Mr. Geo. W. Whitlock and Mr. J. C. McRae and Miss Alice Wells, of the McRae store, were four who were badly injured, the injuries received by Mr. McRae finally causing his death some time after the cyclone.

But for the thoughtfulness of Mr. H. B. Dowling, who, when he saw the electric wires all over the streets and rushed to the plant on Union street, and had the current cut off, there would have been many deaths of electrocution, for it was impossible to walk the streets without getting entangled in wires among the debris on the streets.

Hundreds of men worked all night, extricating the bodies of the men entombed in the capitulated stores. The last was brought out at dawn, and all were found in the cellars where the falling timbers had crushed ceiling and floors to the bottom of cellars.

A triple funeral was held for Messers Dickinson, Adams and Searcy in the First Methodist church and the whole County was in deepest gloom.

The city of Eufaula did not recover from the financial loss by destruction for years.

Even tombs in the cemetery were broken off and century old trees unrooted.

Cyclone at Clayton 1884

On March 25th, 1884, a cyclone passed through the northwest portion of Clayton, going towards Eufaula. The dwelling of Mr. John Buford was damaged severely. The Jones home occuppied by John H. Blair, residence of Bob Stevens and fences, stables, barns and outhouses were destroyed.

Negro cabins were demolished and one negro killed.

Tax Collector Nix and Col. McKay told of the great storm and of A. W. Windman being badly hurt.

In the R. E. Brown settlement, Derrill Blair's near White Oak, Johnathon Thornton, seven miles from Eufaula, R. E. Sanders at Cochran station (now Lugo), Tom Reeves, S. W. Smartt lost houses near Clayton. The tornado was half a mile wide and left destruction in its wake.

FIRES

The year 1884 is a memorable one to the citizenship of Barbour County, and among the many unusual happenings was the destructive fire that swept through the lower part of the County April 8th of that year. Capt. A. A. Walker, who was visiting on the lower edge of the County last Wednesday, states that was the day of the high wind and destructive fire that swept through lower Barbour and upper Henry Counties.

It is unknown how the woods caught fire but it is estimated that 200,000 rails were destroyed and thousands of feet of fine timber, besides the loss of homes. The sufferers in Henry County were W. H. Dinsey, James W. Roberts, on the County line, and B. J. Lindsey.

In Barbour, in the vicinity of "Sandy Bottom" are M. Chestnut, James Vincent, Ab White, John Vincent, William Floyd, James Baker, William Richards, besides homes, lost 400 rails. Hector Daniels, A. Walsh and Tom McIlvane lost everything on and around their farms, John D. Glass and Mrs. McCarroll's losses were slight and Sam MacCarroll, near White Oak, lost 5000 rails.

The wind was so strong that farmers were unable to stand up before it and had to take their mules out and stop, ploughing in the places where there was no fire. In this section, consequently all farm work is coming on poorly and delayed.

April 15th, 1884

The County Commissioners' work last week was devoted to revising the tax collector's list of errors and insolvent taxes, which amounted to $3,484. The treasurer's report of General Fund Railroad Tax and chain gang and were found to be in excellent order. Appropriations of $700 and $500 were made for Clayton and Eufaula courthouses, respectively, and an order was passed for a County bridge inspector.

DR. A. P. BROWN'S DEATH TERRIBLE TRAGEDY

The most terrible accident that ever happened in Barbour County was the tragic death of Dr. A. P. Brown, one of the County's leading and best loved citizens, which brought deep and lasting sorrow to the entire community.

He was born of distinguished ancestry, the son of the late Dr. and Mrs. Pugh H. Brown of Troy, Alabama, where he grew up to splendid manhood and soon after graduating from Dental College with high honors he came to Eufaula, buying out the dental business of Dr. S. G. Robertson, after being associated with that popular dentist for some time.

For twenty-five or more years he rapidly rose professionally until he reached the highest pinnacle. On the afternoon of January 18th, 1927, while serving, he stepped into his laboratory to heat some instrument or device needed, and before he touched the gasoline or gas blow lamp, which had only a few minutes before been lighted, it suddenly exploded and he was so terribly burned all over his body that he died in a few hours in great agony. The patient in the chair, a lady, rushed to his aid, and she, too, was painfully, but not seriously burned.

The entire community was bowed in grief over such a terrible accident taking away the life of such a beloved and useful citizen. He was not only outstanding professionally, but as a man who was valuable in every walk of life—a man of singularly, cultured, artistic tastes and high ideals.

Snatched away, in the very zenith of splendid and successful manhood, it has been hard for his friends, to understand the working of Providence that made it so.

He left his widow (Katie McDowell) and their lovely daughter, Margaret Jean, and his son, Dr. Charles McDowell Brown, who has already reached high and achieved in the practice of medicine as his distinguished father did in the practice of denistry.

THE TERRIBLE TOLL

Of the Cyclone in Barbour County March 5TH, 1919

It was to the First Methodist Church at Eufaula that great throngs, came from all over the County and nearby towns to attend the triple funerals and pay loving tribute to Dr. W. P. Dickinson, the pastor; Dr. J. L. Adams, Sunday School teacher, illustrator and lecturer; and Edward J. Searcy, treasurer, choir singer and cornet player, three of the death toll of the terrible cyclone of Wednesday afternoon.

About the chancel and altar were arranged hundreds of beautiful floral offerings and background for the three grey caskets, literally covered wtih rare flowers of love and friendship.

The vast congregation rose to its feet as the bodies of these beloved and useful men were borne into the church. Dr. Dickinson's body was escorted by the stewards of his church, Dr. Adams' by his Bible class, and Mr. Searcy's by brother Mason members of Harmony Lodge No. 46 F. A. A. M. and the Board of Directors of the Bank of Eufaula.

Dr. A. J. Lamar of Nashville, a very close friend of Dr. Dickinson, gave a beautiful Eulogy on his life.

Dr. A. C. Cornell, presiding elder of the Eufaula District, paid a beautiful tribute to Dr. Adams and Mr. Searcy. Every word spoken by these ministers found response in the hearts of hundreds of listening friends.

On every face was visible the sorrow in the hearts for the loss of these three men to the community.

Visiting ministers were: A. E. Dannelly and H. M. Holt, Montgomery; Dr. A. J. Lamar, Nashville, Tenn.; J. E. Truett, Fitzpatrick; Charles Motley, Louisville; J. F. Feagin, Clayton; L. B. Green, Augusta, Georgia; J. D. McPhail, C. A. Cornell, W. E. Middlebrooks, W. H. Tew, and father Tobin, local pastors.

The body of Dr. Dickinson was carried on the afternoon train to Prattville, Ala., for interment. The bodies of Dr. Adams and Mr. Searcy were interred in the family lots in Fairview cemetery, Harmony Lodge conducting the Masonic burial service at the grave of Mr. Searcy.

Dr. W. P. Dickinson

When the light of heart and home goes out, with the life of the best loved and all is darkness, to our wondering why it all is, there is but one answer—Purpose and Fulfillment. The taking from earth of a man like Dr. Dickinson and in such a tragic manner, surely verifies the fitness of the answer in its every phase.

All his life had been spent in service and when the sudden call came it found him doing his Master's work, in a church business meeting.

Eufaula loved and honored him for his ability as a preacher, his worth as a man and his loveable nature as a friend. When he first came to Eufaula 25 years ago as pastor, in the zenith of life, a brilliant, consecrated man of God, he won the special admiration and love of all He served as pastor of the First Methodist Church two years and when he was sent back, nearly four years ago, there was universal rejoicing over his coming and he has labored as arduously and as successfully for the interest of his charge these later years as he did when a younger man.

He was one of the brightest lights in Southern Methodism and honored and loved in the highest degree. Eufault was proud of him and the church he served so faithfully and loved so much is bowed in sorrow over his death, which it will be hard to lift.

To his heartbroken wife and children a great flood of sympathy goes out.

After the funeral, the body was carried on the 5 p. m. train to Montgomery where it lay in state at the Court Street Methodist Church of which he was for several years the beloved pastor, and Saturday morning was carried to Prattville and interred beside his son, who was killed in Birmingham about 15 years ago.

Dr. John L. Adams

That God moves in a mysterious way, "His lesson to teach, as well as His wonders to perform," and in the teaching always uses an instrument true and tried is strongly illustrated in the death of Dr. John L. Adams—the quiet, dignified, esteemed and loved citizen.

He has spent his life in Eufaula—always weighing the right and wrong of any question in his daily life. He was strong in his convictions, following the straight line of strict integrity and Christian practices that made him conspicious.

He was one of the strongest forces in the First Methodist Sunday School, teacher of one of the largest and most interesting Bible classes in the state—and his blackboard illustrations with lectures on the S. S. lesson weekly were features of the S. S. work.

Such men as Dr. Adams are a city's greatest asset and his taking away brings sorrow, deep and sincere.

He was the son of the late J. L. Adams, an honored pioneer citizen. Besides his stricken wife and one son, John Ball Adams, he leaves two sisters, Mrs. Cora Proctor and Mrs. M. E. Jones, and to them Eufaula's tenderest sympathy goes out in their terrible grief and loss.

Edward J. Searcy

Despite the din and roar of any earthly storm there is always to be heard if the ear listens for it, the far off echo of Heavens music—and Wednesday afternoon when the tornado raged and genial, big souled Ed Searcy was hemmed in under brick and mortar, he caught the echo.

Perhaps it was an echo of his own sweet bugle notes—and as his life went out this echo swelled into the eternal song of the redeemed.

No more will be heard the melody of his cornet in the church and Sunday School, where for long years he has given his talent and his personal service in every line of church work.

In every interest of the city, civic, social, progressive and philanthropic, no citizen was more helpful, more patriotic, or more beloved.

A fine business man, a warm, generous friend, and most

delightful companion, his loss to the city and community is a distinct one.

He was buried in Fairview beside his wife, who was the former Miss Annie Simmons and who died a number of years ago.

Good and true and loved is a fitting epitaph to mark his resting place.

S. F. LAWTON

S. F. Lawton was a traveling man who chanced to be standing in the front door of the store of J. C. McRae, when the cyclone struck and when the top story of the Lampley building topped over, falling on the McRae store, crushing it down into the cellar his body was buried in the debris. It was recovered, prepared for burial and sent on the next night train to his far away home town.

When the last trumpet shall sound and the dead shall be called to come forth, the recording angel will not refer to the records to see whether S. F. Lawton was a Eufaulian, or simply one of His chosen people.

God knows not time, season or location. A day is as a thousand years and Eufaula is only a part of His Kingdom, and it so happened that one of His creatures, made in His own likeness, though living in far off New Bedford, was by some ruling of His Providence in this part of His vineyard when He called him.

Eufaula, though knowing him only slightly, mourned him as one of their own race, far from home, testified to both by the flowers which covered his casket and the tears which were silently falling though feelingly shed by many of her people.

Our sympathy goes to his people, wherever they may be, and we would have them know that though he died "a stranger in a strange land," he died among a people, whose love for humanity is as strong and as lasting as time itself, and who, when they meet him and grasp his hand on the other shore, will recognize him as one of those from Eufaula "for whom Christ Died."

—By M. T. T. from the Eufaula Daily Citizen of March 8, 1919

Miss Sarah King Burned to Death

In the long ago there came to Barbour County a wealthy, cultured lady, Mrs. King, who was a member of the Vandyke family of New York, a granddaughter of the famous old Commodore Van Dyke. With her were her two sons, Joseph and William, and a daughter, Miss Sarah King.

The vicisitudes of the years, depleted the family finances, and the son, Joseph, who had married a French woman, moved to Eufaula where he opened a photographer's studio, remaining for several years, going later to Columbus, Georgia, where he later died. William married Miss Portia Petty, member of the prominent Petty family of Clayton. After Mrs .King died and was buried at Clayton, the fine old home was sold and Miss Sarah came to Eufaula, where for some time she taught a small school, sponsored by ladies of the First Baptist Church and doing fine needle work. The brother, William, and family moved to Troy, Ala., and he and his wife both died at Dothan, Ala., some years ago.

Miss Sarah King was a unique character, tall and queenly, always dressed with exquisite taste, and her every word and movement revealed her culture and the aristocracy from which she was descended.

She was a devout member of the Presbyterian Church, and because of her strict idea of the conventions, was called peculiar. She lived alone near the Presbyterian church, and when her means of support were exhausted and her eyesight failed, she was cared for by the women of the Presbyterian Church. A servant daily looked after her meals, and the church women and neighbors dropped in daily to see after her.

She was 91 years old and had been confined to her bed two or three days, when one day the servant had only left her about a half hour before, when a passerby heard a scream, rushed in and found her standing between the bed and the fire covered with flames. She was rushed to the porch and the fire extinguished, but her clothing was burned entirely off her, and she died in a few minutes in great agony. It was supposed she got out of bed and a spark of fire from the grate set her clothing on fire.

Her terrible fate shocked the community. To the manor born, reared in luxury, a woman of brilliant literary traits, great travel and having been a social queen in her young lady days to come to such an unhappy end was a happening that I hesitate to relate, and am only doing so to make good my assertion that "I am putting into this history EVERY fact, the bad as well as the good."

Joe Sturges BlackSmith Shop Burns and James Barefield and Daughter Burn to Death

For over 75 years Joe Sturges' blacksmith shop on Randolph street near the First Baptist Church was one of the old landmarks of pioneer days, when, about ten years ago, it had been turned into a plumber's shop and the upper story was used as a residence, having been made into apartments after the blacksmith shop had been removed. There was a large wide veranda, that reached over the sidewalk and back of the plumber shop was a warehouse, where much cotton was stored.

Mr. James Barefield and his daughter, Annie, occupied the apartment that faced the street, but the stairway to the apartment was reached by a stair that went up to the front veranda.

One cold winter night, an alarm of fire was sounded and before entrance could be made into the building, Mr. Barefield and daughter, who were awakened by the alarm from outside, were burned to death. He was about 50 years of age and she was 24.

Their double funeral was held at St. James Church next day and the county records again were marked with tragedy of FIRE. The fire was supposed to be of incendiary origin, but there was never proof of that found to establish a fact.

The building was brick and one of the first built in the city.

Chapter Thirty-two
Unique Features In Barbour County

BARBOUR COUNTY'S TALKING JAY BIRD

During the late seventies and early eighties, there lived at Eufaula, Alabama, a Frenchman, Professor Frederick Tufferd, of Daubs, France, who came to America, a refugee from the French Commune. He was a scientist, a naturalist, a socialist (but not an Anarchist in its political terms), was an educator and a man of great ability and perfect culture.

For a term of years he was teacher in Union Female College at Eufaula and in after years, when a private tutor at Eufaula, devoting much time to the collection of rare flowers, plants and butterflies containing many hundred varieties, he hatched and raised a blue jay bird, teaching it to talk more distinctly than any parrot the writer ever heard talk.

He named it "Petite" and the bird called its master 'Cherie."

I have often recited a lesson in French and Greek to Prof. Tufferd, with the bird sitting on his shoulder, listening intently to every word uttered, frequently interrupting to say "Hurry Mattie." This bird was the wonder of the community and all the old residents of that time remember Prof. Tufferd and his pet. He taught it to repeat after him a verse of the French National song "La Marsailliase" and the bird often whistled the tune with perfect accuracy.

Prof. J. C. Van Houten, a blind teacher of music in the same college with Prof. Tufferd, was Prof. Tufferd's warm friend. It was to Prof. Van Houten's playing of the violin that the bird learned to whistle ' La Marsailliase."

On a mid-summer afternoon of 1886, when Prof. Tufferd was in the woods catching butterflies, a storm came up and when he returned "Petite" was dead in his cage on the porch where he had been left.

The grief of his master was pitiful, as was that of young William N. Reeves, Jr., who had helped care for the bird.

Prof. Tufferd pulled out the tail and wing feathers and put them away in a tin box that he chemically prepared for their preservation. The little body he buried in another tin box.

This talking bird could answer any simple question asked if his master was present, and at times, to passers by, would call out "fine day" and would drop its head when he was repeating the song.

When asked, "Petite" wants a cracker?" he ruffled his wings and said ' No." He was fed on carefully selected worms, the yolks of hard boiled eggs, and boiled grits, rice and certain worms and bugs that the Prof. gathered for him off plants in the woods.

One of Prof. Tufferd's pupils was a young German, studying for the ministry, and he being more fond of birds than others of the class, the writer included—took up much time with Petite and at his suggestion Prof. Tufferd taught the bird to bow its head and say "Give Us This Day Our Daily Bread," withholding his meal until he said the sentence.

In 1888 Prof. Tufferd went back to France and in one of his letters later in 1891 said: "I am living in a rose garden in Daubs, writing my book on "Political Economy in the South" in U. S., and have my birds and butterflies few in number now, but I still grieve for "Petite" and think affectionately of my dear friends in Eufaula, where I found birds, flowers and all nature as glorious as it is in my France.

From this little keen-eyed, but big brained man, the writer learned that a jay bird always poisons its offspring, if it can get to them when they are separated from the old birds and caged—also that the jay bird abhors a mocking bird.

During the time that Prof. Tufferd brought his "Petite" to the Thomas home daily, the writer and sister had canaries in separate cages, one a real canary, bought off ship at Charleston, S. C., and the other a "Linnet" bought from a street urchin in Eufaula, who claimed that he picked it up on the street. Prof. Tufferd would stand beside their cages, hung inside the house in a sunny window, and tell ' Petite" to whistle the Marsiallaise and the "Linnet" would begin singing its own notes, but the canary would not chirp.

BARBOUR COUNTY'S "ENOCH ARDEN" STORY

Thirty years ago a stranger, a man about 26 or 28 years of age, rented the residence known as the "Tansey Place," corner of Broad and Livingston streets, less than fifty yards from the Central of Georgia railroad depot in Eufaula. The house had been vacant for some time and was rented to this party for one month only, at a very generous price.

The neighbors saw a hundred amount of furniture carried in and in a few days a beautiful young woman and an old negro servant were seen about the place daily.

Neighbors called, but always an excuse was given, and the girl never received but one visitor, to whom she said,

"My husband is traveling near here and I am here for just a few weeks.

Dr. W. P. Copeland, one of Eufaula's leading physicians, was called to attend her soon after her arrival, and in about three weeks, she gave birth to a little boy. She had every attention and luxury furnished her. Two weeks later, one morning neighbors saw the furniture being hauled back to the furniture store, from which it had been rented and the old negro woman and the girl had disappeared during the night before.

That same morning when old Mr. King, living three from the city, opened his front door, he found a baby boy two or three weeks old and in the basket holding the little waif, a bountiful supply of nice clothes, with a note which asked that "You find a home and a mother for this babe."

Mrs. King adopted the child and named it Jimmie King, but before he was four years old Mrs. King died and her son-in-law and daughter, Mr. and Mrs. R. S. Wasden took him as their own son and reared him.

Today he lives on the same farm with his foster parents, but in the King house. left to him by Mrs. King. He is married and has two children.

He is an industrious young man who has been heard to say often, "I would love to know who my real mother was."

He has been told about the circumstances of his birth and is hoping that some day fate will bring them together. That hope has recently been strengthened by the following fact: A letter was received in Eufaula, mailed at Baltimore, Md., which read, "about 25 years ago a child was born in Eufaula, Barbour County, Alabama, and when about one month old was left on the doorsteps of a farmer near Eufaula. One of this child's parents is anxious to get information concerning this child if it is still living. Write to S. L. C., General Delivery, Baltimore, Md."

This letter was answered by a Eufaula citizen, and the story of the birth of the child, Jimmie King, and his adoption fully given, but nothing further has ever been heard from that letter.

Jimmie King, his wife, and Mr. Wasden are still farming and daily peddle their products in Eufaula, although Mr. Wasden is quite feeble.

But the feature of this story is most unusual, romantic and pathetic, and makes the Wasden farm, near Eufaula, a place of special interest.

For many years, Mr. Wasden, an industrious, esteemed citizen, was manager of the large plantation of Mr. C. A. Locke, located near Barbour Creek in Barbour County.

About 20 years ago, he moved to his own farm near Flagville, a suburb of Eufaula.

Before adopting Jimmie King, Mr. and Mrs. Wasden had adopted another little boy whom they named Richard Wasden, getting him from an Orphan's home, and the two boys grew up together. Richard is now also married and is an employe of the Cowikee Mills.

Mr. and Mrs. Wasden's truck farm was the largest source of vegetables and poultry supply in the community for years, until the chain grocery stores in Eufaula practically killed the trucking business, and the stress of the times and ill health carried Mr. Wasden to Florida for two years.

During this time Mrs. Wasden and the two boys were having a hard time keeping the farm going when there comes along a Mr. Paul Harris from Georgia seeking work at some lumber mills. His search for work brought him by the Wasden place. Mrs. Wasden hired him and in a few months, on the grounds of "desertion" she secured a divorce and married Harris. They had been married nearly two years when Wasden returned, broken in health and at first crushed to find what his wife had done.

The farm belongs to Wasden, but he did not think that turning Harris out, after having been married and lived two years with his former wife, was wise, so he assumed control of his farm again and hired Harris to work.

The former husband and wife had a serious talk over it all and succeeded in adjusting themselves to the situation.

More than 7 years have passed since Wasden's return and they are all living together peaceably, if not happily.

Mr. Wasden says Mr. Harris is a good worker; "I realize I am old and giving out." (When he returned from Florida he was 64 and Harris 42.)

"My former wife is kind to me and considerate of me. I sit at the head of the table as I always did, and there is no difference, only I am no longer the husband, but I am succeeding in being the friend, even though it is kinder hard sometimes. When I am not able to get about Jimmie and his wife do for me and from them and their babies I get happiness.

"I accepted the situation, because I did go off and leave them and sickness kept me, so I see no sense in making a row about her marrying again."

Jimmie told the writer today (Feb. 2nd, 1937), who has been one of the Warsden customers for years, that it was "hard for him to understand how it was possible, but that it was a fact that their family life, since "Dad" Warsden had returned has been without jars at any unpleasantness."

More than 7 years now have passed. While Mr. Warsden lives in his own house with Mr. and Mrs. Harris, he pays Harris regular wages for his work and the Harris' furnish his board, as a part of the contract. Mr. Wasden, while feeble, comes to town every few days, peddling his fruit, vegetables and poultry, Jimmie driving the wagon.

Harris does the farm work, with what help Wasden and Jimmie give him and the extra hired help when needed.

COCHRAN ANECDOTE

Small things sometimes operate heavily against a man in a political campaign said the Macon Telegraph many years ago.

An incident related below recalls a couple of political anecdotes:

Before the war, John Cochran of Eufaula, Barbour County, was a very prominent man, a profound lawyer, a wonderful conversationalist, and one of the brainiest men in the state. He was a secessionist and took the stump in the preliminary campaign.

One day a young countryman from the lower portion of Barbour County strolled into a store in Eufaula. After the salutations of the day, the merchant inquired of him the news of his neighborhood. He replied that the only item of interest that he could recall was that John Cochran was gwine over to Charleston to help South Carolina rebel agin Ameriky."

—Eufaula Times, Feb. 12th, 1904.

It was John Cochran, of Barbour County, who stated to the House that the "banks had proved themselves financial volcanoes, sweeping prosperity from the land and desolating it of virtue itself," and although there was sentiment favoring the abolition of the state banking system, there was danger of the Whigs, meanacing the Democratic party and the Governor deemed it wise to urge caution. The bad debt figure was so large that Governor Fitzhugh's reform idea was blocked by the majority of Whigs over Democrats.

THE FAMOUS "LANE CAKE" A PRODUCT OF BARBOUR COUNTY

The "Lane Cake" so often acclaimed the most popular and delicious of all layer cakes, is distinctively a Barbour County production.

The recipe by which it is correctly made, is one of the original Southern recipes in the splendid cook book of Mrs. Emma Rylander Lane, wife of Dave T. Lane, who was local agent fo rthe Central of Georgia Railroad Company at Clayton, Barbour County, Alabama, over forty years ago.

Mrs. Lane was an expert in fine cooking, and devoted much time, thought and labor to the making of a collection of recipes of her own and other ladies of Clayton into a book that bears her name. She proved the par excellence of these by personal application of them.

During a state fair held at Columbus, Georgia, in the eighties, Mrs. Lane won the prize for the best cake, which was named for her, not as she stated, by any conceit of her own, but through the courtesy of Mrs. Janie McKay Pruett, wife of Judge W. H. Pruett, one of Barbour's most distinguished and valuable citizens.

The collection of prize cakes carried to this fair by Mrs. Lane made her famous and when she won the grand prize, both she and her "Lane Cake" became famous.

At this fair she demonstrated for the Buck Range Company, their ranges, in making other Lane cakes, but the one that won her the prize was baked on an ordinary wood stove at her home in Clayton.

Here is the recipe:

Lane Cake

Five egg whites, 1 cup butter, 1 cup sweet milk, two cups sugar (1 sifted twice), three and one-third cups sifted flour. Two teaspoons baking powder, 1 teaspoon vanilla.

Sift flour and baking powder together three times, cream butter and sugar, until light, add to it (little at a time), flour, milk, eggs and one teaspoon vanilla. This makes four layers. Have medium soft and bake in ungreased pans lined with brown paper.

Filling

Yolks of 8 eggs, 1 large cup sugar and one-half cup butter. Pour into a stew pan and cook on top of stove until thick, stirring all the time. While hot, stir in one cup chopped raisins, one glass good whiskey or brandy and one spoonful vanilla. Spread thick.

Chapter Thirty-three
Ten Lovely Old Ladies

TEN OLD LADIES

A few years ago, Mrs. Gertha Long Couric invited ten old lady friends of hers to a birthday party on St. Valentines Day, at the Blue Bird tea room, of which she was proprietor, and after the birthday dinner and the beautiful program of toasts that interspersed it, the above picture was taken.

Reading left to right: Mrs. S. G. Robertson (Rachel Davis); Victoria Hoole; Bessie McTyer; Mrs. Charles A. Martin (Alice Brunson).

Front row: Mrs. Jonathon Thornton (Fanny Sylvester); Mrs. B. B. McKenzie (Bettie Flournoy); Mrs. Alex McKay Mary Douglas); Mrs. C. F. Massey (Fredonia Sparks); Mrs. Willis B. Butts (Julia Treutlen).

Rachel Davis Robertson

Rachael Davis Robertson daughter of W. B. and Cynthia Davis, was born in Lumpkin, Georgia, 1840, she was educated at Cotton Hill Seminary, Cotton Hill, Ga., the president of that Institution being N. F. Coolidge, brother of John Coolidge, the father of President Calvin Coolidge.

She married Dr. S. G. Robertson at Cuthbert, Ga. They lived several years in Memphis, Tenn., and came to Eufaula from a yellow fever epidemic in the eighties and resided here the rest of their lives. Dr. Robertson was a prominent dentist of Barbour County.

She died July, 1933, from the effects of a fall in her room, greatly beloved by everyone in the community for her kindness, generosity to the poor and thoughtfulness of others. One of the strong forces of the First Bapttist Church, through her long life (the nearest and dearest friend the writer ever had) "none knew her, but to love her."

Miss Victoria Moole

Miss Victoria Hoole, daughter of Bertram and Violetta Hoole, pioneer citizens of Barbour County. A lifelong worker for the interests of St. James Church. She was educated at Old Union Female College, Eufaula, and was a life long school teacher. She taught the first public school in Eufaula, established in the seventies, and was a woman of brilliant literary attainments. She was the granddaughter of John Lingard Hunter, one of the pioneer settlers of Barbour County. The later years of her life were spent with her nephew, Rev. Bertram E. Brown at Tarosboro, N. C., coming back to the old home here, when her sight began failing.

She died in 1935, a Southern woman of rare patriotic type and greatly beloved.

Misses Maggie and Bessie McTyer

Misses Maggie and Bessie McTyer, known affectionately by their friends as "The Girls," were not twins, but it was often supposed that they were. They always dressed alike, were always together, had ideas alike, and were loved and admired by every one.

They were daughters of the late Sumpter McTyer, pioneer citizens of Barbour County. They were musicians of the long ago, were educated at Union Female College, and kept up their music until their death.

They were charter members of Barbour County Chapter U. D. C., members of the Presbyterian Church and always active, enthusiastic and enjoyed life. They were so charming and lovely that they were really famous. They lived together in the old family plot in Fairview Cemetery.

Alice Brunson Martin

In the long ago, Alice Brunson Martin, daughter of Major and Mrs. M. A. Brunson, was the beautiful, sunny haired, bright-eyed girl, that was always the belle of the ball. She married Charles A. Martin, son of J. G. L. and Adele Besson Martin. They spent some years of their married life at Birmingham, some years at Comer, Alabama, coming back home to Eufaula in the late nineties, where they resided on Barbour street. She was for many years a widow, until she, too, passed on, a greatly beloved woman of the old Southern type, that all the world bows in reverence to. She was educated at Union Female College, Eufaula, a member of the First Methodist Church and active in all its interests.

Fanny Sylvester Thornton

Fanny Sylvester Thornton was born in Barbour County at the old historic Sylvester home in the Pine Grove settlement northwest of Eufaula and she grew up to noble womanhood, graduated from Union Female College, married first Mr. Jonathon Thornton, and after his death, she married, second, a cousin of his, also Mr. Thornton, the latter of Union Springs, Alabama. After his death, she came back to Eufaula, where she resided until her death, over 80 years of age.

She was honored and beloved as a woman of rare enthusiasm and personal qualities. She grew beautiful flowers at her home and for many years furnished and arranged flowers every Sunday at the First Baptist Church of which she was a devoted member, taking part in all its activities. She has been beautifully memorialized on the pages of the record books of this church.

Her declining days were cheered by the devotion of her niece, Mrs. Carlton Engram Love, the affection between them being that of mother and daughter.

Bettie Flournoy McKenzie

Bettie Flournoy McKenzie was born in Barbour County at the old historic Flournoy-Toney home, "Roseland," 5 miles north of Eufaula, but grew up in Eufaula at the old Flournoy-McKay-McDowell-Pruett-Lee home on Randolph street, and was there married Oct. 14th, 1858, to Bethune B. McKenzie.

She was a member of the first graduating class of Old Union Female College.

After her marriage she lived 17 years at Durham, Alabama, and was far and wide known and beloved mistress of "Liberty Hall," the name given the hospitable McKenzie home there.

In 1899 Capt. and Mrs. McKenzie moved to Eufaula where she lived until her death in 1928, one of the best beloved women who ever lived in the community, a sweet, lovely Christian whose children "rise up to call her blessed. She was an active member of the First Baptist Church, a member of Barbour County Chapter U. D. C.

Fredonia Sparks Massey

Fredonia Sparks Massey lived the early years of her life in Quitman County, Georgia, coming to Pine Grove in Barbour County with her husband, Capt. C. F. Massey, moving to Eufaula in 1890, where she has since lived, loved and admired by hosts of friends, for her sweet, loveable Christian character, that drew friends to her.

Quiet, reserved, she was the cultured old-time lady who is a joy to know under all circumstances.

Through all the years, she has been a faithful member of the First Baptist Church, which she loved and served.

She passed on to her reward April 19th, 1937, her life a blessing and a benediction to all who have known her.

Julia Treutlen Butt

Julia Treutlen Butt, member of the illustrious Treutlen family and wife of Maj. Willis Butt, was born at Glennvile, Ala., grew up there, attending the famous old Female College at Glennville.

The early years of her married life were spent at Hurtsboro, Alabama, moving to Eufaula in the eighties. During all the years here, she has been beloved to a most unusual degree by everyone in the Community, and was affectionately called "Aunt Jule" by every one.

She was the very crown and flower of the First Methodist church for over 40 years, going about doing good whereever she found a need.

Few women have held the place in the hearts of their friends that she did, and when she passed on the church and the community suffered a great loss. One of the most beautiful and thougtful acts of her life was her habit of always greeting the "stranger in our midst" and bidding them a cordial welcome.

She was the old-time Christian gentlewoman, who leaves the world better for her having lived in it.

She was a patriotic member of Barbour County Chapter U. D. C. and loved the Confederate cause. She died in 1930.

Mary Douglass McKay

Mary Douglass McKay, daughter of John Douglass of North Carolina, was born in North Carolina, but came, when a child, to Oron, near Troy, Alabama, where she grew up.

After her marriage to Alex McKay of Louisville she came to Eufaula and has since resided here, beloved and admired for all the graces that adorn noble womanhood. She has been the Queen Mother, who is always the enobling inspiration of her children, and whose home is her castle and their joy. She is a devoted member of the Presbyterian Church and is an example of the true woman of the old South and all it means today. She is the only member of the birthday party in the above picture who is living today, the other nine, one by one, having passed on. They were all intimate friends and each one has left a blessed memory for the one still living to hold dear as their other friends do. Mrs. McKay died February 10, 1938.

Chapter Thirty-four
Old Settlers' Tea

From Centennial Edition of Eufaula Citizen June 15th, 1923

If some of the early settlers, Wiliams, Thomas, Ledbetter, Lee or others who first landed on the banks of the Chattahoochee could have been present at the Settlers' Tea on Thursday afternoon at the bluff, they would have felt that they were very much at home.

There were the settlers' tents and all about were the settlers' wives and daughters, entertaining the guests and serving ginger ale and ginger snaps and taffy candy from pots hung on trivots in front of the wigwams.

Among the guests of honor were the Governor of the state, W. P. Brandon; Lieut. Governor McDowell, four elderly ladies who knew Eufaula in the early settlers times: Mrs. B. B. McKenzie, and sister, Mrs. B. F. Eidson of Louisville; Mrs. L. W. McLaughlin (Belle Hart); and Mrs. T. W. Brannon (Florida Copeland) who arrived in an old-fashioned phaeton, while Mr. and Mrs. Fern Wood Ham of Glennville came in an old fashioned closed carriage.

Mrs. H. Bathman, a direct descendant of Mark Williams, one of the two who discovered Eufaula, rode on horseback, wearing a riding suit one hundred years old in which was strapped a pistol to ward off possible attacks of the Indians. Indeed, quite a few young Indians did arrive on the scene, with threatening war whoops, but the charm of the Camp Fire girls in old fashioned costumes, quieted their warring spirit. Miss Frances Marshall and others also arrived on horseback.

The stunt of the afternoon, if such a twentieth century word can be used in telling of an early settlers' tea, came when Hortman's orchestra arrived in a covered wagon to play for the tea. Inside the wagon was an old-fashioned organ on which was played the sweetest songs of Dixie while stringed instruments were also used.

On the curve of the bluff, where far below the river has wended its way to the Gulf for hundreds of years, was placed seats for the guests and an invocation was given by Dr. Frank Willis Barnett of Birmingham followed by the reading of a letter dated 1834, by W. H. Merrill, written by his grandfather, A. K. Merrill, who moved to Barbour County from Vermont to take charge of the Eufaula Academy.

He also read a beautiful poem on Eufaula by Dr. M. B. Wharton, distinguished former citizen. Beautiful music was furnished by the Cowikee band. To give an idea of how many attended this unique affair, it might be said that the ladies' committees from the Women's clubs had prepared for six hundred, but that the ginger tea gave out before it was over.

At the Country Club, Miss Caroyne Moore, the beautiful daughter of Mr. and Mrs. T. L. Moore, was queen of the Centennial-Homecoming celebration, and her escort consisted of maids, misses Eva Eula Kaigler, now Mrs. P. P. Salter; Sara Bulloch, now Mrs John Parrot, Roanoke, Va.; Henrietta McCormick, now Mrs. Lister Hill, Montgomery; Miss Mabel Johnston, now Mrs. Paul Stephenson, of Mobile. Heralds, Edward Dantzler, Earl Foy. Humphrey Foy, crown bearer. Train bearers, Alice Comer, Leila Johnson. Flower girls, Catherine Smith, Bertha Merrill.

The old fashioned German parade that followed the coronation was led by Lawrence G. Lightfoot, whose name is known and loved in all Barbour County as the big-hearted, genial society leader who after spending many years in Eufaula, always came home from Montgomery to spend Christmas in Eufaula. He died suddenly in December of 1928, leading the Christmas festivities at the Country Club.

The parade on Wednesday morning was witnessed by thousands from all parts of Southeast Alabama. There were 42 floats in the parade.

At the opening exercises Lieutenant Colonel C. S. McDowell was master of ceremonies and chairman of the One Hundredth birthday celebration of Eufaula. Responses to his patriotic opening talk were given by Mayor H. H. Conner, former Governor W. D. Jelks, Judge E. P. Thomas, S. Hugh Dent, Dr. Frank Willis Barnett, M. B. Wellborn, W. T. Sheehan, Judge H. D. Clayton, all former patriotic citizens of Barbour County.

Extract of Talk by William T. Sheehan at 100th Birthday of Eufaula—1923

In Indian days Eufaula was the site of what was probably the most important town of the lower Creeks, a place for their feats, celebrations and assemblys. The Creeks had Eufaula towns, one not very far from the present site of Montgomery; but the town on the high bluff overlooking the then flowered rock bottomed Chattahoochee river was the largest and the favorite.

When the white settlers came they settled the site of Eufaula for the same reason that the Indians had, it being healthy, and natural beauty made it restful, its hills and valleys sparkling springs of water.

Long sustained history behind it and its well considered and established traditions, which were a part and parcel of the history of Anti-bellum period, by word of mouth. The social habits and customs upon which the people have not fluctuated in hectic days of any short, feverish commercial boom by which the city's ideas, may have been corrupted by a selfish and vicious commercialism.

Barbour County has produced men and women of distinction and culture. Other towns have been well satisfied with men sent forth from Barbour and this county is proud of the number who have attained distinction in varying and different walks of life.

The intellectual life of Barbour County was given tone and color by its earliest settlers and that color has maintained through generations until today.

Barbour has played a conspicuous part in the life of all commercial, financial, industrial, and an influential part in the political affairs of the state that is most remarkable.

Chapter Thirty-five

Pap Speight

In all this community, there is no familiar personage, or unique character than Daniel McLeod (better known as "Pap Speight") the sixty-five year old darkey, who is now porter for P. D. Schaub's book store—after having been porter for J. W. Speight's meat market and grocery store.

When a mere lad, Mr. Speight found him hanging around the courthouse, where his mother, Melisse McLeod, was employed as janitress, often having charge of the keys of the city jail, to carry meals to the inmates.

He went barefooted and wore knee pants until he was more than forty years old and Speight's Market trade made him a daily visitor in the homes to the extent that he was a family fixture in many of these homes.

For many years the Market was next door to the Bluff City Inn and "Pap" became intimately acquainted with the traveling men and was always a source of entertainment with them.

This outburst of wit, that were epigrams of wisdom, have evoked much comment as well as his quaint appearance.

Two years ago Mr. Speight went out of business and his son, Mr. Seth Speight accepted a position as Deputy Sheriff of the County and "Pap" immediately felt his personal responsibility regarding this new job for his former employer, and he was heard to say, in response to the question, "Pap, are you going away?" "No, I ain't going no where. Dare's too much bootlegging going on and I know Mr. Seth'll need me to help him ketch dese niggers and pore white trash what's breaking de law."

When "Pap" became porter for Schaub's bookstore, he immediately took a position of "sentinel" in front of the store, as he had at the market, and daily kept tab on the passersby.

One day he came to the writer's home to bring some magazines. When he handed them to me he said, in the most serious manner, "I'se been bringing you feed for the stomach a mighty long time—now I'se bringing you feed for the head."

He had a reputation for stubbornness that sometimes

got the best of his genial disposition and on one occasion he had to be severely reprimanded by Mr. Speight and one of the butchers gave him a whipping. He was told that for the next similar offense he would be discharged. He looked straight into Mr. Speight's eyes and said, "Mr. Speight, you shore is all wrong—you can't ever turn me off; whip me, or do anything to me but you can't make me quit. I'se gwine to stay here long as dis market runs." And he did.

Thanksgiving week he carried a turkey and other Thanksgiving "goodies," as he called them, to the Schaub home and returning from one of these errands he remarked, "I'se shore gwine to de house Thursday and git some turkey." Mrs. Schaub heard of this remark and put him up a nice plate of Thanksgiving dinner, but he failed to show up and when asked why he did not come for his turkey, he said with significant emphasis, "I went to the funeral" (the interest in a negro funeral overshadowing a good dinner).

Saturday "Pap" delivered a blank bookkeeper's journal to a customer who had phoned his order and when it was received, it was not exactly what had been ordered. He was told to "carry it back and I'll telephone and explain more fully what I wish." In a few minutes "Pap" returned with the book desired and as he handed it in, said: "I don't see why folks don't do the right thing fust time," then he ducked his head, put the money in his pocket and walked out with an air of disgust.

Every one you meet has a story to tell of "Pap" and one heard today was: At the Speight market one day, a package of sausage, out of a box opened each morning and put out on the advertising counter, was noticable by the pile diminishing too rapidly, and Mr. Speight remarked about it to the clerks. "Pap," standing by, spoke up saying, "Mr. Speight, two feets carries dem sausages off," and when Mr. Speight asked: "Where to? he took him by the sleeve and led him to an empty barrel in the rear near the back door, where were found more sausage than on the counter. Then "Pap," silently pointing to one of the small boys that helped deliver meat, he said, "Dat Imp hides dem dare," to slip dem out every night. I'se no meddler, but I'se been watching him and I'se been busting to tell you, kase, he's fixing right now to steal anything he can git his hands on." The boy denied the guilt, trying to fasten the stealing on "Pap," who flew into a rage, jerked the boy up, and but for the interference would have given him a good whipping.

His father, Jim McLeod, was a well-known driver for Skillman's stables in the old days of Eufaula's famous horses and for many years was coachman for Mr. F. M. Gay. He was also a well known and unique character, notable as a horse trainer and skilled race driver.

"Pap" looks exactly as he did thirty years ago and may well be called Eufaula's "Mascot," as there is no more loyal citizen nor is there one who has been more faithful in the performance of duty through the years.

In the early fall of 1896 (exact date not recalled) at 7:30 a. m. in Barbour County and adjacent sections an eclipse of the sun made artificial light necessary for cooking breakfast and it is a memorable fact that all the chickens went back to roost and the darkness at such an early hour was almost appalling.

One amusing incident is recalled. Near the home of the writer were two small churches, branches of the First Methodist and First Baptist Churches, and as she sat under a mulberry tree in the barnward, milking the family cow, near the street, a negro boy "Pap" came in the gate, bringing from the market where he was employed the breakfast steak. Going out, he stopped to ask questions, as to the darkness, and as he talked, it grew so dark, the milking had to be abandoned, and "Pap" (now a porter for a book store) said —"I'se gwine up to one of dese churches to be wid the good folks if Judgment Day is come."

And he did go into the nearest church, just across the street. It is also recalled that a large number of operatives in the cotton mills nearby had gathered in this church.

This boy, now nearly seventy years of age, is a notable character in the town of Eufaula and is unique and really philosophical in many of his sayings.

NOTES

The Ku Klux Klan at Louisville were active and their work effective. It became necessary to kill an anti-Confederate notorious character who was causing trouble and had killed a man on the river.

Cotton was raised prolifically around Louisville before the war, and in 1844, it was noted that everything was raised in abundance in this section.

Mrs. Martin D. Martin, grandmother of Mr. John D. Martin, of Eufaula, was one of the most remarkable women of that time. She was a great factor in the Presbyterian Church, was an artist who wove many beautiful counterpanes that for artistic beauty as well as service were the admiration of every one.

One of the first settlers, Mother McInnis, was the lovely

old Scotch lady whose personality was the joy of the community.

She was the first lady of the large McInnis family distinguished in every way.

At the 100th birthday celebration of Pea River Presbyterian Church there were 600 members present and descen-descendants of past members present.

The first Elders of this church were Martin D. Martin, Mack McEachern, John McNeil, Alex McLendon and others.

In Beat II The Farmers' Alliance was very active and Reuben F. Kolb was popular politically. Mr. John Richards was a factor in the organization.

Beat 6— In the Community known as "Orr's Mill," near Old Judson Church, below Clayton, in the days following reconstruction troubles, continued to be the place of political fights and there was often danger of unexpected blows from bystanders and "smart Alexs" who kept the settlement in a constant state of quarrels and "scraps." It became known as "Bloody Six," and fights and scraps were the order of every day for several years.

Today, things are different, as there is not the political interest and ardor, and the people of the vicinity are more law abiding than in the days when elections always meant bloodshed.

Biographies

Who's who, and what they were,
And DID; is here retold, to show
That there was no blur
On these of the long ago.

JOHN M. ALSTON

John M. Alston was born June 15th, 1850, in Georgia, died in Barbour County, son of James and Rebecca J. (Norwood), great grandson of James Alston, who married a Yancey, a member of the same family to which the Southern statesman and orator belonged; and of John Norwood, who came from Wales and settled in North Carolina. The Alstons are descended from an old Georgia family of Alstons.

Mr. Alston's father was born in 1815 in Elbert County, Georgia, and was taken to Marengo County, where he lived with his family until death in 1853, due to a disease contracted during the Indian war in 1836. Mrs. Alston was born December 8th, 1822, in Charlotte, N. C., and lived in Tennessee, Talbotton, Ga., and Monroe County, Georgia. After her marriage and after her husband's death she moved to Sumpter county, Georgia, and to Spring Hill, Barbour County, in 1874. She farmed five years, owning a plantation of over 3,000 acres in Barbour County.

John Alston was a Democrat, attended every convention during his residence in Barbour County, and was a steward in the Methodist Church.

He married Willie B., daughter of Mrs. McPharland and Jane Norwood. Last residence was in Barbour County.

MOSES ALEXANDER

Among the pioneers of Southeast Alabama who grew up in Barbour County, none was more outstanding and beloved than Moses Alexander, whose home was on the borderline of Henry and Barbour County, called "County Line," and the old home of his father, Ezekiel Alexander, has been notable through several generations.

During reconstruction days, and on down to his death a few years ago, Moses Alexander was enthusiastic in politics, notable as one of the best farmers in all this section and most valuable citizen. His grandchildren were present at the White Oak Church's hundredth year celebration in July, 1938.

Moses Alexander was a weekly visitor (many times over) to Eufaula for a half century. He did his large farm trading in Eufaula, and was a member of the Eufaula Harmony Lodge No. 46, F. A. A. M.

DR. JOHN BALL ADAMS

Dr. John Ball Adams was born in Eufaula November 18th, 1903, the son of the lamented Dr. John L. Adams (see Cyclone Toll page)———and Annie Will (Haliday) Adams, daughter of Marshall Andrews and (Sophie Ball) Halliday, prominent ciitzens of Lumpkin, Georgia.

As a young boy he attended the graded schools of his home town, being unusually studious, and graduated from the University of Alabama, with his A. B. degree in 1926. He graduated from Vanderbilt University, Nashville, Tenn., with his M. D. degree and highest honors in 1930.

Returning from Medical College, he became associated with Dr. W. S. Britt in the practice of medicine, and is on the staff of the Britt Infirmary

He is capable, learned in the intricacies of Modern Medico and enjoys a flattering practice. Personally, he is genial, popular, is rapidly taking his place among the most notable and able physicians of the state. He is a member of Alabama Medical Association, member of Barbour County Medical Society, a leading member of the First Methodist Church and a valuable citizen of whom Barbour County and his home town are very proud.

He married Willie Northrop, daughter of the late Mr. and Mrs. P. D. Northrop, and they have two beautiful children, Mary, aged three, (who has been awarded first prize for baby beauty and perfection in a recent notable beauty contest), and John Ball, Jr., a handsome, acclaimed perfect specimen of babyhood.

GEORGE W. ANDREWS

George W. Andrews, the youngest prosecuting attorney ever known in Alabama, was born in Clayton in 1881, of Scotch ancestry through his grandfather, John Andrews, born in Macon, Georgia. After 40 years he moved to Clayton.

John Z. Andrews was born near Clayton, September 6th, 1843, dying April 17th, 1910. He was a Confederate soldier, serving with distinction with the 9th Alabama Infantry, being severely wounded.

His wife, Maragret McRae, was born April 20th, 1854. Their children: Lula, wife of Dr. Henry E. Peach, Clayton dentist; George W.; Mary; and Irene, wife of Love Ventress. As a youth he attended the City schools and later the University of Alabama, being admitted to the bar in July of his first college year.

Practicing in Clayton until 1909, he located in Union

Springs, where he was a legal light of Bullock County. He married Miss Addie Belle King, daughter of Thomas J. and Sofronia Vining King. Their two sons, George W., Jr., and Thomas.

George W. Andrews, Jr., graduated with honors at the University of Alabama. He was admitted to the Bar and was elected Solicitor of the Third Judicial Circuit. He has made a wonderful record for one so young, and is lauded on all sides for ability of a rare type, his scholarly familiarity with various phases, and is a pleasing speaker with a convincing manner of presenting his arguments. He is a young Democrat, rapidly making for himself an enviable place on the records of the Third Judicial Courts.

ALPHEUS BAKER

Alpheus Baker, teacher, lawyer, Brigadier General Confederate States Army, was born May 23rd, 1825, in Abbeville Courthouse, S. C., son of Alpheus and Eliza (Courtney) Baker, native Cork Ireland, the former born November 31st, 1780 at Athol, Mass.; student at Dartmouth College, New Hampshire, graduating with Daniel Webster, and famous as a teacher and scholar.

General Baker embodied all his father's teachings so thoroughly that at the age of 16 he was holding teachers' chairs at Abbeville, South Carolina, in Lumpkin, Georgia,

PHERIBEE RICKS BAKER   GENERAL ALPHEUS BAKER

and at Glennville, Barbour County, Alabama, where he came in 1848 and settled.

While studying law, he taught music in Eufaula, was admitted to the bar in 1840 and practiced in Eufaula.

In 1856 he accompanied Major J. M. Buford, editor of the 'Spirit of the South," to Kansas. On his return he canvassed the County to arouse the people to the importance of making Kansas a slave state.

In 1861, he represented Barbour County in the State Legislature, but resigned to enter the Confederate Army, as Captain of the Eufaula Rifles which he led to Pensacola.

The Company's flag was presented to him by Miss Ella Pope (Mrs. Dozier Thornton), daughter of Dr. and Mrs. J. C. Pope, in the yard of the Pope home (now the McRae home) on Broad street at Eufaula, as his company was leaving for Pensacola. November, 1861, at Fort Pillow, he was elected Colonel of the 54th Alabama Regiment composed of Tennessee, Mississippi and Alabama troops, the command participating in the seige of New Madrid.

When this regiment was captured at No. 10 Island, Mississippi, River, April 19th, 1862, and sent to Camp Chase, thence to Johnson's Island, the prisoners were exchanged in September and four Alabama companies took the place of the four Mississippi companies in his Regiment.

At Fort Pemberton, on the Zazoo river and Baker's creek he was severely wounded in the foot. His regiment, it was reported, fought gloriously.

On March 4th, 1864, he was promoted to Brigadier General of the 54th Alabama Regiment . On July 28th, he was wounded at the battle of Ezra Church. In September his Brigade was transferred to Mobile and again increased by the addition of the 3rd Reserves and 22nd Louisiana Regiment.

In January, 1865, his Brigade left Mobile to join C. S. A. in the Bentonville Battle, March 19th, 1865.

When the war was over, returning home to Eufaula, he became famous as an attorney and was known as the silver tongued orator of Alabama, as well as the great Confederate hero. In November, 1876, he moved to Louisville, Kentucky, and became associated in the practice of law, with his wife's cousin, Col. Sterling B. Toney, formerly of Barbour County. After a brilliant career in the legal courts of Louisville, Ky., General Baker died at Louisville October 2nd, 1891, and is buried in historic "Cave Hill," said to be the most beautiful—for situation and upkeep—of any cemetery in the world.

General Baker first married Louisa Garvin, daughter of Nelson and Caroline (Cannon) Copeland. Two sons were born to them, Thomas, who died early in childhood, and Alpheus, Jr., (familiarly called "Dogan Baker," who married Cassie Sanders. Their daughter, Rosebud, married Gardner H. Davis, deceased, and with her two sons, Haywood and Albert Davis, reside at their country home two miles north of Eufaula.

General Baker married second Pherebie, daughter of Col. Robert and Eliza Toney Ricks of "Ashland," Clay County, Georgia. Two daughters, Pherebie, Mary, deceased. Eliza Toney married John A. Murray, now residing at Merrimac, New Hampshire;; Robert Ricks married Letitia Harton; Paralee married James A. Edwards; Julia died in infancy; Sterling Toney died young.

Mrs. Baker was a true daughter of the old South, loyal to all the old traditions. She lived to the age of 87, active and interested in doings of the times, and died in 1934 at the home of her daughter, Mrs. Murray.

Among the many honors conferred on General Baker was his selection as pall bearer at the funeral of the Confederate Chieftain Jefferson Davis. During reconstruction days in Barbour County, he took active part in cleaning out the evils attending Republican rule, and was appointed to succeed the notorious Elias Keils as City Judge at Eufaula.

The following campaign song, composed by him was sung on many occasions. It was virtually the song that ran Keils out of the state of Alabama.

CAMPAIGN SONG IN BARBOUR COUNTY, 1874

Written by General Alpheus Baker, who succeeded Judge Keils as City Judge of Eufaula

Keils he sits on de City bench
His nigger juries raise a stench;
He puts white men in the calaboose
And turns black thieves and rascals loose.

Chorus
So clare de kitchen young folks, old folks,
Clare de kitchen, Old Virginia nebber tire.

Manira, born from the brain of **thunder**
A full grown gal, that was a wonder;
But de way Keils burst from an ignaramus
Into a Judge, was much more famous.

Chorus
One Jackass wore a Lion's skin;
Another, a Judge's gown got in;

But the first wus a decent Royal beast
Compared wid de countryfied Judge, at least.

Chorus

Oh, de good nigger works and de bad one steals
But he's got a mighty good friend in Keils.
For what cares de judge, for de stealing of a shoat
If turning de thief loose gains him his vote?

Chorus

I wish I wus back in Old Kaintuck
For since I've left, I've had no luck.
Dere pick dere candidates out ob de jail
And jug de Judge—Kase he can't git bail.

Chorus

Dey play de game of scare and cheat.
Dey bait de nigger wid a slice ob meat,
And shake dere chains in de white men's faces,
And den dey bragged dat dey held four aces.

Chorus

But Uncle Sam, he may took dere bacon
De nigger BIT, but he got mistaken;
Dey fooled de poor blind sons of Ham
And de white folks wouldn't scare worth a Dam.

Chorus

Sor der's in de mountains, run boys run,
We wiregrass wakes to join de fun.
De scalawags' faces all look wry,
Good God, de white man's goose hangs high.

Chorus

De day of nigger rule is past
Dey white man's day is come at last.
De hog will return to de land once more
And de chicken roost low, like it used to roost before.

Note: From official records, "This song ran Keils out the County and State and General Baker was elected Judge of the City Court in his stead.

ROBERT ANDERSON BALLOWE

Backed with an illustrious ancestry of Buckingham, Va., Robert Anderson Ballowe was born in Nashville, Tenn., December 30, 1860, grew up and after he finished his education became an outstanding business man. In 1890 he came to Eufaula as manager of the Eufaula Cotton Oil Co., and quickly became an outstanding citizen. He served as City

Councilman for some years and in 1902 was elected Mayor of Eufaula, serving two terms.

Soon after he established methods that greatly advanced plans and programs that were helpful to the entire community. His genial personality won him warm friends, and when he died in February, 1914, the regret at his passing was a calamity to the city, to his church (First Methodist), to the schools and all the business and social interests. His fine baritone voice in the church choir, and in all the local musical entertainments, was always a joy to hear, and no citizen was ever more honored and beloved.

He married first Nellie Douglass, a lovely girl of Glennville, Ala., and their children were Katie, deceased, who married first Rev. Martin Auld of South Carolina—one son, Fred Auld. She married second John A. DesPortes, and to them was born a son, John A. Des Portes, Jr.

Nellie Ballowe married Edward T. Motley. Children: Robert and John twins, John, deceased, and a daughter, Nellie. Genie and Sarah, deceased.

Mr. Ballowe married second in 1902 Annie Miles, a charming member of the distinguished Miles, Thornton and Estes families. Their children are Anne, who married James T. Slade. Children: Dorothy Ann and James T., Jr. Robert, Jr., married Lula Dunn Ellerbe: Children: two daughters, Susie and Virginia. Martha married B. P. Brooks of Texas. Children: a son, Robert Posie; Miles married Mary Lewis Fort. Children: Hamlin and Sarah Hines.

Louise married Gilder Pate: Children: Martha Louise, Dorothy, who married A. M. Earl.

JULIUS C. BARNETT

Julius C. Barnett was born at Eufaula, son of John and Mary (Davis) Barnett, pioneer citizens of Barbour County, whose home was on Randolph Street in Eufaula, between Broad and Barbour streets.

He went to the War Between the States, when almost a lad, fought through the war and returned a cripple. Soon after his return he had a long illness, but on recovery, he entered the service of the Southwestern railroad (now the Central of Georgia). Mr. D. Philps was agent and soon young Barnett was promoted to treasurer of the Eufaula offices and station. He held this office over a quarter of a century, and during these years, he was known as "a time regulator," who never went anywhere but from his home to the depot to his office, and it was claimed that every employee of the Road relied on him for information and help to every kind, which he most obligingly and graciously gave. In the early nineties he secured a position with the Alabama, Midland railroad, and the family moved to Montgomery. After a few years his health failed (he never recovered entirely from the wounds received in the war) and he was an invalid in the Company's hospital at Waycross, Georgia, where he died, but is buried in the family lot in Eufaula Cemetery. So distinguished was his family and so outstanding was his career as a business man and citizen that he deserves honor mention in this history.

BERTRAM BROWN

Rev. Bertram Brown, D. D., was born in Sumpter, S. C., October 24th, 1871. His grandparents, Bertram J. and Serena Gunter (Hooie), moved to Eufaula during the Indian war of 1934. Early schooling was under Craven and Patterson of the Eufaula Male Academy, and private schools of Capt. Dent, Messrs Philips and Cato. He graduated from the University of Alabama in 1891 and from Sewanee, Tenn., and Virginia Seminary in 1984. He was ordained Rector at St. Johns Church, Montgomery, and Rector of Marion, Ala., Church from 1894 to 1900; Rector Uniontown, Ala., 1900 to 1905; Rector Eufaula, 1905 to 1909; Rector Cavalry Church, North Carolina, 1909 to the present time.

An eloquent, consecrated minister and theological student whose personality has made him outstanding in his childhood County of Barbour, he is greatly beloved.

He married in 1905 Julia Bates, daughter of Francis H. and Addie (Phillips) Bates of Perry County, Alabama. Children: Bertram Hoole Brown, city editor of Evening Telegram, Rocky Mount, N. C., and Julia Bates. He died at Tarboro, May 8th, 1937.

THE RT. REV. WYATT BROWN, D. D., LITT. D

Bishop of Harrisburg

Bishop Wyatt Brown was born in Eufaula, Barbour County, Feb. 14, 1884, son of Eugene and Serena Hoole Brown.

He was educated in the Eufaula schools, attended the University of the South at Sewanee, Tenn.; was very literary and edited the University paper and magazine, also the College Manuel.

He decided to enter the Ministry when quite young, following his brother, Bertram. After graduation he became assistant Rector of St. John's Episcopal Church at Montgomery for a year. He was then Rector of All Saints Church, Mobile, where the membership of his parish increased from 26 to 384.

In 1915 he received honorary degree of Doctor of Letters from the University of Alabama. He then became Rector of Trinity Church, Asheville, N. C., and in less than three years built a new church; rector of the Church of Ascension, Pittsburgh, Pennsylvania, 5 years and while there conducted meetings of College students.

From 1920 to 1928 he was Rector of St. Michael's and All Angels Church, Baltimore. He is a student and scholar, interested in Biography and Poetry and is an enthusiastic peace promoter; has visited Europe and the Holy Land several times; for six years vice president of the Baltimore Federation of Churches; from 1929-31 Dean of St. Paul's Cathedral, Buffalo, N. Y.

On January 23-28 at a Convention of the Diocese of Harrisburg held in York, Pa., he was elected second Bishop of Harrisburg, and on May 1st, 1931, he was consecrated Bishop in St. Stephen's Cathedral, Harrisburg, by the most Reverend James De Wolf Perry, D. D., Presiding Bishop of the Episcopal Church in America, assisted by several other Bishops.

He married Laura Little at Montgomery in 1911.

FRANK WILLIS BARNETT

Frank Willis Barnett was born at Glennville, Barbour County, October 23rd, 1865, son of Augustus William and Celeste (Treutlen) Barnett, the former physician, merchant and Methodist minister, born Aug. 24th, 1825, at Washington, Georgia, grandson of Samuel and Elizabeth (Warsham) Barnett of Washington, Ga., and of Gabriel and Anna (Connor) Treutlen; great grandson of Captain William and Jean (Jack) Barnett, the former of North Carolina, born in 1747; of Lieut. Richard and Mary (Wingfield) Porsham of Washington, Ga.; of John A. T. and Anna (Woolfolk) Connm; great grandson of John and Ann (Spratt) Barnett, the former born in Ireland, in 1700, died in Charlotte, North Carolina in 1871; of Thomas and Elizabeth (Turrell) Wingfield; of Gov. John Adams Truetlen, who was elected first Governor of Georgia in 1777; great, great grandson of John and Sarah (Garlando) Wingfield.

Frank Willis Barnett prepared in the public schools of St. Louis, Mo.; private schools in Paris; University of Berlin; New York Law school and Southern Baptist Theological Seminary at Louisville, Ky.

He read law with Henry D. Clayton of Eufaula, when he lived at Glennville in childhood, practiced law in Birmingham from 1889 until 1892; in New York 1892-1894; in Atlanta 1894-1895.

He was ordained to the Baptist Ministry September 23rd,

1895; pastor Johnson City, Tenn.; assistant pastor First Baptist Church, Nashville, Tenn., 1897; pastor at Forsyth, Ga., 1898-1900; headed a department in the law firm of Frederick-de-Peyster Foster in 1902 and became editor and owner of the Alabama Baptist, the organ of the Baptists of Alabama, January, 1902. Appointed Chaplain of 2nd Regiment of Georgia fo rthe Spanish American war, but declined; a Democrat, a Mason, Kappa Alpha College fraternity.

He married a Forsyth, Ga., girl on June 21st, 1899, Maud Proctor, daughter of David Jesse and Elleen Proctor; has two sons, Frank Willis and Samuel.

He was reared in Eufaula and is an enthusiastic lover of his home town, of which he has written hundreds of feature stories during a period of 30 years with the Birmingham News. His facile pen and happy, genial personality have made him beloved all over the state.

He is Chaplain of the Alabama Writers' Conclave; an eloquent preacher of scholarly force and a man of whom Barbour County is very proud.

He was reared in a Methodist atmosphere, his father a Methodist minister and outstanding churchman and citizen of Barbour County. When he declared for the Baptist faith and was ordained into that ministry, it was a surprise to his family and friends.

A man of most unusual intellect, Dr. J. B. Hawthorne, a distinguished Baptist Divine, with whom he was closely associated, said: "Frank went deep into Theological investigations before he chose the Baptist doctrines and his decision, I know was based on his vast Biblical research and study. The distinguished Barnett family in Barbour County has been "the crown and flower of the Methodist Church in Eufaula nearly an hundred years. Dr. A. W. Barnett, his father, was the beloved man, who "went about doing good" through his life, a prominent, valuable citizen.

His mantle has fallen on his sons. John T. Barnett has taken his father's place in the church and community, ministering to his fellow man in a happy way that makes him beloved and honored, as his saintly father was. The lovely old Barnett home on Barbour street still stands, slightly more modern than formerly, changed by the present owner, Mr. B. L. Bland, but three children of Dr. and Mrs. Barnett are still here.

They are John T., who married Banella Brown, daughter of the late Benjamin F., and Ella E. (Eppes) Brown.

With them reside his two sisters, Miss Caroline Lane Barnett and Mrs. Corneille Barnett Tullis, both lovely women who have come back after 30 years' residence in Washington, D. C., to reside at the old home.

Dr. Frank Willis Barnett resides in Birmingham, as does the older brother, Samuel T. Barnett, retired banker. He married Clara Geary of Union Springs, and their children are Edward, James, Samuel and Claire.

BENJAMIN FRANKLIN BENNETT

Benjamin Franklin Bennett, M. D., son of Benjamin C. Bennett and grandson of James Bennett, native of S. C., who died in Barbour County, having located there in 1837 and becoming one of the leading developers of the County—was born April 27th, nine miles from Louisville.

Benjamin C. Bennett was born in North Carolina in 1836 and was brought by his parents to what was then Barbour County, now Russell, when a few months old.

When less than 21 he entered Tulane University at New Orleans and received his medical education. He located in Barbour County and spent his useful life there as a leading physician, volunteering his services and later was transferred to a hospital at Memphis, Tenn., for expert services.

After the war, he resumed his practice in Barbour County, but ill health caused his retirement and he spent his later years as a Baptist minister, which had long been his desire. He married Amanda Grubbs Huey, September, 1837, and died at Louisville January 10, 1903. Children: James, killed horse gin accident at 14 years of age; Julia, wife of C. M. Capel; Emma Green, deceased; Alaice A., deceased; Sarah Margaret, wife of J. E Horn; Dr. B. F. Bennett; Nancy, wife of W. S. Harris; Carrie, wife of Dr. J. D. Adair of Clayton; Jennie, wife of W. C. Appling; Lillie Mae deceased; Samuel H., pastor of Baptist Church at Washington, Ga., and Clarence C., of Dothan.

Dr. B. F. Bennett received from this distinguished ancestry and enviable background the fine record he has made personally, professionally, educationally and in every other way. He graduated in 1893 from the University of Alabama with his M. D. Degree and began the practice of Medicine at Louisville, going three years after to Clayton, where he built up a large practice over the County. Returning to Louisville, he was a strong factor in the progress of the surrounding territory, and was a leader in building of the fine brick school buildings of Louisville, donating $600 on the fund, besides giving time and influence to the project.

He served on the City Council, was director of the Bank of Louisville and also of the Barbour County Bank at Louisville; Worshipful Master of Louisville Lodge No. 225, F. A. and A. M.; member Clayton Chapter No. 63, R. A. M.; and Liberty Lodge No. III, K. of P., Louisville; member of

Barbour County Medical Association and was life Counselor of that organization; and a "Fellow" of the American Medical Association.

During the World War, Dr. Bennett volunteered his services and was put on Medical Reserve, with rank of First Lieutenant.

He married Dec. 31, 1895, Carrie Eidson, daughter of Frank W. and Fannie Flournoy Eidson, the latter surveyor of Barbour County for over 50 years and tax assessor of Barbour County for several terms.

Children: Emmett, married; Agnes, married Frank Ventress, Clayton; Clarence R., physician, Eufaula; Robert, student University of Alabama.

CLARENCE R. BENNETT

Clarence R. Bennett was born at Louisville, the son of Benjamin F. and Carrie Eidson Bennett, of Louisville.

Coming from a line of distinguished physicians, he began his medical studies at Howard College, Birmingham, where he obtained his A. B. Degree, and also graduated at the University of Virginia, receiving his M. D. degree from Emory College, Oxford, Ga.

A few years ago he came to Eufaula, where he has built up for himself a most enviable reputation as a physician and valuable citizen and a most flattering practice, professionally. For several terms he was president of the County Medical Society and is a member of the State Medical Society.

He is active in the civic and social life of his home town, is a Baptist and member of the Kiwanis Club, and is rapidly reaching the top in his profession, despite the fact that he is one of the younger physicians of the County.

His record is adding luster to that of his distinguished father.

BRAY BROTHERS

Is is a very significant fact of which Barbour County should be and is especially proud that some of the most outstanding and splendid citizens were born in the North, came South to Barbour County before the War Between the States, established businesses, married Southern women and have been an honor to the South.

Among these were four brothers, William M., John W., Nathan M., and Wells J. Bray, who were natives of Fairmonth Conn.

They settled in Eufaula, established the largest Hardware business in Southeast Alabama, carrying an immense stock of firearms ammunition and when the call for volunteers came for the Confederate States Army these brothers promptly answered the call.

Messrs William and John Bray went to the front and Mr. Nathan Bray was detailed to manage the receiving from the manufacturers, and delivering to the Confederate Army, arms and ammunition to help carry on the war. Each one of these were brave soldiers and Mr. Nathan Bray, in his capacity of furnishing the utilities of war was equally as loyal and active.

He received the attached honorable discharge when the war was over, and it is a document of which his children are very proud.

Mr. William Bray's daughters have been enthusiastic United Daughters of the Confederacy (See account of Bray's Hardware stores and Riot prevented).

Mr. William Bray married Miss Mary Sims, of Macon, Georgia, and their children were William, Jr., deceased, who married Mamie McGough.

Tade married Allen H. Merrill: children, Allen K., who married Evelyn Farmer. Children: four sons, Thomas, Bird, Farmer, Allen K. and William Hoadley, who married Bertha Moore. Children: five daughters, Bertha, Harriett, Terese, deceased, Tad, Evelyn, Elizabeth, who married John C. McMae. Children: Elizabeth, who married Winburn Gregory; Tade married J. Via; Mary married A. M. Brown. Children, son, Dr. Hunter Brown, and daughter, Mary married Alex Clark.

Tade, deceased, married R. B. Harrison. Children: two sons, Merrill and Mortimer.

Lila married W. Y. Johnson. Children: daughter, Lula and son, W. Y., Jr.

Sims Bray, deceased, married Ethel Mobley. Children: two sons, Sims and Robert Courtney, deceased.

Lloyd, deceased.

Nina married Edward A. Dantzler. Children: son, Edward, and daughter, Nina.

Mr. John W. Bray married Miss Sarah Whitney. Children: four sons, John W., Frank, Fred, Charles, all deceased and unmarried.

Mr. Nathan Bray married Miss Katherine Wells of Macon, Georgia. Children: Nellie, deceased.

Katie, Ethel and Joseph, deceased, married Miss Jane Goss.

Mr. Wells J. Bray married Miss Martha Caldwell, N. Y., and their daughter, Minnie, married B. Lloyd Guice. Children: a son, Percy Guice.

L. H. BRASSELL

Lenox Hamilton Brassell was born October 28th, 1872, in Coosa County, Alabama, son of William R. Brassell, who was a large land and slave owner in Talladega County. After experiences in the war with the Indians, he served in the Confederacy with great honor, a close personal friend of General John T. Moagan.

L. H. Brassell received his early education at the High schools and at the old Verbena Academy. He studied law under Mac Smith and Thomas W. Sadler of Prattville, Alabama.

After being admitted to the bar he practiced at Eufaula and when the Spanish-American war cry sounded he enlisted in Company G, Volunteer Infantry under General Fitzhugh Lee. Returning to Eufaula after honorable discharge he continued his law practice until 1902 when he moved to Andalusia, Alabama .

From 1907 to 1914 he was County Solicitor for Covington County and in 1914 he was elected to the office of Court Solicitor of the 12th Judicial Circuit. After 4 years, he moved to Montgomery and in 1920 made the race against S. H. Dent and J. R. Tyson for Congressman of the second district. He was defeated by 300 votes, and contested the election.

In 1923 he moved to Troy, Ala., where he is enjoying a a flourishing practice of law. He is a man of most unusual ability, learning and forethought. A Democrat, a Baptist of strong faith and a Christian gentleman of the highest type; a valuable citizen to any community.

He was moderator of the Covington County Baptist Association 8 years; later moderator ofthe Troy-Salem Baptists Association; a Mason; I. O. O. F.; W. O. W.; member of Pike County Bar Association and member of the State Bar Association. He offered for service in the World War but was not called.

He married Winnie E. Stephens, great granddaughter of John DeLoachiou Thomas, the man who settled and named the town of Eufaula, and daughter of Calvin J. Stephens, a Baptist Minister of Eufaula and his wife, Katherine (Barefield) Stephens.

Mrs. Brassell is a talented musician and one of the leading patriotic, church and clubwomen of the state.

Their children: Hamilton Calvin, deceased; Meta Katherine, who married John S. Bankhead, grandson of Senator J. H. Bankhead; Lenox H., deceased; William Perry; Mary Elizabeth; Malcolm, deceased; and John C.

BUNYAN DAVIE

Bunyan Davie was born Dec. 10, 1852, in the Old Spring Hill District in Barbour County, the son of M. C. and Jane E. Davie.

He received his early education at the country home schools of that day and by the time he was college age the War Between the States came on, and he among thousands of other Southern boys, were denied the advantage of College training, but were taught at home some of the most practical needs of a successful business life, which he took advantage of and when quite a young man, accepted a position as local agent for the Southern Express Company at Clayton, Ala., where his long life has been spent, a forceful and appreciated leader in all the best interests of the County.

For a time he also operated his own private telegraph line from Eufaula to Clayton, a connecting line with the Western Union Telegraph lines at Eufaula. The business warranted, after several years, larger wires and heavier poles than those first used, and the Western Union Company built their own line and appointed Mr. Davie, Western Union manager at Clayton in the early seventies, which position he held for many years, resigning to devote his time to state field work for the Alabama Baptist Sunday Schools. He held the position of Sunday School field worker four years and position of Colporter fifteen years, making 19 years of continuous employment to the Baptist Denomination of Alabama.

Mr. Davie is a man of wonderful executive ability, a literary authority and a student who is a deep thinker—a man of the high type of Christian character that won for him a large circle of warm friends and admirers.

Through all the years that he has been a leader in the Baptist denomination of the state, a deacon in his church, his natural leadership, his wide information, religious zeal and strong Christian character has made him outstanding, not only in Barbour County and the state of Alabama, but within all the bounds of the Southern Baptist Convention.

He is easily one of Barbour County's first and most valuable citizens.

He married Miss Hattie Jones of Troy, Alabama, and their attractive home at Clayton is notable for Christian culture and is a place where there is always the atmosphere of that happiness that comes to a home from religious uplift and service.

Their children are, viz: Eunice, Mrs. A. G. Murray, Washington, D. C., Louise, Mrs. J. L. Bennett, Tallahassee, Florida, Lois, Mrs. A. Y. Napier. She and her husband, Rev. A. Y. Napier, were missionaries in China for twenty years. They are now back in the homeland and Dr. Napier is pastor of the Baptist Church at Centerville, Ala.

Hattie (Mrs. John Bracewell), recently married, are making their home with her parents at Clayton.

The two sons of this family, Bunyan, married Louise McCoy, of Birmingham, and with their small son reside in Birmingham.

Joel Davie was employed by the Post Office department at Washingtotn, D. C., and recently died, leaving a widow and little son and daughter.

AMERICUS BERRIAN BUSH

Americus Berrian Bush, better known as "Mac Bush," was born at old "Bushville" in Barbour County, Dec. 29th, 1849 and died July 31st, 1925, at Cotton Hill in Barbour County, where he spent his life.

He was the largest farmer in the County for many years and was a merchant as well.

He was postmaster at Cotton Hill twenty-five years and was a Democrat of the loyal patriotic type that made him outstanding in his state. His opinions on political, agricultural and community affairs were always consulted and had great weight.

He served several years as representative from Barbour in the State Legislature; was a veteran of the War Between the States, who was as enthusiastic over the cause for which he fought, the day he died as he was when he bravely bore the Southern standard on the battlefield.

He attended every annual reunion of the Confederate Veterans that ever assembled during his life, and always carried members of his family with him.

He fought in the battle of Fort Blakely C. S. A. five days, was captured and sent to Shipp Island; imprisoned in a Spanish Fort March 26th to April 8th. He was only a lad when he entered the army and had been crippled when a small child, that caused him to limp through life.

It has been acclaimed that "Mac Bush" had more friends than any farmer who ever lived in the County, and the reason was his big heartedness, his helpfulness to any person in need or cause in need, and he was patterned after because of his wonderful success with his crops.

He farmed on a scientific and technical program and the fortune he amassed from his farm was largely used in philanthropic way.

Education was his hobby and he gave to his children the very best. To educational causes, his purse and heart were always wide open. When his children were too young to attend school and after he employed Miss Victoria Hoole, a brilliant woman of letters, to teach as governess, and later they were all given the best college educations.

He was trustee of Union Female College at Eufaula and while in the Legislature introduced several educational bills.

He married March 4th, 1873, Marthan Ann, daughter of Michaelason and Danie Hays Crawford at their old historic home in Henry County, moving immediately to his home at Cotton Hill where through their long life the most elaborate and charming hospitality was dispensed.

"The Bushes" of Cotton Hill were social leaders and their lovely home was famous for the cordial entertainment—at al times a delightful place to visit.

"Mac Bush" was a prohibition leader in Barbour County whose influence went far, in all efforts to clean County politics and bring about prohibition. He was a valuable, beloved citizen, whose memory will live as long as the County exists.

His children are: Lillie, married to William Stewart; Hattie, who married John D. Martin; Eva, deceased, married to Oscar H. Roberts: Julia, deceased; Dora, married to Robert Roberts; Dr. David R. Bush married Bonalie King, and Comer Lee Bush married Mattie Lee Belcher.

Comer Bush and his family reside at the historic old home at Cotton Hill, and Mr. and Mrs. Robert Roberts, reside nearby in the old Maternal Ancestral home of the Crawford branch of the family.

Among the early settlers of Glennville was Abner Bessey, who came from the Carolinas, his daughter, Mary Bessey, married Dr. Anslem Evans, and to them was born Cynthia Adelle Evans. She married first Warren Goolsbee, and to them were born two sons, Wiley, who died some years ago in Texas, and Warren S., prominent citizen of Eufaula, acclaimed the greatest all-around fox hunter in the County, who always leads the trials, and also acclaimed the finest clothing salesman (which business he was in thirty years or more) in the County.

After Mr. Goolsbee's death, Cynthia Evans Goolsbee married M. O. Dutton, an Englishman, of that old gentility type, that shone out very plainly in his life. His first wife was Sarah Wells and the issue of that marriage was two charming daughters. Addie married James P. Hill, no issue, deceased. Viccie married Warren S. Goolsbee, issue two daughters, Addie and Viccie, and Warren, Jr., deceased.

William Dutton married Kate Hendrix, daughter of Benjamin Hendrix, prominent pioneer citizen of Barbour County, no issue.

There were no children of the marriage of Mr. Dutton and

Mrs. Goolsbee—he the cultured English gentleman and she the brilliant woman of letters and sweet gentle womanliness—made them outstanding in the community, although both were personally modest and unostentious.

ZACHARIAH BUSH

Zachariah Bush and (Polly Dennis), his wife, came to Barbour County about the same time Elliot Thomas and wife, Sallie Berry, came. They were large land owners and slave owners. His brothers, Moses Bush and William Bush also came and settled near New Hope Methodist Church. Three of Zachariah's daughters married three sons of Elliott Thomas and one Thomas daughter married their son, William Bush, issue—

Mariah married Jonathon Thomas, issue,—Herbert married Narcissus Thomas.

Grene Bush married Polly Allen, issue—William married, has issue.

Arreusa Bush married William Wiliams, issue—Francis married William Beasley, and their son, John, died early.

Rettust Emeline Bush married Eli Thomas, issue—Mary Parmelie married William Calhoun. George Hilliard married Mary Walker. Zachory Taylor married Marthelia Carter.

Dennis Bush married Salina DuBose, issue—Zachory Bush Charles married Miss McLeod.

Mary R. Bush married John Watson, issue.

Eason Bush married Betsy Jane Grubbs, issue John Thomas. Jane Thomas married Wilson.

Ruth Bush married Elliott Thomas first and second, John O. Wise of Coffee County, issue—Jerry Wise and others.

Lucinda Bush married first Edward Ward, near Ozark, issue; married second Barney Baldwin, issue—Neally Baldwin and others Eufaula.

Issue of Mariah Bush and Johnathon Thomas: Zachory Thomas; Sarah Jane Thomas married Anderson Crews, issue—Carrie married Dr. Bobbitt; their issue, Carrie, married Asa Willis; Clifford Crews married J. C. Ventriss, issue—Emma and Mary.

Elliott Thomas married, issue—Jennie married John W. Brown; Elizabeth married Kimsey; Fanny unmarried; Edward married Ellen.

W. Hope Thomas married Margaret McCraney, issue—Henry and Oree, both died young; Mamie; Nancy; Richard married Florence Kimbrought; Neil married J. L. Cherry; Lillian McClellan and adopted a son, Alex Thomas.

Alvena Thomas married Harrison Jones, issue—Silas

Ellison Jones married Esther Hale; Ethel married Mr. Jones. Orr Jones died in infancy.

Maggie Jones married Jimmie Martin, issue—Dr. Sterling Martin lives in Coffee.

Col. John James Martin married Beatrice Jones; Margaret Jones married Col. John Peabody, Tuscaloosa; Columbus Arthur married Elizabeth West, Clayton; Clifford Martin; Winn Martin married in Birmingham.

Irma Jean, college student.

Eula Marshall Jones married Claude Leroy Huey, issue—Thomas, Betty Ann, Evelyn, issue—Dr. Thomas Jones married Carrie Ella Stappleton, issue; Claude Leroy married Sarah Stewart, issue—Claude Leroy, Jr., graduate of Georgia Tech and lives in Atlanta, Briarcliff Road.

Alose Elizabeth married Harold Phillips and lives in Birmingham.

Johnathon Thomas killed in railroad accident in Barbour county.

Edna Earl married Harry Burge, Detroit, Mich.

Annie Lee married Arthur Lee Warm Springs, Georgia, issue, Oree married Margaret Fowler; Stewart Lee, student in Detroit; Marshall Palatine married Gerald Noah, issue—Gerald and Nancy Lee.

Emmie Estelle married James Roberts, issue—Theodia married Lloyd Arlege, Birmingham.

William Harrison died age 7; Lily Virginia died infant.

Twins—one died infant, other, Wilbur, married, lives in Washington, D. C.

Callie, daughter of Elliott Thomas, married James Orr, issue—Eula married John Wise, issue—Annie Wade married Wilbur Reeves; Beulah married W. A. Rocher; Mary married G. C. Reid; Georgia married W. M. O'Brian; Prudence married J. D. Stewart; James Orr married Alberta Phillips; J. C. Wise married Bunyan Bowden; Lynn married Louise Price; Eddie Lee married B. F. Rocher; Wade Orr married in Mobile, has issue; Dr. Jimmie Orr, veteran of Spanish-American war, twice married, has issue; Addie Orr married Chche Cowder first and Charles Valertine second. Perlar Orr married Ben McLendon; Robert Orr married Bonnie Dell Smith, issue—Frances, Caroline and Robert. Rufus Orr married and lives in Mobile, Ala.

Jonathan Carter Thomas married Evelyn Virginia Mallard. Addie Thomas died early; Jessie Thomas died early; Crowell Thomas killed in War Between the States; Lee Thomas married Ada Bush.

Eason Bush married Betty Jane Grubbs; Mary married Mr. West, issue—Claudis West and others.

Moses Eason; Anderson; Nora Bush married Mr. Martin

in Dothan, Ala.; Lulu married Relus Rollins, has large family at Dothan.

Ruth Bush married Elliott Thomas, children, John, and Jane Thomas.

John Wise, issue, Jerry Wise; Lucinda Bush married Robert Ward, issue, in Dale County; Barney Ward of Eufaula, issue, Neally Bawlding.

Mary R. Bush married John Watson, issue—Annas Watson, married, has issue in Barbour County; Callie married Mr. Johnson, issue, Mary and others living at Baker Hil, and Wilson's Cross Roads; Mollie married Caphas Rollins; Ward Watson, Eugene Watson and family live in Clayton. "Sissie" Watson married Mr. Stephenson, large and prominent family in Dothan. David Watson, Eufaula, large family. These descendants of Zachariah Bush and wife, Polly Dennis, are numerous and widely scattered and like their forbears are worthwhile people.

—By Rev. Eli A. Thomas, their grandson
Atlanta, Georgia.

MOSE WILEY BRITT

Mose Wiley Britt was born at Eufaula, Alabama, Oct. 28th, 1852, son of Matthew Britt, who was originally from Georgia. His wife, Elizabeth Sinquefield, was born at Marietta, Ga., died at Midway in 1910; had six children, Jennie, wife of Enoch Mills; Matthew, farmer at Eufaula, died at 80 years of age and Sallie, deceased; John T., merchant at Clayton, and Mose W. The latter was educated at Clayton and Eufaula and the University of Alabama. After a year at medical college in 1871 he practiced in Clayton; was a druggist until 1890, after which he gave all his attention to his farms. He moved to Midway in 1892, where he was mayor for many years and justice of the peace for 4 years. He married Mary Hill Roberts, daughter of Thomas and Anne (White) Roberts. Their children were: Mose W., Jr., who married Lucy Sessions; Thomas R. married first Minnie Bledsoe and second Lil Rainer.

Walter Stratten (physician and surgeon) married Kate Comer, daughter of J. F. and Elizabeth (Thornton) Comer; Annie married Charles B. Milner and second Dr. McLauren; Mary married George R. Irvin; Bertha married Samuel P. Wiseman.

BERINGER BROS.

In 1864, there came to Barbour County from New York two brothers, Abraham and Morris W. Beringer. They were born in Bordenheim, Germany, but came to America in early life, and intent on making a success of the mercantile business, cast their lot in Eufaula, Barbour County.

After being in the dry goods business a long time the elder brother, Abraham, was for many years the senior member of the firm of Beringer and Strass, being the brother-in-law of Faust Straus. Mr. Edward R. West, who had long been salesman for S. Lewy, bought an interest, and the firm became Beringer, Strauss and West until in the early nineties, after Mr. Strauss' death, Mr. West withdrew and went into the general mercantile business with his sons, W. R., and E. R. West and the old firm name became A. Beringer until his death.

The Dry Goods history of Barbour County abounds with the activities of these Beringer Brothers for over a half century and their citizenship was one of the best assets of the City of Eufaula, and Barbour County as well as Southwest Georgia.

Mr. "Abe" Beringer married Carrie Goodheart of Cleveland, Ohio, who was acclaimed at that time the most beautiful bride ever brought to Eufaula, her sister, Miss Nellie Goodheart, having been voted the "Queen of Beauty" at Cleveland, Ohio, in the late seventies, and when she visited her sister, Mrs. Beringer in Eufaula, the Alabama papers were full of accounts of her beauty and charm. She made many visits to Eufaula throughout the passing years and was much admired. Mrs. Beringer was one of the most beloved women in all this section. Her home on Barbour street was notable as the home of a rarely loveable woman.

She died several years before her husband, who spent the last months of his life at Britt Infirmary, his sight gone and a patient sufferer who had been one of the leading citizens of the Community and was held in highest esteem. They rest side by side in Fairview cemetery. Mr. Abe Beringer fought for the Southern Confederacy, being one of the number of men from the North, who coming South to make their living, cast their lots in with the South, and were true and loyal Southerners. He wore until his death the Cross of Honor awarded to Southern soldiers for service to the South.

He was a member of Harmony Lodge No. 46 F. A. A. Masons.

The junior brother, Morris M. Beringer, was also closely identified with all the interests of the community.

After the firm of Beringer Brothers was dissolved, Morris

Beringer went into business, the name being M. M. Beringer. His store was unique and he was the personal friend of hosts of customers all over Southeast Alabama and Southwest Georgia.

For many years associated with him were his brothers-in-law, Bert Scheur and Nathan Scheur. After his marriage to Miss Rebecca Scheur of New York, the distinguished Scheur family also came to Eufaula. Mr. Scheur married Miss Lily Denger of the notable Denger family of New York and a friend of Mrs. Abe Beringer, whose guest she was when she met Mr. Scheur. Mr. Nathan Scheur married Etta Friedman, a member of the distinguished old Stern family.

The first home Mr. Beringer owned in Eufaula was a handsome house he built on the corner of Barbour and Livingston streets. Later he purchased the old historic Keils Mansion on Barbour street, where with his sister, Mrs. Schonfield, he lived while a batchelor. After his marriage, he purchased from Mrs. R. J. Woods the Old Laney Home on the hill, now "Photenia Gardens," owned by Mr. J. W. Marshall. It was here that their three splendid sons were born and reared and after they had grown to manhood, married and established homes of their own, Mr. and Mrs. Beringer sold this home and built a modern bungalow on Broad street on College Hill, which they were occupying when death claimed them.

Like Mrs. Abe Beringer, Mrs. M. M. Beringer was a rarely beautiful and charming woman whose friends were legion.

Mr. Beringer was not only an outstanding dry goods merchant, occupying the same store building on Broad street a life time and then turning it over to his two sons, Arthur and Nathan, who likewise carried on the Dry Goods business, until they moved to Montgomery a few years since, purchasing a well known large Ready-to-Wear firm of that city, and are now established and valuable citizens of Montgomery. He was a farmer and cotton dealer as well and was most successful in any business venture he made, and was the personal friend of the citizenship of the surrounding Country. His eldest son, Gerson William Beringer, married Hattie Voss, of New York, and their children are Morris Beringer, Gerson W. Beringer, Jr., and Louise Beringer.

Arthur Bernhardt Beringer married Nellie Wolff, daughter of B. and Sophie Wolff of Montgomery. She is a talented violinist, who studied violin for four years with Franz Wilczek, Austrian, in New York and in Frankfort, Germany with Frantz Rebeer.

She played many times in New York with distinguished artists, taught for a number of years in Montgomery, and while she lived in Eufaula delighted many audiences and her friends, with her brilliant playing. She often plays on the programs of the Federated Clubs in Birmingham and other places. Barbour County lays claim to her by right of her husband's citizenship and the years she lived in Barbour County. Their children are Eleanor, Ruth, Arthur Bernhardt, Jr., and Marjorie Nell Bernhardt.

The youngest son, Nathan Arnold Beringer also married a charming and gifted artist, Miss Erura Ausbrook, of Birmingham. She is a teacher of Interpretation dancing, and over the state the children she has trained and the entertainments that she has directed have been commented on most favorably. Some of her own programs and those given by her pupils are marvelous.

Her interpretations are chiefly the classics.

The moving of Messrs. Arthur and Nathan Beringer was a lost to the County in many ways.

Mr. and Mrs. Beringer are buried in Montgomery, although both died in Eufaula.

B. AND H. BERNSTEIN

Among the prominent Jewish citizens of the long ago in Barbour County were Ben and Henry Bernstein, who had a General Merchandise store.

The elder brother, Ben, kept the Central hotel for many years, and was president of Hebrew Congregation. The resident Rabbi was Rabbi Straus and after he left Eufaula, Mr. Silas Stern was the President and Lay Reader of the Congregation.

In 1874 this Congregation purchased the building that was the First Methodist Church, corner of Barbour and Livingston streets, and it was the Synagogue they worshipped in for many years. Many notable marriages among the Jewish citizens took place there and the organ used was a notable one with, at that time, a chime of bells attached to the reeds.

Mr. B. Bernstein went with his brother to Louisville, Ky., and Mr. J. K. Sams became the resident Rabbi, serving until he moved away, and since then Mr. Jake Oppenheimer has been the President of the Congregation.

Late years so many of the Hebrew faith have moved away from the County that the Synagogue was sold to B. L. Bland Coal Company and the services are now held at the Oppenheimer home on Broad street, when all the days of Obligation and all the festivals and fast days of the Isralites as carried out in the Old Testament are observed

Forty years ago there were over fifty Jewish families in Barbour County. Today there are less than one dozen.

The children of all the old Jewish families are scattered in other states, all prosperous and prominent.

All the Bernsteins went to Louisville, Ky., after leaving the historic old Bernstein home on Barbour street to Orange street.

There were two sons, Benherd and Henry, Jr. They were owners of a large shirt manufacturing business in Louisville, and Benherd, "Benny," as he was called at the old home in Eufaula, travelled for the shirt factory. He married Sarah Kaffman, of Columbus, Georgia; Sarah Bernstein married a Kaffman, also of Columbus, Georgia. Two sisters, Minna and Melinda, died in Louisville and were brought back to Eufaula for burial. Benny and Henry and the parents are dead, while Yetta and Della, the younger sisters, still live in Louisville, Ky.

The beautiful old Bernstein home was purchased by Mrs. Robert Cherry years ago, and after her death, sold by her daughter, Mrs. John M. Little of Baltimore, Md., to Mr. John Hartley, who now occupies it. It is one of the old landmarks of an illustrious Jewish family.

EDWARD COURTNEY BULLOCK

Edward Courtney Bullock, called "the matchless and beloved Bullock," was born in Charleston, S. C., Dec. 1825. His father was a native of Rhode Island and his mother a sister of Edward Courtney of Charleston.

After graduating from Harvard in 1843, he came to Barbour County, taught school at Glennville, and in 1846 began practicing law at Eufaula and editor of the local paper. In 1857, he was elected to the State Senate and after four years, resigned, enlisting as a volunteer in the Confederate army. He was chosen Colonel of the First Alabama Regiment at Pensacola.

While on duty at Mobile, he contracted typhoid fever and died in Dec., 1861, only 36 years of age.

He was a man of striking appearance, cultured taste, and of perfect poise, refined and genial manners. He was a finished scholar and an able lawyer of the highest type of integrity of character.

He married Julia Snipes and their children are Hattie, died young, Edward C., Jr., married Eva Martin, issue, John Martin; Edward C., III; Leila married James Edgar Foy, these three deceased, and Clayton Bullock, married, has issue, Sallie Bullock married first John Anderson Dobbins, children, a son, deceased; married second Robert Moulthrop, son, Albert Moulthrop, married Foy Pitts, no issue; a daughter Willie, married first James E. Obrien, issue, sons Emmett, Edward B.; married second, W. D. Northrup, no issue.

Sallie Bullock-Dobbins-Moulthrop inherited her father's brilliancy of mind and was much beloved. She was elected honorary life Chaplain of the Lewis Chapter Daughters of the American Revolution, after having served that organization in that capacity for over 20 years. Also Chaplain of Barbour County Chapter United Daughters of the Confederacy. She was the victim of an automobile accident a few years ago while out riding with her daughter and some friends and instantly killed.

The eldest daughter of Edward C. and Julia Snipe Bullock was "Miss Eliza" as she was affectionately called. She was a belle of the sixties, and for over 25 years taught in the high schools of Montgomery, making for herself a most enviable reputation as an educator. After she retired from teaching she returned home to Eufaula, and until her death, took active part in all church and patriotic work of the community.

It was her custom to visit the family lot in Fairview cemetery one day in every week carrying flowers to her family graves.

One morning twelve years ago, she did not return for so long, knowing she was not very strong, a neighbor went to meet her and she was found dead, the flowers had slipped from her hands beside her. She had taxed her strength, and succumbed to a heart attack that had been feared.

DR. H. L. BRANNON

Dr. Henry Lee Brannon was born March 19, 1866, at the historic old Brannon home on Eufaula street, Eufaula, the son of William Bradley Brannon, of Edgefield, S. C., who, early in life came to Eufaula and with his wife, Mary Kaigler, helped to build Eufaula. Their lovely home that marks Eufaula's "Five Points" still is one of the beautiful homes of this city.

He grew up to the most splendid manhood. His College career was marked by the fact that he was conspicuous as a student of superior intellect, who went to the top in every undertaking.

He graduated with high honors at Vanderbilt University, Nashville, Tenn., afterwards taking various Post Graduate Courses at Johns Hopkins and other medical institutions.

He began the study of medicine when only a school boy, under that distinguished and greatly beloved Dr. J. W. Drewry whose enviable mantel, as a physician and as a popular man and valuable citizen, fell upon him; and when as the youngest doctor in the community, he took up the large practice of Dr. Drewry when he passed on. Dr. Brannon had already established for himself the reputation and skill that numbered him among the best of his profession.

After giving to Eufaula and the surrounding section 20 years of most faithful service, failing health, caused him to give up the practice of medicine, although he loved it very much, and he moved to Marion, Alabama, going into the drug business.

No citizen ever left a community to make his home elsewhere who was more missed professionally in Church, Civic and social life than he and the great success that was his at Marion was a great source of joy to the old home friends, who loved and appreciated him.

He was not only conspicious as a physician of the most distinguished type, but was a man of brilliant literary and mental atttainments.

He was a scholar and a thinker, whose brilliant mind figured out the best and most pleasing always. His sense of humor was keen and he loved a joke, as only the mind that sparkles with a radiance caught from communion with the written wisdom of the old masters, can.

One of the chief characteristics of Dr. Brannon's life was his loyalty to his old friends, his genuineness and his culture that stamped him the Christian gentleman at all times and under all conditions. His passing took to great reward one whose life had been a blessing and a benediction to all who were fortunate enough to call him friend. To his devoted family, wife (Anna Guice of Eufaula) and two daughters, Julia, Mrs. J. C. Wilkinson, Marion, Alabama, and Mary (Mrs. Julian Parker), Galveston Texas, he left the priceless legacy of a "good name."

H. H. AND L. L. CONNER

Barbour County has not only been fortunate in the citizenry of her pioneer days, but is also singularly fortunate in the citizens who have come in later days to cast their lots and abide here, and chief among these families of note to make it their permanent home are Messrs. Henry Hershel and Lynn Lewis Conner, sons of Thomas and Mary Virginia Covington of Tuskegee, Ala. They were educated in the public schools of their home town, afterwards being students at Howard College, Birmingham, and A. P. I., Auburn, Ala., where both received high degrees of distinction. In 1915 Mr. H. H. Conner came to Eufaula, purchasing cotton oil mills, which he still owns, and a short time thereafter he and his brother, Mr. L. L. Conner, purchased the Glendale Cotton Mills, which they operated for a number of years, finally selling it to the Comer interests of the Cowikee Cotton Mills. Mr. L. L. Conner moved to Enterprise, Alabama, for a few years, returning to Eufaula, where he has since been associated with his brother, Mr. H. H. Conner in the Cotton Oil Mills, one of the leading manufacturing enterprises in the County.

Both are men of fine business qualities and highest type of personal integrity. Leaders in all the activities of the County.

H. H. Conner married first Frances Howard, a charming member of the distinguished Howard family. To them were born Mary Frances, who married Leonard Dean Blackmon, and their two children are Ethel Frances and Lucille; Hershel H., Jr., married Janie Collins.

Mr. H. H. Conner married second Kathleen Corker, daughter of the late Ernest D. Drury Corker. Children: William and John Covington, deceased when babies. Other two children, Clinton and Ernest.

Historic old Good Hope Church in Barbour (now Russell) County was the place of worship in pioneer days (they were possibly among the founders) of the Covington family ancestors of the Conner family, and also of Barney and Aislie Ivey, ancestors of Mrs. H. H. Conner.

Lynn Lewis Conner married Will Ella Hendon, daughter of Mr. and Mrs. W. M. Hendon, her father being tax assessor of Macon County, residing at Tuskegee, Ala., for many years. She is a woman of high literary talent and a leader in Church and philanthropic work in the County. Mesdames Conner are leaders in the First Baptist Church Women's work, while Messrs. Conner, Mr. H. H., Senior Deacon, and Mr. L. L. Conner less enthusiastic, but equally interested in all its activities. Mrs. H. H. leads in Young People's work, while Mrs. L. L. leads in the missionary work of the entire town.

The L. L. Conner children are T. Y., L. L., Jr., and Leon and one daughter, Susie.

Conner brothers and their wives are numbered among the strongest forces for uplift in the County and their coming to Eufaula has proved a blessing in every way.

Mr. H. H. Conner served as mayor several terms and his administration was marked with progress that started the city on new lines of a forward march.

HUGH COMER

The eldest of the illustrious Comer brothers was Hugh Comer, who, although born in Barbour County, spent most of his life at Savannah, Georgia. For many years he was president of the Central of Georgia Railway Company and was one of the South's leaders in "big business," and a broad minded, conservative citizen to whom success was a power that prompted him to doing good to his fellow man.

He was buried in Savannah, Georgia, about 25 years ago. He was married.

J. WALLACE COMER

J. Wallace Comer, one of the Comer brothers born at Old Spring Hill, who became one of the leading cotton men of the state, operating a business at Eufaula and Anniston, Alabama. At the latter place he was interested in several other business organizations and was one of the leading business men of the state. He was a Confederate Veteran and a red hot Democrat. He married Miss Carrie Seay of Barbour County and both died a number of years ago and are buried in Fairview Cemetery, Eufaula.

EDWARD TRIPP COMER

Edward Tripp, youngest of the distinguished Comer brothers, was born at Old Spring Hill, August 1st, 1865, and died March 31st, 1927. For years he resided at Millhaven, Georgia, near Savannah, where he had large cotton mill and farming interests. Like all his brothers he was outstanding, philanthropic and progressive and a most valuable citizen.

In 1919, through the initiative, personal interest and philanthropy of Edward T. Comer a road of 18 miles from Hoboken, a suburb a mile from Eufaula, reaching to old Spring Hill, Ala., known as the Comer Highway, was built at a cost of $100,000, and the perpetual upkeep of this is guaranteed by a trust fund, of which Dr. W. S. Britt, Sr., Mr. Donald Comer, Mr. L. Comer Jennings and the late Col. G. L. Comer were trustees. It was created in 1919, with this generous gift from F. C. Comer.

This stretch of road, ending at the Barbour County line, was used before the right of way of the Montgomery and Eufaula railroad by John Fletcher Comer, Sr., and John W. Drewry and was their private property.

Another of the many generous gifts of E. T. Comer to help humanity was a $7,000 X-ray complete equipment to the Britt Infirmary at Eufaula, besides many generous gifts to help the needs of the communities near his Georgia home.

While E. T. Comer had large interests at Millstead and Savannah, Georgia, and spent most of his life there, the old home at Spring Hill was dearest to him and when the end of his career, made glorious by good deeds, came he was carried back and buried in the family mausoleum near to the old church at "Old Spring Hill."

He married Georgia Collier, sister of Bryan Collier, noted Georgian. Associated with him many years at Millstead was his nephew, Frank Willis Comer, the splendid young son of his brother, G. L. Comer, whose brilliant business career was cut off by his sudden death, as he was returning from his office to breakfast one morning some years since at Milstead, Georgia.

GEORGE LEGARE COMER

George Legare Comer was born January 1st, 1847 at Old Spring Hill, the son of John Fletcher and Catherine Lucinda (Drewry) Comer, the former a native of Chilton, Jones County, Georgia, and grandson of Hugh and Annie (Tripp) Comer, who lived at Clinton, Georgia, the former a soldier in the Revolutionary war, and of John and Elizabeth Drewry of Clinton, Ga. He received his preparatory training at field schools at Old Spring Hill and in Polk County and graduated from the University of Georgia, with A. B. degree, 1869. Admitted to the Bar at Eufaula, May, 1869, he began the practice of law, which continued almost to his death. In 1874, he associated with Captain John M. McKleroy, until 1884. Elected mayor of Eufaula, 1882, and re-elected twelve consecutive years. He was Lieut. Col. of Second Regulars Alabama National Guards 1887 to 1890. Trustee Union Female College; Division Counsel for the Central of Georgia Railroad; vice president of the Bank of Eufaula; Democrat; 25 years member of Baptist State Convention; 30 years Moderator of the Eufaula Baptist Association; many years superintendent of the First Baptist Sunday school, and teacher until a short time before his death of the Men's Bible class of the First Baptist Church, Masons, Odd Fellows, Knights Templar, Knight of Honor, and a member of the National Union. He was also a prohibitionist of power in his community.

Colonel Comer was loved and honored as few men ever are, for the splendid traits of character that have made him Barbour County's big power of strength in everything that needed keen insight, good judgment, and courage. He was a leader, advisor and worker. To the poor a generous hearted philanthropist, and his forceful Christian character has been an example of never ending good. To the First Baptist Church for more than a half century, he has been a veritable backbone.

June 23, 1870, he married Laura Thornton, daughter of Dr. W.H. and Mary (Shorter) Thornton; granddaughter of Reuben and Mary (Gill) Shorter.

Children: William Thornton, deceased, who married first Lillie (Brockett), Atlanta; married second Amanda Holcom.

GEO. LEGARE COMER

Laurie, married Frank Wilkins Jennings, who was one of the leading citizens and outstanding business men of Barbour County, member of the fine old aristocratic Jennings family, who came to Eufaula in his childhood. Besides being a wonderful financier and business man, he was the quiet, cultured gentleman and one of the most valued citizens Eufaula ever had.

Their children are L. Comer Jennings, president and manager of the Cowikee Cotton Mills at Eufaula, and like his lamented father, one of the very best citizens the community can boast of; married Kate Roberts; children: Comer, Jr., and Clarence Roberts. Laurie Jennings married first Elbert Willett. Children: Laurie, Elbert and Frank; married second, Rexford Godwin. Children: Jean, daughter, Frank Jennings, youngest son, unmarried.

John Wallace Comer, deceased, married Sadie Patterson. Children: Mary and Wallace, Jr.

George Legare, Jr., married Clennie Cunningham. Children: No issue.

Edward Tripp Comer married Catherine Jelks, daughter of the late William D. Jelks and Alice Shorter Jelks, both deceased. Children: William Jelks Comer, Dr. Edward B. Comer and Alice Shorter Comer.

James D. Comer married first Mary McCormick, one son, James D. Comer, Jr (who was killed in an automobile accident when coming from a school entertainment, at the age of 15, a few months ago). Married second Anne Moses.

Nell Comer, deceased; Frank, deceased, married Montine Roddenberry. Children: Annie Laurie, Frank W., Jr., married Janet Reeves, issue a son, Jerry LeGare Comer.

Frank W. Comer died suddenly at Hillhaven, Ga., some years ago, in the very zenith of successful young manhood.

Robert, deceased; Nell, deceased, and Walter drowned in the Chattahoochee river, older boys taking him in swimming. He was 11 years old.

Miss Mary Comer for years was her distinguished father's constant companion at the historic old Thornton-Comer home on Randolph street (called in the long ago) of as much importance and because of the people living in it, Eufaula's "replica of Pennsylvania Avenue, Washington, D. C., in beauty and historic valuation.

She still resides there keeping to the fine old traditions of her parents and forbears of many generations.

BRAXTON BRAGG COMER

Braxton Bragg Comer was born Nov. 7th, 1848, at Old Spring Hill in Barbour County, son of John Fletcher and (Catherine Drewery) Comer of Jones County, Ga., the former

Judge of Superior Court of the state, removing in 1837 to Barbour County, settling a plantation, on which his brother preceding him, had cleared land and built saw mill, grist mill and flour mill, which the father later converted into an extensive tearing saw, the type used then.

In 1853-54 he represented Barbour County in the state legislature, dying at the age of 47 years. Was grandson of Hugh Moss Comer, native of Virginia, who moved to Georgia early in the 19th Century, reared a family on a self established plantation; and of John and Elizabeth (Wallace) Drewry, also of Jones County, Ga., who later moved to Old Spring Hill, Barbour County.

This family came from English and Irish stock, early settling in Virginia.

The first Comer ancestors to locate near Petersburg, Va., in the "Old Dominion" was, a follower of Cromwell. It is a coincidence that the Comer family is related to Clement Comer Clay, also a Virginian who was Governor of Alabama in 1835, and also U. S. Senator to fill the vacancy caused by the resignation of John McKinley, serving from 1837-41, then resigning.

Gov. Comer was the fourth of six brothers and their life stories are most remarkable and full of interesting developments. All are noted for superior intelligence, force of character and good judgment.

Reared on a plantation, most of them imbibed a love for farming.

Gov. Comer first attended a county school, his teacher being Prof. E. N. Brown, a noted educator, who later entered politics and was representative from Russel County. He attended the University of Alabama in 1864-65, but the burning of the University by Raider Morgan's Union Army cut short his university career. Watching these buildings burn down, Young Comer little dreamed that in the future years as Governor of the state he would direct the finances that rebuilt the fire destroyed college walls and that to honor his work of restoration one of the new buildings would be called "Comer Hall."

After a year back on the farm, he entered the University but ill health interfered with his education.

June 1st, 1868, he entered Emory and Henry College, Va., graduating in 1869, with A. B. and A. M. honors, and winning a medal for excellency in Natural Science.

After his first term as Governor, recognizing his great accomplishments for the state, the LL. D. was conferred upon him.

In 1872, he moved to Comer the railroad station of Old

Spring Hill and his great farms there are the pride of Barbour County.

He was a member of County Commissioners from 1874 to 1878. In 1885 he moved to Anniston, Alabama, going into the wholesale grocery and commission business.

Five years later he moved to Birmingham, as president of the City National Bank and president of Birmingham Corn and Flour Mills.

In 1904 he was elected president of R. R. Commission, defeating Josh V. Smith. In 1906, he entered the race for governor, on the main issue of railroad regulation, in the Democratic primaries; Aug. 27th, 1906, was elected Lieut. Governor over R. M. Cunningham. His inauguration was elaborate and spectacular.

He married first Eva Harris of Cuthbert, Georgia. Children: Sallie B., married Frank Lathrop; J. C. Comer married Helen Brown; Geo McDonald married Gertrude; Mignonne married Craig Smith.

B. B. Comer married second Mary Carr Gibson of Verbena, Alabama.

DONALD COMER

Since time immemorial, the name Comer has stood out preeminently in Barbour County history and each generation, passing and coming, adds new lustre to the pages illumined with the greatness and goodness of the men and women who bear this enviable name.

Among them are lawyers, doctors, farmers, politicians, governors, judges and business men of note, who have left the impres of their lives in deeds that count for their County and state as well as their town. Barbour County and state as well as their town. Barbour County and Eufaula have been fortunate in claiming the citizenship of many of them and the fact that Eufaula was the home for many years, as well as Old Spring Hill, of Mrs. Katherine Drewry Comer, the lovely and greatly beloved mother of Hugh M. Comer, railroad magnate and Eufaula's own beloved Mayor George LeGare Comer, great lawyer and consecrated Christian citizen; and J. F. Comer, the distinguished father of Mrs. W. S. Britt, who spent much time here, although his home was at Midway; Edward, notable financier of Millhaven, Ga., and J. Wallace, the Alabama cotton factor; and Gov. B. B. Comer, who often came back to Barbour to visit and abide for months at a time at the historic old home at Old Spring Hill in Barbour, all makes this illustrious family belong to Barbour County.

The purpose, however, of this article is to tell what Donald

Comer, son of Governor Braxton Bragg Comer, has done for Barbour County and more directly for Eufaula.

When the Eufaula Cotton Mills, after the death of its Founder and President, Capt. John W. Tullis, was losing ground and was sold to meet its liabilities, members of the Comer family purchased the plant and Col. G. L. Comer became president. In 1919 Mr. Donald Comer was elected president and with his fine executive ability, keen insight into fits and misfits, and his knowledge of cotton mill business —he went to work—did not spare any expense, or curtail any outlay or money to put the plant which he named "Cowikee Mills," into first class, up-to-date condition. For years he has given it his close personal attention and along with the great mill improvement, he has spent hundreds of thousands of dollars in improving and building up the city at the sole expense of the Cowikee Mills. He paved Barbour street fronting the mills, paved the sidewalks from Barbour street across Union street out Eufaula street out to Washington street, built a concrete bridge across the town branch of 100 feet, and ravine on Union street.

Spent something like fifty thousand dollars in landscap gardening, equipment and furnished the Community House, built a school house and maintains all this, which is in charge of a capable superintendent and teacher, Miss Hallie Hartsfield, superintendent and community director; Miss Helen Mitchell, kindergarten teacher and Miss Louise Adcock, assistant teacher.

The Cowikee band of 50 boys and girls, children of the operatives of the mills, with Elbert Beasley, director, is the pride of Barbour County.

In the Mills resident district, a dozen or more modern bungalows were built ten years ago, equipped with every modern convenience.

On Comer street, leading to Comer Athletic Park there is a grandstand and baseball park.

The small children of the mothers working in the mills are cared for during the day at the Community House and the boys and girls have the privilege of night school.

The property of Cowikee Mills Company in Barbour County is estimated at one-half million dollars.

Mr. Comer's wonderful management, his generosity and his thoughtfulness for the comfort and pleasure of the mill employees have made his name a household word among them.

It is worthy of mention that, during all the years that he has been president of Cowikee Mills, his personal Christmas remembrance to each employee has been so generous and timely that the joy it gave is indescribable.

With the past few years Donald Comer has purchased

the historic old home of Col. Hiram Hawkins at Hawkinsville 14 miles north of Eufaula in Barbour County, which he has remodeled and improved and his family spend much time at this beautiful Country home.

It is significant that it should have been the home of two illustrious men who have figured so largely in Barbour County history.

Hawkinsville was the home of the Barbour County Grange, and Farmers' Alliance, and the place of many notable political gatherings in the long ago.

He married Gertrude Miller of Reading, Pa., and their children are: Kate, married Paul Borron, Birmingham; Jane, married Alfred Shook, Birmingham; Donald, Jr., married Isabel Anderson, Montgomery, and Martine, unmarried.

JOHN FLETCHER COMER

John Fletcher Comer, son of John Fletcher and Katherine (Drewry) Comer, was born at the historic old home at Old Spring Hill, where he grew up on the farm deeply interested in agriculture. He attended the University of Alabama. While a man of wonderful executive ability, his taste clung to farm life and his success as a farmer was of the kind that helps not only the farmer himself, but whose example to others is most helpful. In the dark days of reconstruction in Barbour County, Mr. Comer was a force in helping straighten out the terrible conditions brought about by Republican rule, and he, with other members of the Comer family in the County were instrumental in righting many polititcal wrongs.

As the years passed on he married Elizabeth Thornton, a young woman of brilliant intellect, rare and loveable traits of Christian character, and their beautiful home at Midway, Alabama, through all the long years has been one of historical hospitality and Christian culture.

Their one son, Dr. Robert Comer, married May Adams, daughter of Rev. I. O. Adams, one time Rector of St. James Episcopal Church at Eufaula, and he is now a prominent physician of Birmingham, Alabama.

Their four lovely daughters, like their gifted mother, are leaders in social, church and club work in their several homes. Annie married James A. Emory and lives in Mont Clair, New Jersey. She is the mother of a charming family, one of her daughters, Katherine Emory, having become famous as an actress in the great play, "Children's Hour." that has had so many years' popular run on Broadway, New York, and other theatrical honors await her in the future. She already has refused flattering motion pictutre offers.

The next daughter, Kate, married Dr. Walter Stratton

Britt of Eufaula, noted physician and surgeon, who is Barbour County's first citizen from every standpoint. Their children are Elizabeth, married Lewis Moore, son of Thomas L. and Ethel (Dean) Moore, and Walter S., Jr., who like his father is a fine physician just beginning his professional career. He married Julia Bullock, daughter of Mr. and Mrs. S. A. Bullock.

The third daughter, Elizabeth, married Comer Gillmartin, a prominent business man of Texas, and their young son, John Gillmartin, is becoming famous as an aviator and has a promising future before him.

Mr. Comer died Feb. 22nd, 1927, and is buried in the Comer Memorial Mausoleum at the Old Spring Hill Church, where so many of this illustrious family rest.

Mrs. Comer, now in her eighties, is the beautiful, cultured old lady of the South, who despite her age, is still charming, and the delight of her many friends on every occasion that she graces. She is a writer of note and her articles are always eagerly sought.

CLAYTON

Barbour County Chapter U. D. C. was entertained at a recent meeting at the beautiful Clayton home, out a mile from Clayton, nestling amid the wealth of flowers and old trees, and it was recalled that this chapter was founded by Miss Mary Clayton at Eufaula, inspired by the same love of the Confederacy and all that it stood for that made her father, General De Lamar Clayton, the hero and beloved citizen of Barbour County that he was.

When, during the program, it was announced that the sixth District of the Alabama Division U. D. C. had, at the annual Convention in Dothan, May 1st, 1935, been named "Clayton District" to honor this great General, the memory of his brilliant and eventful career was recalled, and the meeting was an event of many delightful, historic memories.

This beautiful, historic old home, from the walls of which this old soldier, patriot and statesman, General Henry D. Clayton, smiles down upon you, from oil paintings and photographs taken at different periods of his life, was a specific pleasure to all present.

The rare antique furnishings are today, just as they were when he glorified this home with his distinguished presence and also when the queen wife and mother who reigned over it, was beautiful, gifted Victoria Hunter Clayton, author of "Black and White Under the Old Regime"—one of the most interesting, vivid and gripping accounts of the war and reconstruction days, reigned over it.

Another distinguished honor paid General Clayton was the selection of his name by the Stone Mountain Memorial Association as one of the outstanding military leaders of Alabama, whose names are to be engraved on the carving into this ' Georgia World Wonder," of hero figures and names, representing the Infantry, Artillery, Cavalry, Naval and Medical departments of the Confederacy.

These five names are, viz: General Joseph Wheeler, Admiral Raphael Semmes; General Henry DeLamar Clayton; John (gallant) Pelham; and Dr. LaFayette Gould.

GENERAL HENRY D. CLAYTON

General Henry DeLamar Clayton was born May 7th, 1827 in Pulaski County, Georgia, the son of Nelson and Sarah (Caruthers) Clayton, the former a farmer, and Representative in the Georgia Legislature many years.

In 1838, he removed to Lee County. He was the grandson of Thomas and Sallie (DeLamar) Clayton, emmigrants from England to Maryland, later locating in South Carolina.

General Clayton was also descended from James Lee, a Revolutionary soldier of Georgia. His Caruthers ancestors were Scotch and French.

He was educated in Vineville near Macon, Georgia, and entered Henry College in Virginia in 1848, after having graduated at Emory college in Georgia.

He studied law in Eufaula under John Gill (Alabama's war-time governor), Eli S. and John Shorter, the law firm of "Shorter Bros." and began the practice of law at Clayton after being admitted to the Bar in 1849.

At the beginning of the War Between the States, he urged Governor Moore to accept the "Clayton Guards" and the "Eufaula Rifles" of the 3rd Alabama Regiment as "Alabama Volunteers" and on Gov. Moore's refusal, he was mustered in as a private in the "Clayton Guards," and the Governor soon saw that he was determined and ordered him to take charge of all Alabama Volunteers and organize them into a Regiment.

He was sent to Pensacola, Florida, on March 28th, 1861, organized the 1st Alabama Regiment and was electetd its Colonel. While commander of this regiment, he was wounded and after his recovery on April 1st, 1863, he was commissioned Brigadier. General, commanding the 18th, 32nd, and 36th, and the 55th Alabama Regiment of Captain Humphrey's Arkansas Battery.

This brigade was the most important in the battle of Rock Face Mountain, New Hope and Chickamauga. July 18th, 1864, he was made Major General commanding troops of the

Army of Tennessee and was wounded several times, his horse being killed under him at Jonesborough.

He covered the retreat of the Confederate army and on December 16th, 1864, his service at Bentonville, N. C., was heroic in every move.

After the war, returning to private life and his law practice in 1866 he was elected Judge for the Third Judicial Circuit of Alabama and served under reconstruction acts of Congress. He was re-elected in 1880 and resigned to become a candidate for Governor, but was defeated, the forces that controlled reconstruction in Alabama, opposing REAL Democracy at that time.

In June, 1886 he was elected President and Professor of International Law of the University of Alabama, receiving the degree of L. L. D. from that institution.

Death came to him in October 1889 while at the acme of his educational service to Alabama and he was buried with high honors at Clayton.

An outstanding churchman of the Episcopal faith, a broad minded, conservative citizen, as well as a brave soldier and wise commander.

About thirty years ago his remains were removed from the cemetery at Clayton and re-interred in Fairview cemetery at Eufaula, most of the family having removed to Eufaula to make their future home. After a few years, however, Miss Mary Clayton and her brother, Jefferson D. Clayton, moved back to the original old home at Clayton, which they have preserved in all its beauty, adding latter day improvements, but not changing any of its former artistic and natural beauty.

Besides this distinguished Confederate General and his wife, his illustrious son and namesake Judge Henry D. Clayton, Jr., rests beside his father and mother.

HENRY DeLAMAR CLAYTON, JR.

Henry D. Clayton, United States District Judge, was born at Clayton in Barbour County February 10th, 1857, son of Major General Henry D. Lamar and Victoria (Hunter) Clayton of the branch of the Clayton family founded by James Clayton who came from England to Maryland and later settled in North Carolina.

Henry Clayton, Jr., was educated at the University of Alabama, graduating in 1877 with A. B. and L. L. B. degrees.

He first practiced law at Clayton, coming to Eufaula in 1880 where he retained Bar Membership until 1924.

He was Register in Chauncery from 1880 to 1884 and a member of the General Assembly 1890-91 and United States

District Attorney for the middle district of Alabama 1893-1896. He was presidential elector in the years 1888 and 1892 and from 1888 to 1908 was member of the Democratic National Committee. In 1896 he was elected to represent the Third Congressional District in Congress and regularly re-elected up to and including the sixty-third Congress from which he resigned his seat May 1st, 1904, to become United States District Judge. He was chairman of the Committee on Judiciary in the house of the Sixty-Second Congress. As chief manager on the part of the House, formulating the articles of impeachment against United States Judge Robert W. Archibald, a circuit judge assigned to the Court of Commerce. This

HENRY DeLAMAR CLAYTON, JR.

famous impeachment trial began in 1912 with Judge Clayton as chief prosecutor.

His conduct of that case as set forth in the public records was most notable.

The Clayton Act, a piece of legislation named to honor Judge Clayton, is a monument to his ability and greatness.

His Federal Bench record places him high in the annals of the states' most weighty measures. Numerous bills, of his have left their impress on the nation.

He married first in 1882, Virginia Ball Allen, daughter of General W. W. Allen, of Montgomery. She died in 1883. He married second Battie Davis, daughter of Samuel M. and Alice (Kenny) Davis of Georgetown, N. Y.

THOMAS M. CLAYTON

Thomas M. Clayton was born at Clayton, Alabama, and grew up and graduated from college. He has spent his entire life, a scientific farmer, on the extensive Clayton Plantations in Barbour County.

He married Nora Jennings and their children were Albert J., who married Marie Feagin; Mary Pugh, deceased; Victoria, who married Elige Lingo; Thomas, married Bates; Elliott, married; Henry, married.

BERTRAM TRACY CLAYTON

Bertram Tracy Clayton was born at the historic Clayton home at Clayton, Alabama, October 19th, 1862, son of Henry DeLamar and Victoria Hunter Clayton. He was a student at the University of Alabama 1180-82 and graduated from the United States Military Academy in 1886.

He was appointed a second lieutenant in the 11th United States Infantry, resigning in April, 1888, to become a civil engineer of Brooklyn, N. Y.

He was adjutant of the 13th Regiment National Guard, New York State in 1890; Major and engineer 2nd brigade 1894, commanding this company during the Spanish-American war and served through the Porto-Rican campaign.

From 1899 to 1901 he was Colonel of the 14th Regiment National Guard, New York State, and served as a member of the fifty-fifth congress, March 4th, 1899-March 3rd, 1901.

He reentered the United States Army and was appointed Captain and Quartermaster March 3rd, 1911, constructing quartermaster in charge of the erection of new riding hall and new Academic building, United States Military Academy, 1911-1913, and chief quartermaster of U. S. troops in Canal Zone to 1917.

[372]

During the European war he was chief quartermaster of the first Division, first Army Corps A. E. F., in France, and was serving in this capacity when killed. (See Barbour County Soldiers killed in France page).

He married first on June 12th, 1887, Louise M. Barasher of Brooklyn, N. Y; married second Sept. 2nd, 1907, Mary D. Watson of New Orleans, La. Children: William Brasher, married to Claud Hill McKenzie, daughter of P. B. and Claudia Hill McKenzie, the former at one time mayor of Eufaula: Bertram Tracy (deceased) married Lucile Hill, Labinia, California.

JEFFERSON DAVIS CLAYTON

Jefferson Davis Clayton was born April 13th, 1869, at Clayton, son of Henry DeLamar and Victoria Hunter Clayton. He graduated in 1890 from the University of Alabama with A. B. degree; from then the Cumberland University, Lebanon, Tenn., with L. L. B. degree in 1892. He practiced law at Eufaula from 1893 to 1903, temporarily giving up law on account of ill health and engaged in farming, which he still follows, being one of the largest and most diversified farmers in Barbour County. In 1919 he was elected to the House of Representatives from Barbour and is deeply interested in political matters of the state and a most valuable citizen.

He is a staunch Democrat, an Episcopalian and is unmarried. He and his sister, Miss Mary Clayton, reside at the old historic Clayton home at Clayton and carry on the traditions of this notable old home. Its flower, fruits, vegetables, stock and poultry are famous.

MISS MARY CLAYTON

One of the most brilliant and beloved women in Barbour County is Mary Clayton, daughter of General Henry D. Clayton (see his biography page) and Victoria Hunter Clayton.

In early life she was a beauty and a belle, and through all the changing years has been a forceful leader in all the Women's work in Church, educational, patriotic, social and civic in the county and in Clayton and Eufaula. All of her life except a few years when she lived with her brother, Judge Henry D. Clayton, Jr., at Eufaula, she has resided at the old Home in Clayton. She is a member of Lewis Chapter D. A. R. and honorary member of Barbour County Chapter U. D. C. (which she organized and founded) of the Service Star Legion at Clayton and of the Clayton Chapter U. D. C., and a power of strength in Grace Episcopal Church at Clayton.

For a number of years she taught in the City Schools at Eufaula and she is greatly beloved.

JUDGE LEE JOHNSTON CLAYTON

Judge Lee J. Clayton was born at the old Clayton home at Clayton, February 10th, 1874, son of Henry DeLamar and Victoria (Hunter) Clayton. He attended the public schools of Clayton and Tuscaloosa (while his father was president of the University of Alabama) and graduated from the University in 1892.

In 1893 he was elected Judge of the Inferior Court of Eufaula, resigning in 1911, when appointed United States attorney from the fifth district of Alabama on September 16. He served two terms as mayor of Eufaula and is now one of the leading lawyers of the state.

He is lay reader and senior Vestryman of St. James Episcopalian church; a "Clayton Democrat"; a Mason; K. of P and I. O. O. F.

He married on July 4th, 1902, Carolyn Elizabeth, daughter of Dr. W. P. and Mary Fontaine (Flewellen) Copeland. Children: Preston Copeland, also an attorney, married Gladys Robertson, Clayton; Mary, married Kenneth Penhallegon, Birmingham; Lee J., Jr., married Margaret Norton, Hurtsboro, Ala.; Victoria, married Vance Custer of Bainbridge; Caroline, married Howard Houston of Eufaula.

Other sons were Joseph A., also a scientific farmer, who married Eugenia Williamson of Birmingham; Julius P., prominent attorney of Ozark, Oklahoma; and Nelson, who died in infancy.

The daughters of General and Mrs. Clayton were: Sarah Elizabeth, who married Andrew Maxwell Walthour of Savannah, Ga.; Victoria Virginia, who married Wiley Williams of Columbus, Ga.; Mary Elliott unmarried; Helen Davis, married Dr. C. H. Rogers of Muscogee, Oklahoma.

All these have been outstanding and representative women in their respective communities and are women of rare culture and higher education.

Humerous Incident of General Clayton's Military Career From Harper's Magazine, March 25th, 1884

"Your story of General Harden," writes an estimable correspondent, brings to my mind another—when the Confederate army was in camp at Tupelo, Miss., after we had run the Federals out of Corinth: (we ran and they ran after us) among the troops which flocked to the standard, came a fine Alabama Regiment of the 39th under Col. Clayton, afterwards General, and who now wears the ermine of an Alabama judge, with the same credit that he wore the grey.

Upon reporting to General Bragg for assignment to a

brigade. Col. Clayton invited General Bragg to ride over and see his troops. General Bragg accepted and invited the staff (of which the writer was one) to accompany him. As we rode on Colonel Clayton with just pride, beguiled the way, with many brags, as to the material and discipline of the Regiment.

As we approached his camp, we saw a soldier sitting on a stump, while his musket rested against a tree across the road.

"Is that one of your men"? said General Bragg to Col. Clayton (addressing the man) "to what regiment do you belong to? The soldier replied "Col. Clayton's." Col. Clayton then said: "What are you doing here"? Soldier: "I'm a sentinel." The Colonel's wrath rose with the peals of laughter from General Bragg and staff and the poor Confederate then and there got a severe lecture on the duties of a sentinel.

As we rode on we heard from the man a loud call—"Mister I say"—As we stopped, he said, "Ain't you Mister Clayton?" "Yes" (very short) said Col. Clayton. "Well," he said, what arrangements have you made for our washing"?

Judge Clayton, when he remembers that of all that large party who enjoyed that scene (as he did) he and the writer only are left alive.

JUDGE LEE J. CLAYTON   F. C. CLAPP

F. C. CLAPP

F. C. Clapp was born July 31st, 1888, at Kasota, Minn., the son of H. W. and Florence Julia Clapp.

He lived on a farm until 1910.

Graduated at the Kasota High School in 1907 from Maukato Normal school (two year course) 1909 and attended college of agriculture in Minnesotao with B. S. degree in 1915; same college M. S. degree in 1916. He taught school one year at Bigelere, Miss., spent 18 months from January to September, 1914, in the Panama Canal Zone.

He joined the U. S. Army on Jan. 1st., 1918, and attended officers' training school at Battle Creek, Mich., February, March and April, 1918.

He was commissioned second lieutenant in Field Artillery June 5th, 1918; was in oversea service as second lieutenant of 316 Field Artillery Battery A, June 1918, to June, 1919, when he was honorably discharged from service.

He was employed in Extensiers service, University of Minnesota in July of 1919; came to Barbour County, Alabama, October, 1920; employed by the Alabama Pecan Company until 1926, and since 1929 has been County farm demonstration agent for Barbour County with office at Clayton.

He married Benito (Baily) and their children are Allen Frederick Clapp, Florence Clapp, Marvin Clapp and Esther Clapp.

Mr. Clapp is an Elder of the Presbyterian Church at Eufaula and teacher of the men's class of the Sunday school. He is also a member of the Kiwanis Club as a high-toned gentleman and a valuable citizen.

He has a beautiful country home six miles from Eufaula and the family are identified with all the higher interests of the community.

His parents, Mr. and Mrs. H. W. Clapp, spend their winters south and are also identified with the social and church life of Barbour County. Mr. Clapp has been, and is, an asset to the agricultural interests of the County.

REV. EUGENE CRAWFORD

Eugene Lowther Crawford, born January 12th, 1871, at Glennville, Barbour County, son of Robert Blakely and Martha Frances (Stephenson) Crawford, who served charges at Montgomery, Mobile, Talladega, White Plains, Glennville, Demopolis, Opelika, died and are both buried at Eufaula.

Eugene Crawford was an outstanding Methodist minister, was secretary of the Alabama Conference for 15 years and was twice delegate to the General Conference. He was the grandson of Robert Blakely and (Olivia) Crawford, who lived at Smith's Station, Lee County, great grandson of Jorick and Martha (Green) Stephenson, the latter a relative of Nathional Green.

He was educated in the Mobile schools at the Barton Academy and at the Southern University at Greensboro, graduating with an A. B. degree in 1891.

He was licensed to preach at the annual conference at Eufaula November 30th, 1893, and was admitted to trial the following December. He was pastor at Washington Street Church, Eufaula; Tuskegee; South Perry Street, Montgomery; presiding elder Pensacola district; Greensboro; Andulusia and Enterprise.

In Texas he was in charge of Central Church at Galveston and Church at Crockett. He was traveling Elder and assistant Secretary of Alabama Conference; was a Democrat; member of Sigma Alpha Eplison fraternity; a Mason and Odd Fellow and Knight of Columbian Woodmen.

He was one time chairman of the Temperance Committee. of Alabama Conference, Trustee of Anti-Saloon League several years and leader of the movement that gave Bullock County Prohibition in 1907, and also leader in the amendment of forces in that county.

He married first on October 30th, Martha Thorington, who died in March, 1911, daughter of Judge William S., and Mary Thorington Montgomery. Children: Francis Lucille; Martha Stephenson.

Married second, Carmichael. Buried in family lot at Eufaula.

LEWIS LEWELLEN CATO

Both in Barbour and Russell Counties the name Cato has figured in agriculture, politics, business, professionally and civically to the extent that the descendants of the pioneer members and down to today have great cause to be proud.

Lewis Lewellen Cato was a lawyer whose ability was known and commented on all over the state.

He practiced at Eufaula many years and it was said that his arguments to a petty jury were as unique as they were emphatic and carried weight.

He built the fine old Cato home on College Hill that is now the home of his daughter-in-law, Mrs. J. C. Cato, and family.

Mr. Cato's farms in former Barbour, now Russell County, were the admiration of all the countryside in those days when he always had from one hundred to a thousand bales of cotton—carried over year to year. He was a lawyer to whom all the young law students of the community sought to secure the advantage of partnership with, because of his reputation, as one of the finest lawyers in the South.

He reared a large family and after his death as each one married and made homes in other sections, the family sold the old home to Mr. Edward B. Young, who made it his home until his death and his family sold it back to Dr. J. C. Cato, the only one of the Cato children who had made Eufaula his permanent home.

Throughout all the years this home has maintained the reputation for culture and family pride that has marked this distinguished family.

He married Martha Jane Richardson of Glennville, Russell (then Barbour) County and to them were born nine children: William Richardson Cato, Leila Conner of Glennville; Sue Cato, married to Mr. Murphy; Lula Cato married to Henry Cobb; Mollie Cato, married; Lewellen Cato Bachelor; Julius Cato married first Lula Kendall, issue: one son, Julius Cato, Jr., deceased, lawyer; married second Louise Knox, issue, Lewis, married.

Annie; Sterling and Carol; Mattie Cato, married; Eugene Cato, married; Floy Cato, married.

MR. AND MRS. ANDERSON CREWS

Anderson A. Crews was born in Barbour County March 1st, 1831. On January 18th, 1857, he married Mariah (Bush) Thomas, who was born at the old Johnathan Thomas home, 12 miles from Clayton, one of the notable hallmarks of the County.

Two children reached maturity. Cynthia Marshall married Dr. G. M. Bobbitt, one of the leading dentists of Southeast Alabama, on March 1st, 1881. Only one child lived from infancy, Carrie C. She married Robert Willis, son of J. J. Willis, tax assessor for the county for many years and a Confederate Veteran of special note—issue, James Arthur Carolyne S. Willis. Clifford Crews married John R. Ventress on March 26th, 1879, of the prominent Ventress family of Barbour County. Their eldest daughter, Emma Marshall, married B. B. Warren, son of a notable Confederate soldier and their son is now 18 years of age. Mary Anderson Ventress married R. L. Fenn, also the son of Confederate Veteran, and member of the dinstinguished Fenn family of Barbour County, being also a great great grandson of Mark Williams, one of the first settlers of the village of Eufaula— L. Fenn being a World War veteran.

Sarah Crews was not only a pious, deeply religious woman but an outstanding clubwoman as well and a strong force in the Clayton Chapter U. D. C., her daughter, Mrs. Ventress also being an enthusiastic U. D. C. worker.

Anderson Crews was quite wealthy, his large farms being known of and praised far and wide. He was a man of that type of character that made him a leader in all the progress of the County. His attractive aind unique home in Clayton was notable for the religious influence that went out from it. Besides their own daughter, Mr. and Mrs. Crews adopted and reared a number of neices and nephews.

Mrs. Crews donated a lot and built a church adjoining their home, and supplied greater part of the salary yearly to maintain this Methodist Protestant Church. Since her death, however, the church organization has been dissolved and the Church has been remodelled into a private residence. This family is the ideal one, leading in kindness, neighborliness, philanthropy and in the citizenry of the County and the descendants still are first among the best ever.

Mr. Crews was a loyal, patriotic Confederate soldier, several times signally honored.

JOHN COLBY

John Colby was born in Stradbaly, Queens County Ireland.

He came to Barbour County in the forties and established the first Merchant-tailoring establishment in this section. He brought a fine bank account with him and was one of the first depositors in the "Bridge Bank" at Eufaula. He bought land and for a number of years had a flourishing farm eight miles from Eufaula. His young son, John Colby, died upon reaching manhood.

His four daughters were all born at the home which he built on Broad street (now owned by Jake Oppenheimer). The new street cut through the Colby property in the early eighties, from Broad street to Garden Lane, and was named Colby Street to honor John Colby.

His wife, Charlotte Colby, was one of the leading pioneer women of the County, and after her husband's death on March 12th, 1858, she kept his tailoring business going for a number of years.

John Colby was a Catholic and his wife a Protestant, but after the Church of the Holy Redeemer was built in Eufaula she became a communicant of that church and moved to the Rectory of the Church with her four young daughters and the pastors of the Church always boarded with her until the late seventies when she moved to Sanfort Street and there died March 15, 1879.

Her daughters were brilliant women, and all took outstanding positions in life. The fortune their father left, giving them every advantage that wealth could procure.

They were Mary, married Dan Rowlette, prominent citizen of Eufaula, who was one of the first from Barbour County to go to Birmingham in 1880. They had one son, John Rowlette, and established a fine business there. Anne married Thomas Carr, the famous "Cracker Manufacturer of Montgomery. They had a son, Dennis Carr, and a daughter, Agnes. Alice married William Rosenstile, a prominent jeweler of Birmingham and a member of the Rosenstile family of Union Springs, Ala.

Sophie married Thomas Thornton, many years a leading groceryman of Birmingham, and to them was born a daughter, Charlotte Colby Thornton, and she is the sole survivor of this large family, except the Carr grandchildren.

The third daughter, Susan, was a brilliant woman of letters, being a teacher at Union Female College at Eufaula, and early in life a special teacher of small children in a private school on Sanford street.

John Colby, wife and son are buried in Fairview cemetery. The others are buried at different places in Birmingham and Montgomery.

AUSTIN C. CARGILL

In the old pioneer days, when settlers were building their homes on the bluff (which gave the town a name of "Bluff City"—one of the best beloved and most unique in character of men was Austin C. Cargill, who spent his life here and who said, with a merry twinkle in his eyes, that were always laughing, "love to live on this bluff because whichever way I look I see beauty—as far as eye can reach." That inate, patriotic love of the beautiful in all things was paramount in his colorful career.

He went about his daily business as contractor and builder, with the cheerful, jolly attitude of life, that from boyhood won friends and held

AUSTIN C. CARGILL

them, throughout a lifetime. To his neighbors and to all whom he could in any way be helpful to, he was always ready, with a cheery word and lending hand, for any service, he could render. His whole life was a song, the melody of which has echoed down the years, and has made his memory blessed.

When the call to arms came, to the sons of Dixie he was among the first to offer himself, and gathering his "Fife" and falling into line gave his musical talent with his patriotism to help swell the martial strains that led to what every true Southerner was—even in defeat, MORE glorious than the victory of the foe, the South resisted so nobly.

That "Fife" is now one of the sacred relics in the Confederate Museum at Richmond, Va.

Throughout the terrors of reconstruction days in Barbour County, Austin Cargill took an active part in all the efforts of the Democratic citizenship, to bring order out of discord, and several times because of his personal, genial manner and ability to convince some of the "hot heads" in political arguments, he was called upon to act as peacemaker—and always succeeded. He was broadminded and genuine and always so fair in all his dealings to the extent that he was sometimes called "precise Austin."

He was a leader in Prof. J. C. Van Houten's famous orchestra over 25 years and every one of his ten children inherited his musical talent, a number of them attaining prominence in the musical world, as members of famous' orchestras and bands, soloists, organists, and pianists, of this large family, those still living being: Mrs. B. F. Fussell (Sallie Cargill), Jacksonville, Fla.; Mrs. G. W. Hinsey (Fanny Cargill), Houston, Texas; Mrs. Edward Moore (Mattie Cargill), Selma, Ala; Mrs. Thomas M. Brannon (Leila Cargill), who is one of Eufaula's sweetest and most gifted soprano singers, whose lovely voice has been heard throughout her life in the choir of the First Baptist Churches at Eufaula and in all the local musical clubs and programs of the community. Her daughter, Mrs. J. C. Blanton (Edith Brannon) of Columbus, Georgia, is a leader in the musical circles of Columbus churches and musical circles of other cities.

Romeo Cargill, Montgomery expert Voincellest, like his father, has been all his life, member of notable orchestras. When a boy he was in the Van Houten orchestra with his father.

Thomas Milton Brannon, Jr., grandson, is now head of the famous "Warner Seven Aces" orchestra of Atlanta, and voted first place as Radio entertainers in America.

Austin Cargill was born in Parish, Ky.

He came to Eufaula in pioneer days; died and is buried in Fairview cemetery in Eufaula.

The writer of this history could not close this article without giving in heartfelt words of love, honor due Amelia Cargill (eldest daughter of Mrs. T. E. W. Callen) one of the dearest, sweetest friends of a lifetime any woman ever had, and the memory of her life, her love for music, her vocal solos, and her unique playing of the organ.

Like her mother (Priscilla Helen Priest) Mrs. Austin Cargill, she was a lovely little woman, whose heart was pure gold and her whole life a sweet song to give the music of joy and love to others.

Appointed Fife Major

Headquarters First Regiment,
Alabama 12-months Volunteers
Barrancas Barracks.

To Austin Columbus Cargill:

Whereas you have been appointed Fife Major of the Alabama Twelve-Months Volunteers, and reposing special trust and confidence in your appointment as such Fife Major: You will dilligently and carefully perform the duties of your office by doing and performing all manner of things, thereto belonging until the Volunteers for 12 months to this place are organized; or for some other cause, I may see proper to cancel this appointment.

You will observe and obey such orders as you may, from time to time receive from me, according to military rule and discipline and all inferior officers and soldiers are enjoined to obey you in your capacity.

Witness my hand this day of Feb., 1861.
Henry D. Clayton, Col.
Aid C. Commander
Alabama 12 Months Volunteers.

B. Lem. Hargrove. ADJ.

JOHN COCHRAN

John Cochran was born in Coke County, Tenn., on a farm; graduated from Greenville College in 1835, and began his career as representative from Calhoun County in 1839.

In 1843 he came to Barbour county and settled in Eufaula and ran for Congress, but was defeated by Herbert Hilliard of Montgomery County.

In 1848 and again in 1851 he was defeated on the Cass Electorial ticket, after a heated canvass with James Abercrombie of Russell County, 1853 to 1857, he represented Barbour County in the General and in 1861, in the Constitutional Convention.

On the resignation of Gov. John Gill Shorter, he was appointed Judge of the Circuit Court until 1865, when he was displaced by Reconstruction troubles

In 1861, he enlisted in the Confederate Army, serving at Pensacola.

He was outstanding, learned, an interesting speaker, full of wit and humor, as well as a logical reasoner. He was the soul of honor and genuine integrity. He was the law partner of U. S. Senator James L. Pugh at Eufaula and it was said, "He came to Barbour County with a Bible in one hand and a dictionary in the other." His brilliant mind, spontaneous wit and ability made him one of the most illustrious men the County boasts of.

He married first Miss Wellborn; second her sister, Miss Wellborn; third cousin of the other, also Miss Wellborn. His fourth wife was Miss Carrie Toney, of Roseland. Their only child, Carolyne, married first Bishop Jackson of the diocese of Alabama, issue: a daughter, Carolyne and a son Mellville, who married.

Carolyne married Dawson McGough of the distinguished Georgia family of Glennville, Barbour County.

Judge Cochran's only son, born of his first wife, was Alfred Wellborn Cochran, also a dinstinguished attorney, was reared at Eufaula and married Teresa, daughter of Senator J. L. Pugh.

In the early eighties they moved to New York where, until he retired from active business, he was counsellor for one of the largest organizations of the state of New York. His wife as Regent of the City of New York, Chapter D. A. R. and president of the New York Chapter U. D. C., was well known and both popular in exclusive New York's society.

About three years ago this fine old couple, rapidly going down the life line, decided to come back to Eufaula and had arranged for their home, when Mrs. Cochran was taken very ill and was never strong enough to make the trip. When she passed away, her husband, 87, brought her remains back to the old home. Their househould furnishings (most beautiful, rare and costly, followed) and were stored and he made his home at a local hotel. Every morning and afternoon, despite his age, he drove his large car to the cemetery and sat for hours beside her grave, always keeping it covered with rare flowers. This beautiful tribute to her was the admiration of the community. In less than a year the call came to him and he quietly passed away at Britt's Infirmary.

During the hours he spent daily at his beloved wife's grave he had planted a weeping willow tree, had placed over the grave also covering the vault he had prepared for himself a most beautiful inscription, verses composed by him, that is a classical gem.

The lesson of love and faithfulness, this distinguished old man (tall and erect to his death) has taught in the months he was left alone is the most touching and beautiful thing that human mind can conceive.

LEONARD YANCEY DEAN

A Memoir of the Life of Captain L. Y. Dean by his wife Carolyne S. Dean

Captain Leonard Yancey Dean was born July 18th, 1844, at "Sycamore Hill," Edgefield, S. C. His father, Aaron Clark Dean, was one of nature's noblemen, of fine family, native intelligence, refined, cultural and of handsome personality. He was scrupulously just, generous to a fault; indeed he was in every respect a gentleman. His mother, Maria Bland, was descended through a long line from John Bland, third son of the illustrious Theodorick, who came to Virginia in 1654. She was the daughter of Pressley Bland, of whom the Honorable George D. Tillman of Edgefield, writes: "I knew him

LEONARD YANCEY DEAN

well; he was a courtly gentleman, a popular and public spirited citizen."

Martha Bland was by heritage of the same courteous nature, dispensing sunshine and happiness in her home and making better all with whom she came in contact. The very name of her home, "Sagamore Hill," was synonimous in all that country with unstinted hospitality; and many a weary traveler would prefer two miles extra travel that he might stop with Uncle Aaron, where there was always a cordial welcome and plenty abounded for man and beast.

With such parents, the childhood of Yancey Dean could have been nothing less than a happy one. Of him as a child his mother says "I cannot say anything half good enough; he was always obedient, rarely ever meriting a reproof; he was thoughtful and conscientious beyond his years and never gave me any trouble. At twelve years of age he professed conversion and connected himself with the Baptist Church. On account of his tender, loving disposition and Christ-like life he won the love of all; even the slaves on the farm loved him more than all the rest."

He was a second son, his brother, John, being the elder, but as the latter died young, Yancey became, as it were, the eldest son in the heart of his father, almost the idol of his mother and the pet of his grandmother(for whom he cherished an unusual devotion, often wishing as a child that she might outlive him) and in his mature years always referring to her as one venerated and whose tender care and untiring administrations to his childish whims could never be forgotten; and on to middle age the remembrance of Katherine Clark was always full of sweet, tender memories in this home and under these benign influence he loved twelve uneventful happy years. He was a big boy of more than usual intelligence and learned rapidly all that was taught in the country schools of that day.

When about thirteen years of age a great desire possessed him to leave the farm and he personally made application to Edmund Penn of Edgefield for a position. There was no vacancy that the little boy could fill, but Mr. Penn remembered his youthful applicant, and being a close friend of the family, soon sent for him and gave him a place in his great Mercantile establishment. His parents allowed it, for as his mother said, "he would not stay away long and treated his going almost as a joke. So the child was carried to the "diner house" and placed in the stage coach, and the battle of life began in earnest. How little thought his parents that they were sending their boy from them, in one sense, never to return. They felt sure that he would tire of his duties and come back. They failed to consider the race from which he sprang, nor did they remember that, although of fragile form, within his veins flowed the blood of men who knew no such word as fail, who never turned back, but whose motto was "Semper Fidelis" to every trust.

Many were the heartaches of that youthful passenger of that stagecoach, even before the village was reached, and as the days went by none will ever know how bravely he fought the battle of homesickness. To use his own wods, "I never came so near dying as I did from homesickness, actually crying (he was only twelve) until I fell asleep, night after night." But he came out victor and established for himself a name and character that still live.

In December, 1860, South Carolina, leading her sister states, seceded, and sent forth the best and bravest of her sons to die if need be for the right. In May, 1861, Yancey Dean, before he was seventeen years of age, enlisted going out with Martin Witherspoon Gary, Company B., Hampton's Legion.

At the first battle of Manassas, he fought with such dauntless courage as to challange the admiration of the entire regiment and he was appointed at once a non commissioned officer by General Gary. Again in 1862, at the terrible battle of Elthams Landing he distinguished himself by his extraordinary courage. Uncomplainingly he endured the hardships and perils of war; always found in the thickest of the fight; he never wearied in the noble struggle of the Southland for freedom.

At "Seven Pines" Yancey Dean did his country honor and made for himself a name which must always be known wherever the details of that memorable battle are preserved. His daring and utter forgetfulness of self during this battle are seldom witnessed in one so young. He was twice wounded in the thigh and his left arm, completely shattered, was amputated May 31st, 1862.

Although he had freely shed his blood and lost an arm and and was entitled to honorable retirement from service, he could not remain at home, but just as soon as he was physically able went back into the service. This time in Jenkins' Brigade he fought around Richmond and Petersburg.

He was elected Captain of Company E., First Regiment, South Carolina State Troops, commanded by Col. James Griffin.

In January, 1865, this brave young soldier resigned his captaincy in order that he might accept an appointment to the State Military School—the Arsenal— at Columbia S. C. Below, we copy accurately a letter written by the gallant Gary.

Gary's Cavalry Brigade
Malvern Hill,
July 21st, 1864

To His Excellency, M. L. Bonham,
Gov. State of Carolina:

I take pleasure in certifying that L. Yancey Dean, who desires to be appointed a cadet to the State Military Academy, under the recent resolution of the General Assembly was a member of Co. B., Hampton's Legion, S. C.

He particularly attracted my attention by his coolness and gallantry at the first Battle of Manassas and at Elthans Landing. At Seven Pines he fought with distinguished courage; he received two wounds, while charging the enemies' Battery, one in the arm and the other in the thigh, his arm being amputated.

I regard him as one of the best and bravest soldiers I have ever seen in the war. I know of no soldier in the Congressional District more worthy of the patronage of the State than Young Dean.

I was Captain of Company B. Hampton's Legion during the engagement referred to above.

He entered the Company as a private, but was promoted to a Sergeant for his excellency as a soldier.

Signed W. M. Gary,
Brigadier General of Cavalry.

Soon after Dean's enrollment at the Arsenal and before he had accomplished anything toward progress in the education he so much desired, Columbia was captured by the relentless Sherman and the Arsenal was burned.

After its destruction Young Dean, together with a number of Cadets, again entered the service, under the command of Col. Thomas, Commandant of State cadets and served under Joseph E. Johnston, in the Quartermaster's department as Sergeant until the close of the war.

While located at Greenville, South Carolina, he was captured by raiders, but fortunately made his escape and was secreted in the house of Dr. Earle.

Now the war was over and the Southern boys—not conquered but overcome by mere brute force, returned to their homes, made desolate by the lawless raiders and plundered by creatures scarcely deserving the name of men.

Young Dean, nothing daunted, went back to his home, the Edgefield Hill; and after taking just time enough to comfort his aged father in the loss of his slaves and whisper in the ears of his idolized mother and grandmother, he bravely began life's battle, and an earnest desire to be educated was uppermost in his mind.

Being without money he associated himself with a man of learning, Henry D. Addison and assisted him in teaching a flourishing school, receiving as part compensation his own instruments. He accumulated some money and in 1867 went to Galahers Commercial College and applied himself with the perseverance so characteristic of him. In 1868 he left Edgefield and went to Baltimore where he graduated at Galahers Commercial College.

In February, 1869, he came to Eufaula, Barbour County, where he engaged in Commercial business. It was then that the gallant Captain, for the first time, acknowledged defeat when he found himself tangled in a mass of golden curls and surrendered unconditionally to a pair of brown eyes scabtilating with mischief.

In 1870, he married Carolyne Simpson, a daughter of one of Barbour County's most prominent citizens, William T. Simpson.

Miss Simpson was a notably brilliant young woman and a direct descendant of the far-famed General Robert Lewis of the Lewis family of America. She did her ancestors honor. The marriage united families, famed in history, the Bland's and Louis' and their children may be proud of their lineage, not only ancient, but pure and good and may they always reflect honor on their escutcheon.

The success of Capt. Dean after his marriage was phenominal and he became one of Alabama's most influential men —one of nature's noblemen, BORN, not made and honored and beloved by all who knew him.

He was a Christian gentleman, and Elder in the Presbyterian Church, a competent man foremost in all good works. His home was a typical Southern Mansion, and not only in the style of Architecture, but in the hospitality extended as is typical of the bounteous days of yore.

Personally, Capt. Dean, like his ancestor, Theodoric Bland, was tall, slender, yet muscularly built with an unusually handsome face. His manners were magnetic and graceful; he was considerate and INATELY polite and refined—in all a courtly man. Much more could be said by those who knew him and loved him, but this much is authentic and will be valued by his posterity.

Captain Dean, after giving up the Mercantile business, served the city of Eufaula as Cotton weigher, a position which he held 13 years and won a reputation for honorable dealing that might be envied by any man. He then became a member of the firm of Simpson and Dean in the Cotton warehouse business and another 13 years of honest, upright dealing, was crowned with success.

Then came to him a call from the London and Lancashire Insurance Company accompanied by a tempting offer to become their special agent for the State of Alabama, and for four years, the company recognizing during the time his great value, secured his services at greatly advanced renumeration as special agent for Alabama and North Georgia with offices at Atlanta, Georgia. This position he held for nine years.

The third day of July, 1911, just as he was taking a train from Oneota for Birmingham, a boy by the name of Kelton threw a high ball which falling struck Captain Dean on his right shoulder. This blow proved to be serious. Neuritis developed and for 18 months he was helpless, not even being able to sign his name. Melancholia seemed inevitable and had it not been for his indomnitable will power and the constant care of his life companion and advisor he would have succumbed to this malady.

Recovering he then determined to enter the industrial field as "Independent Adjustor" of fire losses, but he went out on his first trip with one arm almost helpless to begin work. Business came to him and in the course of the next ten years not a man in Alabama held the record of L. Y. Dean. Independent adjustor in every city, hamlet and town in the state he was beloved and trusted to such extent that it was a matter of great pride to his loved ones.

The Providence that held this manly man in its Divine keeping came again to him and he formed an alliance with that Prince of Insurance men, Albert J. Brame, general agent for six Insurance agencies in Alabama. This position is one to be envied. Captain Dean goes on errands to those who love him and who delight to share their business with him.

Every agent is a personal friend and his labor is one of love; and for this he receives a compensation not enjoyed by many.

Here we leave this incomparable man 85 years of age and just the livest wire on the road. And as we consider the miles in his long career, it is interesting to note that for 13 years he was in the cotton weighing business; for ten years he was adjuster of fire losses and for 13 years he was in the cotton warehouse business and for forty three years in local fire insurance in its highly specialized phase.

It was only a couple of years before her death that Mrs. Dean wrote this beautiful tribute to her distinguished husband who survived her.

He died January 25th, 1934, just a short time before he reached 90 years of age. One of the grand old Southern gentlemen of the kind, whose memory will be blessed through all coming generations.

CAPT. S. H. DENT

Captain Stouten Hubert Dent, lawyer, banker and soldier, was born October 20th, 1833, in Charles County, Md., son of Dr. Stouten Warren and Mary (Smoot) Dent, the former a native of Charles County, Md., where he spent his life.

He was the grandson of Hatch Dent, Revolutionary soldier, and of George and Mary (Dent) Smoot, all of Charles County, Md.

Of English origin the American founders were the brothers who left England under the displeasure of Oliver Cromwell; they had opposed him as adherents of the Stuarts.

They settled in Maryland between the Potomac and Paluxent rivers in Virginia and when the Stuarts were restored, they received a large grant of land in Charles County, Md.

In 1851 he started his career as teacher and in 1856 providence brought him to Eufaula, Alabama, and after teaching a short time in the First Barbour County School at Eufaula now on Broad street he became associated with Pugh and Bullock and the same year was admitted to the bar and full practice of law in the county.

When the first war note of 1861 was sounded, he, then a justice of the Peace, responded to the call and was first lieutenant of the Eufaula Rifles, 1st Alabama Regiment. He acted as Adjutant of the Regiment for several months, but resigned to enter the artillery branch of the service as first lieutenant.

He was wounded in the Battle of Shiloh, but would not leave the field.

In 1863 he was promoted to Captain of the Battery, that from then on bore his name "Dent's Battery" in his honor; and his command was promoted and as a whole was commended for superior and faithful service and gallantry.

He was very seriously wounded at the Battle of Atlanta July 22nd, 1863, and again at Nashville, Tenn., Dec., 16th, 1864.

Captain Dent was also in the memorable Sunday afternoon battle at Chickamauga and at Mission Ridge.

After the war was over and because of Federal Military control there was suspension of the Courts in Barbour County. Captain Dent entered active business, not resuming his law practice until 1866.

In 1879, he was elected president of the Eufaula National Bank and held that office until the bank ceased business in 1890.

Early in the Reconstruction period, he was elected temporary chairman of the state Democratic executive committee.

In 1867 he was elected mayor of Eufaula, but was not allowed to take the office over, because the city was still under Federal Military control and Capt. Dent, had been such a loyal fighter for the cause of the South in Confederacy.

Captain Dent was a man of great literary ability and as one of the leading lay members of the Alabama Methodist Conference, he was known far and wide, denominationally as well as politically and in banking circles. His force of character and worth as a Christian man, made him honored and esteemed in the community to a degree most enviable and his citizenship was one of the County's best assets.

On June 9th, 1860, he married Anna Beall Young, daughter of Edward and Anna Beall Young of Marion, Georgia, and Eufaula.

Children: Edward Young Dent, married Annie McCormick, daughter of Geo. C. and Anna (Beauchamp) McCormick, Eufaula.

Nannie Beall Dent—married first Jackson E. Long, noted lawyer ; married second Dr. William W. Mangum, noted physician, Eufaula.

Stanley Hugh Dent—married Etta Tinsley, Louisville. Ky.

Henry Augustus Dent married Henrietta Copeland McCormick, Eufaula.

Katherine Louise married George N. Hurt.

Caroline married Charles S. McDowell, Jr.

CAPTAIN DENT

(From the Eufaula Times, Jan. 15th, 1884)

A few days ago, the following circular was found posted over the town:

Captain S. H. Dent, of Eufaula, Ala.,

Dear Sir:—

When you went into the Confederate Service, a number of Eufaula boys voted for you, and were eminently satisfied with the manner in which you discharged the duty assigned you.

After the war, they voted for you again and elected you mayor of Eufaula in 1882 and General Pope's U. S. Bayonets prevented you from serving the city as you could and would have done.

Now about four fifths or five sixths of people want to vote for you agin. They want to make you their next mayor and CAN do it without an effort or struggle on your part. All they want is to know is, whether you will serve in that capacity until such time as the people of this Judicial Circuit can say to you, "Come up higher." But they must hear from you, say, now and at once, whether they can honor you and themselves as they wish to and can do.—Signed: Vox Populi Vox Die.

The reporter sought Captain Dent yesterday on the subject of the above circular and asked him if he was a candidate for the Mayoralty and learned from him that he was not and had no thought of being in the field." I did not answer the circular," said Captain Dent, "because it was anonymous; had it borne the signatures of good men, I should have felt called upon to reply to it."

The reporter looked Mr. Comer up and upon being asked if he would be in the field again, replied, "I will."

Mr. Comer has made a first class mayor, faithful and true to the trust. However, should Capt. Dent consent to run, it would be a lively race and to outsiders, full of interest.

THE DENTS IN HISTORY

George Alfred Townsend Gath has an interesting article in the last month's Century Magazine on "How Wilkes Boothe Crossed the Potomac." It is a piece of unwritten history in the flight of the assassin and its details brings in the name of Dr. Stouten Dent, father of Capt. S. H. and George H. Dent and Warren F. Dent of Barbour County.

Referring to Dr. Dent who died in 1913 at the age of 80. Mr. Townsend says in his account of the difficulty of getting mail through the lines, "This old gentlemtn had two sons in the Confederate Army: Captain S. H. Dent and George H. Dent of the firm of (Weedon and Dent) Editor Times and was a practicing physician—riding on his horse from place to place and it seemed to be the case, that some person in Major Watson's family was generally sick.

This good old Dr. would go, wearing a big overcoat with immense pockets and big boots coming high towards his knees.

Everybody liked him, The Federal officers and soldiers as well, as the negroes and neighbors for he was impartial in his cures. At the greatest risk, even of his neck, the old man carried the Rebel mail, which Jones had delivered to him and frequently went all the way to Bryan town, Maryland, with it. He would stuff his pockets and sometimes his boots, with letters and newspapers.

HENRY A. DENT

From the Times—August 4th, 1888

When Capt. H. A. Dent was only 15 years old, his father, Capt. S. H. Dent, carried him into Washington and on a visit to the White House, Capt. Dent had just been presented to President Cleveland, when his son said, "Haven't been presented to the President," at which President Cleveland said, "Yes, I must shake hands with the young man, for he might be noted one day." During President Cleveland's second administration, he appointed Henry A. Dent, paymaster United States Navy.

He served in that capacity 25 years with credit to himself and the high position he held in the Navy and in the government of his country, and is now retired a valuable citizen of Barbour County.

EDWARD YOUNG DENT

The oldest son of Capt. and Mrs. S. H. Dent, Edward Young Dent was born in Eufaula at the historic Young-Dent-Hurt home on College Hill, June 25th, 1861, eldest son of Stouten Hubert and Anna Beall (Young) Dent. His early school days were at the Eufaula Female Academy, just across the street from his home, and he was outstanding as a student, and young boy who early won enviable friendships among his class mates and the highest esteem of his teachers, Craven, Patterson, Prof. Scaife and others.

He later finished in this school and went to the Alabama Southern College at Greensboro, Ala., where he received merited honors.

Entering business in the Eufaula National bank of which his father was president, he was teller and also manager of the insurance department of this bank.

After the bank ceased business, he continued the insurance business, in which he has established a record second to no insurance business in the state.

Today the companies he represents are as popular as they were forty years ago and the "Dent Insurance" is as popular as then.

"Ed Dent" as he is affectionately called by lifelong friends, is the senior steward of the First Methodist Church and a valued member, who has given much of his life to the interests of this church and is a Christian gentleman of the type of aristocracy, as well as integrity of character that he inherits from ancestry on both his paternal and maternal sides.

HUGH DENT

S. Hugh Dent was born at Eufaula in Barbour County, August 16, 1869, son of S. H. and Anna Beall (Young) Dent. Received his early schooling in the Eufaula schools, graduated with A. B. Degree at Southern University, Greensboro, Alabama, June, 1886. Graduated in law from the University of Virginia June, 1889.

Admitted to the Bar at Ozark, Ala., Dale County, in July of 1889. He practiced law in Barbour County and moved to Montgomery, forming legal partnership with W. C. Oates, later being member of the firm of Dent and Weil, Montgomery. He was appointed solicitor to succeed Tenant Lomav by Gov. W. D. Kelks in 1892 and elected in 1904 for a term of six years.

He was nominated by Democrats in a Congressional primary in September, 1908, for member of Congress and successively to that office until 1920; was defeated by J. B. Tyson, former Chief Justice, in the primaries.

During the 12 years in Congress he held membership on important committees and during the World War was chairman on the committee of military affairs, most important of all committees, during that period. His last public service was to codify the laws of Alabama.

Married June, 1897, in Louisville, Ky., Etta Tinsley, daughter of William Henry and Alice (Coke) Tinsley.

One son was born to them, William Dent, of Montgomery

One day in 1895 a circuit court case was being argued before Judge Carmichael at Eufaula. A boyish faced young lawyer was trying to convince a jury that the defendant owed a party $40. And he held in his hand a note, given for it and asked the defendant, "Can you read and write?" To the reply "yes," S. Hugh Dent (the young lawyer) said, "gentlemen of the jury any man who can read and write and tries to evade or break the law by the state, should receive a heavy penalty" and when the case went against the defendant and he had the note, interest and the cost to pay, this defendant said: "Hugh Dent you'll be a great man some day and I'll vote for you for congress." The prediction came true. The man said that was dead before that day came and never voted for him, but his prediction came true, and the Barbour County boy whose eloquence and brain was so noticeable then, to a man in ordinary life, is today, swaying the minds of thinking men and women of the state with his powerful argument of a great issue. He is Congressman from the second Congressional district and his boyhood home friends are very proud of him.

—From the Eufaula Daily Times, Nov., 4th, 1909.

He died suddenly on October 6, 1938. On October 5, 1938, Governor Graves appointed him a special Montgomery County Circuit Judge.

EDMONDSON BROTHERS

Richard Quinn Edmondson was born near Louisville, Ala., in Barbour County, coming to Eufaula with his brother, John M., soon after the War Between the Sates.

They were descendants of Sir Ralph Lane, 1st English Governor in America, who came with Sir Walter Scott in 1585 and who founded the Colony of Roanoke and from Jessie Lane, officer in the 3rd Carolina Continentals, and his three sons who fought at King's Mountain.

This Jessie Lane was a minister in Georgia in 1784 and built the first Methodist church in Georgia. At the age of 17, Quinn Edmondson went into the Confederate Army and fought throught the entire war.

Entering the cotton warehouse, business, Edmondson Brothers were two devoted Christian men who carried their religion all through with their business and were two of the best, business men, and valuable citizens to be found anywhere.

Although entirely different in disposition one offsets the other, and the brotherly love between them, was the admiration of the Community. Both were stewards in the first Methodist church and were a strong force in all the affairs of the Church. R. Q. Edmondson was superintendent of the Sunday school for 25 years and a more faithful, enthusiastic laborer never served in that capacity with more zeal nor has ever been beloved. As business men they stood at the top and were helpers in the making of the County as the years passed.

R. Q. Edmondson married Mary McNeil Heron, daughter of Dr. Henry Heron of Louisville, Ala. Children: Edward L., New Orleans—married Clifford Macon; has one son, Macon Edmondson, U. S. Army. R. Q., Jr., married Tessa Meredith. Sons of R. Q., Jr., and Tessa Edmondson, Quin III and Richard.

Dr. J. H. Edmondson married Mildred Tynes.

John M. Edmondson married Portia Petty of Clayton. Children, one died in infancy.

Leila and Lillie, twins; Leila married W. H. Flowers, Dothan; Lillie married H. W. Flowers, Atlanta.

CHARLES P. S. DANIEL

Charles P. S. Daniel was born in Tuskegee, Alabama, the son of James Lewis and Mathilda (Gandtt) Daniel. After he grew up he spent many years in Midway, Alabama, coming to Eufaula in the early eighties.

Few men have ever been as conspicuous for "Goodness" that made men beloved and honored as Judge Daniel. He was a finished scholar and cultured Christian citizen and a gentle-spirited man in his home, in the church, at the bar, on the bench, in his office, on the streets, his strong personality and genial happy manner made him a man whose every act and word revealed the nobility of his character.

Some of Barbour and Bullock County's brightest history glows with his deeds of kindness, performed in the most modest but most far reaching way.

He married Cornelia (Turner) of Georgia, who for many years was a helpless invalid and his devotion to her was the admiration of the whole community. She died only eight months before he passed away, and they sleep side by side in the family lot in Fairview cemetery.

Their children are Charles Lewis Daniel: married to Mattie Coppedge and their children are Julia Lucile, Ellen Cornelia, Mattie Sue, Robert L. Ridings, issue 2 children, Barbara and Robert Lewis. Cornelius married T. A. Williams. Eloise Mathilda married Frances Golightly, issue two children, William and Frances, wife of William Creight Lloyd, supt. Postal Telegraph Co.

Julia Daniel died in young girlhood.

John Lee Daniel, married Lupe Viccaro, issue Eloise. Eloise Daniel Lloyd, the beautiful daughter of this distinguished family was one of the most brilliant literary women ever reared in Barbour County. She wrote much beautiful poetry and her book of fiction, "The Truth About It," which she wrote, while yet a school girl was greatly praised by literary critics. She was valedictorian of her class of Union Female College, Eufaula in 1892, giving it in beautiful lines of applicable poetry. She was also an eloquent reader and charming actress as a child. She was greatly beloved as her parents were in their home town and admired wherever she went.

Judge Daniel was a direct descendant of Robert Lewis of Revolutionary fame. His wife also descended from illustrous Revolutionary ancestors.

They have left life's sheet, on which is written in years of love and service, that says:

> Life's tasks so well performed,
> The faith so nobly kept,
> All not good, scorned,
> The legacy they have left.
>
> The dearest and the best
> That parents can leave child
> And is the acid test
> Of our Life's afterwhile
>
> The afterwhile of God's
> Long reward to His own
> When there are no returns
> Of fruitage, of Good seed sown.

JOHN DOUGLASS

John Douglass, the oldest citizen of Louisville, was born in North Carolina, the son of a prominent family who came to the Louisville settlement of Barbour County, when he was very young. He grew up and became one of the strongest forces in the progress of the County as the years passed on, and despite his age he is today an enthuiastic, highly honored and valuable citizen.

He is still interested in farming and keeps abreast of all the doings of the day.

He married Fanny Pruett of Midway, Alabama, and reared a large family, each one of whom has occupied important places in the communities.

They are Colin, Stacey, Kate (Mrs. Durden of Columbus, Georgia) Mary (Mrs. Henderson) and Charles.

It is most interesting to hear Mr. Douglass tell of pioneer days in Barbour County, especially during the fifties and sixties, when the eyes of the state were fixed on the County. It was at Louisville, adjacent territory that history was in the making and the Douglass family ranked first in splendid courageous citizenship.

DOUGHTIE

William Doughtie was born in Monroe County, Georgia in 1913 and died in Eufaula in 1882. A soldier of the Indian war of 1836, he married Elizabeth Simpson and operated a farm in Quitman County, Georgia, going to Henry County, Alabama, where he became a large planter, but in 1861 sold out and moved to an estate on the Chattahoochee river 4 miles south of Eufaula in Barbour County. He was a fine manager of his large farms, retiring as age advanced and moved to Eufaula, where his wife died in 1881. The following were his children: Susan, who died in infancy; William A., livestock dealer, died in Montgomery in 1924; James T., livestock dealer, died at Columbus, Ga., 1923; John S. died in Lufkin, Texas, in infancy; and the former at Columbus, Ga., in 1909, the wife of James H. Brown, a farmer at Glennville, Ala., at the time of her death. Edward T. Compress, operator at Opelika, died in 1905; Thaddeus C.; Sarah Amanda married Flavius De Honey of Kansas City, Mo., who died at Eufaula in 1925; Elizabeth Jane married William L. Bass, who died at Sedalia, Miss.; Mittie Culler married John W. Christian, livestock dealer at Montgomery.

Derrill Eugene, commercial traveler, died in 1900 at Manson, Georgia.

THADEUS C. DOUGHTIE

Son of William and Elizabeth (Simpson) Doughtie, born on his father's farm in Henry County, Ala. Attended schools at Eufaula and Eminence, Ky. For many years he was a traveling salesman for Rankin Manufacturing Company, Nashville, Tenn.

He was elected Chief of Police Department of Eufaula and after two years was elected City Clerk and Treasurer which positions he held ten years, retiring when his health failed.

October 25th he married Miss Carrie Malone, daughter of Rev. Green Malone, the former presiding elder of the Eufaula District of the Methodist Church, South. Their Children: Edward Malone Doughtie, who married Mittie McNab, Eufaula; Eugene Rivers, married Fay Groom; Charles Alma McMichael; Claud Lucile Ewing; Porter; Rand, killed in France at Battle of Chateau-Thierry, World War; Julian married Margaret Gamble.

"Thad" Doughty was one of Barbour County's very finest citizens. His wife, "Miss Carrie," as she was lovingly called was notable as a gifted musician with a rarely beautiful soprano voice (see music in Barbour County, this history); Mr. and Mrs. Doughty died only a few years apart and are buried in one grave in Fairview Cemetery.

JUDGE AURELIUS EVANS

Judge Aurelius Evans was born in Barbour County (Now Russell) Dec. 24th, 1862 ,and was reared on the Evans plantation. He was educated in the Glenville, Vidalia and Seale, Ala., schools, graduating at the University of Alabama in 1885, with an A. B. degree.

He taught school and after several years teaching boys whom he prepared for the University as honor for the splendid record made by these pupils of his when they entered the University, the degree of M. A. was conferred upon him by that institution.

"In open court at Ozark, Ala., Nov. 1, 1889, Judge Evans passed the Bar examination before Hon. John A. Foster, Chancellor of the Southeastern Division of Alabama." He served as circuit judge 11 years and resigned to accept appointment by Gov. B. B. Comer as judge of the Supreme Court of Alabama to fill the unexpired term of Hon. N. D. Denson, who had resigned to resume his law practice. After the expiration of that term of office he served 8 years on the tax commission and later was attorney general until his death.

He married December 28th, 1888 Celeste Victoria Waddell, daughter of George and Celeste (Wynne) Waddell: Children: Frances Isabell, Robert Collier, and Aurelius, Jr. Three children of his brother (their mother also a sister of Mrs. Evans) Thomas, Kathleen and Sallier, were reared by Judge and Mrs. Evans.

The family moved from Clayton to Montgomery when Judge Evans was appointed Supreme Judge. He was a brilliant scholar, had the law on the tip of his tongue and was patriotic, just, honorable, loyal and a man whose every day life was an inspiration to the citizenship around him and a great asset to the community as well as an honor to the office he held.

JOHN S. ESPY

John S. Espy was born in Tallapoosa County, Alabama, in 1834, and died in 1902 at the old Espy homestead in Barbour County in 1857.

During the War Between the States he served as a member of Company G, 39th Alabama Volunteer Infantry.

He married Elizabeth White. Their children were John R., deceased; Ludie, married to Dr. John J. Darby; John C., deceased; Seaborn of Dothan, married Ida Helms; Anna married Young J. Smith; William M., Birmingham; Edward F., who owns more real estate than any man in Barbour County, married Pauline Wood, children, Jno. L., married Norma Davidson; Margaret, married Merrill Grant; Grace married William Stokes; Edward married Doris Duke; Polly Ann and James Goodman; Mittie, married Dr. W. G. Lewis, a prominent physician and surgeon of Eufaula, children, Elizabeth; Ethel; Roy; Captain John Lewis, deceased; Dr. Seaborn Sspy, Beaumont, Texas, married Helen Nason; and Goodman Basil, born in Barbour County 12 miles below Eufaula, February 10, 1868.

These are grandchildren of Robert Espy who moved to Tallapoosa County from Georgia, where he was born in 1800. He took part in the Indian battles in Alabama and was very prominent in his section.

He moved to Barbour County in 1854 and established a background for the distinguished Espy family that has succeeded him.

GOODMAN BASIL ESPY

Goodman Basil Espy had his early schooling in the schools at Lawrenceville, Ala., attending the University of Alabama, graduating in 1890 with degree of civil engineering.

He taught school in the public schools of Barbour County,

later engaging in farming, and in the lumber business, moving to Eufaula in 1909. He practiced Civil engineering and since 1894 has served as county surveyor. Being an enthusiastic Democrat, he was elected to serve on the Board of Equalization of Barbour County from 1916 to 1920.

He is a Mason, W. O. W. and local representative of the Federal Land Bank of New Orleans. "Dude" Espy, as he is affectionately called by his close friends, is a popular citizen, probably the best all around educated man in the community, a great reader and thinker, whose memory is most remarkable. He is known as Barbour County's "Bureau of Information," a fluent speaker who has incidents, dates and figures always at his tongue's end.

He is keenly interested in the politics of his county and a valuable citizen. He married Jimmie Gibson July 7, 1897, daughter of the late William Gibson, prominent citizen of Opelika.

Children: Paul, Goodman, Nell and Jamie Gibson, now Professor of the high school of Seale, Alabama.

THADDEUS FLOYD

Dr. Thaddeus Floyd was born Nov. 5th, 1849, coming to Clayton from Harris County, Georgia, when but a school boy. He served the Confederacy, removing to Greenville, Georgia, practiced denistry until 1876 and retired. He was a member of White Lodge No. 10 F. A. M. at Clayton; a leader in the Methodist Church and took active part in all the progress and uplift of the community. His wife, Regina Ellison, was born at Wesleyan College, Macon, Georgia, January 19, 1847. Her father, Rev. W. H. Ellison, then president of that institution. Their six children: William E., dentist, Clayton; Alice, wife of John P. West, died in 1916; Mary, wife of W. T. Wynn, professor State College, Murphreesboro, Tenn.; Julia Capers, wife of W. T. Smith, Durham, N. C.; John Thaddeus; Florence, wife of Howell T. Bently, Brantley, Ala.

The Floyd family is outstanding in Barbour County from every point of view of the best citizenry. Like father like son and the same applies to the woman as well—like father and mother of this distinguished family.

JOHN THAD FLOYD

Hon. John Thaddeus Floyd was born at Clayton August 15th, 1886, son of Dr. Thaddeus and Regina Ellison Floyd, is one of the young men who have carried the enviable reputation that the name Floyd has been honored with for several generations to the highest pinnacles of his undertakings.

In the class of 1904 he graduated from the District Academy at Clayton and entered Emory College at Oxford, Georgia, where his student work and scholarly attainments brought to him well deserved honors.

As book keeper for the Clayton Banking Company honors crowned his career. In 1912 he became cashier and in 1922 president.

He married Miss Elizabeth Paulk of Union Springs and they have a son, Thaddeus, III, who is one of Barbour County's most valuable citizens.

FLOURNOY FAMILY

There are so many members of the distinguished Flournoy family of Barbour County that it would be almost impossible to properly arrange a biography, correctly, the connection is so widespread. So we are giving as near a full list as could be procured.

They have lived mostly at Louisville and Eufaula and the father of the late Mrs. B. B. McKenzie, Mrs. Fanny Edison and Mrs. B. F. Bennett lived many years on Randolph street in Eufaula.

Partial biography of the Flournoy family:

Laurent Flournoy—married Gabrielle Mellin of Lyons, France and refugeed to Genoa, Switzerland in 1562.

Jean Flournoy—born in 1574. Married Frances Mussard. Father of Jacque Flournoy. Born in 1608; married Jacob Flournoy.

Jacob Flournoy—emigrant to Virginia in 1700—married three times; father of Francis Flournoy (wife's name not known). Had nine children; father of Gibson Flournoy; married Mary Farmer; had 12 children; father of John Francis Flournoy who married Mary Ashurst; had 4 children: father of 2 daughters (names unknown); After the father's death the widow with the four children (the girls and the boys, Robert and Josiah) moved to Putnam County, Ga.

Josiah Flournoy married Patsy Manly, the only child of Capt. John Manly of near Petersburg Va.

Thomas Flournoy married Caroline Elizabeth Rogers, daughter of Osborne Rogers, Oxford, Ga. After the birth of the second child they moved to Eufaula, Ala., in 1833 or 1834. They had 10 children, seven growing to manhood and womanhood.

Mary Lou married Robert P. Howard.
Robert Flournoy married Sue McKenzie
Jennie married John C. Moore.
Bettie married Bethune McKenzie.
Fannie married Frank W. Edison.

Osborne Rogers F., married Fletcher Hardin first; then Mattie Flournoy.

Thomas Flournoy married and died in Texas: no children.

WILLIAM HUMPHREY FOY

William Humphrey Foy was born in Wilmington, N. C., and came to Barbour County some time during the early forties locating at Fort Browder in Barbour County, where he soon became outstanding as a successful farmer and valuable citizen.

He married Mary Louise Wilson, daughter of pioneer settlers of the County and their home at Fort Browder, where they reared a family of seven sons and one daughter, was one of the most notable old homes of the County. All the seven sons inherited their father's love for farming, and as the years passed on, despite the fact that they all drifted into various commercial interests they continued their farming interests. In the seventies Mr. Foy moved to Eufaula, establishing a general Merchandise and advancing business under the firm name of Kaigler, Walker, Cherry and Foy. Later the firm was Kaigler, Cherry and Foy, and this large business was handed down from father (Mr. Foy eventually buying out the Cherry and Kaigler interests) to sons, and the business was continued through all the years up to 1930 as Foy Brothers managed principally by L. W. and W. H. Foy. At their death the firm ceased business. During the eighties, Foy Bros established the "Foy Hardware Co," which was managed by younger sons, L. W. and S. R. The eldest, James E., continued farming and also serving the County as treasurer for some time. Later years W. H. retired, turning all his business over to his sons, who had wonderful training under his example.

He had been most successful and when he moved to Eufaula all of the 100 slaves he owned and had remained with him after they had been set free were still on his farms; others coming to the city when he did. He had been the kind and thoughtful master that won their respect and even affection; and their descendants have continued working for the families of the sons and daughter.

JAMES E. FOY

James E. Foy was born at Fort Browder, Ala., the eldest son of William Humphrey and Mary Wilson Foy. He grew up on his father's farm and by actual experience as well as the adoption of scientific methods reached the very acme, as an out standing agriculturist. Early in life he became interested in politics and for several years was chairman of the Democratic executive committee of Barbour County.

He served as treasurer of Barbour County, being reelected term after term for many years, during which time he resided in Clayton, removing to Eufaula in 1889.

At the age of twenty-one while out hunting he accidentalyl shot his hand, so it had to be amputated, and despite the fact that he had no hand or arm to just below the elbow, he was a past master in the art of handling the most spirited horse. He loved horses and it was a familiar sight to see him on horseback driving one and two horses to his buggy, nearly always some little child in front of his saddle or beside him in the buggy.

His fondness for little children and their love for him was beautiful to witness.

The later years of his life were spent looking after his personal and the large agricultural interests of Foy Brothers in which he was equally interested, and "Bud Jimmie" as he was affectionately called, was the older brother, that the other six looked up to as the agricultural authority in the plans for their personal farms.

He was genial, loved a joke and always was ready with some pleasantry that welcomed him wherever you met him.

He married Gertrude Cochran, daughter of Benjamin and Cornelia (Grimes) Cochran. She was one of the most beautiful women in Barbour County, and to the First Methodist Church was an example and influence her personal service has left very sweet and lasting memories.

Their children are Earl H., who married Mary Lou Ware.

Their children are: Simpson, married; Earl; Dorothy, married; Lavinia, married; James.

Mary married Dermot Shemwell of Albany, Ga., and Lexington, N. C. Their daughter, Gertrude, married E. R. Culbertson of Greenville, S. C. Their children are two sons. Robert Dermot and Carey Ulioris.

Mary Shemwell married R. T. Phillips of Lexington, N. C., and they have a son, Thomas Lee.

Dermot Shemwell is unmarried.

James Edgar married Leila Bullock, daughter of E. C. and Eva Martin Bullock.

Their children are Edgar, III, Courtney, Bullock, Elizabeth

JOHN POU FOY

John Pou Foy was born at Fort Browder on May 9th, 1851, son of William H. and Mary (Wilson) Foy, pioneer citizens of Eufaula, the former outstanding farmer and later wholesale and retail merchant at Eufaula. On the shoulders of the second son, John, fell the father's mantle of leadership in business and as soon as the three oldest sons had finished school he took them into business with him and each of these three had the benefit of his example and teaching in farming and the mercantile training as well.

John looked mostly after the clerical parts of the large business interests and in the late eighties he organized and was made President of the East Alabama National Bank. He was president until he sold out his interests in this bank to his brother-in-law, Mr. J. L. Pitts, who had been cashier of the Citizens' Bank at Clayton. Later Mr. Foy organized and was president, until his death, of the Commercial National bank in the late eighties.

He was a man of marked executive ability and gave his personal attention to the large farming interests; was notable for his strong convictions as to right and wrong and was an example of that type of Christian character that always stood for the noblest and best. He was not only a leader in business circles in his community, but as the senior steward of the First Methodist church and leading member. He was its most liberal contributor and a most valuable citizen whose death was a calamity to the county in every sense of the word.

The large number of colored tenants and laborers on his farms and the old family servants who gathered at his funeral expressed by their presense and visible sorrow their friendship for and appreciation of the many kindnesses to them at his hands.

He married first Carrie Drewry, daughter of Dr. John W. and Mrs. Anne (Etheridge) Foy, who was one of the best beloved women in all the Community, known far and wide for her ministering generosity and help to the needy, the poor and suffering at all times.

She was the very crown and flower of the First Methodist Church and gentle sweet homemaker whose children rise up and call her blessed.

They are: Stella, married S. Oscar Williams (deceased) their daughter, Eleanor Williams married Webb Thomas of California; John Drewry married Irene Quick of Tennessee. Their children are: Drewry, Benton and Dorothy. Humphrey Foy married Mary Ross and their children are Norma, Carrie who married Thomas Moorer, U. S.. Navy; Humphrey, Jr., and Ross Foy.

May Wilson Foy married James M. Smith, their children: Caroline married Richard Boyett and their young son is Richard III, and Catherine Smith. He married second Belle Scott Nance, who survives him. Widow of Robert F. Nance, leading Barbour County citizen and notable bank accountant.

SIMPSON R. FOY

Simpson R. Foy, third son of William Humphrey and Mary Wilson Foy, was born at Fort Browder and was educated at the University of Alabama and went into the general merchandise store of his father, where he soon developed splendid business qualities, and when death claimed him in the very zenith of his young manhood he was associated with his brothers in business in Eufaula.

He married Carrie Treutlen, daughter of Col. J. F. Treutlen and his wife, Carrie, of Glennville.

His children are Louise, who married Frank C. Petry, and their children are Frank C., Jr., Caroline and Louise; Treutlen married Neela Sloan of South Carolina and their child is Jean Foy.

LEVY W. FOY

Levy W. Foy, fourth son of William Humphrey and Mary Wilson Foy, was born at Fort Browder March 4th, 1866. He was educated in the Barbour County preparatory schools and graduated at the famous Culleoka College, Tenn., under the special tutorage of the distinguished Prof. Webb.

Like the other Foy Brothers he went into farming, but was also associated actively in the Mercantile business. Later reorganized the Foy Hardware Company and had successful period in that line, sold the Hardware business and again became associated with his brothers in the General Mercantile business and the agricultural interests.

He was a man of lofty instincts, a warm hearted friend and took great interest in his church affiliations. He was genial and always affiable and a most valuable citizen in every way.

He married Frankie Alderman, daughter of the late Mr. and Mrs. A. S. Alderman of Wewauhitchica, Florida, and their children are: Sidney A., married to Martha Ferrell; Mary R. E. Ragan, their children, Ellis and Francis. James married Mary Perkinson; John Pou married Josephine Hurt; Clara married Archibald B. Roberts; Edward married Ruth Newton, and their children are Edward and Jane Loring.

WILLIAM HUMPHREY FOY, JR.

William Humphrey Foy, fifth son of W. H. and Mary Wilson Foy, was born at Fort Browder in 1865 and attended the Eufaula schools and graduated. Afterwards he went into the general merchandise store of Foy Brothers, successors to "Cherry, Walker and Foy." As the years went on the was head of the grocery department of the business, as well as the advancing feature of the large concern. He also looked after his individual farms.

He was of most genial personality, greatly beloved by children to whom he always had time to show consideration. He was kind hearted and generous and always ready to do a favor for a friend. The last years of his life he suffered poor health, but was, even when feeble and strength failing, ready with a smile and a cheery word to children.

He was a useful citizen and a worthy representative of a fine old family.

He married first lovely Nellie Beall Dent, daughter of George H. and Helden Dent. To them were born two sons, Levy W., now a major in the United States Army, and Fred H., a fine young business man of Birmingham. He married second Florence Kirvin of Columbus, Ga., and to them were born a daughter, Florence, who married Carl Strang of Atlanta, Georgia. He married third Marie Lewis, daughter of Mr. and Mrs. W. G. Lewis, of Eufaula. He died a few years since, when Barbour County lost a valuable citizen.

Levie W. Foy was born at Eufaula Dec. 9th, 1895. He graduated from the Infantry school Officers Course 23 Virginia Military Institute. He is the son of William Foy, Jr., and wife Nellie Beall Dent, daughter of George H. and Helen Young Dent.

He is now a major, serving at Fort Benning, Georgia.

Cliff A. Foy, sixth son of William Humphrey, Sr., and Mary Wilson Foy, was born at Fort Browder October, 1872. He attended the Eufaula Male Academy and finished his education at Alabama Polytechnic Institute at Auburn.

He had first hand experience in Foy Brothers General Merchandise business, and then went into business for himself. He had a general merchandise store at Abbeville, Ala., and was a large dealer in livestock, having fine stables there.

Afterwards he was in business at Tifton, Georgia, and while conducting a large General Merchandise business at Criddle's Mill, fifteen miles from Eufaula on the Georgia side of the Chattahoochee river, the flood of 1914 washed away his store, residence and warehouses of tons of peanuts. It was after this that he went in business at Tifton, Georgia, and now for several years has been in business in Zoarville, Ohio. At this time, Feb. 23rd, he is visiting his old home at Eufaula on a 30-days's vacation) and is being cordially welcomed by his many home friends. He has never married. He is notable for interest in his friends and is a fine business man of force of character and integrity.

ROBERT C. FOY

Brigadier General Robert C. Foy, youngest son of William H. and Mary Wilson Foy, was born August 20th, 1876, at the old Foy home on Sanford street in Eufaula (the only member of this distinguished family, not born at the historic old home at Fort Browder.

Unlike the other six brothers, his thoughts early took to the United States Army. He was the youngest graduate of the A. P. I., Auburn, Ala., and also at High Point, New York. where she studied before going to West Point. He served in the Army of Occupation in Cuba during the Spanish-American War.

He graduated from the Infantry school G. S. C. eligible list.

Graduated Army War College 23; General Staff 22nd; distinguished graduate Army School of the Line 16.

Graduate Military Service School, five year Course 15.

His promotions in the Army have been rapid. Several years at Fort Sill, Oklahoma; and has been two years Brigadier General, receiving this promotion at Fort Sam Houston, Texas.

He is now on three months leave of absence, before leaving for his appointment for foreign service in the Hawaiian Islands.

He is the typical, courtly, cultured Army officer who, wherever he goes, carried with him the earmarks of the gentleman soldier that he is. He married Helene Hummel and is now located in Chicago.

JOHN ARTHUR FOSTER

John Arthur Foster was born November 11th, 1828 in Jasper County, Georgia, son of John L. S. and Susan (Hollifield) Foster. He was instructed by Rev. E. B. Teague, afterwards graduating from the University in 1847. He began studying law under Judge Harry I. Thornton of Eutaw. He taught school in Mississippi. He was admitted to the bar at Clayton, Ala., after having been president of the Southern Female College at LaGrange, Georgia, 1855-59.

In 1861 he enlisted in the Confederate Army and in 1864 while acting as Colonel of his regiment he and his regiment were captured at Nashville, Tenn., and held as prisoners until the war ended.

In 1865, he resumed the practice of law. In 1875 he was a delegate to the Constitutional Convention and was made a trustee of the University of Alabama in 1876-78.

He represented Barbour County in the Legislatures of

1878-80 and in 1880 was made Chancellor of the Southern Division of Alabama.

The honorary degree of L. L. D. was conferred upon him by the Alabama Polytechnic Institute in 1883.

He was a loyal Democrat, a Mason, Knights Templar and a "deep water" Baptist.

He married first in 1858, Mary Webb, of LaGrange. Their children were John Webb; Emma married Toole of LaGrange, Ga. He married second Mary Borders. Children: Mary, married Dr. W. H. Robertson, Pearl Married T. C. Guice, of Dawson, Ga.; Arthur Borders.

John Arthur Foster was a lawyer and jurist who stood high in the County of Barbour

JOHN WEBB FOSTER

John Webb Foster was a lawyer and member of the Alabama Legislature and Register in Chancery. He was born on October 14th, 1850, at Lownes County, Miss., son of John Arthur and Mary Webb Foster. He was educated partly in the schools of Clayton, Ala., and by his distinguished father's private instruction. He studied law and was admitted to the bar in 1868.

In 1870 he removed to Abbeville, Ala., having been appointed Register in Chancery of Henry County. Served as County superintendent in 1871 to 1881 and represented Henry County in the legislature from 1884-1886; married May Kate Petty, daughter of B. F. Petty, Confederate soldier, who served under General Henry D. Clayton. Children: Lola, Emma, and Kate.

HENRY BAXTER FLORENCE

Henry Baxter Florence, son of Thomas Jefferson and Mary Sewell Frazier Florence, was born August 31st, 1848, at the plantation home near Old Spring Hill. He received his early education in the local schools, finishing at Marion Military Institute and Howard College.

At the age of fifteen he enlisted in the Home guards, serving as messenger in his home County of Barbour at Mobile and in North Alabama.

He was married Dec. 14th, 1867, to Sarah King Goree, of Marion, Alabama, granddaughter of General Edward Davis King, co-founder of Judson College.

Of this union there were born, Thomas Henry who married Annie Mallory; their daughter, Annette; Porter Frazier Florence married Pauline Ramsey and their son, Porter, Jr., is a distinguished Episcopal minister. Annette Florence married Donald Hobson of Tallahassee; Helen Florence married Mr. Winters and their daughter married Thayer Richets, Madison, Wis.

Henry Florence spent his life on his farms near Comer, and was known as a capable farmer and useful citizen. He was a lover of horses and a fine rider. He was greatly beloved by both races for his charity. He was a member of Ramer Baptist Church and through his generosity and tireless efforts the Methodist Church at Comer was erected, the congregation presenting him with a diamond studded watch fob in recognition of his services. He died March 25th, 1934, at the home of his son, Thomas Florence, Comer, Ala., and is buried in Midway, Ala.

GLENN

The Glenn family who settled and named the town of Glennville, is one of the most illustrious in America, tracing its ancestry back to King John 1st of England and there is also historical records in the possession of the members of this family now residing in Barbour County that show a direct line of ancestry, a line so interestingly and minutely followed back to the primitive days of Adam and Eve. Certainly something that few families can boast of in any country. Sir Dudley Diggs of Childham Castle, Kent, England, was the father of Sir Edward Diggs, born in England March 1st, 1620. He was governor of Virginia by the House of Burgeses, 1670 to 1675; he was auditor general, 1672 to 1675; receiver general; member of council date of appointment 1654. Records say: Edward Diggs of "Bellfield," York County, died in Virginia in 1675. The following is the inscription on his tomb: "To the memory of Edward Diggs Esquire, son of Sir Dudley Diggs, of Childham in Kent; knight and baronet; master of the rolls in the reign of King Charles 1st. He departed this life the 15th of March 1675, 55th year of his age, one of His majesty's council for this his country of Virginia. A gentleman of most commendable parts, an ingenuity and the only introducer and promoter in this Colony of the silk manufacture and in everything else, a pattern worthy of all pious imitation. He had issue, six sons and seven daughters, by the body of Elizabeth his wife, who of her conjugal affection hath dedicated to him this memorial."—(Copied from Meade's old Churches).

These tombs, shipped from England, were made of iron, stone and black marble and are in a perfect state of preservation, with the engraving plainly visible after all the passing centuries

He built Chilham Castle, over the door of which is engraved in marble, "The Lord is my defense and my Castle.—Dudley Diggs and Marp Kemp." He was ambassador to Russia in 1618 and in 1619 was on the "Committee of Colleges of Virginia." This was one of the great honors of Kent.

Of the 25 Barons who were instrumental in receiving the first great Charter of English Rights and Liberties, properly called the "Magna Charter," which was ratified by King John and delivered to them in a meadow called "Runny Mede" June 15th, 1215 A. D.—four of these were ancestors of Governor Edward Diggs.

Other ancestors in England and Scotland, Edward 1st, King of England, and other of the Plantagent House and also Duncan and Malcolm of Scotland featured in Shakespeare's "Macbeth."

Sir Dudley Diggs was a public spirited man and aided Henry Hudson when he sailed for the Northwest, and "Cape Diggs" was named for him. He also was one of the several who purchased the Bermuda Islands from the Virginia Company. We was a member of Parliament 1614-24-25.

His daughter, Katherine, married William Herndon in 1677, of New Kent, Va. Their son, William, married Mary Waller, daughter of Col. John Waller of Kent County, England, whose ancestors came over with William the Conquerer, and their son, Edward, married Anne Drysdale in 1730, daughter of Lieut. Gov. Hugh Drysdale of Virginia. Their son Joseph Herndon; his son Col. Bryan Herndon of the Revolutions, James Elizabeth Glenn, father of Massimillion McHenrdee Glenn of the Methodist conference of Virginia named the town of Cokesbury for Bishop Coke and Bishop Abbury, but settled it.

In 1882 he removed to 4 miles from Eufaula on the Georgia side of the river, then in 1834, moved to one mile from Pittsview, Ala. In 1855 he moved to the site that he settled and named Glennville. Gave land for a M. E. Church and cemetery there. In May 1837, he was forced to move his family back to Georgia, escape the Indians, who had burned his house. He rebuilt it at the same place, but later moved two miles east and died therein March 1851. His wife died in 1869. His children were:

Massillon McKendree Glenn was born March 8th, 1815. He married Barbara Herndon, daughter of Stephen Decatur Herndon, son of Lt. Col Banjamin Herndon of the Revolution, of the Herndon family, who patented lands in St. Stephens' Parish, New Kent County, Virginia, February 16, 1674.

Algernon Sidney Glenn; Doceiuc V. Glenn; Lucious Glenn; James W. Glenn; Mrs. Angelina Screws; Mrs. Elvira Brown.

Massillon McKendree Glenn's Children

Ellen married Patrick Edward Barnett; Eugent Herndon married Sallie Evans; Sallie married Mack Caldwell; Henry

Clarence married Lucy Curtis Cotten; Jule married Alex P. Burch; Addie married Asbury Dowling; Edgar Massillon married Mamie Arrington; Claud married Charles Williamson; Lucy unmarried; Walter died in infancy.

LEVY CLARENCE GLENN

HENRY CLARENCE GLENN

This brings the family down to Henry Clarence, fourth son of Massillon and Barbara (Herndon) who was born on October 27th, 1848, at Glennville.

He grew up and was educated at the historic old Glennville Male Academy and early in manhood went into active business, moving to Eufaula where he was a warehouseman and cotton buyer, notable for business ability, and an expert cotton classer.

He was a leading member of the First Methodist Church, where his magnificent tenor voice in the choir was the delight of his friends and the congregations. Its volume and rare timbre, which it retained to the close of his life at 83, made his singing a joy to the community.

Clarence Glenn possessed not only the gift of an unusually fine tenor voice, but he was a scholar and thinker as well, and it was often said of him that "he was the best read man in Alabama." He was perfectly familiar with all the classics, and his ready store of information proved him the student as well as the scholar.

He married Lucy Curtis Cotten, daughter of Dr. James L. and Lucy Curtis Cotton, the latter being a composer of music, and this lovely bride, also a gifted singer, brought with her the fragrance of Old Cahaba, the first capital of the state of Alabama, to the social life of Eufaula. Like their parents their children are all gifted musicians and singers.

They are, viz: Walter, bookkeeper for Cowikee Mills; Ellene, married Guy Winn, prominent attorney of Barbour

County—their children are: James, United States Army; Mary, librarian in New York; Lucy, newspaper writer and Journalist; Knox, young business man; and Ellene and Elizabeth.

Martha Glenn, famous teacher of piano in New York.

Henry Clarence, Jr., business man of Eufaula, married Carrie Spurlock; their children, Henry, Clarence III, youngest Glenn preacher, ordained by Methodist Conference of Alabama M. E. Church South, and is finishing his ministerial education at Duke University, N. C.

Annie Barbara, student at Brenau College, Gainesville, Georgia.

Hilda, Colarature-Soprano singer, student of New York Operatic studios of famous instructors.

Louise married Philip Johnson, Montgomery. She was a student of New York's famous vocal studios of classic instruction.

Henry Clarence, II and his wife, Carrie, are both gifted singers. It is interesting to know that Henry Clarence Glenn, Sr., traces his lineage back six generations to the same English-Scotch ancestry, Glenn and Herndon, both dating from Malcolm, King of Scotland, and Mathilda, crowned Queen of England Nov., 1100, mother of King John and wife of Henry 1st of England, descended from Alfred the Great.

Lucy Glenn, youngest daughter of Massillon and Barbara Herndon Glenn, is also a gifted musician. She has been organist of the First Methodist Church at Eufaula over 40 years and is a notable music teacher. "Miss Lucy," as she is affectionately called, is greatly beloved.

James Elizabeth Glenn had three brothers, Gideon, John and Thomas D., who married the widow Gallery, sister of Bishop Capers. The North Carolina records show several preachers in the family, and for fifty years there has been two or more Glenn preachers in the Alabama Conference of the First Methodist Church. Thomas D. was the grandfather of Bascom Glenn, distinguished preacher. James M. Glenn, Tallassee, Ala., was direct in line of the noted Glenns of the Alabama Conference. One of the Glenn sisters married Nathaniel Macon, congressman from North Carolina, for whom Macon, Georgia, and Macon County, Alabama, were both named.

H. Clarence Glenn, III, of Eufaula, Barbour County, now a student at Duke University, is the last Glenn preacher to be licensed by the Alabama Conference, recently. He is a superior young man with a bright future before him, indicating that he is to carry out the enviable reputation of this fine old family, famous in history, and in the Religious cause of Barbour County and the state.

Note—In 1840 John Boles Glenn went from Glennville to Auburn, Ala., founded the college there, and for a hundred years there has been a member of this illustrious Glenn family a member of the faculty of this college. Thomas Glenn is today a professor of the A. P. I. at Auburn.

The Glenn name originated from the Lordship of Glen Renfrewshire, so called from a historic Vale in Lochwimnac, in 1180. They were of Norman extraction and the name was originally deNess, of the powerful house of l'Estrange. The family in Scotland assumed the name of Glen by grant of the Steward from the Lordship of Renfrewshire to Henry de Ness and when members of the family came to the Carolinas, another "n" was added to the spelling of the name.

They were of Royal lineage through King Robert Bruce's daughter, Margaret by his second wife, being the wife of Robert de Glen and through these Glen and Herndon lines the Glenns have Malcolmn Canmore (of Shakespeare) and his wife, Mathilda, Queen of England, as common ancestors.

Through the Diggs-Herndon line is descended three Scotish kings, Edgar, Alexander, and greatest of all, King David 1st, 1124-1153.

They prize also Edgar Atherling, nephew of Edward the Conquerer, who was a representative of the old Saxon Dynasty, as these lines give to the Glenns paternal lineage through the Scotish kings and on maternal lines, English kings.

It is also gratifying to trace the Glenns of South Carolina and Barbour County, Alabama, back to LinlithGow, Scotland, and to the ancient family of Bar. Their coat of arms are identical with those of LinlithGow and Bar. This coat of Arms bears on one crest a martlet and on the other an arm, the hand grasping the heart of King Robert Bruce of Scotland to the Holy Land. Robert De Glen was one of the family accompanying those carrying this human heart on this historic journey.

This Glenn family are also in possession of the Sword of King Robert Bruce of Scotland. It was carried to Ireland in 1606, where it was recently seen, the inscription on the blade, proving its ownership. Forest and King David II granted to Robert de Glen lands that included Glascow Forest Thanedom of Kintore, Aberdeen.

From the authentic research of Martha Glenn of New York.

EUGENE HERNDON GLENN

Eugene Herndon Glenn, lawyer and judge, was born at Glennville (then Barbour County) October 26th, son of Massilon McKendree and Barbara Herndon Glenn, the same natives of Abbeville District, S. C. Lived at Glennville from 1834 until his death in 1889; was in the creek war of 1836-37 on General Scott's staff and member of State Convention in 1865; was great grandson of James E. and Elizabeth (Robinson) Glenn, a Methodist preacher, who immigrated from Abbeville, S. C., to Randolph County, Georgia, thence to Barbour County, Alabama, and of Stephen and Sarah (Conner) Herndon of Cokesbury, S. C. Judge Glenn was educated in Glennville College and Military Institute, at that time one of the leading colleges of the state; at University of Alabama 1861 to 1862, and in June, 1862 was detailed by Governor John Gill Shorter to drill Confederate Army Recruits and Auburn Cadets, Auburn station; Auburn drill master, afterwards served as major and later adjutant of the 45th Alabama Infantry Regiment, when General Johnson surrendered at Greensboro, N. C., and formed the Regiment on its colors for its surrender to the Federal officer.

For twelve years, he was Probate Judge of Russell County (formerly Barbour) and represented the 27th Senatorial District in the Senate of 1907. Trustee of the University of Alabama; Democrat; Mason; and Methodist; married Feb. 8th, 1887, Virginia, daughter of John G. and Frances (Collier) Evans. Children: Evans, Herndon, Lucious, Francis. Res. Seale, Ala., deceased.

JASON G. GUICE

Jason G. Guice was born in Talbot County, Georgia, and his parents moved to Barbour County when he was a lad of ten years. He was educated at the schools of Columbus, Georgia, and Barbour County.

When the war cry of the Confederacy sounded, he aided in the organization of a Military Company, but for lack of armaments he joined Co. K, Barbour Rangers Regiment 31, Georgia. Clement A. Adams Co. of Sharpshooters. He was wounded at Gaines Mill, below Richmond, August 31st and wounded again at Fredericksburg. At the battle of the Wilderness May 5th, 1864, while in charge of Gordon's Georgia Brigade was wounded; at Fort Stead a grapeshot from Fort New York struck his wrist. Leading three disabled men (himself disabled) he volunteered to meet Stoneman. He attacked the Federal line and drove them across the road nearby. In the skirmishes Guice was taken from his horse and made prisoner. For this the Federal officer presented him with a pair of buckskin gauntlets.

The wounded wrist caused the amputation of his arm just below the elbow, and after the war he walked home June, 1865.

In 1866 he moved to Eufaula, where he established a large farming interest in Barbour County and built up a cotton shipping business, associating with him his brother, Charles Wood Guice. The firm, which was one of the most outstanding enterprises of the County, was "Guice Bros." Also associated with him in later years were his younger brothers, B. Loyd and Tandy Guice. The latter two, now are prominent citizens of Birmingham. In 1873, he married beautiful, beloved Stella, daughter of Dr. John W. and Anne Ethredge Drewry.

She was the untiring leader in all the Patriotic and Church interests of the Community; for 6 years president of the Barbour County chapter Daughters of the Confederacy, during which time she was the principal factor in the purchase and erection of the $3000 Confederate Monument that stands on Broad street at Eufaula. Most of the money was raised by barbecues, given at "Guice's Lake" on the Guice plantation on the banks of the Chattahoochee river.

Mr. Guice and his wife who were outstanding for generous benevolent and charitable work, and despite the fact that his character was unique and he often had and expressed views at variance with those of his friends, he was broad and genuine. His closest friend said of him, ' It took me 15 years to learn how to handle "Jas", but when I did understand him, I found him to be true blue, and the friend that always stuck closer than a brother."

Mr. and Mrs. Guice had no children, but it was the admiration of the community that in the most modest way he paid the tuition of several orphan girls in the community—the fact known only to the board of trustees of the college—the girls themselves not knowing the name of the generous friends who was seeing that they got an education.

This writer learned of this from the school board of Trustees' records, accidentally falling into her hands in later years.

He died at the historic old Drewry-Guice home in Eufaula and is buried in Fairview Cemetery, Eufaula.—One of the most valuable citizens Barbour County ever had.

ROBERT LONG HOBDY

Robert Long Hobdy, was born 1840 at Hobdy's bridge, Pike County, on what is now Barbour County; son of Harrell and Jennie Hobdy (McNeille) Hobdy, natives of South Carolina; came to Barbour County as children and married. The former fought in the Indian battles of 1836 and at the battle of Pea River. One of Pike's first sheriffs and representatives to the state legislature 1844-45 and Senator during 1853-1855. Died 1862 from wounds received during military service.

He was the grandson of Edmund and Nancy (Harrell) Hobdy, natives of South Carolina. He was a native of Scotch-Irish descent, Pike, now part of Bullock County. At the beginning of the Confederate war in 1861, mustered into service at Montgomery. Served as 4th Corporal Louisville Blues 8th Alabama Regiment S. M. Woods commanding. Stationed at Pensacla 8 months, then transferred to Corinth, Miss., where the regiment disbanded. Returning home, he assisted in raising another Company; was elected its 4th lieutenant; was ordered to Tupelo and there was attached to 39th Alabama Regiment as Co. H served throughout the war; in army of Tennessee and badly wounded July 22nd, 1864 at the Battle of Atlanta. Surrendered at Goldsboro, N. C., April 26th, 1865, when Captain of his company.

After the war he returned to Pike County, and engaged in farming on the Hobdy place, moving to Union Springs in 1880 and there had a large plantation of many hundred acres

He married Mary Buford, born in Barbour County, educated at Eufaula, U. F. College, daughter of Jefferson and Mary Ann Rebecca (White) Buford. Children: Robert Long, planter, Jan. 3, 1870; John Buford, Union Springs; buried at Eufaula.

HIRAM HAWKINS

Hiram Hawkins was born in Bath County, Ky., September, 1826, son of Thomas and (Mary Dean) Hawkins, who were farmers in Bath County, the former a merchant and miller, who died of cholera in Mayesville, Ky., on return from a visit to Baltimore, Md., where he went to purchase goods for his store.

His ancestors came from the Coast of the British Channel to Maryland soon after the American Colonies began settling, having been driven from England by political and religious oppression. Many members of the family were active in the war for independence and at the close of the Revolution, Col. Hiram Hawkins' grandfather moved from Maryland to Kentucky, a member of a band of settlers that redeemed Kentucky from wilderness and savagery.

He left school before graduating to manage his father's estate and gained the most of his education by study and reading, and he was a finished scholar by personal effort.

At the age of 26, he was chosen Colonel by the Militia Regiment of his county, the Governor of Kentucky endorsing him.

In 1854, he was nominated high sheriff for the newly organized Democratic party, but was defeated by the Whig candidate by only 30 votes.

The next year Col. Hawkins was elected by an enormous majority to the state Legislature from Bath County, the only County in Kentucky to go Democratic.

In 1857 he sold his farms, made investments in Texas, establishing a sheep ranch, intending to locate there, but the oncoming war changed his plans and at the beginning of the war he joined forces with his state which was then neutral.

As soon as hostilities began, he raised, drilled and disciplined a company of Cavalry, which he tendered to the governor, to be used in sustaining the state policy. After the state was occupied by Federal troops and Marshals, Col. Hawkins, with part of the Volunteers he had raised, left Bath to join the Confederate army. He was mustered in as a private; three days later appointed Captain of a Company, and promoted to Major of his Company.

In 1862, he was made Commander of the Fifth Kentucky Infantry. He took part in battles of Princeton, Va., Reasaca, Chickamauga ,Mission Ridge, Rocky Face, Gap Dallas, Intrenchment Creek, and took part in harrassing "Sherman's March to the Sea."

After the war, he located in Barbour County, becoming a leading farmer and in 1872 was elected President of Union Female College at Eufaula. He was famous for the organization of the "Farmers' Grange" of Barbour County; took part in politics and his lovely home "Hawkinsville," 12 miles from Eufaula, was one of the show places of the County as well as most hospitable.

He married the widow Boykin, a brilliant woman of letters, musician and an artist. They adopted a little girl, Sallie, the daughter of a relative, who grew to lovely womanhood, a pupil of Prof. J. C. Van Houten, whose lovely soprano voice was the wonder and pride of the community.

She married Mr. Daniel Bradley of Russell County, adjoining Barbour. Col. Hawkins was president of the East Alabama Fair Association, and the great fairs held by this organization in the late seventies and early eighties owed their success to him and are bright pages on Barbour County History.

"Hawkinsville" is now owned by Mr. and Mrs. Donald Comer of Alabama, as their summer country home. Over the parlor mantel still hangs a large handsome oil painting, a portrait of Col. Hawkins, painted by Mrs. Hawkins, who was a brilliant woman, a leader in all the interests of the community; highly accomplished in all the higher arts and activities.

DR. J. L. HOUSTON

DR. J. L. HOUSTON

For many years, one of Barbour County's most outstanding, learned and valuable citizens, was Dr. J. L. Houston, of Comer, Clayton and Eufaula, Alabama.

He was born in Barbour County and received his early education in the famous old Joe Espy school at Abbeville, Alabama, receiving a first grade license at the age of 17 years and immediately accepting a position as teacher, during which time he diligently pursued a line of Medical study, and was later licensed to practice. In 1895, he graduated, going to Vanderbilt Medical University at Nashville, Tenn. So fine were the examinations that he stood and the average that he made, that he put two years in one before graduating there.

He took a post graduate course in the New York Polyclinic, New York; for some time since 1925 served as surgeon for the Alabama Power Company.

In 1899 he went to Texas, practicing medicine, but returning to Alabama, he located at Comer, purchasing the historic old Comer home; went into farming on an extensive scale, being one of the largest land owners in the state.

In addition to his duties as a physician, he organized the Bank at Comer and was its president for eight years and to him is due the fact that when the depression and financial crisis came and the bank ceased to do business, Dr. Houston liquidated the assets, paying every depositor, dollar for every dollar due them, plus the accumulated surplus.

He later purchased a large interest in the Advance Banking Company of Clayton, changing the name to the Bank of Commerce, and this institution paid an annual dividend at the end of the 4th year, the stock being worth $1.30.

Dr. Houston was a fine cautious financier. He was a member of the Board of Stewards of First Methodist Church;

member of the Agricultural Committee of the Bankers Association in 1921.

He was owner of plantations of several thousand acres and owner of a large herd of Whitefaced cattle and gave his personal attention to his large business interests, relinquishing his large practice as a physician (which he loved) only to serve, in vital cases, and answer calls to those needing immediate attention—and so popular was he that these calls were frequent. Later he purchased the Bluff City Inn and other large buildings in Eufaula, moving his family to Eufaula, himself and his three sons personally looking after their home at the hotel. The several departments of their large business interests.

He was deeply interested in and took active part in the politics of the state, county and city. He was a man of broad vision and of much business ability, a most substantial, progressive and useful citizen; a leader in the Educational factors of the County and, busy as he was, at all times he loved his profession and was a leading physician of ability; was member of state and County Medical Societies.

On the 23rd day of May 1938, while enroute to Panama City in his car he turned over and was thrown down a precipice and fatally injured. He died enroute to a Dothan, Alabama, hospital. His body was badly crushed.

Dr. Houston married Belle McCarroll, daughter of the late Mr. and Mrs. Samuel McCarroll, prominent and greatly beloved pioneer citizens of Terese, Barbour County. To them were born three splendid sons, Howard D., Gorman, and J. L., Jr., splendid young business men, who with the help and advice of their mother, are carrying on his programs and plans in handling his large estate.

The eldest son, Howard, married Carolyn Clayton, daughter of Judge and Mrs. Lee J. Clayton. Gorman married Mildred, daughter of Mr. and Mrs. E. W. Vance; J. L. married Frances, daughter of Mr. and Mrs. K. B. McKenzie. All living there in their several homes in Eufaula are contributing to the betterment and uplift of the Community, progressive and valuable citizens like their father.

HART FAMILY

When John Hart came to Barbour County from Rhode Island in the fifties he was owner of many slaves. He was an intimate friend of James Buford, editor of the "Spirit of the South," and from that friendship Mr. Hart imbibed the principles of the Confederacy, from which he became one of the staunchest Southerners. Mr. Buford foretold the War Between the States more than five years before the first gun at Fort Sumpter sounded. He said that war was imminent and Mr. Hart was far seeing enough to sell his large number of slaves, and thereby was not bankrupted when the Emancipation Proclamation decree went into effect, as the majority of Southern slave owners were.

In 1866 he built historic Hart's Block of 8 stores, large stables and warehouse, reaching from Broad to Barbour streets, on Eufaula street east. He was a financial leader in those pioneer days, and a most valuable citizen of the County.

His eldest son, Capt. Henry C. Hart, was one of the first to respond to the Confederate call and went forth with Company G, Alabama Regiment. He was severely wounded at Atlanta and later enlisted in the Eufaula Light Artillery and served during the entire war.

Another son of John Hart, Harrison, fell on the battlefield, and another brother, Charles Hart, asked Capt. Mac Oliver for the use of a wagon to remove him. Capt. Oliver replied: "I have no time for the dead," and ten minutes later Oliver himself was dead. Charlie Hart succeeded in removing the body and found that he was not quite dead, but recovered and lived many years at Eufaula.

Charlie Hart was also badly wounded and was a cripple for life. He lived and died at Eufaula.

Henry C. Hart married first Sarah Corker, and to them were born Sallie, who married first Charles Jackson and had two children, Charles A. and Lillian who married Mr. Coleman.

Sallie Hart Jackson married second Fred Thornton of Barbour County—issue, 3 daughters. Fred Thornton died February, 1937, at Montgomery hospital.

Henry C. Hart married second Paralee Ricks Oliver, widow of Capt. Mac Oliver, who died on the field of battle beside the supposed dead body of Chas. Hart. Their children are Pet, married Victor M. Milton, issue two daughters; Louise who died in infancy, and Emily, married Mr. Boone, issue son.

Lila married Charles J. R. Dalbey, her son Capt. Josiah Toney Dalbey, U. S. Army.

Henry C. Hart, Rhode Island, married, issue.

B. Frank Hart married Lucy Price, daughter of H. W. B. Price, pioneer citizen of Clayton, issue, Olivia married Mr. Bell; Hart married Miss Smith, issue, two sons, Tom Hall and Frank.

B. Frank Hart, Jr., married Janie Doughtie, issue.

B. Frank Hart, Sr., was sheriff of Barbour County 1874-1876, and was a loyal Democrat and an enthusiastic politician; a man of most genial nature and popular as a County official

William Hart married Annie McGough, daughter of Col. and Mrs. Thomas McGough, pioneer citizens of Glennville.

Their only child, Annie, Will, named for both mother and father, married Maj. W. G. Lewis, and they reside at Glennville. She is one of the most active and valuable U. D. C. women in the County and state.

William Hart, another son, was a large farmer in Russell (now Barbour) county; also a politician, who was valuable to the county as a staunch Democrat. He also served in the Confederate army, loyal to the South.

Harrison, the youngest brother, was the Beaux Brummel of this group of brothers. He was a fine musician and an artistic dancing master whose large classes of young men and women annually were his pride and, to whom they were due, the joy of many social occasions as the years passed.

He married in Henry County, Ala., issue, three daughters. See Old Historic Homes—Hart-Milton home.

Capt. Henry C. Hart married third Miss Mollie McGruder, a cousin of his second wife, no issue, but she reared the children of the second marriage.

N. M. HYATT

Among the men who came from the North in the pioneer days and cast their lot in Barbour County, making good and becoming outstanding citizens was N. M. Hyatt, a jeweler, a cultured Christian gentleman. He came from New York when Eufaula was yet a village, and the cottage he resided in on Randolph street, on the site where later years the old McNab-Reeves-McSweeney and later Schamealing Bakery, has made the lot notable. In the store adjoining his residence (one of the first few attractive pioneer homes built) he had Eufaula's first jewelry store and watch and clock repairing establishment.

After a portion of this block, from Barbour street, to the brick wall of the McNab building, was burned to the ground in 1874, Mr. Hyatt moved his Jewelry store, under the old Central hotel (now the Bluff City Inn) with the firm of Matthews and Petry, book sellers.

The files of the Eufaula newspaper, "The Spirit of the South," during the late sixties show many references to the handsome store of Mathews and Petry and the elaborate array of Jewelry of N. M. Hyatt on the opposite side of this store.

Mr. Hyatt was for many years a Justice of the Peace in Barbour County and his unique and very beautiful handwriting is on many of the most important (many very notable) papers attested by him.

Personally, he was a man among men; of splendid physique, his grey hair and grey sideburn whiskers giving him a most distinguished appearance. He was a cultured gentleman of that old Presbyterian code of living that acclaimed him "to the Manor born." He was one of the most distinguished citizens Eufaula ever had. He married a girl from New York and their children were: Mollie, who married William Petry, also one of the most valuable and highly esteemed citizens Barbour County ever had. He came to Eufaula from Apalachicola, Florida. His sister, Miss Mina Petry, who made her home with him, is living today 84 years old, and is the lovely old lady in years only, for she is active, enthusiastic, about all the better ennobling things of the day and time, whose presence it is a joy to be in, and who is greatly beloved by everyone.

The Petry children are Louis, married; Edith, Newham, Natalie, married Hampton Stewart, issue, Hampton, Jr., married Margaret Bunn; Dr. William Stewart married Elizabeth White, Troy, Ala.; Mary, married J. C. Carter of the Rockefeller Foundation, living in Egypt.

Natalie married Mathew Homan, March 29, 1939.

William Petry of White Plains, N. Y., unmarried.

Clifford Petry, deceased.

Lottie Petry married C. B. Boland, Washington, D. C.

Frank C. Petry married Louise Foy, issue, son, Treutlen Foy Petry, Louise and Carolyn Petry.

After the burning of the beautiful and unique Hyatt cottage, Mr. Hyatt built the lovely home on North Randolph street, where, with his wife, who was a very queenly and most cultured woman of the born aristocratic poise and dignity spent their life and reared their children.

The second Hyatt daughter was Emma, who married G. B. Burbank, a very noted Civil Engineer of New York, issue a daughter, Marjorie, and son, Clifford.

Trauss Hyatt, the only son, died a few years ago, in the zenith of splendid manhood.

HENRY C. HOLLEMAN

Henry C. Holleman was born in Eufaula, August 5th, 1864, son of Ely C. and Samantha Holleman, pioneer settlers of Eufaula.

He received his education under Profs. John Dobbins and C. A. Craven and at Rusk-Hinton Male Academy, Eufaula.

When a lad he began his business career as a messenger for the Western Union Telegraph Company and was notable for efficiency and promptness in that capacity. When about 20 years old, he bought out the Photograph business of Photographer Watson for whom he had worked and remained in this business a number of years, selling out to John W. Flournoy. He purchased from Dozier Thornton the Eufaula Dray and Transfer Business and soon thereafter added to it a Coal and Feed business, in which he was most successful.

After a few years he bought from F. W. Jennings, successor to R. J. Woofs, the Eufaula Wharf, and in those days the river traffic was immense, and most profitable. After many years he sold the Wharf to Mr. W. C. Bradley of Columbus, Ga., who was a stockholder in boats running the river.

After selling the wharf, Mr. Holleman organized the Eufaula Hardman Company, selling his interest as a stockholder some years later to the present owners, to engage in other business. For some time he has been Judge of the City (or Inferior Court) and is engaged in looking after large real estate and farming interests.

He is recognized as one of the outstanding native Eufaula citizens who has wrought well and is notable for sterling integrity, sound judgment, that integrity of character, and through his long life has been conspicuous as one of Barbour's leading and highly esteemed citizens. He is a Democrat, a Mason and a steward of the First Methodist Church, in every way dependable and worthy of the friendship that is his in the entire County. He married February 1892, Mamie Watson, daughter of Hinton Watson and Lucy Ming Watson, of Marianna, Florida.

A beautiful woman of the South, she was beloved for personal charm; womanliness, and many traits of Christian character.

Children: Gatra, married Harmon Lampley; Marie, married J. T. Kendall; Hinton Watson, killed in action in France during World War; Henry C., Jr., married Mabel Pomeroy.

J. G. HORTMAN

John Gosper Hortman was born in Germany in a Province called "Dutch Fork" and died in Eufaula November 10th, 1884.

When a young man he came to America and settled in South Carolina, thence to Georgia and then came to Barbour County, homesteading 640 acres known as No. 30, Section 640, the government grant to him, bearing the signature of President Martin Van Buren. It was written on sheepskin, and is an interesting document.

There Mr. Hortman had one of the finest farms in all the County. It adjoined the famous Ott plantation, which today is owned by the Alston family, grandchildren of Col. Edward S. Ott.

In the seventies Mr. Hortman moved into the city of Eufaula, where he owned valuable property, residences, store house and large warehouses.

For many years he operated a wagon yard in the rear of his warehouse and daily drove to his farm at Batesville.

He was a man of forethought, wisdom and understanding

and was a success at every thing he undertook. During the War Between the States he managed a large salting manufactory, exclusively for the Confederate soldiers, and his service to the Confederacy was outstanding and far reaching.

He married first Lennie Metz, and to them was born a son, Harry, who when he grew up, settled at Clayton, Ala., and for years operated the famous old Hortman's Mills four miles from Clayton. This mill was on a great pond that was annually covered with thousands of georgeous water lilies that is another pointed feature of the many notable things that have made Barbour County known of the world over. This lily pond is one of the beauty spots of Alabama.

J. G. HORTMAN

J. G. Hortman married second, Frances Reese, and their children were: Belle, a famous singer and violinist (of whom Prof. Van Houten, her teacher said, "A rare muscial artist in every sense.") She married Daniel Brown and died in Texas; twins, Della and Lulu, who married Dandifer of Louisiana, and Della married Thomas McRae. She also was a gifted pianist, and although 40 years an invalid was until her death still as proficient in music and loved it, as when a girl. She died two years ago and is buried at Pea River Churchyard near Louisville, Ala., beside her husband, both members of most distinguished Barbour County families.

Her daughter, Mabel (McRae) Bush, is the wife of John Bunyan Bush, a member of the prominent Bush family of Barbour, and they are valuable and beloved citizens of Eufaula. Mabel Bush is also a most accomplished musician and a charming woman, who gives much of her time to all of the helpful activities of the County. She has raised hundreds upon hundreds of dollars as the years have passed along, with her musical and dramatic talent, giving amateur shows, concerts and plays, using the money of every one for charitable, church and various benevolent purposes.

Recently she raised money to put a roof on the home of an unfortunate family in the community. She is often seen in her car carrying trays of food she has prepared for the sick and needy. Her son, John B., Jr., is also a musician who during his college terms at Gulfport, La., was Captain of the G. M. C. A. College band.

Her nephew, James Sims (whom she reared after his parents died) is also another musical Hortman descendant, who was slide trombone player in the U. S. Army and in the Canal Zone, but on account of his health finally had to leave that climate. Since then (several years ago) he has been with the College band of the Alabama Polytechnic Institute of Auburn, Ala. He is rated the very highest class slide trombone player; also cornetist.

A daughter, Leila, married a Daniel and they are now prominent citizens of Smithville, Ga. Mrs. Daniel is also a musician and Manager of the Telephone Exchange at Smithville, a position she has held for many years.

Emma married Dr. J. Cleveland and resides at Columbus. She is a musician, too.

Edna is married.

James Wesley was born in 1863 at the old Hortman home at Batesville (as were all the children), grew up there and like his father became a fine farmer, which profession he has spent his life in, and is today still farming though on a smaller scale at his suburban home farm out on College hill. He not only has the finest cotton and corn crops, but his truck gardens are famous, and despite his declining health, he still oversees all the work personally, and cannot resist overdoing it some times, when the urge to lend a hand overcomes him. He is a remarkable citizen in every way, and stands high in the esteem of his friends. He also is a fine musician, and possibly the most finished violinist in all the County.

He married Agnes Cleveland, daughter of Dr. James Cleveland of Cuthbert, Ga., whose brother was the father of president of the U. S., Grover Cleveland. It happened that these brothers when they grew up in Essex County, New Jersey, but one remained North and the other came South. She is a brilliant pianist, and the piano and violin duets they play are the delight of their friends.

Two sons are the children of Mr. and Mrs. James W. Hortman, Hobart Cleveland married Willie Joe Patterson and they have one son, Hobart, Junior. Ambrose C. married Solida Kirvin and they have two daughters, Solida and Gwendolyn and one son. These two sons are also famous musicians, Hobart a pianist, Ambrose a violinist and both saxaphone players. For ten or more years Hortman's orchestra, H. C. Hortman, leader, travelled the South and always met ovations. Both James Sims and J. B. Bush were members of this ten-piece orchestra, which had a wonderful reputation.

It was abandoned because Hortman Brothers became tired of travelling and preferred a business life at home.

The young son, A. C., occupies the old Hortman home on Broad street (which happens to be the house in which the writer of this history was born, and also the home from which the horse owned by the Howe Telegraph Co. (The Columbus and Apalachicolan Telegraph Co.) was stolen the night of the day the "Yankees" passed through Barbour County, and through Eufaula over the Chattahoochee river into Georgia to camp. (See Grierson's March Through Eufaula and "The Story of Yellow Martha".)

The Hortman name is famous for music, literature, farming, trucking and for outstanding citizenship generally.

JOHN LINGUARD HUNTER

John Linguard Hunter was born Nov. 18th, 1794, at Charleston, S. C., and died at Eufaula, Alabama, February 15th, 1869; son of Thomas and Mary (Wyatt) Hunter, the former a native of Scotland who came to Charleston, S. C., grand son of John and Violetta (Linguard) Wyatt of Charleston.

Gov. William Aiken's mother who was a Miss Wyatt was of that city.

He graduated from S. C. College, Columbia, in law, but did not actively engage in practice.

He moved to Barbour County in 1835; was a trustee of the University of Alabama and a member of the Alabama Legislature in 1841 from Barbour County.

He was elected Major General of Militia; rated a specimen of the old school; raised in South Carolina from Huguenot ancestry; highly intelligent, he was a scientific agriculturist and was always made leader in the farming organizations. He was notable for culture and good breeding; was an Episcopalian; a Democrat, and a Mason; married July 8th Sarah Bradwell (Ferguson) Bowler of Godfrey, S. C., and granddaughter of James Wilson Coplain of the Revolutionary War, from S. C., and a signer of the Declaration of Independence. Children: James Linguard, married Sarah Shorter, daughter of Reuben C., and Martha Gill Shorter; Elizabeth Aiken, married Henry D. Clayton; Charles Bradwell; Teresa Wilson, married William Andrew McTyer, buried at old family cemetery near the old Hunter-Pugh home.

R. D. JONES

Robert Dallas Jones, superintendent of Cowikee Mills, Eufaula, was born in Person County, N .C., September 19th,

1868, son of Robert Jones and grandson of William Jones. He attended the school of Orange (now Durham) leaving school at 16 years of age to commence working in the cotton mills of Burlington. He learned the business from the bottom up, being employed in the mills of North and South Carolina, Virginia and Superintendent of Anchor Mills, Huntersville, N. C., from 1901 to 1905, was superintendent of the Nantucket Mills at Spray, N. C., and then to Brown Manufacturing Company, Concord, N. C., 1907 to 1909 when he was made superintendent of Cowikee Mills until his death at Eufaula April 24th, 1929.

During these years he also was Supt. of two (Comer Mills) at Eufaula and one Comer Mill at Union Springs, Ala.

He was for several terms member of City Council of Eufaula and chairman of the Committee of Public Works and Civic Committees; member of Harmon Lodge No. 46, F. A. A.; member the W. O. W. and Eufaula Camp Red Men; was charter member of the Eufaula Kiwanis club and a progressive, leading citizen; married Anna Pearl Laney, daughter of Samuel L. and Laura (Johnson) Laney.

The following are their children: Pearl, married Willis Whitlock, Hillsboro, Ill.; Walter L. married Lena Schmaeling, one daughter, Barbara, Albany, Ga. He was the hero of the great Labam flood at Elba, Ala., in 1929, rescuing from a house garret a mother and new born baby, in the night in a boat; Robert D. married Margaret Ross, Montgomery, Ala.; Mabel married William Davis, Pensacola, Fla.; Lois married J. H. Horne, Eufaula; James married Susie Lee Thompson, Columbus, Ga.; Herman married Lucile Clark, Pensacola, Fla.; Mary married E. M. Heron, Gadsden, Alabama.

WILLIAM THOMAS JOINER

William Thomas Joiner, M. D., was born near Skipperville, Dale County, Nov. 6th, 1869, son of Rev. William D. Joiner, a notable Baptist Minister, and also an extensive farmer. He preached all over Southwest Georgia and Southeast Alabama, moving to Dale County, Ala., in 1855 and later locating back in Georgia at the town of Omaha. He filled various pastorates and died at the home of his son, Dr. Joiner, at Pittsview, Alabama, October 3rd, 1902. He was a most distinguished personage, a Confederate veteran of the War Between the States.

His son, Dr. William Joiner, graduated from Atlanta Medical College in 1891 and began practicing at once. At Loftin, Russell County, he worked up a large country practice, and since 1895, has resided at Pittsview, where he has made an enviable reputation in his large Rural practice.

He is a member of the Russell (formerly Barbour) County and State of Alabama Medical Societies, is a deacon of the Baptist Church and an enthusiastic Democrat.

He married Miss Laura McMichael July, 1891. She was the mother of four children: William Howard, World War veteran, who is still captain of Infantry in the Regular Army; Asa G. and Cary P., business men of Atlanta, Georgia; Reuben C., also World War veteran, and has been many years cashier and director of the Bank of Eufaula, and one of Barbour County's leading, progressive citizens. The first Mrs. Joiner died Jan. 27th, 1913.

Dr. Joiner's second wife was Mrs. Dora B. Pitts, daughter of William M. Burt of Pittsfield, Ala. The three children of this Union are Wilson Marshall; Dorcas, and Mary Jane. Mrs. Joiner died July, 1937.

HENRY JONES

The subject of this sketch was a grandson of Major Peter Jones, for whom the City of Petersberg, Va., was named, and whose progeny is so numerous, especially in the South.

Major Peter Jones, son of Abram Jones, married Mary Wood, daughter of General Abram Wood, once commanded a fort that was located at the falls of the Appomattox. His will, dated Jan. 19, 1721, probated Jan. 10, 1726, recorded in Prince County, Va., names 10 children, as follows: Peter, William, Thomas, John, Wood, Abraham, Mary, Ann, Margaret and Martha. He devises 100 acres of land lying on the Great Creek on Nottoway River to his son, Wood Jones, grandfather of Henry Jones, the subject of this sketch. It is not known whom Wood Jones married nor the names of his children, except his son, Henry Jones, who married Winnie Elder, by whom he had two children: Susannah and Henry, the subject of this sketch. Henry died before his son, Henry, was born. His widow, Winnie Elder Jones, married a second husband, Robert Lenoir, to whom she bore several children.

Now we come to Henry Jones, the subject of this sketch. He was born near the Nottoway River in Dinwiddie County, Va., Feb. 9, 1762. After his mother's second marriage his stepfather, Robert Lenoir, became his guardian. Though under age he served in the Revolutionary army, enlisting three times for short periods, under Col. James Lucas, Captains Binns Jones, Thomas Threadgill and Harrelson. He took part in the Battle of Camden. He married three times: (a) Sallie Lightfoot, daughter of Henry and Mary Lightfoot, Dec.

16, 1786, in Brunswick County, Virginia. (b) Mary Hogan in North Carolina. (c) Nellie Payne at Montezuma, Covington County, Ala. He moved from Virginia to North Carolina in the Vicinity of Guilford; he moved from there to Georgia and lived in different places in the eastern part of the state: in Oglethorpe, Greene and probably in Hancock and Jones Counties. He moved to Alabama before it became a state, and settled at the falls of the Conecuh River in what is now Covington County. He opened up a farm and built a mill, the first corn mill in that section of the territory. He was thrifty Industrious and sober. He accumulated some property in land and slaves. Of the latter he probably had a goodly number, judging from a deed recorded in Butler County, Alabama, showing that he gave to his daughter, Sallie in 1826, six negro slaves," as a part of her patrimony." Since there were 12 of his children, he must have been pretty well-to-do for that period. That he was a man of some consequence in his community is shown by the fact that he was named by the legislature as one of the commissioners in the Act to organize Covington County, "to fix and designate a suitable place for a seat of justice, and to contract for and superintend the erection of such public buildings, etc." and again on a commission to hold the first election of county officers, etc. He moved to Barbour County, near Louisville, about 1830 where he lived until his death, which occurred May 15, 1851. His remains lie in the Cemetery at Louisville, Barbour County, Ala.

His children were:

William Jones, born March 26, 1789; Henry Lightfoot Jones, born Sept. 16, 1791; Thomas Jones, born March 8, 1793.

By second marriage: Cannon Jones, born 1796; Seaborn Jones, born March 17, 1799; Allen Jones, Reuben Lindsey Jones, John Elder Jones, Nancy Jones, Polly Jones, Sallie Saires Jones, born March 7, 1809.

By third marriage: Winnie Elder Jones, born Nov. 3, 1835; Joseph Jones, born June 5, 1838; Benjamin Jones, born Nov. 26, 1841.

William and Thomas, by the first marriage, died in childhood. All the others grew up, married and had families.

A Brief Genealogy of the Descendants of Henry Jones To the Third Generation

Henry Lightfoot Jones—born Sept. 16, 1791, married Mary Elizabeth Marcus, daughter of Daniel Marcus, a veteran of the Revolutionary War. The marriage occurred in Georgia; probably in Jones County. He lived in Meriwether County, Ga., Barbour County and Pike County, Ala.; Ouachita County, Ark., and Bienville Parrish, La., where he died probably about 1860, near Ringgold.

His children—Louisa Daniel Jones, William Henry Jones, Sarah Lightfoot Jones, born Nov. 22, 1882; Martha Jones, born July, 1824; John Hollinger Jones, born Dec. 28, 1826; Mary Elizabeth Jones, born March 2, 1931; Emily Jane Jones, born Dec. 16, 1832.

Louisa Daniel Jones— born in Georgia, probably in Meriwether County, married Thomas Williams; died a year or two after her marriage. One child: Elizabeth. After her mother's death, was brought up by her maternal grandparents. Moved with them to Arkansas, where she married Jan. 30, 1856, John J. Ross, in Ouachita County; died September 17, 1897.

Her children—John Thomas, William Franklin, Henry Calvin, Albert Newton, Virginia Frances, Robert DeWitt, James Wiley, Hattie and Cattie (twins), Anna May, Oscar Israel. Of these there are numerous descendants, mostly in South Arkansas.

William Henry Jones—married Rebecca Westbrook in Barbour County, Ala. Lived in that County a few miles from Louisville. He was a member of Bethlehem Baptist Church; was a private soldier in the Confederate army; was in the battles of Shiloh, New Hope, Atlanta and Peachtree Creek. Died in federal prison at Camp Chase, Ohio.

His children—Louisa, Hollinger Brown, Henry Manuel, Addie, Mary, Lucy, Zilphie, William Thomas, James White.

Sarah Lightfoot Jones Wilkes—born Feb. 22, 1822, in Meriwether County, Ga., just 90 years after the birth of George Washington; married William Usher Wilkes in Barbour County, Ala. Lived in the fork of Pea River and Pea Creek, 5 miles from Louisville. Died Nov. 9, 1900. Buried at Old Ephesus Church Cemetery on Hobdy Bridge road.

Her children—William Henry Wilkes, born July 10, 1845 in Barbour County, Ala.; Laura Ann Wilkes, born Oct. 1, 1849, in Barbour County, Ala.; John Calhoun Wilkes, born Nov. 8, 1852, in Barbour County, Ala.; Sarah Jane Wilkes, born Septerber 15, 1858, in Barbour County, Ala.

William Henry Wilkes—born July 10, 1845, in Barbour County, Ala. Lived in Barbour and Pike Counties. Married (a) in Pike County, Ala., Susannah Missouri Lawson, daughter of Adam and Lavinia (Wheeless) Lawson; (b) Sarah Frances Gause, daughter of Jesse Smith and Martha (Bates) Gause. For more than 40 years he was a justice of the peace at Josie, Pike County, Ala.

His children: Laura Malissa, Alto Monroe, John Adam, Susannah Nancy, Florence Stacy, William Pugh, Katie Luelle, Sarah Frances, Ethel May, Joel Davis, Martha Vernon. Most of these married and have families. William Pugh is a prominent Baptist minister. An interesting branch of the family. deserve more extended notice.

Laura Ann Wilkes Lawson—born Oct. 1, 1849, in Barbour County, Ala., married Joseph Winwright Lawson, son of Adam and Lavinia (Wheeless) Lawson. Lived at Josie, Pike County, Ala. Died there.

Her children—Vernon Davis Lawson, William Adam Lawson, Josie Emma Lawson Salter. An important branch of the family tree.

John Calhoun Wilkes—born Nov. 8, 1862, in Barbour County, Ala., married May 14, 1876, Cydia Antoinette Sellers, daughter of Cornelius and Cydia Eason (Thigpen) Sellers.

His children—William Russell Wilkes, Johnnie and Jodie Wilkes (twins), Ruth Wilkes, Cornelius Sellers Wilkes, Effie Dee Wilkes, Essie Lee Wilkes, Shannon Davis Wilkes.

Sarah Jane Wilkes Price—born Sept. 15, 1858, in Barbour County, Ala., married Jan. 22, 1882, John Patterson Price, son of Burrell and Rebecca (Tomberlin) Price; died Dec. 29, 1904, at Louisville, Barbour County, Ala.

Her children: Laura Viola Price, Leona Permelia Price Tyler, Rosa Maye Price Spires, William Ezra Price, Leah Alice Price Spires, Maggie Corinne Price.

Martha Ann Jones McDowell—daughter of Henry Lightfoot Jones, born in 1824 in Meriwether County, Georgia, married Dec., 1847, in Barbour County, Ala, John G. McDowell. Moved from Brundidge, Ala., to Bienville Parrish, La.; died there Dec. 14, 1907.

Her children—Emma Isabella McDowell Bailey, Edward Thomas McDowell, Warren Montgomery McDowell, George Clinton McDowell, Robert Hamilton McDowell, Mary Elizabeth McDowell Bryan, Fannie Melissa McDowell Waters.

John Hollinger Jones—son of Henry Lightfoot Jones—born Dec. 28, 1826, in Meriwether County, Ga., married Lurana Stewart, daughter of James Madison and Ann (Laws) Stewart at Brundidge, Pike County, Ala., March 30, 1852. Soldier in the Confederate Army, Co. E. 1st Alabama Vols. Died Oct. 3, 1873, near Rose Hil, Covington Co., Ala.

His children—Mary Elizabeth Jones Straughn, Catherine Jones, died in youth; Ella Jane and John Franklin, died in infancy; Morgan Davis Jones, John Isham Jones, Richard Henry Jones.

Morgan Davis Jones—son of John Hollinger Jones, born at Brundidge, Ala., Dec. 8, 1862. Lawyer, civil engineer, abstractor. Pioneer in hydro-electric power development; held offices of tax collector, County Supt. Education; member of legislature, all in Covington County, Ala.; married May 2, 1886, at Dozier, Ala., Melita Dozier, daughter of Green Berry and Arrena (Rowell) Dozier.

His children—Melita Morgana Jones Lowry, John Herbert Jones, Greene Henry Jones, Leola Leslie Jones, Mary Laura Jones, Thomas Kent Jones, Morgan Dozier Jones, Ethel Ruth Jones Black. Leola Leslie and Mary Laura died in childhood. The four sons all served in the World War.

John Isham Jones—son of John Hollinger Jones, born April 15, 1866, near Brundidge, Ala., married January 8, 1891, Isie Ola Straughn, daughter Travis Wendell and Sallie (Cook) Straughn, at Rose Hill, Ala.; died without issue February 14, 1897, at Rose Hill, Ala.

Richard Henry Jones—son of John Hollinger Jones, born near Brundidge, Ala., Jan. 24, 1869. Educated at Normal College at Troy, Ala., Peabody Normal College, Nashville, Tenn., Georgetown University Law School and Columbia University Law School, Washington, D. C. Served several years in U. S. Pension Office. Practiced law in Montgomery, and Andalusia, Ala.; served as Judge and also as Solicitor of Circuit Court; abstractor of titles; served also as member of state legislature; married Jan. 24, 1901, at Ozark, Ala., Mary Zenobia Dillard, daughter of Edmund Dillard.

His children—Annie Lurana Jones Flowers, Henry Edward Jones, Richard Hollinger Jones.

Mary Elizabeth Jones (Watts) (McFarland)—daughter of Henry Lightfoot Jones, born March 3, 1831, in Meriwether County, Ga., married (a) William Barnett Watts, at Brundidge, Ala. (b) married near Coushatta, La., John Porter McFarland; died September 20, 1893, in Red River Parrish, La.

Her children—Robert Walter Watts, Emily Marian Rebecca Watts Cannon, Mary Emma Watts Teer, Almira Josephine Watts Cummings, Joseph Barnett Watts, William Henry McFarland, Irene Louisiana McFarland Horney. A numerous progeny in Louisiana and Texas.

Emily Jane Jones Young Riley—born Dec. 16, 1832, in Meriwether County, Ga., married (a) Bunyan Young, (b) Craddock Riley. Spent her married life and died near Perote, Bullock County, Ala.

Her children: Martha Lucy Elizabeth Riley Edge, Lela Eleanora Riley Ross Green.

Cannon Jones—son of Henry Jones, born in Oglethorpe County, Ga., Aug. 20, 1813. Military record: Served as a private in Capt. Jett Thomas' Company, Colonel Norman's Reg., Ga. Mil. Artillery, Gen. Floyd's Brigade; was in the battle of Caliba in which several of his comrades were killed. Discharged at Ft. Mitchell, Ga., Mar. 14, 1814. Served also in the Florida War under Capt. Danielly, Col. Wimberly, Ga. Mil. Enlisted Nov. 3, 1817 at Milledgeville, Ga.; discharged at Hartford, Ga., June 31, 1818; married Elizabeth Talbot Simpson in Conecuh or Lownes County, Ala., now Lowndes.

Moved back to near Milledgeville, Ga., for two years; then to Conecuh County, Ala., four or five years; to Pike County, to Montgomery, then to Macon County (1856-57). He and his wife were charter members of the First Baptist Church, Montgomery, Ala. He died June 6, 1860, near Notasulga, Ala. Only one child to live to maturity, viz: Henry Simpson Jones.

Henry Simpson Jones—son of Cannon Jones, born Dec. 9, 1820, at Milledgeville, Ga.; served in Confederate Army as a farrier for a cavary outfit; married (a) Rosa E. Lee, an English girl; ((b) Rhoda Angie Arnold, daughter of Robert and Mary (Gordon) rnold, near Gordonsville, Lowndes County, Ala.; died Oct. 3, 1885.

His children by first marriage—Edwin Henry Jones, Mary Elizabeth Jones; died in childhood), Laura. Laura never married.

By second marriage: Caroline Jones Spann, Frankie Rachel Jones McMillan, Rosa Lyon Jones Folmar, Sarah Caroline Jones Johnson, Lula Angie Jones Gardner.

Edwin Henry Jones—son of Henry Simpson Jones, born Sept. 16, 1843, in Montgomery, Ala.; was in Confederate service in the Quartermaster's Department, at Camp Watts, near Notasulga, Ala. m. June 20, 1865, Margaret Rebecca Thompson, dau. of Alfred and Mary Jane (Wagner) Thompson, a relative of the late Congressman Thompson. Lived near Union Springs until 1873, when he moved to Eufaula where he lived until his death, Jan. 18, 1908.

Seaborn Jones— son of Henry Jones, born Mar. 17, 1799 in Georgia. Served in Indian War, but it is not known in what war nor what command. He married August 1, 1822, Eliza Lang, daughter of William and Feraby Lang, probably in Covington County, Ala. He owned land there and his first child was born there. He moved from there to Louisville, Barbour County, where he lived until about 1832, when he moved to Yalobusha County, Mississippi. He died January 31, 1881.

His children—Sarah Amanda Jones McCormick, Mary Elizabeth Jones Atkinson, Martha Margaret Jones Creekmore, William Cowin Jones, John Washington Jones, Nancy Ann Jones Weaver, Andrew Jackson Jones, Rosannah Louisa Brett. (This branch if the Henry Jones family is very numerous, and they live in the northwest Mississippi counties, in Memphis, Tennessee, Arkansas and Louisiana.

Allen Jones—son of Henry Jones, born in Georgia about the year 1800; married Mary Jane Moody, daughter of William Moody; lived near Mt. Meigs, Montgomery County, Alabama. When his first child was about 15 years old he moved to Barbour County in the Skipperville neighborhood; thence to Milton, Florida, where he died January 18, 1881.

His children—Elizabeth Elder Jones Sutton, Mary Eliza Jones Henderson, Sarah Alice Jones Keogh, Susan Jane Jones Ward, Emily Carter Jones Ward, William Henry Jones, Allen Roberson Jones, Johnathan Jones. (This branch of the Henry Jones family are found principally in West Florida. One sub-branch, the Keogha, went to New York City.

Reuben Lindsey Jones—son of Henry Jones, born in Georgia, date not known; married in Covington County, Ala., Cyrenia Brewer, daughter of William and Mary (Harp) Brewer. Lived in Conecuh County; moved thence to Sumter County; died Sept., 1844 at Livingston, Ala.

His children: Mary Ann, Elizabeth Jones Mundy, William Henry Jones.

John Elder Jones—son of Henry Jones; married Rosanna Douglas of Orange, N. C. He was a merchant at Louisville, Barbour County, Ala., for several years. He moved thence to Ouachita County, Ark., in 1884. He owned 1000 acres of land, which was in the heart of what afterwards became the Smackover oil fields.

His children: William Floyd Jones, John Walker Jones, Sarah Ann Jones McLaughlin, Caroline Beuford Jones, Reuben Young Jones. (This branch of the Henry Jones family is not very numerous. There are still a few members in Ouachita County, Ark.

Mary (Polly) Jones Drakeford—married at Louisville, Barbour County, Ala., James Drakeford. Lived in Tuskegee, Ala.; died there, 1863.

Her children: James Jackson Drakeford, Henry Drakeford. (Henry Drakeford never married).

Children of James Jackson Drakeford: Haden Dick Drakeford, James Jackson Drakeford, Mary Lou (Ludie) Drakeford Dugger.

Mary Lou Drakeford Dugger—born Nov. 7, 1871, at Tuskegee, Robert Bolling Dugger, son of Henry Bellfield and Sarah Winifred (Williams) Duggar. Her husband was postmaster at Tuscaloosa, Ala., for several years.

Her children—Louise Lawson Dugger, Henry Bellfield Duggar, Robert Bolling Duggar.

Nancy Jones George—daughter of Henry Jones, born in Georgia; married at Montezuma, Ala, Wiley George. Moved to Louisville, Barbour County, Ala.; thence to Texas; died at Rock Springs, Tex., about 1867-8. She had three children. All died in childhood the same year, and while she lived in Louisville. Her husband became wealthy in Texas. Her branch of the Henry Jones family is extinct.

Harah Saires Jones Feagin—daughter of Henry Jones, born January 7, 1809 in Jones County, Georgia; married February 16, 1826, at Montezuma, Ala., William Richardson Feagin.

Her children: Mary Pheraby Feagin, Samuel James Feagin, Thomas Jefferson Feagin, Aaron Pinson Feagin, Henry Jones Feagin, John Elder Feagin, William Richardson Feagin.

Winnie Elder Jones McRae—daughter of Henry Jones, born Nov. 3, 1835, near Louisville, Barbour County, Alabama, married about 14, Alexander Keane McRae, son of John R. and Comfort (Keane) McRae. Her entire life was spent in the home where she was born.

Her children: John Henry McRae, Laura McRae, Mourning Victoria McRae Wynn, Mary Alice McRae Myers, Gussie McRae, William Alexander McRae, Elizabeth McRae, George Washington McRae, Winnie Elder McRae Patterson, Joseph Benjamin McRae, Margaret McRae Jernigan

Joseph Jones—son of Henry Jones, born June 5, near Louisville, Barbour County, Ala.; married October 1, 1866 Mattie Parker, daughter of Seth and Evie (Ball) Parker at Louisville, Ala.; died May 6, 1912, at Hampton, Ga. He served in the Confederate Army; enlisted April 8, 1861, in Company E, 7th Alabama Regiment; was discharged a year later. Reenlisted soon after in Company G, 21st Alabama Regiment. Taken prisoner at Ft. Gaines Aug. 6, 1864; was in prison at New Orleans and Ship Island.

His children: Mary Belle Jones Vining, William Henry Jones, Joseph Leonard Jones, Alabama Evie Jones Hancock, Benjamin Seth Jones, Lily Ann Jones, Bessie Lee Jones, Katie Lou Jones, Charles Parker Jones.

Benjamin Jones—son of Henry Jones, born near Louisville, Barbour County, Ala., Nov. 26, 1841; married (a) Ann McGuire, who died about two years after her marriage, leaving no children. (b) Sarah Fenn, daughter, Matthew and Matilda Williams Fenn. He was a business man; lived at Louisville, Montgomery, Ala., and Cincinnati, Ohio; died at Montgomery, June 29, 1893.

His children: Travis Glenn Jones, Henry Clay Jones, Katie Jones. Travis Glenn and Katie died in childhood

Henry Clay Jones—son of Benjamin Jones, born August 2, 1874 at Montgomery, Ala.; married at Montgomery July 12, 1898, Mary (called Mamie) Emma Dickinson, daughter of Rev. Walter Phelan and Virginia (Orr) Dickinson; civil and electrical engineer; pioneer in hydro-electric power development, promoting the first large hydro-electric power development in the South.

His children: Henry Clay Jones, Virginia Jones, Benjamin Jones, Mary Elizabeth Jones and Walter Dickinson Jones.

WILLIAM THOMAS JOINER

William Thomas Joiner was born near Skipperville, Dale County, Nov. 4th, a notable Baptist minister, and an extensive farmer. He preached all over southwest Georgia and southeast Alabama, moving to Dale county in 1855, later locating back in Georgia at the town of Omaha. He filled various pastorates and died at the home of his son, Dr. Joiner, at Pittsview, Alabama, October 3rd, 1902, a distinguished Confederate Veteran.

His son, Dr. William Joiner, graduated from Atlanta Medical College in 1891 and began practicing at Loflin, Russell County, working up a large country practice, and since 1895 has resided at Pittsview where he has made an enviable reputation in his large practice. He is a member of the state and county Medical Societies of Alabama; a deacon in the Baptist Church and an enthusiastic Democrat. He married Miss Laura McMitchael in July, 1891. She was the mother of four children, William Howard, World War veteran who is still Captain in the Regular Army; Asa G. and Cary P., of Atlanta; Reuben C., also World War veteran, who has for many years been director and cashier of the Eufaula Bank and Trust Company and one of Barbour County's leading progressive citizens.

Dr. Joiner's second wife was Mrs. Sara B. Pitts, daughter of W. B. Burt of Pittsfield, Ala. The three children of this union are Wilson Marshall; Dorcas and Mary Jane. Mrs. Joiner died July, 1937.

ROBERT SAMUEL JONES

.... Robert Samuel Jones was born September 7th, 1837, at Uchee, Barbour County (now Russell County). When seven years of age his parents moved to Hawkinsville in Barbour County, where he grew to manhood.

He attended school in Old Spring Hill and in Hellican in Lowndes County. Me was married January 25th, 1866, to Miss Elizabeth Florence. They located at Hawkinsville, where they lived 9 years, engaging in stock raising and farming. In 1861 he moved to Eufaula to educate his children, where he died January 2nd., 1927. He was a Veteran of the Confederate Army, attending every reunion as the years passed of the old Veterans, and was an outstanding and valuable citizen.

His parents were Samuel Jones, born July 4th, 1807, near Savannah, Georgia, and Salina Ramsey, born April 1st, 1811, at Columbus, Georgia.

"Sam" Jones, as he was familiarly called, was perhaps the

most enthusiastic Confederate Soldier who marched forth from Barbour County.

His war record shows that he fought from 1861 to 1865, a member of Company D., 15th Alabama Regiment, Sewell's Brigade, Second Brigade, Critenden; third Brigade Trimble Ewell's Division—Jacksons Corps, up to the reorganization of the Alabama troops—Law's Brigade; Hood's Division in Longstreet's Corps.

Afterwards he served in Field Division, army of northern Virginia; Winchester, May, 1862; Battle Port Republic June of 1862.

He was wounded in the seven days fight around Richmond and wounded on the 25th day of June, 1862, at Gaines Mill.

ROBERT SAMUEL JONES

At the battle of Sharpsburg, September 17th, 1862 he was wounded and also at Port Royal, Virginia, while tearing up railroads.

He Joined Longstreet's command in 1863 when the Corps was at Knoxville; was in all the battles of 1861, including the Wilderness May 6th and at Spottslvania Courthouse May 12th.

He was in the battle of Hanover Junction June 3rd, 1864, an dall the battles around Richmond an dPetersburg until the evacuation of Richmond April 2nd, 1865. He surrendered at Appotomax courthouse April 9th, 1865—paroled April 14th, 1865, and reached home May 5th, 1865.

He was badly wounded in the left foot, tearing up a railroad and also received a severe shoulder wound at Gaines Hill.

He was a most unique and interesting character; a man with a broad vision and thoughtful conservative mind and generous heart.

At every meeting for years on Memorial Day, he attended the Memorial exercises, sat with the old Veterans, wearing his Confederate uniform of grey, and always when "Dixie" was played he threw up his hat and gave the "Rebel yell," to which evoryone in the audience joined in.

He never tired of telling interesting stories of the war,

and was a delightful entertainer. On one occasion he told that he "was never made prisoner" and often boasted that "if they'd just give him a 'shirt-tail' distance, he could outrun any ———Yankee."

He told thrilling accounts of camping in Pennsylvania, hungry and being denied food at a farm house when he and several comrades raided the fowl house that night and had a great feast.

Reaching Atlanta on his way home from the war— cold, hungry and ragged, he and a comrade broke a big window and helped themselves to good, warm clothes ,after being refused, and he told these stories in a manner both tragic and humorous. They held you spellbound.

The Jones home, two miles from the city of Eufaula, has been notable for its hospitality for a half century. His wife is over 90 years old, but, although in a rolling chair, is the Queen Mother and head of the beautiful home life on one of the largest and finest farms in Barbour County.

R. S. Jones the only son of the family, grew up a farmer and stepped into his father's shoes, and is the same success that his father was.

He married Lulie Bell Barton, of Southwest Georgia and their three young sons, college graduates, are already carrying out the family traditions and programs of usefulness.

R. S., III, is assisting his father on the farm. Thomas William holds a fine position in Akron Ohio, where his grandmother, Mrs. Barton, resides, and Walter Britt is a senior at A. P. I. in Auburn, where he is majoring in Agriculture.

The daughters are Lillie who married Rev. T. J. Head. Atlanta, Ga—children: Robert Frazier Head, married Katie White—children: Robert, Jr., Kathleen and Clark.

Henry married Emma Kesler; Frances Head married Pauline Womach. They have one son, John, of Macon, Ga.

Mary Head, deceased; Rebecca and Lillian Head; second Jones daughter Mary; third, Ella; fourth, Florence, unmarried; fifth, Mildred, married O. W. Haines, Winston-Salem, N. C.—children: Henry, Thomas, Rebecca and Robert Haines.

Their sixth daughter, Sewell, married T. Leonard Taylor. Their children: Raymond, married Kathleen Rogers, N. C.; Herbert; Thelma Thaylor married Arthur Roberts; Walker, student Mobile College; Samuel and Mary Ella.

WILLIAM DORSEY JELKS

William Dorsey Jelks was born November 7th 1855, at Warrior Stand, Macon County, son of Joseph William Dorsey and Jane Goodrum (Frazer) Jelks—the former killed June, 1862, while captain in the 3rd Alabama Infantry Regiment C.

S. A.; grandson of Robert and Matilda (Crowell) Jelks, the former a native of Halifax County, N. C.; the latter a sister of John Crowell, the first representative in the Congress of the Alabama Territory. His mother was a daughter of Thomas and Martha (Bass) of Warrior Stand.

On his father's side, he was related to the Crowells of England and having been originally "Cromwell," the M was dropped when the Cromwells fled from England to escape the Stuarts.

His father died when he was only 6 years old and his early life was spent in Union Springs in the Bullock County Schools.

WILLIAM DORSEY JELKS

He entered Mercer University, Macon, Georgia, in 1876 on money borrowed from relatives, which he returned in after years.

He received his A. M. degree at Mercer and L. L. D. at the University of Alabama but refused to accept, asking that his name be left off.

In 1876, returning to Union Springs, he kept books and in 1879 purchased an interest in the Union Springs Herald. Soon after that he moved to Eufaula and bought the Times and News, which soon reached such circulation that it was proclaimed the newspaper with the largest circulation in Alabama and was probably the most often quoted paper.

Mr. Jelk's paper fought for Democracy and stood for the editor's convictions, fearlessly. His broad field of information, his insight into political and commercial affairs put his paper at the top.

At 22 years of age he was a councilman of Union Springs and it was while he was acting superintendent of the school board, the fine Public School building at Eufaula was built.

In 1898 he was elected state senator from Barbour and while a candidate for president of the Senate, Gov. Samford became ill. There were five contestants for the election, but all withdrew before the vote was taken.

Gov. Jelks served five years and 8 months during the illness of Gov. Samford, but he took up his duties again and after six months he died.

He became governor June 11th, 1901, but not long after was stricken with illness and spent a long time in Mexico in search of health, during which time Lieut. Gov. R. M. Cunningham served the state in his stead.

During his notable administration, the uniform "school book" law was passed, saving the state thousands of dollars.

He was able to sell bonds at an aggregate premium of over $300,000, thereby decreasing the outstanding obligations of the state.

They were retired and in the same transaction the state saved some $1000,000 a year of interest, over that which had been paid out previously. This reduced the bonded indebtedness of the state, while small, was still the first reduction in the state's indebtedness since Governor Houston's time and the readjustment period. Gov. Jelks went out of office with a cash balance of about $1,800,000 and there was no surplus in the treasurer when he went into office.

He reduced the taxes, increased the school pension appropriation, the Capitol was enlarged during his administration and during this period there was a demand for lower railroad rates in the state. To facilitate action to help this situation, a railroad commission elected by the people was established.

In 1912, Gov. Jelks was elected delegate to the Baltimore Convention that nominated President Wilson and it was while he was National Committeeman on a visit to Governor Wilson at Seagirt, N. J., that the close observer of things that have been are, and yet to be, saw more than was told, but what showed up with the passing years, to prove that William D. Jelks was recognized along with his force of character, its uniqueness, also. The iron in his makeup that did him credit was equalled by tenderness and gentleness as well and the keynote of his life being "results," he balanced cause, effects, needs and results as few men ever did.

His insight into National conditions was into the hearts of the people that his own unique nature, read easily, and his frankness of speech, along with his wonderful brain did things in every campaign that set other Democratic leaders not only thinking, but doing.

While the eye of the Nation has always been and always will be founded on Barbour County, Alabama—it having been three times—because of her distinguished politicians and illustrious citizens—voted the greatest County in the state—is, where the searchlight is lingering and the prophecy is daily being fulfilled.

William Dorsey Jelks' name shines immortally, one of the brightest stars in all the great galaxy of glorious achievement that adorns Barbour County and Alabama history. The brilliant dazzle of glory, softened with the silver and gold, toned to theetherial shades of love, reverence, friendship and hope.

William Dorsey Jelks married Alice Shorter, daughter of Major Henry R. and Addie (Kitt) Shorter on June 7th, 1883. Their only child, a beautiful daughter, Catherine, married Edward Tripp Comer, son of George Legare and Laura (Thornton) Comer. To them were born first, William Jelks Comer; second, Edward Comer and Alice Shorter Comer.

REUBEN F. KOLB

Reuben Francis Kolb was born April 16th at Eufaula, Barbour County, son of David C. and Emily Francis (Shorter) Kolb, the former a native of Cheron, Cheron District, S. C., who lived in Eufaula and at Apalachicola, Florida; grandson of Jessie and Susan Kolb and of Reuben C. and Mary Gill Shorter of Eufaula. His great grandfather Kolb came from Germany when very young. He was a major in the army and was killed in the Revolutionary War on Pedee River in South Carolina, on which spot a monument was erected by the government, stands today, a memorial of his devotion to his adopted country.

Capt. Kolb was educated in the Eufaula schools and at the University of North Carolina, graduating June, 1859. He enlisted in the Confederate Army as Sergeant in Company B, First Alabama Regiment; then raised and commanded "Kolb's Battery" of artillery, through the remainder of the war, during the last being in command of a battalion.

After the war he was engaged in farming in Barbour County; was commissioner of agriculture from 1886 to 1890; was a Democrat on the executive committee of Barbour County; was one of the organizers of the Barbour County Farmers Alliance and in 1892 was candidate for Governor against Thomas G. Jones. That campaign is a memorable one.

There was a consolidation of three candidates and numerous political tricks that counted Kolb out, although citizens of Barbour County were strong and sincere in their belief that Kolb was elected, but counted out by the scheming political actors in the great political drama staged during that campaign. Entering the agricultural field after the financial business panic of 1873, he was appointed commissioner of agriculture in 1887 and later president of the Farmers' Alliance National Congress. He was given authority to employ, at the state's expense, lecturers and prominent persons to assist him.

Some Democratic papers, being alarmed over his growing influence, gave him much publicity and he became known as the best canvasser and one of the most prominent men in Alabama.

He had joined forces with the "Populists" and Democrats, knowing his personal magnetism and popularity, naturally were greatly alarmed over his political influence.

At the convention of the Farmers' Alliance at Auburn, August, 1889, practically the entire delegation endorsed Kolb for governor and he went into the race wholeheartedly and with a strong following.

He led the ticket on the first ballot by a majority. On the 34th the vote stood 269 for Jones and 256 for Kolb.

Later he entered the race aaginst William C. Oated, the latter winning the majority.

Kolb's friends and followers claimed that he carried 40 out of 41 counties and Kolb men threatened to go to Montgomery and seat him by force as Governor and on the day of Gov. Oates' inauguration some of Kolb's friends went through the form of iniugurating Kolb governor on Dexter avenue in front of the Capitol.

Captain Kolb's fame as a farmer went far and wide. He originated the famous "Kolb Gem" watermelon, introduced the LeConte Pear to his section and shipped thousands of car loads of these over the country for many years.

He was a man of strong convictions and force of character, married January 3, 1860, at Eufaula, Calledonia, daughter of Thomas and Louisa Cargill, their children being Emily Francis, who married Lucious Richardson; Reuben, married Pearl Hollifield, and Howard married Edith May Snow at Montgomery. He was a Baptist and a southern gentleman to the core.

JAMES TURNER KENDALL (1826-1892)

James Turner Kendall, an outstanding merchant, farmer and progressive citizen of Barbour County, Ala. was born in Wilminfiton, N. C., in 1826 and died at Eufaula in 1893.

His life was rich in honor, kindness, gallantry, trust and faithful service, both in peace and war. His record throughout the War Between the States was an honorable one and he served gallantly to the end.

His grandfather came to this country from Kentdale, England, and settled in Virginia. As a conservative, progressive citizen, he sponsored every enterprise for the upbuilding of Barbour County.

He was a valuable member of the First Methodist Church and is remembered for his Christian deeds and his public works among which was his great aid in heading the finance committee that raised money to build the fine and beautiful old Methodist Church.

The old General Merchandise store, known as the firm of Kendall and Company, is remembered not only throughout Barbour County but other counties as well for the quaint wagon trains that came to this store twice a week for supplies. These wagon trains came from a radius of 75 to 100 miles.

Kendall had a high code of honor in business and it was said that "Salesmen trained in Kendall's store received a background that would never yield to failure." He was friend and advocate to all who worked for him.

As a farmer he was a success, owning large plantations near White Oak and he not only raised the best of crops, but grew corn, which ranked first in the county, and was known as the "Kendall corn."

On these plantations, barns, graneries and storehouses bacon and lards were cured in the smoke houses with hickory logs.

Orchards, pastures and cotton fields lay on ever side and in the wooded section and in the streams, on his lands were found game and fish. He raised fancy chickens and turkeys, especially making a hobby of raising the peafowl.

He built "Homewood Acres," now the home of his granddaughter, Mrs. Leonard Yancey Dean, Jr. (Jennie Kendall). Here most gracious hospitality has always been dispensed. Just over the hill from this historic mansion is beautiful Kendallwood Park," named in honor of Mrs. Dean, who also was recently presented, "An orchid to you" by the Birmingham News, for her many activities in civic, social, church and philanthropic life in the community.

His eldest son, John Marshall Kendall, made life insurance his life work and was easily acclaimed one of the foremost district managers of the Mutual Life Insurance Company of New York, receiving many honors from this Company for his outstanding record.

And carrying on the work of his father, John M. Kendall, Joseph Jennie Kendall has succeeded him as Dist. Mgr. of the Mutual Life Insurance Co., and by his genial personality and honesty of purpose in all his work.

James Turner Kendall married Mary Jane McRae daughter of John C. McRae, one of Barbour County's pioneer leaders.

Born to them were: Jennie Turner Kendall who married Samuel W. Goode, lawyer, whose children were Mary Kendall, who married Henry Porter Williams of Charleston, S. C., and born to them were four children, Henry Porter, Jr., Elizabeth, Winifred and Samuel Goode.

Martha Goode married Dr. A. M. Anderson, a distinguished surgeon of London, England.

John M. Kendall married lovely Sallie Jennings. Five children were born to them. Jennie married Edward Bancroft Eppes, who had oen son, John Kendall Eppes; married second Leonard Yancey Dean, Jr.

Effie Battle, daughter of John and Sallie Kendall, married Robert W. Dodgen, Spartanburg, S. C., and one son was born to them, William McGuire, Jr.

Mary Reid married Joseph Few, Greer, S. C.

Joseph Jennings Kendall married Terese Merrill born to them one son Joseph Jenning Kendall, Jr.

James T. Kendall married Marie Holleman, born to them a daughter Marie Kendall; John Marshall Kendall, Jr., married Roberta Haynes. Florrie Kendall, daughter of James Turner Kendall and Mary Jane McRae, married Charles R. Ross. Born to them were four children. Kendall Ross married Charlie Kaigler, born to them Kendall, Jr., and Joyce. Charles R. Ross, Jr., not married; Julia married Gordon Wilson of Atlanta. Two boys were born to them.

James Turner Kendall, Jr., married Rose Murray of New Orleans, two children were born to them Mary and James Turner IC.

Marie Belle married Walter McKinney of Gainesville, Ga., two daughters born to them: Mary Florence married Fred Craig of Dalonega, Georgia. Lula Kendall McKinney not married.

Lula Kendall married Dr. J. C. Cato of Eufaula, Ala; born to them one son, Julius C. Cato, lawyer.

JOHN BENJAMIN LASETER

John Benjamin Laseter was born in Barbour county and was for over 50 years, possibly the best known official the county ever had. He was highly honored and respected for his clean politics and the splendid traits of character that marked all his personal and official acts.

In early life he was an extensive farmer, but when he went into service for the state, county and city of Clayton he was so capable that his popularity was soon established.

He served six years as chief of police of Clayton, then served a long time as deputy sheriff of Barbour County; was elected sheriff, and served two terms consecutively. Then, during the administration of Governor B. B. Comer, he was appointed warden of the convict camp at Pond City. On his return to Clayton at the close of the Comer administration he was again elected sheriff of Barbour County.

He was a man of high ideals, genial always thoughtful to

the prisoners under his charge, yet strict to the letter in carrying out the mandates of the law.

He married Lucinda Bennett and their children are, viz.: W. Ray Laseter, who like his father, is of high type character and is a prominent business man of Jackson, Miss., where he went after the ceasing business of the Old Schloss Clothing Store of Eufaula, with whom he was salesman for many years, and a popular leader in the social life of Eufaula.

Rev. James Laster, prominent Baptist minister, who stands at the very top in the Southern Baptist Convention's denominational work. His wife was Miss Ina Neilson, and they have one son, Neilson.

JOHN BENJAMIN LASETER

The younger son, John Foy Laseter, is now serving his first term as Judge of Probate of Barbour County. He followed his distinguished father in the liking for politics, and like him has long established a reputation of good judgment, clean political dealing.

He married Lola Millborn and they have two sons, Foy, Jr., Thomas and a daughter, Lucinda. These three splendid sons and one daughter, Miss Mamie Laseter, one of the outstanding young women of the County, taking part in all the activities for the uplift of the Community, are an honor to their distinguished parents.

LAWRENCE LEE

Lawrence Lee, son of Alto V. Lee, was born at Clayton, August 2nd, 1867; attended the Clayton schools and the University of Alabama, graduating with A. B. Degree and Law in 1888; practiced law at Clayton with his father, and later moved to Gadsden, Ala., and later to Montgomery, where he was reporter of Appellate and Supreme Courts.

He was solicitor of Barbour County from 1889 to 1890; alderman and representative from Barbour County to the legislature 1888-1899. Served as Gov. Graves' legal advisor during both Graves administrations.

He was a highest degree Mason and was often honored by that order; served as grand master of the Grand Lodge of Alabama. Grand Commander of Knight Templar; 33-degree Scotish Right Mason and Noble of Mystic Shrine; married October, 1889, Augusta Alston, daughter of A. H. and Anne Ott Alston. Children: Lillie, Mildred Alston, Theodosia, Lawrence H. and Edward Alston. Lawrence Lee, Jr., is a well known writer of poetry that has made him famous among writers. Died October, 1938.

HENRY FITZHUGH LEE

Fitzhugh Lee was born at Clayton August 31st, 1874, the son of Alto Vela and Lee, and is a member of one of the oldest and most distinguished families of the state.

He attended the local schools at Clayton and later took business courses.

In 1909 he was chief clerk in the Barbour County Probate office at Eufaula. He served as examiner of public accounts under Governor Jelks and Governor Comer in 1911; was chief clerk in the office of the state auditor from 1911-1915; and served as secretary of the state board of equilization from 1915 to 1919 and later was elected state auditor.

Fitzhugh Lee was first elected to the Public Service Commission in November, 1922, and was reelected in 1927.

He is one of the best known and most popular public officials of the state, a man whom everybody likes. His record for service i nall the offices he has held is an enviable one.

Like his distinguished father, he has a personality that wins friends. He is a Royal Arch Mason, A. W. O. W. and a member of Knights of Pythias, a Methodist and a loyal, true blue Democrat.

He married Wyllannie Pruett, daughter of Judge William and Annie (Browder) Pruett. Their eldest son, Browder, a most promising youth, was accidentally drowned.

Another younger son, Fitzhugh, Jr., is a college student, just reaching manhood. The family resides at Montgomery, where Mrs. Lee, carrying out the program of her distinguished ancestors, is a leader in all the betterments of the community's socail life and is active in church work. She is greatly beloved in Barbour County, where she was born and reared

ROBERT M. LEE

Robert M. Lee was born on his father's, Needham Lee, plantation near Louisville, August 19, 1846, spending his life at the same old home. He was a representative citizen who invested largely in lands, owning about 9000 acres in Barbour and Pike Counties, residing at Clio.

For several years he represented the County in the state Legislature.

During the War between the States he served as a member of 45th Alabama Volunteer Infantry, C. S. A.; was wounded at the battle of Atlanta, receiving severe wounds when he advanced into the very front of the storming of the breast works. He has been a most loyal Confederate Veteran, always attending the reunions and notable as the one who always led the "rebel yell."

He was a Methodist Churchman of rare zeal and a valuable beloved citizen whose death was a distinct loss to the community.

He married Annie Reynolds, and the children born to them are: Robert, died in infancy; Greer, who like his father, is an enthusiastic farmer and looks after the large farming interests; and Huey R., who despite his political, Civic, and other interests, still leans to the farms, and gives much time to them.

Mr. Lee has been an outstanding feature of many of the Confederate Veteran's reunions, particularly recalled is the one of 1895 at Louisville, Ky., when this writer traveled from Eufaula to Louisville in company with Mr. R. M. Lee, Col. W. C. Oates and Mr. R. S. Jones. The long rides were made really joyous by the many interesting and realistic stories of the war told by Mr. Lee. And when at breakfast at the Maxwell house in Nashville, when 13 strawberries topped the cereal served to each of the four at the table, he took note of it and followed up several incidents that happened during the next three days in Louisville which were significant enough to call forth an article he afterwards wrote entitled, "Thirteen Berries—Thirteen Bowls."

ALTO VELA LEE

Alto Vela Lee was born at Louisville, Ala., December 24, 1844, being descended from the distinguished old Virginia family of Lees who were of Norman lineage, from William the Conqueror, receiving land grants from the crown.

He was the son of Lovard Lee and Susan Emeline, who came from Georgia to Barbour County in 1832 and fought in the Indian war.

He was also a hero in the Confederate Army. He was educated in the common schools of Clayton, entering the University of Alabama on January 7, 1861. He enlisted and was made orderly Sergeant of the Clayton Guards, one of the first Companys organized in Barbour County serving first at Pensacola, Florida. Later he organized the Lee Guards and was First Lieutenant of the Company. In 1863 his health forced him to resign spending nearly a year as Military Cadet at the University of Alabama, where he raised a "Boys' Company" and was elected their Captain. Rushing them to the front on the Coast, they were captured and imprisoned at Ship Island.

He studied law in the office of Col. D. M. Seals and was admitted to the Bar at Clayton, 1867. Was Solicitor of Barbour County 1868 to 1872, and from 1874 to 1876 was Solicitor of the Judicial Circuit serving in that capacity 16 years. He was acclaimed the most able Solicitor in Alabama at that time. Was just to the fullest degree, but strong in his prosecutions, was brilliant in his arguments and always drew great crowds to hear him argue. Some of his interesting assertions to jurors often were most romatic and unique. On one occasion he was prosecuting a man for "obtaining money on false pretense" and he said, "Gentlemen you have heard the evidence, and you have heard the defendant's statement. I depend on your convicting, on the motive, find it." It was a sensational case, but the defendant was acquitted and a bystander friend said to Solicitor, "Lee was that Jury dumbells or liars?" and he answered, "Just conscious stricken thieves perhaps." In June, 1894, he was succeeded by John V. Smith and in 1902 moved to Gadsden and entered into partnership with his son, L. H. Lee.

Was elected Judge of the Circuit Court of Gadsden. Was a most efficient Judge. His knowledge of the law, long years of experience as a Solicitor made him a fine judge of juries, and gave him insight into legal conditions. He always maintained a dignity that stamped him the gentleman of the old Royal school from which he was descended.

A trustee of the University of Alabama for many years; a Scottish Right Mason and Knights Templar.

Married Lillie Lawrence, daughter of William Haywood and Lucy (Anthony) Lawrence and granddaughter of Josih and Charity (Haywood) Lawrence. Children: Lawrenc, married H. Augusta Alston, daughter of Augustus Holmes and Anne Ott Alston; Vela, married George W. Peach; William, married; Chas. W. married; H. Fitzhugh, married Wilyanne Browder Pruett, daughter of W. H. and Ann Browder; Alto. Jr., married; and Lucien Tenent, married.

SIMON LEWY

Simon Lewy was born in Berlin, Germany, and came to Eufaula, Barbour County, after the War between the States, in which he served in the Confederate Army, receiving injuries, among which was the loss of the fore finger of his left hand, besides injuries to his arm, from which he suffered through life.

He came from New York to Eufaula to be salesman for Waxelbaum Bros., extensive dry goods dealers and leaders in the County.

In the early seventies Mr. Lewy purchased the business and from then, until today, this business has been carried on in the same building it was begun in, in the sixties

When Mr. Lewy died some 15 years ago his three sons, Dave, Henry and Max, took the business over, inheriting with the business, the store house; and it is interesting to know that, through all the passing years, "Lewy's" have featured (as their father did) the high class of goods that distinguished his business, carrying out the enviable reputation, established by their father.

After a few years, Dave, the elder brother, withdrew from the firm and since then, it is also a most interesting as well as unusual fact, that "Lewy's" is the oldest dry goods firm (Lewy Bros., Henry and Max) have owned the business which is the oldest dry goods establishment in Barbour County, and has owned and occupied the same building much over a half century.

In this historic store are large oval mirrors on pedestals bought when the business was established and they have stood as sentinels as the store is entered, and today one of these mirrors reflects you as you enter Lewy's, bringing a thought of long ago, to the older citizens, who have been familiar with them through a half dozen generations.

Simon Lewy's wife, Mary Friedlender, of Posen, Germany, came to Eufaula a bride and all their children were born at the historic home corner of Cherry and Sanford Streets, Eufaula, where Henry, Max and the younger sister, Miss Adele Lewy reside, maintaining the old family traditions.

The other children are: Dave, deceased, married Miss Belle Oppenheimer; Jennie, married Isaac Meyrivitvz; and Hortense, married M. D. Katz.

Simon Lewy was a leader of the Hebrew faith, a member of Binia Braith, Treas. of Harminy Lodge No. 46, F. A. A. M. and Treas. of the Knights of Honor. He was highly esteemed and valuable citizen of the County and his home town. Max Levy married in April, 1938, Minnie Trout.

HARMON LAMPLEY

Harmon Lampley was born July 26, 1849, at Louisville, Barbour County, Alabama, son of Morman and Millie (Warren) Lampley, the former a large land owner, born May 19, 1819, and became one of Barbour's outstanding citizens. Harmon Lampley received his education at the University of Alabama, and while a student there in 1864, he enlisted in the Cadets, Corps, Alabama Company A, under Captain Eugene Smith and Colonel J. T. Murphree.

This Company of young Military Cadets in the Confederate service, were sent to Blue Mountain, Ala., thence to Pollard, Ala., and then marched across the Bay at Mobile to Sibley's mill, back to Spring Hill and back to Tuscaloosa, April 3, 1865. There was fighting on the streets at Tuscaloosa and from there they were sent to Marion, Ala., where they were dismantled and sent home. Young Lampley, Dr. W. P. Copeland, Chappell, Joe Ballard and John Copeland walking from Marion to Eufaula.

Mr. Lampley was a man of wonderful executive and business ability. As a member of the cotton firm of J. W. Tullis and Co., was a recognized power in the cotton business of this section.

He amassed a large fortune, which he invested in lands, real estate and his farms in Barbour County and across the river in Quitman County, Ga., where the finest land to be found anywhere.

He was a Steward in the First Methodist Church and a genial, whole souled friend and valuable citizen, esteemed and cordially liked, by every one who came in contact with him. A public spirited and progressive but quiet and unostentatious in all his affairs.

He married February 25, 1887, Islay Reeves, daughter of Dr. William N. and Flora (McNab) Reeves, the wedding taking place in the First Baptist church and was followed by a brilliant reception at "Mont McNab" the beautiful mansion built the year before on historic "Flake Hill" overlooking the City of Eufaula, and later called "Mt. McNab". This handsome home was burned some years later.

Their children were Harmon, married Gatra Holleman children Harmon III and Hinton Hollemon. William Reeves and Ira Tullis, all three deceased.

ROBERT H. MOULTHROP

Robert H. Moulthrop, son of Robert and Sarah (Daniel) born across the river in Quitman County, Georgia, while the Moulthrop home was being built on the bluff (now Riverside Drive) in Eufaula, on April 29, 1865, the day that General Grierson's Federal Army passed through Eufaula camping on the Georgia side of the Chattahoochee river.

His father, Robert Moulthrop, came from Connecticut,

to superintend the laying of the brick pillars of the Old Rail Road bridge across the Chattahoochee, cast his lot here, and for years, was owner of the largest brick manufacturing plant in the state, situated just across the river from Eufaula, on the same site, or very near, the present McKenkie Brick yard.

The first home Mr. Moulthrop built is still standing and used as a Nurses home by Salter hospital. The second home built was the beautiful brick home that is now the hospital adjoining the first modest home, and the third home built is beautiful "Longview" just a short distance further down Riverside Drive, where his widow and youngest son now reside.

Like father, like son, Robert H. Moulthrop followed in the business of his distinguished father. Robert Moulthrop married first Sarah Daniel, one of the most beautiful women in this section, who was the daughter of James Daniel, a distinguished citizen of Macon, Georgia. To them was born Robert H. He married second, Sallie Bullock Dobbins, daughter of the late Jno. Bullock, one of Eufaula's distinguished earliest settlers. To them was born Albert Moulthrop, a prominent valuable citizen of Eufaula, who married Foy Pitts, daughter of the late lamented Clayton and Eufaula Banker and prominent citizen, Joseph L. Pitts and his wife, Ida Foy Pitts, daughter of the late W. H. Foy, one of Barbour County's most prominent farmers and merchants, Robert H. Moulthrop, was educated at the Eufaula grammar schools and Academy, then graduating at Pio-Nono College, Macon, Georgia.

He was scholarly and exact in all his dealings, and a business man of the highest sense of honor. Inheriting the ability and precision of his distinguished father, he made good in all his undertakings.

Was a student of higher literature, was conversant with all the information of the day and time, and was a delightfully interesting conversationalist. From boyhood, a bright faced, happy hearted lad, whom every one loved. When he grew to manhood, his popularity even increased and no Barbour County man was ever more esteemed and loved than Bob Moulthrop.

While Senator from Barbour County he introduced a bill for the removal of Convicts from labor in the state mines and placing them on the highways, to work the roads, a plan that has shown how practical it was.

His good judgment, his fairness, and uprightness, made his interest in politics, effective for good, in matters of state and locally. Following his father, in Masonic interests, he early joined Harmony Lodge F. A. A. M. and was the youngest man in the state to become a Knights Templar and Shriner. He was widely known over the state fraternally, and personally was one of the most popular Masons in Alabama. His courtly, polished, gentlemanly manner at all times, stamped him "to the Manor born" and his friends held him very dear.

In 1882, he was happily married to lovely (of face and character) Kate Moss, where at the lovely Riverside home, she reigns the beloved mother and grandmother, as charming and beloved in the declining years, as when she was in the zenith of lovely young womanhood.

Their children are: Charles W. of Montgomery, one of the leading insurance men of the South, married Knoxie Walker, has one daughter, (Lucy) married James A. Alexander, Lexington, Ky.; William H., Denver Col., married Lillian Lindley, no children; and M. Moss, one of Eufaula's most prominent young citizens, who is already following in his father's footsteps, as an asset to Eufaula, is member of the city council, has a great poultry business and carries on the farming interests at the historic Moulthrop home on the bluff, married Elizabeth Duncan Gardner of Atlanta, children, Lucie Elizabeth, Susanne Borden and Robert Moss, twins, Francis Katherine, Martha Lassette and Charles Wales II, twins.

JAMES MILTON

James Milton was born in London, England, the only son of an illustrious old English family, who had been watchmakers and jewelers for several generations, but the father died leaving one son, James, and a daughter, Helen Faulkner, who was a widow with three daughters, Hannah, Sarah and Nellie Faulkner.

Young James Milton came to the U. S. early in the fifties, and in New York was soon established in his trade as a watch maker. In the meantime he had sent to England and his sister and her daughters joined him in New York. One one of the trips to the Northern Jewelry markets, Mr. N. M. Hyatt Jeweler in the town of Eufaula, came in contact with the young Englishman, and the result of their acquaintance was, he accompanied Mr. Hyatt to Eufaula and for a number of years was watchmaker, engraver and repairer, for the Hyatt Jewelry store.

Later he purchased the business, and established a business of his own, in the building on Broad Street, now occupied by Neal Logue, Clothier. The building at that time was a very large one, and for nearly a half century, was the home of a Drug Co. and Milton's Jewelry, on the other side

It was the place where everybody stopped in to "get the time" from the large Western Union Regulator that had its pendulum attached to the regulator in the Observatory at Washington and was the official "time" of all this section.

Mr. Milton was the cultured Englishman whose fine character was displayed in every word he ever uttered, and so distinguished in personal appearance that he was notable in any assembly.

He was one of the outstanding Masons of Alabama, being for many years, Worshipful Master of Lodge No. 46, Eufaula.

For about twenty years he was President of the Board of Trustees of Union Female College.

He was a man of recognized superior wisdom to whom the younger of the community always went for advice on weighty matters. He was one of the leaders in the project of building the Presbyterian Church at Eufaula of which he was a leading member, and lived strict to the letter of true religion and the tenits of his church.

He married Lula Crawford, a daughter of distinguished Crawford family of Henry County, Alabama, and built the old English type "Milton Home" on East Broad Street, which has retained its unique beauty from that time, until now. It is owned and occupied by M. Braswell. Later he built the Colonial home adjoining "Milton's Grove" on North Randolph Street in Eufaula, where their children were reared and is now the home of Mr. E. E. Farrell.

Mrs. Milton died when her youngest son, was only a few months old, and it, and the other children were reared by the eldest daughter, Lulu, then only 11 years of age. Her care of the family, and ability as a home maker throughout the years, was the admiration of the community. Capable, unselfish, thoughtful and enduring always. The man who was her father's cloest friend, whose children grew up in intimate association with the Milton children, was often heard to say, "If there is an angel on earth, Lulu Milton is one." She passed away only a few years since.

May Milton, the second daughter, died in the full zenith of young womanhood. The four sons, after finishing their education, all started life as Pharmacists, although their father had tried to make Jewelers out of them. They all made the effort, to please him, but urge of the drug business held to them. The eldest, Victor M. and John M., were prescriptionists in the leading drug firms of the County, and then they purchased the largest of these firms, and as "Milton and Milton, spent their lives in Eufaula. John M. dying about ten years ago and Victor M. only two years ago. The third son, James, Jr., also became a druggist and moved to Kentucky, where his son still resides. The youngest son, Walter S., was a pharmicist in Eufaula many years, married Maud Doughtie. Poor health carried him to Denver Col. for the climatic benefits and for a long time was connected with a Railroad Company. He died three years ago, and was brought to the old home here for the funeral.

Victor, the eldest son, married Pet Hart, daughter of the late Captain Henry C. Hart, and his wife, Paralee (Riks) Hart, daughter of Col. Robert G. Ricks of Clay County, Georgia, one of the South's leading citizens. Their daughter, Emily Milton, married Mr. Boone of Memphis, Tenn., with whom her mother now resides, and the beautiful historic old Hart-Milton home on Eufaula Street, with its wealth of handsome antiques, is now occupied as an apartment house, as are several other handsome houses in Eufaula belonging to the Milton estate.

James Milton and J. H. Whitlock were both jewelers who came to Barbour County from the North, neither of them took any special interest in politics, but both espoused the Southern cause, and were loyal Southern citizens, and while they were competitors in business for a half century they were very close friends. In 1891, when a friend of both (the three having been the most intimate friends possible) was dying, they were seated on one side of the bed and the other across from him, and neither of them had left that bedside for 48 hours. Their friendship was so beautifully evident on this occasion that it was commented on by those who witnessed the scene and spoke of it as a sacred demonstration of "man's love for a friend and fellow man." The Milton and Whitlock memories in Barbour County will forever be thrice blessed.

After he had been established in Eufaula for some time, he sent for one of his neices Miss Nellie Faulkner, who made her home with his family, and married a prominent Eufaula citizen W. Judson Brannon, and their children born and raised in Eufaula, are Thomas M. Brannon, Eufaula; Judson Brannon, Hubert Brannon, and Mrs. Nellie Brannon Wilde of Mount Vernon, New York, with whom Mrs. Nellie Faulkner Brannon now makes her home. She was one of Eufaula's beloved women during the long years of her residence here, only going to New York a few years ago.

CHARLES F. MASSEY

Charles F. Massey was born in Muscogee County, Georgia, in 1837, but was brought to Barbour County by his parents when a small boy, the family locating at Pine Grove, a flourishing settlement between Fort Browder and Mount Andrew. From early young manhood he was interested in politics, and was a staunch Democrat; and a leader in all the best interests of the County. His farm was one of the best, and he was one of the first in the community to introduce scientific methods in his farming.

When the call for Volunteers came from the Confederacy, he patriotically responded and served through the struggle soon rising to the rank of Captain of his company. He was a loyal Southerner who never tired of giving the true facts of the War between the States' stories and his memory and faculty of description was marvelous.

He was a deacon in the First Baptist Church, after the family moved to Eufaula in 1892.

Married Saphronia Sparks. Children, Della, married first Alext Thomas, second J. S. Winter; Charles, deceased; Stella, deceased; Julia, married Edwin McKay, their daughter, Julia, deceased; Mattie, deceased, married Jones, their son is Charles Massey Jones; Laurie, unmarried.

The Massey homes both at "Pine Grove" and in Eufaula, have been notable for rare old Southern hospitality. At "Pine Grove" in the long ago, social history in Barbour County reveals many functions where the Massey home was conspicuous for elegance and culture.

Mrs. Massey, in the evening of life, was greatly beloved by her friends and was the idol of her devoted daughters. She died in 1938.

A. H. MERRILL

Allen Hunter Merrill was born November 29, 1845, in Barbour County. His grandparents, Thos. Abbot and Eliza (Allen) Merrill, who moved from Andover, Mass., to Middlebury, Vermont. Allen Kent (Merrill) father, was a native of Middlebury, Vermont, a graduate of Dartmouth College at Hanover, New Hampshire.

Came South, taught school in Georgia, moved to Eufaula and studied law and was admitted to the Bar practicing until his death in 1847. Married Elizabeth Aiken Hunter, born in South Carolina, daughter of John Linguard and Sarah (Bohler) Hunter.

Allen Merrill attended School at Eufaula and his Collegiate course was thawarted by the Confederate war, in which he enlisted in 1863, a member of the Eufaula Light Infantry, taking part in the Dalton and Atlanta campaigns. Was in all the battles of the Army of Tenn. until the war ended.

On his return from war he was associated in the practice of law with James L. Pugh, and admitted to the bar January, 1869. He was a staunch Democrat, member of the Legislature from Barbour County, 1890, and several times member of the State Democratic Executive Committee. Delegate to the National Convention that nominated Pres. Cleveland for second term and also delegate to Kansas Convention that nominated William Jennings Bryan second time.

A mason; an Episcopal vestryman and a splendid type of manhood physically and mentally; a clean politician and valuable citizen.

Married Tade Sims Bray, daughter of William H. and Mary Bullock Bray. Children: Elizabeth, married John C. McRae; Tade. married R. Buford Harrison, deceased; Mary, married A. M. Brown; Allen K., married Evelyn Farmer; William Hoadley, married Bertha Moore; Lila, married W. J. Johnston; Terese, married Joseph J. Kendall.

Tade Bray Merrill, after her husband's death, January 11, 1922, lived quietly and surrounded by her children at the lovely home on Randolph street, where she delighted to minister to her grandchildren all of whom were devoted to her. Until invalidism prevented, she took active part in all the patriotic and church work of the county, a lovely and beloved "lady of love."

WILLIAM HOADLEY MERRILL

William Hoadley Merrill, son of Col. Allen Hunter and Tade (Bray) Merrill, was born in Eufaula, October 11, 1887. and graduated from the Eufaula High School in 1904 with honors. In 1911 he graduated from the University of Alabama from both the Collegiate and Law departments with honors, and was immediately admitted to the Bar, beginning his practice at Eufaula associated with his father and brother, the firm being A. H. Merrill and Sons.

After the death of his father, and his brother, Allen K. Merrill, moving to Dothan, Alabama, he handled a large practice at Eufaula alone. He was a member of the Third Judicial Bar Association, State Bar Association and The American Bar Association; was a member of Phi Delta Theta and Theta Nu Epislon fraternities and honorary member of Phi Delta Phi Legal fraternity.

He was Governor of the Twenty-sixth District Rotary International and was a Past President of the Eufaula Rotary Club, which he practically organized. Was president of the Commercial Club of Eufaula and took active part in all the civic and progressive interests of the County.

During the World War, he took great interest in and was active as Chairman for Barbour County of the Liberty Loan Campaign, and also arranged the programs of four minute speakers for the Liberty Loan. He was also a member of the Exemption board.

He was Senior Warden of the Vestry of St. James Episcopal Church and one of the County's most highly esteemed and valuable citizens.

In 1915 he married Bertha Moore, daughter of the late John M. and Hattie (Wharton) Moore of Atlanta, Georgia. To them were born five lovely daughters, Betha, Harriet, Terese (deceased) Tade and Evelyn.

While in the very zenith of his fine manhood, he was stricken with pneumonia and died, when just in the happy achievement of his high and noble endeavors, March 23, 1931.

He rated high as a lawyer and was a loyal Democrat whose example of example in politics, was to keep clean the political record of his County and State. Was an eloquent speaker who never failed, when opportunity offered, to laud the heroes of the Confederacy, and was a true son of the old South.

ALLEN K. MERRILL

Allen K. Merrill, son of Allen H. and Tade (Bray) Merrill was born in Eufaula, March 26, 1885, was educated first in the Eufaula High Schools and after graduating from the University of Alabama, where like his brother William H. he distinguished himself, both in his Collegiate course and as a Law student.

A member of the Eufaula law firm of A. H. Merrill and Sons, he was outstanding, as an attorney and business man.

Removing to Dothan later years, he has become actively identified with interests of Henry County and member of the law firm of Farmer, Merrill and Farmer. He is still interested in Barbour County and often is called to cases in the Barbour County courts, being a most capable lawyer.

He is one of Dothan's leading citizens.

Holding fast to the traditions of the distinguished family he represents, he is a loyal Democrat and a Southerner in all the word implies, and is a genial, affiable gentleman, who is an asset to Dothan and Henry County. He married Evelyn Farmer, daughter of Bird G., and (Cowerdry Merrill) of Dothan, and they have four promising young sons, all in college: Allen Hunter, Bird Farmer, Cowdery Kent and William H. Merrill, II.

CHARLES S. McDOWELL, SR

Charles Samuel McDowell, Sr., was born March 8th, 1845, at Greenville, Tenn., and was educated in the schools of the state of Tennessee and was a student who aimed high and wrought well.

When quite young he joined Lynch's Battery of East Tennessee, the organizer of that company being Captain Lynch, a friend of the McDwoell family.

Throughout the four years' struggle of the War Between the States he fought with courage and valor that comes of genuine patriotism.

After the close of the war, he came to Eufaula, Barbour County, and from then until his death on November 23rd, 1926, was a valuable, honored citizen, taking a leading part in all the uplifting interests of the Community.

He was a polished, cultured gentleman of old Scotish ancestry that live by a code of morals that elevates and ennobles.

Mr. McDowell was a man of high literary attainments, a scholar who had history at his tongue's tip and could tell a most delightfully interesting story to meet the need of any occasion.

Throughout his life, he was the very crown and flower of the Presbyterian Church of which he was elder, until his death.

In 1913 he was appointed postmaster at Eufaula by President Wilson and his business ability and daily example to his clerks and assistants was an influence that helped to make the service given to the public, commented on daily, as perfect.

Mr. McDowell was a patriotic Southerner, who though loyal to the American flag, never once forgot that the blood splashed stars and bars is as glorious in the memory of loyal honest Southern hearts today as it was during the four years it waved over Southern heroes fighting for their homes and their all.

A quiet, cultured, educated gentleman whom it was a joy to know and call friend; the legacy he has left his children is a casket of jewels of rare price—honor, character, piety, good will and loyalty.

He married Margaret McKay, the lovely "Queen mother," who ruled her household with a sceptre of love and devotion and like her husband was a loyal Southerner, a leader in church and patriotic and civic activities and was beloved as only one of her lovely type could be.

Charles S. Jr., married Caroline (Dent); C. Annie, deceased; Caroline Joy married John Allen Crook and they have one son, John Allen Crook, Jr.

Katie married Dr. Alfred P. Brown. Children: Charles Pugh Brown and Mary Wood Murphy. Children: a son, Chas. P., Jr.

Edkin K. married Susie May, no children.

Dr. William Patton McDowell married first Cornelia Sylvester. Children: William Patton, Jr., married Gabrella Van-Patton, daughter Gabrella. He married second Loula Rees Deen.

Archibald M. McDonald is unmarried.

Janette married Huey H. Lee. Children: Margaret, deceased; Huey H., Jr., and MacDowell Lee.

CHARLES S. McDOWELL, JR.

CHARLES S. McDOWELL, JR.

Charles S. McDowell, Jr., was born at the old maternal McKay home on Randolph street in Eufaula, Barbour County, son of Charles S., and Margaret McKay. Received his early education at the male schools of the city and was graduated from the University of Alabama and was admitted to the Bar. During his clerkship in the Probate Office at Clayton during the administration of W. H. Pruett, Probate Judge of Barbour County, he began a career that has been marked in every way by clean, high minded principles of honesty of purpose and integrity of character. By right of ability and loyal patriotism he has been a leader in all the best interests of Barbour county, his home town and his state.

He is a Democrat of the kind that is an ethical concept of all the word Democrat embodies.

For thirty years he has easily been Barbour County's first citizen. His genial, accommodating and always happy manner has made him the friend on whom everybody relied for advice; he being a capable leader in all the progressive, political, civic, financial and moral interests of the County. As mayor of Eufaula he built the parks of the city except the two in the business center of the city, those two being built through the efforts of the late Harry R. Shorter, lamented young attorney and beloved citizen of Eufaula.

He brought about the building of the municipal Electric Light Plant, his little daughter, Joy McDowell, turning on the first light this plant gave to Eufaula.

In 1912 he improved and added to Fairview cemetery, personally laying off the plots of the addition purchased at a cost of two thousand dollars, that comprises the 37 new lots this purchase gave to the cemetery, and were sold at $75.00 each to personal parties. Had the Iron fence that came from U.

F. College, built up around the cemetery, and had trees planted in the park.

He put in a filling basin at the City water works. He also saw that the Money for the Dispensary, then in operation, was used to finance the City, in the best interest cases.

As United States Senator from Borbour County from 1923 to 1927 he built the McDowell steel and concrete bridge across the Chattahoochee river. This bridge was directly the result of the planning and working of Senator McDowell. It was dedicated Dec. 15th, 1925, built at a cost of about two hundred and fifty thousand dollars. He introduced and had passed the following bill in the state legislature by which the present board of revenue of Barbour County functions.

As trustee of the Alabama Polytechnic Institute at Auburn, serving 16 years in that capacity he was an honor to the Institution he served.

He was elected president of the Alabama Bar Association from 1915 to 1916; has been a member of the American Bar Association 26 years; was elected some years ago by the Board of Trustees of the University of Alabama (his alumnus) —member of the Board for life.

On his watch chain he wears his proud possession of his Phi Beta Kappa emblem.

Barbour County's Board of Revenue

No. 221   An Act   (365-McDowell)

To divide Barbour county into six districts to be known as Board of Revenue Districts, and to provide for the election of a member of the Board of Revenue of Barbour County from each district, by the qualified voters of each district, and also one member of the Board of Revenue from the County at large. Be it enacted by the legislature of Alabama:

Section I. That Barbour County be and is hereby divided into six districts to be known as Board of Revenue districts, composed respectively as follows: The first district to be composed of Beats 2, 3, and 4. The second district to be composed of Beats 6, 7, and 8. The fourth district to be composed of Beats 9, 10, and 15. The fifth district to be composed of Beats 11 and 16. The sixth district to be composed of Beats 12 and 13. Each district shall have one member of the Board of Revenue of Barbour County, who shall be elected by the qualified voters of the several districts, each district electing its own member of the Board of Revenue.

Section 2. At the general election to be held in 1920, and every six years thereafter, there shall be elected by the qualified voters in districts number one, two, five and six, a member each from their respective districts, each district voting separately for its own representative and at the general election to be held in 1924 and every six years thereafter there shall be elected by the qualified voters in districts three and four a member of each from their respective districts that in the general election to be held in 1920 and every six years thereafter there shall be elected by th qualified voters in the county one member from the county at large and these several members shall constitute the members of the Board of Revenue of Barbour County. Those members of the said board of Revenue that are elected at the General election of 1920 shall be successors are elected and qualified.

Section 4. That members of the Board of Revenue from the several districts as herein provided shall actually reside in the district from which they are elected during their continuance in office—on removal from the district for which they were elected they will vacate their office. The member from the county at large may reside anywhere in the county. Time Board of Revenue of Barbour County shall consist of the seven members to be elected by the qualified voters of the districts and one from the county at large, to be elected by the qualified voters of Barbour County.

Section 5. Provided, however, there shall be no change in the districts as they are now constituted, untl the time for the induction into the office of the members elected in 1920.

Section 6. Any vacancy occurring by death or resignation or other cause shall be filled by appointment by the Governor.

Section 7. That all laws and parts of laws in conflict with the provisions of this Act are hereby repealed. Approved August 15th, 1919.

He was delegate to the National Democratic Convention at Baltimore in 1912 and to New York in 1924. He was elected delegate to the Philadelphia Democratic National Convention in 1936, but found it was not convenient to go at that date. As Elder in the Presbyterian Church he is one of its strongest forces—the churchman who lives strictly to the letter of his faith and gives out a helpful influence.

As candidate for governor of Alabama in 1926, through his campaign, he maintained that dignity of the cultured gentelman and true statesman, holding fast to the code of principles that has marked his political career; and he was more glorious in his defeat for the governorship than the majority of candidates for high office have been in victory. He was Lieutenant Governor of Alabama from 1923 to 1927 and distinguished that office.

Retiring from active political life to resume his large law practice, he was rated Barbour County's leading attorney.

Mr. McDowell's campaign for governer was a memorable

and colorful one. His personal popularity over the state made it so.

He was defeated by a small majority that voted under the influence of some very unusual and unexpected doctoring of some political prophets, and bewildered the minds of weak-kneed voters.

The proudest day of Barbour County's history was in 1926 when Charlie McDowell, at the courthouse in Eufaula, publicly opened his campaign for governor with the following address, in which it will be noted he made no campaign promises to voters:

He married October 15th, 1902, Caroline Dent, daughter of Capt. and Mrs. S. H. Dent, one of Alabama's most brilliant and beloved women.

Born to Mr. and Mrs. McDowell were Annie Beall, died at the age of two years; Caroline Joy, married John Allen Crook and to them have been born sons, John Allen, Jr., and Charles McDowell Crook.

McDowell's Opening Campaign Speech

The courthouse was packed and hundreds could not get inside on the afternoon when Lieut. Gov. Charles S. McDowell, Jr., officially opened his campaign for governor. Hundreds of cars from southeast Alabama filled the streets and it was a memorable occasion.

The city was decorated with banners reaching across the streets and flying from the top of the courthouse on which was painted in great letters, "McDowell for Governor."

When Mr. McDowell, accompanied by his wife, entered a wild applause rang out and the vast throng arose to their feet.

Mayor H. H. Conner, silenced the applause by rising and began the opening talk by saying that "the occasion had aroused the loyalty of these people to one whose record called forth the highest honor.

He closed his talk with the statement that "during his administration as mayor, whenever he had called upon Charlie McDowell to do anything to help his town or community his answer was always to "take off his coat and go to work."

Following Mayor Conner, Judge Lee J. Clayton, in presenting Mr. McDowell to the gathering, said, "fellow Democrats, as you know his views upon public questions, you know his past and private life, and this ovation shows that you are solidly behind him."

Mr. McDowell prefaced his speech with a heart to heart talk to his homefolks as he called them, that brought deafening applause. He stated that for thirty years he had made speeches to them and to others, but never before had he read his speech; but on this occasion, knowing that there would be hostile camps within the bounds of this Commonwealth, and he, for protection, would read what he had to say to his friends and fellow citizens.

On this speech he said "I stand." He first took up highways; turning to Governor Brandon, he said, "And we are going to build them, Governor." He clearly explained why he was for the bond issue for state roads and bridges.

He pointed out why he is opposed to Convict Lease System and he proposed that if he were elected governor to see that it was destroyed so it could never be revived again.

Affirming that education was his first consideration, his plea was "equal chance for every boy an girl"—nine months' school and better pay for the teachers.

Equalization of taxes, enforcement of the Prohibition Law, law enforcement, municipal taxation and other matters he pointed out his views on; but the climax of his speech came when he cried out, "The Port of Mobile," and after plainly explaining his stand on this, going into detail as to what he personally and officially did to secure the appropriation for this Port, he read a letter from appreciative citizens of Mobile thanking and lauding him for his work in this, and the impression prevailed that when the Press of the state gave this letter to the public it would fall like a bombshell in the camps of Mr. McDowell's opponents.

He was given an ovation after the speech and Eufaula and all Barbour County was well satisfied as to whom would be Alabama's next governor.

—Signed M. T. Thompson, Cor. Associated Press.

Note: Ten years later—

It turned out, however, that the "hostile campers were an organization of followers of a doubtful Klan (not the old K. K. K. of the sixties and seventies, who were made up of Democrats, out of a band of the new political Klan, who were rallying to doubtful tents, set up by this political group for the sole purpose of defeating the man of the hour. Results showed how the state suffered through an administration of waste and financial and political errors.

CAROLINE DENT McDOWELL

Caroline (Dent) McDowell, daughter of Captain S. H. and Anna (Beall) Dent, and wife of Charles S. McDowell, Jr., was born in Eufaula, grew up in Eufaula, attended Union Female College, graduating from that institution, which was one of the first 1-A Grade Colleges, established in the South. She completed her musical education under special instructors in

Washington, D. C., and is today the leader in Musical circles in Barbour County. The daughter of Capt. S. H. and (Anna Beall Young) Dent, she inherited the inate culture and refinement that has been so marked in her busy, enthusiastic and useful life.

The wife of Charles S. McDowell, Jr., of Barbour County (see biography), she has always been a leader in the club, social, civic, patriotic and church life of the county.

She is a charter member of the Lanier (Literary) Club; music Lovers Club; for about 11 years was president of Barbour County chapter U. D. C.; two years president Alabama Division United Daughters of the Confederacy; member Parent Teachers Association; and seven years president of the Woman's Missionary Auxiliary; First Methodist Church, Eufaula.

She has served as president of both Lanier and Music Lovers' Clubs; as state officer Alabama Federation of Music Clubs and state officer, Alabama Federation of Woman's Clubs.

She is a gifted pianist and organist, and her lovely soprano voice is at all times the pride of her many home friends.

She has long been justly called Barbour County's "First Lady."

She is interested in all the affairs of the County, Chairman of the Democratic Woman's Organizations of the County, and for several years has served as a member of the Registration of voters board of the County. She is capable, untiring, charming and greatly beloved.

R. M. McEACHERN

Richard Malcolm McEachern, born at Eufaula Feb. 7th, 1872, son of John C., and Victoria (Williams) McEachern. His father was a loyal Confederate soldier. He enlisted in the Clayton Guards 1st Alabama Infantry, then transferred to Pensacola and served throughout the War Between the States.

Grandson of Gilbert McEachern and Katie (Cameron) McEachern, who came from Scotland to Carolina, just before the Revolution.

Malcolm McEachern is possibly the best known man in Barbour County; was educated in the Eufaula schools of which W. H. Patterson and C. A. Craven were principals. His mother an assistant teacher in their school. He was an apt pupil and soon overreached his age in his studies.

While still a school boy, he began working for the Eufaula Times, and his newspaper career took the place of college days and he reached the high plane of citizenship he has attained, practically getting a classical education self taught, with the great assistance of his mother, who was a brilliant woman of letters and highly gifted as a literary authority and her daily influence and help brought to him even more than a college course.

In 1900 he was elected tax assessor of Barbour County and held that office until 1935, when he was defeated, it being easily seen that a strategic effort was put forth at noon on the day of the election to defeat him, on a promise by his opponent to "move the tax assessor's office from Eufaula to Clayton," which although deemed not wise or practical, by many of the real estate owners, voters and leading citizens of the county.

His record in office reveals the splendid type of man he is and his citizenship and personnel is an honor to the County and to the community.

He is a Presbyterian of the strict, old blue stock, King type; an Elder in his church and genuine "good fellow" whose hosts of friends love and honor him.

RUBY DUNBAR McEACHERN

Ruby Dunbar McEachern

He married September 4th, 1907, Ruby Dunbar, at Jackson, Tenn., daughter of William and Elizabeth (Cato) Dunbar, a charming woman of brilliant mental and business attainments, who during her 12 years as Clerk of the Court of the City of Eufaula, has been acclaimed the most accurate and proficient bookkeeper, whose accounts of that office have been audited by experts who readily saw and recognized her super ability.

The lovely McEachern home on Browder street, is one of the old historic homes of the County, and although they have no children, their home is a gathering place for the little folks of the neighborhood and this popular couple are never happier than when contributing to the pleasure of these children.

Enjoying the most unusual distinction of being one of, if not the only woman city clerk in the state of Alabama, Mrs. Ruby McEachern has had a splendid political career in Barbour county.

Born at Newnan, Georgia, she moved to this county when only a small girl, and was educated in the schools of Eufaula. Soon after graduation from high school, her family moved to Jackson, Tennessee, where she was married about a year later to R. M. McEachern, tax assessor of Barbour County.

In January, 1919, she was appointed Probate Clerk of Eufaula by Honorable B. T. Roberts, then Probate Judge, serving throughout the remainder of his term of office. When Honorable Huey R. Lee was elected Probate Judge in 1923, she was appointed clerk under him, in which she served until elected to the office of City Clerk.

Mrs. McEachern was appointed Deputy Clerk of the Circuit Court of Barbour County in September, 1919, by Honorable B. F. Petty, who was then Circuit Clerk. She served under him throughout his term of office and was appointed to the same position by Honorable B. H. Baker, who succeeded him. Mrs. McEachern has served a term of six years under Mr. Baker, and is now serving through his second term of office.

In 1925, she was appointed Registrar of Vital Statistics of Beat 5, by Dr. E. M. Moore, County Health officer, which position she held until 1926 when appointed to the office of City Clerk of Eufaula necessitated her entire time.

She was offered the position of City Clerk in January, 1926, due to the illness of Mr. T. C. Doughtie. She was acting clerk until October, 1920, when she was elected for two years under H. H. Conner, Mayor. She was re-elected to this office for a term of four years under Lee J. Clayton, mayor and is now serving under Ernest Jarrell, who is mayor.

Mrs. McEachern has the distinction of being the first woman in Eufaula to register when women were granted suffrage and the first to be appointed registrar for Beat 5.

She is the first woman to hold the office of Probate Clerk and Deputy Circuit Clerk, in Barbour County and the first ever to be elected City Clerk and treasurer, which honor she now shares with very few other women in the state.

She is a member of the Methodist Church of the Symposium Club, a member of the Chamber of Commerce.

She is the wife of R. M. McEachern who held the office of tax assessor of Barbour County over 30 years and is the happy minded, charming woman whose courtesy, efficiency, executive ability and her accuracy and competency have made her outstanding and popular in business as well as a social favorite.

DR. WILLIAM P. McDOWELL

Dr. William P. McDowell, son of Charles S. and Maggie (McKay) McDowell, was born Dec. 22nd, 1875, at the old McKay-McDowell home on Randolph street, and soon after finishing school, went into business, being clerk in a large department store, when a mere youth, where he soon showed splendid business qualities. But the call of the Medico came to him, and he went the Medical College in Mobile, graduating with honors and then taking post graduate courses in surgery and children's diseases at several of the leading New York hospitals and Medical colleges.

He began the practice of Medicine in his home town, Eufaula, and for a time was associated with Dr. W. S. Britt-McDowell infirmary at Eufaula. In 1906 he married Miss Cornelia Sylvester, and a son and daughter were born to them.

After about ten years of successful practice in Barbour County he removed to Norfolk, Virginia, where his success in all lines has been phenomenal.

Not only has his general practice been most flattering, but he has built up for himself a reputation as "Children's Specialist," but is one of the leading citizens of Norfolk.

His wife died four years ago, and in February, 1937, he married Mrs. Lula Dean Rees of Eufaula.

He is one of the most notable physicians of the South.

EDWIN K. McDOWELL

Edwin K. McDowell, son of Charles S. and Margaret (McKay) McDowell, was also born at the historic McKay-McDowell home on Randolph at Eufaula and grew up, attending the home town schools, afterwards attending the University of Alabama. In early young manhood he entered the Insurance business, and through the years has been successful to a degree most flattering.

For a number of years he was located in Atlanta with leading companies as special agent, then for a time in Texas, holding a fine position in the Insurance business of that state, and now for several years he has held a most important and responsible position, with the U. S. government in insurance, being located in Washington, D. C.

He is a fine business man, and one of the splendid four brothers that have gone out from a fine old family into fields of a a life work that have been notably successful for each one of them.

He married Susie May, of Montgomery, Alabama.

ARCHIBALD M. McDOWELL

The youngest of the four splendid sons of the distinguished McDowell family of Barbour County is Senator A. M. McDowell, familiarly called by his hosts of friends, "Arch."

He was born at the historic home on Sanford street June 29th, and grew up in the shadow of the City schools across the street, afterwards grauduating from the University of Alabama, and then taking post graduate courses—specializing at Law at Havard University.

He went into partnership with his brother, Charles S. McDowell, who had already established an enviable reputation as an attorney at law in Barbour County.

ARCHIBALD M. McDOWELL

Through the passing years, the firm has been one of the most popular and successful legal firms in the state. The Senior member, handling most of the criminal cases, and the junior member, most of the civil cases of routine work; both giving undivided service in cases of special import.

The volume of their business is immense.

Personally "Arch" McDowell is an asset to any business, and in the courtroom his dignity, discretion and ability is noticable under any condition that arises. As a speaker he is entertaining, convincing and has the knack of carrying his point of argument to a jury with force that has effect.

Representing the County of Barbour in the State Senate, he has been author of a number of bills, most helpful to the county. His judgment is sound; he is tactful, and a valuable citizen of whom his home town and County is very proud.

He is the kind of Democrat that embodies an ehtical concept infinitely higher than the propaganda that attempts to emphasize the economic and material factors of the day and time, and whose personal efforts daily are for keeping clean the political pot, that is sometimes boiling over with the petty slime of the political programs of the day.

He began his early career in the Commercial National Bank and was a director and vice president of that bank.

He is a member of the County Democratic Executive committee; was member of the City Council for several terms.

He is a charter member of the Kiwanis Club and was its president at one time and is a member of the Chamber of Commerce.

Mr. McDowell is a Presbyterian of that strict type that shows its influence in the daily life, and is an Elder of the Presbyterian Church of Eufaula. For a long time he was superintendent of the Sunday School.

DR. E. M. MOORE

Dr. E. M. Moore was born in Wetumpka, Alabama, and there received his early education, receiving his B. S. degree from the University of Alabama and post graduate courses at Philadelphia, Penn. For the past 8 years he has been County Health officer of Barbour county, residing at Clayton and is one of the most popular physicians of the County. He is a member of the Methodist Church, of the Eufaula Rotary Club and gives much time to Welfare work for the children of the schools of the County, and is also a member of the Commercial Club.

He pays weekly visits to the schools in the County, observing and caring for the health of the school children.

DR. E. M. MOORE

REV. P. P. MARGART, D. D.

Dr. J. P. Margart was the brilliant churchman of pioneer days who came to Barbour County from the Pastorate of the Lutheran Presbyterian Church at Savannah, Georgia, and located between Barnesville and Eufaula; married Nancy Treadwell, sister of B. F. Treadwell, famous as an outstanding soldier and officer of the Confederacy. He organized four Lutheran Churches in different sections, serving them with the methods of real religion that stamped the pious man of God, who had given his life to doing good.

To him and his equally fine and popular wife were born two sons, Frank, who married first Nella Norman; second Myrtle Slease, no issue, and Samuel T., married Camilla Powell, daughter of Joseph Sidney Powell, and wife, Antoinette (Stovall Powell), distinguished pioneer citizens, issue one daughter, Nettie, married Jerry H. Reeves, Jr., son of J. H. Reeves, Sr., and wife, Elizabeth Reeves, daughter of John McNab, pioneer banker of Barbour County, issue Jerry H., III, married Zeadora Breckenridge of Birmingham, issue three sons, John and Jerry, IV.

Daughters of J. H. and Nettie Reeves were Camilla, Elizabeth and Janet, who married Frank W. Comer, III, issue, son, Jerry Legare Comer, V.

Carrie Margaret married Col. J. W. Otis.

Dr. Margart built a handsome home which was a show place for years and the plantations of S. T. Magart and his large general merchandise store were the most important in the Batesville community. He was rated a most excellent farmer and business man. For many years Batesville was one of the important trading points for miles and the Margart store notable as were the farms.

The family came from long lines of distinguished ancestry and the third and fourth generations are upholding the fine old traditions of culture that follows all "to the Manor born."

B. B. McKENZIE

Bethune Beaton McKenzie, born October 11, 1837, at Louisville, son of Daniel and Amanda (Birch) McKenzie, who came to Barbour County from North Carolina in 1828.

He received his early education in the schools at Louisville and entered Harvard University, graduating in 1858.

In 1861 he enlisted in the Confederate Army, private in Company H, 7th Alabama Regiment. In 1862, he entered 39th Alabama Regiment as First Lieutenant Company C. Was not strong physically and was ordered to the Virginia Department as a part of the J. D. Legion, being present when General Johnson surrendered to General Sherman. During the long strife, he was a loyal, patriotic soldier.

After the war he was elected delegate to the Constitutional Convention, being the youngest member.

Taking up civil engineering, he surveyed and built the Vicksburg and Brunswick railroad from Eufaula to Clayton.

Later he was chief engineer for the Central of Georgia railroad.

In 1881 he went into the lumber business, organizing the Durham Lumber Company, moving to Eufaula some time later, he purchased the Chewalla Cotton Mills, operating them until his death in 1913. Mr. McKenzie was a man of highest principles an character, a consecrated Christian man of commanding appearance and personality, and outstanding in Barbour County, as one of its most valuable citizens; a deacon in the First Baptist Church and a power of strength in that denomination in the County.

He married Bettie Flournoy, lovely Christian woman, and their beautiful home, "Liberty Hall," was for years one of the most hospitable homes in the state, as was their lovely Eufaula home.

Their children were:

Edgar F. married Lena Lampley, both deceased; their children: Howard, Walter and Kenneth.

Anna married S. T. Surrat, deceased; Caroline Elizabeth married W. C. Vinson, deceased. Children: E. C. H., McKenzie, Paul and W. C., Jr.,; Amanda Birch married Dr. W. W. Mangum, deceased. Children: Annie Will and Elizabeth.

Fannie M. married E. M. Lovelace; children, Edwin McKenzie and William Yancey. Mary Lou married first Edward H. Roberts. Their daughter, Caroline Roberts, married J. R. Williams—one son, J. R., married second James E. Methvin. Their daughter, Mary Lou, married O. D. Blinov of Russia.

Daniel B. married Esther Downing, two sons, Daniel, Jr., and Robert. Kenneth B. married Clyde Methvin, children, Emma Gay; Francis married J. L. Houston.

Kenneth, Jr., and James Methvin.

Susie married John C. Copeland, children John Alexander, McKenzie, Caroline and Elizabeth.

In 1783 his great grandfather with his wife and three sons sailed from the Island of Sky off the Scottish coast. He died enroute to America and was buried at sea. His wife and sons landed at Baltimore, later going to Richmond County, N. C., and from this original branch of the family have sprung the five brothers, one of whom was the father of B. B. McKenzie who came to Barbour in 1828.

There were three Daniels in the family, and the line, direct down from the Isles of the North British seas, make Dan B., eldest son of Mr. and Mrs. Dan B. McKenzie the lineage bearer. Another Dan McKenzie of this distinguished family was one of the heroes of the Confederacy, being on the staff of General Johnston at the surrender of the Confederate forces.

JOHN C. McRAE—J. M. McRAE

John C. McRae came to Barbour County from South Carolina, where he was born, and was among the first pioneers of the Louisville settlement, being of that fine old Scotch stock of which the County has boasted since those early days.

He married Janet McLeod, also of this enviable Scotch blood, and they were leaders in the progress of the County.

He was a farmer, who used the scientific plans, and personally experimented along lines that brought to him well earned success.

After living for some time in the Louisville settlement he moved to a settlement between Clayton and Eufaula, near White Oak, where his children grew up, moving into the city of Eufaula in the seventies.

The eldest son, John McLeod McRae, graduated from Chapel Hill College, N. C., and entered the Confederate army, and while in this service was a member of the company that was the honor escort of President Jefferson Davis, when he was inaugurated chieftain of the Confederacy at Montgomery.

He married Amanda Williams and their children were: Julia, who married John W. Drewry, both deceased; Fanny, deceased; John C., II, died from effects of injuries received received in the Cyclone of March 5th, 1919; married Elizabeth Merrill; Louis M., now of New York; Amma married Samuel Allen Bulloch; Jennie, librarian of Carnegie Library, Eufaula.

The eldest daughter of John C. McRae was Maria, married to Henry A. Young, who was killed in the War Between the States when a bridge his company was crossing went down. Their children were Julia, who married Albert C. Barnett, both deceased, and William H. Young of Anniston, Alabama.

Mary Jane, second daughter, married James T. Kendall, and their children are: Jennie, married Samuel W. Goode; John M., married Sallie Jennings; Forrie, married Charles R. Ross, both deceased; James T., Jr., married Rose Mooneyham, both deceased; Maribeel married W. E. McKenney; Lula married Dr. J. C. Cato, both deceased.

John M. McRae and his wife were the home makers that make the world better for having lived in it, and their country home was notable as one of the finest farms anywhere in the county and it is also notable that the slaves on this farm were loath to leave it and a number of them remained in the employ of Mr. John C. McRae and the families of his son and daughters all their lives.

Mr. J. C. McRae made his home with his son until his

death after his daughter, Mrs. Young, moved to Anniston, Ala., and he was the beloved grandfather to whom all his grandchildren were devoted.

The McRae home in the City was and is still equally as notable as the old historic country home. It is the place where General Alpheus Baker received the flag tht led his Volunteer company to fight for the South. See historic homes.

All the children of this distinguished family have and are still filling important places in the life of whatever community their lot has been cast in and are an honor to Barbour county.

James McRae, son of J. C., and Janet (McLeod) McRae, married Josejhine McKay, of the distinguished CcRae family of Barbour County, and their home was one of the notable ones of Barbour County.

WILLIAM McLEOD—JAMES McLEOD

In the days of "Bonnie Scotland's glory, the greatest achivemenets were at the hands of "ye farmers" and the products of the fields were the yields that have emblazoned and recorded that glory.

The name McLeod was written high on the role of citi-

WM. McLEOD   JAMES McLEOD

zens, who dwelt "where the blue bells and the heather grow." From those old days, through many generations in song and story until now this McLeod name has carried with it fortune and fame.

In Barbour County, two men of this good old Scotch name and inheritance, keeping true to tradition, all that it has stood for, were William McLeod, born in South Carolina, but came to Barbour County in early manhood, taking active part, until his death in 1910, in all local, agricultural, progressive and political interests.

His large farms near Batesville were notable for their splendid yields and the system by which they were produced.

Mr. McLeod had a splendid program of his own, the carrying out of which brought him success that put him foremost in the state as a high class farmer. He did not take readily to new and untried plans, but used his own ideas, and acted on his own experience, discarding new and suggested but untried innovations.

A man of integrity and high code of principles, he won for himself many friends, and his industry and good management brought him a neat fortune that was the reward of "well doing," and the community mourned his passing genuinely.

On his only son, James McLeod, fell the mantle of what, so often is the blessing of "like father, like son," and the story of young James McLeod's career as one of the outstanding citizens of the County, is one that is as bright with good works as the story of his death is tragic and lamentable. He was struck down by the hand of a negro laborer and a road hand, when he was breaking up a quarrel between two negro road workers on the farm roads. His death deprived the County of a most valuable citizen.

The old McLeod home was one of most delightful hospitality and the large family of sisters who grew up with one idolized brother have during the passing years scattered and made new homes of their own.

The eldest (Alice) Mrs. J. W. Grubbs, wife of the late J. W. Grubbs, one of Barbour County's most prominent and beloved citizens, lives quietly on College hill in Eufaula surrounded by her flowers and sweet memories of the past, and devotes her time to active work in all the interests of the First Methodist Church. Her younger sister (Ruby) Mrs. Robert Dunbar, is also a Methodist church worker, giving her interest mostly to the Sunday School in which both she and her husband take leading parts of helpful work.

Miss Sallie still holds to the old Scotch Presbyterian

faith, and is a faithful, useful member of the Presbyterian church at Eufaula.

(Kate) Mrs. W. W. Stanton, Sylacauga, Ala.

(Mary Leonora) Mrs. James W. Watson.

(Marion) Mrs. William Rose, deceased.

(Rosa) Mrs. C. A. Davis, Atlanta, Georgia.

(Willie) Mrs. R. E. Calhoun, Columbus, Georgia.

Two McLeod sisters, Miss Sallie and Mrs. Robert Dunbar (Ruby) after the death of their brother entered business life. Opening with a millinery establishment at Eufaula, they soon added dry goods, and are now under the firm name of McLeod and McLeod, carrying on one of the largest department store trades in the County, and one of the largest in southeast Alabama.

They are also interested in real estate, owning four of the finest business buildings on Broad street in Eufaula, besides a number of the most desirable residences in Eufaula.

At the June meeting of Barbour County Chapter U. D. C., celebrating Jefferson Davis' birthday, a cross of honor awarded to William McLeod, deceased, was presented to his eldest daughter, Miss Sallie McLeod, by the chapter registrar, Mrs. Erin McCormick Jones.

JOHN McNAB

It was December 2nd, when the Heather covered fields of Argyleshire Province were russet and red under the winter sky over the little town of Islay in Scotland—when John McNab was born, the cultured, courtly gentleman who bore all the earmarks of a "Prince among men."

In the early summer of 1818, he came to America and married Janie Graham of Charleston, S. C., and in the forties they came to Barbour County. He was a man of wealth and influence and was one of the main forces that engineered the progress of the town of Eufaula in pioneer days.

He built a beautiful home, cornor of Eufaula and Barbour streets, where his children were reared. In the early fifties he built the John McNab bank, corner of Broad and Randolph streets, which is a magnificent fire-proof building (now owned by Mrs. Eli S. Shorter III), and at the time it was built it was the finest bank building in the state. It was used as the John McNab Bank from 1853 to April 1st, 1891, when it ceased business after Mr. McNab's death. Other fine buildings and stores he built were the original Central Hotel, afterwards the Bluff City Inn; the very large office and stores building at the corner of Broad and Randolph streets, opposite the McNab Bank; and the two stores and second story office building adjoining the bank, one occupied the past 35 years by the Schaub Book Store.

In 1884 Mr. McNab, together with his-in-law, Dr. W. N. Reeves, who succeeded him as president of the bank, built the elegant Mansion "Mont McNab," which was most notable. (see Historic Old Homes).

Mr. McNab was the instigator of and largest contributor to the building of the Presbyterian Church that now stands on the corner of Randolph and Church streets, and throughout his long and useful life its mainstay, and his personal influence, as well as financal aid, one of its best assets.

He was a Presbyterian who lived by a code that has made the Scotish Isle famous through all time for religious observance of the noblest in every lifetime.

Before the town of Eufaula was chartered as a city he presided for many years over it as "Intendent" and was the first leader in all the progress that led to making it a city in 1857.

Mr. McNab was a large land owner and his farming interests were extensive. As president of the John McNab Bank, he was tactfully conservative, always obliging and the Eufaula of today and other parts of the County owe much to his labors in the old days.

He was a man of scholarly abilities and wide information, with an artistic mind that gloried in the beautiful and cultural.

Among his personal papers after his death were found many beautiful poems he had written during idle moments in his office.

On Christmas morning, 1889, he was bed ridden and unable to go to the home of his daughter, whose husband —Prof. J. C. Van Houten—had died that morning; but lying in bed (over 80 years old) he wrote her a most beautiful letter of sympathy and comfort in verse, which was pronounced a masterpiece of literature.

Mr. McNab was so gentle, thoughtful and so cultured that his very presence created an atmosphere that breathed out the highest and noblest always, and in all things.

He died in April, 1890, at the age of 85.

His children were: Four sons, Graham, Franklin, these dying early in life, and John, who married Jennie Singer, of Lumpkin, Georgia, and the children are: Mittie, married E. Malone Doughtie, and Janie, unmarried. He died in the zenith of manhood.

His daughters were Flora, married Dr. W. M. Reeves (see biography) and their children were Islay, married Harmon Lampley, John M., William R., married Fanny Tennelle, David, and Charles, married, all deceased.

Mattie married Prof. J. C. Van Houten. Children: James Essie, deceased; Moselle and John M., deceased, and Mattie, who for many years was privae secretary to Senator Hoar, both at Worcester, Mass., and at Washington, D. C.

Elizabeth McNab married Jerry H. Reeves (see biography) and their children are Janie, married Robert M. Jennings, Lily, deceased, Malcolm M., deceased, married Mathide Copeland. Jerry H., Jr., married Nettie Margart, and Janie.

ANGUS McINNIS OF SCOTLAND AND BARBOUR COUNTY AND WIFE, CATHERINE OF SCOTLAND

Angus McInnis was born in Scotland before the Revolutionary War and with his wife, whose maiden name was Catherine McInnis, came to America with their daughters and lived in North Carolina. They were devout Presbyterian church members and when a colony of Scotch Presbyterians came to Barbour County, Alabama, about 1825, they settled fourteen miles from Eufaula. From this couple many descendants have lived and blessed the church and their country. Catherine McInnis and son, Miles, are buried in the old McGilvary cemetery and Augus McLnnis and youngest daughter, Margaret, are buried in the upper part of Dale County. Angus McInnis and wife and daughters spoke the Gaelic language and were people of the highest type. Their grandchildren and great-great grand children are prominent in the church and in the political world.

To this union was born the following children:

Mary (Polly) McInnis married George Keahey, Scotch Presbyterian Elder.

Nancy McInnis (born 1810) married in 1831, Lewis Walker, son of Solomon Walker.

Catherine McInnis married William Berry Thomas, son son of Elliott Thomas and wife, Sallie Berry.

Christian McInnis married William French.

Miles McInnis died as a child.

Margaret McInnis died young.

The descendants of Nancy (Polly) McInnis and husband, William Keahey, were: George Keahey, married Sallie Wiggins, issue:

William Hardee Keahey, also two daughters.

James Keahey, died young.

Nancy Emiline Keahey died about 1916, about 80 years old.

James Keahey, killed in Confederate army.

Miles Keahey, moved to Texas about 1870, Confederate soldier.

John Keahey, killed in Confederate Army.
Greene Keahey killed in Confederate Army.
Martha Keahey married Levi Foxworth.
Issue: Angus, John, Mary and two other boys and fiirls. They live in Houston County.

Nancy McInnis was born March 23, 1810, died March 29, 1893; she married Lewis walker, son of Solomon Walker. Note: See Solomon Walker line and George Hilliard Thomas Esquire line.

Catherine McInnis married William Berry Thomas, son of Elliott Thomas and his wife, Sally Berry, of Barbour County. Soon after their marriage they moved with their slaves to a large plantation near Bloodworth bridge. Their children were:

Eliza Jane married Silas Bush, of Enterprise, Alabama; before the Civil War.

Nancy Caroline Thomas married Wyatt Snow in Dale County; Sarah Elizabeth married Frances Marion Pridgen, Confederate soldier of Dale County, the year after the Civil War.

William Marion married Mrs. Catherine Chancy Brewer; Lewis Bryan died young; Mary Ann married William Carroll and moved to Texas. They have issue: Marcus LaFayette, married Lora Clarke of Clopton, Ala, issue:

Issue of Eliza Jane and her her husband, Silas Bush, of Enterprise, Alabama, Coffee County:

Henry, Matilda, Fletcher, Richard, John; Charles married Miss Maggie Garner Ozark; no issue, Enterprise, Ala., Robert married Miss Garner of Ozark; they have issue: Harriett Lillie, Naomi Eugene married Miss Chapman of Enterprise, Alabama, and have issue.

Sarah Elizabeth Thomas and Frances Marion Pridgen have issue as follows:

Cassie Pridgen and her husband, Thomas Latimer, Lakeland, Fla.; Otto Latimer, Lakeland, Fla., issue:

Otto Latimer, Bradentown, Florida.

Cleo, married Rev. Griffin, pastor of First Baptst Church of Winter Haven, Florida.

Other children were Clare Bell, Ruby, Tollie, Una and Teddy Roosevelt—all of Lakeland, Florida; and Lewey Frank.

Frances Malisea Pridgen married Young D. Dowling, Ozark, Ala., issue: Alonzo Gills, died when grown; Bertie Mae married Dr. William Palmar, issue: Margaret; Katie Florence married Fred E. Inslen, Birmingham; Frederick Tolbert married Sally McWilliams, issue: Sarah, Jule, Nell, Fred and Tolbert, Jr., Ozark.

Pauline died young; Samuel Marion, world war veteran, married Fannie Henderson of Virginia; Erin died young;

Jesse Bryan died in 1926; Grace married Kirck Enzor and lives in Massachusetts; Robert Lewis lives in New York.

Annie Pridgen married Henry A. W. Martin, Ozark. Issuie: Henry Pridgen and Maxie Pridgen.

Mosella Pridgen, married Mr. Pettus, Dothan. Issue: Francis Pridgen Pettus.

Marcellus Pridgeon, married Lena Dowling, Ozark; Marcellus Pridgeon was a prominent business man in Dothan, Ala.; issue: J. Francis Pridgen, lawyer, Dothan, Alabama; Miss Elsa Pridgen, Dothan, Alabama.

Arlue Prigden married Joseph Edmondson, Daleville, Alabama. Issue: Rosa Bell, married Dr. J. B. Woodall, issue, Sollie, married Agnes Terry; issue: Joseps Francis, and a daughter.

Other children were Troy, Dade, Joseph Burley, Maxie, Pauline, who married Lewis Brock Thomas, no issue; Haley, Woodrow Wilson.

William Marion Thomas married Mrs. Catherine Chancey Brewer; issue: Arnold Alonzo, James, William, Colie, all of Troy, Ala.

Mary Ann married William Carroll and went to Texas soon after the Civil War. Have issue:

Marcus LaFayette married Lora Clarke, Clopton. Issue: (a) Mary, married James Preston; ten children, Ozark, Ala.;

William Augustus Thomas married Ila Dykes, Ozark. He was a prominent merchant in Ozark. Issue: Dewey Thomas, died young; Marcus Thomas, Perry Thomas, in United States Navy; daughter.

Barney Thomas is married and lives in Florida. Has children.

Angus, married, one child in Texas.

Malcomb; Bunyan, died while young; Shelley married Miss Kelley and have children in Midland City.

Annie Bell married Mr. McKinnon of Clio, postmistress, two children, Marvin and Catherine, married at Enterprise, Alabama.

Grady is married and has issue:

Christian McInnis, daughter of Angus McInnis and wife, Catherine, married William French. Issue: James Edward, Jefferson, Nancy Jane, Angus and Frances.

James Edward married Mrs. Nancy Stimson Goff, Brundidge, Ala. Issue, William, Charles, Lena and Fox.

Nancy Jane, married Mr. Jones and died early, no issue.

Angus married Miss Vickers, of Elba, Ala. Issue:

Frances married Mr. Clowers, Troy, Alabama, issue: 6.

These descendants of Angus McInnis and wife, Catherine McInnis, are many and all worthwhile citizens. They are intermarried into the Thomas, Bush and Walker families of Barbour County and Dale County.

McKAY BROTHERS

Among the splendid men who were reared at Louisville in Barbour County none have been more notable or worthy of rememberance in a history of that County than the three McKay brothers, sons of the fine old Scotch ancestry of which they could boast, but being the cultured ,well bred gentlemen that they were, were unostentatious and retiring in their daily life. They all grew to manhood at the fine old home near Louisville and in the late seventies they came to Eufaula first, the eldest of whom was Philip McKay.

PHILIP McKAY

He was remarkable for his business ability. He went into the wagon and buggy business, at first representing a Tennessee company and later having the wagons made in Eufaula. He served in the Confederate army and was cited for special acts of bravery; was member of Louisville Blues. Personally he was handsome, stood erect and commanded attention in any assembly. He was a Presbyterian of the strict old type that observes the conventions. He was a social leader and possibly was more popular than any other young man of that day in Eufaula.

He married Leila Felder, of Americus, Georgia, daughter of Colonel Felder, a notoable attorney of Georgia. In the nineties they moved to Middlesboro, Ky., where some years ago he died, and his widow still makes her home there.

ALEXANDER McKAY

Alexander McKay came to Eufaula shortly after his elder brother and was associated with him in the wagon business. He built and operated an ice factory in Eufaula for many years, and for a long time was superintendent of the Eufaula waterworks.

He was one of the best citizens Eufaula ever had; married Mary Douglas of Louisville, who survives him, and is one of the best beloved women of the community (see photo on page of ten old ladies).

Their children are: Edwin McKay, expert electrician of Asheville, N. C., married Julia Massey, issue one daughter, Julia, deceased.

Minnie, married Julius D. Schaub, Eufaula, issue Douglas, married Arbella Paulson, of Minnesota, now living in Los Angeles, Cal.

Mary Denie Schaub, married John A. Ward, issue a son, John A., Jr.; Alex Schaub; Julius Schaub.

Annie Belle McKay married Clarence Worrill; issue, Elizabeth Worrill, married M. C. McDonald; and sons Clarence Worrill and Thomas Worrill, Asheville, N. C.

Nora McKay married Samuel McCarroll, both deceased. Their children: Samuel, William and Julius McCarroll.

FARQUAR McKAY

Farquar McKay, the youngest of the three brothers, came ot Eufaula from Louisville several years later than the elder brothers and went in business with his brother, Alex, remaining here some years, then going to Russellville, Alabama, where he died.

He married first, Rosa Fasen, issue two sons, Phil and Donald, married second Lonnie Green, issue two girls, Winnie and Louise.

Only the children of this brother are now living, and are prominent citizens of Alabama.

All the McKay family were leaders in the Presbyterian church, and all the descendants, high toned gentlemen and ladies of the highest type of Christians and citizens.

McCORMICK BROTHERS

Barbour County never had three more outstanding and valuable citizens than **John D., George C.,** and **William E. McCormick,** sons of William and Ann (McKigney). Born September 8th, 1817; died Sept. 17th, 1866. He was born in Richmond County, N. C., Sept. 8th, 1817. His father was John Mac McCormick, a native of Appin Argyleshire, Scotland. He came to America very young and died in 1837 at the age of 75 years.

His wife, Mary McCormick, was born January 14th, 1828, and died Nov. 24th, 1884. She was also a native of Scotland.

This father and son are buried at Pea River cemetery, notable as being over a hundred years old.

John Duncan McCormick, the eldest son, was born at Louisville, Dec. 22nd, 1840, died at Eufaula May 29th, 1881.

He grew up loyal to the South and enlisted with the volunteers at Louisville, becoming captain of Company D, 59th Alabama Regiment. He married Sarah E. Hawkins October 14th, 1871, at Americus, Georgia.

He resided in Eufaula until his death during which time he was one of the leading men of the city of Eufaula, being in the grocery and general merchandise business.

His children were: Roy; John; Julia; Cornelia; the latter marrying John Stow.

George Chalmers, born at Louisville, July 25th, 1843, and died at Eufaula July 8th, 1913. He was first Lieutenant of Company D, 59th Alabama Regiment.

He was Senior member of the firm of McCormick and Richardson, which had previously been Cox-McCormick and Company, and at his death he was president of the Eufaula Grocery Company, of which his grandson, George McCormick Dent, is now president.

He married Catherine Love Allen, Feb. 17th, 1867; their children were I. William Love McCormick, born August 12th, 1868; married Etta Fountaine Copeland, issue, Mary McCormick; married first James D. Comer, issue, son, James D., Jr., deceased; married second Warren Andrews, issue, a son, Warren McCormick Andrews. Henrietta McCormick married Congressman J. Lister Hill, issue, a daughter, Henrietta Fountaine Hill, and a son, L. L. Hill, II. Annie Stuart McCormick married Edward Young Dent, son of Captain S. H. Dent, children: George McCormick Dent, married Helen Mittman May 3rd, 1919, daughter of Rev. S. U. Mittman, issue, three daughters, Sarah, Marguerite, Annie McCormick and one son, George McCormick Dent.

Nana Bell Dent married George E. McGough, a member of the distinguished old McGough family of Glennville, Alabama, issue two sons, George E., Jr., and Edward McCormick.

Catherine Dent is unmarried, died May 22, 1939.

Stuart Dent married Bibb Walker of Jacksonville, Fla., issue a daughter, Catherine Anna Dent; George Rossiter McCormick was born July 12th, 1873, and died April 13th, 1899.

The third son, **William Emmett McCormick,** was born at Louisville, March 17th, 1848. He went into the Confederate army, Company D, 59th Alabama Regiment, and was seriously wounded several times—one time so terribly that his life was despaired of.

After the War Between the States was over, the McCormick Brothers were strong forces in the terrible fight made to readjust reconstruction troubles in Barbour County. They were mostly business men and not interested in politics, but being loyal Southerners, they joined in the struggle to build up the break down of the Southland, and their native County.

He was also a groceryman and the leading broker of the county.

In the eighties, responding to the Texas boom lure, he left with his partner, Mr. Clifford Asbury Locke. They were in business there for about a year when the home lure urged stronger and they came back to Eufaula. Mr. McCormick continued in the brokerage business, retiring when his health failed. Mr. Locke went into the retail fancy grocery business and until his death his store was the pride of Barbour County, rated with any extra fine fancy grocery store of any large city.

"Will McCormick," as he was affectionately called, was a most genial and especially intellectual man, a veritable encylopedia of information, loved a joke, and his dry wit was the delight of his friends.

He married Clara Elizabeth Beauchamp, daughter of Andree Hamille and his wife, Margaret (Allen) Beauchamp, pioneer citizens of Barbour County. Their children: Helen died when a beautiful little girl; Erin married J. H. Jones, June 12th, 1912, and one son, William Emmett, unmarried.

There were two other sons of William McCormick, Henry Lang McCormick, born at Louisville Dec. 20th, 1854, and James Allen McCormick, also born at Louisville on July 12th, 1857, both deceased many years ago.

JULIA MASSEY McKAY

JULIA MASSEY McKAY

From January, 1926, to January, 1935, Mrs. Julia Massey McKay held the office of Probate Clerk at Eufaula, appointed by Probate Judge Huey R. Lee, and serving through the administrations of Judges Lee and G. O. Wallace, being succeeded when Judge J. F. Laseter went in office by Clerk George H. Dent, 3rd, present incumbent.

During these years it was ontable that Mrs. McKay was an A No. 1 accountant and efficient and capable to a degree that was most flattering to her and valuable to the county.

Personally she was accomodating, untiring and painstaking, holding an office that required the daily handling of documents that demanded perfect accuracy on her part. She never failed to meet this requirement.

The past year or more she has held a newly created office at Eufaula, that of deputy circuit clerk of Barbour County, appointed by Circuit Clerk, Ben Baker. The creation of this office is of great convenience to the citizens of this section.

Mrs. McKay is the daughter of the late Captain Charles F. and Fredonia (Sparks) Massey. She is a woman of culture and executive ability and does credit to the position she holds and to the County. Married Edwin McKay, deceased.

EDWARD S. OTT

Among the earliest settlers of Barbour County who came to Barbour County with his father, William Ott, from Orange District, South Carolina, more than a hundred years ago. William Alston owned and lived on what is now known as the Shorter place near Batesville, Alabama, now owned by Mrs. W. D. Jelks. The son, Edward S. Ott, married Anne Amanda Alston, then living at Columbus, Georgia, and whose uncle, Philip H. Alston, was one of the five commissioners appointed by the legislature of Georgia to survey lands acquired from the Indians to lay off a town site and sell lots in what was to be known as Columbue, Georgia, which was done in 1828. Mr. Edward S. Ott lived near Batesville and his plantation is still owned by his grandchildren.

He was a member of the Alabama legislature and was a colonel of militia. He was an outstanding wealthy citizen whose descendants have honored him by holding to the high principles of citizenship that has made the Ott-Alston name through generations, distinguished.

The old notable home both at Fort Browder and at Clayton have colorful histories that brighten Alabama records— made so by them who have gone from the homes to take some of the highest places in the annals of the country.

It is notable, however, that the War between the states which brought havoc, wreck and ruin to Barbour County destroyed much of the wealth of these families, but undaunted, these men had in the makeup all the traits needed to meet situations and with effort put forth by young Augustus Alston, after his return from the war every one of the family has achieved in most notable lines of endeavor.

Edward S. Ott married and children were: Anna Maria, married A. H. Alston; Elizabeth married Drake; Addies marriedfirst Keitt; married second B. F. Treadwell.

Col. Edward Ott was the son of William and Charity Alston Ott, the former a member of the Provincial Congress and grandson of James and Christian Lillington Alston.

The chief characteristic of the Ott family has been personal integrity and culture. "To the manor born" every one who has borne the name carried the marks of nobility that throughout each generation has been definite. At Fort Browder the Ott-Alston homes were typical of refinement, good taste ,industry and progress that as the years have passed, although the families have gone elsewhere to abide, the memory of their personality and citizenship is one of the blessings left to the community.

STERN-OPPENHEIMER

When "Hart's Block" composed of 8 stores and an immense public hall and auditorium above, was the most attractive business center of this section, the most outstanding and attractive of all was "Stern's Temple of Fashion."

It was the first attempt on the part of any merchant in Barbour County to bring South a reproduction of New York styles and ideas.

Mr. David G. Stern was the head of this firm, but his son, Gabe, was manager and it was his artistic, progressive ideas, with his father's judgment and good business methods that made this dry goods and notion store the most famous Eufaula ever had. Nothing so elaborate has ever been attempted by any other merchant here through all the years—and with the record of all the fine stores since then and now one can imagine how beautiful this outlay and display of goods of the "Temple of Fashion" was.

DAVID G. STERN

JACOB OPPENHEIMER

But the population of Eufaula and Barbour County was not equal to the support of such a fine store and Mr. Gabe Stern, after a few years, moved it to New Orleans, where he carried on on a much larger scale.

The mantle of grandfather and uncle, however, fell on Jacob Oppenheimer, then a mere lad, but from boyhood he has been one of Barbour County's most valuable citizens. a leader in every progressive movement, for the uplift of the community. Few men have been as highly esteemed by the citizenship generally and beloved by his hosts of warm friends.

His personal charity and his influence have made philanthropic history in Barbour County.

His store in Eufaula is a meeting place for politicians and headquarters for farmers and is the place to which everybody (white or black) goes when in trouble, or want a favor, for they know that "Jake" will always be ready to help them out. He has served many years on the City Council as its president and for years was president of the County Board of Revenue, of which he is a most active member and is always the true blue.

He has headed every benevolent project in the County and his influence and work for Barbour County roads is both old and new histoy.

The Stern family record for community helpfulness is still being carried on by those who still reside here. Mr. and Mrs. Oppenheimer (Rebecca Bloom), daughter of Mr. and Mrs. A. M .Bloom, who moved here from Louisville, Ky., to be with their daughter and son, Mr. Seigman Bloom who married Minna Stern of the illustrious Stern family—coming originally from Alsace Loraine France where the former was a distinguished officer in the Franco-Prussian war—living here until his death. Daisy Oppenheimer now Mrs. J. M. Barr her husband a member of the distinguished Weedon and Barr families; and Mrs. Belle Oppenheimer Lewy her late husband, son of Mr. and Mrs. Simon Lewy, and one of the most prominent young men ever reared in the County, women who are equally as well beloved as "Jake," the husband, father and brother, for personal charm and well known charity.

This family has been notable in Barbour County since the early seventies, coming here from New York.

Mr. David G. Stern was the courtly gentleman of the old school type and his wife the queenly mother whose home was a kingdom and their children have played important parts in every phase of history in the building up of the community.

The eldest son, Silas, was a prominent broker and cotton dealer and a leading citizen. For many years he served as Justice of the Peace, and was a most capable and just officer of the law.

The next son, Gabe, went from here to New Orleans, and reached the highest pinnacle of success in his business.

The third son, Benjamin, spent much of his time in Mississippi, where he died, as did the youngest son, Henry.

The fourth son, Seigman Stern, went to Mississippi in the early eighties, married Alice Hart of Woodville, Miss., and lived for a time at Lake Charles, Mississippi, and after and since the death of his wife in recent years has returned to Eufaula to reside with his daughter, Mrs. Seigman Bloom (Minna Stern) and although 84 years old, still recalls with great pleasure the old home here and is enjoying being at the old home again. Despite his advanced age, he is down town daily and takes interest in the daily life about him. He and his one sister are the only living members of that group of sons and daughters of this family. He died July 4, 1938.

The Stern daughters were Mary, married first J. Oppenheimer, issue a son, Jake, and a daughter, Belle, now Mrs. Dave Lewy; married second Samuel Baer, issue, Jennie, married Herman Dearman, Dothan, Alabama, died February 15, 1939, and Dora, married Gus Seligman, Jacksonville, Fla.

The next daughter married Jacob Friedman of Midway, Alabama. They also established a large Dry Goods business at Eufaula, moving about 12 years ago to Montgomery after Mr. Friedman's death, where she had died some years later. Their children: Were Benjamin, married Matilda Meyer, and residing in New Orleans, La.; and Etta married Nathan Scheuer, also a prominent citizen, now of Montgomery, and member of the distinguished Scheuer family, formerly of Eufaula, their only child, Edith, is married and lives in Montgomery.

Hannah Stern married Jake Stern and since his death she resides with her daughter (Gertrude Stern) Mrs. Abe Strauss of Columbus, Georgia, and (Rosye Stern) Mrs. Joe Watterman.

Sarah Stern married Henry Bloom, both deceased, but lived in Eufaula always. He came here from Louisville, Ky., where the Bloom family was prominent in business and socially. Their children are (Retta) Bloom, married Abe Greenfield of Atlanta, her wedding being one of the most brilliant that ever took place in Barbour County. Minna Bloom married Edward Kahlman of New Orleans and has a son named David G., for his grandfather Stern. He married Marjorie Kaufman of Columbus, Georgia. Emma Stern married J. K. Sams and lived for many years at Eufaula; was prominent as leader of the Hebrew faith and greatly beloved in Barbour County, both deceased; left a son, Gabe Sams.

All these sisters were the true type of the most loveable womanhood and were an honor to Barbour county.

In the days of Eufaula's greatest prosperity this large family were foremost in all that has made the civic, benevolent, business and social life history great as it is.

The Oppenheimer home on Broad street is one of the beautiful old landmarks as is the fine old family representatives, housed within its historic walls. Mr. and Mrs. J. Oppenheimer and their daughter, Mrs. J. M. Barr, Mrs. Belle Oppenheimer Lewy, being the direct representatives ,still carrying out the fine old Stern family principles.

The "Red Star" store of today is one of the long unbroken lines from his grandfather's "Temple of Fashion" of the long ago.

PARISH BROTHERS

Chief among the most progressive, wealthy and valuable citizens of Barbour County were Parish Brothers. They laid the foundations for many of the enterprises of the County and were leaders in all the projects that have made the town of Clayton and surrounding country.

Thomas R. Parish was born in Pike County, March 4th, 1847. He served in the War Between the States in the 64th Company B, Alabama Infantry; was with Lee in Northern Virginia and was captured at the battle of the Wilderness. He was a corporal, acting sergeant, and was in prison at Elmira, New York; served under two captains, Capt. McCaslan and Captain Joiner. He was in the mercantile business at Clayton and at Eufaula, Ala., one of the firm names being Parish and Lillienthal; had large farming interests, and his mercantile business was on a very large scale.

Mr. Parish was a man of dignity, and depth of character that marked all his dealings, and his success was typical of integrity that made him an esteemed and valuable citizen of the County. He married Margie (Hill) of Clayton and their elegant home is notable in the social history of Clayton. Their children are Ida May, married A. B. Carlisle; Ella Hill married first Browder Pruett married second Ponserler. Joseph married Hattie Seay. T. R., Jr., married Elizabeth Green; and Emmett O. married Lucile Guest of Mobile.

J. E. Parish, the second brother, was born the son of Thomas E. and Rebecca (Sellars) Parish. Like his brother he was in the mercantile business and after his brother, Thomas, was active in the banking business he enlarged the other stores and was a factor in the building up of the extensive Parish interests in the County.

The Dry Goods department of the business was a feature and Mr. Parish who was the personification of personal neat-ness, brought to his customers the most fashionable of all wearing apparel and notions.

He was a gentleman of the school of "Chesterfield" type and an asset to the town and community.

He married Lucy Walker of Union Springs, who survives him, and is a beloved woman of the culture that always radiates a woman's life. Their children are Walter, who married Levinia Dismukes of Columbus, president of the Richland, Georgia Bank; Rebecca, also cashier of the same bank, and Thomas of Clayton, of the Clayton Banking Company.

The third brother, **Martin Parish**, was manager of the large hardware store that for many years was the largest business in the County.

He was a man of much ability, broad minded and far seeing, and a most valuable and esteemed citizen.

GREGORY PAPPAS

GREGORY PAPPAS

While Barbour County history is glorified with the records of the lives of the citizens of the past it has been deemed wise to glorify it with the lives and accomplishments of a younger generation of men who are doing things worth while for their home and community today.

25 years ago there came to Eufaula a young man, Gregory Pappas, who has proved himself a true son of the Grecian Isle "where Marathon slept" and whose industry, perseverance and integrity have won for him new County and home friends, who value his friendship.

When fourteen years of age he embarked on his uncle's merchant ship and with him made voyages around the world, gaining from this life experiences that have helped him in his business successes.

He established a restaurant in this city, went hard to work and today is one of the County and city's most successful and prominent citizens.

Besides his up-to-date cafe, which is modern in all its methods, he is a large real estate owner and his property is all kept in perfect condition, revealing the civic pride that governs all his business.

From a modest beginning in business, his splendid management and hard work has brought to him returns that have enabled him to attain enviable success.

He stands for progress and is always on the alert to help an all civic undertakings.

Mr. Pappas is a fluent writer and his stories of Greece and other countries, as well as his articles on timely American subjects that have appeared in the newspapers are most interesting, showing him to be a man of superior education and serious thought.

His interesting family consists of his charming wife (who was Miss Bessie Smith of Abbeville, Ala.) and the following splendid boys and girls: Venezelus, age 13; Zafero, 10; Sistie, 8; William, 6; Hellene, Frances, 4, and Alonza, 2.

The eldest, Venizelus, is a high school lad who last year honored himself, his parents and teachers by making the best marks of any pupil in the school of eight hundred. His record was commented on as most unusual in excellency for a boy of his age.

Note: As student at University, 1938-1939, Venezelus Poppas has made a phenominal record and received special commendation from that faculty.

JAMES L. PUGH

James Lawrence Pugh was born Dec. 12th, 1820, in Pike County; died March 9th, 1907, at Washington, D. C., and was buried at Eufaula.

At the age of 11 he was an orphan and began carrying the mail between Louisville, Ala., in Barbour County and Franklin in Henry County, making and saving money to pay his school tuition.

At the age of 21 he was admitted to the bar at Eufaula after clerking in a Eufaula store and studying his law books at night.

In 1860 he delivered a speech in Congress, which, although brief, it clearly brought out the fact that Senator Pugh was a secessonist, and the ability with which he presented his views showed that he did not believe the Constitution could survive the tests that had been heaped upon it, or that we could ever get back to the real patritoism of our fathers.

His speech was a clarion note that echoed long after the telegram came that told of South Carolina seceding.

Senator Pugh wrote the Resolution, which embodied the plank drawing the race line, which was accepted by the Democratic Convention of 1874, with memorable enthusiasm, and was the first step taken in Alabama towards bringing about Democratic conditions that now prevail.

He was far seeing, conservative, loyal to his convictions; was most notable for accuracy in all his statements and during his 25 years in the United States Congress was an honor to the state and county he represented.

He was always conservative in his views and moderate in his expression of opinion, yet, at the same time he was staunch in the defense of the cases he enlisted.

As a jurist he occupied a high position in the Senate and his service to the state he represented "and protected from mal-administration of Justice, by reforming the loose code of procedure in the Department of Justice often vexed and annoyed many of his contemporaries."

He was a senator who won high position in the esteem of his fellow Senators, however, and showed his usefulness in giving counsel and advice to his Constituents, as well as personal assistance. He showed a practical mind, especially in a time when theories were so often rapidly rushed aside, before the rush of a few facts.

He was a statesman who kept on the alert for happenings and coming events of the day, and who had the will and capacity to test new ideas that began to be needed more than ever before in our national government.

He married Terese Hunter, daughter of John Linguard Hunter, one of the most prominent of the pioneer settlers, and built the beautiful home known as the "Pugh Place" in the Southern Suburbs of Eufaula. Surrounding it was one of the finest farms in the County and on the estate is the old Hunter family cemetery where lie many of that illustrious family, although Senator Pugh himself and wife are buried in Fairview cemetery, Eufaula. Their children: Teresa married Alfred W. Cochran, no issue; James, Edward, John, married Inez Powell; Sallie, married Albert Elliott, children, Mary, married Fred Kyle; Pugh Elliott of Birmingham.

In 1847 the Whigs elected Henry W. Hillard to Congress without opposition. In 1849 one Whig opposed another in the famous campaign of "The War of the Roses." James L. Pugh of Barbour County was an independent Whig candidate against Hilliard and was supported by Democrats. Colonel Yancey took the stump for Pugh. The regular Whigs attempted to discredit Yancey by associating his name with Calhoun and the secession movement in South Carolina. J. J. Hooper claimed that Yancey, the chunky statesman, had brought back to Alabama from South Carolina the latest orders from headquarters at "Fort Hill."

Pugh swept the "Cow" counties and won by getting larger majorities in the Black Belt in the upper part of the District.

He and other leaders of Barbour County made a strong Southern Rights group. They were principally from Eufaula and were, viz: Eli S. Shorter elected to Congress from 1850 to 1857. John Gill Shorter, 1861; John Cochran, candidate for Congress, 1851; Jefferson Buford; Alpheus Baker; E. C. Bullock; L. L. Cato; Sterling G. Cato; Jere N. Williams; H. D. Clayton, called the "Eufaula Regency."

In 1851 the disruption of the two old parties, the Whigs and Democrats and the formation of the Party Union and the Southern Rights Party, which differed over the acceptance or rejection of the compromise measures which Congress was debating in 1850, the Union Party won in 1851, but the Democrats reorganized their old party after the election and by 1852 the two old parties were opposed to each other as much as they had been before 1850.

The Whig party gradually declined after 1852 and in 1855 a new party, known as the "American Party" sprang up, succeeding it as the opponent of the Democratic party.

The issues which separated the Whigs and Democrats in Alabama in 1850 were not clearly defined or ever understood.

Senator James Lawrence Pugh in 1882 traveled through New England as a member of the Senate Labor Committee and expressed himself as pleased with the activities of New Englanders. He said he hardly saw an acre of land that Southern people could live on.

JOSEPH L. PITTS

Joseph L. Pitts was born near Union Springs, Ala, son of Joseph and Emeline (Sessions) Pitts, pioneer citizens. He was educated in the Union Springs schools and immediately after graduation went into the drug business with his uncle, Dr. Sessions at Union Springs.

From there he went to Clayton, Alabama, going into the banking business first as cashier and later as president of the Citizens Bank at Clayton. In the late nineties Mr. Pitts bought an interest in the East Alabama National Bank at Eufaula of which he was president.

Mr. Pitts built two of the finest homes in Barbour County —one at Clayton, now owned by Mrs. J. E. Parish, and one at Eufaula, now owned by Mrs. E. E. Stafford. While a citizen of both Clayton and Eufaula, he was deeply interested in the civic progress and his homes at both places were monuments to his good judgment and fine ideas.

He was a man of business qualities that only accepted the best and gave out the best. His executive ability was notable and as a banker his methods were wise and accurate.

He was genial and highly esteemed in the business and social world, and when he died in 1900 in the full flush of life's activities the Community lost a valuable citizen.

IDA FOY PITTS

He married Ida Foy, daughter of William Humphrey and Mary Wilson Foy.

The only sister of this distinguished Foy Family, Ida Foy Pitts, was also born at Fort Browder.

She was educated at Union Female College, Eufaula, finhising at Dr. Price's select school for young women at Nashville, Tenn.

She married Joseph L. Pitts, distinguished Alabamian and their two children are Foy, who married Albert Moulthrop, and Mingnon Pitts.

"Miss Ida" as she is affectionately called by three generations of Eufaula school children was the most efficient and well beloved teacher in the Eufaula schools for 25 years, accepting this position after her husband's death. She taught the higher branches and the languages and her record as an educator placed at the top of the lists of the very best.

Both her daughters have also achieved the high rating of superior teacher. Both Mrs. Pitts and Mrs. Moulthrop have resigned their positions after many years of high class service, but Miss Mingnon Pitts is now a teacher of most capable and efficient merit at the Livingston, Alabama, Normal school.

T. F. PITTS

Thomas Frederick Pitts was born at Union Springs, Alabama, June 12th, 1865, son of Joseph and Emeline J. (Sessions) Pitts.

He was educated in the schools of Union Springs and his career as associate member of the state tax commission has been marked with splendid service.

He served as tax collector of Bullock County (adjoining Barbour) for many years and resided in Clayton, Barbour County, where he was one of the largest and leading cotton buyers in southeast Alabama.

He was appointed to the Tax Commission by Governor Brandon in 1923 and his record was very flattering to him as a state official.

He was a Mason, a Democrat and Methodist churchman of prominence.

He married Victoria M. Walker, daughter of Captain M. W. and Josephine Walker of Bullock County. Mrs. Pitts is one of the most charming women of the old regime type, whose life is emblematic of the old traditions and romances.

Their children are: Lucy, married Edward B. Freeman of Eufaula, one son, Edward B., Jr.; Annie, married William Thomas Davis of Hurtsboro, and Joseph, who enlisted and fought in the World War, member of Company B, National Guards; saw active service on the Mexican Border in 1916 and later his command was made a part of the 167th Alabama Rainbow Division, and he is one of the heroes that glorified that division in the battle of the Marne, in which he was wounded by a shell from which he is still suffering in a government hospital.

THOMAS M. PATTERSON

THOMAS M. PATTERSON

Thomas M. Patterson was born at Louisville, Ala., and received his early education at the Louisville schools after which he attended the Southern University at Greensboro, Alabama, a member of Sigma Alpha Epsylom fraternity. He served as a member of the state legislature from 1898 to 1899 and for over fifteen years was solicitor, Third Judicial Circuit.

As a prosecutor he was far reaching in the intricacies of evidence and always ready with a technicality to emphasize the law as he saw that it fitted the case in hand. He was a capable official with a clean cut explanation to meet every assertion.

Personally he was genial, brim full of dry wit and a citizen of whom the County was well proud. He is a Presbyterian of the strictist type and a prominent citizen of Clayton.

He married Miss Mamie Appling of Columbia, Ala.

GEORGE W. PEACH

George W. Peach was born at Perote, Bullock County, in 1859 and died at Clayton December 25th, 1928.

He never went actively into politics, but was a brilliant lawyer, who gave his attention to the clean thought and honest purpose of the law, under all circumstances and conditions. It was said of him often that "he knew the law in all its intracacies, better than any lawyer in the state, judging by the attitude of justice and honesty he always made paramount in his cases.

He was the clean gentleman of the type that won admiration and friends. He practiced the religion he professed in his daily life, and was a citizen who is always an asset to his community, and as superintendent of the Methodist Sunday School for many years, his church held him in high regard as an example of Christian manhood.

He married Vela Lee, daughter of Mr. and Mrs. Alto Vela Lee of Clayton. Their only child is Ildergerte, who married Otis Taylor of Birmingham (deceased) and the issue of this marrige is a son, George Peach Taylor. His widow is one of the outstanding women of the state in patriotic, church and club work and is greatly beloved for her Christian character.

BENJAMIN FRANKLIN PETTY

Benjamin Franklin Petty, one of the pioneer citizens of Barbour County, residing at Clayton, was three times married and reared a large family, all of whom were leaders in the County in all the business, social, Church and civic interests of the County.

He was a dealer in general merchandise and carried a large stock of buggys and wagons.

The Petty family was distinctive in every way and the historic hom,e built right in the heart of the town (now the home of Judge and Mrs. B. T. Roberts) is one of the most attractive and unique anywhere to be found.

It is built Octagon shape two, two storied with the stairs going up from the outside gallery that surrounds the house.

It was in this home that the Petty family entertained General Grierson of the Union Army, when his regiment marched through Barbour County enroute to camps in Quitman County, Georgia.

As the years passed along until the the family sold this home it was notable as a gathering place for the Belles and Beaux of the Community.

This Octagon shaped house is one of the three only like it in America, the other two being one in Michigan and the other in Ohio, so the writer has been told.

The children of this family were:

Frank Petty, deceased; Elizabeth, married John M. Edmondson, Eufaula; Juliette married Dan Hixon, Perote; Portia married William King of Clayton and Dothan; Lula, deceased; Robert L. married Alma Peach; Walter, deceased; Jennie, deceased; Nannie married Cornelius Herlong; Benjamin F., Jr., many years clerk of the court of Barbour County, now residing at Clayton, with his sister, Nannie Herlong, they being the only surviving members of the family.

E. R. QUILLIAN

One of the most conspicious men in Barbour County for many years was Edgar R. Quillan during the years he edited the Clayton Courier. He was born in Suffolk, Virginia in 1834 where he lived until 1848, coming to Alabama at the age of 18 as a journeyman printer. He located in Troy. In 1867 he moved to Abbeville in Henry County and lived there for six years. He served in the Confederate Army, being in General Hood's Command. He left Abbeville to locate at Clayton in Barbour County and was founder and publisher of the Clayton Courier until his death in 1924.

Served as County Commissioner of Barbour County and member of the City Council of Clayton for several terms.

He was an Episcopal Church Vestryman, a Democrat, a Mason, Knight of Honor, and Pythian Knight.

He and his wife were the very crown and flower of Grace Episcopal Church, Clayton, and were greatly beloved citizens.

He married Mollie Helms of Henry County and their children were: Jefferson, married Belle McRae; James C.; Mollied, married Alexander L. Blizzard; Maggie, deceased; Robert, druggist, Miami, Florida, and Edgar O., druggist, Montgomery, Ala.

RICHARDS FAMILY

Since time immemorial in Barbour County the name Richards has been outstanding and through all the years "Richards' Cross Roads" has been an important place in the County and state.

This large family, distinguished as expert farmers, patriotic Democrats and prominent and valuable citizens of the County.

James Richards was born in Coosa County, Alabama, in 1811; married his cousin, Louisa Richards, and her father, Robert Richards settled "Richards' Cross Roads" about 1850 This place is fifteen miles from Eufaula, 17 miles from Clayton, 13 from Abbeville, and 17 from Fort Gaines, Georgia.

It was formerly Beat 11, but is now Beat 16. James Richards enlisted as a "Minute Man" and was the instigator of ordering the families in that section to move to Abbeville for protection. In 1836 his daughter, Harriet Richards, married S. J. Belcher and when her first son was less than two weeks old her husband led a horse that she rode the distance from Richard sCross Roads to Abbeville, the point to which they were fleeing. That was Dr. W. R. Belcher of Abbeville, father of Dr. W. R. Belcher now of Abbeville and Eufaula.

This large family have married and intermarried among

the leading families of Alabama and their place in the life of Barbour County is unique and most creditable in many ways.

"Richards Cross Roads" is known far and wide for the hospitality of the old days there, the great barbecues and political speakings, all made possible by the Richards family.

The children of J. B. Richards (known as "County Line Richards," are viz: Harriet, married S. J. Belcher; William A. married Emma Tyler (a cousin of President of the United States Tyler.

R. D. Richards married Ursurla Tyler; James L. (called Pork) married Cynthia Ray; A. J. Richards married Jerusa Baker; Nancy Richards married Rev. J. W. Malone (presiding Elder of the Eufaula District M. E. Church, South; Mathilda, unmarried.

Children of James L. Richards:

James Benson Richards, not married.

W. E. Richards, married first Rosa Warr; married second Jennie Lee, daughter of Rev. R. B. Lee.

M. B. Richards married Mamie Ray.

Maggie Richards married Dr. W. R. Belcher.

Dr. A. M. Richards married Anna Shreeve and now lives in Texas.

R. J. Richards married Cora Davis; J. C. Richards married Myrtle Birdshaw.

This notable family has in its possession a number of land grants that are written and printed on sheep skin.

One of these certificates, No. 5989, issued to Robert Richards seventy nine acres of land east quarter of section 19 township (signed by President of the United States Martin Van Buren; also a grant to James Richards of Barbour County, southwest quarter of Section 20 in township (containing forty acres and two twelve hundredths of an acre) signed by President of the United States Taylor, May 1st, 1850; also one issuing to Asa H. Webb, musician in Captain Watson's Company Alabama Militia, Florida War, northwest corner section 20, township 9, forty and twelve one hundredths of an acre to Leonard C. Harrison and Ransom Godwin, their heirs and assigns, signed by President of the United States Franklin Pierce, April 15th, 1853.

In 1875, Governor H. Houston of Alabama appointed James Richards census taker for Barbour County.

Many other County offices of trust have been held by members of this old and prominent family.

ROBERTSON

Dr. William H. Robertson was born at China Grove, Pike County, May. 1861. He graduated from the University of Alabama Medical College at Mobile where he won his degrees. He spent his life at Clayton where his professional and farming activities, were large and successful. He went high in the medical profession and was a man of great personal worth and ability; was a member of the Barbour County Medical Society; and of the Alabama state Medical Association.

He was a member of Royal White Heart Lodge No. 10 F. A. A. M. at Clayton and a valuable and active member of the Baptist Church.

He married Mary Foster, daughter of John Arthur and Mary (Webb) Foster. Children: William H. Robertson, Jr., president of the Bank of Commerce of Clayton, and like his father a land owner and farmer. He was born August 10th, 1891, the second son of Dr. Robertson; Arthur B., who is in business at Clayton; a daughter, Mary Lee, graduated from Cox College and from the Boston School of Physical Education, taking post graduate courses at Columbia University and Barnard College.

Miss Ruth Robertson was graduated from the University of Alabama, class of 1925, with degree of A. B.. Both these daughters have attained educational heights, that place them at the top among the outstanding women of letters in America. Aristocrats, born, they are most charming women in every way.

William H. Robertson, Jr., married Alice Street, daughter of Rev. W. H. and Florida Hutchinson Street, both deceased. He is a member of Eufaula Lodge 912 B. P. O. E. and Clayton Camp M. W. A. For many years he served on the Barbour County Board of Revenue.

His handsome home at Clayton is one of the show places of the County. The home of his mother and late father, Dr. W. H. Robertson, is also one of the old historic homes of Clayton, around which clusters much of the glory of the long ago.

CHAUNCEY RHODES—WILLIAM T. SIMPSON

Chauncey Rhodes was born in Weathersfield, Connecticut, and came to Barbour County when a young man. His family was composed of Puritans of the strict type, and he was reared in a religious atmosphere that was revealed throughout his long life and in his Southern home he was honored and beloved by everyone for his culture, integrity, generosity to the poor and his example of humble Christianity.

He was perhaps the finest accountant who ever handled "big business" in Barbour County. He was cashier of the John McNab Bank and such an expert whose services were badly needed, that when he volunteered and entered the Confederate army and was on his way to the front, a strong plea was made, and it was shown so clearly that his services to the South and Barbour County could be of more worth, handling grave finances at home, and in order for him to turn back, was sent to Fort Gaines, Georgia, and he came back to do special work for the community and for the Confederacy. Although born and reared in the North, when he cast his lot with the South, he was loyal to the core and one of the most valuable citizens the South ever had. For nearly 50 years he was deacon and Chorister of the First Baptist Church, his splendid tenor voice was heard in the choir at every service of that Church. He was always promptly in his place, a joy and inspiration to the membership of that Church, and always a personal strength and help to the pastors.

He married Elizabeth (Daniel), daughter of James L. and Mathilda (Hantt) Daniel, and reared a large family, which has been outstanding in life. They were: Chauncey, Jr., who was associated with his father in the John McNab bank as teller, and accountant until his death when in the very zenith of young manhood.

Florence married first Ernest Brannon and their daughter, Claudia Brannon married Major Cooper D. Winn, U. S. Army.

Florence married second Homer Dickenson. Their children: Florence and Chauncey Rhodes Dickinson.

Janie D. Rhodes married Mamie Harcourt. Children: Chancey and Mattie Lee (Rhodes) the latter married Gene Adams.

Charles L. Rhodes died unmarried.

Mamie Rhodes married Edgar T. Long and their children are Gertha, married William Roy Couric, one daughter, Mamie Long, and one son, Alex, died when six years of age.

Edgar T. married Edna Blair; Marjorie married Alex Lewis, children, Anne and Alex.

William, married Patsy Howard, daughter, Patricia.

Elizabeth Daniel Rhodes was the twin sister of Mollie Daniel Simpson, and at their double wedding they were so much alike that as they started to walk out on the floor before the minister Mr. Simpson took Elizabeth instead of Mollie whom he was to marry and the mistake created peals of laughter.

After they were married they lived side by side and were the beautiful and beloved sisters who spent their lives in charitable work in the community. Elizabeth Rhodes was a Baptist and was the very "crown and flower" of the womanhood of that church, while Mollie Simpson was the factor in the Presbyterian Church that her sister was in the Baptist. Both the sweet, gentle, Christian women, spending their lives doing good that made them greatly beloved.

WILLIAM T. SIMPSON

William T. Simpson was born in Sparta, Georgia, coming to Barbour County when quite young. He went into the General Merchandise business and was highly successful. In later years he was associated in the warehouse business with his son-in-law, L. Y. Dean, under the firm name of Simpson and Dean. When Capt. Dent came to Eufaula after the War Between the States he was bookkeeper for William T. Simpson and afterwards married his daughter, Carolyne.

Mr. Simpson was a man of strong character, determined ideas, and strict to the letter of right and wrong, and was outstanding as a churchman of piety and a citizen of value that made the community better for his having lived in it.

Mr. and Mrs. Rhodes and Mr. and Mrs. Simpson were looked upon as the examples of the highest and noblest in manhood and womanhood.

The Simpson children were:

Carolyne married Leonard Yancey Dean; their children were Melanie, married Frank F. Bakewell; Loula, married first John Reese; married second Dr. William P. McDowell; Leonard Yancy, Jr., married first Madye Threatt; married second Jennie Kendall Epps; Ethel married Thomas L. Moore; Evie married Keese; Lula, who married J. E. Fitzgerald, died two weeks after marriage. Dr. J. L. Simpson married Alice Fitzgerald. William Simpson, deceased. Bessie Simpson married Edward K. Cargill.

WILLIAM N. REEVES

Dr. William N. Reeves was born in Dallas County near Selma, Alabama, and was educated at Howard College and took theological courses at several institutions. He came to Barbour County in the late fifties and in 1864 married Flora McNab, daughter of John M. McNab, banker and large real estate owner.

When the war Between the states was declared, he was pastor of the First Baptist Church at Eufaula, but responded to his country's need and went forth with the first Barbour County company. He served throughout the war, returning a Major. He resumed his pastorate and served the Church until 1866, then went into the banking business with his father-in-law, but again in 1864 accepted the call to the pastorate of the same church and served through 1876.

He was a man of most magnetic personality, a brilliant

scholar and an eloquent speaker, with a smile and happy greeting for everyone whom he met. After resigning the pastorate of the Church, he accepted the superintendency of the Sunday School, and for more than ten years his Sunday School was repeatedly declared the finest Sunday School in Alabama from every standpoint.

Dr. Reeves was one of the most picturesque preachers; his peculiar way of painting with words and metaphors his descriptive and mind pictures was most fascinating.

On one occasion he took for his subject "Belshazzar's Feast" and it was pronounced a gem that shone in the Church life of the community for many years.

On another occasion he described to his congregation a terrific storm that encountered the steamship he was returning from a trip to Europe on. By request he repeated the sermon, the subject of which was, "God," and the church could not hold the people, so he preached it a third time, in the Opera House. He was a man of broad vision, keen perception and a scholar who delved deep into his subjects, giving to his hearers the essence of what his quick and powerful mind caught and held.

For many years he was president of the John McNab Bank and had large farming interests.

He built a beautiful home on Old Flake's Hill, naming it "Mount McNab," which was one of the most beautiful homes ever built in Barbour County, but soon after the death of Dr. and Mrs. Reeves it was destroyed by fire, and in that fire were lost many handsome furnishings and old family treasures.

The children born to Dr. and Mrs. Reeves were Islay, married Harmon Lampley, Feb. 22nd, 1887. To them were born three sons, Harmon, Jr., William Reeves, and Ira Tullis, all deceased. The eldest, Harmon, married Gara Hollemon and to them were born two sons, Harmon, III, and Hinton C. Harmon is a Cadet at West Point Military Academy and Hinton a high school boy.

All the other children of Dr. and Mrs. Reeves were sons: Dr. John M. Reeves, dentist, deceased; William N., Jr., married Fannie Tennille, and to them were born two daughters, Florine and Lillian.

The third son, David, and the youngest, Charles, all now deceased.

JERRY H. REEVES

Jerry Heeland Reeves was born in Dallas County near Selma, Ala., July 26th, 1847, and came to Eufaula immediately after graduating at the University of Virginia in 1871. He was one of the most prominent, progressive and enterprising citizens of Barbour County, a man of much learning and marked business ability.

For many years he was engaged in the mercantile business and was manager of the large farming interests of John McNab Bank of which he was vice president, when his brother, Dr. W. N. Reeves, succeeded their father-in-law, John McNab, as president of that institution.

He was an enthusiastic lover of Eufaula and took the lead in every project for the upbuilding of the town and county in the days of her glorious past.

During the later years of his life he was manager of the large insurance business of W. N. and J. H. Reeves. Personally he was beloved for many traits of character that made him outstanding. He was jovial, happy hearted and was appreciated by many to whom he ministered in many helpful ways throughout his life.

He was always active and enjoyed fine health, until the accident that caused his death. He was thrown from his buggy as he drove down town from his home out on the hill, receiving internal injuries that culminated in his death.

Mr. Reeves was the first man in Barbour County to ride a bicycle and he presented a unique and most imposing picture riding along on one of the big one-wheel bicycles, with the very small wheel at the bottom of the large one, as he was tall and stout, but he was a fine rider. He was a consistent and valuable member of the First Baptist Church; a deacon and a Bible Class Sunday School teacher.

In 1872 he married Elizabeth McNab, daughter of John M. McNab, pioneer banker of Eufaula, and intendant of the town, before it was made a city, and for a long time the wealthiest citizen in Barbour County. Children: Janie, married Robert M. Jennings; Malcolm McNab, married Mathilda Copeland. Their children: Janie, married Benjamin Campbell Blake, III; Malcolm married Virginia Chapman of Ripley, Tenn.; Fontaine Flewellen Reeves, married Marie Carroll, son, Fontaine, Jr.; John Morris Reeves; Bettie Reeves; Mathilda Reeves, deceased (killed by automobile running over her at 6 years of age) and Virginia Reeves.

Third child of J. H. and Elizabeth McNab Reeves, Lily, deceased; Jerry H., Jr., married Nettie Margart. Their children: Jerry H., III, married Dedora Breckenridge; Misses

Camilla, married Floy Radney; Elizabeth Reeves; Janet Reeves, married Frank W. Comer, II.

Jamie F. Reeves, son of J. H. and Elizabeth Reeves.

The Reeves home on Weston Heights, famous as one of the most hospitable in all this section, was burned down many years ago, but rebuilt, a facsmile of the original. It is on a high hill and overlooks the City of Eufaula and the Chattahoochee Valley below.

FATHER ABRAM J. RYAN
Poet Priest of the South

While Father Ryan was not born in Barbour County, the fact that he lived in the County while serving as Parish Priest at Eufaula during the year, 1867, and then twenty years after, in the eighties, made several visits back to Eufaula, and the hold that he had upon the hearts of the people of the County of all denominations, make it quite proper that he be included in the Biographical sketches of this History. The fact that Father Ryan made history wherever he abided, places him among Barbour County's most distinguished citizens.

Biographers have differed over the place of his birth—some claiming Norfolk, Va., some Hagerstown, Md., and it also has been claimed that he was born in Limerick, Ireland, in 1834 or 1936. coming to America with his parents when about seven years of age, being reared at St. Louis, Mo., where he attended the Christian Brothers College.

He early showed traits of character that foretold the moulding into the superior manhood that maturity found him —possibly not without some fault, but a man among men— not cold or selfish, but generous and kind. One who communed with God and sought for the higher and nobler things.

With a genuine and strong zeal for piety, his lofty ideas and principles lifted him above the world's narrow findings, and kept him broad minded.

His verses show his broad character. A Southerner to the core, he was unwilling to make any concession to the North, and keenly felt the sufferings of the South, yet when the War was over and peace was restored, unlike most Southerners he rejoiced in the reunited country, with charity and brotherly love and wrote more beautifully of it, than was ever penned by any other writer.

The South justly claims Father Ryan as an inspiration to the World's Religion, poetical and higher ideal life and the whole character of the man is so genuine, so romantic and idealistic that naturally he is a figure most unique.

In his career, he brought to light the elements that made

one of the old masters assert that "The love of God, the love of woman and the love of Country exemplify all the spiritual, all the romantic and material and political feelings of the world."

As an orator he had no superior in his day and his personal popularity as well as his gift of golden thought and silver tongue made him sought on all occasions as a notable personage.

It was during this period that he came again to Eufaula several times, spending weeks at a time. One time he served in place of the late Monsigner D. Savage, then pastor at Eufaula. On these occasions he was the guest of the Colby family ,next door neighbors of the writer, and although I was only a girl of 14 years, I formed a warm attachment for this man of God around whom all the children of the neighborhood flocked daily.

I recall his unique appearance—long auburn hair, eyes of genuine Irish grey-blue, with the kindliest expression of face one can conceive, large frame.

He often sat on the Colby porch and told us stories of Ireland—of the ctiy of Mobile, the Cathedral there, and the children on Sanford street loved to listen to his stories, or hear him read one of his poems.

One day Miss Susan Colby, who had been our school teacher, sitting with us said, "Father, read them "Their Story Runneth Thus," and I never hear the great beloved poet's name mentioned—but I see (with memory's eye) him sitting there in the Autumn afternoon ,the boys and girls on the steps and hte unshed tears in his eyes as he told us his own love story.

Daily, during his visits, he went to Church, which was just up the hill on Broad street and he would stop for the roses to put on the altar as he passed my home.

There was a quaint old lady, Mrs. James Sherry, who rode to church behind her husband on his mule.

She always wore a little green hat tied onto the large Chignon in which her hair was fashioned, and her shawl was wrapped around her in typical rural Irish way.

Although Father Ryan was graduated from a Seminary at Niagara Falls, N. Y., but little is known of him until the War Between the States. His love for the South and all her institutions suddenly blazed forth in his sermons, on the battle fields and his snatches of verse suggested to him by the incidents of the war.

His brother, Captain David Ryan, was slain by the bullet of a northern soldier, and this set afiire the flame of wrath smouldering in his make-up and his hatred of every phase of war incited him to often give vent to his indignation.

While serving at New Orleans, history tells that he was brought before General Butler of the Union forces on a charge of having refused to bury a dead soldier, because he was a Yankee. General Butler was very ironic in his remarks and angrily said to him: "I am told that you refused to bury a dead soldier because he was a Yankee." Why, answered Father Ryan in feigned surprise, "I was never asked to bury him and never refused. The fact is, General, it would give me great pleasure to bury the whole lot of you."

Early in the eighties (to make retreat) he retired to a Franciscan Monastery in Louisville, Ky., and finished there the "Life of Christ," that he had been engaged in writing for some time, but illness overtook him and he quietly passed away April 23rd, 1886.

His remains were carried to Mobile, Alabama.

In Father Ryan were the nappy combinations of deep piety, a high class wit and humor, and a philosophy of spiritual and material things that made him great and good. His patriotism of that God given kind that ennobled and uplifted and has left itself emblazoned on every phase of history that recalls Father Ryan.

JAMES ROSS

Among the prominent citizens of Barbour County who came from afar, and casting their lots here, became builders of the town and county was James Ross, a typical Englishman, whose personality was as strong as his judgment as fruit bearing as is only seen in results of superior citizenship.

His parents came from England to Canada, and the vicissitudes of the years brought him to Midway, Ala., in Bullock County, adjoining Barbour.

He married Miss Sarah English of Barbour County and it was about 1861 that the family moved to Eufaula, where from the small beginning of a wagon shop, he established what became the largest manufacturing plant in Barbour County for many years—a carriage, buggy and wagon factory.

He built the handsome four-story Ross building which housed these three industries and which is now owned by Edmond Foy.

This factory turned out the vast number of vehicles that supplied Southeast Alabama and Southwest Georgia, for many years as well as the many carloads shipped annually to farther off points.

The carriage department an dthe undertaking department of the business, superintended by Mr. Harry Sasser, son of the man for whom the town of Sasser, Georgia, was named. This man who was an expert made with his own hands a handsome burial casket that proved to be so large it did not readily sell, and was stored away.

Twelve years afterward, when Mr. Sasser died, he had grown so stout that he was buried in this casket, made with special care by his own hands.

Mr. Ross' business ventures were all successful and his personal influence and civic interest had a large part in the progress of Barbour County and the glory of the Eufaula of that day. Mr. Ross purchased "Monterey," the home of Barbour County's war Governor, John Gill Shorter, and the family lived in this old mansion until it was burned, moving to the home on Randolph street, which was the family home until after his death, and the children all married and were established in other homes.

He was a leading member of St. James Episcopal church, a master Mason and a valuable citizen in every way.

His children and grandchildren have all carried out the family traditions and are carrying on to interest of the County and town in which they have and now lived and now live.

They were, viz: Ida, married Robert C. Ross, issue daughter, Alice, married W. A. Medlock, sons, Frank, James, deceased.

Alice married Theodore Pruden, issue Ida, married Henry Weil, issue, daughter, Alice; Nell married John deTreville, issue, son, Pruden.

Eugene married Bonny Brown; Theodore, Jr., married Ludie Johnson; Charles R. married Florrie Kendall, issue, sons, Kendall H., married Charlie Kaigler; Charles R., Jr., bachelor; Julia married Gordon Wilson, issue, Robert Gordon, Jr.

William, deceased; Henry deceased.

James L. married Mary Weedon, issue daughters Mary, married Humphrey Foy; Sarah married A. S. Dozier.

Edward Hill married Eugenie Poston, issue, Margaret, married Robert Jones; Charles Robert married Hazel Coleman, issue, Charles Robert; William Poston married Mildred Sauls; James Lidden; Sarah; John, married Venie McInnis; and H. E. H., Jr.

Sallie Ross married Frank L. Bloodworth, deceased; Clara, deceased, married Dr. Frank Bloodworth; Clifford, unmarried.

JACOB RAMSER

Jacob Ramser and his wife (Singer) Ramser, were natives of Germany, coming from Lumpkin, Georgia, to Barbour County in pioneer days and locating at Eufaula.

He was a furniture dealer and undertaker and amassed a fortune from his integrity of character and personal industry.

He was progressive and built five or six store houses on Broad street in Eufaula. Two of these were made into the Lee theatre some years ago, two were made into the commodious three-story Ramser building, now owned by R. M. McEachern, and is still used as a furniture store. Other Ramser buildings were purchased by Dean and Moore years ago.

He built the old Colonial Ramser home, corner Barbour and Forsythe streets and it was there that this hospitable couple, with all the traditions of the "Fatherland" that made the German homes notable in song and story, reared their large family.

With Jacob Ramser came his brother, Ursus who also was a progressive and honored citizen many years. He never married, but was greatly attached to his nephews and nieces who were devoted to him.

Jacob Ramser was a philanthropic man and gave large of his means to every cause of the community. He was an enthusiastic Mason and a man of much learning and wide information. It was a treat to listen to his stories of his childhood.

His children were, viz: Pauline, married Daniel McNeill, issue Ursus, married Anna Carroll.

Jacob, married; Oscar, married; Mamie, married.

Mary married Bowers, issue; Fanny married F. H. Tripp, deceased; Jacob S., bachelor; Major, deceased, married Annie Ogletree.

Laura married Edward P. Blair, issue; Marie married Joe Holland, deceased; Orsie married Charles; Edna married Edgar T. Long; Charles Blair, married.

Anna married J. B. Crawford, issue, Dr. Ramser Crawford, prominent physician, New York City. Anderson Crawford and Fulmore Crawford, issue, one daughter, Annie Laurie, married Duard Lagrand, issue, son, Duard, and daughter, Annie Laurie.

Thomas J. married Annie Dozier, issue, Mary, married Arthur E. Stanbury, their children, Ann and Ramser, two sons, Julian and Dozier Ramser.

Emma married Luther Bell, issue, daughter, Mary married Leonard, one son, deceased.

GEORGE ALBERT ROBERTS

George Albert Roberts was a member of the distnguished Roberts family of Culpepper County, Va., and a number of this family have had a part in making Barbour County famous for illustrious families.

He married Ann Oliver from Twiggs County, Georgia, and their home on North Eufaula street in Eufaula was notable as the years passed. Albert Roberts was a man of that force of character that leaves impressions for good wherever its influence reaches and in Barbour County it went far and was effective. As Mayor of the city of Eufaula he was honored and his judgment respected and in private life his genuineness and high principles wrought for good in all conditions and emergencies. He was a Christian gentleman, a substantial and valuable citizen. The sons and only daughter of this family were devoted to the historic old home town, their parents helped to make notable.

They were: Anna who married Judge W. H. Pruett, issue one son, Albert Roberts Pruett.

The eldest son, Noah W. Roberts, married Carrie Young, uniting two of the first old families and were both loved to a degree most unusual.

Mac S., like his older brother, spent his life, an attachee of Eufaula banks and knew the business like he knew the alphabet.

William R., a merchant, died in the zenith of manhood, Clarence Pope was bank cashier and also president of the Commercial National Bank until his health forced him to retire from business. He was like his brothers, a superior business man and a valuable citizen.

Clarence P. Roberts was not only a man of wonderful business ability and accuracy in all he attempted to do as a busy man of affairs, but he was conservative in judgment and was a great help in the bringing of success to all local undertakings. Not only was he an asset to the banks of which he was both cashier and treasurer, but to the First Baptist Church he was a power of material and spiritual strength.

After the burning of the First Baptist Church in 1907 and its subsequent rebuilding, Mr. Roberts was chairman of the building Committee, and to his untiring efforts and daily work was due the result of a tremendous job. As deacon of this church, he was of that number who was most valuable.

He married Georgia Archibald, a member of the distinguished Archibald family of Oxford, Miss., and was a granddaughter of David Reese of Revolutionary fame, issue, Elmir, married Charles Frank Pleas; Archibald B. Roberts married Clara Foy, issue, Frankie and Georgianna, and a son.

Kate Roberts married L. Comer Jennings, issue two sons, Comer, Jr., and Robert.

Edward H. Roberts grew up, finished college and entered

the U. S. Navy as assistant paymaster. While at home on leave, he infected his hand with an electric wire, which caused blood poison from which he died, leaving a young wife, Mary Lou (MacKenzie) and a baby daughter, Caroline, who married J. R. Williams and they have a son, Junior Williams.

JOHN D. ROQUEMORE

John D. Roquemore was born in Barbour County August 27th 1846, son of Zackarah and Julia McGifory of Alabama. He attended the County schools at home and when a Cadet at the University of Alabama at 17 years of age, dropped his studies, shouldered his musket for the Confederacy, became a member of "Nelson's Rangers" and was personal escort for Stephen D. Lee.

In 1867, he was admitted to the Bar at Clayton, Ala., but practiced law at Eufaula.

In 1876 he was appointed one of a commission to revise and codify the statutes of the state, which was a most important work, requiring much wisdom and forethought.

In 1878 he was elected to represent Barbour County in the State Senate and was made member of the Judiciary committee and Senate leader.

He declined to offer for reelection and in 1886 formed a law partnership with Joe M. White of Clayton and Jackson E. Long, of Eufaula. After Mr. Long's death he was with Mr. S. H. Dent, Jr., as member of the firm in Montgomery, Ala.

He was attorney for the Central of Georgia Railway Company and director of the Decatur Land Company. He was president of the first White Man's Club ever organized in Barbour County. This club was a great organization and featured in activities for the best interests of the state and County.

A man of high ideals, integrity and Christian character, he was for many years teacher of the Young People's Bible class of the First Baptist church (of which this writer was a member). His weekly letcures were gems of thought, words and eloquence that have been "memories to bliss" and uplift.

In 1886 he was appointed Adjutant General of Alabama and received his B. A. degree from the University of Alabama.

In 1876 he married Mary Hunter, daughter of John Lingard, II, and Sarah Shorter Hunter. To them were born Hunter, Mary Annie, John and Zack. In 1887 he married Henrietta Brown of Boston, Mass., a charming young woman who came South to teach the special features of higher education to the children of Prof. J. C. Van Houten, and the marriage of these two unusually distinguished persons was the happy fruition of a romance begun when, to Prof. Van Houten's wonderful playing, Miss Brown at a concert recited and danced the "Money Musk," a highly classical number. Col. Roquemore, in the audience, was charmed and entranced. (See Reveries of Prof. Van Houten's Old Violin). Before many months there came the marriage, and not long after, removal of the family to Montgomery. To this second marriage was born one lovely daughter.

Colonel Roquemore died in the very zenith of a brilliant career, but his lovely wife and daughter spend their time divided between Boston and Montgomery, and the elder sons and daughters all reside in Montgomery.

SWANSON

William C. Swanson, perhaps more than any man in the state, has the reputation for ready information on most any call for accuracy and efficiency, and is looked upon as "Barbour County's obliging bureau of information."

He was born in Barbour County in Dec., 1866, the son of Thomas and Ann (Cobb) Swanson, pioneer settlers of Old Spring Hill.

He attended the Public schools of Midway, the Male Academy of Craven and Patterson at Eufaula and the Southern University at Greenville, Ala.

After two years as clerk for Probate Judge A. H. Alston at Clayton, he was Congressional clerk, under Congressman William C. Oates at Washington, 1888 and 1889; took law courses at University of Alabama, where he received his L. L. B. degree.

In 1890 he was appointed Register in Chauncery at Eufaula, holding this office nine or ten years. In 1902, he was appointed by his personal friend, Gov. Jelks, auditing clerk in the State Superintendent of Education's office at Montgomery.

In 1909 he was supervisor of United States Census; 1910 employed in the General Auditing offices of the Southern Express Company, Chattanooga, Tenn; 1918 in the Fiscal Agency Div., Federal Reserve Bank, Atlanta, Georgia; 1919-1923 chief clerk in the state auditor's office at Montgomery, and since 1925 has been chief assistant of the Judge of Probates' office at Clayton.

During his varied career of holding intricate and high class positions of great responsibility, he has maintained a program of procedure where accuracy, ability and faithful service have won for him an enviable reputation as a business man and broad-minded citizen.

He is a scholar, a reader and a thinker, and a versatile writer, whose newspaper and magazine articles are not only delightfully interesting to read, but are full of the highest standards of thinking and living. His memory of dates and happenings is most remarkable, and his genial personality, displayed to the large number of different types of human beings he deals wtih daily, furnishing them information on almost every subject conceivable has stamped him a man of wonderful patience with consideration for others.

HUGO SCHLOSS

Hugh Schlos was born in Oppach, Barvaria, Germany, coming to New York when very young. In 1871 he came to Eufaula, Barbour County, as cutter and manager of the tailoring department of Isaac Steurman, later Steurman and Schold, clothiers.

Soon after this time, the business was purchased by H. Schloss and J. W. Huddleston, and in 1895 Mr. Schloss bought the Huddleston interest.

Until 1910, when he retired, Mr. Schloss has owned the largest wholesale and retail clothing and tailoring business in Southeast Alabama and Southwest Georgia, selling to to Mr. S. D. Roth, who occupies the same building with his clothing business of today.

Through all those years Mr. Schloss was a business success in all the assertion implies. Socially he was the man with a smile, with the roses on lips, their fragrance penetrating his own life and the lives of all with whom he came in contact. Courteous, affable, his influence was given to and his purse was always generously open to every cause for the betterment of the community. No call for help was ever turned down by him and his familiar presence about the streets was one of the daily pleasures of his many warm friends. No man was better known in Southeast Alabama and Southwest Georgia; was member of Board of Trustees Union Female College; city schools; director of the East Alabama National Bank; member of City Council; Harmony Lodge 46, F. A. A. M. Lodge 912; I. O. O. F. He was big hearted, progressive, philanthropic, enthusiastic and useful. A man whom everyone who knew him honored and loved.

He loved Barbour County with a patriotic devotion and felt a strong personal pride in her welfare.

Broad in his views in all things, he always contributed liberally, annually to the support of every church in the City of Eufaula.

His death was a serious blow to Barbour County's every interest.

Hugo Schloss married first Jennie Steuerman, who died before the end of their first year of wedded life; married second Rachael Menderson, daughter of M. Menderson, capitalist of Cincinnati, Ohio. She was, like her husband, a power for good in all the benevolent and helpful activities of the Community. Her carriage for many years was seen daily carrying her about the ctiy, looking after the sick and needy, and her charitable work in Barbour County is a monument to the good works of a good woman, greatly beloved.

After Mr. Schloss' death the family moved to New York, and never has a family left a community, who has been more missed in every circle, than this distinguished and beloved family.

They are Mrs. Rachael Menderson Schloss, New York City, children, Dr. Oscar Menderson Schloss, nationally famous baby specialist, Bellview, N. Y., married Roberta Cornell.

Nettie Schloss married H. A. Moses, Sumpter, S. C.; Florence Schloss married Raymond Smith, New York; Nathan Schloss, unmarried.

WILLIAM GREENE SUTLIVE

One of the outstanding newspaper men and fine citizens, who is proud that Barbour County is his birthplace, is William Greene Sutlive, who was born at Clayton, Alabama, March 18th, 1873. He is the son of John W. and Etta Kirkland Sutlive, prominent citizens of that day. As a boy he worked on the Cuthbert Georgia Liberal for a time. He went to Savannah, Georgia, as a youth and worked for the Savannah Evening Times and later for the Savannah Evening Press. He was gradually promoted on the Evening Press from cub reporter to editor; is a past president of the Georgia Press Association, and was the first daily newspaper editor to be elected to office in the Georgia Press Association.

He is a Past Grand Chancellor of the Knights of Pythias of Georgia and is affiliated with the Odd Fellows, Masons and other fraternal orders. He is a Past Commandant of Francis Bartow Camp Sons of Confederate Veterans at Savannah, eligible for membership, through the record of his father in the Army, 9th Georgia Regiment C. S. A.

He served two terms as president of the Savannah Chamber of Commerce and nearly 20 years as a member of the Board of Education of Savannah and is a member of the Presbyterian Church at Savannah. Mr. Sutlive is a scholarly and forceful writer, whose editorials go straight to the point and his articles always bear the earmarks of the deep thinker. Personally he is of genial, gracious manner and is an enviable asset to every feature of the papers he has so long been serving.

He married Josephine Laffiteau in Savannah and they have four sons, John Kirkland, Carey and Charles, and one daughter, Josephine. Kirkland is a citizen of Blackshear, Ga., and Carey of Brunswick, Ga.

Ten years ago, when this history was first begun, and mentioned in the newspapers as likely to be written, Mr. Sutlive was the first person to order a copy, saying "My childhood love for Barbour County has grown with the years, and I want to see a history of the grand old state of Barbour."

WILLIAM CHAPPELL STANDIFER

WILLIAM CHAPPELL STANDIFER

William Chappell Standifer was born in Barbour County, on a farm which he bought in the late years because of sentiment, and has made it into a modern 100-acre farm 9 miles from Eufaula. His wife has planted over a thousand roses and many hundred fruit trees and grape vines, turning it into a beautiful show place. He is the son of William and Eliza (Hatfield) Standifer, pioneer citizen of Barbour County.

When a youth he began teaching a country school. Coming to the city, he began clerking for the Foy Hardware store, which position he held 18 years, and for the past 25 years he has been division distributor for the Gulf Refining Co. He is a highly self educated man who has spent his life in strenuous effort to accomplish for himself and family the nobler and better things of life, and although he had no college training, he is one of the most scholarly and best informed men of the community.

He and his wife (Leonora Hughes) who is an enthusiastic home maker and a woman of superior qualities, have reared a large family, each one a credit to their parents. They are Bessie Louise, married Joseph H. Hall, Brooklyn, N. Y., and is one of the outstanding women of the literary world and a practicing attorney in New York. Luther married Louise Steele. He was manager of Rich's Shoe Department, Atlanta, when killed by an automobile enroute to Atlanta. He leaves a daughter Leonora, a son, Luther, the former a gifted reader and elocutionist; Guy, drowned at Newport News, while in the U. S. Navy, doing his routine work; John married Louise Palmer, two children, Vivian and Rannie Will; Cornelia married Bates, who holds a position in Montgomery; one daughter, Edna.

REUBEN C. SHORTER

When Reuben C. Shorter was born in Culpepper County, Virginia, there was recorded on the pages of American history a descendant of Sir John Shorter, Lord Mayor of London, and it is interesting to know that Lady Catherine of Walpole, Sir John's oldest daughter, was his mother.

When he graduated from the Medical University of Philidelphia, he settled in Twigs County, Georgia, and there he married Mary Gill, daughter of John and Martha Gill.

He had become a General in the United States Army; had amassed a fortune and, hearing through Georgia bankers, of the boom in the lands on the Chattahoochee river, he came to the village of Eufaula in Barbour County, bought much land and built the beautiful, historic old Shorter mansion, overlooking the high Chattahoochee bluff. There, in the most beautiful and picturesque home, one can conceive, he reared a large family; but in the early seventies the lure of the Western hills enticed and this home was torn away and the fine material used in the building of Shorter Opera House, on Broad street, by Kolb, Couric and Hayes, a large Cotton firm. Kolb and Couric were descendants and heirs of Reuben Shorter.

This opera house had years of interesting history, and today the Eufaula Hardware Company occupies its historic site.

Children: The eldest daughter, Sarah E. Shorter, married James Linguard Hunter and to them were born two daughters.

Sarah Hunter, who married first Dr. J. K. Battle and their one child was Dr. Julius K. Battle, Jr., who married Effie Jennings, no issue; Mary Hunter married John D. Roquemore and to them were born four children: Mary ,deceased, John D., Jr., Sarah; Annie; Jack. Emily Francis Shorter married David C. Kolb and to them was born Reuben F. Kolb, who married Callie Cargill. Their children were: Emily F. and Reuben F., and Howard Kolb.

Emily Kolb married Luscious Richardson, Reuben F. married Ruth Scott; Howard married; Martha Gill Shorter married Captain William H. McKleroy, and to them was born

William H. McKleroy, II. He married Martha Woods, daughter of William Henry Woods. To them was born a son, William H., III, and a daughter, Hattie.

Mittie McKleroy married Rev. J. Stratten Pauling, a distinguished Baptist minister, to them was born a son, John.

Mary McKleroy married Randall Flewellen, had no children, but after the death of her sister, Mittie, adopted her little son and changed his name to John Flewellen.

Sarah McKleroy married Alfred Alexis Couric, and to them was born Alfred Alexis, who married first Nettie Nix, to them was born a daughter, Martha Gill, deceased in infancy; married second Willie Copeland, daughter of Dr. W. P. and Mary Fountaine Flewellen Copeland, and to them have been born, Alfred Copeland, married Leola Swann, issue a son Alfred Copeland Jr. Milliam unmarried and Charles married Marie Shackelford.

William McKleroy Couric married Gertha Long daughter of E. T. and Mamie Rhodes Long, to whom two children were born, Mamie Long, and Alec, deceased.

John Martin Couric married Wildie Hibbler; children, Charlotte and John Martin, Jr.

Carl M. Couric, deceased, married Mary Wagner, children, Mary O'Neil; Edmundson, Jr.

Junius Battle Couric married Bessie Welch, children, William Battle and Robert.

Katherine Couric (deceased) married W. J. Willingham, one child, died in infancy, and a son, W. J. Willingham, Jr.

Misses Mollie and Pauline Couric, other two daughters still live at the historic old Couric home on Eufaula street.

Laura Shorter married Thomas W. Cowles, son of the General Thomas Cowles of the illustrious Cowles family of Montgomery, Ala.

Their children were John Shorter Cowles, married Elizabeth Pattillo, children, Laura, Sallie, Alton.

William Thornton Cowles married first Edith Pope and second Annie Pope. Children, William and John Cowles, attorneys of Jacksonville, Fla. John Cowles was assassinated at Jacksonville, Fla., in 1926, when he was protecting a lady who was living in an apartment in his home.

Thomas W. Cowles, deceased, before reaching manhood; Mary Butler Shorter, second daughter of Reuben Shorter, married Dr. William Horatio Thornton, first mayor of Eufaula, and beloved physician.

The four lovely daughters of this couple grew up in Eufaula, belles of Eufaula's glorious days.

Laurt, the eldest, married George Legare Comer, brilliant lawyer and mayor of Eufaula ten years. He was outstanding citizen of Barbour County and of the state of Alabama. Their children, William Thornton, deceased, married first Lily Brockett; second Alamada Holcombe, Atlanta; John Wallace, deceased, married Sadie Patterson of Anniston, Ala.; George Legare, II, married Glennie Cunningham, Nashville, Tenn.; Laurie, eldest daughter, married Frank Wilkins Jennings, deceased; Frank Willis, deceased, married Montine Roddenberry; Edward Tripp, deceased, married Catherine Jelks, deceased; Robert and (Nell, deceased), and little Walter, 11 years old, was drowned in the Chattahoochee river May, 1886, when some larger boys enticed him in bathing.

James Drewry Comer married first Mary McCormick. Born to them, James D., Jr., deceased; married second, Annie Moses, Atlanta, Ga.

Miss Mary Comer resides at the old home in Eufaula.

Anna Thornton, the second daughter, married George Henson Estes, of Georgia, but who spent many years in Barbour County. Their children: Brigadier General Henson Estes, U. S. Army, retired, married Fanny Sparrow; Mary married Bardwell, Atlanta; Edith married William Stokely; Martha married Lesese DeWitt; Thornton married Julia somebody of Blount Springs.

Charles married Margaret Sylvester, daughter of J. Asbury Sysvester of the distinguished Sylvester family of Barbour County.

Claud a man from Swann, Tennessee, and Thomas Estes married a girl from Birmingham.

Sallie Thornton married Edward Edward T. Graham many years Mayor of Montgomery, and distinguished Alabama attorney.

Their children were: Amelia, married first Stokely; married second W. J. Sanford of Knoxville, Tenn.

Annie married Rev. Eugene L. Hill, pastor of the Presbyterian Church at Athens, Ga., the past 25 years and has been elected to that pastorate for life. (Was pastor of the Presbyterian Church at Eufaula from 1901 to 1906, when called to Athens).

Mary (deceased) married T. J. Wood.

Dorothy married George Deaderick of the U. S. Army.

Edward Thornton is married and is a prominent citizen of Montgomery   Willie Thornton and Rebecca died when a young girl.

Retta Fayne Thornton married first Thomas G. Berry, to them was born a daughter, who married James Callaway of the distinguished Callaway family of Georgia. They reside in Columbus, Ga. Children: May Shorter, Caroline and James. Married second Clifford A. Locke of the Locke and Sylvester families of Barbour County. Born to them were Marie, deceased, married Carl Strang, left a son, Shorter Thornton

Strang; Retta married Bushman H. Jackson, born to them a daughter, Retta and a son, Bushman, J. They reside in New Orleans, La.

Clifford A., Jr., married Julia Cargill, daughter of E. K. Cargill and Bessie Simpson Cargill. They reside at Miami, Fla, children, Bettie.

The old Thornton-Comer home presided over by Miss Mary Comer is full of sacred memories of the years that Mary Shorter Thornton reigned queen mother of this large family and later her eldest daughter, Laura Comer, taking her place.

JOHN GILL SHORTER

The new Shorter home, "Monterey," built out on the hill, was Alabama's war governor's home. John Gill Shorter was born in Jasper County, Ga., April 23, 1818. After graduating at the University of Virginia, he came to his new home in Eufaula. His father, General Reuben Clarke Shorter, had not long been located at his new home, and his career, up to his election, to the governorship of Alabama, had been eventful.

He had served Barbour County in every official capacity and it was during the three terms of his judgeship that the crisis of secession came on and he was appointed a commissioner to the secession Convention of Georgia to secure the co-operation of Alabama in the movement contemplated.

JOHN GILL SHORTER

In 1861 he resigned his judgeship to accept a seat in the Provincial Congress of Confederate States and served in that capacity both in Montgomery and Richmond, until elected governor of Alabama.

His record throughout the war, says several biographers, was notable for moral courage, and nobility of character, and few public men have been so beloved."

His wife, Mary (Battle Shorter), daughter of Dr. Archibald Battle, of Georgia, and their daughter and only child, Mollie Shorter, married first T. J. Perkins at the new home "Monterey" out on the hill, and the wedding was the most brilliant affair in the social history of the county. A widow many years, she was happily married to B. L. Willingham of Macon, Georgia. After his death she returned to Eufaula, making her home with the Couric family. When she died a few years ago she was buried in the old Shorter family cemetery overlooking the Chattahoochee river, near where the old Mansion stood on the bluff, beside her distinguished parents and grandparents.

ELI SIMS SHORTER

Eli Sims Shorter, third son of General and Mrs. Reuben C. Shorter, graduated at Yale College in 1884, delivering the Salutatory address.

The Congressional District, of which Barbour County was a part, had always been the stronghold of the "Whiggs," a Democrat never having represented it. The political records show that in 1855 there was a strong determination to change this if possible.

Col. Shorter was elected to the next Congress and when he took his seat in the National Congress he acted in the Southern Rights wing of his party and was reelected in 1857.

During his Congressional experiences, he made a National reputation as a brilliant, forceful and effective speaker, who held his audience with influence.

During the presidential campaign of 1868, he canvassed for the ticket, as he did again in 1876. His friend, Thomas A. Hendrix, had intentions for him a cabinet portfolio, but his death in 1879 prevented this.

His wife, Marietta Fannin, daughter of Col. Fannin of LaGrange, Georgia, was greatly beloved in Eufaula and the beautiful home out on the hill across the (now Country Club Road) from "Monterey" was where she reared her children, and until it was burned was one of Barbour's grand old homes, where Shorter culture was paramount.

Adjoining this still stands "Highland View," owned by Mrs. C. P. Roberts, the beautiful home Col. Shorter built and presented to his daughter, Annie Shorter Leftwich, who married Col. J. H. Leftwich, a distinguished citizen of Virginia, and a prominent figure in the Cotton business of Barbour County for some years. Children: Reta, Annie, Elizabeth and Clement Shorter.

On the shoulders of the eldest son, Clement Clay Shorter fell the political mantle of his father, and when death claimed him he was representing Barbour County as Speaker of the House. A bright future loomed before him when the dark winged reaped suddenly cut him down. Eli Sims Shorter, II, was known as the silver tongued orator of Alabama, and was a scholar of highest merit, an orator whose speeches held you tensely and a man among men, much loved for a unique personality.

He married Wylena Lamar, daughter of Col. Henry J. Lamar of Macon, Ga.; and the romance of their life is one of the most beautiful ever known to a family or friends. She was a brilliant woman of letters, and to her friends was the generous, sincere "Lady O' Love" and beauty of thought and action, always.

To them were born, Alberta, married N. D. Eubank, Atlanta, Ga.; Fanny, married Herman L. Upshaw, Eufaula, issue Wylena Shorter, 1937 debutante.

ELI SIMS SHORTER III

Like the predecessors bearing his name, he was an outstanding and beloved citizen carrying out the personal and business plans of his parents and notable for charity and the lending of a helping hand, whereever he saw or heard of any need. His death Dec. 3rd, 1934, claimed a most valuable citizen. He embodied all the traits that had made his illustrious ancestors honored and beloved. Few Young men ever find the place in the hearts of the communiy that he did for kindness and usefulness to a community.

He married Orline O'Daniel, daughter of Dr. William and Mattie (Carswell) O'Daniel of Milledgeville and Bullock, Georgia.

These three daughters of his branch of the family, Mrs. Eubank, Mrs. Upshaw and Mrs. Eli S. Shorter, III, are exceptionally fine young women, whose personality, generosity and philanthropy has made them greatly beloved. They are holding up the old traditions of the family in a way that gives joy that will bear fruit through all time.

HENRY R. SHORTER

Henry Russell Shorter was a citizen who was a credit not only to Barbour County and the state of Alabama, but to the entire South and to the Shorter name. For many years he was a leader in the political life of Barbour County and added to the list of Barbour Statesmen, one of the brightest stars that has beamed down the years.

For many years he was railroad commissioner of Alabama, and one of the best known civil and criminal lawyers in the state   In Barbour County he was always sought for advice on weighty matters.

He married Addie Keitt, daughter of Mrs. A. B. Treadwell and "Buena Vista," the beloved old home built by her, is now the home of Major and Mrs. Shorter's second daughter, Alice Keitt Shorter Jelks, where she lives surrounded by beautiful flowers, and the rare and sacred old family relics that adorn this home—spending her time as beloved mother and grandmother, supplying the vacancies death has caused in their home and cherished the memories of former gloriously happy days.

She is loved for her generosity and thoughtfulness for the poor and distressed and the first thought of lovely woman, who was a queen in her young days, now finds her greatest joy in "helpfulness" to someone else.

She married William Dorsey Jelks, Barbour County's second gubernatorial gift to the State of Alabama.

First came the loss of her young sister, beautiful, beloved Louise, the youngest child of the home, cut down 'ere she was twenty years of age; then her brother, Harry R., Jr., just beginning a brilliant law career; following in a few years her elder sister, Dellie Shorter Hanson; then her beloved and distinguished husband, Gov. Jelks; and just recently her only child, winsome, lovely, admired and beloved Catherine Jelks Comer whose passing wrapped in gloom a community where all her life this generous hearted, benevolent young woman, following in the footsteps of her mother, grandmother and great grandmother, had looked after the needs of all the poor and affflicted in the Community.

The son, Harry R., married Loula Fendley of Alabama, and his widow, and the widow of Eli S. Shorter, III, both childless, are the only two living today who bear the illustrious Shorter name of this family.

Catherine Shorter Jelks married Edward Tripp Comer, son of Col. G. L. and Laura Thornton Comer. To them were born William Jelks Comer, Edward T. Comer, Jr., and Alice Shorter Comer.

Dellie Shorter married Charles Clinton Hanson, prominent business man and most of their married life was spent in Memphis, Tenn. She is buried in the family lot in Fairview cemetery.

Major and Mrs. H. R. Shorter and his sister, Laura Shorter, who married Thomas W. Cowles, were married at beautiful weddings in March of 1854.

Mrs. Shorter and her mother, Mrs. Treadwell, were the leading "Good Samaritans."

SPARKS

Judge Chauncey Sparks was born October 8th, 1884, in Barbour County, son of George W. Sparks and Sarah (Castellow) Sparks. When a lad the family moved to the Sparks plantation near Morris, Georgia, in Quitman County, Georgia.

He attended the public schools of Quitman County, graduated from Mercer University with A. B. degree in 1907; was Valedictorian of his class and received his L. L. B. degree from Mercer University in 1910.

The family moved to Eufaula where he began the practice of law; was appointed by Governor O'Neal, Judge of the Inferior Court, Precinct five, Barbour County, serving from July, 1911, to December, 1916.

He was 2nd Lieut. of Co. G. Second Infantry National Guards from April, 1912, to April 1915.

JUDGE CHAUNCEY SPARKS

He represented the legislature in 1918; was reelected in 1930, and is a valued member of the Third Judicial Circuit Bar Association, Alabama, and State Bar Association.

He is a member of the Baptist Church; vice president of the Eufaula Bank and Trust Co.; a fine lawyer, who knows the law to every letter, and a student and thinker; a most eloquent speaker and entertainer; a man of civic and patriotic pride and a most valuable citizen. He is one of the foremost politicians of the County and State.

It was clearly evident in the Alabama State Senate sessions, Judge Sparks was the man of the hour. He was a leader in all the important measures and his opinions had weight. He is broadminded, conservative and has shown good, sound judgment in his opinions.

JOHN JOSHUA SPEIGHT

John Joshua Speight was born in Eufaula, Barbour County, July 24th, 1885, son of John W. and Emma Cobb

Speight, the former born in Georgia, February, 1848 and the latter born in Barbour County, July 19th, 1859.

The Speight family is of Scotch-Irish ancestry, one of whom was Richard Dobbs Speight, one of the signers of the Constitution of the United States, from North Carolina, and

JOHN JOSHUA SPEIGHT

was the grandfather of John Seth Speight of North Carolina, who came to Randolph County, Ga., and later to Eufaula, Barbour County, Ala., where he died some years ago. During the War Between the States, he was a conscript officer of the Confederate Army. His second wife was a Miss Williams of Georgia.

John W. Speight moved to Barbour County from Cuthbert, Georgia, in 1884, and is today one of the most distinguished looking men, despite his 86 years. He is tall and erect, with flowing snowwhite beard, a polished gentleman of the old school type, whom it is a joy to converse with. He is active and interested and since retiring from active business, only two years ago, he spends his time visiting among his children. Until his retirement he rode his horse daily to his farm several miles from town, sometimes several times daily. He was engaged in the mercantile and cattle business, besides his farming, for over fifty years.

His children are Oscar Cobb, Captain in 116th Infantry, Rainbow Division, World War, who married Beatrice Johnson of Dallas, Tex., has several children; Seth, who has always been associated with his father in the mercantile business and now heads the farming and cattle business. He married Posey Jones, daughter of Mr. and Mrs. E. H. Jones of Barbour County. Maro married Lester Boothe of Dallas, Texas, associated with Journal and News, Dallas, Texas.

Jesse Earl, secretary of Alabama State Senate, married Lois Colquitt. One child was born to them, Thomas, field secretary of the Farm and Loan Company, Dothan, Ala., married Martha Clark of St. Louis, two children.

John Joshua, after graduating in high school at the age of 16, went to Washington, D. C., with Congressman H. D. Clayton as private secretary from 1902 to 1914. From 1919 to 1914 he was minute reference clerk on the floor of the House of Representatives, and from 1911 to 1914 was clerk of the Judiciary Committee of the House. During all this time Young Speight studied dilligently the higher educational branches his early secretarial work prevented. He attended Washington and Lee University at Lexinfiton, Va., and in 1911 took his law degree from Georgetown University at Washington. He is a Phi Delta Phi and Phi Kamma Delta fraternity man; was admitted to the Bar in 1913 at Ozark, Ala., Aug. 16, 1913 and leaving Washington practiced law at Ozark. He was appointed Referee in Bankruptcy for Southern Division of the Middle Judicial District of Alabama and is still serving in that capacity.

He is a Democrat, a Baptist; a Kiwanian and a member of Dothan Camp W. O. W. and member of Alabama State Bar Association.

He married Ruth Wood, daughter of Edward and Ella Wood, of West Webster, New York. Children, Betty Clayton, married, and John J., Jr.

THOMAS J. SEARCEY

Conceding the fact that a collector of Public Funds must needs be a man of superior ability, when Barbour County voters chose T. J. Searcey for Tax Collector, their act was most wise. During his long service in this capacity, his books and every act of his administration proved him peculiarly fitted for this office. His annual calls on the tax payers were occasions of pleasure, rather than annoying, because he went about his duties in an affable manner.

A leading citizen of the county, personally as well as officially, he made his term of office notable in the County's annals.

THOMAS J. SEARCEY

SPURLOCK FAMILY

There is no family in Barbour County more worthy of special biography than the Spurlock family. James Madison and Tabatha (Hawthorn) Spurlock were pioneer citizens of Barbour County, the old Spurlock home four and a half miles north of Eufaula, being one of the historic old hospitable homes of the long ago. There this interesting couple reared their children and while their home was in the country, they were an important part of the church, school and social life of the city.

The eldest son, James M., Jr., died in the early days of splendid young manhood; the eldest daughter, Ella, married Robert E. Greir, one of Eufaula's expert accountants, and prominent Eufaula business men. The younger daughter, Eula, also died in the full flush of beautiful young womanhood and the second son, Osburn R. Spurlock, Sr., (of whom this sketch directly treats) married Annie Freeman, daughter of

Tandy R. and Eliza (Roquemore) Freeman, also prominent pioneer citizens of Barbour County, who many years ago moved to Texas.

O. R. Spurlock was born at the country home north of Eufaula and received his education in the schools of Eufaula, making a record of splendid marks and reports as a student.

He was from boyhood an enthusiast, and whatever he undertook he carried to a finish of perfection.

For a long time he was associated in the general merchandise business with J. B. Searcy at Eufaula, after which has was associated with the W. C. Bradley Company of Columbus, Ga., as traveling salesman and as a "knight of the grip," he had no superior. He is well known in Southeast Alabama and Southwest Georgia, and esteemed for his genial personality, sterling integrity and business ability.

Just a few years since poor health caused him to give up traveling, and he opened a fancy grocery business in Eufaula, where his son, Eugene Spurlock and his wife, assist him.

An interesting feature of the Spurlock family is the fact that four of the five sons are engaged in the grocery business.

The eldest son, Tady R, was for many years associated with the W. C. Bradley Grocery Company at Columbus also, but late years has been in the retail grocery and market business in Eufaula.

MRS. O. R. SPURLOCK   MR. O. R. SPURLOCK

James M. is a member of the firm of Marshall-Spurlock Wholesale Grocers.

Osborn, Jr., is proprietor of the Spurlock Wholesale Grocery Company, while W. Eugene is associated with the McCormick Grocery Company.

The two daughters, Mrs. H. C. Glenn (Carrie Spurlock) and Mrs. W. K. Hogan (Annie Spurlock) are both brilliant women, who are leaders in Church, educational, literary and musical circles. Like their mother, they are interested in all the patriotic, benevolent uplifting interests of the community. Mrs. Spurlock served several terms as president of Barbour County Chapter United Daughters of the Confederacy, as did Mrs. Glenn, and President of the Woman's Auxiliary of the First Methodist Church.

The fifth son of this popular family, Hugh Spurlock, holds a responsible position with the engineering department of the Southern Telephone and Telegraph Company at Birmingham. He married Ollie Kendrick, children, son, Hugh and daughter, Betty Green; Tandy R. married Fedora Hill, Columbus. Their children, one daughter, Fedora. James married Mary Louise Britt, and has one daughter, Lucy and one son, James, Jr. Osborn R., Jr., married Esther Rish and has two daughters, Barbara Sue and Esther, and one son, Ben Rish.

Mr. and Mrs. H. C. Glenn, Jr., have one daughter, Anna Barbara, and one son, H. C., II a theological student at Duke University. He has already been licensed to preach by the Methodist Conference. Mr. and Mrs. W. K. Hogan have one little daughter, Carrie Spurlock Hogan.

DR. PAUL PULLEN SALTER

Dr. Paul Pullen Salter was born at Evergreen, Alabama, August 25, 1891, son of Mitchell B. Salter and grandson of John Buford Salter—the entire family connection being prominent pioneer citizens of Evergreen and people of wealth and culture, owning extensive lands and many slaves.

The Salter family are of Scotch descent, coming to the Carolinas prior to the Revolution.

Mitchell B. Salter was an educator of note; he answered the first call of the Confederacy; left an arm on the field at Gettysburg. After the war he served his county, Conecuh, as tax collector one term and as treasurer three consecutive terms. He married Miss Eugenia Pullen of Monroeville, and their children are—Dr. Wilbur M. Salter, Anniston, Ala.; Julia, wife of Dr. Joseph Sellar of Anniston, Alabama; Mary Dent Salter, wife of Fred E. Mills, and Dr. Paul Pullen Salter of this sketch.

He attended the Southern Agricultural College after Evergreen; was student at the University of Alabama, graduating in 1911 with a degree of Bachelor of Science, and in 1912, took his masters degree in Science. He then went to Tulane University in New Orleans and graduated in professional training from Tulane University, in 1916.

He was Phi Gamma Delta Academic, Greek fraternity to Kappa Phi Medical Greek letter fraternity to the Honorary Medical Greek letter Alpha Omega Alpha and also to the Greek Letter fraternity, Phi Beta Kappa at Tulane. He was made an interne in 1914 of Physiology and Anatomy and held this position until 1916. In 1916-1917 he was interne at the Charity Hospital in New Orleans and later at Montgomery was field director for the Alabama State Board of Health.

DR. PAUL PULLEN SALTER

He was then made director of State Laboratories and Pasteur institute.

He volunteered for the World War in 1918 receiving the rank of First Lieutenant. Received honorable discharge in November, 1918.

Following this he was instructor of Bacteriaology and Pathology at the Army and Navy Medical School in Washington, D. C.

He took a post graduate course in New York Polytechnic Institute, specalizing in Surgery. He came to Eufaula, Barbour County May 24th, 1920, where he has since remained, enjoying a large practice.

In September, 1923, he established Salter hospital, accomodating patients from a large territory, subsidiary of Eufaula.

Dr. Salter is a Democrat, a steward in the First Methodist church at Eufaula; a Mason; member of the County Medical Society and a Fellow of the American Medical Society; also a member of the Alabama State Medical Association; a Rotarian and a most valuable citizen of Barbour County.

Married first Grace Pulliam, daughter of Stonewall Jackson and Nell (Mullins) Pulliam.

Children: Louise ,Leonora and Paul, Jr.

Married second Eula Kaigler, daughter of David and Lena (Duskin) Kaigler of Stewart and Randolph Counties, Georgia.

Personally Dr. Salter is genial and of that sunny nature that has made him many admiring friends, socially as well as professionally.

BENJAMIN HARRISON SCREWS

Benjamin Harrison Screws was born at Glennville, Barbour County (now Russell) County, Alabama, April 11, 1843, and was the son of Benjamin Screws of Glennville, and wife, Mourning Jones Drake. His grandchildren were respectively John Screws of Washington County, North Carolina, and James Drake, an early Alabama settler who was killed by the Indians.

The career of Captain Screws was full of interest as it was full of honors. He was educated in the common schools of Barbour County.

Due to the vicissitudes of war, his education was not completed. He inherited mental equipment which he improved by studious habits. It was said of him that he was one of the most widely informed men in Alabama and his brilliancy of mind was a matter of current comment.

He enlisted in the Confederate Army January 20, 1861, and served continuously until April 26, 1865. He was first lieutenant and Captain of Company K, 29th Alabama infantry and served as adjutant of that regiment which saw hard service. He was affectionately called "the boy Captain of the Confederacy," having been one of the youngest officers of that rank in the army. Although he displayed heroism on many battlefields, Captain Screws was wounded but once and that he received during the fighting around Atlanta. It was a desperate wound from the effects of which he never fully recovered.

At the close of the war, Captain Screws located in Montgomery and devoted himself to journalism and the law, studying law under Thomas H. Watts, Alabama's governor. He was for sometime associated with the Advertiser and his writings were ever keen, incisive and graphic.

Always a Democrat, fearless and straightforward in his convictions, Captain Screws achieved unusual success in public life. As a legislator he was loyal to the interests of his people. As a speaker in that interest he was peerless.

Before the reconstruction period, Capain Screws was selected by Governor Patton in 1865 as his private secretary; this, his fiirst official position, he displayed the tact and wisdom which marked his course throught life.

When the Constitutional Convention of 1875 was organized, Captain Screws was elected Secretary of that great body. It was his pride that he took a part in the framing of the organic law which redeemed Alabama from the misrule of the Republican Party.

Before this time and while engaged in newspaper work, Captain Screws wrote a burlesque, "The Loil Legislature of Alabama," purporting to be a history of the so-called Legislature composed of ignorant negroes and alien white men who met under military protection at the Capitol in 1868. This burlesque was widely circulated and attracted much attention for its satirical finish.

Captain Screws represented Montgomery County in the House of Representatives of 1890-91, of 1894-95, of 1898-99, and of 1900-01. In 1902 he was elected to the state senate and was a member of that body when he died.

It is doubtful if Captain Screws had an equal in the state as a speaker. In the use of poetic metaphor he was incomparably gifted. Whenever he raised his voice to speak of his comrades of the Confederacy and the cause he loved so well, the veil which concealed his soul seemed to be lifted and he spoke with the fire of genius. Wherever he went he was in great demand as an orator and he frequently had more invitations than he could accept.

Captain Screws achieved national fame in June of 1876 through a speech he made to General Grant, then president of the United States, on the occasion of the visit of the Alabama Press Association to Washington. This speech constituted a Bible of Southern Democracy to Reconstruction Days and in its viewpoint is vital today.

In every walk of civic life Captain Screws was prominent and popular. He had been a magistrate many years and his decisions were always just and without fear or favor. Lawyers, clients and litigants were his friends because they honored his integrity and knew his intellect.

A man of such unusual popularity, it was but natural that Captain Screws should have taken a leading part in the fraternal organizations of men. In none of these organizations did he play the part of a laggard. He knew the merits of each of them and on many occasions these merits were publicly exploited by his eloquent speech.

October 8, 1863, at Wetumpka, Captain Screws married Emma McNeill, a daughter of Dr. Daniel S. McNeill, and his wife, Mrs. Elizabeth Jeffries McNeill.

Captain Screws died in Montgomery, February 22, 1905. He was a Methodist and believed in the teaching of his religious faith and he died secure in the salvation offered by the Redeemer of Mankind.

Captain Screws had one son, Major Michel Hamilton Screws, who served in the World War as a Major in the 82nd Division, 319th Field Artillery; six daughters as follows:

Mrs. Walter Thomas, Mrs. Gustave Mertins, Mrs. Thornton W. Garrett, Mrs. Cassidy A. Garrett, Mrs. Meriwether N. Gilmer, Mrs. Charles W. Abbott.

EDWARD STOW

Owner of Many Business Industries of Barbour County

The man who personally owned and operated at the same time more industries and enterprises than any man in Barbour County was Edward Stow, wholesale and retail grocery man. His stores occupied the four buildings on Broad street, west from the old "Stow's corner" Broad and Randolph streets; upstairs over one store was the candy factory; over another the large bakery; and in Hobokan (a mile from the city) was the ice factory, the knitting factory (hosiery) and the grist mill, all supplied with water from Chewalla creek. "Stow's water ground meal" was famous all over Southeast Alabama and Southwest Georgia.

Mr. Stow came to Barbour from New York accompanied by his uncle, Mr. Anthony Stow, and his sister, Miss Katie Stow. He married Miss Reyburn Brantley, niece and foster daughter of Dr. and Mrs. Mark Shivers of the old historic town of Cotton Hill in Clay County, 15 miles from Eufaula.

Their ten children were born and reared at the old Stow home on Randolph street, which was the site of the old Indian Stockade of Early settlement days, when the Indians were the problem of the settlers.

For over 15 years Mr. Stow employed three expert bookkeepers for his extensive businesses, two for the daily work and one to audit their work daily (or rather nightly, from ten to twelve o'clock).

He was a man of ability, and managed his large businesses by his own personal programs that fit into each other splendidly.

He had two grocery delivery wagons, a bread wagon, and an ice wagon and in those days the City of Eufaula, so far as business was concerned, was far more of a real live city than it is now.

Mr. Stow, although from a northern state cast his lot in the South and was loyal to the Confederacy. He was a man of few words, but of much doing and was one of Barbour County's leading and most valuable citizens; a Mason and a Presbyterian churchman.

Their children: Raburn, died in infancy; Edward died in 1937, after being with Atl. Constitution many years; Lula married Benjamin Amzi Beach; Arthur deceased; Mary Elizabeth married William A. Davies, deceased; Anthony married Mamie Mamie May, Ensley, Alabama; Kate married E. H. Fell, Atlanta, deceased; Ruth married A. T. Porter, Atlanta; Walter married Jennis Charles, Greenville, S. C.; Norman married; D. G.; Charles; and Addie married Oliver T. Roberts.

GEORGE HILLIARD THOMAS, ESQ. AND WIFE

George Hilliard Thomas was born in Barbour County, July 16, 1845, the son of Eli Thomas and his wife, Retense Emiline Bush. His grandfather, Elliott Thomas, whose wife was Sally Berry, was one of the pioneer settlers of Barbour County, coming in about 1822, from South Carolina with his wife, slaves, cattle, settling in the community where old New Hope Methodist church was later built. This church was built by the Elliott Thomases, Zachary Bush, and Arthur Crews and other families, many of whom lie buried in the churchyard. After Elliott Thomas' second marriage to Annie Bolyston he owned and moved to the spot where Clayton, Alabama, now stands. He built and ran a tavern there. He

MARY P. CALHOUN   GEO. H. THOMAS AND FAMILY

and his second wife are buried near the entrance of Clayton cemetery. Sallie Thomas, his sister, married David Heidt.

The children of Elliott Thomas and his first wife, Sally Berry, were:

Joseph, married first, Jane Taylor, second Sarah Baker, Philingain.

Jonathan. married Mariam Bush.

James married Darkness Herring.

William Berry married Catherine McInnis (see Augus McInnis line).

Eliza married William Bush.

Sarah Jane married James McGilvary.

Aaron married Almira Herdct.

Eli married first Retense Emiline Bush; second, Annie Zorn; third, Jane Zorn.

Elliott married Ruth Bush.

Charity married John Waterson.

George Hilliard Thomas' father, Eli Thomas, son of Elliott Thomas and wife of Salley Berry, his first wife, married Retense Emiiine Bush, daughter of Zachary Bush and wife, Polly Dennis. Issue:

John Thomas, who died early.

Mary Parnelia Thomas, who married Marion Calhoun, Confederate soldier.

George Hillard Thomas, born July 16, 1845, died February 1, 1897, married Mary Walker.

Zachary Taylor Thomas married Martha Carter, daughter of Henry Carter and his wife, Sarah, of Henry County.

Retense Emiline Bush, their mother, was the daughter of Zachary Bush and his wife, Polly Dennis, and came with their family, slaves about the same time the Thomas family came to Barbour and were large land owners. Moses and William Bush, his brothers, came at the same time the Thomas family came to Barbour and were large land owners. Moses and William Bush, his brothers, came at the same time. Three daughters of this family married three sons of the Thomas family, and one son married Thomas' daughter.

The children were as follows:

Mariah Bush married Jonathan Thomas.

Greenberry Bush married Polly Allen, issue Arrense Bush married William Williams; Retense Bush married Eli Thomas; Dennis Bush married Salina Dubose.

Mary R. Bush married John Watson.

Eason Bush married Betsy Jane Grubbs.

Ruth Bush married Elliott Thomas, and second, John Q. Wise, of Dale County.

Lucinda Bush married Robert, issue, Barney Baldwin of Eufaula, second issue.

Mary Parmelie Thomas (daughter of Eli Thomas and wife, Retensa (Emeline Bush) married Dec. 7, 1859, Marion Calhoun, a Confederate soldier who was killed in the Confederate War. They had one son, Rev. George Marion Calhoun (member of Texas Conference and later of Alabama conference. He married Miss Minnie Locke of Barbour County, April 9th, 1890.

Their children: Col. Velo Alto Calhoun, born January 14, 1892, a prominent lawyer of Alabama, was studying law at the University of Alabama and when the World War started he became an airplane pilot and is still one. He married Marie Williams of Greenboro, Ala., and lives at College Park, near Atlanta, Georgia.

Eli Thomas Calhoun who was killed along with three others in San Diego, California; was Lieut. 47th Field Artillery during the World War, and is buried at Brundidge, Ala. He war born Dec. 29, 1893.

Miss Beulah Calhoun, prominent teacher in Montgomery.

Prof. Wallace Calhoun, born September 7, 1918, is present principal of schools at Clayton. His children are Wallace Eli Thomas and Mamie Elise Calhoun.

Mary Parmelie Thomas Calhoun is buried in Waxahatchie, Texas, and Rev. George Marion Calhoun is buried in Curbville, Ala., where he was pastor.

The children of George Hilliard Thomas, Esq., and wife, Mary Walker are:

William Lewis married Jennie Lee Brock, Clio.

James Walker married first Eudore Payne, Ozark; second Sarah Jane Dykes, Ozark.

Nall Thomas died as a child.

Frank Leonidas married Linnie Mathews, Monroe, La.

David Tilden married Willie Ophelia Folkes, of Dothan, Ala.

Rev. Eli Adolphus married Ruby Felder Ray of Newnan and Atlanta, Ga.

George Hilliard married Vivian Mitchell of Ozark.

Their children: Lewis Thomas and Wife, Denny Bock of Clio, Ala.

Fred Hilliard Thomas, World War Veteran, who is married and lives in San Monica, California.

Mary Joe Thomas married Calvin Lawrence Messer, Scotch Canadian and lives in Indianapolis, Indiana.

Lewis Brock married Pauline Edmondson, both great grandchildren of Elliott Thomas and wife, Sally Berry and both great grandchildren of Angus McInnis and wife, Catherine McInnis, formerly of Barbour County.

Edith Ophelia, business woman of Jacksonville, Florida, issue of James Walker Thomas and wife, Sarah Jane Dykes.

Mary Kate married Willie W. Adkins, Ozark. Issue, James William Adkins, 3 years old.

Pauline, Ozark, issue of Frank L. Thomas and wife, Linnie Matthews, Monroe, La.

Elsie Louise, teacher in Monroe, La.

Ina Merle, teacher in Monroe, La.

George Willis, business in Monroe La.

Frank Leonidas, business in Monroe, La.

Albert, high school, Monroe, La.

Issue of David Tilden Thomas and wife, Willie Ophelia Folkes, Ozark:

Mary Martha married Col. Howell McLendon, Abbeville, Alabama.

Maud Helen, Ozark, Alabama.

Thomas Howell McLendon, 3 years old is grandson.

Rev. Eli A. Thomas and wife, Ruby Felder Ray—no issue.

Issue of George Hilliard Thomas, Jr., and wife, Vivian, Ozark, Ala:

Mary Alice, Vivian Mitchell, Richard Ewell, Fred Thomas.

The children of Zachary Taylor Thomas and wife, Martha Carter, daughter of Henry Carter and wife, Sarah:

Sarah Retensa married Thaddeus O. Hutto, World War Veteran, Ozark.

Footnote: See Sollomon Walker line and Angus McInnis line.

Thadeus O. Hutto, Jr., Birmingham, Alabama.

Zachary Taylor, who is an actor and married an actress.

Hartsford Hutto, Birmingham.

These three brothers are married and have issue:

Annie Laurie Thomas died as a young lady in Ozark.

Henry Ross, prominent merchant of Ozark, married Grace Mixon, Ozark.

Henry Ross, Jr. Ozark, Alabama; Zachary Taylor, Ozark, Grace Thomas, Ozark, Alabma.

George Hillard Thomas Esquire's parents died young and he and his brother, Zachary Taylor, and sister, Mary Parmelia, went to live with their uncle, Jonathan Thomas. His wife, Mariah Bush, was their aunt. He was their guardian and lived in an immense two story log house, which was built by Elliott Thomas, their grand father in the early history of Barbour County. The house remodeled, still stands. Jonathan Thomas had eleven children of his own, and was the guardian also of four children of Sarah Jane McGilvary, and three children of Charity Waterson's. These McGilvary,

Waterson and Thomas boys and girls were all his nieces and nephews.

George Hilliard Thomas was educated in the school in the neighborhood of old New Hope Methodist church and was taught for years by "Old Captan Henry," a famous school master. Later he was sent to the famous Espy school at Lawrenceville in Henry County. At the age of seventeen, young George joined the "Barbour Greys," the first company for the duration of the war. The late Dr. Winn, of Clayton, was in this company. Captain Eugene Blackford was their captain, who later lived in "Sudbrook Park," Baltimore. He corresponded with George H. Thomas as late as 1896, when he was invited and visited Captain Blackford. These interesting letters are in the possession of Rev. Eli A. Thomas of Atlanta, Georgia—his son. After being wounded four times in Virginia, George Hilliard Thomas, was honorably discharged by Stonewall Jackson and came back to Eufaula where he served as enrolling officer 'till the close of the War.

On February 12, 1866, he was married to Mary Walker, daughter of Lewis Walker and his wife, Nancy McInnis. (See Solomon Walker and Angus McInnis' Lines.

In 1873, he moved with his family to Dale County, and for two years was a merchant at Skipperville, Alabama. He was a justice of the peace and moved to and operated his own farm. His wife was a most estimable Christian wife and mother. They were loyal members of Pleasant View Presbyterian church in Barbour County—in Dale County of "Union Presbyterian church" and later in 1892 his family moved to Ozark—having been elected a clerk of Circut Court, which office he held until his death, February 1, 1887. They were charter members of the Ozark Presbyterian church.

Mary Walker, wife of George Hilliad Thomas, Esq., was born October 6, 1838, the daughter of Lewis Walker and his wife, Nancy McInnis. Lewis Walker was the son of Solomon Walker, born Virginia in 1757. He was a Revolutionary soldier, a pioneer settler, who came from Cumberland County, North Carolina, to Barbour County, Alabama, before the Indians were gone. Solomon Walker's wife was Goodwin Cox of of Richmond County, N. C.

Her brothers and sisters were:

Maisy Catherine Walker, Nancy Jane Walker, Solomon Miles Walker, Mary Walker, John Alexander Walker, Amanda Walker, David Lewis Walker, James Franklin Walker,

Her mother, Nancy McInnis, was the daughter of Augus McInnis and his wife, Catherine McInnis (her maiden name was also McInnis). They were married in Scotland. He was one of the founders of old Pea River Presbyterian church. Their issue:

Mary Polly, married George Keehey; Nancy, married Lewis Walker; Katherine married William Berry Thomas, son of Elliott Thomas; Christian married William French; Miles died young; Margaret died young.

Rev. Eli Adolphus Thomas, 6th son of George Hilliard Thomas, Esquire, and wife, Mary Walker, was born in Dale County, Alabama, Nov. 17, 1881.

Graduated at Ozark High School in 1900, attended Troy Normal College and held a first grade certificate to teach in Alabama. Bachelor of Arts degree at Southwestern Presbyterian University, Tennessee, in 1907; Bachelor of Divinity Degree at Princeton Theological Seminary in 1911; member of "Benham Club" at Princeton. He is a Presbyterian minister, having served churches in Alabma, in Georgia at Cedartown, and in Atlanta. During the World he was religious secretary of the Y. M. C. A. at Camp Grey in Atlanta; at Fort McPherson and War Prison Camp where German prisoners were kept near Fort McPherson. He placed a beautiful Baptismal Fort in the Ozark Presbyterian church in memory of George Hilliard Thomas and Mary Walker) Thomas, his parents. He organized two churche in Atlanta and was their first pastor—Capitol View Presbyterian and the Oakhurst Presbyterian church. He and his wife are members of Atlanta Historical Society. He is still active in the church and is pastor of Salem Presbyterian church which unveiled a beautiful art glass window in his honor in 1934.

On December 21, 1916, he was married to Ruby Felder Ray, daughter of Col. Lavender R. Ray of Newnan and Atlanta, Georgia, and his wife, Annie Felder, of Americus, Georgia. She is active in church and patriotic societies—authoress of "Historic Spots and Places of Interest in Georgia." Her name is on Bronze Tablet in the Georgia Capitol—the tablet observing the Bicentenial of Georgia, 1933.

Footnote: See Solomon Walker and Angus McGinnis.

E. PERRY THOMAS

Elias Thomas was born in Henry County, Alabama, August 26th, 1872, son of Elias Hugh and Nancy A. (Hays) Thomas. His grandparents were Alexander and Polly (Harris) Hays, all of Georgia.

Elias Hugh Thomas moved to Henry County, Ala., from Laurens County, Georgia, in 1836, and took part in the Creek Indian battles.

He settled on the river near Otho, Alabama, 11 miles below Eufaula and during the war between the states he was Major in the 3rd battalion of Reserves.

Perry Thomas grew up at Clayton after his father's

death and attended school at the agricultural school at Abbeville, Ala., and then attended the University of Alabama.

In 1892 he studied law at Clayton with his older brother, Alex H. Thomas, and was admitted to the bar in 1893, practicing there some years.

During this time he was mayor of Clayton two terms and was elected state senator from Barbour and reelected in 1906. During his last term he served as president of the senate.

In 1914 he moved to Eufaula and formed a partnership in law with Charles S. McDowell and George W. Peach. October 1912 he was appointed associate judge of the Court of Appeals of Alabama by Governor O'Neal, to succeed Judge Edward de Graflenried, and was reappointed in Octover of 1914.

He resigned to enter into partnership with George W. Jones as district attorney for the L. and N. railroad.

He was a polished gentleman, a scholar and notable as an attorney in weighty civil matters, also in the criminal courts he was acclaimed superior.

He was a Mason, Vestryman of the Episcopal church and member of the Elks and W. O. W.

He married Nell, daughter of Dr. Edward Hill and Elizabeth (Swanson) Pritchett of Haynesville, Ala.

Children: Nell and Edward Perry and an infant who died.

JOHN DELOCHIOU THOMAS

John Delochiou Thomas was born in Charleston, S. C., son of Elliott and grandson of Dr. John Thomas of Marshfield, Mass., who succeeded General Montgomery of the American Army at the battle of Quebec, off "Abraham Heights" on the St. Lawrence river. He was brigadier general.

He died of smallpox on June 3rd, and is buried at Fort Chambly—and his wife, Eugenia Delochiou, who was born in Arcadia, Nova Scotia, with her parents refugeed down the Atlantic coast to Charleston.

At the age of 17 young Thomas enlisted in the war of 1812-1814 and fought under General Coffee, of Jackson's Army in the battle of New Orleans, where he distinguished himself by jumping over the ramparts and catching up the company's flag and rushing to the front bearing it, when he saw the color bearer shot down.

He fought through the war, and returning to South Carolina with Jackson's army, when a half dozen or more families were leaving South Carolina to immigrate to Florida, he joined them and while enroute he camped in Twiggs County, Georgia. While there he married Nancy Williams, daughter of Mark Williams, the leader of the company of immigrants.

They were over three years enroute, and while still in Twiggs County their first child, Winifred Thomas, was born.

On February 2nd., 1823, Mark Williams, Floyd Lee, William Ledbetter and John Delochiou Thomas paddled down the Chattahoochee river in a canoe from their camp and travvelled on nearer the Florida sought destination.

When they saw the high bluff they landed and explored and were charmed. The result was the settling and subsequent naming of Eufaula, the village they thus started.

They went back and brought their families in a few weeks.

JOHN DELOCHIOU THOMAS LINE

In a few months their second child, Emeline Thomas was born, the first white child there is record of being born in Barbour County. She married Jasper Lawyer of Pike County, Ala., adjoining Barbour. He fought through the War Between the states and was killed by John Brady, another Confederate soldier in Eufaula in 1865 in a dispute over the issuing of food out of the commissary to widows of soldiers, according to war regulations.

Years after Brady was drowned in the river near Bradenton, Florida, where he had large real estate interests.

Emeline Thomas Sawyer lived to be 86 years old, with not a grey hair in her head and her eyesight was perfect. She is buried in Fairview cemetery beside her husband at Eufaula.

John D. Thomas bought much land from the Indians and procured land grants from the government. These deeds are unique in writing and wording. He was practically the leader in the village of Eufaula, reared a large family and died in 1859 before he saw much of the development of the town he settled and named. (See Call of Blood and Naming of Eufaula in this volume).

He owned much land in the Clayton community and he and his brothers owned many slaves, purchased after they came from South Carolina.

His children were: Winifred, married John Barefield of Clayton, isslue, John, married; Cynthia Vaughan, issue John Charles, and William.

Charity married George Hudson. Children: Two sons, who now live at Chipley, Florida.

George Washington married Minerva Courtney, issue, Edwin, who married Katie Harrison, issue, son, Carl, U. S. Navy. Thelma married Johnston; Quinn married Maggie Browne; issue Cullis; Marion and Marguerite; Mather deceased, U. S. Army.

Emory H. married Lucy Shannon, issue Ermine married Alton Hobbs, issue, son, Alton, Jr.

E. H. married Eugenia Page, issue daughter Charline; Wliliam, unmarried.

Fourth, Katherine, married Rev. C. J. Stephens, Baptist minister, issue. Winnifred married L. Brassell (see biography). Hamilton Calvin deceased; Meta Katherine married John S. Bankhead grandson of Senator J. H. Bankhead; Lenox H., deceased; William Perry; Elizabeth; Malcolm, deceased, and John C.

Mary Ann married James Baker, a northerner, who came South and entered the Confederate army, in which he lost his sight. He was a finished musician and a brilliant violinist. Issue: son, Grady, and daughter, Mary, who married Thomas Watts of Floride, issue, three sons.

James Barefield married Mary Clements, issue, daughter, Annie and son, Emmett.

Children of Emeline Thomas Sawyer:

Walter W. married Sallie Thomas, issue, Walter Jr., married Maria Smith, issue a son, Thomas.

Louise Sawyer, unmarried, Katherine married Earl Seals, issue son and daughter.

James Sawyer, deceased, and Corsica, married Bertha Parpasino, issue three sons.

Cassibianca married Mattie Folsom, no issue.

Henry A. Thomas, son of John D. Thomas, married Pheribee Hunt, no issue, but adopted a son and daughter. He was a soldier in the Confederate Army, belonging to the company of Captain S. H. Dent. He died in the late nineties in Dale county.

His children were Sallie, married W. W. Sawyer; Fanny, deceased; John Delochiou, II, married Lily Kendrick, issue, Judson, deceased, Mildred married Joseph Rinker, Augusta, Georgia.

Roderick married Juanita McClintoch, Washington, D. C.

Milton married; Claudia married; Alexander, married.

John Delochiou, II, and Elliott V. were both Number 1 telegraph operators, both holding responsible positions as operators at the age of 14. Both went to the top as Associated Press expert operators. Elliott, deceased; John D., II, retired and pensioned by Postal Telegraph Company.

Mamie Thomas married Paul Bostwick, Washington, D. C. Issue two daughters, Evelyn and Hattie and a son, Paul.

Hattie Thomas, unmarried ,residence Eufaula.

John Curtis Thomas, 7th son of John Delochiou and Nancy (Williams) Thomas, born Feb. 27th, 1842, in Eufaula. When 9 years of age he was employed as messenger at the Telegraph office at Eufaula, and when 18 was made manager, which position he held until 1887 when he resigned, because of ill health.

He married Mattie Virginia Aldee, daughter of William and Mary (Crocker) Aldee of Lumpkin, Georgia, issue Mattie Crocker, born June 23, 1865, married Charles Mallory Thompson, no issue; second Annie Virginia, born Nov. 12, 1867, married William Marcellus Tully, born in Carlow, Ireland, August 8th, 1857, issue:

Daniel Thomas Tully, sergeant first class 35th Service Co. Signal Corps, killed at Tours, France, September 4th, 1919. Reinterred Arlington National Cemetery September 8th, 1921. William Mallory Tully, born March 10, 1898, died June 28th, 1904. Olivia Thomas Tully born April 14th, 1903; married Capt. George Garvin, issue, Danile Tully Garvin, born at Fort Benning, Ga., March 9th, 1824; Ford Morris Garvin, born at Fort McKinley, Philippine Islands, January 11, 1926; Kathleen Virginia Garvin, Jefferson Barracks, Missouri, Nov. 5th, 1929; George Thomas Garvin born at Fort McPherson, Dec. 21st, 1934.

Agatha was born September 8, 1866; died in infancy. Annie Thomas Tully was born Dec. 8, 1887; died at the age of three. Kathleen Curtis Tully was born September 1, 1889. She married David Hooper, first lieutenant 38th Infantry, 3rd division U. S. Army during World War; died in 1936; buried in Arlington National Cemetery.

Edmund Mooney Tully was born at Eufaula July 30th, 1906. He married Betty Wendlan of Nebraska, no issue.

John Cortez Thomas, son of J. C. and M. V. Thomas, was born March 3rd, 1874, and married Egletine Boyleston, issue, a son, John C., III. all deceased.

Edith Curtis Thomas, born March 1st, 1872, deceased in infancy, Arthur Morse, deceased June 3rd, 1877; and Nelly Feb. 22nd, 1879. Herbert Spencer Thomas, son of J. C. and M. V. Thomas, born Nov. 17, 1882. Now lives in New York.

Randolph Rusk Thomas, youngest son, was born April 12th, 1889. He married Willie May May Hinton, daughter of Emmett and Mary Hinton, issue, Randolph Hinton Thomas; married Maysie Azile Joyce, daughter of Henry Lee and Eunice Lampley Joyce of Norwood, N. C.

John Curtis Thomas, II, deceased in infancy; Mary Virginia Thomas; and twins, William J., and Julian J. Thomas.

JOHNATHAN THOMAS

Johnathon Thomas, son of Elliott and (Sally Berry) Thomas, was born in Barbour County.

He married Mariah Bush, and their children were: Sarah, married Anderson Crews, one of Barbour County's leading citizens. She was a woman of great force of character, a consecrated Christian, and her brilliant intellect made her a leader in all the uplifting activities of the community. She gave generously of her wealth to missionary work, and all church work and was one of the strongest forces in the Daughters of the Confederacy during her life. She built a Church on her home lot and supported it for many years, and was greatly beloved for her philanthropy.

Her children, Clifford, married J. R. Ventress, issue Mary, married Warren; and Emma marred second Dr. Bobbitt, issue, Carrie, married Robert A. Willis.

Zachariah was born in 1834 in Barbour County; married, issue, Jessie, unmarried, and Mittie later married E. P. Clarke of Eufaula and resided at Clayton, issue, a son.

William Hamilton married Margaret McCraney, children, Henry Calvin, born 1869, died 1890; Oree Baker, born 1871, died 1890; Minnie deceased; Mary Ida; Nancy Campbell; Neille Maria, married John Lemuel Cherry; Malcolm Alexander, married. was born in 1878, and died in 1936. He married Lillian McClellan, daughter of Andrew Jackson McClellan, one son, Alexander Malcolm.

Richard David, born in 1880 married Florence Kimbrough, daughter of B. L. and Cordelia Kimbrough (a cousin of Archibald Butt, attachee to three presidents and who was drowned on a ship).

Their children are William Hamilton, born July 29th, 1906, and is now a prominent business man of Birmingham, Ala.

Florence married Blucher M. Cooper, and they have one son, Blucher, III. Richard Erle, of Tuscaloosa, Ala.

Alvenia Thomas married William Harrison Jones, issue, A. Silas Allison, married Esther Hale, issue, Beatrice, married Mr. Martin of Birmingham; Willie Ray; Margaret died in infancy.

(See George Hilliard Thomas line); Maggie Jones married James Martin of Clayton, issue, Dr. Sterling Martin, married and lives in Texas.

Col. John James Martin married Beatrice Jones, and lives in Birmingham.

Margaret Jones married Col. John Pearson, Tuscaloosa, Ala.

Columbus Arthur married Elizabeth West in Clayton.

Clifford Martin; Winn Martin married in Birmingham; Irma and Jean are students at Montevallo College; Sarah Ellen.

Children: Eula Marshall Jones married Claude Ella Appleton, issue, A Thomas Jones; Betty Ann; and C. Evelyn.

Claude Leroy married Sarah Stewart in Fitzgerald, Ga., issue A. Claude Leroy, Jr., graduate of Georgia Tech and lives at Briarcliff Road, N. E., Atlanta.

Alice Elizabeth married Harold Phillips and lives in Birmingham.

Jonathan Thomas was killed in a railway accident in Barbour.

Edna Earl married Harry Burge in Detroit, issue Rev. Harry Burge, Jr.; Catherine is married.

Annie Lee married Arthur Lee, Warm Springs, Georgia, issue, Creel Lee, married Margaret Fowler; Stewart Lee, student in Detroit; Marshall Palatine married Gerald Noah, issue, Theodosia married Lloyd Arlege, Postal Telegraph Company, Birmingham.

William Harrison died at the age of 7.

Lilly Virginia died in infancy.

Twins: Fred, died in infancy; Wilbur Leonidas Jones married and lives in Washington, D. C.

Callie Thomas married James Orr, Barbour County, issue, James, deceased; Eula married John Wise, issue:

Annie Wade married Wilbur Reeves in Eufaula.

Beulah married W. A. Rocker.

Mary C. married G. C. Reid, Eufaula; Georgia married W. M. O'Brien, Birmingham.

Prudence married J. D. Stewart.

James Orr married Alberta Phillips.

J. B. Wise married Bunyan Bowden.

Alberta.

Lem married Louise Price.

Eddie Lee married B. F. Richards.

William Wise, unmarried and Maud.

Wade Orr is in Mobile and has issue, son Lyman.

Dr. James Orr, veteran of Spanish-American war, married twice, has issue and lives in Texas.

Addie Orr married Jesse Hinson, Abbeville, Ala—issue, Prof. Jesse James Hinson, married and lives in Maryland; Dr. Angus Hinson; Rev. Hinson and three daughters, all college graduates; Lorene, Hettie Carolyn; Lutie.

Annie Orr married first Cody Crawford, married second Charles Valentine, issue, Jocebed and Mary Charles.

Perla Orr, deceased, married Ben McLendon, issue Al Perry, Bemie Lou.

Robert Orr married Bonnie Bell Smith, issue, Frances Caroline and Robert L. Merchant in Birmingham.

Rufus Orr, married and lives in Mobile, has issue.

Jonathan Carter Thomas married Evelyn Virginia Mallard.

Addie Thomas died early.

Crowell Thomas killed in the War Between the States.

Lee Thomas married first Ada Bush; second Ella Bush and married a third time, issue by each.

Eason Bush married Batty Jane Grubbs.

Mary married Mr. West, issue, Claude West and others lives in Texas.

Moses Eason.

Anderson.

Nora Bush married Mr. Martin of Dothan, has issue.

Lula Bush married Relus Rollins, large family in Dothan.

(See Jonathon Carter Thomas line.)

ELLIOTT THOMAS IV LINE

Elliott Thomas, third son of Johnathon and Mariah Bush Thomas, was born in Barbour County, and spent his life at the old Thomas Home,, known as the "Mile Branch," Wool Factory, "Thomas Place." He married Ruth Bush, and the following are his issue: viz:

Edward, whose store near the Barbour Bridge in Barbour County, was swept away by the floods of July, 1914. He married Ellen Statham, no issue.

Jennie married John W. Brown, and while this is being written she is lying at death's door at Britt's infirmary.

Elizabeth married Mr. Lindsay. She is deceased, and left one son.

Preston is deceased.

Fanny resides with her sister Jennie.

David Thomas was the fourth son of Johnathan Thomas and Mariah Bush Thomas. He married Anne Floyd, and their son, Floyd, died when a prominent young business man of the County. His mother is still living, over 88 years old at her home in Clayton.

JONATHAN CARTER THOMAS

Johnathan Carter Thomas was born February 22nd, 1847. His parents were Johnathan and Mariah Bush Thomas. His father, Johnathan Thomas, was a soldier against the Indians in the Creek War.

Johnathan Carter Thomas joined the Confederate Army at the age of sixteen with his double first cousin, Zachary Taylor Thomas, and David Louis Walker, from New Hope Methodist Church Community; was assigned to Company D, 39th Alabama Regiment, and stationed in the vicinity of Mobile, Alabama. All were finally taken prisoners and held on Ship Island, after he was wounded in battle.

Jonathan Carter Thomas was married to Evaline Virginia Mallard, on January 24th, 1871. They were the parents of four sons and one daughter, Jonathan Carleton Thomas,

Robert Elliott Thomas, Ivy Anderson Thomas, Hattie May Thomas and Marvin Thomas. Died May 18th, 1914, at Clayton, Alabama.

Jonathan Carleton Thomas was born February 2nd, 1872, and married Fannie Kennedy about 1894; was the father of two boys, Fred Thomas and Bart Thomas, died March 24th, 1903.

Robert Elliott Thomas was born August 21st, 1875, enlisted in the United States Army July 28th, 1899, and served two years in Cuba, in Troop D, 7th U. S. Calvary. He married Mattie Belle Chapman, September 30th, 1906, and is the father of two daughters and three sons: Elizabeth Ayer Thomas, Evelyn Virginia Thomas, Robert Glynn Thomas, Ivy Arliss Thomas and Carleton Wheeler Thomas. They now live at 1357 Grant street, Atlanta, Georgia.

Elizabeth Ayer Thomas was born March 2nd, 1908, married Leland S. Miller, November 19th, 1932, and is the mother of one son, Rogert Leland Miller, address, 206 Stovall street, Atlanta, Georgia.

Evelyn Virginia Thomas was born April 26th, 1911.

Robert Glynn Thomas was born July 29th, 1913.

Ivy Arliss Thomas was born April 25th, 1916.

Carleton Wheeler Thomas was born July 7th, 1918.

Hattie Mae Thomas was born May 31st, 1878, died September 9th, 1885.

Marvin Thomas was born March 17th, 1885, died August 7th, 1865.

HERMAN L. UPSHAW

Herman L. Upshaw was born in Alexander City, Alabama, and received his early education in the schools of Tallapoosa County, graduating from State Normal school at Troy with the degree of B. Ph. He also was a student at Columbia University, New York; Chicago University and Peabody University at Nashville.

He was elected a first assistant in the public schools at Midway, Ala., and in 1908 was elected superintendent of the city schools at Eufaula, which position he held for twelve years, resigning to accept a position with the McMillian Publishing Company, his territory being Alabama and Tennessee.

In 1929 he jointly with Mr. Carl Strang of the same Company, established the Eufaula Daily Tribune, afterwards purchasing from T. G. Wilkinson the Daily Citizen which they merged into the present Daily Tribune, which he is now sole owner and publisher of.

Mr. Upshaw is also postmaster at Eufaula, having been

appointed by President Roosevelt soon after his first inauguration. He is a man of letters, a scholar and a writer whose facile pen carries with it's every tracing, some forceful thought that he weaves into articles carried on his editorial page that deal with the problems, for the betterment of his paper.

As a citizen he is always first to take part in all progressive movements, and is the leading philanthropist of the community, generously giving financial help wherever needed.

He is a Rotarian, member of the Commercial Club, a deacon of the First Baptist Church and one of its strongest forces.

He is the citizen who is always ready to promote the progress of the community.

He does not engage actively in politics, but is a Democrat of the type whose influence has weight.

He married Fanny Shorter, daughter of Eli S. and Wylena Lamar Shorter. Their only child is a charming daughter, now at College in New York.

THE WHITLOCKS

A singular fact that has been commented on often during the passing years is that of the many Northern citizens who came to the Southland just before the war cry between the states was sounded, and cast their lots here, a large number of them espoused the Southern cause, and became loyal to the South.

Among this number was John H. Whitlock, who in 1854 came from New Jersey and opened a jewelry store in Perry, Georgia, remaining there for some time, then removing to Columbia in Henry County, Ala., where he became manager of the Telegraph office of the Georgia and Florida Telegraph Company. When his office was seized by the United States government and abandoned, at the instance of the manager of the Eufaula office—a warm friendship having sprung up between them over the wires, several years before they met, and continued, growing stronger. He came to Eufaula in 1865, and established the Whitlock Jewelry store, that has been the pride of Barbour County for 72 years and is still today one of the largest Jewelry firms in the South.

Mr. Whitlock was a remarkable man—handsome physically, cultured, polished and the quiet, dignified type of gentleman it is refreshing to know.

With an aesthetic mind, and artistic eye, and an ear for the classic music of the old masters, he was for years organist at St. James Episcopal church. A vestryman of the Church and a hightoned Christian gentleman, and a citizen of whom the community was justly very proud.

In 1863, he married lovely Clara Griffith, daughter of Col.

Griffith of Columbia, Ala., and their home is one of the most beautiful and artistic to be found anywhere. Their only child, Dr. John B. Whitlock, so like his mother in feature, has inherited from both parents the superior qualities that made them beloved and honored in their section.

Dr. J. B. Whitlock

Dr. Whitlock sold his jewelry business in recent years and devotes himself to the practice of Optometrist. He has never married, but is a social favorite with every one, of all ages.

His greatest joy is to gather a group of little girls together and contribute to their happiness, by giving them rides, picnics or parties.

"Mr. Johnnie," the dear friend of several generations who were the life long friends of the parents, and the friends of the children of the day as well. They represent as well, a most valuable, progressive citizen, whose heart, hand and purse is wide open to any cause, that is for the uplift and happness of his home town and friends. He is widely known all over Southeast Alabama and Southwest Georgia.

He has travelled extensively and is a delightful story teller, whom his friends enjoy hearing tell of his travels through Europe.

He is a scholar and one of the leading literary lights of the community. Over the front entrance of the Whitlock Jewelry store hangs a large bronze watch that has hung there ever since the day the store first opened in 1865, and is Eufaula's oldest public antique.

The Whitlock Jewelry store is the oldest jewelry store in Alabama, possibly in the entire south, and a notable feature of this jewelry business is that there never has gone to press a single issue of the Eufaula newspaper since the day the business opened here that they did not carry the ad of the firm.

Associated with Mr. J. H. Whitlock and son, Dr. J. B. Whitlock for many years was his brother, Mr. George W. Whitlock, who was the manager of the jewelry department, while Dr. Whitlock managed the Optical department.

Mr. George Whitlock was also a talented musician like his father, playing the violin and flute, his brother the organ and piano, while Dr. J. B. Whitlock also played the cello and base violin.

He was born in Vermont May 17, 1837, and was educated in New York.

JOHN ABSALOM WALKER

John Absalom Walker was born May 9th, in Putnam County, Georgia, son of Elizabeth Hunter Woolridge, and

John Hedge Walker; left an orphan, he began working for himself when a boy and before twenty years old, having moved to Glennville, Barbour County, Ala., from there enlisting in the Confederate Army, helped organize Company C, a part of the Thirty First Georgia Regiment. He fought at the battle of Cedar Creek; the battle of Manassas, and was at Chancellersville when General Jackson received the wounds that ended his career; was also at the "Seven Days Fight" when seven hundred out of over twelve hundred were killed; fought at Sharpsburg and Harper's Ferry, under Brigadier General John B. Gordon, Captain Walker was appointed Assistant Commisary General of his brigade, being promoted over five Majors, for efficiency.

He was with the army that was so glorious at Gettysburg and fought in all the battles in the Virginia valley. He stood beside General Lee at Appomattox, when he surrendered. Previous to this he had received from General Lee many details of special service, due to his ability and faithfulness to duty. One was to go to Richmond to secure one thousand dollars with which to purchase supplies for the Army.

At the close of the war Captain Walker went into the General Merchandise busines at Eufaula, became a large plantation owner in Barbour County, and spent the rest of his life in active business, reaching old age, the perfect specimen of vigorous manhood. Was Deacon of the First Baptist Church, and progressive, valuable citizen and a gentleman of the old school type, who was an honor and asset to the Community. Moved to Birmingham a few years before his death, where like in his home town, he was beloved for the genial, kindly, generous friendship, and sterling worth as a man. Is buried in the family lot in Fairview Cemetery, Eufaula.

He married first Mary Elizabeth Pitts, to them were born John Thomas and Robert Humphry Walker, married second, Eliza Kendrick (Lewis) Annie Kendrick Walker, their daughter, being the charming, and brilliant writer, whose facile pen in Journalism, both in Alabama and New York City, has made her notable.

HISTORIC WELLBORN HOME

This picture was taken in 1936, when the Parade of the Barbour County Fair, formed in front of the Old Colonial Wellborn Home on Livingston street in Eufaula. The handsome old home looms up in the background while the Queen of the fair, Miss Carrie Foy, now Mrs. Thomas R. Moorer, sits in the old Foy Phaeton painted white, with her pages, Dick Williams, Jr., and Horace Cade, the driver is Mr. R. S. Jones, Jr. (See R. S. Jones, Sr., biography), holding the ribbons over his two beautiful white horses, that are the pride of this section.

The occasion, the carriage, its occupants and the horses, are a fitting frontice-piece for the Wellborn home that was the home years ago of the illustrious Wellborn family. It is now the home of Miss Alice Wells.

WELLBORN FAMILY

One of the outstanding members of the Wellborn family, (which originated in England, was Thomas W. Wellborn, who in 1702 was a member of the House of Burgesses.

His son, William Wellborn, was a soldier of the Revolutionary war and was one of Barbour County's earliest citizens.

Maximilian Bethune Wellborn was a lawyer of great and rare ability, graduating from the University of Alabama in 1846. Practiced law at Eufaula, where his father had come, when he was a small boy. After ten years he moved to Lewisville, Ark., and served the Trans, Miss. Dept. of the Confederate Army, as Colonel of staff of General Magruder, and during the last year of the war was judge of Military Court.

Returning to Eufaula in 1867, he was nominated for Congress in 1870. From 1878 to 1880 he served as Registrar in Chanvery and during 1880-1881 represented his District in the State Assembly.

He married Emma Julia Dent of Morgan County, Georgia. He died at Eufaula, 1885, his wife surviving until 1919. Their children Maximilian, Jr., married Mary Hinton Graves; Elizabeth, deceased, married Warren F. Dent; Walter D., deceased, married a New Orleans, La., girl of prominent family.

Maximilian Bethune, Jr., born at Lewisville, Ark., January 22, 1863, graduated from the Eufaula Male Academy of Craven and Patterson, entered business and in 1887 went to Anniston, Ala., where he was highly successful in the real estate business. In 1891 he established the Anniston banking and Loan Co.; organized the first Building and Loan of Anniston and was its President in 1905, was elected President of the First National Bank of Anniston. In 1904 he organized the First National Bank of Piedmont, of which he was President; the Cherokee County Bank of Center and was President of the First National Bank of Jacksonville, Alabama.

It was 1914 when the Federal Reserve Bank was established and he was appointed Chairman of the Federal Reserve Bank of Atlanta, Georgia, and in 1919, he was elected Governor of this institution by its board of Directors.

For some years he served as County Commissioner of Calhoun County and Governor O'Neal appointed him temporary President of the Convict Dept. of the State, because of his ability to straighten out a tangle of its finances. In 1912 he was Delegate to the Democratic National Convention at Baltimore, Md.

A man of wonderful ability in handling the finances of any great measure, and a true gentleman of the old school, "to the manor born" he honored any position he filled.

When he resigned the Presidency of four banking institutions, at a financial sacrifice, moved to Atlanta where he made History and gave aid to the South in setting up and operating that portion of the Federal reserve system, embracing Alabama, Georgia, Florida, and parts of Louisiana, Mississippi and Tennessee.

Governor Wellborn never sought political office but was always interested in the politics of his County.

He married Mary Hinton Graves of Rome Georgia. Children, Margaret (Wellborn) Matthews, Anniston; Walter Harry Wellborn and William Bethune Wellborn, Atlanta; Mary Graves Wellborn.

He retired from the Federal Reserve Bank, 1928, and

resides at his "Tallasshatchee" farm at "Maxwellborn" near Anniston, Ala.

One of the bright shining lights of the Wellborn family, was Mrs. Roxanna Wellborn, wife of Levi Wellborn, a distinguished Barbour County citizen, who rendered great service during the War between the States. She presided over the beautiful historic old Wellborn home at Eufaula, which is situated on Livingston Street, and faces also Orange Street, reaching with its long avenues of thousands of spring blooming flowers, from Livingston to Orange. With its two double verandas, with imposing Colonial Columns.

It was here where the Wellborn children of two generations were reared and its queenly Misstresses, reigned in the old days.

"Aunt Roxanna", as she was lovingly called, turned her home into a hospital to nurse wounded Confederate Soldiers, and during those bloody four years, gave her time, her money and constant service, in the Confederate Cause.

She was the first President of the Women's Memorial Association in Barbour County, and on every Memorial Day, April 26, her grave in Fairview receives the decoration given to the Confederate Soldiers buried all about her.

The three Wellborn brothers, Max, Walter and Marshall, were among the gallant "beaux" of the early eighties, that honored Eufaula society with their presence at all the ultra fashionable affairs and they were popular with the debutantes.

JOHN EDWARD WARD

The crowning glory of any life is always found in record of achievement and service rendered by an individual to his fellow man in the community in which he lives.

John Edward Ward was born in Barbour County, his parents among the first settlers of that section near the old "Wool Factory", famous many years as one of the first industries of the County. He grew up a lover and student of the soil, a deep thinker, wide reader and early began laying the foundation for the success that came to him as a large, scientific farmer and capable business man.

His farms always produced the best and the great droves of fine hogs, that he raised and marketed annually were the wonder and pride of his neighbors, and the citizenship of all this section.

His fame as a watermelon grower spread over the large section of Southeast Alabama and Southwest Georgia, when he shipped car loads of his beautiful lucious loing grey "Rattle Snake melons.

He reared a large family who have in their lives emulated

the doctrines and programs of their father, and are following in line with the fine examples he has left them of the best citizenship.

They are, viz.: Robert and Ulric, two elder sons, have succeeded their father as A-No. 1 farmers, both living on the old plantations, and carrying out the old plans and policies of farming, with pronounced success. Robert Ward, living at the old family home place; Ulric Ward, making his home on another section of the old plantation, in the family division of lands. This old place being one of the most historic in the County, situated about two miles from Eufaula.

JOHN EDWARD WARD

Bartow and Arthur are both prominent merchants with flourishing businesses while the younger brother, Julien, is associated in business with older brothers. Two other brothers, Edward and Grover, both Veterans of the World War, have died since the war.

The sisters are: Mrs. C. W. Strippling of Atlanta, Georgia, (Eva Ward); Mrs. Geo. Thompson (Ella Corine), Richland; Mrs. N. L. Pruett (Manola Ward), Eufaula; Mrs. Else Floyd (Mary Ward), Eufaula. All representative citizens who take active part in the civic, business, Church and social life of the community.

Mr. Ward's first wife was Julia Elizabeth Statham of Preston, Georgia, and mother of all his children. His second wife, who survived him only a few years, was Mrs. Pearl Ingram, both superior women of the old regime who were true and faithful helpmeets in the career of one of Barbour's outstanding citizens.

MORTON BRYAN WHARTON

> His memory lives in Barbour County's heart
> And ever blessed will be,
> When the scroll of Time's chart
> The coming generations shall see.

Preacher, poet, patriot, statesman, scholar, consecrated Christian.

Morton Bryan Wharton was born in Orange County, Virginia, April 5, 1839, where he grew up and received his early education.

After graduating at the University of Virginia he attended Theological Seminaries and soon after his ordination to the Ministry accepted a call to the Pastorate of the First Baptist Church at Eufaula, Alabama, in 1867. Serving this Church through 1871, he personally supervised the building of the former handsome church which was built at a cost of $37,000.00. More than thirty years later he returned to the pastorate of this Church and during that time the Church building was destroyed by lightening and the present fine structure was erected at a cost of $20,000.00, so that to him was given the unique distinction of having supervised the construction of two edifices of this congregation, nearly forty years apart. It is a pathetic fact, however, that he never was permitted to preach in the latest structure, on account of a delay in the new pews being placed before declining health carried him to Gainesville, Georgia, for the summer and he died after being brought to the Tabernacle Baptist Hospital at Atlanta, Georgia, July 20, 1908. However his body was brought home immediately and lay in state in his Church from the arrival of the train from Atlanta until the hour for the funeral, with a military guard of honor.

The funeral took place from the First Methodist Church, every place of business in the city closed for the half day, and several hundred people were unable to get inside the crowded church. He was buried in Fairview Cemetery at Eufaula, at his own request.

Besides the beautiful church he twice built—which is a significant monument to him—there stands in front of the church a beautiful white marble sixteen foot monument, topped with a life size, standing statue of Dr. Wharton. On the monument is the following inscription:

Morton Bryan Wharton, D. D. Born April 5, 1839, Orange County, Va. Died July 20, 1908, Atlanta, Ga.

Erected by appreciative friends in memory of Eufaula's helpful and well beloved citizen.

Preacher, Poet, Patriotic Philanthropist, Statesman, Scholar, Consecrated Christian. He was great and broad and good.

And on the opposite side: "A life that all the muses decked, with gifts of grace, that might express, all comprehensing tenderness, all subtelizing intellect."

This monument was built under the direction of the Wharton Memorial Association, composed of eight or ten women of various denominations and the money (over a thousand dollars) was voluntarily sent in by friends from all parts of the South. It was carved in Italy and is a splendid likeness of Dr. Wharton.

His lifelong friend, Dr. Langsing Burroughs of Georgia, made the dedication address in the Church where an appropriate program of his own songs set to popular airs, were used and Mayor Charles S. McDowell paid a glowing tribute, when he accepted the monument in the name of the City, while in and around the church there stood in the street about 1500 people. The Second Alabama Regiment Band played and 25 little girls sang. The monument was unveiled by his granddaughter, Miss Bertha Moore, of Atlanta, now Mrs. W. H. Merrill of Eufaula, and his great grand daughter, Bessie Mitchell, now Mrs. H. Clay Moore, Jr., of Atlanta.

Dr. Wharton was distinguished because of his great service to his people as a citizen, as a statesman, and as a Gospel preacher, and Eufaula claimed him more than any other part of the country, for here, he spent 12 years and six months of the most active and useful part of his life, as a personal laborer for mankind, his acts being acts of pure love for a people.

He chose and accepted the Call to Eufaula, because his help was needed here. For a number of years he was Editor of the Christian Index, published in Atlanta.

His balance and poise gave him a singular power and influence in any crisis and a steady hand at the helm to steer the Church he loved over any difficulties.

Among the many interesting facts of his colorful career, is that when the money was being raised to build the first Baptist Church here, under his pastorate—the women of the Church planned a great Bazaar, to last a week in "Hart's Hall" the largest hall in the city.

Dr. Wharton wrote letters asking for donations to some of the largest business firms in the U. S. selecting those to address, among his acquaintances. Replies to some of these letters brought donations totaling over $6,000.00 in Bazaar receipts.

On Dr. Wharton's return from Germany as soon as he learned that the Church at Eufaula still owed notes on borrowed money, that completed the building of the church, he came for a two-day visit. Preaching in his old pulpit on a bitter cold January morning, and after the sermon called a church Conference. He remained in the pulpit until after two P. M., not a person in the large congregation left the church until the benediction was pronounced, and when it was, every note against the church had been taken over by persons present. In thirty days time every cent of the debt of over $3000.00 had been cancelled. Voluntary donations were quickly called out to offset these notes, which were promptly burned.

Not one held against the church, Dr. Wharton's appeal going to the hearts and pockets of his hearers, showing the power of his personality.

Biography Of Living Descendants

His descendants are one daughter, Mrs. John McDowell Moore (Hattie Wharton), her daughter married William H. Merrill (Bertha Moore), Eufaula, and her four daughters, Bertha, Harriet, Tade and Evelyn; and her daughter, Mrs. I. S. Mitchell, Jr. (Bessie Moore), and her daughter, Mrs. H. Clay Moore, Jr. (Bessie Mitchell); and son, Wharton Mitchell, Atlanta, and her two children, Bessie Moore and H. Clay Moore, III, Atlanta. The children of his only son, Morton, deceased, are Mrs. Douglass Malcolm (Catherine Wharton), of Scarsdale, New York, brother, Thomas Holt Wharton, died in Raleigh, N. C., November, 1934.

DR. JAMES J. WINN

Dr. J. J. Winn was born in Dekalb County, Georgia, near Decatur, and as early in life as his educational courses would permit, he began the practice of Medicine at Clayton in Barbour County, where he spent his life, rated one of the finest physicians in the state.

He coupled the title of "old time Dr.", with the later year "new method expert," because, espousing the new, he never dropped any of the old time "better ways," but combined the two into a perfection, in the medical world, that counted greatly.

Dr. Winn, was a man of pronounced ideas, a learned scholar, a thinker and a doer. He was strict to his standards and principles and no man ever had a stronger hold in the estimations and the hearts of his friends. He held every office in the County Medical Society, was a prominent member of the State Medical Association, and was eagerly sought authority on all weighty subjects that concerned the Medico of Barbour County.

He was also a business man. President of the Citizens Bank of Clayton and farmer, who ran his large farms on scientific plans. He was a man of poise and prominence whose memory is thrice blessed.

He married May Crews and they reared a large family of children, who have each been an honor to their parents.

They are, viz.: Mamie, married Richard Fryer; Pauline, Public Welfare Director of Barbour County; Dr. Lock Winn, married Mary Bryan, prominent physician of Birmingham; Guy, married Allene Glenn; and James J., Jr., prominent attorney of Clayton and Politician of the County; Condy, physician of New York; Mary, Samuel and Minnie, deceased; and Hattie, teacher in the City school of Florence, Alabama. Dr. Nannie Winn, deceased. (See biography).

DR. MONROE WARREN

Dr. Monroe Warren was one of the outstanding physicians of Barbour County and a man prominent and useful in the community.

He married Mary Francis Lawson and their children have been notable in the history of the County. The name Warren standing for all that implied good citizenship and personal integrity.

The eldest daughter, "Miss Weedie," as she was affectionately called, was one of the cultured women of the South, who dispensed joy wherever she went. She was a leader in all the Women's activities of her home town and County and was greatly beloved.

Monroe Warren is a valuable citizen of Clayton today, never married; Bates, married Lisette Ball, Washington, D. C.; Ben, married Leella Underwood; John L., married Kirkland Waddell. Late years the Warren family moved to Washington, D. C., where they are carrying on in various fields of high endeavor.

DR. HAMILTON M. WEEDON

Dr. Hamilton M. Weedon was born at Tallahassee, Florida, May 15, 1834, came to Eufaula in 1864 to take charge of the Military hospital, which was located at the Old Howard House on Broad and Livingston Streets.

He came to Eufaula from St. Augustine, Florida, where he was first Health Officer at that Fort of the Confederate army.

July 1, 1868, associated with Mr. Geo. H. Dent, he entered the Drug business, the firm name being Weedon and Dent, and this firm continued in business in the same building on Broad Street until 1897, when the business was taken over and continued until 1935, by his son, Edward B. Weedon, who is now associated with the firm of Milton and Milton, as prescriptionist. Dr. Weedon was a man of brilliant attainments, a polished gentleman of the type that is outstanding by right of genuine worth. An able physician, a most valuable citizen, and socially, a man whom it was a delight to associate with. He was always a "Chesterfield" wherever you came in contact with him.

He married, first Mary Young, daughter of Edward B. and Anna Beall Young, and after living several years out on the hill, in a vineclad cottage, he built the handsome Weedon home on Barbour street, where this distinguished couple reared their large family, all of whom are prominent in all the progress and uplift of the Community.

They were Hampton M., Jr., married Julia Henderson of Troy, daughter Mildred Weedon, married Mr. Blont; Annie, married John R. Barr, children Hampton Barr, married Julia Simpson, Lumpkin, Ga., Weedon Barr married Annie Laurie Talberg; James M. Barr, married Daisy Oppenheimer, children, son, Billie Barr; John R. Barr, Jr., married Nan Dent Hurt; Lucious Barr, married Aubyn Coleman; Ross Barr, deceased; Mary Weedon married James L. Ross, children, Mary, married Humphrey Foy, children, Humphrey Ross; Norma Carrie, married T. H. Moorer; Sarah, married Albert S. Dozier, children, Mary, Sarah, married Alex Williams, son, Alex William, III, Albert Dozier, Jr.

Edward B. Weedon married Mary Garland, children, Garland, prescriptionist Maxwell Field, Alabama; Edward B., Jr., married Virginia Lewis, Boston, Mass.

Walter W. Weedon, deceased; Herbert Weedon.

Dr. Weedon married second in 1895, Bessie Fanning of Raleigh, N. C., to them were born a son, Fanning Weedon.

JUDGE J. S. WILLIAMS

Judge J. S. Williams was born at Clayton, Alabama, in the beautiful picturesque and historic old home in which he still resides. He is the son of the late Judge Jere N. Williams, who was the first white representative in Congress, after the War Between the States, from this District and whose fearless leadership and courage, resulted in the defeat of the negro Rapier, the overthrow of Republicans and carpet baggers.

Judge Williams is of English-Scotch ancestry, his mother being Elizabeth Screws, and a product of the type of manhood that is genuine and stands for the noblest.

He studied in the common schools of his home town, and graduated with distinction at the University of Alabama receiving his A. B. Degree; studied law under his distinguished father and Judge A. A. Evans. He was appointed to the Judgeship of the Third Judicial Circuit, by Governor Charles Henderson and following the expiration of this appointment, was elected by the people, three terms, consecutively, and is still holding that office.

He is learned in all the phases of the law and strictly just and honest in all his rulings. He is outstanding as being no respector of persons, when on the bench, other than to enforce the law and deal justly. His charges to the grand juries of his court sessions, are being so keen clear cut, that the effect of his personal influence, in many cases that are grave, is felt.

Judge Williams began his political career, as enrolling clerk in the House of Representatives of Alabama and was twice a member of that body representing Barbour County.

He served the City of Clayton several terms as Mayor and is a popular and patriotic and a most valuable citizen of the County.

He married Martha Crawford, daughter of Dr. R. B. Crawford, a distinguished minister of the Methodist Alabama Conference and his wife, Martha Stevenson Crawford, and together this greatly beloved couple are still carrying out at the lovely old Williams home, all the programs and traditions of their ancestry.

Few public men have attained the genuine popularity in the political world that has been Judge Williams' portion.

Personally he is genial, kind and generous hearted and lives by the code of principles that make the esteem of his friends as genuine as it is universal.

EDWARD R. WEST

Edward R. West was born in Baldwin County, Georgia, March 28, 1843. Enlisting in the War Between the States April 26, 1861, Company H, 4th Regiment, Georgia Volunteers from Baldwin County. He was discharged at Appomattox Company H. Va., April 9, 1865, with rank of 2nd Sergeant, Company H, Baldwin Blues, 4th Georgia Regiment. At the time of surrender, he was in charge of Ambulance Corps.

On November 13, 1867, he married Mary J. Brannon, daughter of the distinguished old Brannon family of Alabama and Georgia, and throughout their life and up to today the historic old West home on Eufaula street, where all their children were born and reared, has been one of the most historic in the Community.

Mr. West early entered the Dry Goods business, for many years being a member of the firm of Beringer, Straus and West. When the evening of life came on and this popular old firm has ceased business, he established a Dry Goods and Shoe Department, in one of the stores owned by him and adjoining the Grocery store of his sons, William and Edward West. The former, also having been connected with Beringer Strauss and West, and the latter, Edward, going into the Grocery business. The firm being West and Brothers.

William is now head of the Dry Goods Dept. of a local Department store, while Edward has been with a local furniture store ever since they closed the old business after the fater's death, December ?, 1907.

Mr. West was a most valuable citizen, of marked business ability, of dignified personality, that commanded respect and won friends. H occupied a very enviable position in all the circles of the life of the town and surrounding country. He was an outstanding Mason, holding high offices during his life as a member of Harmony Lodge No. 46 F. A. A. M. The sons and daughters of this notable West Family are Sallie, married William L. Lott, of Columbus, Georgia, their children are: Sarah Elizabeth, married Gordon Hale, and they have a son, Gordon Hale, Jr.; William Lott, Jr.; William S. West and Edward R. West, Jr., both unmarried, and three sisters, Misses Mamie, Leah and Julia, still keep the tradition of the family alive at the old home. Miss Annie, another sister, having died several years ago.

JERE N. WILLIAMS

The subject of this sketch was distinctly a son of Barbour County and one of whom its citizens were justly proud.

His people were pioneers in the Louisville Country, having gone there in the very early days when the Indians were numerous and in charge. His father, Judge S. Williams, of Virginia and Georgia, emigrated to Alabama with older brothers when he was a very young child, and his mother, Effie McNeill Williams, whose ancestors were pure Scotch, were from North Carolina. It is said that her grandfather was the first white person buried in the country near Louisville, and that, at that time, Fort Gaines, Ga., was the nearest market place, so the old Scotch pioneer was buried in a coffin hewn by his slaves and the Indians from a poplar tree. The Williams were of English descent, and the grandfather of Jere N. Williams was a Captain of Militia in the Continental Army.

The early education of Judge Jere N. Williams was derived from the schools of this County, and he finished at Columbia College, South Carolina, which was then one of the foremost educational institutions in the United States. He chose the practice of law as his profession and studied in Montgomery and Tuskegee, being admitted to practice before the Supreme Court in 1855. When Alabama seceded, he was among the first to volunteer his services and assisted in raising the First Alabama Regiment, in which he was Captain and subsequently Major. He remained with his regiment for an entire year, but was forced by physical infirmities and ill health to retire from active service. He came home from the army to his people, returning as often to his command as his physical condition would permit. It was after the War, in the trying days of Reconstruction that his charcater and courage shone most resplendently and that he contributed so largely to restore this government to the white people, and wrest it from negro and Republican and Scalawag misrule. At the risk of his own life and great personal peril, he campaigned alone from one end of this Congressional District to the other, going into the remotest precincts and into those filled with deserters from the Confederate Army and local renegades, arousing his people. Those were days that tried the souls of men, and Judge Williams met the emergency. This District was then represented in Congress by a negro named Rapier until Jere N. Williams defeated him in the memorable campaign of 1874. Until 1878, Jere Williams was the creditable and distinguished Congressman from the Third District, the first white man to occupy the place after the War Between the States. Retiring from Congress, he returned to the practice of law at Clayton, where he enjoyed a large practice and was recognized as one of the leaders at the Bar in Alabama. He, with two other Confederate Soldiers, Captain S. H. Dent and Captain Michael Cody, were nominated by the white people to represent them in the Alabama Legislature shortly after the War. Together they went to Montgomery, then in the hands of Union Soldiers, to become Legislators. Federal warrants had been issued for their arrest, and they were kept at the home of Captain Walker for several days. Having faced Yankee bullets on the battle field and being unafraid they could endure their confinement no longer, when one morning, they went boldly to the Capitol to present their credentials. They were denied admission, were sent back to Barbour County and in their stead were seated three black Republicans who participated in that wild orgy of Reconstruction.

Judge Williams was made Chancellor of this Division, and in that capacity served with distinction and satisfaction, for his honesty, courage and ability were always dominant and controlled him. He was highly educated, a gifted linguist and writer, and no more fluent and graceful speaker could be found. In private life, he was above reproach and furnished an example that shone as a beacon light to all who sought the right way. In December, 1864, when at home on leave from the army, he married Mary Elizabeth Screws, the sister of Major Wallace Screws and Captain Ben Screws, both illustrious products of Barbour County.

Of this union, there were born five children who are: Mrs. W. M. Wilkerson, widow of Dr. W. M. Wilkerson, of Montgomery; Mrs. W. A. Leland, Widow of W. A. Leland, Charleston, S. C.; Mrs. Geo. W. Feagin, Athens, Alabama;

Mrs. T. C. Stevenson, Charleston, S. C.;and Judge J. S. Williams, the present occupant of the Bench of the Third Judicial Circuit of Alabama. Judge Jere Williams' father was Probate Judge of this County during and after the War, until ousted by the negroes and Republicans, and his record was notable for its achievements and his personal character was so high and pure that he, too, is revered and his memory blessed.

Barbour County has had no sons who gave more unstintedly of their time, talents, energy and loyalty to her welfare than did Jere N. Williams and his name will always occupy a lofty place in its history.

He was one of the framers of the present Constitution of the State of Alabama, being a delegate to the Convention from the Third Congressional District, and his knowledge of the law and his judgment of men and affairs were contributing factors to the success of that instrument under which we, as a State, live and function.

Among the many notable experiences of Judge Williams is the following: A certain part of Dale and Barbour County, was simply alive with deserters from the Confederate Army, who had become Republicans, and who controlled Civil affairs. Judge Williams was denouncing such characters with all vehemence and skill that he could command—and he was a master in the use of English and as a speaker. Those wretches had threatened his life if he made one of his characteristic speeches in their community, or sought to interfere with them.

When he reached Ozark, he was met by a Committee headed by Judge Carmichael who advised him of the threats and the extreme danger that existed, and insisted that he be accompanied by a body guard, as he stood in dire need of protection. Judge Williams spurned the offer, insisting that he would not involve others in danger on his account, and he went, as he thought, alone and made one of the most vigorous speeches which some yet remember and which did arouse our people to their situation. It so happened, however, that a body guard, or guard did go to the meeting, and were present without Judge Williams' knowledge to assist if needed. Such examples of courage and fidelity could be multiplied, and goes to show the fibre of the man's nature and his courage and devotion.

EDWARD B. YOUNG, SR.

Edward B. Young was born in New York, N. Y., August 24, 1802. He married Anna Fendell of Warren County, Georgia, and came to Barbour County when a very young man. He first established at Eufaula what was the first Iron and Foundry works in all this section, and his son, William Young was Owner and Manager of this large enterprise, for many years, going, after the War Between the States, to Newton, New Jersey, where he died. His son, Charles Young, often visited the old ancestral home at Eufaula. Another son, Henry A. Young, was one of the earliest Barbour County men to go into the Confederate Army and was killed February 19, 1863, at Chunkey Bridge, Miss. At the same time his friend, also a former Eufaulian, Prof. Cliff Muiller, who had been a Music Professor in Union Female College, was killed and the Young family, brought the two bodies home to Eufaula together and buried them side by side, in the historic old Young family lot in Fairview Cemetery. Henry A. Young married Maria McRae, daughter of John C. McRae, one of Barbour County's outstanding citizens, their children were Julia, who married Albert Barnett, and William H. Young, and is now a prominent citizen of Anniston, Alabama.

The third son of Edward Brown and Anne Fendell Young was Edward Billops Young, who grew in the banking business with his father, who established at Eufaula the first Bank, known as the "Bridge Bank" which for a long time was one of the only four banks in Alabama (so unverified tradition says). Edward Young, Jr., was Cashier of the Eufaula National Bank, which his father laid the foundation for, and throughout his life he was a leader in all the financial projects of the county, and a man of spotless character, and rare ability, a chesterfield, and a pattern of citizenship that was held up to and admired by all.

He married Mamie Jennings, and their children, Annie married Thos. Holt of Macon, Ga.; Mabel, Hubert, Flora, Edward B. Young, III, married Meta Baldwin of Dawson, Ga. (now lives at Albany, Ga.).

This illustrious family grew up at the Young home on College Hill adjoining the old historic mansion built by Mr. Young in the early fifties.

The daughters were: Mary, married Dr. H. M. Weedon.
Second daughter, Anna Bealle, married Capt. S. H. Dent.
Third daughter, Ada, married James G. H. Martin.
Fourth daughter, Helen, married George H. Dent.
Fifth daughter, Carrie, married Noah W. Roberts, deceased.

The first Edward Young was the first moneyed man to cast his lot in this section of Barbour County, and his progressive ideas and his facilities for carrying them out were large factors in the building up of this community.

SOLOMON WALKERS—REVOLUTIONARY SOLDIER

Solomon Walker, Revolutionary soldier, was born in Virginia in 1757, and with his parents and brother, David Walker, and sister, Susan Walker and another sister came to Cumberland County, N. C., and lived there and fought in defense of his country. The Walker family had probably been in Virginia since its earliest settlement. The family owned a large and handsome collection of Pewert platters and Baisins which authorities say were early brought from England.

The vessels were in the Walker family in Barbour County until a few years ago when the old Walker home was burned and all were melted but one which is owned by his great grandson, Rev. Eli A. Thomas, of Atlanta, Georgia. David Walker never married and died in Cumberland County, N. C. Susan Walker married a Mr. Blanchett in North Carolina and later came to South Alabama—the other sister married a Mr. Jarman of North Carolina." In 1778, Solomon Walker in company with Richard Taylor was sent to join the American army which was stationed on the North side of the Savannah River, opposite Augusta, then occupied by the British. A detachment under General Ashe was ordered across the river to take their station at the point where Briar Creek flows into the Savannah. To avoid being captured, Lieutenant Solomon Walker swam the Savannah River.

—State Records of North Carolina Bq Clarke, Vol. XXII, page 125.

Solomon Waker, wife and son, Lewis Walker, came to

DAVID A. WILSON   JOHN A. WALKER

Barbour County before the Indians had gone—settled 13 miles from Eufaula. The home place is still owned by his great granddaughter, Mrs. Maud Wilson Howell, and her mother, Cynthia Caroline (Walker) Wilson. The deed to this place was signed on sheepskin by President Andrew Jackson. They were study, long-lived people and lived by the side of the road and were the friends to man." It is said that Solomon Walker in Barbour would swap corn to the Indians for wild honey in raw deer hides, when he had plenty of his own in order to live on friendly terms with them. His batchelor brother, David Walker, of Cumberland County, N. C., died soon after they reached Barbour County, and the executor sent $1000 in gold to Solomon Walker on August 11, 1837. Solomon Walker died and was buried on his own land and on November 5, 1938, Godin Cox Walker, his wife, died and was buried by his side.

Nancy McInnis Walker spoke the Gaelic language and was said by the late Dr. Crews to be the best Bible student in Barbour County.

In this home was found worthwhile books and a Presbyteian religious paper fiirst published in Philadelphia and nearby lay her Bible Dictionary—a devoted Christian wife and mother. Her daughters and sons were fine women and men. It is said she had a regular time of day to go to her room for prayer. Her home was full of beautiful woolen Scotch plaid spreads and coverlets done in patterns of the spreading eagle, symbolic of the new American Independence. She kept carefully Solomon Walker's long linen stockings and silver knee buckles which are now owned by his granddaughter, Mrs. Cynthia Wilson. This family was an outstanding representative of the pioneers who have contributed much in the founding of this county from Revolutionary days to the present. Louis Walker died November 23, 1877, and Nancy McInnis Walker died March 29, 1893, and were buried in the Walker cemetery.

Their issue: Maisy Catherine Walker, born March 23, 1832; died Jan. 17, 1889; Nancy Jane Walker, born March 16,1835; died August 23, 1929; Solomon Miles Walker, born Aug. 14, 1837; died Nov. 10, 1937; Mary Walker, born October 6, 1838; died March 18, 1925. John Alexander Walker, born March 14, 1851; died Nov. 9, 1862. Amanda Walker, born January 1, 1844; died October 13, 1931.

Footnote: See George Hilliard Thomas Esq., and Mary Walker line—"Angus McInnis—Scotland."

David Lewis Walker was born September 1, 1846; died March 20, 1935.

James Franklin Walker was born March 30, 1849; died September 25, 1933.

Cynthia Caroline Walker, born December 19, 1851.

Maisy Catherine Walker was marrie dto Arthur Crews about 1861. Issue—

Mary Victoria Crews, born August 25, 1864; died July 21, 1865.

Ellie Corine Crews married Ewell Glover and they lefet the following issue:

Judge Arthur Crews Glover, World War veteran, Wetumka, Alabama.

Edward Glover, of Birmingham, Ala.

Robert Tombs Glover died while young.

Mary Glover; Helen Glover; Peggy Glover, teacher in Alabama school; Thomas Heflin Glover.

Andrew Johnson Crews died when grown.

Nancy Jane Walker was one of those unusual high type women, like her mother and sister, who for almost 94 years made the world brighter for everyone.—"Many daughters have done virtuously but thou excellest them all."

Mary Walker married George Hilliard Thomas, Esq., on February 12, 1866, and leaves the following issue. See the (George Hillard Thomas, Esk., and Mary Walker Thomas line).

John Alexander Walker was a stalwart soldier of the Confederacy and died of fever and was burried in Cleveland, Tenn., November 9, 1862. Company B.—39th Alabama Regiment.

Amanda Walker married James Mitchell Keahey, a Scotch Presbyterian elder. She is buried in Walker cemetery.

James Franklin Walker married first June 25, 1876, Nancy A. Cictoria McCraney; second Clara Rogers, June 17, 1884.

By the first marriage, issue, one daughter, Nancy Jane Walker, born November 2, 1876.

Nancy Jane Walker married William H. McEachern, April 30, 1893 of Louisville, Alabama. Issue:

James Daniel McEeachern, married Erin Massey Munn, live in Birmingham.

Nancy Victoria (Viccie) married James Calvin Stievender, D. D., pastor of Ruhemer Church, Howard College.

William H., Jr., married Dr. Wyatt Barnes, Ariton, Alabama.

Lloyd Franklin married Louisa Tyler Wheeler, Macon, Georgia.

Mary Mildred married Edward Anthony Kilinski, Washnigton, D. C.

Annie Catherine married Rev. Brady Richmond, Justice, Fort Payne, Ala.

John Rogers Walker married Virginia Slemp—no issue.

James Franklin died young.

William Cullen married Sadie Cargill, Eufaula. Issue: Sarah, Pauline and Rogers.

Robert Emmett Walker married Annie Laura Shaw. Issue —Robert Emmett, Jack Knox, Elsie 7Catherine, John Lewis, twins, Clara Adina and Ann Elizabeth.

Cynthia Caroline Walker married January 25, 1870, David A .Wilson, son of David and Nancy Wilson, of Wilson Cross Roads. He was a Confederate Soldier, Company B, 39th Regiment. Their children:

Leon Lewis Wilson, born January 15, 1871, married Clara Hawkins. Issue, Hattie Wilson, married and has issue:

Lela Leon married Mr. Owens, issue ,one daughter.

Augusta Wilson, born March 28, 1874—died March, 1926.

Maud Wilson married Mr. Howell, Barbour County.

David Patrick Wilson, born December 25, 1893, married Lucinde West ,issue:

Edgar Wilson, Douglas Wilson, Mary Helen Wilson, Dorothy Mae Wilson.

The Walker home place is 13 miles from Eufaula and has been in the Walker family since 1821.

THE END

www.ingramcontent.com/pod-product-compliance
Lightning Source LLC
Chambersburg PA
CBHW020632300426
44112CB00007B/87